Lecture Notes in Computer Science

Lecture Notes in Artificial Intelligence   15281

Founding Editor

Jörg Siekmann

Series Editors

Randy Goebel, *University of Alberta, Edmonton, Canada*
Wolfgang Wahlster, *DFKI, Berlin, Germany*
Zhi-Hua Zhou, *Nanjing University, Nanjing, China*

The series Lecture Notes in Artificial Intelligence (LNAI) was established in 1988 as a topical subseries of LNCS devoted to artificial intelligence.

The series publishes state-of-the-art research results at a high level. As with the LNCS mother series, the mission of the series is to serve the international R & D community by providing an invaluable service, mainly focused on the publication of conference and workshop proceedings and postproceedings.

Rafik Hadfi · Patricia Anthony · Alok Sharma ·
Takayuki Ito · Quan Bai

Editors

PRICAI 2024: Trends in Artificial Intelligence

21st Pacific Rim International Conference
on Artificial Intelligence, PRICAI 2024
Kyoto, Japan, November 18–24, 2024
Proceedings, Part I

Springer

Editors
Rafik Hadfi 🆔
Kyoto University
Kyoto, Japan

Patricia Anthony 🆔
Lincoln University
Christchurch, New Zealand

Alok Sharma 🆔
RIKEN Center for Integrative Medical
Sciences
Yokohama, Japan

Takayuki Ito 🆔
Kyoto University
Kyoto, Japan

Quan Bai 🆔
University of Tasmania
Tasmania, TAS, Australia

ISSN 0302-9743   ISSN 1611-3349 (electronic)
Lecture Notes in Artificial Intelligence
ISBN 978-981-96-0115-8   ISBN 978-981-96-0116-5 (eBook)
https://doi.org/10.1007/978-981-96-0116-5

LNCS Sublibrary: SL7 – Artificial Intelligence

Preface

These proceedings, presented in five volumes, contain the papers from the 21st Pacific Rim International Conference on Artificial Intelligence (PRICAI 2024), held from November 18 to 24, 2024, in Kyoto, Japan. The papers in these volumes reflect the richness and diversity of the discussions held during the conference, encompassing topics such as machine learning, computer vision, generative artificial intelligence (AI), large language models, and innovative applications of AI in various domains.

PRICAI was inaugurated in Tokyo in 1990 as a biennial international conference focused on AI theories, technologies, and AI applications that hold social and economic significance for the Pacific Rim countries. Since its inception, PRICAI has provided a common platform for researchers and practitioners across different AI fields to exchange new ideas and share expertise across AI disciplines. Over the years, the conference has grown in both participation and scope, establishing itself as a leading international AI event for the Pacific Rim nations and the global AI community. The conference has been held annually since 2019.

This year, PRICAI 2024 received an overwhelming number of 543 submissions--the highest in the conference's history. Each submission underwent a rigorous double-blind peer-review process, ensuring the highest quality standards. Each paper received three reviews, and some even five. Program Committee members engaged in discussions and, when necessary, sought additional reviews to ensure thorough and fair evaluations. After careful deliberation, the Program Chairs evaluated the reviews and comments, and reconciled any discrepancies in individual reviews and ratings to ensure consistency in the final decisions. We eventually accepted 145 regular papers and 35 short papers for oral presentation. This gives a regular paper acceptance rate of 27% and an overall acceptance rate of 33%. Additionally, a comprehensive quality control process was implemented for camera-ready papers. Authors were required to incorporate the feedback provided by reviewers into their final submissions. Content similarity checks were also performed to ensure the similarity rate remained below 15%. Due to the large number of high-quality submissions, a few papers were accepted as posters, with the understanding that they would not be included in the proceedings.

The papers are organized into five volumes, covering several broad themes, such as machine learning, computer vision, natural language processing, and general applications of AI. The technical program consisted of eight workshops, six tutorials, one panel session, and the main conference sessions. All regular and short papers at the main conference were orally presented across multiple parallel thematically organized sessions. We were honoured to have five outstanding keynote speakers share their insights with the conference attendants: Bo An (Nanyang Technological University, Singapore), Long Tran-Thanh (University of Warwick, UK), Sadao Kurohashi (Kyoto University, Japan), Milind Tambe (Harvard University, USA), and Noa Garcia (Osaka University, Japan).

The success of PRICAI 2024 would not have been possible without the effort and support of numerous individuals worldwide. First and foremost, we extend our gratitude to the Program Committee members and external reviewers for their commitment to providing thorough and timely reviews. We would also like to acknowledge the workshop and tutorial organizers, who played a pivotal role in shaping the core of the technical program.

We are deeply grateful to the organising committee for their tireless and unwavering efforts which made this event a success. Our appreciation also goes to the advisory board members for their invaluable guidance during the planning stages. We also extend our gratitude to the PRICAI Steering Committee for entrusting us with the honour of hosting this significant conference.

Our gratitude extends to our sponsors, whose support has been instrumental in making PRICAI 2024 possible and enabled us to continue pushing boundaries. We particularly thank the Telecommunication Advancement Foundation (TAF), the Japanese Society for Artificial Intelligence (JSAI), the Information Processing Society of Japan (IPSJ), and OMRON Corporation. Last but not least, we extend our heartfelt thanks to all authors and conference participants for their contributions and support. We hope everyone took advantage of this valuable opportunity to share and exchange ideas, and that participants enjoyed their time at PRICAI 2024. We look forward to the continued contributions of students, researchers, scientists, academicians, and industry professionals in future editions of PRICAI.

November 2024

Rafik Hadfi
Patricia Anthony
Alok Sharma
Takayuki Ito
Quan Bai

Organization

Program Committee

Tooba Aamir	CSIRO, Data61, Australia
Azizi Ab Aziz	Universiti Utara Malaysia, Malaysia
Taufik Abidin	Universitas Syiah Kuala, Indonesia
Amit Agarwal	Oracle, USA
Hissah Alotaibi	Jazan University, Saudi Arabia
Patricia Anthony	Lincoln University, New Zealand
Ryuta Arisaka	Kyoto University, Japan
Mansour Assaf	University of the South Pacific, Fiji
James Atlas	University of Canterbury, New Zealand
Quan Bai	Auckland University of Technology, New Zealand
Thirunavukarasu Balasubramaniam	Queensland University of Technology, Australia
Debabrota Basu	Inria, France
Diana Benavides Prado	University of Auckland, New Zealand
Thilini Bhagya	Lincoln University, New Zealand
Ateet Bhalla	Independent Technology Consultant, India
Radhakrishna Bhat	Manipal Institute of Technology, India
Ran Bi	Northeastern Technology, China
Aida Brankovic	Australian e-Health Research Centre, CSIRO, Australia
Chenyang Bu	Hefei University of Technology, China
Francesco Busolin	Università Ca Foscari, Italy
Jian Cao	Shanghai Jiao Tong University, China
Tru Cao	University of Texas Health Science Center at Houston, USA
Zehong Cao	University of South Australia, Australia
M. A. P. Chamikara	CSIRO Data61, Australia
Hutchatai Chanlekha	Kasetsart University, Thailand
Gang Chen	Victoria University of Wellington, New Zealand
Jianxia Chen	Hubei University of Technology, China
Liangyu Chen	East China Normal University, China
Qi Chen	Victoria University of Wellington, New Zealand
Siqi Chen	Chongqing Jiaotong University, China
Songcan Chen	Nanjing University of Aeronautics & Astronautics, China

Tingxuan Chen	Central South University, China
Weiwei Chen	Sun Yat-sen University, China
Wu Chen	Southwest University, China
Yingke Chen	Northumbria University, UK
Yihang Cheng	Tianjin University, China
Cody Christopher	CSIRO's Data61, Australia
Zhi Churan	University of California San Diego, USA
Jinmiao Cong	Dalian University of Technology, China
Dan Corbett	University of Sydney, Australia
Zhihong Cui	Shandong University, China
Jirapun Daengdej	Innocop Co., Ltd, Australia
Iman Dehzangi	Rutgers University, USA
Chandra Kusuma Dewa	Universitas Islam Indonesia, Indonesia
Shiyao Ding	Kyoto University, Japan
Zheng Dong	ByteDance, China
Karan Dua	Oracle Corporation, India
Atilla Elci	Hasan Kalyoncu University, Turkey
Eduardo Fermé	Universidade da Madeira, Portugal
Xiaoxuan Fu	China University of Political Science and Law, China
Katsuhide Fujita	Tokyo University of Agriculture and Technology, Japan
Naoki Fukuta	Shizuoka University, Japan
Hiroaki Furukawa	University of Kitakyushu, Japan
Hua Leong Fwa	Singapore Management University, Singapore
Dragan Gamberger	Ruđer Bošković Institute, Croatia
Wei Gao	Nanjing University, China
Carlos Rodrigo Garibay Rubio	Kyoto University, Japan
Manolis Gergatsoulis	Ionian University, Greece
Akbar Ghobakhlou	Auckland University of Technology, New Zealand
Nicola Gigante	Free University of Bozen-Bolzano, Italy
Maria Gini	University of Minnesota, USA
Takaaki Goto	Toyo University, Japan
Guido Governatori	Central Queensland University, Australia
Alban Grastien	CEA-List, France
Jinjin Guo	JD.com, Inc., China
Avisek Gupta	TCG CREST, India
Rafik Hadfi	Kyoto University, Japan
Mourad Hakem	Université de Franche-Comté, France
Bavly Hanna	University of Technology Sydney, Australia
Mehedi Hasan	BRAC University, Bangladesh

Shinobu Hasegawa	Japan Advanced Institute of Science and Technology, Tokyo
Hamed Hassanzadeh	Australian e-Health Research Centre, CSIRO, Australia
Tessai Hayama	Nagaoka University of Technology, Japan
Yang He	A*STAR, Singapore
Ryuichiro Higashinaka	Nagoya University/NTT, Japan
Linlin Hou	Zhejiang Lab, China
Siyi Hu	University of South Australia, Australia
Junhao Huang	Victoria University of Wellington, New Zealand
Xiaodi Huang	Charles Sturt University, Australia
Nguyen Duy Hung	Sirindhorn International Institute of Technology, Thammasat University, Thailand
Huan Huo	University of Technology Sydney, Australia
Habibi Husain Arifin	Assumption University, Thailand
Du Huynh	University of Western Australia, Australia
Van Nam Huynh	JAIST, Japan
Masashi Inoue	Tohoku Institute of Technology, Japan
Naohiro Ishii	Advanced Institute of Industrial Technology, Japan
Md Khaled Ben Islam	Griffith University, Australia
Md. Saiful Islam	University of Newcastle, Australia
Takayuki Ito	Kyoto University, Japan
Kiyoshi Izumi	University of Tokyo, Japan
Sanjay Jain	National University of Singapore, Singapore
Fatemeh Jalalvand	CSIRO's Data61, Australia
Ziyu Jia	Institute of Automation, Chinese Academy of Sciences, China
Yuncheng Jiang	South China Normal University, China
Nattagit Jiteurtragool	King Mongkut's University of Technology North Bangkok, Thailand
Rui-Yang Ju	National Taiwan University, Taiwan
Hideaki Kanai	Japan Advanced Institute of Science and Technology, Japan
Ryo Kanamori	Nagoya University, Japan
Natsuda Kaothanthong	Thammasat University, Thailand
Shohei Kato	Nagoya Institute of Technology, Japan
Takahiro Kawaji	Kurume University, Japan
Satoshi Kawase	Kobe Gakuin University, Japan
Yi Wen Kerk	Universiti Kebangsaan Malaysia, Malaysia
Gabriele Kern-Isberner	Technische Universität Dortmund, Germany
Natthawut Kertkeidkachorn	Japan Advanced Institute of Science and Technology, Japan

Yue Liu	Data61, CSIRO, Australia
Man Fung Lo	University of Hong Kong, China
Emiliano Lorini	IRIT, France
Dickson Lukose	Tabcorp Holdings Ltd., Australia
Sreenivasan M.	International Institute of Information Technology Hyderabad, India
Hui Ma	Victoria University of Wellington, New Zealand
Eric Martin	University of New South Wales, Australia
Brendan McCane	University of Otago, New Zealand
Md Humaion Kabir Mehedi	BRAC University, Bangladesh
Arne Meier	Leibniz Universität Hannover, Germany
Thomas Meyer	University of Cape Town and CAIR, South Africa
Lynn Miller	Monash University, Australia
Muhammad Syafiq Mohd Pozi	Universiti Utara Malaysia, Malaysia
Jose M. Molina	Universidad Carlos III de Madrid, Spain
Kristen Moore	CSIRO Data61, Australia
Lailil Muflikhah	Brawijaya University, Indonesia
Toyohisa Nakada	Niigata University of International and Information Studies, Japan
Parma Nand	Auckland University of Technology, New Zealand
Pavel Naumov	University of Southampton, UK
M. A. Hakim Newton	University of Newcastle, Australia
Binh P. Nguyen	Victoria University of Wellington, New Zealand
Minh Nguyen	Auckland University of Technology, New Zealand
Phi Le Nguyen	Hanoi University of Science and Technology, Vietnam
Trung Nguyen	University of Auckland, New Zealand
Nianwen Ning	Henan University, China
Anto Satriyo Nugroho	National Research and Innovation Agency, Indonesia
Kouzou Ohara	Aoyama Gakuin University, Japan
Takanobu Otsuka	Nagoya Institute of Technology, Japan
Maurice Pagnucco	University of New South Wales, Australia
Hitesh Patel	New York University/Oracle, USA
Priyaranjan Pattnayak	Oracle Cloud, USA
Songwen Pei	University of Shanghai for Science and Technology, China
Chang-Shyh Peng	California Lutheran University, USA
Tao Peng	Soochow University, China
Isidoros Perikos	University of Patras, Greece
Bernhard Pfahringer	University of Waikato, New Zealand
Ioannis Pierros	Aristotle University of Thessaloniki, Greece

Przemyslaw Pukocz	AGH, Poland
Qi Qi	Hainan University, China
Shiyou Qian	Shanghai Jiao Tong University, China
Jianglin Qiao	University of South Australia, Australia
Teeradaj Racharak	Japan Advanced Institute of Science and Technology, Japan
Annajiat Alim Rasel	BRAC University, Bangladesh
Wandeep Kaur Ratan Singh	Universiti Kebangsaan Malaysia, Malaysia
Md Saifullah Razali	University of Wollongong, Australia
Fenghui Ren	University of Wollongong, Australia
Jiankang Ren	Dalian University of Technology, China
Yuheng Ren	Digital Industry College of Jimei University, China
Jandson S. Ribeiro	Cardiff University, UK
Jia Rong	Monash University, Australia
Yi Rong	Wuhan University of Technology, China
Taufik Roni Sahroni	Bina Nusantara University, Indonesia
Sanjukta Roy	University of Leeds, UK
Ji Ruan	Auckland University of Technology, New Zealand
Khairun Saddami	Universitas Syiah Kuala, Indonesia
Payel Sadhukhan	Neotia University, India
Chiaki Sakama	Wakayama University, Japan
Ario Santoso	Independent, Indonesia
Yunita Sari	Universitas Gadjah Mada, Indonesia
Abdul Sattar	Griffith University, Australia
Nicolas Schwind	National Institute of Advanced Industrial Science and Technology, Japan
Nazha Selmaoui-Folcher	University of New Caledonia, New Caledonia
Lin Shang	Nanjing University, China
Alok Sharma	RIKEN Center for Integrative Medical Sciences, Japan
Bibhya Sharma	University of the South Pacific, Fiji
Nandita Sharma	Australian Government, Australia
Ronesh Sharma	Fiji National University, Fiji
Swakkhar Shatabda	BRAC University, Bangladesh
Yifan Shen	University of Illinois at Urbana-Champaign, USA
Kaize Shi	University of Technology Sydney, Australia
Yanfeng Shu	CSIRO, Australia
Ronal Singh	Data61@CSIRO, Australia
Chan Sixian	Zhejiang University of Technology, China
Chattrakul Sombattheera	Mahasarakham University, Thailand
Insu Song	James Cook University, Australia

Pokpong Songmuang	Thammasat University, Thailand
Giancarlo Sperlì	University of Naples Federico II, Italy
Markus Stumptner	University of South Australia, Australia
Guoxin Su	University of Wollongong, Australia
Ruidan Su	Shanghai Jiao Tong University, China
Xing Su	Beijing University of Technology, China
Toshiharu Sugawara	Waseda University, Japan
Jie Sun	Nanjing Xiaozhuang University, China
Junping Sun	Nova Southeastern University, USA
Andrew Sung	University of Southern Mississippi, USA
Boontawee Suntisrivaraporn	SparkBeyond, USA
Luis Martín Sánchez-Adame	FES-Acatlán, UNAM, Mexico
Jose Paolo Talusan	Vanderbilt University, USA
Tse Guan Tan	Universiti Malaysia Kelantan, Malaysia
Aparna Taneja	Google, USA
Xijin Tang	CAS Academy of Mathematics & Systems Science, China
Michiaki Tatsubori	IBM Research - Africa/Tokyo, Japan
Sotarat Thammaboosadee	Mahidol University, Thailand
Bui Thi-Mai-Anh	Hanoi University of Science and Technology, Vietnam
Michael Thielscher	University of New South Wales, Australia
Kar-Ann Toh	Yonsei University, South Korea
Dang Hung Tran	Hanoi National University of Education, Vietnam
Jarrod Trevathan	Griffith University, Australia
Masateru Tsunoda	Kindai University, Japan
Ayad Turky	University of Sharjah, UAE
Takahiro Uchiya	Nagoya Institute of Technology, Japan
Qurrat Ul-Ain	Victoria University of Wellington, New Zealand
Fumito Uwano	Okayama University, Japan
Khimji Vaghjiani	Torrens University Australia, Adelaide, Australia
Miroslav Velev	Aries Design Automation, USA
Alberto Veneri	Ca' Foscari University of Venice & ISTI-CNR, Italy
Toby Walsh	University of New South Wales, Australia
Agustinus Waluyo	La Trobe University, Australia
Chen Wang	National Institute of Water and Atmospheric Research, New Zealand
Yuchen Wang	Zhejiang University of Science and Technology, China
Yuxin Wang	Dalian University of Technology, China
Xiao Wei	Shanghai University, China

Guilherme Weigert Cassales   University of Waikato, New Zealand
Paul Weng   Duke Kunshan University, China
Peter Whigham   University of Otago, New Zealand
Arie Wahyu Wijayanto   Politeknik Statistika STIS, Indonesia
Wayne Wobcke   University of New South Wales, Australia
Sartra Wongthanavasu   Khon Kaen University, Thailand
Brendon J. Woodford   University of Otago, New Zealand
Huiwen Wu   Zhejiang Laboratory, China
Ou Wu   Tianjin University, China
Shiqing Wu   University of Technology Sydney, Australia
Yutong Wu   Australian e-Health Research Center, CSIRO,
                                  Australia
Yin Xian   Hong Kong Baptist University, China
Liang Xiao   Hubei University of Technology, China
Ming Xu   Xi'an Jiaotong-Liverpool University, China
Shuxiang Xu   University of Tasmania, Australia
Yongxiu Xu   Institute of Information Engineering, Chinese
                                  Academy of Sciences, China
Hui Xue   Southeast University, China
Chunming Yang   Southwest University of Science and Technology,
                                  China
Chunsheng Yang   National Research Council Canada, Canada
Fengyu Yang   Nanchang Hangkong University, China
Yi Yang   Hefei University of Technology, China
Yuan Yao   University of Nottingham Ningbo China, China
Kun Yi   Beijing Institute of Technology, China
Vithya Yogarajan   University of Waikato, New Zealand
Sira Yongchareon   Auckland University of Technology, New Zealand
Dianer Yu   University of Technology Sydney, Australia
Hang Yu   Shanghai University, China
Lin Yue   University of Adelaide, Australia
Takaya Yuizono   Japan Advanced Institute of Science and
                                  Technology, Japan
Intan Nurma Yulita   Padjadjaran University, Indonesia
Chengwei Zhang   Dalian Maritime University, China
Daokun Zhang   University of Nottingham Ningbo China, China
Fangfang Zhang   Victoria University of Wellington, New Zealand
Haibo Zhang   Kyushu Institute of Technology, Japan
Hengzhe Zhang   Victoria University of Wellington, New Zealand
Huan Zhang   Zhengzhou University, China
John Z. Zhang   University of Lethbridge, Canada
Leo Yu Zhang   Griffith University, Australia

Liying Zhang	China University of Petroleum, Beijing, China
Min-Ling Zhang	Southeast University, China
Mingyue Zhang	Southwest University, China
Shenglin Zhang	Nankai University, China
Wei Emma Zhang	University of Adelaide, Australia
Wen Zhang	Beijing University of Technology, China
Xinghua Zhang	Institute of Information Engineering, Chinese Academy of Sciences, China
Yaqian Zhang	University of Waikato, New Zealand
Zili Zhang	Deakin University, Australia
Dengji Zhao	ShanghaiTech University, China
Jennifer Zhao	CMIC, New Zealand
Yijing Zhao	Institute of Software, Chinese Academy of Sciences, China
Zhilin Zhao	Macquarie University, Australia
Xin Zhou	Nanyang Technological University, Singapore
Ye Zhou	Universiti Sains Malaysia, Malaysia
Guohun Zhu	University of Queensland, Australia
Liang Zhu	Hebei University, China
Nengjun Zhu	Shanghai University, China

Conference Organizing Committee

General Chairs

Takayuki Ito	Kyoto University, Japan
Quan Bai	University of Tasmania, Australia

Program Chairs

Rafik Hadfi	Kyoto University, Japan
Patricia Anthony	Lincoln University, New Zealand
Alok Sharma	RIKEN Center for Integrative Medical Sciences, Japan

Local Arrangements Chairs

Tokuro Matsuo	Advanced Institute of Industrial Technology, Japan
Shiyao Ding	Kyoto University, Japan

Jawad Haqbeen	Kyoto University, Japan
Shun Shiramatsu	Nagoya Institute of Technology, Japan

Publication Chair

Sofia Sahab	Kyoto University, Japan

Workshop Chairs

Takahiro Uchiya	Nagoya Institute of Technology, Japan
Yuncheng Jiang	South China Normal University, China

Tutorial Chairs

Wen Gu	Japan Advanced Institute of Science and Technology, Japan
Sankalp Khanna	CSIRO Australian e-Health Research Centre, Australia

Publicity Chairs

Thepchai Supnithi	NECTEC, Thailand
Jimmy Cao	University of South Australia, Australia
Shun Okuhara	Mie University, Japan

Sponsorship Chairs

Takayuki Ito	Kyoto University, Japan
Shohei Kato	Nagoya Institute of Technology, Japan

Student Sponsorship Committee

Quan Bai	University of Tasmania, Australia
Takayuki Ito	Kyoto University, Japan
Tokuro Matsuo	Advanced Institute of Industrial Technology, Japan

Advisory Committee

Abdul Sattar	Griffith University, Australia
Sankalp Khanna	CSIRO Australian e-Health Research Centre, Australia

Hideyuki Nakashima	Sapporo City University, Japan
Chengqi Zhang	UTS, Australia
Dickson Lukose	Tabcorp Holdings Ltd., Australia

PRICAI Steering Committee

Active Members

Quan Bai	University of Tasmania, Australia
Jian Cao	Shanghai Jiao Tong University, China
Tru Hoang Cao	University of Texas Health Science Center at Houston, USA
Xin Geng	Southeast University, China
Guido Governatori	Central Queensland University, Australia
Takayuki Ito	Kyoto University, Japan
Byeong-Ho Kang	University of Tasmania, Australia
M. G. M. Khan	University of the South Pacific, Fiji
Sankalp Khanna	CSIRO Australian e-Health Research Centre, Australia
Satoshi Kurihara	Keio University, Japan
Fenrong Liu	Tsinghua University, China
Dickson Lukose	Tabcorp Holdings Ltd., Australia
Hideyuki Nakashima	Sapporo City University, Japan
Abhaya Nayak	Macquarie University, Australia
Seong Bae Park	Kyung Hee University, South Korea
Duc Nghia Pham	Tabcorp Holdings Ltd., Australia
Hammam Riza	National Research and Innovation Agency (BRIN), Indonesia
Abdul Sattar	Griffith University, Australia
Alok Sharma	RIKEN Center for Integrative Medical Sciences, Japan
Thanaruk Theeramunkong	Thammasat University, Thailand
Guandong Xu	University of Technology Sydney, Australia
Zhi-Hua Zhou	Nanjing University, China

Honorary Members

Randy Goebel	University of Alberta, Canada
Tu-Bao Ho*	Advanced Institute of Science and Technology, Japan
Mitsuru Ishizuka*	University of Tokyo, Japan

Hiroshi Motoda*	Osaka University, Japan
Geoff Webb	Monash University, Australia
Albert Yeap	Auckland University of Technology, New Zealand
Byoung-Tak Zhang	Seoul National University, South Korea
Chengqi Zhang	University of Technology Sydney, Australia

* Emeritus Professor

Additional Reviewers

An, Yuexuan
Bali, Kavitesh
Bao, Qiming
Burigana, Alessandro
Cai, Songtao
Chandra, Abel
Chandra, Rohitash
Chang, Wui Lee
Chaw, Jun Kit
Chin, Kui Fern
Damigos, Matthew
Duan, Jinglong
Fan, Qinglan
Feng, Ji
Francis Lothai, Florence
Ge, Yaoxin
Han, Aiyang
Hanna, Bavly
Haruta, Shuichiro
He, Yifan
He, Yonghou
Jain, Manish
Jong, Chian Haur
Josling, Gabrielle
Jou, Jianhou
Kalogeros, Eleftherios
Khalid, Mohd Nor Akmal
Kojima, Ryoichi
Kok, Ven Jyn
Kongyoung, Sarawoot
Konishi, Tatsuya
Kumar, Dinesh
Kumar, Rahul

Lau, See Hung
Le, Hung
Li, Xiang
Li, Zhibin
Liang, Dong
Liang, Qin
Ling, Cheng
Liu, Dingbang
Liu, Yusen
Lopez, Yosvany
Ma, Jiaxue
Newton, M. A. Hakim
Nguyen, Van Tinh
Nguy~ên, Dũng
Ni, Haowei
Riahi, Vahid
Roy, Sudeshna
Shakeri, Ali
Shang, Junhui
Sharma, Priynka
Shi, Qiuying
Singh, Anuradha
Song, Xinwei
Su, Yuxin
Takeda, Naoto
Tan, Choo Jun
Tan, Hongwei
Tian, Jinyue
Tran, Anh Tu
Trung, Giang Thanh
Vaghjiani, Dr Khimji
Viriyavisuthisakul, Supatta
Wang, Mao

Wang, Minggang
Wang, Qinyu
Wang, Qiyang
Wang, Xinrui
Wang, Yunyun
Wang, Zhe
Wang, Ziyu
Wu, Tong
Wu, Weijie
Wu, Yixin
Xia, Yi
Xiaoqin, Tang
Yan, Jialiang
Yang, Lishan

Yang, Qianyi
Yang, Qikai
Yao, Naimeng
Ye, Xuesong
Yin, Yifan
Yuan, Minghuan
Yuhan, Zhao
Zhang, Junyu
Zhang, Justin
Zhao, Zhiguang
Zhao, Ziying
Zhao, Zuoyan
Zheng, Hui

Contents – Part I

Machine Learning

Quantitative Analysis of Training Methods, Data Size, and User-Specific
Effectiveness in DL-Based Personalized Aesthetic Evaluation 3
    Yoshia Abe, Tatsuya Daikoku, and Yasuo Kuniyoshi

EQUISCALE: Equitable Scaling for Abstention Learning 16
    Tejas Chaudhari and Naresh Manwani

Unsupervised Clustering Using a Variational Autoencoder
with Constrained Mixtures for Posterior and Prior 29
    Mashfiqul Huq Chowdhury, Yuichi Hirose, Stephen Marsland,
    and Yuan Yao

UTBoost: Gradient Boosted Decision Trees for Uplift Modeling 41
    Junjie Gao, Xiangyu Zheng, DongDong Wang, Zhixiang Huang,
    and Bangqi Zheng

CodeMosaic Patch: Physical Adversarial Attacks Against Infrared Aerial
Object Detectors 54
    Hangwei He, Libing Wu, Enshu Wang, Yizhou Wang, and Yu Zhao

Sequential Clustering for Real-World Datasets 69
    Chongwei Huang, Jian Hou, and Huaqiang Yuan

Dual-Mode Contrastive Learning-Enhanced Knowledge Tracing 81
    Danni Huang, Jicheng Yu, Shun Mao, Jiawei Li, and Yuncheng Jiang

Leveraging Information Consistency in Frequency and Spatial Domain
for Adversarial Attacks 93
    Zhibo Jin, Jiayu Zhang, Zhiyu Zhu, Xinyi Wang, Yiyun Huang,
    and Huaming Chen

Characterization of Similarity Metrics in Epistemic Logic 106
    Xiaolong Liang and Yì N. Wáng

A Relaxed Symmetric Non-negative Matrix Factorization Approach
for Community Discovery 119
    Zhigang Liu, Hao Yan, Yurong Zhong, and Weiling Li

Enhanced Cognitive Distortions Detection and Classification Through
Data Augmentation Techniques 134
    Mohamad Rasmy, Caroline Sabty, Nourhan Sakr, and Alia El Bolock

Enhancing Music Genre Classification Using Augmented Features
Ensemble Learning Technique 146
    Raad Shariat and John Z. Zhang

A Multi-layer Network Community Detection Method via Network
Feature Augmentation and Contrastive Learning 158
    Min Teng, Chao Gao, Zhen Wang, and Tanimoto Jun

Scene Text Recognition Based on Corner Point and Attention Mechanism 170
    Hui Wang, Tao Hu, Xiaoke Geng, and Kai Li

A Comprehensive Framework for Debiased Sample Selection Across All
Noise Types 182
    Naihao Wang and Ruirui Li

A Traffic Flow Prediction Model Integrating Dynamic Implicit Graph
Information 194
    You Wu, Jingfeng Guo, Xiao Chen, Xiao Pan, and Bin Liu

A Recursive Learning Algorithm for the Least Squares SVM 209
    Xiao-Lei Xia and Mingxing Ouyang

BDEL: A Backdoor Attack Defense Method Based on Ensemble Learning 221
    *Zhihuan Xing, Yuqing Lan, Yin Yu, Yong Cao, Xiaoyi Yang, Yichun Yu,
    and Dan Yu*

Customizing Spatial-Temporal Graph Mamba Networks for Pandemic
Forecasting 236
    Haowei Xu, Chao Gao, Xianghua Li, Zhen Wang, and Tanimoto Jun

Distribution-Aligned Sequential Counterfactual Explanation with Local
Outlier Factor 243
    *Shoki Yamao, Ken Kobayashi, Kentaro Kanamori, Takuya Takagi,
    Yuichi Ike, and Kazuhide Nakata*

T-FIA: Temporal-Frequency Interactive Attention Network for Long-Term
Time Series Forecasting 257
    Haoning Yang, Yimin Wang, Yixi Wang, and Jun Chen

Multi-modal Food Recommendation Using Clustering and Self-supervised
Learning 269
  Yixin Zhang, Xin Zhou, Qianwen Meng, Fanglin Zhu, Yonghui Xu,
  Zhiqi Shen, and Lizhen Cui

A Quality Assessment Method of Few-Shot Datasets Based on the Fusion
of Quantity and Quality 282
  Zhengchao Zhang, Lianke Zhou, Junzheng Sun, and Nianbin Wang

Deep Learning

CSDCNet: A Semantic Segmentation Network for Tubular Structures 297
  Feiyang Dong, Jizhong Jin, Lei Li, Heyang Li, and Yucheng Zhang

Neural Network Surrogate Based on Binary Classification for Assisting
Genetic Programming in Searching Scheduling Heuristic 309
  Ruiqi Chen, Yi Mei, Fangfang Zhang, and Mengjie Zhang

HN-Darts:Hybrid Network Differentiable Architecture Search
for Industrial Scenarios 322
  Jie Li, Yuxia Wang, Yifan Wang, Ruiyun Yu, and Xingwei Wang

High-Order Structure Enhanced Graph Clustering Network 328
  Yangfan Zhang and Bing Guo

CAFGO: Confidence-Adaptive Factor Graph Optimization Algorithm
for Fusion Localization 341
  Fan Wu, Zineng Zhou, Haiyong Luo, Fang Zhao, and Bo Zhou

MFNAS: Multi-fidelity Exploration in Neural Architecture Search
with Stable Zero-Shot Proxy 348
  Wei Fu, Wenqi Lou, Yunji Qin, Lei Gong, Chao Wang, and Xuehai Zhou

DyAGL: A Dynamic-Aware Adaptive Graph Learning Network for Next
POI Recommendation 361
  Tianci Wang, Yantong Lai, Yiyuan Wang, and Ji Xiang

Acoustic Classification of Bird Species Using Improved Pre-trained Models ... 375
  Jie Xie, Mingying Zhu, and Juan Gabriel Colonna

Aspect Term Extraction via Dynamic Attention and a Densely Connected
Graph Convolutional Network 383
  Xin Sun, Yongqing Mi, Jia Liu, and Hongao Li

NLDF: Neural Light Dynamic Fields for 3D Talking Head Generation 396
  Guanchen Niu, Songsong Cheng, and Teng Li

Enhanced Knowledge Tracing via Frequency Integration and Order
Sensitivity 403
  Songtao Cai and Li Li

Position-Aware Dynamic Graph Convolutional Recurrent Network
for Traffic Forecasting 416
  Rui Mao, Xufei Zhuang, Xudong Gao, Haitao Zhang,
  Qing-Dao-Er-Ji Ren, Bao Shi, Yatu Ji, and Nier Wu

Pose Preserving Landmark Guided Neural Radiation Fields for Talking
Portrait Synthesis 429
  Zhen Xiong, Haozhi Huang, Jundong Tan, and Guanghua Yang

Adaptive Optimisation of PyTorch Memory Pools for DNNs 441
  Leilei Li, Jun Luo, Pan Dong, Xiaoxiang Fang, Axin Yu, and Zhe Jiang

Detaching Range from Depth: Personalized Recommendation Meets
Personalized PageRank 454
  Jiahui Hu, Jie Xu, Jiakun Chen, Liqiang Qiao, Jilu Wang,
  Feiran Huang, and Chaozhuo Li

Context-Aware Structural Adaptive Graph Neural Networks 467
  Jiakun Chen, Jie Xu, Jiahui Hu, Liqiang Qiao, Shuo Wang,
  Feiran Huang, and Chaozhuo Li

multi-GAT: Integrative Analysis of scRNA-seq and scATAC-seq Data
Using Graph Attention Networks for Cell Annotation 480
  Shangru Jia, Tatsuhiko Tsunoda, and Alok Sharma

Author Index 487

Machine Learning

Quantitative Analysis of Training Methods, Data Size, and User-Specific Effectiveness in DL-Based Personalized Aesthetic Evaluation

Yoshia Abe[(⊠)][iD], Tatsuya Daikoku[iD], and Yasuo Kuniyoshi[iD]

The University of Tokyo, Tokyo, Japan
`{y-abe,daikoku,kuniyosh}@isi.imi.i.u-tokyo.ac.jp`

Abstract. The perception of beauty is a highly subjective phenomenon that varies among individuals. In the past decade, advancements in deep learning technologies have led to numerous studies proposing AI models capable of predicting human aesthetic evaluations of images. Furthermore, several of these studies have focused on personalizing AI models for specific individuals. However, there have been challenges in collecting sufficient data required for deep learning. Recently, a large-scale image dataset for individual aesthetic evaluation has been proposed, enabling the quantitative analysis of the performance of deep learning-based personalized prediction models. The present study addresses this issue by focusing on training methods, data size, and effectiveness for individuals with different characteristics. The results demonstrate both the effectiveness and limitations of current deep learning-based training methods. Additionally, the analysis reveals the potential of AI as a promising entity that can deeply understand an individual's aesthetic preferences. This study provides valuable insights and suggestions for developing superior personalized aesthetic evaluation models.

Keywords: Aesthetic Evaluation · Personalization · Deep Learning

1 Introduction

To what extent can Artificial Intelligence (AI) learn human aesthetic evaluations? In the past decade, numerous methods have been proposed for predicting aesthetic evaluations of images rated by human raters based on deep learning (DL) technologies [2,10]. Typically, these methods aim to predict the average score given by multiple raters for a particular image, a task known as Generic Image Aesthetics Assessment (GIAA) [7].

However, the perception of beauty is a highly subjective phenomenon that varies among individuals. Utilizing the average score of the public's aesthetic evaluations risks discarding the important aspect of individual differences in aesthetic experience. Consequently, recent research has emerged that addresses

R. Hadfi et al. (Eds.): PRICAI 2024, LNAI 15281, pp. 3–15, 2025.
https://doi.org/10.1007/978-981-96-0116-5_1

the task of learning the aesthetic evaluations of specific individuals, known as Personalized Image Aesthetics Assessment (PIAA) [7].

Obtaining the large amount of training data required for deep learning from specific individuals (referred to hereafter as users) has been challenging. Therefore, various strategies have been proposed to overcome this issue. Recently, a large-scale PIAA dataset named Personalized image Aesthetics database with Rich Attributes (PARA) [11] has been proposed, which collects aesthetic evaluations for thousands of images per individual and includes rich information about personal attributes. By utilizing this extensive dataset, this study quantitatively evaluates previously unexplored aspects of training methods, data size, and the effectiveness for users with different characteristics in the domain of deep learning technology for the PIAA task.

The contributions of this paper are as follows:

1. Compare PIAA training methods under unified experimental conditions.
2. Quantitatively investigate the data size required per user for PIAA training.
3. Quantitatively analyze whether the effectiveness of PIAA training varies based on individual user attributes.
4. Demonstrate the potential of AI as a promising entity for deeply understanding personal aesthetic evaluations by comparing the predictive accuracy of DL models with the evaluation discrepancies among users.

2   Related Works

Numerous studies have attempted to enable machines to learn human visual aesthetic evaluations. Historically, various approaches have been proposed, ranging from manually designing image features to using classical machine learning methods [2,10]. About a decade ago, with the widespread adoption of deep learning technologies, research began to emerge on learning aesthetic evaluations using neural networks [5]. These studies have been supported by the proposals of large-scale datasets crucial for deep learning. AVA [8] is one of the most famous datasets in this domain.

Most of these studies deal with tasks of predicting the average aesthetic evaluation score given by multiple raters for a particular image, known as GIAA tasks. However, it is known that human aesthetic evaluations differ significantly from the average behavior derived from multiple others' evaluations [4,9,10,12]. Consequently, recent research has begun to address the task of learning the aesthetic evaluations of specific individuals, known as the PIAA task.

In PIAA tasks, there is a challenge of obtaining large amounts of aesthetic evaluation data from specific individuals. For example, the PIAA datasets used in [12] (FLICKR-AES [9], AADB [6], REAL-CUR [9]) contained up to about 200 evaluations per individual at most. Various methods have been devised to overcome this limitation. For example, a method has been developed that trains both a predictor for the average evaluation score and a predictor for the personal attributes of individuals, and integrates them by fine-tuning with a small amount of individual evaluation data [7]. Additionally, there are methods that infer aesthetic evaluations from individual behavior on social media platforms

[1], or predict the difference between the average evaluation scores and personal evaluation scores using a Support Vector Regressor [9]. These studies address the issue of insufficient training data required for deep learning by using inferred individual attribute information, alternative evaluations of aesthetics, or classical machine learning methods.

Recently, a large-scale PIAA dataset named PARA [11] has been proposed, which collects aesthetic evaluations for thousands of images per individual and includes rich information about personal and image attributes. Using PARA, it has become possible to quantitatively analyze DL-based methods for the PIAA task, which previously could not be conducted due to data limitations. Therefore, this study aims to quantitatively evaluate the effectiveness of learning methods, data size, and the influence of characteristics of target users in the domain of deep learning technology for the PIAA task by adopting this extensive dataset.

3   Methods

3.1   Datasets for the GIAA Task and the PIAA Task

In this experiment, we use the PARA dataset [11], which contains aesthetic evaluation scores for 31220 photograph images provided by 438 users. Each user has provided information on personal characteristics such as age, gender, education level, experience level in photography and art, and Big-Five personality traits. For experience level in photography and art, users choose from one of four levels: Beginner, Competent, Proficient, and Expert. The photographs are categorized into ten semantic categories: Animal, Building, Food, Indoor, Night Scene, Plant, Portrait, Scene, Still Life, and Others. The aesthetic evaluation scores range from 1.0 to 5.0 in increments of 0.5. Details on the annotation method can be found in [11].

In the experiments, the model will be trained for two tasks: the GIAA task, which involves predicting the average aesthetic evaluation score across multiple users, and the PIAA task, which involves predicting the aesthetic evaluation score for each individual user. In the PARA dataset, 283, 202, and 125 users have evaluated more than 1000, 2000, and 3000 images, respectively. Since deep learning methods benefit from large amounts of training data, we focus on users who have evaluated more than 3000 images as the target users in the PIAA task. This criterion allows us to select a subset of 125 users out of 438 users.

In this paper, we will refer to the dataset where the ground truth labels are the average aesthetic evaluation scores from multiple users as the GIAA dataset. Conversely, the dataset where the ground truth labels are the aesthetic evaluation scores from each of the 125 users will be referred to as the PIAA dataset. Since the PIAA dataset is a subset of the GIAA dataset, there may be overlap in the images used, but the ground truth labels are different.

3.2   Training Methods for the PIAA Task

For the PIAA task of predicting the aesthetic evaluation scores rated by a specific user (referred to here as User A), various methods can be considered. Based on

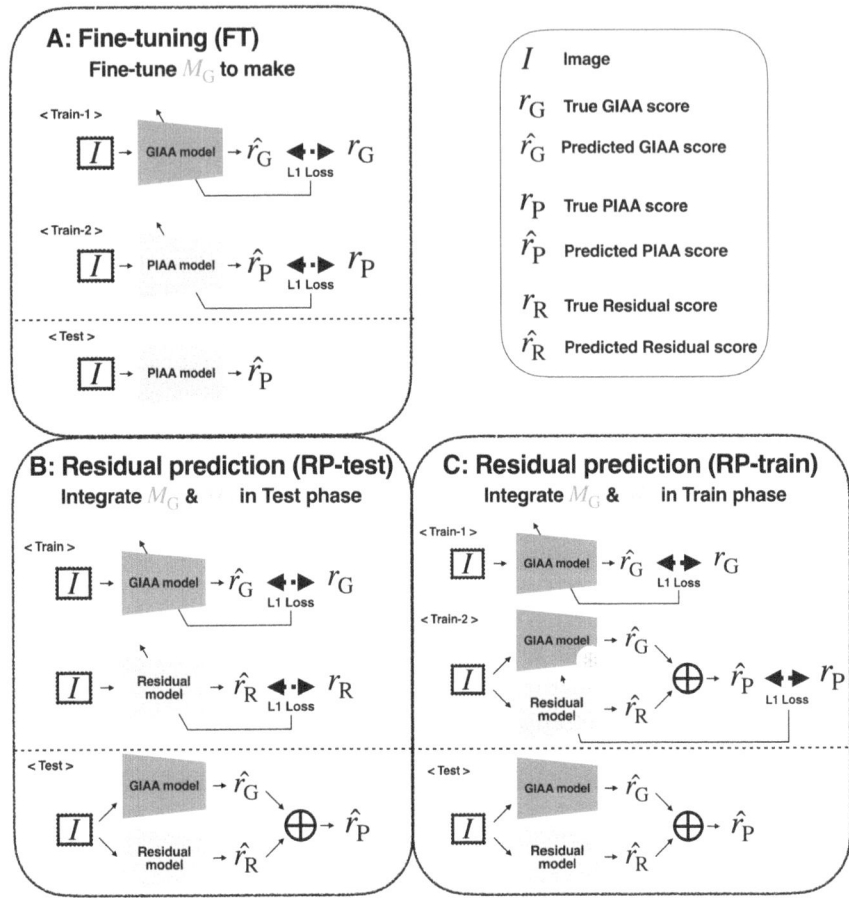

Fig. 1. The diagram of PIAA training method A, B, and C.

these, this experiment examines three methods: Method A: Fine-tuning (FT), Method B: Residual Prediction (RP-test), Method C: Residual Prediction (RP-train) (see Fig. 1). Method A is based on [11], and Method B and C are based on [9]. In this experiment, we refer to neural networks trained with GIAA scores, PIAA scores, and Residual scores (details provided later) as GIAA models, PIAA models, and Residual models, respectively. The final model obtained by using the PIAA model or integrating the GIAA model and the Residual model to predict a specific user's PIAA score is referred to as the User model (the structure below the dotted lines in the blocks of each method in Fig. 1 corresponds to it).

Method A: Fine-tuning (FT) involves first training a GIAA model using the GIAA dataset and then fine-tuning it with User A's PIAA dataset to obtain a PIAA model.

Method B: Residual Prediction (RP-test) involves the following approach. Given the average aesthetic evaluation scores from multiple users for each image in the individual's PIAA dataset, the differences (referred to as Residual scores) are computed. For each image, let r_G be the average aesthetic evaluation score from multiple users, and r_P be the aesthetic evaluation score assigned by User A. The Residual score is calculated as $r_R = r_P - r_G$. This Residual score serves as the target label, and the objective function during training minimizes the error between the true Residual score r_R and the predicted Residual score $\hat{r_R}$. At test time, the predicted aesthetic evaluation score for User A is obtained by summing the predicted Residual score $\hat{r_R}$ from the trained Residual model with the predicted average score $\hat{r_G}$ from the GIAA model trained on the GIAA dataset ($\hat{r_P} = \hat{r_G} + \hat{r_R}$).

Method C: Residual Prediction (RP-train) also uses separate GIAA and Residual models like Method B. However, the target label during training differs: this method uses User A's aesthetic evaluation score r_P as the target label. Specifically, during training, the sum of the predictions from the GIAA model and the Residual model ($\hat{r_P} = \hat{r_G} + \hat{r_R}$) is compared against r_P in the objective function. During this training phase, the weights of the GIAA model are kept frozen. The difference between Methods B and C lies in their training approach. Method B separately trains the GIAA model and the Residual model, which may simplify training but may accumulate errors from both models during test time. In contrast, Method C, although more complex in its training structure and processing, trains the Residual model in consideration of the GIAA model's behavior, potentially absorbing errors from the GIAA model.

3.3   Experimental Conditions

In all three methods A, B, and C, the GIAA models and Residual models are fine-tuned from ResNet-50 pre-trained on the ImageNet dataset [3]. The output of the final layer is adjusted to a single dimension for score output.

The GIAA and PIAA scores range from 1 to 5, and the Residual score ranges from -4 to 4. When used as ground truth labels for error calculation, these scores are normalized to a range from 0 to 1. The loss function used for training is L1 loss, and the optimizer is Adam with a learning rate set to 0.0001. Early stopping is employed during training, halting the process if the validation loss does not improve for 5 epochs.

In the GIAA dataset, 3000 images are fixed as the test set, while the remaining 28220 images are randomly split into 22576 images for training and 5644 images for validation in an 8:2 ratio. In the PIAA dataset, the total number of images varies for each user (all having at least 3000 images), but the ratio of images for training, validation, and testing is fixed at 8:1:1.

The training algorithm follows Algorithm 1. Let u_i denote the users, where $i = 1, 2, \ldots, 125$. Let D_G be the GIAA dataset, and $D_{P,i}$ be the PIAA dataset for user u_i. We denote M_G as the GIAA model, $M_{P,i}$ as the PIAA model for user u_i, $M_{R,i}$ as the Residual model for user u_i, and $M_{U,i}$ as the User model for user u_i. To account for variability due to random initialization, trainings and evaluations are performed with 5 different seeds.

Algorithm 1. Training and Evaluation of User Models

1: **procedure** TRAINING PHASE
2:      Train M_G using D_G.
3:      **for** $i = 1$ to 125 **do**
4:          Train $M_{\mathrm{P},i}$ or $M_{\mathrm{R},i}$ using $D_{\mathrm{P},i}$.   *
5:      **end for**
6: **end procedure**
7: **procedure** TESTING PHASE
8:      **for** $i = 1$ to 125 **do**
9:          Make $M_{\mathrm{U},i}$ by integrating M_G, $M_{\mathrm{P},i}$, or $M_{\mathrm{R},i}$.   *
10:          Evaluate the performance of $M_{\mathrm{U},i}$ on $D_{\mathrm{P},i}$.
11:      **end for**
12: **end procedure**

* The method selection (A, B, or C) affects how $M_{\mathrm{P},i}$ and $M_{\mathrm{R},i}$ are trained and how they are integrated into $M_{\mathrm{U},i}$.

---

4 Experiments and Results

4.1 Exp. 1: Comparison of Training Methods

In this Sect. 4.1, we quantitatively evaluate which of the learning methods A, B, and C is the most effective under consistent experimental conditions.

Methods. The trained User model's PIAA performance is measured using the mean absolute error (MAE) and the coefficient of determination (R^2) on the test set of each user's PIAA dataset. These two metrics are averaged across the 125 users within each seed and then averaged across the 5 seeds.

The MAE value is calculated as follows, where N_P is the number of images in the test data, $\hat{r_{\mathrm{P},n}}$ is the predicted score by the model, and $r_{\mathrm{P},n}$ is the ground truth label: $\mathrm{MAE} = \frac{1}{N_\mathrm{P}} \sum_{n=1}^{N_\mathrm{P}} |\hat{r_{\mathrm{P},n}} - r_{\mathrm{P},n}|$

The R^2 value ranges from 1 or below, where a value closer to 1 indicates better performance of the prediction model, and a value of 0 signifies that the model's performance is equivalent to predicting the mean of the ground truth labels. The R^2 value is calculated as follows, where $\bar{r_\mathrm{P}}$ is the mean of the ground truth labels: $R^2 = 1 - \sum_{n=1}^{N_\mathrm{P}} (r_{\mathrm{P},n} - \hat{r_{\mathrm{P},n}})^2 / \sum_{n=1}^{N_\mathrm{P}} (r_{\mathrm{P},n} - \bar{r_\mathrm{P}})^2$.

Results. The average PIAA performance for each method A, B, and C is shown in Fig. 2. From this result, it is evident that Method A: Fine-tuning (FT) is more effective than separately learning the Residual score. A paired t-test was conducted to compare Method A with B and A with C, in terms of MAE, at a significance level of 0.05. The resulting p-values were 5.81×10^{-7} and 1.08×10^{-6}, respectively, indicating that Method A performs significantly better than both Method B and C.

Possible reasons for this outcome are that learning individual aesthetic evaluations benefits from the insights gained from learning public aesthetic evaluations. For example, the focus points acquired during the GIAA training can be directly utilized in PIAA training. Also, learning Residual scores might be challenging, especially with only 3000 PIAA data points.

Additionally, as shown in Fig. 2, contrary to expectations, Method B outperforms Method C. A paired t-test was conducted to compare them, in terms of MAE, at a significance level of 0.05. The resulting p-value was 2.95×10^{-4}, indicating that Method B performs significantly better than Method C. The instability in the GIAA model outputs might have negatively impacted the learning of the Residual model in Method C.

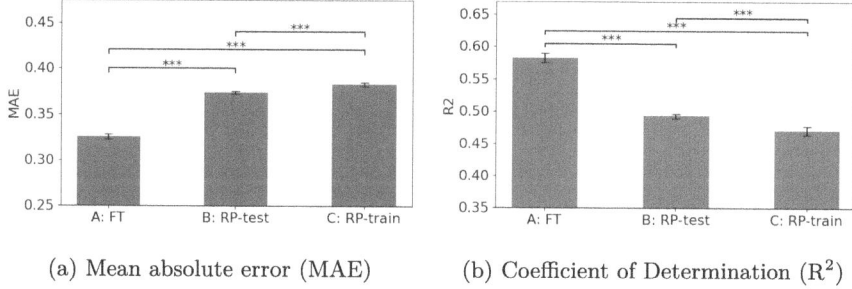

(a) Mean absolute error (MAE)   (b) Coefficient of Determination (R^2)

Fig. 2. The result of comparison of method A, B, and C. The bars represent the mean values across the 5 seeds, and the error bars indicate the interval of 1 standard deviation. *** indicates $p < 0.001$ from paird t-tests between methods.

4.2 Exp. 2: Comparison of Data Size for PIAA Training

In this Sect. 4.2, we investigate how the performance of PIAA degrades when the number of images used for PIAA training is restricted. This analysis provides valuable insights for the PIAA task, where collecting data is challenging.

Methods. We restrict the number of images used from each user's PIAA dataset N_P. We use eight cases ($N_P = 10, 25, 50, 100, 250, 500, 1000, 2000$). The images are divided into training, validation, and test sets with a ratio of 8:1:1. The training method adopted is Method A (Fine-tuning).

Results. The average PIAA performance for different numbers of images N_P is shown in Fig. 3. The results indicate that as N_P decreases, the PIAA performance degrades. When N_P is 50, the R^2 value drops to around 0, indicating performance comparable to predicting the mean value.

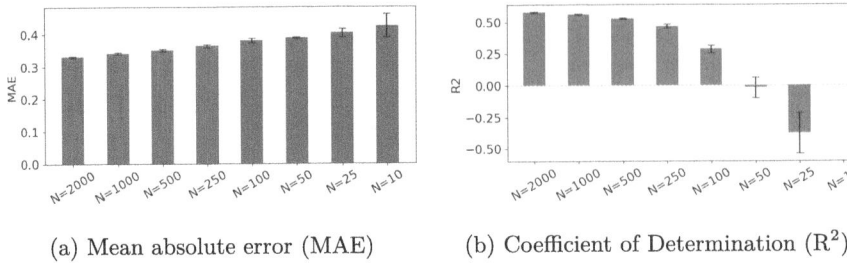

(a) Mean absolute error (MAE)   (b) Coefficient of Determination (R^2)

Fig. 3. The result of comparison of PIAA dataset size N_P. The bars represent the mean values across the 5 seeds, and the error bars indicate the interval of 1 standard deviation. Since the test set for $N_P = 10$ contains only a single image, the R^2 value cannot be calculated; therefore no plot is presented for this case.

Additionally, in Fig. 4, we plotted the PIAA performance of the User model on each user's PIAA test dataset with green bars, along with the PIAA performance of the GIAA model on the same PIAA test datasets with blue bars. The only difference between the experimental conditions is the number of images in the PIAA dataset N_P, while the number of images in the GIAA dataset remains constant. Therefore, the performance of the GIAA model on the PIAA dataset shows little variation. (However, the variance increases due to the number of images used for evaluation N_P decreasing.) When N_P decreases, the PIAA performance converges to that of the GIAA model, meaning that the performance becomes similar to the scenario where no individual-specific training is performed.

These results suggest that to gain any benefit from PIAA training, at least 50 to 100 images are needed. Furthermore, the more images used, the better the PIAA performance becomes. The likely causes of these results include the difficulty in obtaining sufficient information for effective PIAA training, and the negative impact on early stopping decisions due to validation instability when N_P is too small.

4.3   Exp. 3: Experience Level and Effectiveness of PIAA Training

In this Sect. 4.3, we investigate whether the effectiveness of PIAA training varies according to the characteristics of the target users, particularly their experience level in photography and art. Insights from this analysis could help make PIAA models to better suit individual user profiles based on their expertise.

PARA dataset includes information on each user's experience level in photography and art. The number of users in each experience level among the 125 users is as follows: Beginner: 42/ Competent: 42/ Proficient: 39/ Expert: 2 for photography, and Beginner: 44/ Competent: 38/ Proficient: 30/ Expert: 13 for art. For these users, we apply Method A (Fine-tuning) for PIAA training. In this experiment, the experience levels are converted into intensity indices for the analysis (Beginner: 1, Competent: 2, Proficient: 3, Expert: 4).

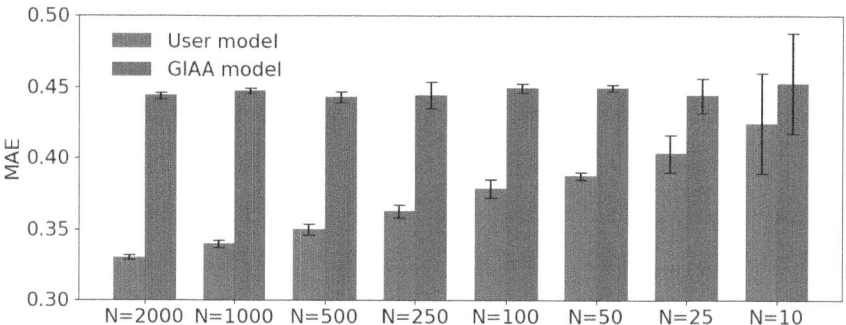

Fig. 4. PIAA performances of User models and GIAA models. The bars represent the mean values across the 5 seeds, and the error bars indicate the interval of 1 standard deviation.

Preliminary Analysis. For each of the 125 users selected in this experiment, we calculated the mean GIAA score, PIAA score, and Residual score across the more than 3000 images they evaluated. Then we tested for correlations between these mean GIAA/PIAA/Residual scores and the users' experience levels, using Spearman's rank correlation test (significance level 0.05), but no significant correlations were found. This indicates that differences in experience levels do not lead to significant variations in the aesthetic evaluation scores themselves, at least when averaged across images.

Methods. We define a metric called Effectiveness as follows. For a user $u_i (i = 1, 2, \ldots, 125)$, we use the GIAA model M_G, trained with GIAA dataset D_G to evaluate the test loss $l_{P,i}$ on the PIAA dataset $D_{P,i}$ before starting PIAA training. Then, after completing the PIAA training, we evaluate the test loss $L_{P,i}$ of the resulting PIAA model $M_{P,i}$ on the same PIAA dataset $D_{P,i}$. The Effectiveness E_i is defined as the improvement in PIAA performance $l_{P,i} - L_{P,i}$ relative to the initial test loss $l_{P,i}$: $E_i = (l_{P,i} - L_{P,i})/l_{P,i}$.

Results. The Effectiveness of PIAA training based on differences in experience levels in photography and art is shown in Fig. 5. Spearman's rank correlation test (significance level 0.05) was conducted. For photography experience, the p-value was 0.045, indicating a significant correlation, while for art experience, the p-value was 0.134, indicating no significant correlation.

As described above, while no correlation was found between experience levels and the Residual scores, a correlation was observed between experience levels in photography and the Effectiveness values of PIAA training. This indicates that although differences in experience levels in photography do not affect the aesthetic evaluation scores themselves, they do influence the ease of learning the aesthetic evaluations.

4.4   Exp. 4: Proximity Between Models and Users

How well do the User models understand the aesthetic evaluation tendencies of the target users? In this Sect. 4.4, we compare the distance between the trained User models and the target users with the distance between the target users and other users.

Methods. For each of the 125 target users, we calculate the following metrics:

$d_{U,M}$: The distance between the target user's actual aesthetic evaluations and those predicted by the User model; this is measured by averaging the MAE scores of the User model across five different seeds.

$d_{U,U}$: The distance between the target user's aesthetic evaluations and those of other users. For example, for two users u_1 and u_2 who have both evaluated N_{u_1,u_2} overlapping images, the distance is calculated as the average of the absolute error in their evaluations across these N_{u_1,u_2} images.

Results. As a representative example, the plot comparing the two distances $d_{U,M}$ and $d_{U,U}$ for a user A2ce68c is shown in Fig. 6. The black dashed line represents $d_{U,M}$ while the light blue to blue bar graphs represent $d_{U,U}$ between the user A2ce68c and the other 124 users. The color intensity of the bars indicates the number of overlapping images N_{u_1,u_2}. The graph shows that for the user A2ce68c, the User model's aesthetic evaluation tendency is closer to his/her own than those of any of the other 124 users.

To ensure fairness in comparison, we excluded user pairs with fewer than 200 overlapping images N_{u_1,u_2} and performed the same comparison as described above. As a result, for 84 out of the 125 users, the User model demonstrated aesthetic evaluation tendencies closer to each user's own than those of any other user. (More than 100 other users remained as comparison subjects for each user.)

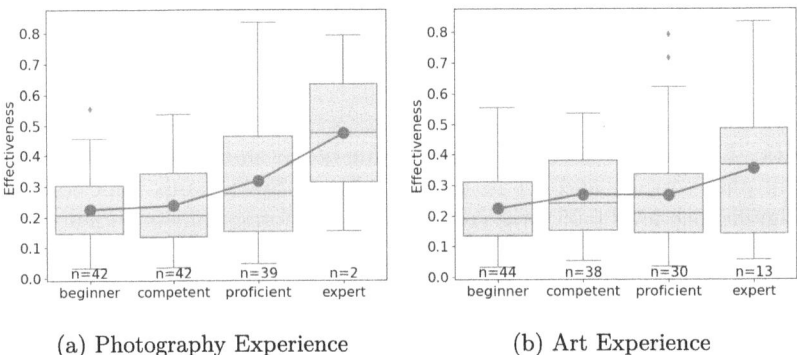

(a) Photography Experience   (b) Art Experience

Fig. 5. Box plots showing relationship between experience level and effectiveness. The whiskers extend 1.5 times the interquartile range from the quartiles, with outliers shown as black diamonds. The red circles indicate mean values. (Color figure online)

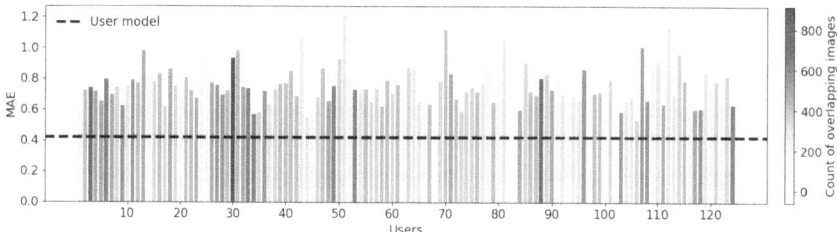

Fig. 6. Comparison of $d_{U,M}$ and $d_{U,U}$ for User A2ce68c.

5   Discussion and Conclusion

In this study, we quantitatively investigated the performance of PIAA models based on deep learning using the large-scale PARA dataset.

Exp. 1 demonstrated that, when there is a sufficiently large PIAA dataset per user, fine-tuning a GIAA model into a PIAA model yields better PIAA performance than training a separate Residual model. In this experiment, the Residual model was fine-tuned from a ResNet-50 model, but it may be worth investigating whether fine-tuning the Residual model from a GIAA model might improve its predictive performance in future work.

Exp. 2 compared the PIAA performance for the different sizes of the PIAA dataset per user. The results showed that PIAA performance deteriorates as the number of images decreases, with the determination coefficient dropping to 0 around the range of 50 to 100 images. This suggests that at least a few hundred images are required, and the more images there are, the better. However, even with 2000 images per user, the MAE remains above 0.3 on a scale of 1 to 5 points, indicating that further improvements are necessary to close this gap.

Exp. 3 examined whether the effectiveness of PIAA training varies according to the user's characteristics, particularly their level of experience in photography and art. It was found that the effectiveness of PIAA training increases with higher levels of experience in photography. This suggests that people with less experience in photography may have lower consistency in their aesthetic evaluations, while those with higher experience tend to have more consistency, possibly due to the formation of specific focal points or evaluation criteria. This aligns with the understanding that differences in experience lead to variations in aesthetic evaluation behaviors [10]. Although no correlation was found between the effectiveness score and art experience, this could be attributed to the fact that the PARA dataset consists of photography images rather than art images. Therefore, the possibility that the effectiveness of training using a dataset of art images might be correlated with art experience is not ruled out. This finding suggests the importance of considering the target user's characteristics as in [7,11]. Developing effective methods for it should be addressed in future work.

Exp. 4 investigated how well the User model, which learned the user's aesthetic evaluations, performed compared to the deviations in aesthetic evaluations between the user and others. For 84 out of 125 target users, the User model's aesthetic evaluation tendencies were closer to their own than to those of any other user. Humans have strong subjective aspects based on knowledge, emotions, and physicality that may hinder deep mutual understanding of aesthetic tastes. In contrast, AI initially does not have these subjective aspects. Therefore, by effectively reproducing the target user's subjective aspects, AI could become the entity that understands the user's aesthetic preferences most deeply.

In this study, we used models that predict individual aesthetic evaluations based only on image inputs. However, factors such as the individual's personality traits, emotional responses, and physical reactions likely play a role in shaping their aesthetic perception. Therefore, it may be necessary to develop predictive models that incorporate such information, for example, through conditioning. Additionally, investigating the internal responses of the trained models could provide valuable insights into the relationship between PIAA predictions and image features, as well as between focal points and individuals' characteristics.

In conclusion, this study conducted a quantitative analysis of training deep learning-based models for the Personalized Image Aesthetics Assessment (PIAA) task and provided insights and suggestions for improvement, highlighting the importance of user-specific training. These findings could be valuable for developing superior personalized aesthetic evaluation models in the future.

Acknowledgments. This research was supported by Next Generation AI Research Center of The University of Tokyo and JST SPRING GX project (Grant Number JPMJSP2108).

Disclosure of Interests. The authors have no competing interests to declare that are relevant to the content of this article.

References

1. Cui, C., Yang, W., Shi, C., Wang, M., Nie, X., Yin, Y.: Personalized image quality assessment with social-sensed aesthetic preference. Inf. Sci. **512**, 780–794 (2020)
2. Deng, Y., Loy, C.C., Tang, X.: Image aesthetic assessment: an experimental survey. IEEE Signal Process. Mag. **34**(4), 80–106 (2017)
3. He, K., Zhang, X., Ren, S., Sun, J.: Deep residual learning for image recognition (2015). arXiv:1512.03385
4. Iigaya, K., Yi, S., Wahle, I.A., Tanwisuth, K., O'Doherty, J.P.: Aesthetic preference for art can be predicted from a mixture of low- and high-level visual features. Nat. Hum. Behav. **5**(6), 743–755 (2021)
5. Kao, Y., Wang, C., Huang, K.: Visual aesthetic quality assessment with a regression model. In: 2015 IEEE International Conference on Image Processing, pp. 1583–1587 (2015)
6. Kong, S., Shen, X., Lin, Z., Mech, R., Fowlkes, C.: Photo aesthetics ranking network with attributes and content adaptation. In: Leibe, B., Matas, J., Sebe, N., Welling, M. (eds.) ECCV 2016. LNCS, vol. 9905, pp. 662–679. Springer, Cham (2016). https://doi.org/10.1007/978-3-319-46448-0_40

7. Li, L., Zhu, H., Zhao, S., Ding, G., Lin, W.: Personality-assisted multi-task learning for generic and personalized image aesthetics assessment. IEEE Trans. Image Process. **29**, 3898–3910 (2020)
8. Murray, N., Marchesotti, L., Perronnin, F.: AVA: a large-scale database for aesthetic visual analysis. In: 2012 IEEE Conference on Computer Vision and Pattern Recognition, pp. 2408–2415 (2012)
9. Ren, J., Shen, X., Lin, Z., Mech, R., Foran, D.J.: Personalized image aesthetics. In: Proceedings of the IEEE International Conference on Computer Vision (2017)
10. Valenzise, G., Kang, C., Dufaux, F.: Advances and challenges in computational image aesthetics. In: Ionescu, B., Bainbridge, W.A., Murray, N. (eds.) Human Perception of Visual Information, pp. 133–181. Springer, Cham (2022). https://doi.org/10.1007/978-3-030-81465-6_6
11. Yang, Y., et al.: Personalized image aesthetics assessment with rich attributes. In: Proceedings of the IEEE/CVF Conference on Computer Vision and Pattern Recognition, pp. 19861–19869 (2022)
12. Zhu, H., Li, L., Wu, J., Zhao, S., Ding, G., Shi, G.: Personalized image aesthetics assessment via meta-learning with bilevel gradient optimization. IEEE Trans. Cybern. **52**(3), 1798–1811 (2022)

EQUISCALE: Equitable Scaling for Abstention Learning

Tejas Chaudhari$^{(\boxtimes)}$ and Naresh Manwani

International Institute of Information Technology, Hyderabad, Hyderabad, India
tejas.chaudhari@research.iiit.ac.in, naresh.manwani@iiit.ac.in

Abstract. We propose an approach to train a fair cost-based abstain option classifier. Existing literature on fairness in classification with abstention is limited, covering only coverage-based abstention models. In coverage-based abstention models, the target coverage is decided beforehand and is kept the same for all the groups. In contrast, cost-based approaches introduce a cost for abstention, which can cause uneven abstention rates between different groups, leading to an unfair system. We extend the independence and separation fairness criteria to consider abstention. We provide a model-agnostic in-processing algorithm to incorporate these constraints in the models. We demonstrate the algorithm's efficacy by experimenting with two different cost-based abstain option classifiers. Additionally, we explore mixing constraints from independence and separation criteria into one model, which is impossible in a binary classification task.

Keywords: Fairness · Reject option classification

1 Introduction

Machine learning systems are used for decision making in various fields, such as job applications, judiciary, and healthcare systems. This high dependence on automation has led to concerns of unfairness and bias in the systems [6,15, 16,20]. Fairness in machine learning aims to remove this bias. Fairness criteria are broadly divided into two categories: individual fairness, which follows the paradigm of "similar individuals should receive similar treatments," and group fairness, which aims to remove disparities between different groups identified by specific sensitive attributes. We shall be dealing with group fairness in this paper. The research on fairness in abstain option classification is minimal. [11] showed that abstention can magnify group disparities by demonstrating that at lower coverage's the difference between the group's accuracies increases. [14] studied a closely related problem of fair learning to defer, where a decision maker is used to make decisions on abstained samples. [13] introduces an algorithm to train the sufficiency fairness criterion, which ensures the equality of GroupWise accuracy over all coverages.

© The Author(s), under exclusive license to Springer Nature Singapore Pte Ltd. 2025
R. Hadfi et al. (Eds.): PRICAI 2024, LNAI 15281, pp. 16–28, 2025.
https://doi.org/10.1007/978-981-96-0116-5_2

However, there are cases where the rejection rate of one group can be very high compared to the others. For example, suppose a medical diagnosis system abstains more for women than for men. In that case, women will have to wait longer to receive treatments, which can cause further complications [21], or judiciary systems where abstention translates to a longer custody time, which negatively affects black people [10]. [18] proposed an algorithm for the independence fairness criterion, which fixed an abstention rate for all groups and then constrained the positive rates to be equal for all groups. Note that both [13,18] are based on coverage-based abstention models, while our proposed approach is the **first algorithm to consider fairness in a cost-based abstention setting**. We make the following contributions in this paper (Table 1):

1. We introduce a simple approach for obtaining classwise prediction probabilities for confidence-based abstain option classifiers.
2. We propose fairness constraints for demographic parity and equalized odds in the context of abstain option classifiers.
3. We propose a model agnostic in-processing algorithm to learn a fair abstain option classifier using the fairness constraints.
4. We verify the models' performance based on accuracy and fairness metrics.
5. We extend a fairness impossibility theorem (both independence and separation cannot hold) from binary classification to binary classification with abstain option classification.
6. We explore mixing the constraints from the demographic parity and equalized odds constraints to obtain fair classifiers for mixed fairness constraints.

Table 1. Differences between existing approaches and our approach (EQUISCALE). DP and EO refer to demographic parity (independence fairness constraint) and equalized odds (separation fairness constraint). DP+EO refers to a combination of constraints from DP and EO.

Approach	Cost/Cov	In/Post	DP	EO	Sufficiency	DP+EO
DPABST [18]	Cov	Post	Yes	No	No	No
SUFSEL [13]	Cov	In	No	No	Yes	No
EQUISCALE	**Cost**	In	Yes	Yes	No	**Yes**

2 Related Work

2.1 Abstain Option Classifier

There are two broad categories of approaches for abstain/reject option classifiers: coverage-based and cost-based. In coverage based models such as [7,8], learning is based on optimizing risk-coverage trade-offs, and no cost is associated with abstaining. Meanwhile, cost-based approaches have a cost of abstention and the model learns to minimize the cost incurred by abstention and misclassification.

Cost-based models are further divided into confidence-based and classifier-rejector methods. In a confidence-based approach, the classifier outputs a confidence value, and a threshold is learned to obtain the abstention region. [12] proposed a confidence-based approach for a deep neural network setting that can learn instance-dependent abstention thresholds. Classifier-rejector combines the rejector and predictor into a single model. [4] proposed consistent multiclass loss functions for the abstain option classifier, which can be used to form a surrogate loss function using certain calibrated loss functions and then treat the problem as learning a $k + 1$ class classifier.

2.2   Fairness in Machine Learning

Group fairness has three main criteria: independence, separation, and sufficiency. Independence criterion [3] requires the prediction to be independent of the sensitive attribute. Separation criterion [9] requires the prediction to be conditionally independent of the sensitive attribute when conditioned on the true label. Sufficiency criterion [5] requires the label to be conditionally independent of the sensitive attribute when conditioned on the prediction. Various constraints exist for each criteria, such as demographic parity and disparate impact for independence, equalized odds for separation, and calibration within groups for sufficiency. Various in-processing approaches exist for fair binary classification. [1] proposed a classifier agnostic approach. They reduced the optimization problem to a sequence of cost-sensitive classification problems based on the fairness criterion. A limitation of the proposed approach was that the fairness criterion needed to be linear inequalities. [17] introduced a general framework that could be used for any differentiable fairness constraint, including nonlinear constraints. They achieved this by framing the problem as a constrained optimization problem and then using Lagrange multipliers to solve it during training.

3   Preliminaries

3.1   Abstain Option Classifier

We consider the cost-based abstention in binary classification setting. The input space is $\mathcal{X} \subseteq \mathbb{R}^n$, the label space is $\mathcal{Y} = \{+1, -1\}$, the prediction space is $\hat{\mathcal{Y}} = \{+1, 0, -1\}$ where 0 denotes that the classifier has chosen to abstain from making a decision. The training set consists of N samples drawn i.i.d. from an unknown distribution on $\mathcal{X} \times \mathcal{Y}$. The performance is measured using the L_{0d1} loss, where d is the cost of abstention.

$$L_{0d1} = d * \mathbb{I}[\hat{Y} = 0] + \mathbb{I}[\hat{Y} \neq 0] \cdot \mathbb{I}[\hat{Y} \neq Y].$$

Confidence Based Method: We use the formulation from [12]. The classifier is modeled using a deep neural network having a single output node. The network output is a function $f : \mathcal{X} \times \Theta \to \mathbb{R}$, where Θ is the parameter space of the network. The abstention bandwidth $\rho \in \mathbb{R}_+$ is a learnable parameter. The final prediction is done as follows.

$$h(f(\mathbf{x}; \boldsymbol{\theta}), \rho) = 1 \, \mathbb{I}[f(\mathbf{x}) > \rho] \; + \; 0 \, \mathbb{I}[|f(\mathbf{x})| \leq \rho] \; - \; 1 \, \mathbb{I}[f(\mathbf{x}) < -\rho] \qquad (1)$$

where $\boldsymbol{\theta} \in \Theta$ represent network parameters. We use double sigmoid loss L_{ds} function [19] to train the classifier in a deep neural network setting. We represent the network output as $f(\mathbf{x}; \boldsymbol{\theta})$. Double sigmoid loss L_{ds}^ρ is computed as follows.

$$L_{ds}^\rho(f(\mathbf{x}; \boldsymbol{\theta}), y) = 2d\sigma(yf(\mathbf{x}; \boldsymbol{\theta}) - \rho) + 2(1 - d)\sigma(yf(\mathbf{x}; \boldsymbol{\theta}) + \rho) \qquad (2)$$

where $\sigma(a) = \frac{1}{1+e^{\gamma a}}$ and $\gamma > 0$. Double sigmoid loss is consistent with L_{0d1} [12].

Classifier-Rejector Method. In this method, rejection is considered as a new class [4] during the prediction. Thus, the classifier-rejector model outputs a function $f(\mathbf{x}; \boldsymbol{\theta}) \in \mathbb{R}^3$, where two outputs corresponding to each class and the third node is for rejection. The surrogate loss function $L_c^\phi : \mathbb{R}^3 \times \mathcal{Y} \to \mathbb{R}_+$ used in this classifier-rejector setting is described as follows.

$$L_c^\phi(f(\mathbf{x}; \boldsymbol{\theta}), y) = \phi(f(\mathbf{x}; \boldsymbol{\theta}), y) + (1 - d)\phi(f(\mathbf{x}; \boldsymbol{\theta}), \, 3) \qquad$$

where $\phi : \mathbb{R}^{k+1} \times \mathcal{Y} \cup \{3\} \to \mathbb{R}_+$. Here ϕ is a l_{01} calibrated loss as mentioned in [4]. We use the generalized cross entropy (GCE) as ϕ [4], defined as follows.

$$GCE(f(\mathbf{x}; \boldsymbol{\theta}), y) = (1 - S(f(\mathbf{x}; \boldsymbol{\theta}))_y^\gamma)/\gamma$$

Here, $\gamma \in (0, 1]$, S is the softmax transformation, and the subscript y indicates we are choosing the value corresponding to the correct label, similar to how cross-entropy works. Note that in GCE, the labels are expected to be $\tilde{\mathcal{Y}} = \{0, 1\}$. We transform labels $\mathcal{Y}$ to $\tilde{\mathcal{Y}}$ using the transformation $\tilde{\mathcal{Y}} = (1 + \mathcal{Y})/2$.

3.2   Fairness

There are two group fairness criteria we are going to focus on in this work: Independence and Separation. A classifier satisfies **independence** criteria [2] if the score is statistically independent of the sensitive attribute, i.e., $R \perp A$. A classifier satisfies **separation** criteria [2] if the score is statistically independent of the sensitive attribute given the target variable, i.e., $R \perp A|Y$. In the binary classification case, the Impossibility Theorem [2] states that independence and separation cannot be held together.

4   EQUISCALE: Proposed Approach

Here, we extend demographic parity (independence) and equalized odds (separation) to the binary classification with an abstention setting. We first require a score vector denoting the classwise prediction probabilities for a sample.

4.1   Outcome Score Vector

Let the outcome score vector be $\mathbf{r}(\mathbf{x}; \boldsymbol{\theta})$ such that $r_i = \mathbb{P}[\hat{Y} = i \mid \mathbf{x}]$ for $i \in \{+1, 0, -1\}$, and R_1, R_0, R_{-1} be the corresponding random variables.

Confidence Based Method: Given $f(\mathbf{x}; \boldsymbol{\theta})$ and ρ, we can define $r_i(\mathbf{x}; \boldsymbol{\theta})$, $i \in \{+1, 0, -1\}$ as follows.

$$r_{-1}(\mathbf{x}; \boldsymbol{\theta}) = \frac{e^{-f(\mathbf{x};\boldsymbol{\theta})-\rho}}{Z}, \quad r_0(\mathbf{x}; \boldsymbol{\theta}) = \frac{e^{\rho-|f(\mathbf{x};\boldsymbol{\theta})|}}{Z}, \quad r_1(\mathbf{x}; \boldsymbol{\theta}) = \frac{e^{f(\mathbf{x};\boldsymbol{\theta})-\rho}}{Z}$$

where $Z = e^{-f(\mathbf{x};\boldsymbol{\theta})-\rho} + e^{\rho-|f(\mathbf{x};\boldsymbol{\theta})|} + e^{f(\mathbf{x};\boldsymbol{\theta})-\rho}$. The prediction will then be $\arg\max_{i \in \{+1, 0, -1\}} r_i(\mathbf{x}; \boldsymbol{\theta})$. Note that only one of $-f(\mathbf{x}; \boldsymbol{\theta}) - \rho$, $\rho - |f(\mathbf{x}; \boldsymbol{\theta})|$ and $f(\mathbf{x}) - \rho$ will be positive at a time, so the corresponding $r_i(\mathbf{x}; \boldsymbol{\theta})$ will be maximum. This ensures that the predictions from $\mathbf{r}(\mathbf{x}; \boldsymbol{\theta})$ and $h(f(\mathbf{x}; \boldsymbol{\theta}), \rho)$ match.

Classifier-Rejector Method: Since $f(\mathbf{x}; \boldsymbol{\theta})$ in classifier-rejector is already a classwise prediction probability vector, this will simply mean $r_1(\mathbf{x}; \boldsymbol{\theta}) = f_1(\mathbf{x}; \boldsymbol{\theta})$, $r_{-1}(\mathbf{x}; \boldsymbol{\theta}) = f_2(\mathbf{x}; \boldsymbol{\theta})$ and $r_0(\mathbf{x}; \boldsymbol{\theta}) = f_3(\mathbf{x}; \boldsymbol{\theta})$.

4.2   Fairness Constraints

We now derive the fairness constraints for the abstain option classifier corresponding to independence and separation. Since talking about group fairness constraints on a single sample is meaningless, we consider fairness constraints derived over a mini-batch. Let B_k denote the kth minibatch during the training. Samples from B_k will be indexed by j. Let r_0^j, r_{-1}^j and r_1^j be the score values for j^{th} example in the mini-batch B_k. a_j is the value of sensitive attribute for j^{th} example in B_k. $y_j \in \{-1, 1\}$ is the class label of the jth example, and $\hat{y}_j$ denotes the prediction on j^{th} example. Let A and Y be the random variables corresponding to a and y, respectively. We extend the independence and equalized odds definitions in the context of the abstain option classifier.

Definition 1. Independence for Abstain Option Classifier: *An abstain option classifier satisfies independence if scores R_1, R_0 and R_{-1} are statistically independent of the sensitive attribute A, i.e., $R_1 \perp A$, $R_0 \perp A$ and $R_{-1} \perp A$.*

To achieve independence, we use demographic parity (also known as disparate impact) for abstaining option classifiers. Fairness constraints to achieve demographic parity for abstain option classification are described as follows. There is one constraint corresponding to each predicted outcome.

1. **Equalized Abstention Rate (ABS):**

$$\mathbb{E}[R_0 | A = 0] = \mathbb{E}[R_0 | A = 1] \Rightarrow \frac{\sum\limits_{j \in B_k} (1 - a_j) r_0^j}{\sum\limits_{j \in B_k} (1 - a_j)} = \frac{\sum\limits_{j \in B_k} a_j r_0^j}{\sum\limits_{j \in B_k} a_j}.$$

2. **Equalized Negative Rate (NEG):**

$$\mathbb{E}[R_{-1} | A = 0] = \mathbb{E}[R_{-1} | A = 1] \Rightarrow \frac{\sum\limits_{j \in B_k} (1 - a_j) r_{-1}^j}{\sum\limits_{j \in B_k} (1 - a_j)} = \frac{\sum\limits_{j \in B_k} a_j r_{-1}^j}{\sum\limits_{j \in B_k} a_j}$$

3. Equalized Positive Rate (POS):

$$\mathbb{E}[R_1|A=0] = \mathbb{E}[R_1|A=1] \Rightarrow \frac{\sum\limits_{j \in B_i}(1-a_j)r_1^j}{\sum\limits_{j \in B_i}(1-a_j)} = \frac{\sum\limits_{j \in B_i}a_j r_1^j}{\sum\limits_{j \in B_i}a_j}.$$

Definition 2. Equalized Odds Conditions for Abstain Option Classifier: *An abstain option classifier satisfies equalized odds if the scores $(R_1, R_0,$ and $R_{-1})$ are statistically independent of the sensitive attribute A given the target variable Y. Thus, $R_1 \perp A|Y$, $R_0 \perp A|Y$ and $R_{-1} \perp A|Y$.*

This paper focuses on achieving equalized odds for abstaining option classifiers. The following six constraints are required to achieve equalized odds.

1. **Equalized True Negative Rate (TNR):** $\mathbb{E}[R_{-1}|A=0,Y=-1] =$
$$\mathbb{E}[R_{-1}|A=1,Y=-1] \Rightarrow \frac{\sum\limits_{j \in B_i}(1-a_j)r_{-1}^j(\frac{1-y_j}{2})}{\sum\limits_{j \in B_i}(1-a_j)(\frac{1-y_j}{2})} = \frac{\sum\limits_{j \in B_i}a_j r_{-1}^j(\frac{1-y_j}{2})}{\sum\limits_{j \in B_i}a_j(\frac{1-y_j}{2})}.$$

2. **Equalized Negative Abstention Rate (NAR):** $\mathbb{E}[R_0|A=0,Y=-1] =$
$$\mathbb{E}[R_0|A=1,Y=-1] \Rightarrow \frac{\sum\limits_{j \in B_i}(1-a_j)r_0^j(\frac{1-y_j}{2})}{\sum\limits_{j \in B_i}(1-a_j)(\frac{1-y_j}{2})} = \frac{\sum\limits_{j \in B_i}a_j r_0^j(\frac{1-y_j}{2})}{\sum\limits_{j \in B_i}a_j(\frac{1-y_j}{2})}.$$

3. **Equalized False Positive Rate (FPR):** $\mathbb{E}[R_1|A=0,Y=-1] =$
$$\mathbb{E}[R_1|A=1,Y=-1] \Rightarrow \frac{\sum\limits_{j \in B_i}(1-a_j)r_1^j(\frac{1-y_j}{2})}{\sum\limits_{j \in B_i}(1-a_j)(\frac{1-y_j}{2})} = \frac{\sum\limits_{j \in B_i}a_j r_1^j(\frac{1-y_j}{2})}{\sum\limits_{j \in B_i}a_j(\frac{1-y_j}{2})}.$$

4. **Equalized False Negative Rate (FNR):** $\mathbb{E}[R_{-1}|A=0,Y=1] =$
$$\mathbb{E}[R_{-1}|A=1,Y=1] \Rightarrow \frac{\sum\limits_{j \in B_i}(1-a_j)r_{-1}^j(\frac{1+y_j}{2})}{\sum\limits_{j \in B_i}(1-a_j)(\frac{1+y_j}{2})} = \frac{\sum\limits_{j \in B_i}a_j r_{-1}^j(\frac{1+y_j}{2})}{\sum\limits_{j \in B_i}a_j(\frac{1+y_j}{2})}.$$

5. **Equalized Positive Abstention Rate (PAR):** $\mathbb{E}[R_0|A=0,Y=1] =$
$$\mathbb{E}[R_0|A=1,Y=1] \Rightarrow \frac{\sum\limits_{j \in B_i}(1-a_j)r_0^j(\frac{1+y_j}{2})}{\sum\limits_{j \in B_i}(1-a_j)(\frac{1+y_j}{2})} = \frac{\sum\limits_{j \in B_i}a_j r_0^j(\frac{1+y_j}{2})}{\sum\limits_{j \in B_i}a_j(\frac{1+y_j}{2})}.$$

6. **Equalized True Positive Rate (TPR):** $\mathbb{E}[R_1|A=0,Y=1] = \mathbb{E}[R_1|A=$
$$1,Y=1] \Rightarrow \frac{\sum\limits_{j \in B_i}(1-a_j)r_1^j(\frac{1+y_j}{2})}{\sum\limits_{j \in B_i}(1-a_j)(\frac{1+y_j}{2})} = \frac{\sum\limits_{j \in B_i}a_j r_1^j(\frac{1+y_j}{2})}{\sum\limits_{j \in B_i}a_j(\frac{1+y_j}{2})}.$$

Theorem 1. *[Impossibility Theorem: DP and EO cannot hold together] Consider binary classification with a reject option setting. The target label Y is binary. Let the sensitive attribute A be dependent on Y, and R_i, $i \in \{-1,0,1\}$ is not independent of Y. Then, DP and EO cannot both hold together.*

The proof is skipped due to the space constraints. If $A \perp Y$, then the group membership does not affect the statistics of the target variable. If $R_i \perp Y \; \forall I \in \{-1,0,1\}$, then the score function is independent of the target variable, which makes it a bad score function.

Objective for Demographic Parity (DP). Given a minibatch B_k, we solve the following optimization problem to find a reject option classifier that satisfies DP conditions. The classifier is modeled using a deep neural network.

$$\textbf{(DP)} \quad \min_{\theta} \sum_{j \in B_k} L_{ds}(y_j f(\mathbf{x}_j; \boldsymbol{\theta}), \rho(\mathbf{x}_j; \boldsymbol{\theta})) \text{ s.t. } h_i(\boldsymbol{\theta}) = 0, \ i \in \{+1, -1, 0\}$$

where $\boldsymbol{\theta}$ are the parameters of the neural network representing the classifier, $h_i(\boldsymbol{\theta}) = \mathbb{E}[R_i | A = 0] - \mathbb{E}[R_i | A = 1]$. To represent functions h_1, h_0 and h_{-1} in the vector form, we use $\mathbf{h}(\boldsymbol{\theta}) = \begin{bmatrix} h_1(\boldsymbol{\theta}) & h_0(\boldsymbol{\theta}) & h_{-1}(\boldsymbol{\theta}) \end{bmatrix}^{\top}$. For DP, we only need to add two constraints: an equalized negative rate, an equalized positive rate, and an equalized rejection rate. The third constraint will be satisfied automatically. For the sake of completeness, we have included all three constraints here. The Lagrangian for the above problem is as follows.

$$\mathcal{L}_{DP}(B_k; \boldsymbol{\theta}, \boldsymbol{\lambda}) = \sum_{j \in B_k} L(f(\mathbf{x}_j; \boldsymbol{\theta}), y_j) + \sum_{i \in \{-1, 0, 1\}} \lambda_i h_i(\boldsymbol{\theta})$$

Where L is the loss function used, $\boldsymbol{\lambda} = (\lambda_{-1}, \lambda_0, \lambda_1)$ are dual variables. We learn $\boldsymbol{\theta}$ and $\boldsymbol{\lambda}$ by solving the optimization problem $\min_{\theta} \max_{\lambda} \ \mathcal{L}_{DP}(B_k; \boldsymbol{\theta}, \boldsymbol{\lambda})$.

Objective for Equalized Odds (EO). Given a minibatch B_k, we solve the following optimization problem to implement equalized odds in the reject option classifier.

$$\textbf{(EO)} \quad \min_{\theta} \sum_{j \in B_k} L(f(\mathbf{x}_j; \boldsymbol{\theta}), y_j) \text{s.t. } h_{i,y}(\boldsymbol{\theta}) = 0; \ i \in \{+1, -1, 0\}, \ y \in \{+1, -1\}$$

where $h_{i,y}(\boldsymbol{\theta}) = \mathbb{E}[R_i | A = 0, Y = y] - \mathbb{E}[R_i | A = 1, Y = y]$. In vector form, the constraints are represented as $\mathbf{h}(\boldsymbol{\theta}) = \begin{bmatrix} h_{+1,+1} & h_{+1,-1} & h_{-1,+1} & h_{-1,-1} & h_{0,+1} & h_{0,-1} \end{bmatrix}^{\top}$. We form the Lagrangian for the above problem.

$$\mathcal{L}_{EO}(B_k; \boldsymbol{\theta}, \boldsymbol{\lambda}) = \sum_{j \in B_i} L(f(\mathbf{x}_j; \boldsymbol{\theta}), y_j) + \sum_{i \in \{-1, 0, 1\}} \sum_{y \in \{-1, 1\}} \lambda_{i,y} h_{i,y}(\boldsymbol{\theta})$$

where $\boldsymbol{\lambda} = \begin{bmatrix} \lambda_{+1,+1} & \lambda_{+1,-1} & \lambda_{-1,+1} & \lambda_{-1,-1} & \lambda_{0,+1} & \lambda_{0,-1} \end{bmatrix}^{\top}$. We learn $\boldsymbol{\theta}$ and $\boldsymbol{\lambda}$ by solving the following problem $\min_{\theta} \max_{\lambda} \ \mathcal{L}_{EO}(B_k; \boldsymbol{\theta}, \boldsymbol{\lambda})$.

4.3   Possibility of Mixed Constraints in Reject Option Setting

In the reject option classifier, our prediction space is $\hat{\mathcal{Y}} = \{-1, 0, +1\}$. Thus, we have three conditions for demographic parity (DP) and six for equalized odds (EO). This allows for mixed constraints (few from DP and few from EO). We now analyze the mixing possibilities. From Theorem 1, we can directly infer the impossibility of the following combinations. (a) Combination of Equalized POS, Equalized TPR, and Equalized FPR is impossible. (b) Combination of Equalized

NEG, Equalized FNR, and Equalized TNR is impossible. (c) Combination of Equalized ABS, Equalized PAR, and Equalized NAR is impossible. Any other combination than these three is possible. To empirically verify if mixing fairness constraints work, we use Equalized ABS, Equalized TPR, and Equalized TNR as our fairness constraints to obtain a mixed fairness constraint setting.

Table 2. Demographic parity results on Adult, German and Compas dataset

Model	Adult				German				Compas			
	Acc	ΔPos	ΔNeg	ΔAbs	Acc	ΔPos	ΔNeg	ΔAbs	Acc	ΔPos	ΔNeg	ΔAbs
	Cov = 41.5				**Cov = 45.5**				**Cov = 41**			
RN	98.04	1.58	43.49	41.92	86.71	0.23	11.09	10.86	77.6	10.43	12.66	2.23
EQ RN	95.5	1.24	0.09	1.15	86.33	0.13	0.98	1.11	72.05	1.83	1.14	0.69
KP1	97.63	0	44.57	44.57	87.08	0	9.27	9.27	75.52	3.46	12.15	8.69
EQ KP1	91.81	0	0.37	0.37	87.44	0	1.18	1.18	74.72	1.24	1.44	2.67
DPABST	89.05	0.12	0.18	0.3	85.08	1.86	1.73	3.6	72.08	0.51	3.15	3.66
	Cov = 65.5				**Cov = 66**				**Cov = 51**			
RN	93.57	3.06	36.77	33.71	82.25	2.25	15.12	12.87	76.3	13.19	15.65	2.46
EQ RN	89.8	1.08	0.76	0.32	81.87	0.77	5.06	4.28	73.34	2.28	0.19	2.48
KP1	92.03	0	33.39	33.39	82.47	0.12	12.76	12.64	74.27	8.61	17.03	8.42
EQ KP1	87.85	0	0.38	0.38	81.84	0	3.11	3.11	73.46	2.27	1.74	4.01
DPABST	84.46	0.06	0.32	0.26	81.22	1.42	4.07	5.49	69.68	0.26	1.28	1.55
	Cov = 79.5				**Cov = 78**				**Cov = 60**			
RN	88.95	6.27	24.34	18.07	79.5	5.09	13.01	7.92	76.3	13.19	15.65	2.46
EQ RN	86.33	1.3	1.02	0.28	78.81	0.23	2.38	2.61	73.34	2.28	0.19	2.48
KP1	86.9	0	21.36	21.36	78.6	2.37	11.06	8.69	74.27	8.61	17.03	8.42
EQ KP1	83.98	0.35	1.7	1.35	77.94	0.01	1.49	1.48	73.46	2.27	1.74	4.01
DPABST	81.9	0.17	0.48	0.31	79.48	1.42	1.51	2.93	69.68	0.26	1.28	1.55

5 Experiments

5.1 Setting

Datasets: We use German credit, Compas and Adult datasets in our experiments. In the German dataset, the task is to predict if a person is a good or bad credit risk. In the Compas dataset, the task is to predict if a person will recidivate in two years. In the Adult dataset, the task is to predict if a person's income exceeds $50k/yr. The sensitive attribute in German and Adult datasets is the gender, and the sensitive attribute in Compas dataset is the race. Categorical variables were replace with numeric values. Features were normalized to the range $[-1, 1]$.

Table 3. Equalized odds results on Adult, German and Compas dataset

	Model	Acc	ΔTpr	ΔFnr	ΔPar	ΔFpr	ΔTnr	ΔNar
Adult dataset	**Cov = 40.5**							
	RN	98.04	0.41	12.76	12.35	0.01	40.1	40.11
	EQ RN	94.29	0.06	1.49	1.42	0.01	0.77	0.78
	KP1	97.63	0	15.44	15.44	0	40.54	40.54
	EQ KP1	95.27	0	2.1	2.1	0	1.33	1.33
	Cov = 63							
	RN	93.93	2.44	22.05	19.6	0.06	28.54	28.49
	EQ RN	89.28	0.03	2.64	2.61	0.02	1.22	1.21
	KP1	92.86	0	20.77	20.77	0	25.64	25.64
	EQ KP1	89.81	0	3.06	3.06	0	4.95	4.95
	Cov = 77.5							
	RN	89.78	7.17	16.25	9.08	0.78	16.21	15.43
	EQ RN	85.42	0.38	1.52	1.14	0.04	2.6	2.56
	KP1	87.5	0	16.65	16.65	0	12.24	12.24
	EQ KP1	85.63	0	0.9	0.9	0	5.21	5.21
German dataset	**Cov = 40.5**							
	RN	87.01	1.75	5.41	3.66	0.12	11.45	11.57
	EQ RN	87.61	0.91	0.01	0.9	0	1.14	1.14
	KP1	87.9	0	4.01	4.01	0	14.11	14.11
	EQ KP1	88.52	0	0.27	0.27	0	0.77	0.77
	Cov = 55							
	RN	84.83	2.54	11.61	9.07	0.04	8.61	8.65
	EQ RN	84.85	0.15	2.2	2.36	0.02	0.01	0.03
	KP1	85.4	0	6.76	6.76	0	3.82	3.82
	EQ KP1	84.97	0	2.26	2.26	0	0.3	0.3
	Cov = 69							
	RN	81.67	5.93	12.92	6.99	1.05	9.92	8.87
	EQ RN	81.71	0.57	9.21	8.64	0.02	1.74	1.75
	KP1	81.17	0.36	15.63	15.99	0.02	9.15	9.13
	EQ KP1	81.23	0.23	2.84	3.07	0.11	2.15	2.04
Compas dataset	**Cov = 48**							
	RN	76.66	18.26	13.89	4.37	5.42	12.56	7.15
	EQ RN	66.29	3.66	4.4	0.74	0.06	1.24	1.18
	KP1	74.79	8.9	16.02	7.12	3.39	13.06	9.67
	EQ KP1	62.11	2.48	1.26	1.22	0.76	3.74	4.5
	Cov = 61							
	RN	74.7	19.96	19.76	0.21	7.68	15.97	8.29
	EQ RN	71.17	2.39	4.41	2.02	0.49	1.35	0.85
	KP1	73.24	15.9	20.8	4.9	6.45	15.4	8.95
	EQ KP1	60.07	1.93	2.48	0.55	0.31	2.49	2.81
	Cov = 79							
	RN	71.49	23.97	24.39	0.41	10.94	17.18	6.24
	EQ RN	67.25	3.16	2.45	0.7	0.04	1.82	1.86
	KP1	70.94	22.07	24.58	2.52	10.36	16.21	5.85
	EQ KP1	66.83	1.09	2.34	1.25	0.56	1.94	1.38

Baselines: We are using three models for our baselines. **RISAN/RN** [12] and **KP1** [4] are the biased baseline models in all experiments. **DPABST** [18] is the state-of-the-art fairness model for the independence criterion. There are no baseline models for the separation criterion in the fair binary classification with abstention setting. **EQUISCALE RISAN/EQ RN** and **EQUISCALE KP1/EQ KP1** are the fair versions of RISAN and KP1.

Model Architecture. We use a single hidden layer with 32 neurons for all the models. The output layer for RN/EQ RN is a single neuron while for KP1/EQ KP1 it is a three neuron output layer. Between the hidden layer and output layer, a batch norm, ReLU activation and dropout layer is used in that order. For RN/EQ RN, ρ is a learnable parameter constrained to be always positive by using softplus on the parameter.

Experiments on all datasets are conducted for five runs, and we report the average and standard deviation over the runs. We track the positive rate, negative rate, abstention rate, TPR, FNR, PAR, FPR, TNR, NAR, accuracy, and coverage. For RN, EQ RN, KP1, EQ KP1, abstention costs are varied in the range [0.00625, 0.49375]. For DPABST, the abstention rate is varied from 40% to 80%, using step size of 2%.

Table 4. Mixed constraints results on Adult, German and Compas dataset

Model	Adult				German				Compas			
	Acc	ΔAbs	ΔTpr	ΔTnr	Acc	ΔAbs	ΔTpr	ΔTnr	Acc	ΔAbs	ΔTpr	ΔTnr
	Cov = 40				**Cov = 44.5**				**Cov = 42.5**			
RN	98.04	41.92	0.41	40.1	86.68	12.34	0.86	11.08	77.6	2.23	15.7	9.72
EQ RN	96	5.96	0.76	1.48	86.67	2.05	0.34	1.73	75.62	1.21	2.81	0.47
KP1	97.63	44.57	0	40.54	87.08	9.27	0	8.33	75.09	7.54	7.55	8.9
EQ KP1	94.64	6.11	0	1.89	87.09	2.55	0	0.4	71	1.46	3.66	3.34
	Cov = 65				**Cov = 60**				**Cov = 67.5**			
RN	93.57	33.71	3.05	27.09	84.14	13.04	3.81	9.9	73.65	3.84	21.65	14.96
EQ RN	90.81	5.65	1.87	0.53	83.54	5.7	0.01	2.65	71.61	1.8	2.57	0.93
KP1	92.03	33.39	0	23.46	84.69	10.58	0	6.51	71.61	8.51	15.99	15.06
EQ KP1	89.06	5.58	0	1.66	84.04	3.11	0	0.08	70.59	2.05	3.93	0.51
	Cov = 77				**Cov = 71**				**Cov = 80**			
RN	89.78	20.69	7.17	16.21	80.77	10.8	5.46	9.93	71.49	4.17	23.97	17.18
EQ RN	87.95	4.08	2.1	0.41	80.5	5.21	1.08	1.65	69.12	1.96	2.87	0.23
KP1	86.9	21.36	0	11.36	81.29	12.24	0.25	7.47	70.24	2.35	25.9	16.04
EQ KP1	86.3	2.56	0.87	2.65	81.26	2.7	0.23	0.44	68.19	3.34	4.86	2.08

5.2   Results

Demographic Parity: From Table 2, we observe the following. In Adult dataset, on all three coverages, EQ RN and EQ KP1 achieve higher accuracy than DPABST. Compared to RN and KP1, EQ RN and EQ KP1 reduce fairness violations in ΔNeg and ΔAbs from 40% to less than 1.5% on coverage 41%, 30% to less than 0.5% on coverage 65.5%, and 20% to less than 1.75% on coverage 79.5%. In German dataset, all the models achieve similar accuracies, yet compared to RN and KP1, EQ RN and EQ KP1 reduce the fairness violations in ΔNeg and ΔAbs by around 8%–10% across all the coverages. In Compas dataset, EQ RN and EQ KP1 achieve higher accuracies than DPABST, epecially on higher coverages. EQ RN and EQ KP1 reduce the fairness violations in ΔPos and ΔNeg by around 10% across all the coverages. In all instances, EQ KP1 and EQ RN perform worse compared to KP1 and RN on accuracies, since there is a fairness-accuracy tradeoff. In no instance did EQ KP1 and EQ RN increase the fairness violation compared to KP1 and RN, even if the initial violations were extremely small.

Equalized Odds: From Table 3, EQ RN and EQ KP1 exhibit significant accuracy drop compared to RN and KP1, except on the German dataset. In Adult dataset, we observe that EQ KP1 and EQ RNredice the fairness violations from 40% in ΔTNR and ΔNAR to less than 1.5%, and from 12% in ΔFNR and ΔPAR to around 2%. The trend continues as the coverage increases, where it reduced violations from around 10%, 20% or 30% to less than 5% at coverages 63% and 77.5%. Note that the fairness violation reductions aren't as stable or low as obtained in demographic parity. This is due to optimizing equalized odds being harder than optimizing demographic parity, since equalized odds requires six Lagrange multipliers, whereas demographic parity requires only three Lagrange multipliers. This leads to instability in the algorithm, leading to cases such as EQ RN increasing the fairness violation for ΔPAR at coverage 69% on the German dataset while reducing all other fairness violations. EQ RN and EQ KP1 manage to consistently reduce the fairness violations to less than 5%.

Mixed Constraints: Referring to Table 4, EQ RN and EQ KP1 do indeed work with mixed constraints. Specifically, looking at Adult dataset, we can see that the most fairness violation occurs in ΔAbs and ΔTnr, which are constraints from demographic parity and equalized odds respectively. Both the fairness violations are reduced from violations over 20% to violations around or less than 5%. Due to the fairness-accuracy trade off, we observe drops in accuracy in the performance of EQ RN and EQ KP1 across both the Adult and Compas dataset, but the drop in German dataset is not significant. All fairness violations have been reduced to be less than 5% across all settings.

6   Conclusions

We provided fairness criteria for the binary classification with abstain option setting by extending the fairness constraints. We then formulated a model-agnostic in-processing approach as a Lagrange multiplier problem. Since the constraints are differentiable, we solved the problem using the dual ascent method. We then demonstrated the effectiveness of the models by performing on par or better than DPABST for demographic parity and obtained fair classifiers satisfying equalized odds. We experimented on mixing constraints from demographic parity and equalized odds, which is not possible in the binary classification setting.

References

1. Agarwal, A., Beygelzimer, A., Dudik, M., Langford, J., Wallach, H.: A reductions approach to fair classification. In: Proceedings of the 35th ICML. PMLR, vol. 80, pp. 60–69 (2018)
2. Barocas, S., Hardt, M., Narayanan, A.: Fairness in Machine Learning: Limitations and Opportunities. MIT Press, Cambridge (2023). https://fairmlbook.org/
3. Calders, T., Kamiran, F., Pechenizkiy, M.: Building classifiers with independency constraints. In: 2009 IEEE ICDM Workshops, pp. 13–18 (2009)
4. Cao, Y., et al.: Generalizing consistent multi-class classification with rejection to be compatible with arbitrary losses. In: NeurIPS, vol. 35, pp. 521–534. Curran Associates, Inc. (2022)
5. Chouldechova, A.: Fair prediction with disparate impact: a study of bias in recidivism prediction instruments. Big Data 5(2), 153–163 (2017)
6. Dastin, J.: Amazon scraps secret AI recruiting tool that showed bias against women. Reuters News Paper (2018). https://www.reuters.com/article/us-amazon-com-jobs-automation-insight-idUSKCN1MK08G
7. Geifman, Y., El-Yaniv, R.: Selective classification for deep neural networks. In: NIPS, pp. 4878–4887 (2017)
8. Geifman, Y., El-Yaniv, R.: Selectivenet: a deep neural network with an integrated reject option. In: International Conference on Machine Learning, pp. 2151–2159. PMLR (2019)
9. Hardt, M., Price, E., Srebro, N.: Equality of opportunity in supervised learning. In: NeurIPS, NIPS 2016, Red Hook, NY, USA, pp. 3323–3331 (2016)
10. Huang, H.: Racial disparities in pre-trial detention (2017). http://fingfx.thomsonreuters.com/gfx/rngs/CANADA-JAILS-RACE/0100516D2N4/index.html
11. Jones, E., Sagawa, S., Koh, P.W., Kumar, A., Liang, P.: Selective classification can magnify disparities across groups. In: ICLR (2021)
12. Kalra, B., Shah, K., Manwani, N.: RISAN: robust instance specific deep abstention network. In: UAI, pp. 1525–1534. PMLR (2021)
13. Lee, J.K., et al.: Fair selective classification via sufficiency. In: Proceedings of the 38th ICML. PMLR, vol. 139, pp. 6076–6086 (2021)
14. Madras, D., Pitassi, T., Zemel, R.: Predict responsibly: improving fairness and accuracy by learning to defer. In: NeurIPS, vol. 31 (2018)
15. Mattu, Angwin, J., Larson, J., Kirchner, L., Surya: Machine bias. ProPublica (2016). https://www.propublica.org/article/machine-bias-risk-assessments-in-criminal-sentencing
16. Mittermaier, M., Raza, M.M., Kvedar, J.C.: Bias in AI-based models for medical applications: challenges and mitigation strategies. NPJ Digit. Med. 6(1) (2023)
17. Padala, M., Gujar, S.: FNNC: achieving fairness through neural networks. In: Proceedings of the Twenty-Ninth IJCAI. IJCAI 2020 (2021)

18. Schreuder, N., Chzhen, E.: Classification with abstention but without disparities. In: UAI. PMLR, vol. 161, pp. 1227–1236 (2021)
19. Shah, K., Manwani, N.: Online active learning of reject option classifiers. In: AAAI, pp. 5652–5659 (2020)
20. Vokinger, K.N., Feuerriegel, S., Kesselheim, A.S.: Mitigating bias in machine learning for medicine. Commun. Med. **1**(1), 1–3 (2021)
21. Westergaard, D., Moseley, P., Sørup, F.K.H., Baldi, P., Brunak, S.: Population-wide analysis of differences in disease progression patterns in men and women. Nat. Commun. **10**, 666 (2019)

Unsupervised Clustering Using a Variational Autoencoder with Constrained Mixtures for Posterior and Prior

Mashfiqul Huq Chowdhury$^{(\boxtimes)}$ [ID], Yuichi Hirose [ID], Stephen Marsland [ID], and Yuan Yao [ID]

School of Mathematics and Statistics, Victoria University of Wellington, Wellington, New Zealand
{mashfiq.chowdhury,yuichi.hirose,stephen.marsland,yuan.yao}@vuw.ac.nz

Abstract. Clustering high-dimensional unlabelled data is a challenging task. We propose a probabilistic generative model based on the variational autoencoder (VAE) that learns the underlying statistical distribution of the dataset and performs cluster analysis. We assume a mixture distribution for both the posterior and prior components and derive the evidence lower bound of our mixtures VAE algorithm, which integrates the clustering distribution within each component of the VAE framework. We explicitly use the EM algorithm to find the clustering assignment estimate and model parameters. We also propose a constrained version of the mixtures VAE model to balance the reconstruction and regularization components during optimization. The experimental results of our proposed model demonstrate superior clustering performance compared to baseline algorithms. Moreover, the proposed model generates realistic examples from specified clusters in the latent space.

Keywords: Clustering · GMM · Latent Space · Mixture VAE · Representation Learning

1 Introduction

Cluster analysis aims to group similar objects in an unsupervised manner. Unsupervised cluster analysis of high-dimensional complex datasets, such as images, audio, and text, is challenging [18]. Standard algorithms such as k-means and the Gaussian mixture model (GMM) perform poorly with high-dimensional data [21].

Representation learning seeks to find a useful low-dimensional latent space representation of high-dimensional data points. These latent embeddings can be applied to unsupervised cluster analysis. Several state-of-the-art algorithms [5,10,26] have used the variational autoencoder (VAE) [12] framework for representation learning and clustering tasks. These algorithms used the unimodal Gaussian distribution as variational posterior to derive the evidence lower bound

© The Author(s), under exclusive license to Springer Nature Singapore Pte Ltd. 2025
R. Hadfi et al. (Eds.): PRICAI 2024, LNAI 15281, pp. 29–40, 2025.
https://doi.org/10.1007/978-981-96-0116-5_3

(ELBO) of the marginal log-likelihood function. Some studies [5, 17, 22, 27] have highlighted that simplistic choices for the prior and posterior distributions may not sufficiently address the underlying structures in latent space and could result in over-regularization [8].

In general, mixture distributions are often useful for approximating complex relationships within datasets [2]. In this work, we assume a mixture distribution for both the variational posterior and prior components within the VAE framework to model complicated latent space representations. We derive the ELBO objective function, where the clustering distribution is integrated into both reconstruction error and regularization terms. Our proposed mixtures VAE method utilizes the EM algorithm to find a solution for the clustering assignment estimate and optimize the model parameters, which we refer to as the MVAE(EM) algorithm. Additionally, we modify the objective function of the MVAE(EM) model by including a hyper-parameter β in the regularization term, and we refer to this constrained method as the β-MVAE(EM) algorithm. We implement our proposed methods to a set of benchmark datasets and evaluate the clustering performance based on test datasets. The empirical results of our proposed models demonstrate good clustering performance compared to state-of-the-art deep clustering methods.

2   Related Works

Several deep generative models are proposed based on the autoencoder (AE) and VAE framework for clustering tasks. The deep embedded clustering (DEC) method [25] and improved deep embedded clustering (IDEC) [6] method uses the AE framework for unsupervised clustering. The VAE model [12] assumes a Gaussian distribution for both the variational posterior and prior components and its ELBO function consists of reconstruction and regularization terms, where the regularization component drives the variational posterior to match the prior distribution. The VADE [10], GMVAE [5], and DGG [26] methods modify the prior distribution assumption from a standard Gaussian to a Gaussian mixture model (GMM) over the continuous latent variables, enabling clustering in the latent space. The clustering assignment estimate in these algorithms is associated only with the prior term. In the LTVAE algorithm [16], latent features are assumed to be generated from tree-structured Bayesian networks. The k-DVAE [3] method derives the ELBO function by assuming an isotropic Gaussian as the prior and a mixture distribution as the variational posterior distribution. This method optimizes the ELBO without explicitly finding the clustering assignment estimate.

Our proposed model extends the VADE, and k-DVAE methods by assuming a mixture of Gaussians for both the prior and posterior distributions. Unlike previous models, the clustering assignment estimate of our proposed MVAE(EM) model is associated with both the variational posterior and prior components. Furthermore, the β-MVAE(EM) model includes a regularisation parameter to the MVAE(EM) model to trade-off between the reconstruction error and regularization in the latent space. The training procedure for both the MVAE(EM) and β-MVAE(EM) methods involves iterative optimization of both clustering assignment probabilities and model parameters. Additionally, the proposed methods can be trained using two approaches (Sect. 3.3): optimizing the weighted form of the ELBO that utilizes the full distribution over the classes (soft optimization), or selecting a simpler ELBO function for optimization based on the maximum a posteriori probability (MAP) estimate (hard optimization).

3   The Mixtures VAE Model

Given a dataset of D-dimensional vectors $\mathcal{D} = \{\mathbf{x}_i\}_{i=1}^{N} \in \mathbb{R}^D$ or $\mathbb{Z}^D$ where each datapoint $\mathbf{x}_i$ belongs to one of K predefined clusters. Our goal is to model the distribution of a dataset by fitting a non-linear latent variable model $p(\mathbf{x}, \mathbf{z}, \mathbf{y})$ (where $\mathbf{z} \in \mathbb{R}^M$ ($M << D$) and $\mathbf{y} = (y_1, \cdots, y_K)$) of the following form:

$$p(\mathbf{x}, \mathbf{z}, \mathbf{y}) = p_\theta(\mathbf{x}|\mathbf{z}) p(\mathbf{z}|\mathbf{y}) p(\mathbf{y}). \tag{1}$$

Writing y_k as an indicator variable for $\mathbf{x}_i$ belonging to class k (so $y_k = 1$ and $y_j = 0, j \neq k$) the terms of (1) are:

$$p(\mathbf{y}) = \prod_{k=1}^{K} \pi_k^{y_k}, \tag{2}$$

$$p(\mathbf{z}|\mathbf{y}) = \prod_{k=1}^{K} p(\mathbf{z}|y_k)^{y_k} = \prod_{k=1}^{K} \left[\mathcal{N}(\mathbf{z}; \boldsymbol{\mu}_k, \mathrm{diag}(\boldsymbol{\sigma}_k^2)) \right]^{y_k}, \tag{3}$$

$$p_\theta(\mathbf{x}|\mathbf{z}) = \begin{cases} \mathcal{N}(\mathbf{x}; \boldsymbol{\mu}_\theta(\mathbf{z}), \mathbf{I}); & \mathbf{x} \in \mathbb{R}^D, \\ \mathrm{Ber}(\mathbf{x}; \boldsymbol{\mu}_\theta(\mathbf{z})); & \mathbf{x} \in \{0,1\}^D, \\ \mathrm{Cat}(\mathbf{x}; \boldsymbol{\mu}_\theta(\mathbf{z})); & \mathbf{x} \in (\mathbb{Z}^+)^D, \end{cases} \tag{4}$$

where π_k is the prior probability for k^{th} component ($0 \leq \pi_k \leq 1$, $\sum_{k=1}^{K} \pi_k = 1$), $\boldsymbol{\mu}_k \in \mathbb{R}^M$ and $\boldsymbol{\sigma}_k^2 \in \mathbb{R}_+^M$ denote the mean and variance of the kth component Gaussian distribution (prior). For brevity, we use y_k instead of $y_k = 1$. The conditional likelihood distribution, $p_\theta(\mathbf{x}|\mathbf{z})$, depends on the data type: a normal distribution for continuous data, a Bernoulli distribution for binary data, or a categorical distribution for multinomial data.

3.1   Likelihood Function and Evidence Lower Bound

The marginal density of the observed variables $\mathbf{x}$ is given by:

$$p(\mathbf{x}) = \sum_{\mathbf{y}} \int p_\theta(\mathbf{x}|\mathbf{z}) \, p(\mathbf{z}|\mathbf{y}) \, p(\mathbf{y}) \, d\mathbf{z}. \tag{5}$$

However, the integral over $\mathbf{z}$ in (5) cannot be analytically computed, so the marginal distribution $p(\mathbf{x})$ and posterior distribution $p_\theta(\mathbf{z}|\mathbf{x}, \mathbf{y})$ are intractable.

Variational inference provides an analytical approximation to the posterior probability density over the latent variables. We introduce $q_\phi(\mathbf{z}|\mathbf{x}, \mathbf{y})$ as an approximate posterior distribution over the continuous latent variables $\mathbf{z}$ with parameters ϕ and $q(\mathbf{y})$ as the arbitrary distribution over a discrete latent variable $\mathbf{y}$. Now for a single data point $\mathbf{x}$, the lower bound of the marginal log-likelihood is derived as follows:

$$
\begin{aligned}
\log p(\mathbf{x}) &= \log \sum_{\mathbf{y}} \int p_\theta(\mathbf{x}|\mathbf{z})p(\mathbf{z}|\mathbf{y})p(\mathbf{y})\ d\mathbf{z} \\
&= \log \sum_{\mathbf{y}} \int q_\phi(\mathbf{z}|\mathbf{x}, \mathbf{y})q(\mathbf{y}) \frac{p_\theta(\mathbf{x}|\mathbf{z})p(\mathbf{z}|\mathbf{y})p(\mathbf{y})}{q_\phi(\mathbf{z}|\mathbf{x}, \mathbf{y})q(\mathbf{y})}\ d\mathbf{z} \\
&\geq \sum_{\mathbf{y}} \int q_\phi(\mathbf{z}|\mathbf{x}, \mathbf{y})q(\mathbf{y}) \log\left[\frac{p_\theta(\mathbf{x}|\mathbf{z})p(\mathbf{z}|\mathbf{y})p(\mathbf{y})}{q_\phi(\mathbf{z}|\mathbf{x}, \mathbf{y})q(\mathbf{y})}\right]\ d\mathbf{z} \quad \text{[Jensen's inequality]} \\
&= \sum_{k=1}^{K} \int q_\phi(\mathbf{z}|\mathbf{x}, y_k)q(y_k) \log p_\theta(\mathbf{x}|\mathbf{z})d\mathbf{z}- \\
&\qquad\qquad \sum_{k=1}^{K} \int q_\phi(\mathbf{z}|\mathbf{x}, y_k)q(y_k) \log \frac{q_\phi(\mathbf{z}|\mathbf{x}, y_k)q(y_k)}{p(\mathbf{z}|y_k)p(y_k)}d\mathbf{z} \qquad (6) \\
&\equiv \mathcal{L}_{\phi,\theta,\psi,q(\mathbf{y})}(\mathbf{x}).
\end{aligned}
$$

This is the evidence lower bound (ELBO) of the marginal log-likelihood with parameters ϕ, θ, ψ, and $q(\mathbf{y})$, where $\phi = \{\phi_k\}_{k=1}^{K}$ and $\theta = \{\theta_k\}_{k=1}^{K}$ specify the parameter set of the mixtures of the variational posterior distribution (encoder) and conditional likelihood distribution $p_\theta(\mathbf{x}|\mathbf{z})$ (decoder), respectively, and $\psi = \{\pi_k, \mu_k, \sigma_k^2\}_{k=1}^{K}$ denotes the parameters of the prior distribution. For each $\mathbf{y}$, $q_\phi(\mathbf{z}|\mathbf{x}, \mathbf{y})$ is assumed to follow a multivariate Gaussian distribution with a diagonal covariance matrix:

$$
q_\phi(\mathbf{z}|y_k,\ \mathbf{x}) = \mathcal{N}(\mathbf{z};\ \mu_{\phi k}(\mathbf{x}),\ \mathrm{diag}(\sigma_{\phi k}^2(\mathbf{x}))),
$$

where $\mu_{\phi k}(\mathbf{x}) \in \mathbb{R}^M$ and $\sigma_{\phi k}^2(\mathbf{x}) \in \mathbb{R}_+^M$ represent the means and variances of the kth component Gaussian distribution. The encoder neural network (NN) approximates this distribution with parameters ϕ. Similarly, the decoder NN parameterizes the conditional likelihood $p_\theta(\mathbf{x}|\mathbf{z})$ with parameters θ. We treat $q(\mathbf{y})$ as a functional parameter that is integrated with the mixtures of the prior, posterior, and conditional likelihood distributions. The following section presents the non-parametric estimation of $q(\mathbf{y})$.

3.2   MVAE(EM)

The ELBO in (6) can also be expressed as:

$$
\mathcal{L}_{\phi,\theta,\psi,q(\mathbf{y})}(\mathbf{x}) = \mathbb{E}_{(\mathbf{z},\mathbf{y})\sim q_\phi(\mathbf{z}|\mathbf{x},\mathbf{y})q(\mathbf{y})} \log p_\theta(\mathbf{x}|\mathbf{z})-
$$
$$
\mathrm{D_{KL}}[q_\phi(\mathbf{z}|\mathbf{x}, \mathbf{y})q(\mathbf{y}) \parallel p(\mathbf{z}|\mathbf{y})p(\mathbf{y})], \quad (7)
$$

where the first term of the ELBO is the reconstruction error and the second is the Kullback-Leibler (K-L) divergence, which can be written as:

$$D_{KL}[q_\phi(\mathbf{z}|\mathbf{x},\mathbf{y})q(\mathbf{y}) \| p(\mathbf{z}|\mathbf{y})p(\mathbf{y})] = \sum_{k=1}^{K} q(y_k)\mathbb{E}_{\mathbf{z}\sim q_\phi(\mathbf{z}|\mathbf{x},y_k)} \log \frac{q_\phi(\mathbf{z}|\mathbf{x},y_k)q(y_k)}{p(\mathbf{z}|y_k)p(y_k)}.$$

(8)

The expectation-maximization (EM) algorithm can be used to optimize (7), providing an analytical form of $q(\mathbf{y})$ and estimate the model parameters (ϕ, θ, ψ) using:

– E-step: Estimate $q(\mathbf{y})$ by minimizing the K-L divergence:

$$\underset{q(\mathbf{y})}{\arg\max}\, D_{KL}\left[q_\phi(\mathbf{z}|\mathbf{x},\mathbf{y})q(\mathbf{y}) \| p(\mathbf{z}|\mathbf{y})p(\mathbf{y})\right].$$

– M-step: Estimate the model parameters by maximizing:

$$\underset{\phi,\theta,\psi}{\arg\max}\left[\mathbb{E}_{(\mathbf{z},\mathbf{y})\sim q_\phi(\mathbf{z}|\mathbf{x},\mathbf{y})\hat{q}(\mathbf{y})} \log p_\theta(\mathbf{x}|\mathbf{z}) - D_{KL}[q_\phi(\mathbf{z}|\mathbf{x},\mathbf{y})\hat{q}(\mathbf{y}) \| p(\mathbf{z}|\mathbf{y})p(\mathbf{y})]\right].$$

We apply the reparameterization (RP) trick [12,20] to compute the expectation over $\mathbf{z}$ in (8):

$$\mathbf{z}_k^{(l)} = \boldsymbol{\mu}_{\phi k}(\mathbf{x}) + \boldsymbol{\sigma}_{\phi k}(\mathbf{x}) \odot \boldsymbol{\epsilon}^{(l)}; \quad l = 1, \cdots, L; \quad k = 1, \cdots, K;$$

(9)

where L denotes the number of Monte Carlo samples, $\odot$ is the element-wise Hadamard product and $\boldsymbol{\epsilon}^{(l)} \overset{\text{i.i.d.}}{\sim} p(\boldsymbol{\epsilon}) = \mathcal{N}(\boldsymbol{\epsilon}; \mathbf{0}, \mathbf{I})$. The K-L divergence can be approximated as:

$$\tilde{D}_{KL}[q_\phi(\mathbf{z}|\mathbf{x},\mathbf{y})q(\mathbf{y}) \| p(\mathbf{z}|\mathbf{y})p(\mathbf{y})] = \frac{1}{L}\sum_{k=1}^{K} q(y_k) \sum_{l=1}^{L} \log \left[\frac{q_\phi(z_k^{(l)}|\mathbf{x},y_k)q(y_k)}{p(z_k^{(l)}|y_k)p(y_k)}\right].$$

(10)

To find an estimate of $q(y_k)$ under the constraints: $q(y_k) \geq 0$ and $\sum_{k=1}^{K} q(y_k) = 1$, we introduce a Lagrange multiplier λ and solve:

$$\frac{1}{L}\sum_{k=1}^{K} q(y_k) \sum_{l=1}^{L} \log \left[\frac{q_\phi(z_k^{(l)}|\mathbf{x},y_k)q(y_k)}{p(z_k^{(l)}|y_k)p(y_k)}\right] + \lambda\left[1 - \sum_{k=1}^{K} q(y_k)\right].$$

(11)

Differentiating (11) w.r.t. $q(y_k)$ and setting the derivative equal to 0 gives an analytical solution of $q(y_k)$[1]:

$$\hat{q}(y_k) = \frac{\prod_{l=1}^{L}\left[\frac{p(y_k)p(z_k^{(l)}|y_k)}{q_\phi(z_k^{(l)}|\mathbf{x},y_k)}\right]}{\sum_{j=1}^{K}\prod_{l=1}^{L}\left[\frac{p(y_j)p(\mathbf{z}_j^{(l)}|y_j)}{q_\phi(\mathbf{z}_j^{(l)}|\mathbf{x},y_j)}\right]}.$$

(12)

---

[1] Detailed derivation is provided in the supplementary files on GitHub.

In (12), $\hat{q}(y_k)$ is the clustering assignment estimate, which gives the probability of an observation belonging to a particular class given latent vector $\mathbf{z}$, i.e., $\hat{q}(y_k) = p(y_k = 1|\mathbf{z})$. This estimate is associated with both the prior and variational posterior distributions. Now using $\hat{q}(y_k)$, we maximize the following Monte Carlo ELBO estimator of our proposed MVAE(EM) model (M-step):

$$\tilde{\mathcal{L}}_{\phi,\theta,\psi,\hat{q}(y)}(\mathbf{x}) = \frac{1}{L} \sum_{k=1}^{K} \hat{q}(y_k) \sum_{l=1}^{L} \log p_\theta(\mathbf{x}|\mathbf{z}_k^{(l)}) -$$

$$\frac{1}{L} \sum_{k=1}^{K} \hat{q}(y_{ik}) \sum_{l=1}^{L} \log \frac{q_\phi(\mathbf{z}_k^{(l)}|\mathbf{x}, y_k)\hat{q}(y_k)}{p(\mathbf{z}_k^{(l)}|y_k)p(y_k)}. \quad (13)$$

3.3 β-MVAE(EM)

The choice of how to weigh the two terms of the ELBO in (7) will significantly affect the results, placing more emphasis on either the regularization or the reconstruction. Therefore, we added a hyper-parameter $\beta > 0$ to control this balance:

$$\mathcal{L}_{\phi,\theta,\psi,q(\mathbf{y})}(\mathbf{x}) = \mathbb{E}_{(\mathbf{z},\mathbf{y}) \sim q_\phi(\mathbf{z}|\mathbf{x},\mathbf{y})q(\mathbf{y})} \log p_\theta(\mathbf{x}|\mathbf{z}) -$$

$$\beta\, D_{KL}\left[q_\phi(\mathbf{z}|\mathbf{x}, \mathbf{y})q(\mathbf{y}) \,\|\, p(\mathbf{z}|\mathbf{y})p(\mathbf{y}) \right]. \quad (14)$$

When $\beta = 1$, the objective function of the β-MVAE(EM) model turns to the MVAE(EM) model[2]. The Monte Carlo ELBO estimator of this model can be written as:

$$\tilde{\mathcal{L}}_{\phi,\theta,\psi,\hat{q}(\mathbf{y})}(\mathbf{x}) = \frac{1}{L} \sum_{k=1}^{K} \hat{q}(y_k) \sum_{l=1}^{L} \log p_\theta(\mathbf{x}|\mathbf{z}_k^{(l)}) -$$

$$\beta\frac{1}{L} \sum_{k=1}^{K} \hat{q}(y_k) \sum_{l=1}^{L} \log \frac{q_\phi(\mathbf{z}_k^{(l)}|\mathbf{x}, y_k)\hat{q}(y_k)}{p(\mathbf{z}_k^{(l)}|y_k)p(y_k)}. \quad (15)$$

We train the model using mini-batch stochastic gradient descent (SGD) to iteratively update the encoder NN (ϕ), decoder NN (θ), and prior distribution parameters $\psi = \{\pi_k, \mu_k, \text{diag}(\sigma_k^2)\}_{k=1}^{K}$. By incorporating a sum over mini-batch samples $\mathcal{B} = \{\mathbf{x}_1, \cdots, \mathbf{x}_B\}$ (where B is the mini-batch size) in (15), we obtain a soft optimization ELBO. By using the MAP estimate in $\hat{q}(y_k)$ from (12), we obtain a hard optimization ELBO function:

$$\tilde{\mathcal{L}}_{\phi,\theta,\psi,\hat{q}(\mathbf{y})}(\mathcal{B}) = \sum_{i=1}^{B} \tilde{l}_{i\hat{k}}; \hat{k} = \arg\max_k q(y_{ik}) \quad \text{and} \quad (16)$$

$$\tilde{l}_{ik} = \frac{1}{L} \sum_{l=1}^{L} \left[\log p_\theta(\mathbf{x}_i|\mathbf{z}_{ik}^{(l)}) - \beta\left\{ \log q_\phi(\mathbf{z}_{ik}^{(l)}|\mathbf{x}_i, y_{ik}) - \log p(\mathbf{z}_{ik}^{(l)}|y_{ik}) - \log p(y_{ik}) \right\} \right].$$

---

[2] Algorithm of MVAE and β-MVAE is provided in the supplementary files on GitHub.

4 Experiments and Results

In this section, we evaluate the clustering performance of our proposed models, MVAE(EM) and β-MVAE(EM), and compare them with the baseline algorithms: VAE [12], VADE [10], and k-DVAE [3]. We implemented all models in Python using the PyTorch library[3]. Experiments used 24-GB GPUs, specifically the NVIDIA RTX A5000 and Quadro RTX 6000, with CUDA version 12.3.

4.1 Datasets

We trained all the models on seven benchmark datasets, including images, text, and motion data. The MNIST [14], Fashion-MNIST [24], Digits [1], and USPS [9] dataset contain grayscale images of sizes 28×28, 28×28, 8×8, and 16×16 pixels, respectively. We flattened each dataset into a 1D vector and scaled the values to the range $[0, 1]$. The STL-10 dataset [4] comprises 10 different types of images of size 96×96 pixels. We extracted features using a pre-trained ResNet-50 model [7] and applied an average pooling operation to produce 2,048-dimensional inputs. The Reuters dataset [15] consists of text documents from 4 news categories. The input is based on TF-IDF feature vectors representing the most frequent words in the articles producing a 2,000-dimensional vector. The human activity recognition (HAR) dataset [19] contains measurements of six different activities. All features were scaled to the range $[-1, 1]$. Table 1 summarizes these datasets.

Table 1. Summary of the datasets.

Datasets	Dimension	No. of Samples		No. of Classes
		Training	Test	
MNIST	784	60,000	10,000	10
Fashion-MNIST	784	60,000	10,000	10
STL-10	2,048	8,000	5,000	10
USPS	256	7,291	2,007	10
Digits	64	1,527	270	10
Reuters	2,000	9,000	1,000	4
HAR	561	7,352	2,947	6

4.2 Experimental Setup

We used the same NN architecture for all datasets: $D - 500 - 500 - 2000 - M$ for the encoder and $M - 2000 - 500 - 500 - D$ for the decoder, where D and M represent the dimensionality of the input and the latent space, respectively, except for the Digits dataset, which is small, and where we used $D - 256 - 256 - M$ for the

---

[3] The code is available online at https://github.com/Mashfiqul/Beta_MVAE.

encoder and $M-256-256-D$ for the decoder. All NN layers were fully connected and used ReLU activation functions for the hidden layers. We performed hyper-parameter tuning for $M = \{5, 6, 7, 8, 9, 10\}$ and $\beta = \{0.1, 0.2, 0.3, 0.4, 0.5\}$, selecting these parameters based on the optimum clustering performance achieved by the model[4]. The activation function at the output layer varied by dataset, being tanh for HAR, linear for Reuters and STL-10, and sigmoid for the rest. We set the mini-batch size to 50 observations for the Digits dataset and 100 for the others. We draw a single Monte Carlo sample $(L = 1)$ to apply the RP trick. We used the ADAM [11] optimizer with an initial learning rate of 10^{-4} and a decay schedule of 9% every 20 epochs for the MNIST, STL-10, Reuters, Digits, and HAR datasets and every 30 epochs for the other datasets. A Dirichlet distribution initializes the mixing coefficient (π_k), and a standard normal distribution initializes both the mean $(\boldsymbol{\mu}_k)$ and log variance $(\log \boldsymbol{\sigma}_k^2)$ parameters. Each algorithm was trained for each dataset from five random seeds and latent embeddings extracted from the test data. A GMM with a full covariance structure was applied to the latent embeddings for cluster analysis, with 20 different parameter initializations, selecting the one that achieved the highest clustering accuracy. The results reported are the best test accuracy of the five trained algorithms, where accuracy is evaluated using the Hungarian algorithm [13] to give the unsupervised clustering accuracy (ACC):

$$\text{ACC} = \max_{m \in \mathcal{M}} \frac{1}{N} \sum_{i=1}^{N} \mathbf{I}\{y_i = m(\hat{y}(\mathbf{x}_i))\}, \tag{17}$$

where N is the total number of samples, y_i and $\hat{y}(\mathbf{x}_i)$ are the ground truth label and clustering assignment obtained by the model for a sample $\mathbf{x}_i$, $\mathcal{M}$ is the set of all permutations $\{1, \cdots, K\}$ between true and predicted labels, and $\mathbf{I}(.)$ denotes indicator function. ACC ranges between 0 and 1, with higher values indicating better clustering performance. Algorithm 1 presents the clustering procedure of the MVAE model.

4.3 Experimental Results

Table 2 presents the comparisons of all evaluated algorithms, indicating that our proposed models outperform state-of-the-art methods across most benchmark datasets. The constrained β-MVAE(EM) model demonstrates superior clustering performance compared to other models except for with the significantly smaller Digits dataset, where VADE outperforms it. We also conducted experiments to assess the clustering performance for higher values of the regularization coefficient. Table 3 shows that for $\beta > 1$, the clustering performance decreases, which is to be expected since this places a higher weight on the regularization term in (16).

Figures 1 and 2 show the original images and their reconstructions by the MVAE(EM) and β-MVAE(EM) for the MNIST and Fashion-MNIST datasets.

---

[4] The optimal M for each dataset are in the supplementary files on GitHub.

Algorithm 1: Clustering algorithm of MVAE(EM) and β-MVAE(EM)

Input: $\mathcal{D}_{\text{Test}} = \{\mathbf{x}_1, \cdots, \mathbf{x}_N\}$ and ground truth labels $(y_1, \cdots, y_N)$.
Output: Clustering accuracy (on test dataset).
for *each* $\mathbf{x}_i \in \{\mathbf{x}_1, \cdots, \mathbf{x}_N\}$ *from* $\mathcal{D}_{\text{Test}}$ **do**
    for *each* $k \in \{1, \cdots, K\}$ **do**
        $\tilde{\mathbf{z}}_{ik} \leftarrow \boldsymbol{\mu}_{\phi k}(\mathbf{x}_i)$.
        Compute the clustering assignment estimate $\hat{q}(y_{ik})$ using (12).
    Choose the representations based on the MAP estimate of $\hat{q}(y_{ik})$:
$$\mathbf{z}_i = \tilde{\mathbf{z}}_{i\hat{k}}; \hat{k} = \arg\max_k \hat{q}(y_{ik})$$

- N latent embeddings: $\mathbf{Z} = \{\mathbf{z}_1, \cdots, \mathbf{z}_N\}$.
- Apply the GMM method to $\mathbf{Z}$ and determine the predicted labels $(\hat{y})$.
- Use the Hungarian algorithm [13] to calculate the clustering accuracy.

Table 2. Best clustering accuracy (%) for different models over five random initializations. The best performance is highlighted in bold. The optimum β value for which the model achieves the highest accuracy is reported in parenthesis.

Datasets				Models			
	VAE	VADE	k-DVAE	MVAE (EM)		β-MVAE(EM)	
				Soft	Hard	Soft (β)	Hard (β)
Digits	84.44	**88.15**	74.44	66.67	71.48	84.44 (0.3)	81.48 (0.1)
MNIST	93.60	93.65	93.80	94.95	93.19	**96.42** (0.2)	95.49 (0.2)
USPS	67.66	78.33	74.14	81.12	78.57	85.80 (0.3)	**87.84** (0.1)
STL-10	87.62	89.16	89.32	94.54	87.66	**95.06** (0.1)	93.50 (0.1)
Fashion-MNIST	61.56	64.76	59.66	64.84	66.00	67.15 (0.1)	**67.57** (0.2)
Reuters	69.80	68.70	72.50	81.00	81.40	**82.70** (0.5)	78.50 (0.4)
HAR	74.38	74.92	70.31	70.95	74.79	79.64 (0.5)	**80.49** (0.1)

Table 3. Impact of β using β-MVAE(EM) model on MNIST. The best clustering accuracy is reported over five randomly initialized training sessions.

β	Clustering accuracy (%)	
	Soft optimization	Hard optimization
0.1	96.20	94.07
0.2	96.42	95.49
1.0	93.26	93.19
3.0	84.90	74.09
5.0	80.04	67.11
10.0	75.49	65.01

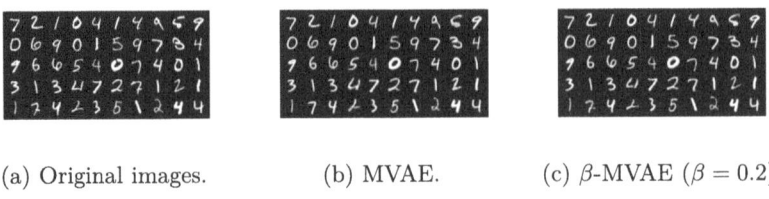

(a) Original images.   (b) MVAE.   (c) β-MVAE ($\beta = 0.2$)

Fig. 1. Original and reconstructed images of MNIST (test datasets).

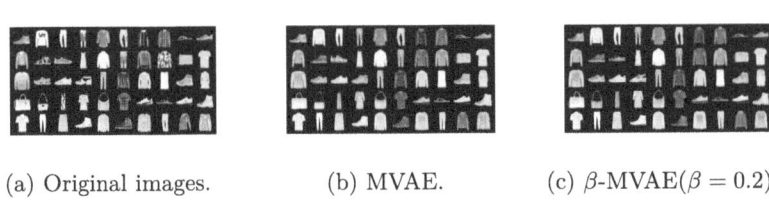

(a) Original images.   (b) MVAE.   (c) β-MVAE($\beta = 0.2$).

Fig. 2. Original and reconstructed images of Fashion-MNIST (test datasets).

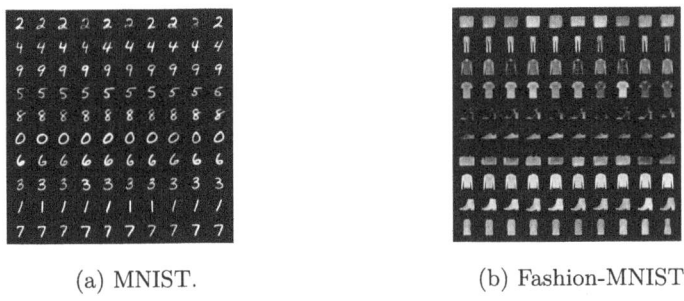

(a) MNIST.   (b) Fashion-MNIST.

Fig. 3. Generated images using the β-MVAE model ($\beta = 0.2$).

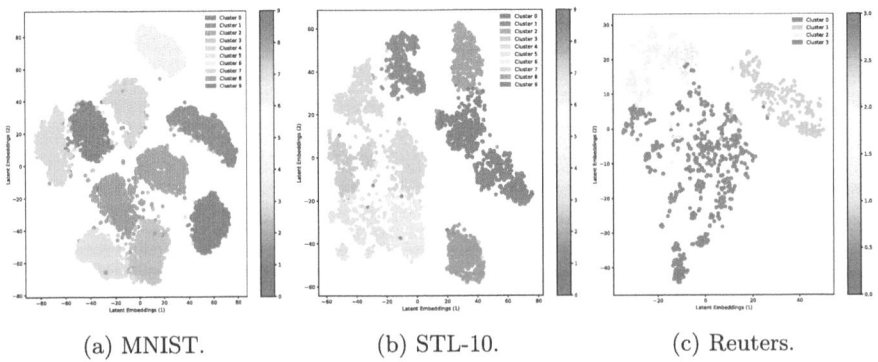

(a) MNIST.   (b) STL-10.   (c) Reuters.

Fig. 4. t-SNE representations using β-MVAE(EM) algorithm.

The original and reconstructed images are nearly identical. Figure 3 presents the generated images of the MNIST and Fashion-MNIST datasets using the trained constrained model with $\beta = 0.2$. The images of each row in Fig. 3 are generated by using samples from each cluster in the latent space. The samples $\mathbf{z}$ are drawn using the mean and variance of each cluster from the GMM model and then passed into a trained decoder NN. The generated images appear realistic. Figure 4 visualizes the learned latent embeddings of the test sets from the MNIST, STL-10, and Reuters datasets using t-SNE plots [23] with the β-MVAE(EM) algorithm. The t-SNE reduces the dimensionality of the latent space to 2, demonstrating a clear separation of the latent embeddings across clusters.

5   Conclusion

This paper presents a probabilistic mixture model for cluster analysis using the VAE framework. Our proposed model assumes a mixture distribution for both the variational posterior and prior components. The objective function integrates the clustering assignment estimate with all components of the VAE framework; here we use the EM algorithm to optimize the model parameters. The model is trained using either hard or soft optimization approaches. Experimental results on benchmark datasets demonstrate the superior clustering performance of our proposed mixtures VAE and constrained mixtures VAE methods compared to the baseline algorithms. The proposed models also exhibit good reconstruction performance and generate realistic examples from samples in the latent space.

References

1. Alpaydin, E., Kaynak, C.: Optical recognition of handwritten digits data set. UCI Mach. Learn. Repos. **64**, 5620 (1998)
2. Bishop, C.M.: Pattern Recognition and Machine Learning, vol. 4. Springer, New York (2006)
3. Caciularu, A., Goldberger, J.: An entangled mixture of variational autoencoders approach to deep clustering. Neurocomputing **529**, 182–189 (2023)
4. Coates, A., Ng, A., Lee, H.: An analysis of single-layer networks in unsupervised feature learning. In: Proceedings of the 14th AISTATS Conference. JMLR Workshop and Conference Proceedings, pp. 215–223 (2011)
5. Dilokthanakul, N., et al.: Deep unsupervised clustering with Gaussian mixture variational autoencoders. arXiv:1611.02648 (2016)
6. Guo, X., Gao, L., Liu, X., Yin, J.: Improved deep embedded clustering with local structure preservation. In: International Joint Conferences on Artificial Intelligence, vol. 17, pp. 1753–1759 (2017)
7. He, K., Zhang, X., Ren, S., Sun, J.: Deep residual learning for image recognition. In: Proceedings of the IEEE Conference on Computer Vision and Pattern Recognition, pp. 770–778 (2016)
8. Hoffman, M.D., Johnson, M.J.: Elbo surgery: yet another way to carve up the variational evidence lower bound. In: Workshop in Advances in Approximate Bayesian Inference, NIPS, vol. 1 (2016)

9. Hull, J.J.: A database for handwritten text recognition research. IEEE Trans. Pattern Anal. Mach. Intell. **16**(5), 550–554 (1994)
10. Jiang, Z., Zheng, Y., Tan, H., Tang, B., Zhou, H.: Variational deep embedding: a generative approach to clustering. CoRR, abs/1611.05148 1 (2016)
11. Kingma, D.P., Ba, J.: Adam: a method for stochastic optimization. In: International Conference on Learning Representations (2015)
12. Kingma, D.P., Welling, M.: Auto-encoding variational Bayes. In: International Conference on Learning Representations (2014)
13. Kuhn, H.W.: The Hungarian method for the assignment problem. Naval Res. Logist. Q. **2**(1–2), 83–97 (1955)
14. LeCun, Y., Bottou, L., Bengio, Y., Haffner, P.: Gradient-based learning applied to document recognition. IEEE Proc. **86**(11), 2278–2324 (1998)
15. Lewis, D.D., Yang, Y., Russell-Rose, T., Li, F.: RCV1: a new benchmark collection for text categorization research. J. Mach. Learn. Res. **5**, 361–397 (2004)
16. Li, X., Chen, Z., Poon, L.K., Zhang, N.L.: Learning latent superstructures in variational autoencoders for deep multidimensional clustering. In: International Conference on Learning Representations (2019)
17. Morningstar, W., Vikram, S., Ham, C., Gallagher, A., Dillon, J.: Automatic differentiation variational inference with mixtures. In: International Conference on Artificial Intelligence and Statistics, pp. 3250–3258. PMLR (2021)
18. Prasad, V., Das, D., Bhowmick, B.: Variational clustering: leveraging variational autoencoders for image clustering. In: 2020 International Joint Conference on Neural Networks (IJCNN), pp. 1–10. IEEE (2020)
19. Reyes-Ortiz, J., Anguita, D., Ghio, A., Oneto, L., Parra, X.: Human activity recognition using smartphones. UCI Mach. Learn. Repos. (2012). https://doi.org/10.24432/C54S4K
20. Rezende, D.J., Mohamed, S., Wierstra, D.: Stochastic backpropagation and approximate inference in deep generative models. In: International Conference on Machine Learning, pp. 1278–1286. PMLR (2014)
21. Steinbach, M., Ertöz, L., Kumar, V.: The challenges of clustering high dimensional data. In: Wille, L.T. (ed.) New Directions in Statistical Physics: Econophysics. Bioinformatics, and Pattern Recognition, pp. 273–309. Springer, Heidelberg (2004). https://doi.org/10.1007/978-3-662-08968-2_16
22. Tomczak, J., Welling, M.: VAE with a VampPrior. In: International Conference on Artificial Intelligence and Statistics, pp. 1214–1223. PMLR (2018)
23. Van der Maaten, L., Hinton, G.: Visualizing data using t-SNE. J. Mach. Learn. Res. **9**, 11 (2008)
24. Xiao, H., Rasul, K., Vollgraf, R.: Fashion-mnist: a novel image dataset for benchmarking machine learning algorithms. arXiv:1708.07747 (2017)
25. Xie, J., Girshick, R., Farhadi, A.: Unsupervised deep embedding for clustering analysis. In: International Conference on Machine Learning, pp. 478–487. PMLR (2016)
26. Yang, L., Cheung, N.-M., Li, J., Fang, J.: Deep clustering by Gaussian mixture variational autoencoders with graph embedding. In: Proceedings of the IEEE/CVF International Conference on Computer Vision, pp. 6440–6449 (2019)
27. Ye, F., Bors, A.G.: Deep mixture generative autoencoders. IEEE Trans. Neural Netw. Learn. Syst. **33**(10), 5789–5803 (2021)

UTBoost: Gradient Boosted Decision Trees for Uplift Modeling

Junjie Gao$^{(\boxtimes)}$, Xiangyu Zheng, DongDong Wang, Zhixiang Huang, and Bangqi Zheng

JD Technology, Beijing, China
{gaojunjie10,zhengxiangyu8,wangdongdong9,huangzhixiang,
zhengbangqi}@jd.com

Abstract. Uplift modeling comprises a collection of machine learning techniques designed for managers to predict the incremental impact of specific actions on customer outcomes. However, accurately estimating this incremental impact poses significant challenges due to the necessity of determining the difference between two mutually exclusive outcomes for each individual. In our study, we introduce two novel modifications to the established Gradient Boosting Decision Trees (GBDT) technique. These modifications sequentially learn the causal effect, addressing the counterfactual dilemma. Each modification innovates upon the existing technique in terms of the ensemble learning method and the learning objective, respectively. Experiments with large-scale datasets validate the effectiveness of our methods, consistently achieving substantial improvements over baseline models.

Keywords: Uplift modeling · Causal inference · Boosting trees

1 Introduction

Uplift modeling, a machine learning technique used to estimate the net effect of a particular action, has recently drawn considerable attention. In contrast to traditional supervised learning, uplift models concentrate on modeling the effect of a treatment on individual outcomes and generate uplift scores that show the probability of persuasion for each instance. This technique has proven particularly useful in personalized medicine, performance marketing, and social science.

However, a notable challenge in uplift modeling is the absence of observations for both treated and control conditions for an individual within the same context. Various uplift tree-based studies have tackled this challenge by creating measures of outcome differences between treated and untreated observations and maximizing heterogeneity between groups [1,16]. Several research studies provide further generalization to bagging ensemble methods on the idea of random forests [5,6], which aim to address the challenges of tree model performance decay with an increasing number of covariates. Despite the success of these nonparametric methods in prediction, we have experimentally discovered that random-forest

R. Hadfi et al. (Eds.): PRICAI 2024, LNAI 15281, pp. 41–53, 2025.
https://doi.org/10.1007/978-981-96-0116-5_4

based methods still suffer from significant degradation of power in predicting causal effects as the number of variables increases.

Boosted trees, with their iterative refinement capabilities, offer a promising solution. By sequentially fitting trees to residuals from previous models, boosting methods can effectively capture intricate patterns in the data, leading to more accurate uplift estimates. In this paper, we propose an innovative approach to the uplift tree method, which employs gradient boosting as the ensemble technique. Subsequent trees are fitted based on the causal effect learned by preceding models. Our findings indicate that while both ensemble learning methods perform comparably in low-dimensional settings, boosting exhibits significant advantages in handling high-dimensional data.

However, the split criterion employed in uplift tree fails to consider the learning of outcomes and instead focuses solely on uplift signals. An alternative approach is to utilise the outcomes observed under different treatments as a fitting objective, with meta-learning, in particular, gaining traction for its versatility in employing any machine learning estimator as a base model. The Single-Model [2] and Two-Model [13] approaches represent two prevalent strategies. The first method is trained over an entire space, with the treatment indicator serving as an additive input feature. However, this method's drawback is that a model may not select the treatment indicator if it only uses a subset of features for predictions, such as a tree model. Consequently, the causal effect is estimated as zero for all subjects. An enhancement over the Single-Model method involves using two separate models to represent the two potential outcomes. However, this dual-model approach does not leverage the shared information between control and treated subjects, resulting in cumulative errors [14]. Furthermore, additional model training also incurs higher training resource consumption and model deployment costs.

In this paper, we propose CausalGBM (Causal Gradient Boosting Machine), a new nonparametric method that utilizes tree models as base learners to simultaneously learn causal effects and potential outcomes through loss optimization. Our method explicitly computes the contribution of causal effects to the loss function at each split selection, avoiding the defect that the treatment indicator may not be picked up in some scenarios where the causal effects are weak. We further enhance the model's convergence speed by incorporating second-order gradient information. Experimental comparisons on four datasets demonstrate that our model outperforms baseline methods and shows better robustness. We have implemented our novel techniques in the UTBoost (Uplift Tree Boosting system) software[1], available under the MIT license. We highlight our contributions as follows:

1. We innovate the uplift tree method that focuses on maximizing heterogeneity by extending the ensemble of trees from bagging to boosting.
2. For the first time, we integrate potential outcomes and causal effects within the classical GBDT framework, employing a second-order method to fit the multi-objective function. In the context of randomized trials, we propose an

---

[1] https://github.com/jd-opensource/UTBoost.

approximation method that significantly reduces the computational complexity of the algorithm.
3. Through extensive experimentation on real-world and public datasets, we demonstrate that our models outperform baseline methods and exhibit superior robustness.

2   Uplift Problem Formulation

Uplift modeling seeks to quantify the incremental causal effect of interventions on individual outcomes. Given n independent and identically distributed samples $\{(\mathbf{X}_i, y_i, w_i)\}_{i=1}^n$, where each sample comprises p features $\mathbf{X}_i \in \mathbb{R}^p$, an observed outcome $y_i \in \mathbb{R}$, and a binary treatment indicator w_i, which indicates whether unit i received treatment ($w_i = 1$) or control ($w_i = 0$). Let $y_i(1)$ and $y_i(0)$ be the potential outcomes that would be observed for unit i when $w_i = 1$ and 0, respectively. The uplift of an individual i, denoted by τ_i, is denoted as: $\tau_i = y_i(1) - y_i(0)$.

In practice, we will never observe both $y_i(1)$ and $y_i(0)$ for a same individual and thus τ_i cannot be directly calculated. Fortunately, we can use the conditional average treatment effect (CATE) as an estimator for the uplift. In the uplift modeling literature [19], it is typical to assume that the treatment w_i is randomly assigned and CATE is defined as:

$$\tau(\mathbf{x}) = \mathbb{E}[y|w=1, \mathbf{X}=\mathbf{x}] - \mathbb{E}[y|w=0, \mathbf{X}=\mathbf{x}], \tag{1}$$

which signifies the uplift on y caused by the treatment w for the subject with feature $\mathbf{x}$. Uplift can be empirically estimated by considering two groups: a treatment group and a control group (without treatment).

3   Tree Boosting for Treatment Effect Estimation

Our first proposed method adopts a sequential learning approach to fit uplift directly. This method extends the ensemble learning approach of uplift tree, and it has better performance on high-dimensional data compared to the uplift random forest method. As the splitting criterion in the training process is similar to the standard delta-delta-p (DDP) algorithm [8], which aims to maximize the difference of uplift between the left and right child nodes. We refer to this method as TDDP (Transformed DDP). It enables incremental training of subsequent uplift trees by transforming the sample labels in each iteration.

3.1   Ensemble Learning with Transformed Labels

Taking the decision tree as the base learner, we use a sequence of decision trees to predict the uplift $\tau(\mathbf{x})$. As the uplift cannot be observed for each sample unit, the ensemble method for $\tau(\mathbf{x})$ differs from the common supervised-learning scenarios. We explicitly derive the optimization target for uplift estimation in each iteration of the boosting.

Denoting a tree model by $T(\mathbf{x}; \theta_j)$, where θ_j encapsulates the model's parameters, including partitioning and leaf node estimation, our goal is to predict the uplift through the equation: $\hat{\tau}(\mathbf{x}) = \sum_{j=1}^{M} T(\mathbf{x}; \theta_j)$. We sequentially optimize $T(\mathbf{x}; \theta_j)$ to minimize the loss associated with $\hat{\tau}(\mathbf{x})$.

Let $u_m = \sum_{j=1}^{m} T(\mathbf{x}; \theta_j)$ represent the cumulative prediction of the first m trees. At step m, with the current prediction u_m, the loss is denoted by $\mathcal{L}(\tau(\mathbf{x}), u_m(\mathbf{x}))$. The gradient, then, is defined as $\boldsymbol{g}_m := \frac{\partial \mathcal{L}(\tau(\mathbf{x}), u_m(\mathbf{x}))}{\partial u_m(\mathbf{x})}$, where $-\boldsymbol{g}_m$ indicates a local direction for further decreasing the loss at u_m. Thus, in a greedy manner, we fit $T(\mathbf{x}; \theta_{m+1})$ to approximate $\boldsymbol{g}_m$. Specifically, for uplift modeling, the quadratic loss at step m can be expressed as:

$$\mathcal{L}(\tau(\mathbf{x}), u_m(\mathbf{x})) = \frac{1}{2} \Big\{ \mathbb{E}[y|\mathbf{X} = \mathbf{x}, w = 1] - \mathbb{E}[y|\mathbf{X} = \mathbf{x}, w = 0] - u_m(\mathbf{x}) \Big\}^2$$

with the coefficient $\frac{1}{2}$ simplifying gradient computation. The negative gradient then becomes:

$$-\frac{\partial \mathcal{L}(\tau(\mathbf{x}), u_m(\mathbf{x}))}{\partial u_m(\mathbf{x})} = \mathbb{E}[y - u_m(\mathbf{x})|\mathbf{X} = \mathbf{x}, w = 1] - \mathbb{E}[y|\mathbf{X} = \mathbf{x}, w = 0].$$

Thus, in constructing the $(m+1)$-th tree, $T(\mathbf{x}; \theta_{m+1})$, we transform the outcome y_i to $y_i - u_m(\mathbf{X}_i)$ for treated units, while maintaining the original outcome for the control group. This approach allows for tree construction based on these transformed outcomes. Algorithm 1 outlines the overall training procedures for TDDP, where the *split criterion* temporarily serves as a placeholder and the details will be introduced in the following Subsect. 3.2.

3.2   Tree Construction Method

Here, we delve into the split criterion, a pivotal component of our tree construction methodology.

Split Criterion. Traditional CART algorithms select splits to minimize mean squared errors (MSE) in regression trees. However, this approach is not directly applicable in uplift modeling due to the unobservability of unit-level uplift (τ_i). In our context, we adapt this criterion to leverage aggregated uplift statistics, such as averages or variances, available within groups of units.

In the next, we will show that minimizing the MSE is equivalent to maximizing the gaps between the average uplift within the split nodes. Consider the split selection at an internal root node t with data $D_t := \{\mathbf{X}_i, y_i, w_i\}_{i=1}^{n_t}$. Let s denote a split, s_L and s_R denote the indices set in the left and right child nodes with sub-sample size n_L and n_R, respectively, under the split s. For example, suppose $s = \{x_j = a\}$ for a numeric variable x_j, then $s_L = \{i|X_{ij} \leq a\}$ and $s_R = \{i|X_{ij} > a\}$. Let $\bar{\tau}_L := \sum_{i \in s_L} \frac{\tau_i}{n_L}$ and $\bar{\tau}_R := \sum_{i \in s_R} \frac{\tau_i}{n_R}$ denote the average uplift in the left and right child nodes, respectively. Then we have the following proposition:

Algorithm 1. Gradient Tree Boosting for Uplift Modeling

Input: Data: $\mathcal{D} = \{(\mathbf{X}_i, y_i, w_i)\}_{i=1}^N$, Shrinkage rate: α
Output: $u_M = \sum_{m=1}^M T(\mathbf{x}; \theta_m)$
1: Set $u_0(\mathbf{x}) = 0$.
2: **for** $m = 1, \cdots, M$ **do**
3:     Set $y_i = y_i - T(\mathbf{x}, \theta_{m-1})$ for $\{i \mid w_i = 1\}$.
4:     **Build Tree Structure:** Recursively partition $\mathcal{D}^m$:
5:     **while** the *stopping rule* is not satisfied **do**
6:         Select the optimal split s^* in the candidate splits by criterion (*split criterion*).
7:         Split the current node into child nodes by s^*.
8:     **end while**
9:     Output the Tree Structure T_m
10:    **Obtain the Estimator** $T(\mathbf{x}; \theta_m)$:
11:    **for** each leaf node t_i of T_m **do**
12:        Get $D^m(t_i)$: the sample units in D^m that fall into t_i.
13:        Estimate Weight: $\hat{\tau}_m(t_i) = \bar{Y}_1(D^m(t_i)) - \bar{Y}_0(D^m(t_i))$.
14:        Output the m-th predictor: $T(\mathbf{x}; \theta_m) = \alpha \hat{\tau}_m(t_{T_m}(\mathbf{x}))$, where $t_{T_m}(x)$ denotes the leaf node that x belongs to in T_m.
15:    **end for**
16: **end for**

Proposition 1. *Minimizing the mean squared errors of τ_i in the split nodes is equivalent to maximizing the difference between the average uplift within the left and right child nodes, i.e.,*

$$argmin_s \left\{ \sum_{i|i \in s_L} (\tau_i - \bar{\tau}_L)^2 + \sum_{i|i \in s_R} (\tau_i - \bar{\tau}_R)^2 \right\} = argmax_s \left\{ \frac{n_L n_R}{n} (\bar{\tau}_L - \bar{\tau}_R)^2 \right\}.$$

Proposition 1 guides us to a practical split criterion for the uplift modeling as both $\bar{\tau}_L$ and $\bar{\tau}_R$ are aggregated values that can be estimated from data. Taking $\bar{\tau}_L$ as an example, the definition of $\bar{\tau}_L$ involves $\{y_i(1), y_i(0)\}$ as shown in equation (2),

$$\bar{\tau}_L = \frac{\sum_{i \in s_L} y_i(1) - y_i(0)}{n_L} = \bar{Y}_L(1) - \bar{Y}_L(0). \tag{2}$$

Under randomly assigned treatment, $\bar{Y}(1)$ and $\bar{Y}(0)$ can be estimated by the sample average of y in the treatment and control groups, respectively. Therefore, the optimal split s^* is selected by the following rule:

$$s^* = \arg \max_s \left\{ \frac{n_L n_R}{n} \left[(\bar{Y}_L^1 - \bar{Y}_L^0) - (\bar{Y}_R^1 - \bar{Y}_R^0) \right]^2 \right\}, \qquad (split\ criterion)$$

where $Y_L^1 := \frac{\sum_{i|i \in s_L; w_i = 1} y_i}{n_L^1}$ with n_L^1 denoting the number of treated units in the left child node, and Y_L^0, Y_R^1, Y_R^0 are defined similarly.

It's important to note that TDDP, while inspired by gradient boosting, diverges from it by focusing on observed outcomes and directing weak learners towards uncovering heterogeneities in treatment effects rather than strictly following a gradient descent path. Moreover, as TDDP is exclusively concerned with uplift as the learning objective, this method is unsuitable for estimating potential outcomes. In the following section, we put forward an alternative gradient boosting method which takes both causal effects and potential outcomes as dual learning objectives and adheres strictly to the gradient descent path.

4   Causal Gradient Boosting Machine

Single-Model and Two-Model are two widely used strategies. However, Single-Model suffers from model invalidation due to unselected treatment indicator variables, while Two-Model's dual model incurs accumulated errors [14] and doubled training and deployment costs. In order to alleviate the shortcomings of the two approaches, we propose a Causal Gradient Boosting Machine (CausalGBM) to fit causal effects and outcomes in a single learner. This approach extends the standard gradient boosting algorithm to the field of causal effect estimation, thus bridging the gap between the two classes of methods. Since this technique calculates the contribution of causal effects to the loss separately at each split, it does not suffer from the problem of model failure that may occur in Single-Model, and compared with the Two-Model method, it can train a single model using the information of the whole samples set, avoiding the accumulation of errors by multiple models.

4.1   Learning Objective

In order to realize the simultaneous estimation of the two objectives, we split the original single learning task. We can conduct that:

$$y_i = y_i(1)w_i + y_i(0)(1 - w_i) = w_i \tau_i + y_i(0) \tag{3}$$

which indicates that for treated instances, observed outcomes are the sum of potential outcomes and individual causal effects, while for control instances, they equate to the potential outcomes alone. This relationship facilitates the indirect learning of both potential outcomes and individual causal effects from the observed data.

We employ a tree ensemble model with $2M$ additive functions to predict the output for a dataset with n samples and p features:

$$\hat{y}_i = \sum_{m=1}^{M} f_m(\mathbf{X}_i) + w_i \tau_m(\mathbf{X}_i), \ f_m, \tau_m \in \mathcal{F}$$

where $\mathcal{F} = \{f(\mathbf{X}) = v_{q(\mathbf{X})}, \tau(\mathbf{X}) = u_{q(\mathbf{X})}\}(q : \mathbb{R}^p \to T, v \in \mathbb{R}^T, u \in \mathbb{R}^T)$ represents the regression trees space. Here q maps each example to the corresponding leaf index in each tree, and T refers to the number of leaves in the tree. Note that leaf weights comprise both u and v in this framework, which is significantly different from the classical regression tree. We will use the decision rules in the trees (given by q) to classify instances to leaves and compute the final predictions by summing up the scores by (3) in the corresponding leaves (given by u, v). To learn the set of functions that are employed in the ensemble model, we minimize the following objective function: $\mathcal{L}(\theta) = \sum_i l(y_i, \hat{y}_i)$. Here l is a differentiable convex loss function that measures the difference between the prediction and the observed label. Using the binary decision tree as a meta-learner, we train the ensemble model sequentially to minimize loss. In other words, let $\hat{y}_i^t$ be the prediction of the i-th instance at the t-th iteration, we add $f_t + w_i \tau_t$ to minimize the following objective:

$$\mathcal{L}^{(t)} = \sum_{i=1}^{n} l(y_i, \hat{y}_i(0)^{(t-1)} + f_t(\mathbf{X}_i) + w_i(\hat{\tau}_i^{(t-1)} + \tau_t(\mathbf{X}_i)))$$

We employ a second-order approximation to expedite the optimization process.

Under the setting that $w_i \in [0,1]$, we can remove the constant terms to obtain the following simplified objective at step t:

$$\tilde{\mathcal{L}}^{(t)} = \sum_{i=1}^{n} [w_i g_i \tau_t(\mathbf{X}_i) + \frac{1}{2} w_i h_i \tau_t^2(\mathbf{X}_i) + g_i f_t(\mathbf{X}_i) + \frac{1}{2} h_i f_t^2(\mathbf{X}_i) + w_i h_i \tau_t(\mathbf{X}_i) f_t(\mathbf{X}_i)]$$

where $g_i = \partial_{\hat{y}^{(t-1)}} l(y_i, \hat{y}^{(t-1)})$ and $h_i = \partial^2_{\hat{y}^{(t-1)}} l(y_i, \hat{y}^{(t-1)})$ are first and second order gradient statistics on the loss function. Note that they are defined in the same way as standard gradient trees.

Define $I_j = \{i | q(\mathbf{X}_i) = j\}$ as the instance set of leaf j, we can rewrite the above equation as:

$$\tilde{\mathcal{L}}^{(t)} = \sum_{j=1}^{T} [(\sum_{i \in I_j} w_i g_i + w_i h_i f_j) \tau_j + \frac{1}{2}(\sum_{i \in I_j} w_i h_i) \tau_j^2 + (\sum_{i \in I_j} g_i) f_j + \frac{1}{2}(\sum_{i \in I_j} h_i) f_j^2]$$

We can further derive the optimal values for f_j and τ_j of this dual quadratic function and the corresponding optimal weights v^* and u^*. However, it is important to note that solving for both weights simultaneously will result in a significant decrease in the computing efficiency of the algorithm, compared to the standard regression tree, which has a simpler analytic solution for the quadratic function, during training process. We will introduce an approximation method to solve this difficulty in the next section.

4.2   Multi-objective Approximation

We point that if all w_i are equal to 0, i.e., the data set contains only control samples, the above equation is identical to the optimization objective of the regression tree, and we can compute the optimal v_0^* in that specific context.

Under the setting that treatments are assigned randomly, we further assume that $v^* = v_0^*$ on each leaf, which enables us to derive the optimal weights v^* with control instances. After that, the objective function degenerates to a simple quadratic function with one variable and we can solve optimal u^*. We can compute the optimal weights by

$$v_j^* = -\frac{\sum_{i \in I_j^0} g_i}{\sum_{i \in I_j^0} h_i}, \quad u_j^* = -\frac{\sum_{i \in I_j} w_i g_i + w_i h_i v_j^*}{\sum_{i \in I_j} w_i h_i} = -\frac{\sum_{i \in I_j^1} g_i + h_i v_j^*}{\sum_{i \in I_j^1} h_i}$$

where $I_j^0 = \{i | q(\mathbf{X}_i) = j, w_i = 0\}$ is the control instance set and $I_j^1 = \{i | q(\mathbf{X}_i) = j, w_i = 1\}$ is the treated instance set of leaf j. It is obvious that, after obtaining v^* from the control group, u^* is only related to the treated samples. This innovation simplifies the original solution process to sequentially solving two quadratic equations in one variable. It also enables the CausalGBM algorithm to scale to multiple treatment scenarios with minimal additional computational resources, as u^* is computed based on the samples of the corresponding group independently of other groups. We then calculate the corresponding optimal loss by:

$$\tilde{\mathcal{L}}_{global}^{(t)}(q) = \sum_{j=1}^{T} [(\sum_{i \in I_j} g_i) v_j^* + \frac{1}{2} (\sum_{i \in I_j} h_i)(v_j^*)^2 - \frac{(\sum_{i \in I_j^1} g_i + h_i v_j^*)^2}{2 \sum_{i \in I_j^1} h_i}]$$

Note that the value is obtained by computing all instances on leaf I_j to ensure the global loss is optimized under this approximation method.

4.3　Greedy Algorithm for Tree Construction

Enumerating all possible tree structures to find the minimum loss is infeasible due to the combinatorial explosion. Instead, we employ a greedy algorithm that recursively bifurcates nodes, starting with a single parent node. We define the loss of a leaf as:

$$\tilde{\mathcal{L}}_{leaf}^{(t)} = (\sum_{i \in I_{leaf}} g_i) f_j^* + \frac{1}{2} (\sum_{i \in I_{leaf}} h_i)(f_j^*)^2 - \frac{(\sum_{i \in I_{leaf}^1} g_i + h_i f_j^*)^2}{2 \sum_{i \in I_{leaf}^1} h_i}$$

Assume that I_L and I_R are the instance sets of left and right nodes after the split. Letting $I = I_L \cup I_R$, then the loss reduction after the split is given by:

$$\tilde{\mathcal{L}}_{split} = \tilde{\mathcal{L}}_I^{(t)} - (\tilde{\mathcal{L}}_L^{(t)} + \tilde{\mathcal{L}}_R^{(t)})$$

The above function will be used to evaluate the candidate split points. Compared with the gbm algorithm, CausalGBM redefines the computation formulas for weights and evaluation functions in uplift modeling problems. As for the construction of the tree, we follow the computational framework of lightgbm but have adjusted the calculation methods pertaining to weights and evaluations.

5   Experiments

In this section we present an experimental evaluation of the two proposed algorithms and compare their performance with performance of the base models and bagging. To comprehensively evaluate our proposed methods, extensive experiments were conducted on three large-scale real-world datasets [4,9] and a synthetic dataset [3]. A summary of these datasets is given in Table 1.

Table 1. The basic statistics of datasets used in the paper.

Metrics	CRITEO	HILLSTROM	VOUCHER	SYNTHETIC$_m$
Size	1,000,000	42,693	371,730	200,000
Features	12	8	2076	m
Avg. Label	0.047	0.129	0.356	0.600
Treatment Ratio	0.85	0.50	0.85	0.50
Relative Uplift (%)	26.7	42.6	2.0	50.0

Evaluation Protocols. We perform 10-fold cross-validation and use Qini coefficient [4,7,19] (normalized by prefect Qini score) for evaluation, and we perform a grid search for hyperparameters to search for an optimal parameter set that achieved the best performance on the validation dataset, which consisted of 25% of the training dataset in each fold.

5.1   Overall Performance Comparison

To verify that our proposed methods can make the uplift prediction model more accurate, we compare TDDP and CausalGBM with different types of baselines and show their prediction performance on four large-scale datasets in Table 2. Here, we summarize key observations and insights as follows:

CausalGBM's Superior Performance: Our proposed model CausalGBM outperforms all different baseline methods across all datasets. Specifically, it achieves relative performance gains of 1.1%, 1.3%, 22.7%, and 1.5% on four datasets, respectively, comparing to the best baseline. Further, Qini reflects the model's ability to give high predicted probabilities of persuasion to those who are actually more likely to be persuaded, and the improvement implies that our proposed model more accurately finds the target population for which the treatment is effective.

CausalGBM's Robustness Across Different Scenarios: Comparing results across four datasets of varying scales, many baseline models lack robustness. For instance, URF-based methods excel on HILLSTROM and CRITEO but

Table 2. Model performance evaluated by Qini coefficient on four datasets with corresponding mean and standard error. "S-", "T-", "TO-" and "URF-" stands for instantiations of single-model [2], two-model [13], transformed outcome [10] and uplift random forest [5], respectively. The base learner for the methods in the first part of the table is Lightgbm. For methods of "URF-", we select four splitting criteria based on KL divergence, χ^2 divergence, Euclidean and the difference of uplift (DDP) between the two leaves for decision trees.

Model	HILLSTROM	CRITEO	VOUCHER	SYNTHETIC$_{100}$
	Qini Coefficient ($mean \pm s.e.$)			
S-LGB	0.0616 ± 0.018	0.0933 ± 0.016	0.0032 ± 0.005	0.1812 ± 0.003
T-LGB	0.0567 ± 0.018	0.0900 ± 0.018	0.0014 ± 0.005	0.1831 ± 0.002
TO-LGB	0.0377 ± 0.020	0.0941 ± 0.020	0.0048 ± 0.006	0.1832 ± 0.004
X-Learner [11]	0.0619 ± 0.015	0.0929 ± 0.025	0.0029 ± 0.007	0.1824 ± 0.003
R-Learner [12]	0.0621 ± 0.021	0.0936 ± 0.020	0.0033 ± 0.007	0.1829 ± 0.003
TARNet [17]	$\underline{0.0636 \pm 0.020}$	0.0935 ± 0.011	0.0045 ± 0.008	0.1803 ± 0.005
CFRNet [17]	0.0635 ± 0.022	0.0909 ± 0.017	0.0042 ± 0.008	0.1829 ± 0.004
CForest [18]	0.0617 ± 0.014	0.0933 ± 0.011	0.0055 ± 0.004	0.1395 ± 0.004
UB-RF [15]	0.0595 ± 0.013	$\underline{0.0959 \pm 0.019}$	0.0081 ± 0.009	0.1775 ± 0.005
URF-Chi	0.0623 ± 0.017	0.0925 ± 0.013	0.0062 ± 0.007	0.1003 ± 0.005
URF-ED	0.0613 ± 0.018	0.0942 ± 0.014	0.0070 ± 0.006	0.1657 ± 0.006
URF-KL	0.0605 ± 0.016	0.0926 ± 0.012	0.0060 ± 0.006	0.1457 ± 0.004
URF-DDP	0.0599 ± 0.016	0.0938 ± 0.014	0.0072 ± 0.006	0.1661 ± 0.005
TDDP	0.0576 ± 0.012	0.0884 ± 0.018	$\underline{0.0088 \pm 0.006}$	$\underline{0.1836 \pm 0.005}$
CausalGBM	$\mathbf{0.0643 \pm 0.025}$	$\mathbf{0.0971 \pm 0.014}$	$\mathbf{0.0108 \pm 0.004}$	$\mathbf{0.1863 \pm 0.004}$

perform poorly on SYNTHETIC$_{100}$, likely due to the smaller feature dimensions of the first two datasets. In contrast, CausalGBM consistently achieves the best performance across all datasets, demonstrating its robustness.

On the VOUCHER dataset, deep learning and some meta-learning methods, which focus on fitting potential outcomes, are weaker than tree models that emphasize causal effect heterogeneity. This dataset has the weakest causal effect significance, challenging methods that only consider potential outcomes, resulting in predicted causal effects close to zero. URF-based methods still perform well by minimizing heterogeneous differences. CausalGBM, trained to compute both potential outcomes and causal effects simultaneously, remains robust on the weak causal effect dataset compared to methods driven solely by potential outcomes. However, on the HILLSTROM dataset, CausalGBM exhibited high variance, which was not observed on other datasets. This indicates that the algorithm shows some performance fluctuations on smaller-scale data.

An Analysis of the Volatility for TDDP on Different Datasets: The difference between TDDP and URF-DDP lies in the ensemble learning method.

Comparing the performances of the two methods on four datasets, TDDP performs better on the dataset with high-dimensional features, while URF-DDP performs better on the dataset consisting of low-dimensional features. A plausible reason is that TDDP overfits the data in datasets with low-dimensional features, meanwhile, URF-DDP does not fit the data in high-dimensional datasets adequately.

5.2 Analysis of Ensemble Method

We will study how the ensemble learning method contributes to the predictive performance of the model in this section. In order to better visualize the experimental findings and prevent the derivation of conclusions from misleading information, we select the synthetic dataset and divide 50% as the training set and the remaining part as the test (Fig. 1).

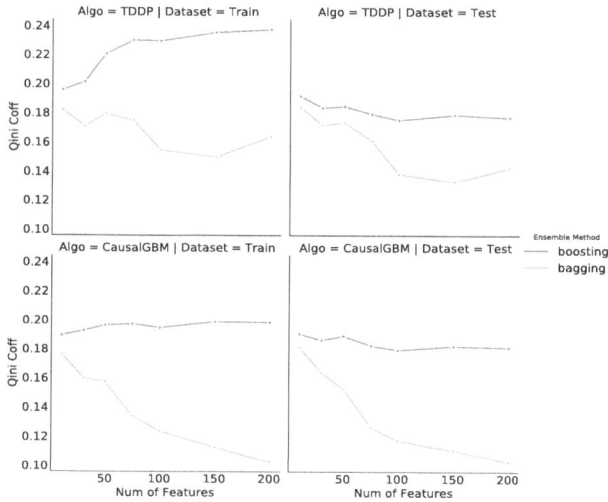

Fig. 1. The result on different ensemble methods. The upper and lower parts are the results of TDDP and CasualGBM respectively, while the left and right parts represent the training and testing datasets. Two ensemble methods are distinguished by color.

We compare the prediction results of TDDP and CausalGBM with an ablation version using bagging instead of boosting. In this version, the gradient is computed only once before training and remains constant. We find that boosted trees significantly enhances the model's ability to fit the training data compared to bagging, especially as feature dimensionality increases. This improvement is also evident in the test dataset, indicating that boosting is particularly effective for high-dimensional datasets. On low-dimensional datasets, the difference between the methods is minimal. Additionally, the boosting version of TDDP tends to overfit with increasing feature size, leading to weaker generalization compared to CausalGBM.

In light of this finding, we suggest that tree models, which focus on the heterogeneity of local causal effects, require regularization methods to avoid overfitting, compared to the GBM approach that optimizes the global loss function.

6   Conclusion

In this paper, we formulate two novel boosting methods for the uplift modeling problem. The first algorithm we propose follows the idea of maximizing the heterogeneity of causal effects. In contrast, the second algorithm we proposed, CausalGBM, fits both potential outcomes and causal effects by optimizing the loss function. We demonstrate that our proposed techniques outperform the baseline model on large-scale real datasets, where the CausalGBM algorithm shows excellent robustness, while the TDDP algorithm needs to blend in some regularization methods to prevent the model from overfitting the training data.

References

1. Athey, S., Imbens, G.: Recursive partitioning for heterogeneous causal effects: table 1. Proc. Natl. Acad. Sci. **113**(27), 7353–7360 (2016)
2. Athey, S., Imbens, G.W.: Machine learning methods for estimating heterogeneous causal effects. Stat **1050**(5), 1–26 (2015)
3. Chen, H., Harinen, T., Lee, J.Y., Yung, M., Zhao, Z.: Causalml: python package for causal machine learning (2020)
4. Diemert, E., Betlei, A., Renaudin, C., Amini, M.R.: A large scale benchmark for uplift modeling. In: KDD (2018)
5. Guelman, L., Guillén, M., Pérez-Marín, A.M.: Random forests for uplift modeling: an insurance customer retention case. In: Engemann, K.J., Gil-Lafuente, A.M., Merigó, J.M. (eds.) MS 2012. LNBIP, vol. 115, pp. 123–133. Springer, Heidelberg (2012). https://doi.org/10.1007/978-3-642-30433-0_13
6. Guelman, L., Guillén, M., Pérez-Marín, A.M.: Uplift random forests. Cybern. Syst. **46**(3–4), 230–248 (2015)
7. Gutierrez, P., Gérardy, J.Y.: Causal inference and uplift modelling: a review of the literature. In: International Conference on Predictive Applications and APIs, pp. 1–13. PMLR (2017)
8. Hansotia, B., Rukstales, B.: Incremental value modeling. J. Interact. Mark. **16**(3), 35–46 (2002)
9. Hillstrom, K.: The minethatdata e-mail analytics and data mining challenge. MineThatData blog (2008)
10. Jaskowski, M., Jaroszewicz, S.: Uplift modeling for clinical trial data. In: ICML Workshop on Clinical Data Analysis, vol. 46, pp. 79–95 (2012)
11. Künzel, S.R., Sekhon, J.S., Bickel, P.J., Yu, B.: Metalearners for estimating heterogeneous treatment effects using machine learning. Proc. Natl. Acad. Sci. **116**(10), 4156–4165 (2019)
12. Nie, X., Wager, S.: Quasi-oracle estimation of heterogeneous treatment effects. Biometrika **108**(2), 299–319 (2021)

13. Radcliffe, N.: Using control groups to target on predicted lift: building and assessing uplift model. Direct Mark. Anal. J. 14–21 (2007)
14. Radcliffe, N.J., Surry, P.D.: Real-world uplift modelling with significance-based uplift trees. White Paper TR-2011-1, Stochastic Solutions, pp. 1–33 (2011)
15. Rafla, M., Voisine, N., Crémilleux, B.: Parameter-free Bayesian decision trees for uplift modeling. In: Kashima, H., Ide, T., Peng, W.C. (eds.) PAKDD 2023. LNCS, vol. 13936, pp. 309–321. Springer, Cham (2023). https://doi.org/10.1007/978-3-031-33377-4_24
16. Rzepakowski, P., Jaroszewicz, S.: Decision trees for uplift modeling with single and multiple treatments. Knowl. Inf. Syst. **32**(2), 303–327 (2012)
17. Shalit, U., Johansson, F.D., Sontag, D.: Estimating individual treatment effect: generalization bounds and algorithms. In: International Conference on Machine Learning, pp. 3076–3085. PMLR (2017)
18. Wager, S., Athey, S.: Estimation and inference of heterogeneous treatment effects using random forests. J. Am. Stat. Assoc. **113**(523), 1228–1242 (2018)
19. Zhang, W., Li, J., Liu, L.: A unified survey of treatment effect heterogeneity modelling and uplift modelling. ACM Comput. Surv. (CSUR) (2021)

CodeMosaic Patch: Physical Adversarial Attacks Against Infrared Aerial Object Detectors

Hangwei He, Libing Wu$^{(\boxtimes)}$, Enshu Wang$^{(\boxtimes)}$, Yizhou Wang, and Yu Zhao

School of Cyber Science and Engineering, Wuhan University, Wuhan 430072, China
{wu,wanges17}@whu.edu.cn

Abstract. In recent years, drones illegally spy on military bases and steal military secrets, especially in dark scenes. In the face of illegal detection by drones, physical infrared adversarial patches can play a defensive role. Existing methods are either hard to implement physically or lose effectiveness over time. They also overlook that the target may be positioned at various angles. To solve this problem, we design the CodeMosaic Patch (CMP) method for attacks on infrared remote sensing object detectors, which combines remote sensing attacks and infrared attacks to hide non-live targets like vehicles. The CMP utilizes differential evolutionary algorithms to train the patch's structure, texture, size, position, and rotation angle. We use aluminum foil as the reproduction material for infrared patches, successfully concealing the target object from infrared detectors in the real world. Experimental results show that the average digital and physical domain attack success rates (ASR) are 84.2% and 81.02%, respectively. Notably, our CMP can transition from infrared to visible light, achieving a 92.42% ASR and demonstrating cross-modality generalization. This represents the first instance of a patch with cross-modality attack performance being proposed.

Keywords: Infrared adversarial attacks · Physical adversarial patches · Infrared aerial object detectors · Cross-modality generalization capabilities

1 Introduction

With the rapid increase in the number of drones worldwide [1], remote sensing data applications are playing an increasingly important role in the fields of military security and environmental monitoring and protection [2]. It follows that automatic analysis, for example, deep neural networks(DNN) are used for image classification, object detection, and semantic segmentation of images collected from drones.

While the practicality of deep learning is well-recognized, the vulnerability of DNNs to adversarial examples is increasingly under scrutiny. DNNs are susceptible to digital perturbations, but these are hard to implement in real life due

R. Hadfi et al. (Eds.): PRICAI 2024, LNAI 15281, pp. 54–68, 2025.
https://doi.org/10.1007/978-981-96-0116-5_5

to their pixel-level changes [3]. Consequently, research is shifting to adversarial patches [4–7]. For example, colorful physical patches on traffic signs can mislead autonomous vehicles, causing accidents [5,8]. Similarly, patches on vehicles can help them evade camera tracking, creating 'stealth cars' [9].

The security of DNNs has attracted a great deal of attention in the visible light field [10–13], but it has not been fully explored in infrared imaging. Infrared images are not affected by weather conditions such as atmosphere, temperature and light. They have strong anti-interference capabilities, making them suitable for security monitoring [14], remote sensing [15] and other safety-critical tasks. Therefore, it is necessary to study the robustness of physical adversarial patches against infrared target detectors. The aforementioned adversarial patches do not work well in infrared images because they are adversarial perturbations generated by the RGB appearance view [16]. Therefore, training an infrared physical patch that is applicable to infrared images is of great significance.

Few have addressed this problem, and existing methods have significant limitations. For instance, adversarial bulbs [17] are complex to implement and lack stealth due to heat generation. Adversarial clothing [18] using thermal insulation materials remains difficult to translate from digital to physical. The HOTCOLD Block [19] is time-sensitive, losing attack efficacy over time. Additionally, all these methods have a single attack approach, lacking multi-angle and cross-modality generalization capabilities.

To address the aforementioned limitations, we propose the CodeMosaic Patch (CMP). This patch can hide target objects in infrared aerial object detectors and remains effective in visible light through environmental migration. For physical implementation, we use easily obtainable and cut low-emissivity aluminum foil, which is shaped and assembled based on digital training. CMP is simpler than other methods, easier to implement, and offers superior attack effectiveness.

Our main contributions are summarized below: (1) We propose CodeMosaic Patch(CMP), an infrared remote sensing attack method for non-live targets. Compared to existing methods, CMP is simpler, easier to implement physically, and more effective. Notably, this is the first infrared physical patch proven to work across both visible and infrared light environments, showcasing its cross-modal capabilities. (2) We integrate an Infrared Remote Sensing Vehicle Dataset(IR-RSVD) to address the lack of an authoritative dataset available for vehicle infrared adversarial attacks. IR-RSVD features diverse target angles and panoramic views, with 836 images in the training set and 386 images in the test set. (3) We are the first to use aluminum foil as the reproduction material for infrared patches, successfully concealing the target object from infrared detectors in the real world. Experiments in both digital and physical environments confirm the high effectiveness and robustness of our CMPs.

2   Related Works

Existing physical attacks are mainly performed on low-field-of-view images taken from a flat parallel viewpoint, at relatively short distances, i.e., within the sensing range of a camera in a self-driving car or a security system. Physical attacks on aerial drones and satellite imagery have not been extensively studied. The few exceptions are Czaja et al. [20], Den Hollander et al. [21] and Du et al. [22], who generate adversarial patches for the classification and detection of aerial images. However, the works in [20,21] only evaluated their attacks in the digital domain, meaning that they did not make physical patches and deploy them in the real world. Du et al. [22] developed a physical patch effective only in visible light/daytime conditions, where extreme weather, visibility, light, and seasonal effects significantly reduce its attack success rate. We develop a remote sensing attack method with high ASR in night/infrared environments, demonstrating strong effectiveness in both digital and physical domains.

Unlike the extensive research on adversarial attacks in visible light, there is very little research on thermal infrared images. Below are recent explorations of adversarial attacks on thermal infrared images. Edwards et al. [23] investigated adversarial attacks on ship detection using thermal infrared imagery. Osahor et al. [24] focused on generating visually imperceptible adversarial infrared examples, making DNN-based target detectors unable to detect targets. These methods generated perturbations by changing pixel values within the infrared image and were not applicable to the physical world. Zhu et al.(2021) [17] proposed a patch-based adversarial attack that uses small light-emitting bulbs to create special infrared patterns. The following year, Zhu et al. (2022) [18] designed infrared clothing based on a new material, aerogel. Obviously, light-emitting bulbs and clothes made from aerogel material share a common disadvantage: they are particularly noticeable during an attack, which contradicts the inherent stealth of adversarial examples. Wei et al. [19] proposed an infrared patch, HOTCOLD Block, which did not thoroughly explore the patch's structure, placement, or angle. Made from Warming Paste and Cooling Paste, it is difficult to implement physically due to its complex material that cannot be easily cut. Additionally, its attack effects are time-limited, ceasing once the materials' heating and cooling periods end.

Our approach stands out from existing methods in several ways: (1) Compared to Zhu et al.(2022) [18], our design of adversarial infrared patches is simpler, focusing only on the patch's structure and position rather than complex patterns. (2) Unlike Zhu et al. (2021) [17], which enhances thermal radiation for pedestrians, our method uses insulation to reduce the thermal radiation of the target, making it less conspicuous in real-world scenarios. (3) In contrast to Wei et al. [19], CMP uses easily cut and assembled aluminum foil, simplifying implementation while providing effective attack capabilities. Most importantly, CMP offers permanent attack performance. (4) Previous studies have only validated their methods on live target detection, e.g., pedestrians, which are easier to detect and attack due to their high temperature and clear imaging in infrared. Our method, however, demonstrates strong attack performance on non-live detection, showcasing CMP's excellent capabilities. (5) Unlike previous methods that are only effective in the infrared domain, our method retains strong attack effects even when transferred to the visible domain, proving its cross-modality generalization capabilities.

3   Methodology

This section presents our method, CodeMosaic Patch. We describe the properties, construction, and overall flow of the CMP attack methodology.

3.1   Problem Formulation

The goal of this paper is to generate a physical adversarial patch that enables vehicles to avoid detection by pre-trained infrared aerial object detectors. These patches will be placed on the roof of the car, with an infrared camera serving as the image collector (see Fig. 1(c) and Fig. 1(a)).

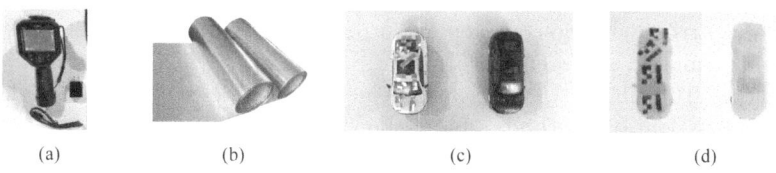

(a)   (b)   (c)   (d)

Fig. 1. (a)(b) Hardware and materials used to carry out a physical attack. (c)(d) Images of vehicles under visible light and infrared conditions

In infrared vehicle detection, given the distribution of all original images $\mathcal{O}$ and an input image $\mathcal{I}$. Let $f(\cdot)$ be the infrared car detector with parameter θ. $\hat{y} = f(\mathcal{I}; \theta)$ represents the output prediction given an unmodified thermal infrared image $\mathcal{I} \in \mathbb{R}^{h \times w}$. And the output $\hat{y}$ contains the car candidate bounding box $\{b_i | i = 1, ..., n\}$ and confidence scores $\{c_i | i = 1, ..., n\}$. Before patch is added, the predicted value $\hat{y}$ roughly matches the real label $\mathcal{Y}$, which contains information such as boundary box position $\mathcal{V}_{pos}$, object probability $\mathcal{V}_{obj}$, and class score $\mathcal{V}_{cls}$:

$$\hat{y} \approx \mathcal{Y} = [\mathcal{V}_{pos}, \mathcal{V}_{obj}, \mathcal{V}_{cls}] = f(\mathcal{I}; \theta) \tag{1}$$

Our goal is to trick the car object detector so that it does not recognize the car, i.e. $\mathcal{V}_{obj} = 0$. We represent the threat image as $\mathcal{I}_{adv}$ as Eq. 3. The target can be described as Eq. 2, where i is the index of the i-th image in $\mathcal{O}$ [6,19]:

$$\arg \min \mathcal{V}_{obj} = \arg \min_i f(\mathcal{I}_{adv}) \tag{2}$$

$$\mathcal{I}_{adv} = \mathcal{I} \odot (1 - M) + \hat{I} \odot M \tag{3}$$

So the operation is to minimize the maximum confidence score in all bounding boxes until it falls below the threshold. In general, the disappear attack loss is defined as follows:

$$\mathcal{L}_{attack}(f(\mathcal{I}_{adv})) = \max_{i \in \{1,\dots,n\}} c_i \tag{4}$$

3.2 Properties of the CodeMosaic Patch

The CodeMosaic attack scheme is essentially patch-based, involving attributes like structure, texture, size, position, and shape. In this paper, we improve the patch's structure, texture, position, and shape. Unlike previous research where the position and rotation angle were manually set, we optimize these parameters to find the most effective CodeMosaic patch and its placement.

The Size of CodeMosaic. The size here is defined as the total area covered by the CMP. CMP's size depends on the number of patches n, the number of occupied grids s, and the length of the sides l of the grids. Larger patches can potentially improve the attack effect by covering more of the target's properties. However, they are too conspicuous in real-life scenarios. Therefore, we aim to generate smaller, more effective patches to enhance concealment and cost-effectiveness. To balance the size and attack effectiveness, we use the elastic network regularization method, adding the size increment as a penalty term in the loss function, expressed as:

$$\mathcal{L}_{attack} = \mathcal{V}_{obj} + \lambda\mathcal{L}_{patch\_tv} + \alpha\mathcal{L}_{mask\_tv} + \overbrace{\beta\Delta_\uparrow\Omega(s)}^{penalty\ term} \tag{5}$$

$$\Omega(s) = \rho\Sigma|s_i| + (1-\rho)s_i^2 \tag{6}$$

where $\Omega(s)$ is the penalty term in Eq. 5, and β determines the balance between the target probability and the area constraint. In this loss function, $\mathcal{L}_{patch\_tv}$ and $\mathcal{L}_{mask\_tv}$ are the total variation loss corresponding to the patch and mask blocks. The purpose of these two components is to maintain the image's smoothness, reduce the noise, and maintain the edge and structural information.

The Structure and Textures of CodeMosaic. For the structure and texture of the patch, we use a 6×6 matrix M to determine, as shown in Fig. 2(b). The 0-1 value of the matrix controls the state of each grid in the thirty-six square grid. For example, the all-zero matrix M_1 represents 6×6 units of all black lattice blocks (Fig. 2(c)). The 6×6 matrix consists of 36 block information elements, which can be randomly converted to 0 or 1. We can use flexible and complex combinations to create various structural textures. The square blocks in mosaic patches are easier to implement physically and can be efficiently cut from physical materials, facilitating direct physical deployment.

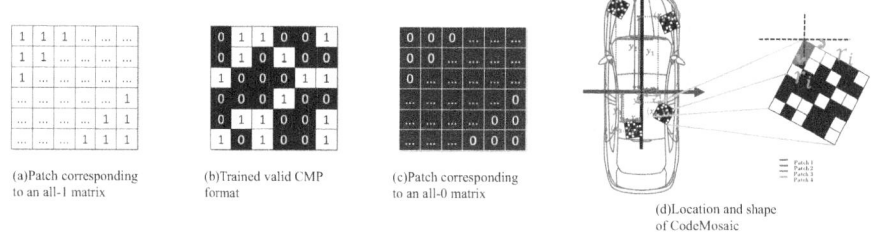

(a)Patch corresponding to an all-1 matrix

(b)Trained valid CMP format

(c)Patch corresponding to an all-0 matrix

(d)Location and shape of CodeMosaic

Fig. 2. Structural texture diagram of a CMP and Location and shape of multi-patch.

Location and Shape of CodeMosaic. To enhance attack efficiency, Code-Mosaic uses a multi-patch joint strategy. We need to determine the location coordinates for each unit in the CMP set. The upper-left vertex of each patch is recorded as a coordinate. For n patch blocks, we find appropriate coordinates $P = \{(x_1, y_1), (x_2, y_2), ..., (x_n, y_n)\}$, making P the optimization parameter. Experiments (see Sect. 4.5) demonstrate that patches trained this way can effectively attack from multiple angles, regardless of vehicle orientation.

This is the first study to include the rotation angle in the optimization parameter set. Previously, the rotation angle was manually set, but we now incorporate it directly into the optimization parameters, changing $O = \{M, P\}$ to $O = \{M, P, R\}$. This enhances the patch definition and properties. Figure 2(d) illustrates CodeMosaic's placement and rotation angle.

3.3   Optimization Algorithm

Thermal infrared images differ significantly from visible images, accepting only grayscale maps and having discrete parameter values in O. Consequently, the optimization process is not continuous, preventing the direct use of gradient descent methods commonly employed in adversarial attacks on visible images [25].

After comparing the time and performance of three optimization algorithms, we chose the gradient-free differential evolutionary algorithm (DE) for CMP-DE patch optimization. The optimization target is $\mathcal{L}_{attack}$ as described in Eq. 4.

Each individual in the population pool comprises $O = \{M, P, R\}$, representing the patch's structure and texture, its position on the target object, and its rotation angle. The differential evolution algorithm initializes the population and iteratively approaches the optimal solution through mutation and crossover operations. Algorithm 1 provides the optimization pseudo-code for CMP-DE.

Algorithm 1. CMP-DE Optimization Algorithm

Input: Initial population Q with N individuals
Output: Best individual from Q
Parameters: Scaling factor F, crossover rate c, termination condition,number of iterations T

1: Initialize population Q
2: **for** $i \leftarrow 1$ to N **do**
3:     Generate random individual v_i
4:     Append v_i to Q
5: **end for**
6: Compute fitness values for individuals in Q
7: $t \leftarrow 1$
8: **while** $t \leq T$ **do**
9:     **for** $i \leftarrow 1$ to N **do**
10:       Randomly select three individuals r_0, r_1, r_2 from Q
11:       Calculate the difference vector $d = r_1 - r_2$
12:       Generate a new candidate solution $q_i = r_0 + F \cdot d$
13:       Apply crossover to q_i and a differential evolution individual x_i to produce a new vector u_i
14:       **for** each dimension j in u_i **do**
15:         **if** $r_{ij} < c$ or $j = J_r$ **then**
16:           $u_{ij} = q_{ij}$
17:         **else**
18:           $u_{ij} = x_{ij}$
19:         **end if**
20:       **end for**
21:       Evaluate the fitness of u_i
22:       **if** fitness of u_i is better than fitness of r_0 **then**
23:         Replace r_0 with u_i in Q
24:       **end if**
25:     **end for**
26:     $t \leftarrow t + 1$
27: **end while**
28: **return** Best individual from Q

3.4 Physical Reproduction Methods

Thermal infrared imaging relies on the varying infrared radiation emitted by an object's surface, which depends on its temperature and emissivity. To simulate black blocks in CMP for infrared imaging, we focus on finding materials with low infrared emissivity that are easy to obtain and cut. Aluminum foil is ideal due to its thin, lightweight nature and high infrared reflectivity with low emissivity (about 0.03 to 0.05). This makes the foil appear darker in infrared images by reflecting most incident thermal radiation. Figure 1(d) shows that the material appears noticeably darker, creating a clear distinction from the target object.

3.5   Overall Algorithm Process

We initialize the CodeMosaic patch as a black patch (all zeros) and adjust it to prevent the target detector from recognizing certain targets. This is achieved by minimizing the loss function containing V_{obj} using CMP-DE based on Differential Evolution. Optimization stops when no relevant targets are detected or when the maximum iterations are reached.

The flowchart in Fig. 3 outlines the process. First, the attacked model is trained on an infrared dataset to achieve high accuracy. Next, a gray two-dimensional code patch is initialized, and clean images with this patch are input into the model. The goal is to minimize V_{obj} in the output, optimizing the loss function as described in Eq. (5). During this process, the patch's structure, texture, rotation angle, position, and size are continuously optimized.

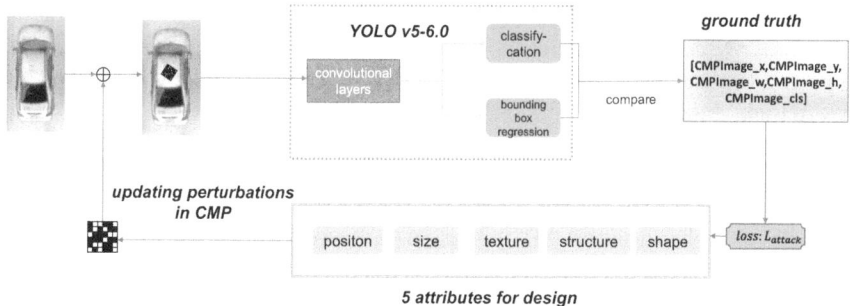

Fig. 3. Complete Flowchart of CodeMosaic Patch Attack Generation.

4   Experiments

4.1   Experiment Settings

Dataset. Due to the lack of previous work on non-live infrared adversarial attacks, there is no authoritative dataset available. We integrate a dataset called IR-RSVD, derived from the "IR" dataset and the "Infrared Aerial Photography Human Vehicle Detection" dataset. IR-RSVD includes various target angles and some non-vehicle panoramic views. The training set has 836 images, and the test set has 386 images. For the physics experiment dataset, we capture infrared images using an H13PRO thermal camera with a resolution of 192 × 144. We record two different scenes at distances of 1 m and 2 m, taking 360-degree views of the vehicle and extracting three frames per second. In total, we capture 282 images and annotate them with 559 labels using LabelImg.

Target Detector. We use YOLOv5 [26] as our target model. For infrared adversarial detection, we use pre-trained weights on the MSCOCO dataset [27] as initialization and fine-tuned the model on the homemade dataset IR-RSVD. The fine-tuned target model achieve an AP score of 91.8% on the test set.

Implementation Details. In the experiment, we set the differential evolution iterations to 10, population size to 100, crossover rate to 0.6, mutation rate to 0.1, and block pixel value to 0.0. The IoU of the target detector is set to automatic hyper-parameter optimization mode with thresholds from 0.1 to 0.7. All experiments are performed on NVIDIA GeForce RTX 4090 GPUs.

Metrics. ASR indicates Attack Success Rate. The higher the ASR, the higher the attack effect. AP indicates the Average Precision, that is, the performance of the object detector on the dataset. The lower the AP, the stronger the attack effect.

4.2   Comparisons with SOTA Methods

Given that the current researches focus on physical adversarial attacks against pedestrians, we compare our method with the most effective pedestrian infrared adversarial attack methods: HOTCOLD Block, Bulb Attack, QR Attack and Wei's Attack. A clear contrast can be seen from Fig. 4. We conduct experiments on the IR-RSVD dataset to evaluate the attack performance. Table 1 presents the ASR and AP reduction rates for various methods. CMP achieves an ASR of 86.75%, significantly higher than the 37.78% of the best other method. In adversarial attacks, greater AP reduction indicates better performance. CMP reduce the AP by 74% (from an initial 91.8% accuracy), while other methods only reduce it by up to 14.76%. These results validate the superiority of our method.

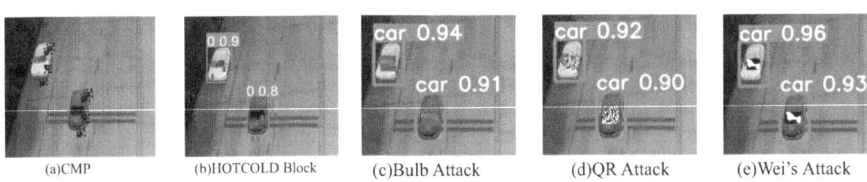

(a)CMP   (b)HOTCOLD Block   (c)Bulb Attack   (d)QR Attack   (e)Wei's Attack

Fig. 4. Qualitative comparison with SOTA method. The boundary box indicates that the infrared detector successfully detected the vehicle.

4.3   Ablation Study

We verify the effectiveness of the unique structure and properties of the Code-Mosaic patch through ablation experiments.

As shown in Table 2, the best results are achieved with a side proportion of 0.2 and 4–5 patches. The side proportion refers to the ratio of the total length of the patches to the target bounding box length. Although 5 patches are slightly more effective than 4 in quantitative analysis, they are harder to implement physically. Therefore, we select 4 patches for the subsequent physical experiments to facilitate modification and realization. Meanwhile, Table 2 shows the performance differences in ASR and AP scores between our CMP patch and pure white and random blocks. Among the comparisons, it is clear that CMP is significantly more effective in attacks.

Table 1. Quantitative comparison with SOTA method.

Metrics	CMP	HOTCOLD Block	Bulb Attack	QR Attack	Wei's Attack
ASR	**86.75%**	37.78%	39.00%	21.20%	23.90%
AP Decline	**74.00%**	14.76%	3.47%	1.80%	2.00%

Regarding the structure and texture of the patch, we also conduct ablation experiments using nine different matrix structures: $2 \times 2, 3 \times 3, 4 \times 4, 8 \times 8, 9 \times 9,$ $12 \times 12, 13 \times 13, 14 \times 14,$ and 16×16. The results show that 6×6 performs best, while 16×16 performs worst. Structures smaller than 6×6 may carry insufficient attack information and lack effective training. Structures larger than 6×6 may reduce the attack effectiveness due to smaller areas allocated to each subcompartment. Therefore, we use 6×6 matrix-sized structural blocks to carry attack information.

Table 2. Quantitative results for the IR-RSVD test set under different settings. We report the AP (%) and ASR (%) of the CodeMosaic Patch(CMP) with randomized block attack(R) and manual randomized block attack(MR).

Num of Patches	Method	patch_size												Average	
n		0.1		0.12		0.14		0.16		0.18		0.2			
		AP(%)	ASR(%)	AP(%)	ASR(%)	AP(%)	ASR(%)	AP(%)	ASR(%)	AP(%)	ASR(%)	AP(%)	ASR(%)	AP(%)	ASR(%)
1	R	54.1	34.89	52.69	36.55	50.67	38.27	49.11	40.67	48.02	43.05	45.77	46.55	50.06	39.99
	MR	54.7	33.16	53.16	34.28	51.34	36.59	49.96	39.16	48.57	41.72	46.8	45.33	50.76	38.37
	CMP	35.39	55.29	34.18	56.63	33.56	57.03	33.22	57.45	32.38	58.18	32.6	58.21	33.56	57.18
2	R	45.8	44.32	44.2	46.67	42.5	48.25	42.1	49.57	41.1	50.36	39.54	53.28	42.54	48.74
	MR	46.76	43.21	45.08	44.78	44.13	47.36	42.89	48.28	41.15	49.95	39.6	51.25	43.27	47.47
	CMP	34.03	56.68	32.2	58.74	30.75	60.73	29.33	62.78	27.92	64.76	26.6	66.56	30.14	61.71
3	R	35.53	54.72	34.9	55.18	34.41	55.55	33.89	56.18	33.1	57.25	32.48	58.03	34.05	56.15
	MR	35.69	55.12	35.34	55.42	34.88	55.61	34.24	56.15	33.67	56.62	32.9	57.66	34.45	56.10
	CMP	30.83	60.63	29.27	62.83	27.23	65.88	24.97	68.92	20.17	75.64	20.3	75.36	25.46	68.21
4	R	34.22	55.79	33.74	56.08	32.44	57.92	30.74	60.42	29.14	62.72	27.02	65.97	31.22	59.82
	MR	34.8	55.85	34.04	56.37	32.92	57.61	31.49	59.55	30.82	60.44	28.79	63.41	32.14	58.87
	CMP	28.73	63.69	25.94	67.77	23.12	71.72	19.23	76.9	17.58	78.94	15.61	81.17	21.70	73.37
5	R	33.11	57.04	31.26	59.4	28.81	62.83	27.19	65.4	24.17	69.75	21.63	73.38	27.66	64.63
	MR	33.62	56.71	32.4	58.31	31.18	59.98	28.55	63.63	25.59	67.99	23.15	71.5	29.08	63.02
	CMP	27.64	65.29	20.23	75.62	18.79	77.52	17.26	79.55	14.21	83.65	13.53	84.2	18.61	77.64

4.4   Evaluation of Attack Generalization

Cross-Modality Generalization. To verify CMP's generalization performance, we transfer the generated infrared patch to a visible light dataset. Despite

CMP's simple shape and single color, it demonstrates remarkably high attack performance in a generalized light environment. Across 32 detection experiments, the average attack success rate is 92.42%. The target detector's lowest AP value is 7.21%, reducing the original accuracy (91.8%) by 84.59% points.

Figure 5(a) shows three vehicles at the top with CMP patches and four vehicles at the bottom without CMP patches. The vehicles without CMP are easily identified by the target detector, while the ones with CMP are not. Similarly, (b) and (c) display the same image with CMP patches applied differently. In (b), CMP is on the right side, and in (c), it's on the left. The visible light domain attack effectiveness of CMP is evident from the clear visual contrast differences.

    (a)   (b)   (c)

Fig. 5. Attack performance effect of CMP in the visible light images.

Evaluation of Robustness. We evaluate CMP's attack robustness on various detectors in a black-box setting, including YOLOv3 [28], YOLOv4 [29], RetinaNet [30], Mask RCNN [31], Faster RCNN [32], and DETR [33]. The parameters of these detectors are pre-trained on the MSCOCO dataset [27] and fine-tuned on the IR-RSVD dataset. Table 3 shows a significant decrease in detector performance with CMP, averaging a 59.06% drop in AP and 49.8% in ASR. Among the models compared, the attack performance migrates best with YOLOv3 and worst with DETR. Overall, our attacks are robust across most models, proving CMP's effectiveness.

Table 3. Evaluation of performance under other detectors in a black box setup.

Object Detector	Before attack		After attack	
	AP (%)	ASR(%)	AP (%)	ASR (%)
YOLOv3	86.60	–	15.71	63.25
YOLOv4	78.07	–	17.17	50.25
RetinaNet	78.27	–	12.07	57.54
Faster RCNN	76.25	–	15.09	46.69
DETR	75.28	–	39.1	31.25
Average	**78.89**	–	**19.83**	**49.8**

4.5   Physical Adversarial Attack

In physical experiments, we assess CMP's attack effectiveness from various angles and distances. Each video features two vehicles: one clean and one with a CMP, as shown in Fig. 1(c). Figure 6(a) displays the target detector's direct output. Simulating overhead target detection by a drone, we move from 1 m to 2 m distance. As shown in Fig. 6(b), the success rate of the attack decreases slightly as the distance increases. However, the attack success rate still reaches 72.96% at the farthest distance, with an average ASR of 81.02% in the physical domain, demonstrating the robustness of our patches.

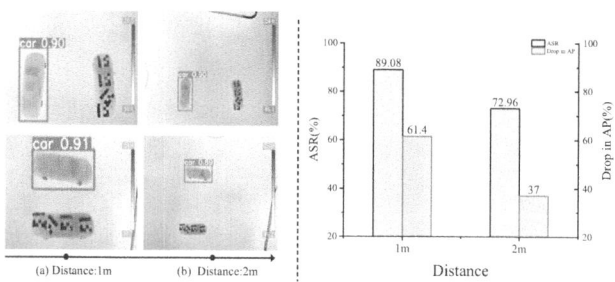

Fig. 6. The effect of distance variation on the efficacy of CMP attacks.

Figure 7 provides a clearer comparison by cropping out the two vehicles. Simulating overhead target detection by a drone, we move angles from 0° to 180°, then from 0° to −180°, demonstrating CMP's effectiveness across multiple angles.

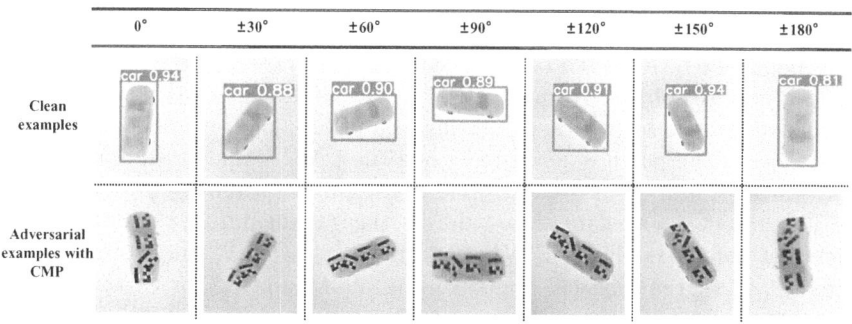

Fig. 7. Comparison plot of attack effectiveness at multiple angles.

The complete quantitative results are presented in Table 4, showing an average attack success rate of 71.43%, which confirms the vulnerability of the target detector to CMP.

Table 4. Quantitative results of attack effectiveness at multiple angles.

Angle	0°	±30°	±60°	±90°	±120°	±150°	180°	Average
ASR	97.87%	75.44%	91.43%	79.17%	81.25%	71.43%	95.87%	84.64%

To demonstrate that the attack effectiveness is due to the structure and texture of the CMP, we re-form the 36 small aluminum sheets of the CMP into a 6×6 large square block (Fig. 8(b)) and two 3×6 rectangular blocks (Fig. 8(c)). Neither configuration has any attack effect, proving the CMP's design is crucial for the attack. The quantitative results in Table 4, along with the comparisons in Fig. 6(a) and Fig. 8, highlight the CMP's excellent attack performance from various angles and distances.

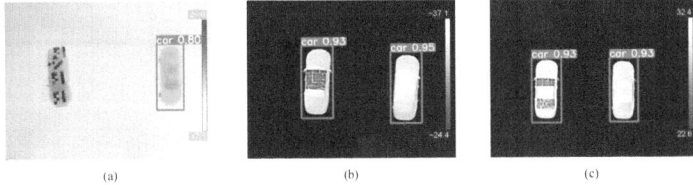

(a)   (b)   (c)

Fig. 8. Comparing the effect of the CMP structure with others under the same number of aluminum sheets. Without CMP's structure and placement, 36 identical-sized aluminum foils (b, c) show no attack effects.

5 Conclusion

In this paper, we have presented the first physical infrared remote sensing attack targeting non-live objects, termed the CodeMosaic Patch (CMP). This method remains unaffected by weather, lighting conditions, or the orientation of the target object. The patches generated using the CMP-DE algorithm are simple, highly efficient, and easily reproducible in the physical world. Furthermore, we have integrated a new dataset to address the gap in infrared remote sensing vehicle datasets, namely IR-RSVD. Additionally, we have successfully implemented CMP in the physical domain using aluminum foil for cutting, assembling, and pasting, achieving lasting attack performance. In both digital and physical domains, CMP demonstrates excellent attack effectiveness across various angles, distances, orientations, and scenarios. Compared to existing SOTA attack methods, CMP exhibits superior performance. Notably, CMP can perform cross-modality attacks in both infrared and visible light conditions, showcasing its cross-modality generalization capabilities. This represents the first instance of a patch with cross-modality attack performance being proposed.

Acknowledgments. This work is supported by the National Key Research and Development Program of China (No. 2022YFB3104502), National Natural Science Foundation of China (No. U20A20177, 62272348, U22B2022), and Wuhan Science and Technology Joint Project for Building a Strong Transportation Country (No. 2023-2-7).

References

1. Zhu, X.X., et al.: Deep learning in remote sensing: a comprehensive review and list of resources. IEEE Geosci. Remote Sens. Mag. **5**(4), 8–36 (2017)
2. Manfreda, S., et al.: On the use of unmanned aerial systems for environmental monitoring. Remote Sens. **10**(4), 641 (2018)
3. Su, J., Vargas, D.V., Sakurai, K.: One pixel attack for fooling deep neural networks. IEEE Trans. Evol. Comput. **23**(5), 828–841 (2019)
4. Brown, T.B., Mané, D., Roy, A., Abadi, M., Gilmer, J.: Adversarial patch. arXiv preprint arXiv:1712.09665 (2017)
5. Eykholt, K., et al.: Robust physical-world attacks on deep learning visual classification. In: Proceedings of the IEEE Conference on Computer Vision and Pattern Recognition, pp. 1625–1634 (2018)
6. Wei, X., Pu, B., Lu, J., Wu, B.: Physically adversarial attacks and defenses in computer vision: a survey. arXiv preprint arXiv:2211.01671, vol. 1, no. 2 (2022)
7. Yang, C., Kortylewski, A., Xie, C., Cao, Y., Yuille, A.: PatchAttack: a black-box texture-based attack with reinforcement learning. In: Vedaldi, A., Bischof, H., Brox, T., Frahm, J.-M. (eds.) ECCV 2020. LNCS, vol. 12371, pp. 681–698. Springer, Cham (2020). https://doi.org/10.1007/978-3-030-58574-7_41
8. Wei, X., Guo, Y., Yu, J., Zhang, B.: Simultaneously optimizing perturbations and positions for black-box adversarial patch attacks. IEEE Trans. Pattern Anal. Mach. Intell. **45**(7), 9041–9054 (2022)
9. Wang, J., Liu, A., Yin, Z., Liu, S., Tang, S., Liu, X.: Dual attention suppression attack: generate adversarial camouflage in physical world. In: Proceedings of the IEEE/CVF Conference on Computer Vision and Pattern Recognition, pp. 8565–8574 (2021)
10. Duan, R., et al.: Adversarial laser beam: effective physical-world attack to DNNs in a blink. In: Proceedings of the IEEE/CVF Conference on Computer Vision and Pattern Recognition, pp. 16062–16071 (2021)
11. Cai, Z., et al.: Context-aware transfer attacks for object detection. In: Proceedings of the AAAI Conference on Artificial Intelligence, vol. 36, pp. 149–157 (2022)
12. Wang, D., et al.: FCA: learning a 3D full-coverage vehicle camouflage for multi-view physical adversarial attack. In: Proceedings of the AAAI Conference on Artificial Intelligence, vol. 36, pp. 2414–2422 (2022)
13. Hu, Z., Huang, S., Zhu, X., Sun, F., Zhang, B., Hu, X.: Adversarial texture for fooling person detectors in the physical world. In: Proceedings of the IEEE/CVF Conference on Computer Vision and Pattern Recognition, pp. 13307–13316 (2022)
14. Suard, F., Rakotomamonjy, A., Bensrhair, A., Broggi, A.: Pedestrian detection using infrared images and histograms of oriented gradients. In: 2006 IEEE Intelligent Vehicles Symposium, pp. 206–212. IEEE (2006)
15. Weng, Q.: Thermal infrared remote sensing for urban climate and environmental studies: methods, applications, and trends. ISPRS J. Photogramm. Remote. Sens. **64**(4), 335–344 (2009)
16. Vollmer, M.: Infrared thermal imaging. In: Computer Vision: A Reference Guide, pp. 666–670. Springer, Cham (2021)

17. Zhu, X., Li, X., Li, J., Wang, Z., Xiaolin, H.: Fooling thermal infrared pedestrian detectors in real world using small bulbs. In: Proceedings of the AAAI Conference on Artificial Intelligence, vol. 35, pp. 3616–3624 (2021)
18. Zhu, X., Hu, Z., Huang, S., Li, J., Hu, X.: Infrared invisible clothing: hiding from infrared detectors at multiple angles in real world. In: Proceedings of the IEEE/CVF Conference on Computer Vision and Pattern Recognition, pp. 13317–13326 (2022)
19. Wei, H., et al.: Hotcold block: fooling thermal infrared detectors with a novel wearable design. In: Proceedings of the AAAI Conference on Artificial Intelligence, vol. 37, pp. 15233–15241 (2023)
20. Czaja, W., Fendley, N., Pekala, M., Ratto, C., Wang, I.-J.: Adversarial examples in remote sensing. In: Proceedings of the 26th ACM SIGSPATIAL International Conference on Advances in Geographic Information Systems, pp. 408–411 (2018)
21. Den Hollander, R., et al.: Adversarial patch camouflage against aerial detection. In: Artificial Intelligence and Machine Learning in Defense Applications II, vol. 11543, pp. 77–86. SPIE (2020)
22. Du, A., et al.: Physical adversarial attacks on an aerial imagery object detector. In: Proceedings of the IEEE/CVF Winter Conference on Applications of Computer Vision, pp. 1796–1806 (2022)
23. Edwards, D.M., Rawat, D.B.: Study of adversarial machine learning with infrared examples for surveillance applications. Electronics $9(8)$, 1284 (2020)
24. Osahor, U.M., Nasrabadi, N.M.: Deep adversarial attack on target detection systems. In: Artificial Intelligence and Machine Learning for Multi-Domain Operations Applications, vol. 11006, pp. 620–628. SPIE (2019)
25. Ruder, S.: An overview of gradient descent optimization algorithms. arXiv preprint arXiv:1609.04747 (2016)
26. Jocher, G., Nishimura, K., Mineeva, T., Vilariño, R.: YOLOv5. Code repository, p. 9 (2020)
27. Lin, T.-Y., et al.: Microsoft COCO: common objects in context. In: Fleet, D., Pajdla, T., Schiele, B., Tuytelaars, T. (eds.) ECCV 2014. LNCS, vol. 8693, pp. 740–755. Springer, Cham (2014). https://doi.org/10.1007/978-3-319-10602-1_48
28. Redmon, J., Farhadi, A.: Yolov3: an incremental improvement. arXiv preprint arXiv:1804.02767 (2018)
29. Bochkovskiy, A., Wang, C.-Y., Liao, H.-Y.M.: Yolov4: optimal speed and accuracy of object detection. arXiv preprint arXiv:2004.10934 (2020)
30. Lin, T.-Y., Goyal, P., Girshick, R., He, K., Dollár, P.: Focal loss for dense object detection. In: Proceedings of the IEEE International Conference on Computer Vision, pp. 2980–2988 (2017)
31. He, K., Gkioxari, G., Dollár, P., Girshick, R.: Mask R-CNN. In: Proceedings of the IEEE International Conference on Computer Vision, pp. 2961–2969 (2017)
32. Girshick, R.: Fast R-CNN. In: Proceedings of the IEEE International Conference on Computer Vision, pp. 1440–1448 (2015)
33. Carion, N., Massa, F., Synnaeve, G., Usunier, N., Kirillov, A., Zagoruyko, S.: End-to-end object detection with transformers. In: Vedaldi, A., Bischof, H., Brox, T., Frahm, J.-M. (eds.) ECCV 2020. LNCS, vol. 12346, pp. 213–229. Springer, Cham (2020). https://doi.org/10.1007/978-3-030-58452-8_13

Sequential Clustering for Real-World Datasets

Chongwei Huang, Jian Hou$^{(\boxtimes)}$, and Huaqiang Yuan

School of Computer Science and Technology, Dongguan University of Technology,
Dongguan 523808, China
houjian@dgut.edu.cn

Abstract. This paper is intended to address two major problems in
data clustering. First, the clustering results of many algorithms depend
heavily on the given number of clusters. Second, while many algorithms
perform well on synthetic datasets, they often generate less satisfactory
results on real datasets. We propose to do clustering sequentially to tackle
these two problems simultaneously. In the first step, we use the dominant
set algorithm together with border-peeling and reverse nearest neighbors to obtain clusters sequentially. In the second step, we estimate the
parameters of Gaussian mixture models (GMM) based on the current
clustering result and then do GMM clustering to obtain the final clustering result, thereby being adapted to clusters of approximate Gaussian
distribution in many real-world datasets. Our algorithm can be used as
both a complete algorithm and a pre-clustering step for estimating the
number of clusters. In experiments on 20 real datasets our algorithm is
demonstrated to be effective in real-world data clustering.

Keywords: Dominant set · Real-world data · Sequential clustering ·
Gaussian Mixture Model · Border-peeling

1 Introduction

Data clustering is used to explore the intrinsic structure of data, facilitating
a deep understanding of the underlying data patterns. Traditional clustering
approaches can be categorized approximately into several types, i.e., partition-
based, hierarchical, density-based [2], and model-based [9] methods.

One popular partition-based clustering approach is the so-called k-means
algorithm. While being simple in its concept and fast to converge, this algorithm depends on the specified number of clusters. The GMM (Gaussian Mixture Model) algorithm assumes that clusters are weighted combinations of Gaussian distributions and fits clusters through the EM (Expectation Maximization)
process. It is able to generate notable clustering results for Gaussian-distributed
clusters, with the help of pre-determined parameters. As a popular density-based
clustering approach, the DBSCAN algorithm [8] involves two parameters, i.e.,
density threshold and neighborhood radius, both of which are specified by the

R. Hadfi et al. (Eds.): PRICAI 2024, LNAI 15281, pp. 69–80, 2025.
https://doi.org/10.1007/978-981-96-0116-5_6

user. Although DBSCAN can identify clusters of any shapes, it performs unsatisfactorily in dealing with non-uniform clusters, due to the fixed parameters. Other important progresses in clustering include mean-shift [6], normalized cut [30], affinity propagation [3], spectral clustering [24], ensemble clustering [16], subspace clustering [32], multi-view clustering [4,23] and others [39].

In reviewing previous works, we notice that existing methods usually involve parameters, e.g., number of clusters. The inappropriate parameters usually lead to unsatisfactory clustering results. In addition, we observe in our own experiments and many works, e.g., [15,20,38], that many algorithms perform well on synthetic datasets, but their results on real datasets are not as good as those on synthetic datasets. In order to tackle these two problems, we exploit the potential of the dominant set (DSet) method [25] and GMM. DSet involves the data similarity matrix as the only input and extracts clusters in a sequential mode, thereby determining the number of clusters in itself. This property can be employed to dealing with the parameter dependence problem. The GMM clustering assumes that clusters follow Gaussian distributions. Noticing that clusters in real-world datasets are often of approximate Gaussian distributions [22], the GMM algorithm is expected to be effective for real datasets. In fact, experiments in [15] shows that the GMM algorithm outperforms some recent algorithms on real datasets. This observation motivates us to make use of the GMM algorithm to deal with real dataset clustering.

We present a hybrid clustering algorithm to deal with the aforementioned problems. In the first step, we peel off the low-density data points which often lie in the border of clusters, thereby separating different clusters apart. By extracting and expanding dominant sets sequentially, we obtain a set of subclusters. Then, we use the data in subclusters to estimate Gaussian distribution parameters, and then do GMM clustering to get the final clusters. While our algorithm is proposed as a complete clustering algorithm, it can also be used as a pre-clustering step for estimating number of clusters. In experiments with 20 real datasets, our algorithm is shown to outperform several recent algorithms with multiple evaluation criteria, and the estimated numbers of clusters are also close to the ground truth.

Compared with previous works, our contributions are as follows. First, we combine the merits of DSet, border-peeling and reverse nearest neighbors to obtain subclusters sequentially, and obtain the number of clusters quite accurately. Second, we use data in subclusters to estimate Gaussian distribution parameters, which are then used in GMM clustering. In this way our algorithm is adapted to clusters of approximate Gaussian distribution, and no user-specified parameters are needed. In summary, our algorithm is adapted to clusters of real datasets while reducing the influence of user-specified parameters as much as possible.

In Sect. 2 we introduce some recent clustering algorithms, some of which will be used in comparison with our algorithm in the experiments. The detailed clustering algorithm is proposed in Sect. 3, and Sect. 4 presents experimental valuation. In the end, Sect. 5 concludes this paper.

2   Related Works

As our algorithm belongs to single-view clustering, we review some of the recent works in this area, and those in multiview clustering, subspace clustering and ensemble clustering are not included.

Density based clustering algorithms have an attractive property, i.e., being able to extract clusters of any shapes. This property is attractive for real datasets where complex data distribution may lead to clusters of irregular shapes. Different from the well-known DBSCAN based on thresholding on density, the DPC (density peak clustering) [27] algorithm regards density peaks as candidates of cluster centers, and allocate non-central data using density relationship between points. Recent DPC-based works mainly focus on density estimation and non-central data allocation.

The original DPC estimates densities using the cutoff and Gaussian kernels. In further developments, DPC-KNN [7] proposes a density kernel with the k-nearest neighbors (kNN) concept [10], which is also adopted in DPC-DLP [29]. The SNN-DPC algorithm [19] proposes to use shared nearest neighbors [5] in local density estimation, and the SFKNN-DPC algorithm [35] uses fuzzy weighted kNN to estimate local density. The 3W-ADPC algorithm [33] presents a parameter-free approach with the concept of natural nearest neighbors. In addition, DPC-DBFN [21] and DPC-FSC [18] define the local density in a fuzzy manner. Other works on improving density estimation also include [26,36].

In non-central data allocation, DPC-DLP assigns labels using graph-based label propagation, and DPC-DBFN propagates labels from cluster centers to nearest neighbors. In 3W-DPET [38], each cluster center includes its kNN into its cluster, and the remaining data points are allocated based on evidence theory and kNN. The VDPC algorithm [34] applies different allocation strategies to different local density hierarchies using the merits of DPC and DBSCAN.

Different from algorithms partitioning data to get clusters simultaneously, DSet extracts clusters sequentially. Being fed with the similarity matrix, this algorithm extracts the first cluster with the replicator dynamics in all the data points. Then with the same method we extracts the next cluster in the remaining data, until all the data points are included into clusters. In this way we obtain all clusters one by one and determine the number of clusters. As the DSet algorithm involves no parameters, it is attractive for our purpose of reducing parameter dependence in data clustering.

While DBSCAN also generates clusters sequentially, it relies on density parameters and the clusters are obtained in the order of core points being visited. In contrast, the DSet algorithm involves no parameters, and the clusters are extracted roughly in the descending order of cluster density. In other words, the first cluster is obtained in the densest area of the whole dataset, and the second one is extracted from the densest area in the dataset excluding the first cluster. With these interesting properties, DSet was used in image segmentation image geo-localization [40], and others [15,31]. A review of DSet and its applications can be found in [28].

3   Our Approach

We intend to address two existing problems in data clustering. First, many algorithms depend heavily on the given number of clusters. Second, existing algorithms are often unable to produce as good results on real datasets as on synthetic datasets.

In dealing with the above-mentioned two problems, we merge the merits of DSet and GMM to present a hybrid clustering algorithm. As the DSet algorithm does not require to know the number of clusters, we intend to use DSet to extract clusters sequentially in the first step, thereby solving the first problem. Noticing that clusters in real datasets are of approximate Gaussian distribution [22] and GMM is shown to be powerful in real dataset clustering [15], we intend to do GMM clustering to obtain final results in the second step, thereby relieving the second problem.

However, the DSet algorithm requires a large intra-cluster similarity and tends to generate small clusters, thereby leading to an over-large number of clusters. To solve this problem, we can expand each cluster before extracting the next one. The cluster expansion needs to be terminated at an appropriate point, so that all points in the same cluster are included and none in other clusters is included. For this purpose, we propose to peel off the low-density data in the boundary between clusters before extracting clusters, so that different clusters are well separated. Furthermore, we use the relationship of reverse k-nearest neighbors (RkNN) [1] in cluster expansion. These two methods together enable us to reduced the possibility of including data from other clusters in cluster expansion. Consequently, we obtain a set of clusters in the first step, which are actually subclusters as some data have been peeled off. In the second step, we do GMM clustering to obtain the final results, where GMM parameters are estimated with the data in subclusters.

We describe our algorithm specifically as follows. Firstly, we peel off the low-density border points from the dataset, extract clusters with the DSet algorithm and expand them based on RkNN sequentially in the remaining data points. Secondly, we use the data in sub-clusters to estimate the Gaussian distribution parameters, based on which we do GMM clustering to obtain the final clusters. Here we see that our algorithm does not require to specify number of clusters, and the GMM clustering in the second step is suitable for many real datasets where clusters are of approximate Gaussian distribution [22].

In summary, our algorithm is composed of three parts, namely peeling off border points, sequential cluster extraction and expansion, and GMM clustering. The detailed descriptions are given below.

3.1   Peeling Off Border Points

As is observed in density based clustering, different clusters are usually separated by low-density border points. If we peel off low-density border points, different clusters will be separated by larger margins, facilitating the subsequent clustering. Many density calculation methods depend on one or more parameters, and inappropriate parameters lead to too large or too small neighborhoods in density calculation, resulting in inaccurate density. To obtain reliable densites, we adopt the reverse k-nearest neighbor (RkNN) relationship to calculate data density.

Definition 1. *Reverse k-nearest neighbors (RkNN). The reverse k-nearest neighbors $RN_k(x_i)$ of a data point x_i are the set of data points whose kNN include x_i, i.e., $RN_k(x_i) = \{x_j \mid x_i \in N_k(x_j)\}$, where $N_k(x_j)$ denotes the kNN of x_j.*

The importance of RkNN lies in that x_i belongs to the kNN of each of its kNN. This relationship guarantees that x_i is really close to its RkNN, and they are very likely to be in the same cluster.

The density ρ_i of each data x_i is then calculated as

$$\rho_i = \sum_{x_j \in RN_k(x_i)} f(x_i, x_j), \tag{1}$$

where $f(x_i, x_j)$ is a local scaling function. The commonly used Gaussian kernel assigns smaller weights to distant neighbors, in contrast to the Cauchy kernel which assigns more importance to distant neighbors. Therefore we adopt the Cauchy kernel to define the scaling function as

$$f(x_i, x_j) = \left(-\frac{\|x_i - x_j\|_2^2}{\sigma_j^2} + 1 \right)^{-1}, \tag{2}$$

where the scaling factor σ_j can be set as the distance between x_j and its kNN.

With the data densities calculated with Eq. (1) and Eq. (2), we can simply peel off data points with the lowest densities. However, in the case that different clusters have significantly different density, the low-density clusters may be peeled off completely. Therefore we adopt an iterative method to peel off low-density data points gradually following [1]. Specifically, we peel off 20% of the data points with the lowest densities, and update the density estimation in each iteration. Let $\overline{\rho}^{(t)}$ be the average density of the peeled-off points in the t-th iteration, if $\frac{\overline{\rho}^{(t)}}{\overline{\rho}^{(t-1)}} - \frac{\overline{\rho}^{(t-1)}}{\overline{\rho}^{(t-2)}} > 0.15$, the iteration terminates. This termination criterion is to avoid large density variance due to over-small clusters.

3.2 Sequential Cluster Extraction and Expansion

Being fed the similarity matrix, DSet groups the densest part of the dataset into a cluster without any parameters. Noticing that low-density border points have been peeled off, DSet is especially suitable for grouping the remaining high-density points. However, if we simply apply DSet to extract clusters sequentially, the obtained number of clusters is probably larger than the ground truth. The reason is that DSet requires large intra-cluster similarities and the obtained clusters tend to be smaller than the real ones. Therefore after we extract a cluster, we need to expand it before extracting the next one.

Recall that we have obtained the RkNN of all data points in calculating data density, here we use the RkNN to expand the cluster. Different from the kNN which may include distant data points with a large k, the RkNN imposes a bi-directional nearest-neighbor constraint and therefore excludes distant data points. For example, one data x_i in the border of a cluster C_1 may include x_j in its kNN, and x_j is in the neighboring cluster C_2. As the data x_j is closer to other points in C_2, its kNN may not include x_i. In this case, x_j belongs to the kNN of x_i, but not in the RkNN of x_i. Therefore one data is usually really close to its RkNN and they are probably to be in the same cluster. In addition, by peeling off the border points, we have separated different clusters well apart. This further reduces the probability of one data point and its RkNN are in different clusters. These observations propel us to expand the cluster based on RkNN.

The expansion of the current cluster C_j is described as follows. With one data point $x_i \notin C_j$, we firstly find its RkNN denoted as $RN_k(x_i)$. If at least one data point in $RN_k(x_i)$ is also in C_j, i.e., $RN_k(x_i) \cap C_j \neq \emptyset$, then we add x_i into C_j. It is worth noting that in expanding the cluster, we must firstly consider the outside points closest to the cluster. Otherwise, if one data x_i is a little distant from the original cluster, all its RkNN may not be in the cluster, and therefore x_i has no chance to be included into the cluster. We use the following method to avoid this problem. For each data $x_i \in C_j$, we identify its nearest neighbor in the set of data not assigned to any cluster, obtaining a set N_{C_j} of these nearest neighbors. Then for each data in N_{C_j}, we check if it can be included into C_j. We update the set N_{C_j} and add data into the cluster C_j, until no data in N_{C_j} can be included into C_j, thereby accomplishing the cluster expansion.

3.3   GMM Clustering

After extracting and expanding the clusters sequentially, all the core points have been grouped into clusters. We can also group the peeled-off data points into clusters based on the RkNN. However, noticing that the GMM clustering shows significant potential in deal with real datasets in [15], here we propose to use GMM to accomplish the final clustering.

GMM clustering models one dataset as the mixture of multiple Gaussian distributions. Since many real datasets consist of clusters of approximate Gaussian distributions [22], this algorithm is promising in real-world data clustering. In GMM clustering, the probability of one data x_i is described by

$$p(x_i) = \sum_{j=1}^{n_c} \alpha_j p(x_i \mid \mu_j, \Sigma_j) \tag{3}$$

where n_c is the number of mixture distributions, μ_j represents the mean of j-th distribution, Σ_j denotes the j-th covariance matrix, and α_j signifies the weight of j-th distribution. In order to maximize the overall probability of the whole dataset, we use the Expectation-Maximization (EM) method as follows.

(1) **Initialization.** The user specifies the number of clusters, the initial mean, covariance matrices and weight of each Gaussian distribution.
(2) **Expectation-Maximization**. The posterior probability of each data point belonging to each Gaussian distribution is computed. Subsequently, the

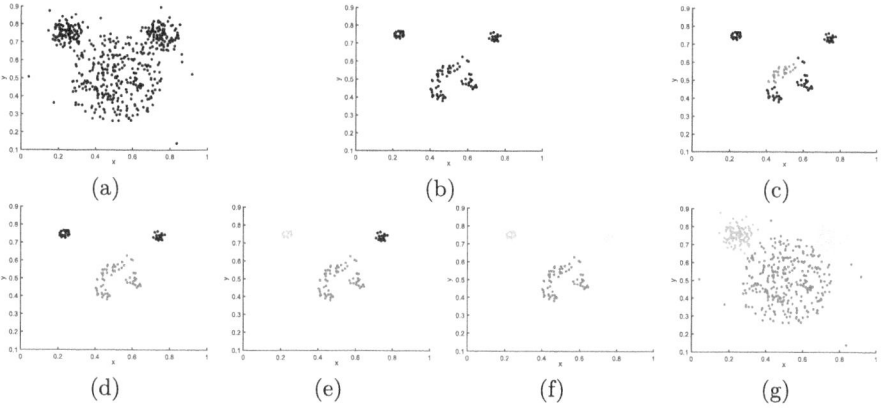

Fig. 1. Demonstration of the clustering process. (a) Original dataset. (b) After peeling-off. (c) First subcluster. (d) First expanded subcluster. (e) Second subcluster. (f) Third subcluster. (g) After GMM clustering.

weights, means, and covariance matrices of the Gaussian distributions are updated based on these posterior probabilities. The EM algorithm iterates until convergence criteria are satisfied.

(3) **Classification**. Each data point is classified into the Gaussian distribution (cluster) with the highest posterior probability for this data point.

The number n_c of clusters have been determined in sequential cluster extraction, and we use the data points in each subcluster to estimate the parameters μ and Σ. As to the parameter α, we set the weight of each distribution based on the ratio of the subcluster size in all the data points. We then do GMM clustering to obtain the final clustering results.

We use the Mouse dataset from the ELKI project[1] to illustrate the process of our algorithm, as shown in the Fig. 1(a) to Fig. 1(g).

4   Experiments

We conduct experiments on 20 real datasets taken from the UCI Repository[2] as shown in Table 1, with NP, ND and NC denoting number of points, data dimensionality and number of clusters, respectively. These datasets vary significantly in number of clusters, data dimensionality and dataset size.

Firstly, our algorithm is compared with traditional algorithms and several recent algorithms. Three criteria are used to evaluate clustering results, i.e. ARI (adjusted rand index), ACC (accuracy) and NMI (normalized mutual information). With all the three criteria, higher values indicate better clustering results. As our approach determines number of clusters in itself, we also compare it with several other algorithms in determining number of clusters.

---

[1] https://elki-project.github.io/datasets/.
[2] https://archive.ics.uci.edu/.

Table 1. Characteristics of datasets.

dataset	NP	ND	NC	dataset	NP	ND	NC	dataset	NP	ND	NC
Thyroid	215	5	3	Waveform	5000	21	3	Rice	3810	7	2
Wine	178	13	3	CNAE9	1080	856	9	Spambase	4601	57	2
Iris	150	4	3	Dermatology	366	33	6	Vehicle	846	18	4
Wdbc	569	30	2	Optdigits	5620	3	10	Isolet	7797	617	26
Breast	699	9	2	SCC	600	60	6	Landmine	338	3	5
Seeds	210	7	3	Pendigits	10992	3	10	Dutchnumeral	2000	649	10
Segmentation	2310	19	7	USPS	11000	256	10				

Table 2. Clustering results (NMI) with best parameters on 20 real datasets.

	kmeans	GMM	3W-DPET	FHC-LPD	FS-DPC	DPC-FSC	LDP-SC	KS-FDPC	ICKDP	BP	Ours
Thyroid	0.60	0.79	0.48	0.27	0.30	0.59	0.53	0.54	0.38	0.46	**0.81**
Wine	0.73	0.59	**0.82**	0.56	0.63	0.74	0.67	0.67	0.76	0.57	0.77
Iris	0.82	0.85	0.76	0.66	0.86	0.83	0.86	0.88	0.86	0.82	**0.90**
Wdbc	0.59	0.71	0.65	0.65	0.04	0.55	0.54	0.68	0.48	0.42	**0.72**
Breast	0.74	0.56	0.70	0.01	0.26	0.05	0.72	0.67	0.04	0.66	**0.78**
Seeds	0.66	0.72	0.63	0.66	0.67	0.70	0.62	0.69	0.71	0.66	**0.82**
Segment	0.62	0.62	0.02	0.69	**0.74**	0.72	0.58	0.66	0.69	0.67	0.73
Waveform	0.36	**0.51**	0.42	0.31	0.27	0.37	0.33	0.29	0.32	0.27	0.46
CNAE9	0.40	0.48	0.42	0.25	0.32	0.33	0.49	0.47	0.42	0.03	**0.52**
Dermatology	0.79	0.74	0.75	0.80	0.78	0.93	0.84	0.92	0.79	0.83	**0.94**
Optdigits	0.00	0.60	0.02	0.86	0.86	0.85	0.91	0.85	0.85	0.87	**0.93**
SCC	0.71	0.70	0.72	0.80	0.71	0.80	0.82	0.86	0.76	0.86	**0.87**
Pendigits	0.68	0.68	0.70	0.71	0.75	0.75	0.78	0.79	0.77	0.82	**0.85**
USPS	0.44	0.38	0.48	0.62	0.46	0.44	0.65	0.66	0.55	0.61	**0.80**
Rice	0.53	0.53	0.59	0.30	0.54	0.53	0.19	0.28	0.10	0.39	**0.61**
Spambase	0.21	0.14	0.00	0.05	0.16	0.05	0.02	0.14	0.03	0.09	**0.19**
Vehicle	0.12	0.20	0.15	0.16	0.15	0.14	0.15	0.15	0.14	0.18	**0.22**
Isolet	0.72	0.72	0.46	0.61	0.57	0.63	0.76	0.76	0.74	0.60	**0.81**
Landmine	0.08	0.23	0.27	0.04	0.05	0.13	0.02	0.20	0.03	0.25	**0.32**
Dutchnumeral	0.74	0.57	0.57	0.89	0.80	0.84	0.90	**0.92**	0.81	0.86	**0.92**
mean	0.53	0.57	0.48	0.49	0.50	0.55	0.57	0.60	0.51	0.55	**0.70**
Friedman	0.00	0.00	0.00	0.00	0.00	0.00	0.00	0.00	0.00	0.00	-

4.1 Comparisons

We firstly make a comparison with 2 traditional methods, namely k-means and GMM, and 8 recent algorithms, including 3W-DPET [38], FHC-LPD [11], FS-DPC [37], DPC-FSC [18], LDPSC [20], KS-FDPC [17], ICKDP [12] and BP [1]. In the parameters of these algorithms, the number of clusters is specified as ground truth, the number of nearest neighbors is selected from 2 to 50, and the other parameters are determined following the respective papers. The experimental results with three criteria are reported in Table 2 to Table 4. As our algorithm involves density estimation, we mainly compare with density-based clustering approaches, and the adopted datasets have no categorical attributes or attribute noises. We will take these issues into account in futher works.

We observe in Table 2 that with the NMI criterion, the results of our algorithm are the best on 17 out of 20 datasets, and second-best on the remaining 3 datasets. The average result of our algorithm is much better than those of all

Table 3. Clustering results (ACC) with best parameters on 20 real datasets.

	kmeans	GMM	3W-DPET	FHC-LPD	FS-DPC	DPC-FSC	LDP-SC	KSF-DPC	ICKDP	BP	Ours
Thyroid	0.89	**0.96**	0.84	0.63	0.53	0.88	0.85	0.87	0.62	0.80	**0.96**
Wine	0.88	0.83	**0.94**	0.79	0.81	0.91	0.88	0.88	0.92	0.69	0.93
Iris	0.87	0.89	0.89	0.55	0.96	0.95	0.96	**0.97**	0.96	0.92	**0.97**
Wdbc	0.92	**0.95**	0.94	0.93	0.61	0.89	0.91	0.94	0.86	0.84	**0.95**
Breast	0.96	0.88	0.95	0.65	0.72	0.62	0.95	0.94	0.65	0.91	**0.97**
Seeds	0.88	0.90	0.87	0.90	0.89	0.91	0.86	0.90	0.91	0.88	**0.94**
Segment	0.64	0.59	0.14	0.64	**0.75**	0.73	0.51	0.55	0.68	0.68	0.70
Waveform	0.50	0.84	0.75	0.58	0.64	0.54	0.53	0.64	0.53	0.58	0.79
CNAE9	0.40	0.50	0.41	0.22	0.35	0.30	0.46	0.51	0.44	0.14	**0.52**
Dermatology	0.68	0.63	0.80	0.74	0.85	0.86	0.76	0.85	0.75	0.77	**0.87**
Optdigits	0.10	0.60	0.10	0.87	0.86	0.89	0.91	0.76	0.85	0.81	**0.92**
SCC	0.58	0.59	0.67	0.57	0.66	0.82	0.61	**0.86**	0.66	0.67	0.81
Pendigits	0.70	0.67	0.70	0.58	0.78	0.76	0.75	0.73	0.80	0.80	**0.82**
USPS	0.43	0.37	0.37	0.66	0.36	0.36	0.60	0.49	0.50	0.52	**0.81**
Rice	0.90	0.89	**0.92**	0.77	0.90	0.89	0.66	0.79	0.52	0.57	**0.92**
Spambase	**0.76**	0.60	0.61	0.58	0.73	0.61	0.60	0.66	0.60	0.58	0.73
Vehicle	0.39	**0.44**	0.41	**0.44**	0.39	0.37	0.36	0.39	0.37	0.38	0.42
Isolet	0.53	0.54	0.31	0.28	0.31	0.35	0.58	0.52	0.57	0.30	**0.60**
Landmine	0.28	0.35	0.34	0.29	0.30	0.34	0.25	0.34	0.28	0.30	**0.36**
Dutchnumeral	0.72	0.54	0.57	0.85	0.71	0.72	0.87	0.96	0.77	0.84	**0.96**
mean	0.65	0.68	0.63	0.63	0.66	0.69	0.69	0.73	0.66	0.65	**0.80**
Friedman	0.00	0.00	0.00	0.00	0.00	0.00	0.00	0.00	0.00	0.00	-

10 competing algorithms. We also do Friedman test between the results of our algorithm and of the 10 competing algorithms, and find that in all the cases the Friedman p values are less than 0.05, indicating an evident difference. All these observations together show that in dealing with real dataset clustering, our algorithm outperforms not only the traditional k-means and GMM algorithms, but also the recent state-of-the-art ones. In addition, the GMM algorithm outperforms some recent algorithms in overall results, indicating that it is indeed suitable for real-world datasets. These observations show that although there is no guarantee that clusters in all real datasets follow the Gaussian distributions approximately, this assumption does hold for many real datasets. We arrive at similar conclusions from Table 3 and Table 4, and skip the discussions for space reason. However, as our hybrid algorithm is composed of multiple processing steps, it is computationally expensive in comparison with some algorithms. We plan to solve this problem in future works.

4.2 Estimating the Number of Clusters

As our algorithm is able to determine the number of clusters, we compare the obtained numbers of clusters from our algorithm with those from other methods, including the eigen-gap [14], LastLeap [13] and LastMajorLeap [13] methods. The comparison is shown in Table 5, where the 20 datasets are denoted by D1, D2, $\cdots$, D20, in the same order as in Table 2. It can be observed that in all the 20 real datasets, our algorithm generates the same numbers of clusters as the ground truth on 10 datasets. In the remaining 10 datasets, our estimated numbers of clusters are the most accurate on 4 datasets (D10, D11, D14 and

Table 4. Clustering results (ARI) with best parameters on 20 real datasets.

	kmeans	GMM	3W-DPET	FHC-LPD	FS-DPC	DPC-FSC	LDP-SC	KSF-DPC	ICKDP	BP	Ours
Thyroid	0.64	0.86	0.45	0.17	0.14	0.61	0.54	0.55	0.20	0.58	**0.88**
Wine	0.72	0.60	**0.83**	0.51	0.55	0.74	0.67	0.67	0.76	0.44	0.78
Iris	0.80	0.82	0.73	0.45	0.89	0.87	0.89	**0.90**	0.89	0.84	**0.90**
Wdbc	0.71	**0.81**	0.76	0.75	−0.02	0.61	0.67	0.77	0.50	0.56	0.80
Breast	0.84	0.57	0.81	−0.00	0.20	−0.03	0.82	0.78	−0.01	0.80	**0.87**
Seeds	0.69	0.73	0.64	0.72	0.71	0.75	0.64	0.72	0.75	0.70	**0.84**
Segment	0.51	0.47	0.00	0.55	**0.63**	0.61	0.38	0.38	0.55	0.58	0.59
Waveform	0.25	0.58	0.44	0.26	0.25	0.27	0.24	0.25	0.27	0.26	**0.47**
CNAE9	0.16	0.29	0.16	0.10	0.14	0.12	0.22	0.30	0.16	0.00	**0.32**
Dermatology	0.63	0.57	0.68	0.66	0.81	0.86	0.70	0.87	0.66	0.73	**0.87**
Optdigits	0.00	0.45	0.00	0.79	0.79	0.81	0.86	0.69	0.77	0.82	**0.90**
SCC	0.53	0.52	0.56	0.62	0.54	0.70	0.63	0.74	0.59	0.68	**0.74**
Pendigits	0.56	0.54	0.57	0.41	0.65	0.62	0.64	0.55	0.66	0.73	**0.75**
USPS	0.28	0.18	0.24	0.47	0.21	0.17	0.50	0.34	0.25	0.40	**0.70**
Rice	0.64	0.61	0.70	0.30	0.64	0.62	0.10	0.33	−0.01	0.33	**0.72**
Spambase	0.28	0.09	0.00	−0.02	**0.21**	0.01	−0.00	0.11	−0.00	0.02	0.20
Vehicle	0.09	**0.15**	0.11	0.12	0.08	0.08	0.10	0.08	0.08	0.10	0.13
Isolet	0.46	0.49	0.21	0.20	0.27	0.32	0.52	0.45	0.48	0.16	**0.55**
Landmine	0.02	**0.12**	0.07	0.03	0.04	0.10	0.00	0.10	0.02	0.08	0.11
Dutchnumeral	0.63	0.42	0.44	0.82	0.63	0.71	0.84	**0.92**	0.70	0.79	0.91
mean	0.47	0.49	0.42	0.39	0.42	0.48	0.50	0.52	0.41	0.48	**0.65**
Friedman	0.00	0.01	0.00	0.00	0.00	0.00	0.00	0.00	0.00	0.00	-

Table 5. Comparison of numbers of clusters.

	D1	D2	D3	D4	D5	D6	D7	D8	D9	D10	D11	D12	D13	D14	D15	D16	D17	D18	D19	D20
Ground truth	3	3	3	2	2	3	7	3	9	6	10	6	10	10	2	2	4	26	5	10
Ours	3	3	3	2	2	3	14	5	9	5	13	6	23	12	2	24	10	22	2	10
eigen-gap	3	2	2	2	2	3	3	2	2	3	4	2	3	2	2	2	2	2	3	2
LastLeap	1	2	2	3	4	2	3	1	1	5	1	3	1	1	2	2	2	1	1	4
LastMajorLeap	1	2	3	3	4	2	3	1	1	5	1	23	1	1	2	2	2	1	1	15

D18). These comparisons indicate that our algorithm performs better than the three methods in estimating the number of clusters.

5   Conclusion

We present a sequential clustering algorithm for real datasets without knowing number of clusters. Firstly, we peel off low-density border points from the dataset, thereby separating different clusters apart and facilitating subsequent clustering. Secondly, we extract clusters sequentially to determine the number of clusters, where each cluster is obtained by extracting a dominant set and then expanding it with reverse nearest neighbors. Finally, we use the data in the clusters to estimate Gaussian distribution parameters and do Gaussian mixture model clustering to obtain the final results. In experiments with 20 real datasets, our algorithm is shown to outperform both traditional algorithms and some recent ones with three criteria. In addition, our algorithm estimates number of clusters rather accurately, and therefore can be used as a preprocessing step of other algorithms.

Acknowledgment. This work is supported by the National Natural Science Foundation of China under Grants No. 62176057.

References

1. Averbuch-Elor, H., Bar, N., Cohen-Or, D.: Border-peeling clustering. IEEE Trans. Pattern Anal. Mach. Intell. **42**(7), 1791–1797 (2019)
2. Bhattacharjee, P., Mitra, P.: A survey of density based clustering algorithms. Front. Comp. Sci. **15**, 1–27 (2021)
3. Brendan, J.F., Delbert, D.: Clustering by passing messages between data points. Science **315**, 972–976 (2007)
4. Chen, M., Wang, C.D., Lai, J.H.: Low-rank tensor based proximity learning for multi-view clustering. IEEE Trans. Knowl. Data Eng. **35**(5), 5076–5090 (2023)
5. Cheng, D., Zhu, Q., Huang, J., Wu, Q., Yang, L.: Clustering with local density peaks-based minimum spanning tree. IEEE Trans. Knowl. Data Eng. **33**(2), 374–387 (2021)
6. Comaniciu, D., Peter, M.: Mean shift: a robust approach toward feature space analysis. IEEE Trans. Pattern Anal. Mach. Intell. **24**(5), 603–619 (2002)
7. Du, M., Ding, S., Jia, H.: Study on density peaks clustering based on k-nearest neighbors and principal component analysis. Knowl.-Based Syst. **99**, 135–145 (2016)
8. Ester, M., Kriegel, H.P., Sander, J., Xu, X.W.: A density-based algorithm for discovering clusters in large spatial databases with noise. In: International Conference on Knowledge Discovery and Data Mining, pp. 226–231 (1996)
9. Gormley, I.C., Murphy, T.B., Raftery, A.E.: Model-based clustering. Ann. Rev. Stat. Appl. **10**, 573–595 (2023)
10. Gou, J., et al.: A representation coefficient-based k-nearest centroid neighbor classifier. Expert Syst. Appl. **194**, 116529 (2022)
11. Guan, J., Li, S., He, X., Zhu, J., Chen, J.: Fast hierarchical clustering of local density peaks via an association degree transfer method. Neurocomputing **455**, 401–418 (2021)
12. Guo, W., Chen, W., Liu, X.: Density peak clustering by local centers and improved connectivity kernel. Inf. Sci. **666**, 120439 (2024)
13. Gupta, A., Datta, S., Das, S.: Fast automatic estimation of the number of clusters from the minimum inter-center distance for k-means clustering. Pattern Recogn. Lett. **116**, 72–79 (2018)
14. Heckel, R., Bölcskei, H.: Robust subspace clustering via thresholding. IEEE Trans. Inf. Theory **61**(11), 6320–6342 (2015)
15. Hou, J., Yuan, H., Pelillo, M.: Towards parameter-free clustering for real-world data. Pattern Recogn. **134**, 109062 (2023)
16. Huang, D., Wang, C.D., Wu, J.S., Lai, J.H., Kwoh, C.K.: Ultra-scalable spectral clustering and ensemble clustering. IEEE Trans. Knowl. Data Eng. **32**(6), 1212–1226 (2020)
17. Li, C., Ding, S., Xu, X., Hou, H., Ding, L.: Fast density peaks clustering algorithm based on improved mutual k-nearest-neighbor and sub-cluster merging. Inf. Sci. **647**, 119470 (2023)
18. Li, Y., Sun, L., Tang, Y.: DPC-FSC: an approach of fuzzy semantic cells to density peaks clustering. Inf. Sci. **616**, 88–107 (2022)
19. Liu, R., Wang, H., Yu, X.: Shared-nearest-neighbor-based clustering by fast search and find of density peaks. Inf. Sci. **450**, 200–226 (2018)

20. Long, Z., Gao, Y., Meng, H., Yao, Y., Li, T.: Clustering based on local density peaks and graph cut. Inf. Sci. **600**, 263–286 (2022)
21. Lotfi, A., Moradi, P., Beigy, H.: Density peaks clustering based on density backbone and fuzzy neighborhood. Pattern Recogn. **107**, 107449 (2020)
22. Lyon, A.: Why are normal distributions normal? Br. J. Philos. Sci. **65**(3), 621–649 (2014)
23. Ma, J., Zhang, Y., Zhang, L.: Discriminative subspace matrix factorization for multiview data clustering. Pattern Recogn. **111**, 107676 (2021)
24. Ng, A., Jordan, M., Weiss, Y.: On spectral clustering: analysis and an algorithm. In: Advances in Neural Information Processing Systems, pp. 849–856 (2002)
25. Pavan, M., Pelillo, M.: Dominant sets and pairwise clustering. IEEE Trans. Pattern Anal. Mach. Intell. **29**(1), 167–172 (2007)
26. Pourbahrami, S.: A neighborhood-based robust clustering algorithm using apollonius function kernel. Expert Syst. Appl. **248**, 123407 (2024)
27. Rodriguez, A., Laio, A.: Clustering by fast search and find of density peaks. Science **344**, 1492–1496 (2014)
28. Rota Bulò, S., Pelillo, M.: Dominant-set clustering: a review. Eur. J. Oper. Res. **262**(1), 1–13 (2017)
29. Seyedi, A., Lotfi, A., Moradi, P., Qader, N.N.: Dynamic graph-based label propagation for density peaks clustering. Expert Syst. Appl. **115**, 314–328 (2019)
30. Shi, J., Malik, J.: Normalized cuts and image segmentation. IEEE Trans. Pattern Anal. Mach. Intell. **22**(8), 167–172 (2000)
31. Vascon, S., Mequanint, E.Z., Cristani, M., Hung, H., Pelillo, M., Murino, V.: Detecting conversational groups in images and sequences: a robust game-theoretic approach. Comput. Vis. Image Underst. **143**, 11–24 (2016)
32. Wang, L., Huang, J., Yin, M., Cai, R., Hao, Z.: Block diagonal representation learning for robust subspace clustering. Inf. Sci. **526**, 54–67 (2020)
33. Wang, P., Wu, T., Yao, Y.: A three-way adaptive density peak clustering (3W-ADPC) method. Appl. Intell. **53**(20), 23966–23982 (2023)
34. Wang, Y., Wang, D., Zhou, Y., Zhang, X., Quek, C.: VDPC: variational density peak clustering algorithm. Inf. Sci. **621**, 627–651 (2023)
35. Xie, J., Liu, X., Wang, M.: SFKNN-DPC: Standard deviation weighted distance based density peak clustering algorithm. Inf. Sci. **653**, 119788 (2024)
36. Xiong, J., Zang, W., Zhao, Y., Liu, X.: Density peaks clustering algorithm with connected local density and punished relative distance. J. Supercomput. **80**, 6140–6168 (2024)
37. Xu, X., Ding, S., Wang, Y., Wang, L., Jia, W.: A fast density peaks clustering algorithm with sparse search. Inf. Sci. **554**, 61–83 (2021)
38. Yu, H., Chen, L., Yao, J.: A three-way density peak clustering method based on evidence theory. Knowl.-Based Syst. **211**, 106532 (2021)
39. Yu, Z., Zhang, Z., Cao, W., Chen, C.L.P., Liu, C., Wong, H.S.: GAN-based enhanced deep subspace clustering networks. IEEE Trans. Knowl. Data Eng. **34**(7), 3267–3281 (2022)
40. Zemene, E., Tesfaye, Y.T., Idrees, H., Prati, A., Pelillo, M., Shah, M.: Large-scale image geo-localization using dominant sets. IEEE Trans. Pattern Anal. Mach. Intell. **41**(1), 148–161 (2019)

Dual-Mode Contrastive Learning-Enhanced Knowledge Tracing

Danni Huang[1], Jicheng Yu[1], Shun Mao[1], Jiawei Li[1], and Yuncheng Jiang[1,2(✉)]

[1] School of Computer Science, South China Normal University,
Guangzhou 510631, China
{dnhuang,jcyu,shunm,lijiawei,jiangyuncheng}@m.scnu.edu.cn
[2] School of Artificial Intelligence and School of Software, South China Normal
University, Foshan 528225, China

Abstract. Knowledge Tracing (KT) aims to model learners' dynamic knowledge states and predict their future response performance. Most of the existing KT models overlook the importance of advanced exercise representations and other beneficial exercise information. Besides, the relationship between exercises and learners is neglected, and difficulty and discrimination differ from exercises to exercises. Therefore, we propose a Dual-mode Contrastive Learning-Enhanced Knowledge Tracing (DEKT) model, which can obtain fine exercise representations and generate better predictions. Specifically, our model incorporates three additional types of heterogeneous nodes: learner, difficulty, and discrimination to explicitly exploit the exercise information. Furthermore, we employ the dual-mode contrastive learning (path-based mode and schema-based mode) to strengthen and complement exercise representations with semantic and structural information. Finally, through the dual-temporal attention mechanism architecture (one for tracing learners' knowledge states and the other for predicting), we acquire the long-term dependencies between exercises between time step 1 and t, as well as between time step 1 and $t+1$, helping us to capture learners' knowledge states in a more effective manner.

Keywords: Knowledge Tracing · Exercise Representation Enhancement · Heterogeneous Contrastive Learning

1 Introduction

Accompanied by the development of Intelligent Tutoring Systems (ITS), many learners choose to learn online. ITS advocates recommending tailored and adaptive educational resources to learners based on their knowledge levels, where Knowledge Tracing (KT) is of great importance in this process [1–4]. The primary purpose of KT is to predict learners' future performance by using learners' historical learning records. Many KT methods can be divided into two categories:

R. Hadfi et al. (Eds.): PRICAI 2024, LNAI 15281, pp. 81–92, 2025.
https://doi.org/10.1007/978-981-96-0116-5_7

traditional technique-based KT and deep learning-based KT (DLKT). Current KT models mainly focus on deep learning methods, as does our model.

Although most DLKT models can predict well, most of them concentrate on learners' historical learning sequences or the relationship between exercises and skills, which overlook the importance of advanced exercise representations and other beneficial exercise information, such as learners, difficulty and discrimination. To be specific, 1) ITS usually has extensive exercises, while each learner may only answer to a limited number of exercises. To address this issue, early sequence-based models often rely on skills rather than exercises as input for predictions [5–7], but they neglect the characteristics of exercises, which can restrict the ability of the model to accurately estimate final performance. 2) Some researchers have proposed the use of exercise features as a supplement to skill input [8–10]. Nonetheless, merely incorporating exercise features might overlook valuable higher-order and structural information. 3) In recent years, inspired by Graph Neural Network (GNN) [11–14], many researchers have proposed GNN-based KT models. Typically, most of them only focus on exercises or skills [15–17], achieving great success in prediction. Nevertheless, they tend to ignore other relevant exercise information about learners, difficulty, and discrimination, which play an essential role in predicting learners' future performance.

DEKT is proposed to deeply explore refined exercise representations and generate more accurate predictions. The key contributions of this research are outlined as follows:

1. For the first and second issues, We develop a heterogeneous graph to represent the intricate relationships among entities within learners' historical learning sequences. Besides, we design dual-mode contrastive learning to strengthen and complement exercise representations with semantic and structural information.
2. For the third issue, we highlight the vital significance of information pertaining to learners, difficulty, and discrimination. By maximally extracting and leveraging them, it is possible to build highly expressive exercise representations for the prediction task.
3. We assess the performance of the proposed DEKT model using four publicly available real-world datasets. The experimental results demonstrate DEKT can better complete the KT task over baseline models, which validates the superiority and effectiveness of DEKT.

2   Related Work

KT models can be commonly categorized into traditional methods [18–20] and deep learning methods [5,6,21–23]. In traditional KT, Bayesian Knowledge Tracing (BKT) [18] uses the Hidden Markov Model (HMM) to simulate learners' learning processes based on Bayesian Network.

In DLKT, one pioneering work is Deep Knowledge Tracing (DKT) [5], which utilizes Recurrent Neural Network (RNN) to model the interactive exercise records. Memory network-based models [6,21] and attention mechanism-based models [22,23] have been proposed to capture long-term dependencies and highlight relevant historical interactions. Subsequently, some KT models have also been proposed by adding time information [24,25]. However, these works face the same problem that it is challenging to greatly improve the prediction performance because of the neglect of exercise information.

In addition to these KT models at skill level, many researchers have also proposed to use the exercise information and improve prediction [8–10], However, the mere addition of exercise features results in the loss of higher-order and structured information. Moreover, it is impractical to collect the exercise information in real scenarios. In our model, we use dual-mode contrastive learning to encode and complement exercise representations with semantic and structural information.

Recently, the potential of GNN has been explored to enhance feature representations, which can be used to fill the gaps in the exercise data to some extent. Previous graph-based models are mainly implemented on the basis of the exercises-skills relationship to construct bipartite or homogeneous graphs [26–29]. Different from them, we construct a heterogeneous graph for KT, considering learners, difficulty and discrimination based on exercises and skills, aiming to generate refined exercise representations for better prediction.

3   Methodology

In this section, we introduce the overall architecture of DEKT, as shown in Fig. 1, which encompasses a dual-mode contrastive learning (DCL) part and a learning process modeling (LPM) part. The DCL part comprises the construction of heterogeneous graph and the dual-mode contrastive learning. The LPM part is further divided into a dual-temporal attention mechanism module, a learner states module and a prediction module.

3.1   Construction of Heterogeneous Graph

We embody the heterogeneous graph upon the KT task. From the left section of Fig. 1a), the heterogeneous graph includes five distinct node types: learner (l), exercise (e), skill (s), difficulty (d), discrimination (d'), and four relational types: l-e, s-e, d-e, d'-e.

More importantly, difficulty and discrimination are crucial exercise information, but they focus on different aspects. Difficulty is concerned with the general easy or difficulty of the exercise j for all learners, which is typically measured by calculating the average incorrect rate of all learners on the exercise j:

$$Diff_j = \begin{cases} \left\lceil \sum_{i \in \mathcal{S}_j} \frac{|r_{ij} == 0|}{|\mathcal{S}_j|} \cdot c \right\rceil, & if |\mathcal{S}_j| \geq 10 \\ c/2, & else \end{cases}, \tag{1}$$

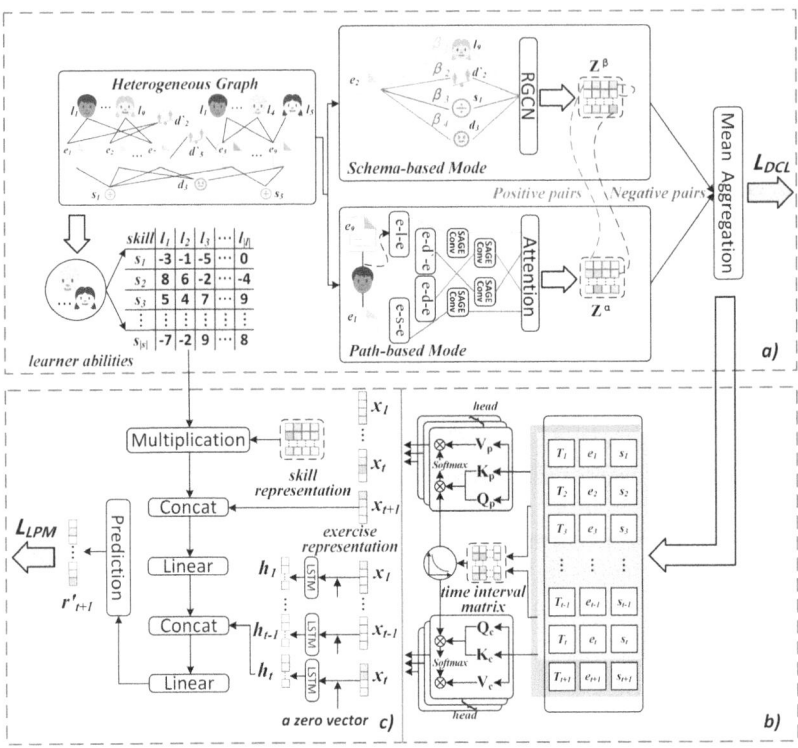

Fig. 1. The architecture of DEKT is divided into two parts: the upper part is the DCL part, and the lower part is the LPM part. (Color figure online)

where $\mathcal{S}_j$ denotes all learners answering the exercise j and $|r_{ij} == 0|$ denotes the number of times learner i answers the exercise j incorrectly. We set the maximum difficulty c to 10 in our paper.

Discrimination is concerned with the capacity of the exercise j to distinguish between learners' abilities differences, which is often evaluated by comparing the average correct rates differences between high-performing and low-performing learners on the exercise j:

$$Disc_j = \left[\sum_{m \in High_j} \frac{|r_{mj} == 1|}{|High_j|} \right] - \left[\sum_{n \in Low_j} \frac{|r_{nj} == 1|}{|Low_j|} \right], \tag{2}$$

where $High_j$ and Low_j denote the high-performing group and low-performing group, which are formed with the top p percent and the bottom p percent of learners after descending sorting all learners' correct rates on the exercise j. p is set to 40 in our paper.

3.2   Dual-Mode Contrastive Learning

Path-Based Mode Learning. As illustrated in Fig. 1a), the two different exercises, designated e_1 and e_2, are associated with the same skill s_1, or e_2 and e_7, which share the same difficulty d_3. These semantic information can be modeled by meta-paths, which are used in the heterogeneous graph to describe composite relationships connecting two objects. Since multiple meta-paths represent various complex semantic information, we can utilize meta-paths to learn exercise embeddings with higher-order semantic information.

Inspired by GraphSAGE [30], we use SAGEConv to sample and aggregate neighbors' information effectively. To be specific, We assume that there are K types of meta-paths starting from the target node i, as $\{\alpha_1, \alpha_2, \ldots, \alpha_K\}$. For each α_k, its neighbors can be marked with $\mathcal{N}_i^{\alpha_k}$. The SAGEConv is defined as follows:

$$\mathcal{Z}_{\mathcal{N}_i^{\alpha_k}}^l = \text{Aggregate}(\{\mathcal{Z}_u^{l-1}, \forall u \in \mathcal{N}_i^{\alpha_k}\}), \tag{3}$$

$$\mathcal{Z}_{i,\alpha_k}^l = \sigma\left(\mathbf{W}_{\alpha_k} \cdot [\mathcal{Z}_{i,\alpha_k}^{l-1} \,||\, \mathcal{Z}_{\mathcal{N}_i^{\alpha_k}}^l] + \mathbf{b}_{\alpha_k}\right), \tag{4}$$

$$\mathcal{Z}_{i,\alpha_k}^l = \text{Norm}(\mathcal{Z}_{i,\alpha_k}^l), \tag{5}$$

where $\mathcal{Z}_{i,\alpha_k}^l$ denotes the representation of the node i output by the layer l of the SAGEConv network on meta-path α_K. $|\cdot|$ stands for the concatenation operation. σ is the ReLU activation function, and *Aggregate* is performed using a mean pooling operation.

Since different meta-paths represent distinct information of the same exercise, we use attention to fuse different representations of the same exercise on all meta-paths. Specifically, after getting different updated representations $\mathcal{Z}_{i,\alpha_k}$ of the exercise node i, we compute the attention value Att_{i,α_k} and obtain the final embedding $\mathcal{Z}_i^\alpha$ of exercise node i from the meta-path mode:

$$Att_{i,\alpha_k} = \text{Softmax}((\mathbf{W}_{\mathbf{att}} \cdot \mathcal{Z}_{i,\alpha_k} + \mathbf{b}_{\mathbf{att}}), \tag{6}$$

$$\mathcal{Z}_i^\alpha = \sum_{k=1}^{K} Att_{i,\alpha_k} \mathcal{Z}_{i,\alpha_k}. \tag{7}$$

Schema-Based Mode Learning. Figure 1a) shows that the learner l_9 answers the exercise e_2 contained the skill s_1 with discrimination d_2' and difficulty d_3. Such simultaneous local relations can be modeled by network schemas, which efficiently describe the intricate structural patterns in the heterogeneous graph. Therefore, we can take advantage of network schemas to ensure that exercise embeddings can accurately reflect local structural information.

To be specific, for a certain exercise node, different types of neighbors contribute differently to it, and the contributions of nodes within the same neighbor type are also different. So, we introduce the Relational Graph Convolutional Network (RGCN) to capture diverse local structures through network schemas. We assume that there are M types of neighbors for target node i, as $\{\beta_1, \beta_2, \ldots, \beta_M\}$. For each β_m, its neighbors can be marked with $\mathcal{N}_i^{\beta_m}$. The RGCN is defined as follows:

$$\mathcal{Z}_i^l = \Psi \left\{ \mathbf{W_i} \mathcal{Z}_i^{l-1} + \frac{1}{M} \cdot \frac{1}{|\mathcal{N}_i^{\beta_m}|} \sum_{m \in M} \sum_{j \in \mathcal{N}_i^{\beta_m}} (\mathbf{W}_{\beta_m} \cdot \mathcal{Z}_j^{l-1}) \right\}, \quad (8)$$

where $\mathbf{W_i}$, $\mathbf{W}_{\beta_m}$ denotes the weight matrices, and Ψ is the LeakyReLU activation function. We treat the representation output by the last layer of the RGCN network as the final exercise representation $\mathcal{Z}_i^\beta$ from the network schema mode.

Contrastive Learning. Finally, we average the sum of $\mathcal{Z}_i^\alpha$ and $\mathcal{Z}_i^\beta$ from the path-based mode and schema-based mode to obtain the final representation $\mathcal{Z}_i$ of the exercise i.

In order to strengthen and complement these two independent representations, we incorporate Graph Contrastive Learning (GCL) into dual-mode learning. The same nodes of two modes are treated as positive pairs, while distinct nodes of the same mode and distinct nodes of two modes are treated as negative pairs. Formally, When the exercise i from the path-based mode serves as the target reference node, the contrastive loss $\mathcal{L}_i^\alpha$ in the path-based mode is calculated as follows:

$$\mathcal{L}_i^\alpha = -\log \left(\frac{\exp(s(\mathcal{Z}_i^\alpha, \mathcal{Z}_i^\beta))}{\exp(s(\mathcal{Z}_i^\alpha, \mathcal{Z}_i^\beta)) + \sum_{j \neq i} \exp(s(\mathcal{Z}_i^\alpha, \mathcal{Z}_j^\alpha)) + \sum_{j \neq i} \exp(s(\mathcal{Z}_i^\alpha, \mathcal{Z}_j^\beta))} \right), \quad (9)$$

where $s(\cdot)$ is the cosine similarity function that measures the similarity between two vectors. Similarly, because of the symmetry of two modes, we can define the contrastive loss $\mathcal{L}_i^\beta$ in the schema-based mode. Finally, the final contrastive loss function is obtained:

$$\mathcal{L}_{DCL} = \frac{1}{|\mathcal{V}|} \sum_{i \in \mathcal{V}} \left(\mathcal{L}_i^\alpha + \mathcal{L}_i^\beta \right). \quad (10)$$

3.3   Dual-Temporal Attention Mechanism Module

To focus on the learner's historical learning interactions being strongly related to the target exercise, we apply two attention mechanisms on the whole sequence in different terms, shown in Fig. 1b), allowing us to acquire learners' knowledge states in a more effective manner.

Dual-Temporal Attention. From the pink section of Fig. 1b), as the attention for tracing, the query is given as $q_t = \mathcal{Z}_{e_t}$, the key as $k_\tau = \mathcal{Z}_{e_\tau}$ and the value as $v_\tau = H_{s_\tau}$ ($\tau \leq t$), where $\mathcal{Z}_{e_t}$ means the embedding of the exercise e_t learned by the DCL part at time step t and H_{s_τ} means the embedding of the skill s_τ. The importance of interactions at time step τ and exercise at time step t is calculated via the application of the softmax function. Similarly, in the light green section of Fig. 1b), as the attention for predicting, t is replaced with $t + 1$ in the query and the value.

Time-Related Decay Term. A time-related exponential decay term is introduced to simulate the learner's forgetting behavior and help exercise embeddings contain useful time-related information. We introduce an exponential decay term $\delta_{t,\tau}$, which takes the time interval $|t - \tau|$ and the decay rate θ into account:

$$Attention_{t,\tau} = \text{Softmax}\left(\frac{q_t k_\tau^T}{\sqrt{d}}\delta_{t,\tau}\right), \delta_{t,\tau} = \exp(-\theta|t - \tau|). \qquad (11)$$

3.4 Learner States Module

For modeling the learner's historical learning sequence and further considering the correctness of the learner's answer to the exercise e_t at time step t, we extend the exercise embedding x_t from attention for tracing ($x_t = x_{e_t}$) by incorporating an entirely zero vector of the same dimension as x_t to obtain the final interaction y_t. The process is as follows:

$$y_t = \begin{cases} [x_t \,\|\, 0], & r_t = 1 \\ [0 \,\|\, x_t], & r_t = 0 \end{cases}. \qquad (12)$$

Like most deep KT models, we employ the Long Short-Term Memory (LSTM) to obtain the learner's knowledge state h_t as follows:

$$h_t = \text{LSTM}(y_t, h_{t-1}). \qquad (13)$$

3.5 Prediction Module

Here, we introduce the embedding representing each learner's learning ability $Ability(s^t)$ at time step t, which differs from discrimination focusing on differences in overall learners' abilities. To illustrate, we assume an arbitrary skill s_j. Then, we obtain the learner's net score $V(s_j^t)$ and the ability $Ability(s_j^t)$ at time step t as follows:

$$Ability(s_j^t) = \begin{cases} g & , & V(s_j^t) \geq g \\ V(s_j^t), & |V(s_j^t)| < g, \\ -g & , & V(s_j^t) \leq -g \end{cases} \qquad (14)$$

$$V(s_j^t) = Correct(s_j^t) - Incorrect(s_j^t) \qquad (15)$$

$$= \sum_{i=1}^{t}(r_{s_j}^i == 1) - \sum_{i=1}^{t}(r_{s_j}^i == 0), \qquad (16)$$

where we set the threshold g to 10 to ensure the rationality of the data. The importance of the skill s_j is adjusted based on $Ability(s_j^t)$ in the skill representation $H_{s_{t+1}}$ at time step $t+1$.

During the prediction phase, we consider the learner's knowledge state h_t, the exercise embedding x_{t+1} from the attention for predicting $(x_{t+1} = x_{e_{t+1}})$, and the skill representation $H_{s_{t+1}}$ considering the learner's ability $Ability(s^t)$ as follows:

$$\gamma_{t+1} = \text{ReLU}(\mathbf{W_2} \cdot [h_t \, || \, (\mathbf{W_1} \cdot [H_{s_{t+1}} \, || \, x_{t+1}] + \mathbf{b_1})] + \mathbf{b_2}), \tag{17}$$

$$r'_{t+1} = \text{Sigmoid}(\mathbf{W_3} \cdot \gamma_{t+1} + \mathbf{b_3}). \tag{18}$$

For training learnable parameters, the following binary cross-entropy loss is used as the objective function of the LPM part:

$$\mathcal{L}_{\text{LPM}} = -\sum_{t=1}^{T} (r_{t+1} \log(r'_{t+1}) + (1 - r_{t+1}) \log(1 - r'_{t+1})), \tag{19}$$

where $r'_{t+1} \in [0,1]$ and $r_{t+1} \in [0,1]$ refer to the predicted value and the true value at time step $t+1$, respectively.

3.6   Model Training

Finally, the total objective function of DEKT is a linear combination of DCL loss and LPM loss:

$$\mathcal{L} = \lambda \mathcal{L}_{\text{DCL}} + \mathcal{L}_{\text{LPM}}, \tag{20}$$

where λ is the hyper-parameter to control the contribution of the DCL task.

4   Experiments

4.1   Setup

The setup of the experiments is introduced, including the four datasets, the compared baselines, and the implementation details.

Datasets. To evaluate the model, we use four public datasets, including ASSISTments2009[1], ASSISTments2017[2], Statics2011[3], and JunyiAcademy[4]. The detailed statistics of these four datasets are summarized in Table 1, where the last column represents the average number of learning records per learner.

---

[1] https://sites.google.com/site/assistmentsdata/home/assistment-2009-2010-data.
[2] https://sites.google.com/view/assistmentsdatamining/dataset.
[3] https://pslcdatashop.web.cmu.edu/DatasetInfo?datasetId=507.
[4] https://pslcdatashop.web.cmu.edu/Files?datasetId=1198.

Table 1. Dataset statistics.

Dataset	Learners	Exercises	Skills	Records	Avg.records
ASSISTments2009	4,161	15,550	121	258,972	62
ASSISTments2017	1,706	1,146	86	249,031	146
Statics2011	331	633	85	112,921	341
JunyiAcademy	5,000	662	39	490,220	98

Baselines. To evaluate the performance of DEKT, we compare the following models as our baselines: DKT [5], SAKT [22], AKT [23], GIKT [17], GASKT [28], CL4KT [31], KSGAN [32], AT-DKT [33] and GLNC [34].

Implementation Details. We evaluate all models using the conventional five-fold cross-validation approach. Our experiments utilize the Adam optimizer to fine-tune the model's learnable parameters and reduce the loss function. During training, we set the embedding dimension to 64, batch size to 32, dropout rate at 0.3, and the learning rate at 0.001. In training loss, hyper-parameters are selected through a search over the range of 0.001, 0.01, 0.05, and 0.1. Additionally, L2 regularization is applied to the weights with a decay rate set to $1e^{-6}$. For other models, their hyper-parameters are set as the original optimal setting in their papers or optimized by grid search. All models were implemented using PyTorch in Python, running on a Linux server.

Table 2. Performance comparison of different models.

Models	ASSISTments2009		ASSISTments2017		Statics2011		JunyiAcademy	
	AUC	ACC	AUC	ACC	AUC	ACC	AUC	ACC
DKT [5]	0.7623	0.7322	0.7288	0.6733	0.8134	0.7724	0.7381	0.8500
SAKT [22]	0.7686	0.7369	0.7646	0.7022	0.8388	0.7898	0.7828	0.8548
AKT [23]	0.7724	0.7410	0.7737	0.7063	0.8455	0.8087	0.7833	0.8548
GIKT [17]	0.7789	0.7489	0.7791	0.7091	0.8462	0.8090	0.7839	0.8549
GASKT [28]	<u>0.7834</u>	<u>0.7521</u>	0.7697	0.7029	<u>0.8488</u>	<u>0.8132</u>	0.7862	0.8552
CL4KT [31]	0.7621	0.7356	0.7269	0.6733	0.8014	0.7651	0.7811	0.8549
KSGAN [32]	0.7781	0.7489	0.7691	0.7028	0.8461	0.8087	0.7878	0.8568
AT-DKT [33]	0.7690	0.7400	0.7721	0.7060	0.8460	0.8088	0.7860	0.8553
GLNC [34]	0.7826	<u>0.7521</u>	<u>0.7801</u>	<u>0.7143</u>	0.8444	0.8086	<u>0.7890</u>	<u>0.8570</u>
DEKT	**0.7874**	**0.7540**	**0.7860**	**0.7182**	**0.8544**	**0.8155**	**0.7942**	**0.8581**

* The best results are bold, and the second best results are underlined.

4.2   Performance Analysis

The Area Under Curve (AUC) and Accuracy (ACC) are employed as the metrics for reporting performance. Table 2 presents the performance of all compared models and DEKT. From the experimental results, we can draw the following conclusion: 1) In comparison to the original DKT approach, which solely uses the skill information, those graph-based models that use the graph method to mine the exercises-skills relations, including GIKT, GASKT, and KSGAN, have achieved notable promotion. 2) When comparing the performance of SAKT and AKT, the better results of AKT can be attributed to its construction of the exercises-skills relations. 3) Compared with graph-based methods, including GIKT, GASKT, and KSGAN, the performance improvements of the proposed DEKT show that fusing heterogeneous information is necessary to build representations for nodes. 4) Although the results of CL4KT reflect the effectiveness of introducing the contrastive learning method, the average performance of CL4KT inputting the skill information is inferior to that of DEKT, indicating that using only skills as input is inadequate, which fails to leverage valuable exercise information. 5) Our DEKT model that employs exercise representation enhancement and dual-mode contrastive learning considering various information about exercise, skill, learner, difficulty and discrimination on a heterogeneous graph to encode and complement exercise embeddings with semantic and structural information, achieves the best performance on all four datasets.

Table 3. Ablation study of DEKT.

Models	ASSISTments2009		ASSISTments2017		Statics2011		JunyiAcademy	
	AUC	ACC	AUC	ACC	AUC	ACC	AUC	ACC
DEKT-RCL	0.7618	0.7433	0.7711	0.7019	0.8354	0.8019	0.7821	0.8492
DEKT-RT	0.7834	0.7530	0.7797	0.7162	0.8477	0.8146	0.7889	0.8567
DEKT-RA	0.7791	0.7511	0.7806	0.7175	0.8437	0.8115	0.7866	0.8521
DEKT	**0.7874**	**0.7540**	**0.7860**	**0.7182**	**0.8544**	**0.8155**	**0.7942**	**0.8581**

* The best results are bold.

4.3   Ablation Study

Table 3 illustrates the distinct roles played by the three components of DEKT. In this section, the dual-mode contrastive learning (RCL) plays a key role in enhancing exercise representations, resulting in improved predictions. The addition of learner, discrimination, and difficulty nodes (RT) refines the model's ability to capture complex relationships, though its impact is more modest. The dual-temporal attention mechanism (RA) is essential for accurately modeling long-term dependencies, and its absence leads to a significant drop in performance. These components work together to enhance DEKT's overall effectiveness.

- **DEKT-RCL**: In order to assess the potential of GCL regardless of the scale of the exercise, the dual-mode contrastive learning method is removed, and the traditional exercise embedding method is adopted.
- **DEKT-RT**: In order to assess the impact of adding three node types in the heterogeneous graph, the learner nodes, discrimination nodes, and difficulty nodes are removed, except for the exercise nodes and skill nodes.
- **DEKT-RA**: In order to assess the role of the dual-temporal attention mechanism module in accurately modeling the learner's learning process, the two attention modules are removed.

5   Conclusion

In this paper, we propose a Dual-mode Contrastive Learning-Enhanced Knowledge Tracing model to sufficiently capture fine exercise representations and enhance KT. To be specific, DEKT contains a dual-mode contrastive learning (DCL) part to deeply explore and complement richer exercise information, and a learning process modeling (LPM) to capture long-term dependencies between exercises and model learners' knowledge states more effectively. During the training phase, the two loss functions generated by these two parts will be jointly minimized. The experimental results on four real-world datasets confirm the effectiveness and the superiority of DEKT.

Acknowledgements. The works described in this paper are supported by The National Natural Science Foundation of China under Grant Nos. 61772210 and U1911201; Key Research and Development Program of Guangdong of China under Grant No. 2023B0303010004; The Innovation Team Project for Universities in Guangdong Province in China under Grant No. 2023KCXTD011.

References

1. Sun, J., et al.: Weighted heterogeneous graph-based three-view contrastive learning for knowledge tracing in personalized e-learning systems. TCE **70**(1), 2838–2847 (2023)
2. Abdelrahman, G., et al.: Knowledge tracing: a survey. CSUR **55**(11), 1–37 (2023)
3. Yang, H., et al.: Heterogeneous graph-based knowledge tracing with spatiotemporal evolution. ESWA **238**, 122249 (2024)
4. Mao, S., et al.: Improving knowledge tracing via considering two types of actual differences from exercises and prior knowledge. IEEE Trans. Learn. Technol. **16**(3), 324–338 (2023)
5. Piech, C., et al.: Deep knowledge tracing. In: NIPS, pp. 505–513 (2015)
6. Zhang, J., et al.: Dynamic key-value memory networks for knowledge tracing. In: WWW, pp. 765–774 (2017)
7. Chen, P., et al.: Prerequisite-driven deep knowledge tracing. In: ICDM, pp. 39–48 (2018)
8. Su, Y., et al.: Exercise-enhanced sequential modeling for student performance prediction. In: AAAI, pp. 2435–2443 (2018)

9. Liu, Q., et al.: EKT: exercise-aware knowledge tracing for student performance prediction. TKDE **33**(1), 100–115 (2019)
10. Pandey, S., Srivastava, J.: RKT: relation-aware self-attention for knowledge tracing. In: CIKM, pp. 1205–1214 (2020)
11. Lu, Y., et al.: Meta-learning on heterogeneous information networks for cold-start recommendation. In: KDD, pp. 1563–1573 (2020)
12. Wang, Y., et al.: Disenhan: disentangled heterogeneous graph attention network for recommendation. In: CIKM, pp. 1605–1614 (2020)
13. Dong, W., et al.: Improving performance and efficiency of graph neural networks by injective aggregation. KBS **254**, 109616 (2022)
14. Dong, W., et al.: Denoising aggregation of graph neural networks by using principal component analysis. TII **19**(3), 2385–2394 (2022)
15. Nakagawa, H., et al.: Graph-based knowledge tracing: modeling student proficiency using graph neural network. In: WI, pp. 156–163 (2019)
16. Liu, Y., et al.: Improving knowledge tracing via pre-training question embeddings. In: IJCAI, pp. 1577–1583 (2020)
17. Yang, Y., et al.: GIKT: a graph-based interaction model for knowledge tracing. In: ECML PKDD, pp. 299–315 (2021)
18. Corbett, A.T., Anderson, J.R.: Knowledge tracing: modeling the acquisition of procedural knowledge. User Model. User-Adap. Inter. **4**, 253–278 (1994)
19. Cen, H., et al.: Learning factors analysis - a general method for cognitive model evaluation and improvement. In: ITS, pp. 164–175 (2006)
20. Pavlik Jr, P.I., et al.: Performance factors analysis - a new alternative to knowledge tracing. In: AIED, pp. 531–538 (2009)
21. Abdelrahman, G., Wang, Q.: Knowledge tracing with sequential key-value memory networks. In: SIGIR, pp. 175–184 (2019)
22. Pandey, S., Karypis, G.: A self attentive model for knowledge tracing. In: EDM, pp. 384–389 (2019)
23. Ghosh, A., et al.: Context-aware attentive knowledge tracing. In: KDD, pp. 2330–2339 (2020)
24. Shin, D., et al.: SAINT+: integrating temporal features for EdNet correctness prediction. In: LAK, pp. 490–496 (2021)
25. Wang, C., et al.: Temporal cross-effects in knowledge tracing. In: WSDM, pp. 517–525 (2021)
26. Tong, S., et al.: Structure-based knowledge tracing: an influence propagation view. In: ICDM, pp. 541–550 (2020)
27. Song, X., et al.: JKT: a joint graph convolutional network based deep knowledge tracing. Inf. Sci. **580**, 510–523 (2021)
28. Wang, M., et al.: GASKT: a graph-based attentive knowledge-search model for knowledge tracing. In: KSEM, pp. 268–279 (2021)
29. Gan, W., et al.: Knowledge structure enhanced graph representation learning model for attentive knowledge tracing. Int. J. Intell. Syst. **37**(3), 2012–2045 (2022)
30. Hamilton, W., et al.: Inductive representation learning on large graphs. In: NIPS, pp. 1024–1034 (2017)
31. Lee, W., et al.: Contrastive learning for knowledge tracing. In: WWW, pp. 2330–2338 (2022)
32. Mao, S., et al.: Knowledge structure-aware graph-attention networks for knowledge tracing. In: KSEM, pp. 309–321 (2022)
33. Liu, Z., et al.: Enhancing deep knowledge tracing with auxiliary tasks. In: WWW, pp. 4178–4187 (2023)
34. Yu, S., et al.: Global and local neural cognitive modeling for student performance prediction. ESWA **237**, 121637 (2024)

Leveraging Information Consistency in Frequency and Spatial Domain for Adversarial Attacks

Zhibo Jin[1], Jiayu Zhang[2], Zhiyu Zhu[1], Xinyi Wang[3], Yiyun Huang[4], and Huaming Chen[1(✉)]

[1] The University of Sydney, Sydney, Australia
{zjin0915,zzhu2018}@uni.sydney.edu.au, huaming.chen@sydney.edu.au
[2] Suzhou Yierqi, Suzhou, China
[3] University of Malaya, Kuala Lumpur, Malaysia
[4] Virginia Polytechnic Institute and State University, Blacksburg, USA

Abstract. Adversarial examples are a key method to exploit deep neural networks. Using gradient information, such examples can be generated in an efficient way without altering the victim model. Recent frequency domain transformation has further enhanced the transferability of such adversarial examples, such as spectrum simulation attack. In this work, we investigate the effectiveness of frequency domain-based attacks, aligning with similar findings in the spatial domain. Furthermore, such consistency between the frequency and spatial domains provides insights into how gradient-based adversarial attacks induce perturbations across different domains, which is yet to be explored. Hence, we propose a simple, effective, and scalable gradient-based adversarial attack algorithm leveraging the information consistency in both frequency and spatial domains. We evaluate the algorithm for its effectiveness against different models. Extensive experiments demonstrate that our algorithm achieves state-of-the-art results compared to other gradient-based algorithms. Our code is available at: https://github.com/LMBTough/FSA.

Keywords: Adversarial Attacks · Frequency Analysis · Transferability

1 Introduction

Deep neural networks (DNNs) are susceptible to subtle perturbations, which can lead to erroneous predictions [26]. The attacks with adversarial examples are generally classified into white-box and black-box attacks based on the level of information accessible to the attacker. In white-box attacks [8], the attacker has access to model information, such as model parameters, network structure, training dataset, and defense mechanisms. This allows for the deliberate construction of adversarial examples. In contrast, black-box attacks limit the access

---

Z. Jin and J. Zhang—These authors contributed equally to this work.

R. Hadfi et al. (Eds.): PRICAI 2024, LNAI 15281, pp. 93–105, 2025.
https://doi.org/10.1007/978-981-96-0116-5_8

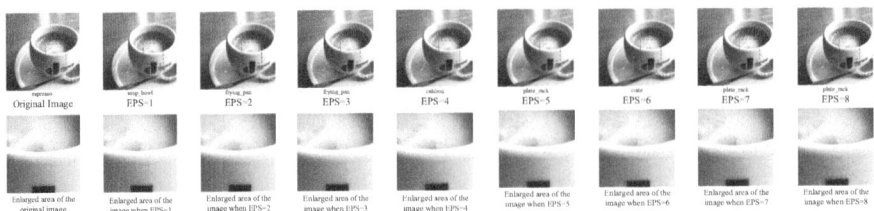

Fig. 1. Attack samples at different perturbation rates (EPS values). The first image, labeled 'espresso' by ResNet-50, is the original. The following images are adversarial examples generated with increasing EPS values, along with their incorrect predictions. The second row shows magnified regions of the images. As EPS increases, the noise becomes more noticeable, starting to be visible at EPS = 3, and becoming increasingly pronounced with higher values.

to model information for the attackers [3,13,15]. Some black-box defense models can restrict or disable external access upon detecting an adversarial attack attempt, significantly reducing the attack success rate.

We focus on white-box attacks in this paper, as they are considered the most straightforward way to construct adversarial examples. With access to model information, it can achieve optimal performance while maintaining minimal perturbation rates. Consequently, white-box attacks play a crucial role in evaluating system performance under adversarial conditions and assessing model robustness. Furthermore, they facilitate the development of adversarial training focused on minimizing perturbations [28].

Gradient-based adversarial methods can achieve substantial performance in most white-box attacks [14,35,38]. These methods use the model's gradient information to generate optimal perturbation vectors that are difficult to defense. The noise is added to the original input to create adversarial examples, thereby manipulating model outputs. However, due to the inherent nature of gradients, current methods typically utilize only the spatial information of images to generate perturbations, neglecting frequency information during the attack process. Studies have shown a strong correlation between DNNs and frequency domain information [7]. DNNs can effectively capture high-frequency information in an image that is invisible to humans [29]. When subjected to human-added perturbations, the sensitivity of DNNs to different frequency regions varies, with high-frequency regions showing high sensitivity [32]. To investigate the effects of adding perturbation solely to the low-frequency image area on the target model, [9] proposed an adversarial algorithm that adds perturbation to the low-frequency domain, confirming the importance of low-frequency information in DNN predictions. Following this, we anticipate that frequency domain is informative for adversarial attacks and can effectively enhance the attack performance.

However, focusing exclusively on frequency information for attacks could result in a loss of spatial information. Combining gradient computation with both spatial and frequency information may address the gradient explosion issue in conventional spatial domain-based attacks and generate perturbations that appear natural in both domains. In Fig. 1, we display the original image and adversarial images under varying levels of perturbation. With a low perturbation rate (EPS = 1), our algorithm effectively induce misclassifications in the model, indicating a higher level of threat in a white-box setting. As the perturbation level increases, the alterations become more visible. Some white-box defense algorithms, such as adversarial training [2], gradient masking [17], and feature transformations [30], have shown promising defense capabilities, prompting us to explore the generation of adversarial examples that are sufficiently concealed.

In this paper, we empirically analyze the information consistency in the frequency and spatial domains for adversarial attacks. Algorithms that utilize only spatial information for adversarial attacks, such as FGSM [8], rely on the spatial gradients to generate perturbations. On the other hand, algorithms that exclusively use frequency information, such as SSA [18], exploit the frequency domain to craft adversarial examples. Exploring the consistency between frequency and spatial domains provides novel insights into how gradient-based adversarial attack algorithms induce perturbations across diverse domains, a perspective that has not been explored with singular domain attacks. Therefore, we aim to combine the frequency and spatial domains for attacks, leveraging this property to enhance the attack effectiveness. We propose a novel algorithm, termed the Frequency and Spatial consistency based adversarial Attack (FSA), to improve the attack success rate. We summarize the key contributions as follows:

- We thoroughly analyse white-box attacks from the perspectives of spatial and frequency domain, confirming information consistency.
- By combining information from the frequency and spatial domain, we propose a simple, effective, and scalable adversarial attack algorithm FSA, which has significantly improved the attack performance in white-box settings.
- We have conducted comprehensive experiments to evaluate the effectiveness of FSA, demonstrating state-of-the-art performance. We also release the replication package of our method publicly.

2   Related Work

2.1   Gradient-Based Adversarial Attacks

Gradient-based adversarial attacks are divided into white-box and black-box categories, with white-box attacks having access to the model's internals. The Fast Gradient Sign Method (FGSM) [8] is a typical white-box approach that enhances adversarial examples with a single gradient ascent step. Iterative FGSM (I-FGSM) [16] refines these examples through multiple iterations. Momentum Iterative FGSM (MI-FGSM) [5] adds momentum to gradient updates, avoiding local maxima and stabilizing the attack. TI-FGSM [6] uses transformation kernels on gradients, while DI-FGSM [31] employs random resizing and padding. Projected Gradient Descent (PGD) [19] and C&W [4] further refine attacks by constraining perturbation sizes and optimizing effectiveness.

2.2   Frequency-Based Adversarial Attacks

Frequency domain analysis presents significant relevance in adversarial attacks. Wang et al. [29] found that DNNs have unique advantages in the frequency domain of images. For high-frequency domain features that are difficult to be recognised by human eyes, DNNs can capture their effective information. Yin et al. [32] noticed that naturally trained models are highly sensitive to high-frequency perturbation information, and the model robustness to high-frequency noise is enhanced by methods such as Gaussian data augmentation and adversarial training.

Guo et al. [9] propose an adversarial attack method with the low-frequency information of images. This verifies that low-frequency information also plays a crucial role in model prediction, even though DNNs are more sensitive in the high-frequency domain. By considering the effect of frequency-domain attacks on adversarial defense, Sharma et al. [22] found that the adversarial training-based defense model is less sensitive to high-frequency perturbations and the defense effect is more susceptible to low-frequency perturbations. Duan et al. [7] proposed the AdvDrop attack algorithm, which discards some details in the frequency domain of pure images to enhance offensiveness. However, these aforementioned gradient-based and frequency-based adversarial attack methods focus only on generating perturbations within singular domain, without taking into account the consistency between frequency information and spatial information.

3   Approach

3.1   Preliminaries of Adversarial Attack

Formally, consider a deep learning network $N : R^n \rightarrow R^c$, where n is the input dimension and c is the number of classes and original image sample $x^0 \in R^n$, if an imperceptible perturbation $\sum_{k=0}^{t-1} \triangle x^k$ is applied to the original sample x^0, this may mislead the network N into classify the manipulated input $x^t = x^0 + \sum_{k=0}^{t-1} \triangle x^k$ as having the label m. This manipulated input can also be denoted as x^{adv}. Assuming the output of the sample x is denoted by $N(x)$, the optimization goal is:

$$\left\| x^t - x^0 \right\|_n < \epsilon \quad subject\ to \quad N(x^t) \neq N(x^0) \tag{1}$$

Here, $\left\| \cdot \right\|_n$ represents the n-norm distance.

3.2   Frequency Transfromation

In this subsection, we introduce the DCT (Discrete Cosine Transform) and IDCT (Inverse Discrete Cosine Transform) transformations [7]. The DCT aims to transform an image from the spatial domain to the frequency domain, while the IDCT

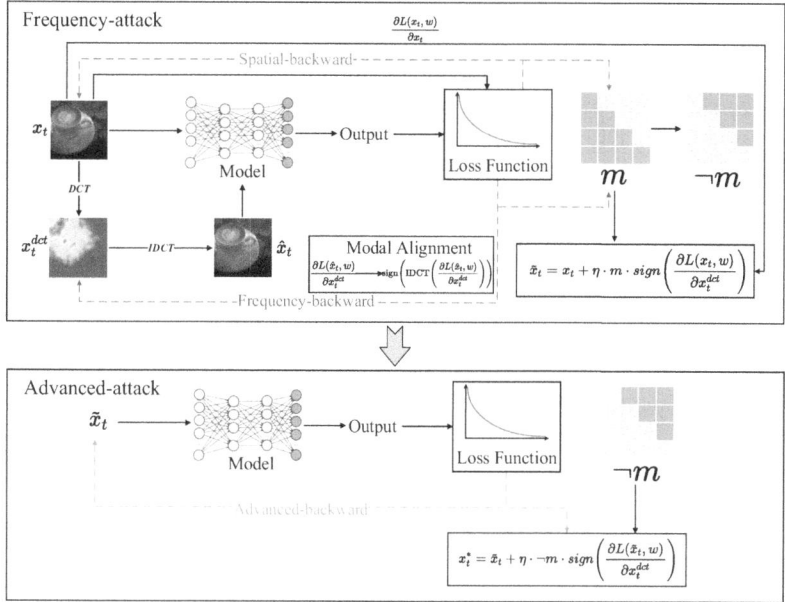

Fig. 2. Schematic diagram of FSA (We first extract gradient information from both the spatial and frequency domains of the original image. The information is then combined through a consistency check, where only gradients with matching directions in both domains are considered valid. To facilitate this, we employ a mask to control the updating of dimensions in the image. This mask is integrated into the adversarial example update process, resulting in the intermediate image $\widetilde{x}_{t+1}$. Following this, the mask is inverted (denoted as $\neg m$) and applied to $\widetilde{x}_{t+1}$ for a subsequent attack iteration, yielding the final adversarial sample x^*_{t+1}. Finally, the gradient information verified for consistency is iterated into previous round of x_t to obtain x_{t+1}.)

transforms the image back to the spatial domain.

$$D(x)_{[u,v]} = \frac{1}{\sqrt{2N}} C(u)C(v) \sum_{x=0}^{N-1} \sum_{y=0}^{N-1} x[k,m]$$
$$\cos\left[\frac{(2k+1)i\pi}{2N}\right] \cos\left[\frac{(2m+1)j\pi}{2N}\right] \tag{2}$$

Here, $D(x)[u, v]$ represents the frequency domain value, $x[k, m]$ is the input image in the spatial domain, and $C(u)$ and $C(v)$ are normalization factors. Equation 2 provides the mathematical definition of DCT transformation. The primary purpose of DCT is to identify the frequency components in the input signal or image. Furthermore, the DCT decomposes the input signal into a weighted combination of a series with cosine functions of increasing frequencies. Low-frequency components are usually located at the front of the DCT coefficient array, and high-frequency components are located at the rear.

IDCT is the inverse operation of DCT and is used to convert signals or images represented in the frequency domain back to the spatial domain. In image compression, a DCT-compressed image can be restored by applying IDCT to obtain a version that is close to the original image. Detailed explanations of the symbols used in the DCT and its inverse form, IDCT, can be referred to [1]. The most important intuition that DCT shows is that operations in the frequency domain(transformed by DCT operation) can be reflected back to the original spatial domain by using IDCT transformation. It is worth noting that both the DCT and IDCT operations are lossless, and they can be used to calculate gradients easily. The definition of discrete cosine transform gives us another perspective on adversarial attacks using the frequency domain information.

3.3   Frequency and Spatial Consistency Based Adversarial Attack

Leveraging DCT and IDCT operations, we propose FSA, which comprises two distinct adversarial attack steps: the spatial attack and the frequency attack.

$$\Delta \text{grad}\,(x_t) = \alpha \cdot \text{sign} \left(\frac{\partial L\,(x_t; y)}{\partial x_t} \right) \tag{3}$$

Equation 3 defines the formula for spatial attack feature changes. $\Delta \text{grad}\,(x_t)$ denotes the original adversarial attack changes, which comprise learning rate α and the gradients $\frac{\partial L(x_t; y)}{\partial x_t}$ under the t-th sample x. Other gradient-based adversarial attacks like PGD [19] can also obtain $\Delta \text{grad}\,(x_t)$, and can use a projection function to constrain the feature changes. Specifically, the *sign* function in Eq. 3 has the following two different properties:

Decoupling the Attack from Model Parameters. Consider a simple neural network $Y = W \cdot X$, where Y is a one-dimensional value, as an example. It can be calculated that the gradients of X can be represented as W^T, which are the model's parameters. The greater value in parameters, the more significant the changes, which is not a desired outcome in the attack progress. This phenomenon can be mitigated by applying the *sign* function.

Balance Spatial Attack and Frequency Attack. With the *sign* function and attack value ranges between $\alpha, -\alpha$, and 0, the consistency between spatial and frequency attacks can be inferred from the similarity of their attack value.

$$\Delta \text{frequency}(x_t) = \alpha \cdot sign \left[IDCT \left(\frac{\partial L(IDCT(DCT(x_t)), y)}{\partial DCT(x_t)} \right) \right] \tag{4}$$

Equation 4 is the formula for frequency attack feature changes. It calculates the gradient in the frequency domain $DCT(x_t)$ and uses the IDCT transformation to convert the attack changes back to the spatial domain. Subsequently, the *sign* function is used to align the attack with the spatial domain.

$$m_t = (\Delta \text{grad}\,(x_t) == \Delta \text{frequency}(x_t)) \tag{5}$$

$$\widetilde{x}_t = x_t + m_t \cdot \Delta \text{grad}\,(x_t) \tag{6}$$

$$x_t^* = \widetilde{x}_t + \neg m_t \cdot \Delta \text{grad}\,(\widetilde{x}_t) \tag{7}$$

Finally, we obtain the consistency mask m_t by aligning the values from two domain attacks and apply it in FSA attack step. It is important to note that m_t is a binary mask, taking values 0 or 1. Equation 5 is used to compute this mask. Here, $==$ indicates that m_t takes the value 1 when the sign of the spatial gradient $\Delta \text{grad}(x_t)$ and the frequency gradient $\Delta \text{frequency}(x_t)$ are the same, and it takes the value 0 when the signs differ. Equation 6 represents the step of the frequency attack, where $\widetilde{x}_t$ is the intermediate state after the frequency attack. Equation 7 represents the step of the advanced attack, where x_t^* denotes the final attack outcome. During the iterative process, the inverse of the obtained consistency mask m_t is calculated as $\neg m_t$. In the subsequent attack phase, the region corresponding to m_t is targeted first, followed by the region associated with $\neg m_t$. This approach is particularly significant since the region corresponding to $\neg m_t$ was not attacked in the previous phase. Specifically, we ensure that the maximum perturbation $max|\Delta x|$ is less than or equal to a predefined disturbance rate α. Given that $m_t \in [0,1]$, the constraint $max|m_t \cdot \Delta x| \le \alpha$ remains valid. Thus, our method complies with the disturbance rate constraint as $max|m \cdot \Delta x + \neg m \cdot \Delta \widetilde{x}| \le \alpha$. Algorithm 1 is the pseudocode based on the example of FGSM algorithm. The schematic diagram of our FSA algorithm is shown in Fig. 2.

Algorithm 1. Frequency and Spatial Consistency Based Adversarial Attack

---

Input: Learning rate η, loss function L, original input feature x_0, label y, step T

Output: x_T^*

1: $x = x_0$
2: **for** i in range T **do**
3:     $\Delta \text{grad}\,(x_t) = \eta \cdot \text{sign}\left(\frac{\partial L(x_t;y)}{\partial x_t}\right)$
4:     Get $\Delta \text{frequency}(x_t)$ by Equ. 4
5:     $m_t = (\Delta \text{grad}\,(x_t) == \Delta \text{frequency}(x_t))$
6:     $\widetilde{x}_t = x_t + m_t \cdot \Delta \text{grad}\,(x_t)$
7:     $\Delta \text{grad}\,(\widetilde{x}_t) = \eta \cdot \text{sign}\left(\frac{\partial L(\widetilde{x}_t;y)}{\partial x_t}\right)$
8:     $x_t^* = \widetilde{x}_t + \neg m_t \cdot \Delta \text{grad}\,(\widetilde{x}_t)$

    The FGSM algorithm is used as a pseudocode to illustrate our FSA, and it is the same in DI-FGSM, MI-FGSM and TI-FGSM.

9: **end for**
10: **return** x_T^*

---

4 Experiments

In the experiment, we have conducted a comparative analysis of nine models, including DenseNet_121 [12], Inception_v3 [25], VGG16 [23], MobileNet_v2 [21], GoogLeNet [24], EfficientNet_B0 [27], VGG19 [23], MobileNet_v3_large [11], and ResNet_50 [10], utilizing five distinct adversarial methods: MI-FGSM [5], DI-FGSM [31], TI-FGSM [6], I-FGSM [16], and PGD [19]. The objective of these comparison experiments is to investigate how FSA method could enhance the attack effectiveness of the aforementioned methods. By integrating the FSA method with the aforementioned adversarial techniques, we provide comprehensive results to demonstrate the improvements in their adversarial capabilities.

Table 1. Comparison table of attack success rate with and without our FSA

Model	MI-FGSM		DI-FGSM		TI-FGSM		I-FGSM		PGD	
	No FSA	FSA	No FSA	FSA	No FSA	FSA	No FSA	FSA	No FSA	FSA
DenseNet121	99.57	99.78(0.21)	92.11	98.27(6.16)	75.89	94.27(18.38)	99.78	99.78(0)	98.81	99.03(0.22)
Inception_v3	87.80	92.32(4.52)	77.71	85.80(8.09)	58.78	77.18(18.40)	89.38	90.75(1.37)	86.75	87.38(0.63)
VGG16	98.83	99.42(0.59)	96.38	98.48(2.10)	75.03	87.86(12.83)	99.30	99.42(0.12)	98.72	98.60(0.12)
MobileNet_v2	99.88	100(0.12)	94.73	98.95(4.22)	72.72	94.26(21.54)	100	100(0)	99.53	99.65(0.12)
GoogLeNet	96.71	98.03(1.32)	83.13	94.30(11.17)	57.06	80.50(23.44)	97.48	97.59(0.11)	94.85	95.29(0.44)
EfficientNet_b0	91.48	93.50(2.02)	84.45	90.95(6.50)	57.51	70.61(13.10)	93.40	93.61(0.21)	90.84	91.27(0.43)
VGG19	97.83	98.63(0.80)	94.52	97.26(2.74)	72.95	88.70(15.75)	98.40	98.52(0.12)	97.60	97.37(0.23)
MobileNet_v3_large	99.88	100(0.12)	96.30	98.85(2.55)	74.48	92.03(17.55)	100	100(0)	99.42	99.42(0)
ResNet_50	99.13	99.67(0.54)	89.32	97.17(7.85)	58.82	87.80(28.98)	99.56	99.56(0)	98.58	98.80(0.22)

4.1   Dataset

The dataset consists of 1000 images, selected in accordance with the settings used in these methods [33, 34, 36, 37, 39–41]. These images were randomly chosen from diverse categories within the ILSVRC 2012 validation set [20], which is widely recognized and extensively utilized for adversarial attacks.

4.2   Evaluation Metrics

This experiment aimed to evaluate various attack methods using the attack success rate as the metric. A higher success rate indicates a more effective adversarial attack. We calculated the difference in success rates before and after applying the FSA method to demonstrate its effectiveness in enhancing attack methods.

4.3   Parameter Setting

The parameters considered in this experiment are the maximum perturbation (Epsilon) and the number of iterations (Steps). The maximum perturbation value was set to 1.0, respectively, while the number of iterations was set to 5.

4.4   Experimental Results

The analysis depicted in Fig. 3 clearly shows variations in the success rate improvements of different attack methods under varying Epsilon and Steps counts, across different models. Nevertheless, the utilization of the FSA method yielded significant enhancements in attack success rates for a considerable number of attack methods across these models. Table 1 shows the attack success rate of our algorithm in various environments. Specifically, employing the FSA method results in a maximum increase in attack success rates of 28.98% across the range of attack methods, with an average increase of 5.23%. Additionally, while a slight decrease in attack success rates was observed for PGD method, the magnitude of the decrease was minimal, only 0.23% and 0.12%. These findings provide substantial evidence supporting the effectiveness of the FSA approach. Moreover, as illustrated in Fig. 3 and Table 1, it is evident that different attack methods experience a substantial enhancement in success rates as the attack

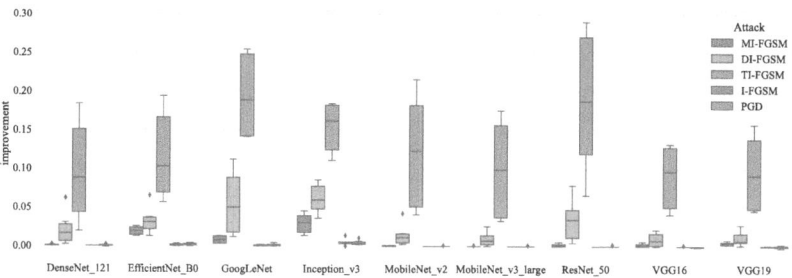

Fig. 3. Box plot of FSA compared to other methods for indicators

Table 2. Mean attack success rate (Improved%) with different EPS

Attack	Steps = 5		Steps = 10		Steps = 16	
	Eps = 1/255	Eps = 2/255	Eps = 1/255	Eps = 2/255	Eps = 1/255	Eps = 2/255
MI-FGSM with FSA	1.14	0.54(−0.6)	1.01	0.38(−0.63)	0.96	0.36(−0.6)
DI-FGSM with FSA	5.71	1.99(−3.72)	3.99	1.01(−2.98)	3.05	0.85(−2.2)
TI-FGSM with FSA	18.89	8.9(−9.99)	18.71	7.16(−11.55)	17.18	6.17(−11.01)
I-FGSM with FSA	0.21	0.09(−0.12)	0.09	0.04(−0.05)	0.08	0(−0.08)
PGD with FSA	0.19	0.08(−0.11)	0.05	−0.06(0.01)	0.16	0.08(−0.08)

perturbation levels increase. However, the effectiveness of the FSA method in improving attack success rates diminishes across various attack methods. This observation suggests that the FSA method exhibits more pronounced improvements when the initial attack success rates are relatively low. Conversely, when the original success rates are already high, the impact of the FSA method in enhancing the success rates becomes limited.

Notably, SSA achieved an attack success rate of 24.02% on the ImageNet dataset with an epsilon constraint set to 1, specifically targeting the Inception_v3 model. This result is attributed to SSA being a black-box transferable method. However, conducting its evaluation within the experimental framework of this paper would not be equitable. Therefore, SSA was not included as a competitive baseline for comparative analysis.

4.5   Ablation Experiments

Effect of Different the Epsilon. We conduct a comparative analysis of the effect of different Epsilon values on the performance of FSA method. Specifically, we investigate the impact of Epsilon values from 1.0 to 2.0 on the FSA method under the Steps settings of 5, 10, and 16, respectively. Figure 4 and Table 2 illustrate the results of a decreasing trend in the attack success rate of the FSA method as the Epsilon value increases. Notably, the TI-FGSM method demonstrates the largest decline in success rate improvement, with a decrease of 10.19%

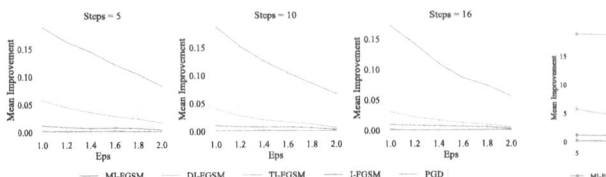 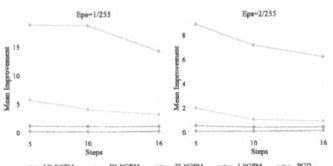

Fig. 4. Mean attack success rate improvement with different Epsilon values

Fig. 5. Mean attack success rate improvement with different Steps

and an average decrease of 3.17% in attack success rate improvement. Moreover, the effectiveness of FSA declines with higher Epsilon values, suggesting that FSA performs better when the Epsilon is set to 1.0.

Table 3. Mean attack success rate (Improved%) with different Steps

Attack	Eps = 1/255			Eps = 2/255		
	Steps = 5	Steps = 10	Steps = 16	Steps = 5	Steps = 10	Steps = 16
MI-FGSM with FSA	1.14	1.01	0.96	0.54	0.38	0.36
DI-FGSM with FSA	5.71	3.99	3.05	1.99	1.01	0.85
TI-FGSM with FSA	18.89	18.71	14.18	8.90	7.16	6.17
I-FGSM with FSA	0.21	0.09	0.08	0.09	0.04	0
PGD with FSA	0.19	0.05	0.16	0.08	0.06	0.08

Effect of Different Steps. We compare the effects of different step parameters on the performance of FSA. We first examine the influence of different step values, namely 5, 10, and 16, on the gain achieved by FSA, with EPS values set to 1.0 and 2.0, respectively. As shown in Fig. 5 and Table 3, it can be observed that with an increase in steps, there is no significant fluctuation in the effectiveness of FSA method across various attack methods, regardless of whether EPS is set to 1.0 or 2.0. The experimental results suggest that different step parameters do not have substantial impact on the effectiveness of FSA.

5   Conclusion

In this paper, we introduce the Frequency and Spatial Consistency-Based Adversarial Attack (FSA) method to enhance the success rate of most white-box algorithms by leveraging consistency in both frequency and spatial domains. Noticing the limitations of using singular domain information for attacks, we extend the frequency transformation using DCT and IDCT operations during training, significantly boosting FSA's performance. Experiments with MI-FGSM, DI-FGSM, TI-FGSM, and I-FGSM demonstrate that our method improves attack success rates and achieves state-of-the-art results.

References

1. Ahmed, N., Natarajan, T., Rao, K.R.: Discrete cosine transform. IEEE Trans. Comput. **100**(1), 90–93 (1974)
2. Bai, T., Luo, J., Zhao, J., Wen, B., Wang, Q.: Recent advances in adversarial training for adversarial robustness. arXiv preprint arXiv:2102.01356 (2021)
3. Brendel, W., Rauber, J., Bethge, M.: Decision-based adversarial attacks: reliable attacks against black-box machine learning models. arXiv:1712.04248 (2017)
4. Carlini, N., Wagner, D.: Towards evaluating the robustness of neural networks. In: 2017 IEEE Symposium on Security and Privacy (SP), pp. 39–57. IEEE (2017)
5. Dong, Y., et al.: Boosting adversarial attacks with momentum. In: Proceedings of the IEEE Conference on Computer Vision and Pattern Recognition, pp. 9185–9193 (2018)
6. Dong, Y., Pang, T., Su, H., Zhu, J.: Evading defenses to transferable adversarial examples by translation-invariant attacks. In: Proceedings of the IEEE/CVF Conference on Computer Vision and Pattern Recognition, pp. 4312–4321 (2019)
7. Duan, R., Chen, Y., Niu, D., Yang, Y., Qin, A.K., He, Y.: AdvDrop: adversarial attack to DNNs by dropping information. In: Proceedings of the IEEE/CVF International Conference on Computer Vision, pp. 7506–7515 (2021)
8. Goodfellow, I.J., Shlens, J., Szegedy, C.: Explaining and harnessing adversarial examples. arXiv preprint arXiv:1412.6572 (2014)
9. Guo, C., Frank, J.S., Weinberger, K.Q.: Low frequency adversarial perturbation. arXiv preprint arXiv:1809.08758 (2018)
10. He, K., Zhang, X., Ren, S., Sun, J.: Deep residual learning for image recognition. In: Proceedings of the IEEE conference on CVPR, pp. 770–778 (2016)
11. Howard, A., et al.: Searching for mobilenetv3. In: Proceedings of the IEEE/CVF International Conference on Computer Vision, pp. 1314–1324 (2019)
12. Huang, G., Liu, Z., Van Der Maaten, L., Weinberger, K.Q.: Densely connected convolutional networks. In: Proceedings of the IEEE Conference on Computer Vision and Pattern Recognition, pp. 4700–4708 (2017)
13. Jin, Z., Zhang, J., Zhu, Z., Chen, H.: Benchmarking transferable adversarial attacks. CoRR (2024)
14. Jin, Z., et al.: Enhancing adversarial attacks via parameter adaptive adversarial attack. arXiv preprint arXiv:2408.07733 (2024)
15. Jin, Z., Zhu, Z., Wang, X., Zhang, J., Shen, J., Chen, H.: DANAA: towards transferable attacks with double adversarial neuron attribution. In: Yang, X., et al. (eds.) ADMA 2023. LNCS, vol. 14177, pp. 456–470. Springer, Cham (2023). https://doi.org/10.1007/978-3-031-46664-9_31
16. Kurakin, A., Goodfellow, I.J., Bengio, S.: Adversarial examples in the physical world. In: Artificial Intelligence Safety and Security, pp. 99–112 (2018)
17. Lee, H., Bae, H., Yoon, S.: Gradient masking of label smoothing in adversarial robustness. IEEE Access **9**, 6453–6464 (2020)
18. Long, Y., et al.: Frequency domain model augmentation for adversarial attack. In: Avidan, S., Brostow, G., Cissé, M., Farinella, G.M., Hassner, T. (eds.) ECCV 2022. LNCS, vol. 13664, pp. 549–566. Springer, Cham (2022). https://doi.org/10.1007/978-3-031-19772-7_32
19. Madry, A., Makelov, A., Schmidt, L., Tsipras, D., Vladu, A.: Towards deep learning models resistant to adversarial attacks. arXiv preprint arXiv:1706.06083 (2017)

20. Russakovsky, O., et al.: Imagenet large scale visual recognition challenge. Int. J. Comput. Vision **115**, 211–252 (2015)
21. Sandler, M., Howard, A., Zhu, M., Zhmoginov, A., Chen, L.C.: Mobilenetv2: inverted residuals and linear bottlenecks. In: Proceedings of the IEEE conference on Computer Vision and Pattern Recognition, pp. 4510–4520 (2018)
22. Sharma, Y., Ding, G.W., Brubaker, M.: On the effectiveness of low frequency perturbations. arXiv preprint arXiv:1903.00073 (2019)
23. Simonyan, K., Zisserman, A.: Very deep convolutional networks for large-scale image recognition. arXiv preprint arXiv:1409.1556 (2014)
24. Szegedy, C., et al.: Going deeper with convolutions. In: Proceedings of the IEEE Conference on Computer Vision and Pattern Recognition, pp. 1–9 (2015)
25. Szegedy, C., Vanhoucke, V., Ioffe, S., Shlens, J., Wojna, Z.: Rethinking the inception architecture for computer vision. In: Proceedings of the IEEE Conference on Computer Vision and Pattern Recognition, pp. 2818–2826 (2016)
26. Szegedy, C., et al.: Intriguing properties of neural networks. arXiv:1312.6199 (2013)
27. Tan, M., Le, Q.: EfficientNet: rethinking model scaling for convolutional neural networks. In: International Conference on Machine Learning, pp. 6105–6114 (2019)
28. Tramèr, F., Kurakin, A., Papernot, N., Goodfellow, I., Boneh, D., McDaniel, P.: Ensemble adversarial training: attacks and defenses. arXiv preprint arXiv:1705.07204 (2017)
29. Wang, H., Wu, X., Huang, Z., Xing, E.P.: High-frequency component helps explain the generalization of convolutional neural networks. In: Proceedings of the IEEE/CVF Conference on CVPR, pp. 8684–8694 (2020)
30. Wu, W., Su, Y., Lyu, M.R., King, I.: Improving the transferability of adversarial samples with adversarial transformations. In: Proceedings of the IEEE/CVF Conference on Computer Vision and Pattern Recognition, pp. 9024–9033 (2021)
31. Xie, C., et al.: Improving transferability of adversarial examples with input diversity. In: Proceedings of the IEEE/CVF Conference on CVPR, pp. 2730–2739 (2019)
32. Yin, D., Gontijo Lopes, R., Shlens, J., Cubuk, E.D., Gilmer, J.: A fourier perspective on model robustness in computer vision. In: NeurIPS, vol. 32 (2019)
33. Zhu, Z., et al.: Ge-advgan: improving the transferability of adversarial samples by gradient editing-based adversarial generative model. In: Proceedings of the 2024 SIAM International Conference on Data Mining (SDM), pp. 706–714. SIAM (2024)
34. Zhu, Z., et al.: Iterative search attribution for deep neural networks. In: Forty-first International Conference on Machine Learning (2024)
35. Zhu, Z., et al.: Improving adversarial transferability via frequency-based stationary point search. In: Proceedings of the 32nd ACM International Conference on Information and Knowledge Management, pp. 3626–3635 (2023)
36. Zhu, Z., et al.: AttExplore: attribution for explanation with model parameters exploration. In: The Twelfth International Conference on Learning Representations (2024)
37. Zhu, Z., et al.: MFABA: a more faithful and accelerated boundary-based attribution method for deep neural networks. In: Proceedings of the AAAI Conference on Artificial Intelligence, vol. 38, pp. 17228–17236 (2024)
38. Zhu, Z., Jin, Z., Wang, X., Zhang, J., Chen, H., Choo, K.K.R.: Rethinking transferable adversarial attacks with double adversarial neuron attribution. IEEE Trans. Artif. Intell. (2024)
39. Zhu, Z., Jin, Z., Zhang, J., Chen, H.: Enhancing model interpretability with local attribution over global exploration. arXiv preprint arXiv:2408.07736 (2024)

40. Zhu, Z., Wang, X., Jin, Z., Zhang, J., Chen, H.: Enhancing transferable adversarial attacks on vision transformers through gradient normalization scaling and high-frequency adaptation. In: The Twelfth International Conference on Learning Representations (2024)
41. Zhu, Z., Zhang, J., Wang, X., Jin, Z., Chen, H.: DMS: addressing information loss with more steps for pragmatic adversarial attacks. arXiv preprint arXiv:2406.07580 (2024)

Characterization of Similarity Metrics in Epistemic Logic

Xiaolong Liang[1] and Yì N. Wáng[2]([⊠]) [ID]

[1] School of Philosophy, Shanxi University, Taiyuan 030006, China
[2] Department of Philosophy (Zhuhai), Sun Yat-sen University, Zhuhai 519082, China
ynw@xixilogic.org

Abstract. The comprehension of similarity metrics lags behind that of distance metrics. This study aims to address this disparity by synthesizing the properties of similarity metrics and examining them through the lens of weighted epistemic logic. By incorporating these metrics, we analyze knowledge systems in terms of their metric properties. Modal logic techniques, including bisimulation and bounded morphism, are employed to investigate the definable and undefinable properties of similarity. Definable alternatives for undefinable properties are proposed.

Keywords: similarity · epistemic logic · definability · model checking

1 Introduction

Distance and similarity metrics are essential concepts in various fields such as machine learning, statistics, data analysis, and information retrieval. These metrics quantify how similar or dissimilar objects—such as vectors, texts, or images—are to one another, and are standard components in textbooks in, e.g., data mining [9,18] and cluster analysis [7,19]. While distance metrics are well-studied with established foundations, the understanding of similarity metrics is less developed. We will first summarize the common properties of distance metrics and their generalization, known as partial metrics. Next, we will link the variants of similarity metrics to the axioms for distance and partial metrics and then organize these axioms. These axioms provide valuable sources for testing characterization problems within the frameworks of weighted epistemic logics [5,16], which will be explained in more detail in subsequent sections.

1.1 Metrics and Partial Metrics of Distance

When considering abstract or various objects, certain properties of a distance metric are widely accepted. Given a set X, the function $d : X \times X \to \mathbb{R}$ is called a *distance metric* (or simply *metric*) over X, if it satisfies the following conditions for any $x, y, z \in X$:

D1 $d(x, y) \geq 0$ *(nonnegativity)*; [1]

Supported by Project of Humanities and Social Sciences, MOE (China).

[1] As observed in [4, p. 4], D1 follows from D3 and D4: by setting $y = x$ in D4, we obtain $0 \leq d(x, x)$, and by letting $x = z$ in D4, we arrive at D1. It remains unclear why the 2016 edition weakens this to suggest that D1 follows from D2 to D4.

D2a $d(x,y) = 0$ implies $x = y$ (*indistancy implies equality*);
D2b $d(x,x) = 0$ (*equality implies indistancy* or *reflexivity*);
D3 $d(x,y) = d(y,x)$ (*symmetry*);
D4 $d(x,z) \leq d(x,y) + d(y,z)$ (*triangularity* or *triangle/triangular inequiality*).

In the above conditions for a distance metric, D2a and D2b together (i.e., $d(x,y) = 0$ if and only if $x = y$) are usually referred to as the *identity of indiscernibles*. The combination of D1, D2a, and D2b is sometimes called *positivity* (see [18]). The property of positivity is often stated in an equivalent form, such as requiring $d(x,x) = 0$ and $d(x,y) > 0$ for $x \neq y$, as in [6].

Matthews [2,13,14] proposes the concept of a *partial metric*, which generalizes the concept of a *metric* by allowing self-distance to be nonzero—a property significant in computing partially defined or incomplete information. Given a set X, the function $p : X \times X \to \mathbb{R}$ is called a *partial metric* over X, if it satisfies the following conditions for any $x, y, z \in X$:

P1 $p(x,y) \geq 0$ (*nonnegativity*);[2]
P2a' $p(x,x) = p(x,y) = p(y,y)$ implies $x = y$ (*indistancy implies equality*);
P2cl $p(x,x) \leq p(x,y)$ (*small self-distance, left unchanged version*);
P3 $p(x,y) = p(y,x)$ (*symmetry*);
P4' $p(x,z) \leq p(x,y) + p(y,z) - p(y,y)$ (*sharp triangularity*[3]).

As pointed out in [2], the above conditions generalize those of a distance metric, with D2a, D2b and D4 weakened to P2a', P2cl and P4', respectively. Specifically, if we treat $p(x,y)$ as $d(x,y)$, then conditions D1–D4 altogether imply P1–P4; conversely, if $d(x,y)$ is considered as $p(x,y)$, then conditions P1–P4', together with the condition that $d(x,x) = 0$ for all x, imply D1–D4.[4]

1.2   Similarity Metrics

We now turn to the concept of a *similarity metric*. While a similarity metric is intuitively the dual concept of a distance metric, its general definition is not as well studied in the literature. According to [18], given a set X, the function $s : X \times X \to \mathbb{R}$ is called a *similarity metric* over X (normalized so that any similarity degree is in the interval $[0,1]$) if it satisfies the following conditions for any $x, y, z \in X$:

S1' $1 \geq s(x,y) \geq 0$ (*normalization*);
S2a $s(x,y) = 1$ implies $x = y$ (*congruence implies equality*);
S3 $s(x,y) = s(y,x)$ (*symmetry*).

In [3], it is proposed that a *similarity metric* (without normalization) must satisfy the following conditions:

---

[2] This condition is not required in an earlier version [14].
[3] It is called "triangularity" in [2], and renamed to "sharp triangle inequality" in [4].
[4] In [2], it is suggested to treat $d(x,y)$ as $2p(x,y) - p(x,x) - p(y,y)$, which enforces that $d(x,x) = 0$.

S1⁻ $s(x, x) \geq 0$ (*nonnegative self-similarity*);
S2a' $s(x, x) = s(x, y) = s(y, y)$ implies $x = y$ (*congruence implies equality*);[5]
S2cl $s(x, x) \geq s(x, y)$ (*high self-similarity, left unchanged version*);
S3 $s(x, y) = s(y, x)$ (*symmetry*);
S4' $s(x, z) \geq s(x, y) + s(y, z) - s(y, y)$ (*sharp triangularity*).

Elzinga and Studer [6] provide a different set of conditions, which removes S2a' and replaces S2cl with S2c':

S1 $s(x, y) \geq 0$ (*nonnegativity*);
S2c' $\min\{s(x, x), s(y, y)\} \geq s(x, y)$ (*bounded self-similarity*);
S3 $s(x, y) = s(y, x)$ (*symmetry*);
S4' $s(x, z) \geq s(x, y) + s(y, z) - s(y, y)$ (*sharp triangularity*[6]).

Given S3, it can be readily shown that S2cl is equivalent to S2c': S2cl implies S2c' through symmetry (S3), while S2c' directly implies S2cl.

Rozinek and Mareš [17] examine the relationship between similarity and partial metrics, introducing an alternative version of the similarity metric. They retain S2a' while removing S2c' by asserting and demonstrating that "bounded self-similarity" follows from S3 and S4'. However, their version of "bounded self-similarity," which we shall call S2c", is distinct:

S2c" $s(x, x) + s(y, y) \geq 2s(x, y)$ (*bounded self-similarity, version 2*).

Their definition of a similarity metric, which includes conditions {S1, S2a', S2c", S3, S4'}, differs from the sets {S1, S2a', S2cl, S3, S4'} and {S1, S2a', S2c', S3, S4'}, as the following counterexample illustrates.

Example 1. Let $X = \{a, b\}$, and let $s : X \times X \to \mathbb{R}$ be such that $s(a, a) = 0$, $s(a, b) = s(b, a) = 0.5$, and $s(b, b) = 1$. We can verify that:

- S1 (also S1⁻ and S1') holds, since the range of s is $\{0, 0.5, 1\}$;
- S2a' holds, as its precondition is met only when $x = y$;
- S3 is straightforward to verify;
- S4' holds: Since the set X contains only two elements, at least two of x, y, z must be equal. When $y = x$ or $y = z$, S4' holds directly. The remaining case is when $x = z$: we get $s(x, x) \geq s(x, y) + s(y, x) - s(y, y)$. In this scenario, if $y = x$, the property holds immediately. Otherwise $y \neq x$, so $x = a$ and $y = b$ (or $x = b$ and $y = a$, which can be verified similarly). Thus, $s(a, a) + s(b, b) \geq s(a, b) + s(b, a)$, which holds true.
- S2c" holds and is easily verifiable (it also follows from S3 and S4');
- However, neither S2cl nor S2c' holds (consider $x = a$ and $y = b$).   □

---

[5] The original definition in [3] uses "if and only if" instead of "implies", however, the other direction is trivial as long as s is a function.

[6] It is called "covering inequality" in [6].

1.3   Our Treatment

The conditions S1 and S1', along with their absence, represent three different ranges for the similarity function: nonnegative real numbers, the interval $[0, 1]$, and the full set of real numbers ($\mathbb{R}$). The condition S1$^-$ suggested by [3] concerns only self-similarities. These conditions are more about the choice of values used—an issue of *normalization*—and are not considered essential in our treatment.

When generalizing from distance metrics to partial metrics, the main concern is to allow self-distance to be nonzero. However, there is an implicit condition not carefully examined when transitioning from {D2a, D2b} to {P2a', P2cl}, as indicated by our naming system. D2b states that self-distance must be 0, implying two properties of self-distance:

> *Self-distance is small*: $d(x, x)$ must be the smallest;
> *Self-distances are equal*: $d(x, x) = d(y, y)$ for any two objects x and y.

When shifting from a distance metric to a partial metric, it is important to lift the condition of nonzeroity. However, it may be advisable to maintain equality of self-distances. By replacing D2b with P2cl, we lose the equality of self-distances. The term S2b' is reserved for this property for a similarity metric (for all $x, y \in X$):

S2b' $s(x, x) = s(y, y)$ (*equality of self-similarities*).

We will examine the various conditions of a similarity metric—including S2a', S2b', S2cl, S2c', S2c", S3, and S4'—from the perspective of epistemic logic. The core idea is to adopt a *similarity relation* between states (i.e., possible worlds) in accordance with a similarity metric, and treat this relation as a form of individual *speculation* or *uncertainty* about states, through which knowledge is understood to transcend this uncertainty.

In classical epistemic logic [8, 10, 15], the statement "Proposition φ is known" (typically written as $K\varphi$ or $\Box\varphi$) is interpreted as "φ is true in all states that is considered possible as the actual state." This interpretation treats the binary relation in an epistemic model as a relation for individual speculation, uncertainty or indistinguishability.

In weighted epistemic logic [5, 16], where both the language and the models are weighted, formulas such as "Proposition φ is known with discernment r" (written as $K^r\varphi$ or $\Box^r\varphi$) are interpreted as "φ is true in all states that is found, based on discernment r, similar to the actual state." Whether two states appear similar to an agent depends on whether their degree of similarity exceeds her discernment r. The uncertainty relation is thus defined by whether the agent can distinguish between the states given her discernment. In summary, *uncertainty arises from similarity* in our models.

The paper is structured as follows. Section 2 introduces an epistemic logic based on inter-state similarity, treating similarity metric conditions as frame conditions for these logics. We also show that the model checking problem for this logic is in P. Section 3 identifies definable and undefinable properties, proposing solutions for the latter. Section 4 concludes with a discussion of potential contributions to theoretical and applied studies of distance and similarity metrics.

2   Weighted Epistemic Logic

We employ the framework of weighted epistemic logic [5,16], which has its origins in a form of weighted modal logic [11]. Let Prop denote a countably infinite set of atomic propositions.

Definition 1 (language $\mathcal{L}$). *The formulas of language $\mathcal{L}$ is given as follows:*

$$\varphi ::= p \mid \neg\varphi \mid (\varphi \rightarrow \varphi) \mid \Box^r\varphi$$

where $p \in$ Prop and $r \in \mathbb{R}$. Conjunction ($\wedge$), disjunction ($\vee$), equivalence ($\leftrightarrow$), verum ($\top$) and falsum ($\bot$) are treated as defined operators in a usual way. Moreover, $\Diamond^r\varphi$ is shortened for $\neg\Box^r\neg\varphi$. The formula $\Box^r\varphi$ stands for "The agent knows φ based on her discernment no less than r."

Definition 2 (frames and models). *A* frame *is defined as a pair (W, E) s.t.:*

- *W is a nonempty set of states/worlds;*
- *$E : (W \times W) \rightarrow \mathbb{R}$ is an edge function, which assigns to every pair of states a real number.*

A model *is a triple (W, E, V) such that (W, E) is a frame and*

- *$V : W \rightarrow \wp(\text{Prop})$ is a valuation assigning a set of true atoms to each state.*

In the above definition, the function E assigns every pair of states a real number that expresses the degree of similarity between them. In other words, we can regard E as a similarity metric over W.

Definition 3 (satisfaction). *Given a model $M = (W, E, V)$, a state $s \in W$ and a formula φ, we say φ is* true *(or* satisfied*) at state s of M, denoted $M, s \models \varphi$, if the following recursive conditions hold:*

$$
\begin{aligned}
M, s &\models p &&\Longleftrightarrow p \in V(s) \\
M, s &\models \neg\psi &&\Longleftrightarrow \text{not } M, s \models \psi \\
M, s &\models (\psi \rightarrow \chi) &&\Longleftrightarrow \text{if } M, s \models \psi \text{ then } M, s \models \chi \\
M, s &\models \Box^r\psi &&\Longleftrightarrow \text{for all } t \in W, \text{if } E(s, t) \geq r \text{ then } M, t \models \psi.
\end{aligned}
$$

Given a frame $F = (W, E)$ and a formula φ, we say φ is valid *on F (denoted as $F \models \varphi$), if for any valuation V and any state $s \in W$, $(W, E, V), s \models \varphi$.*

2.1   Model Checking

In this section, we examine the complexity of the model checking problem for the introduced logic. Given a model $M = (W, E, V)$, a state s of M, and a formula φ, the model checking problem involves determining whether "$M, s \models \varphi$" is true.

We propose a polynomial-time algorithm similar to the one presented in [12] for solving the model checking problem. Specifically, Algorithm 1 computes the *truth set* of a given formula φ in a given model M (i.e., the set

$\{s \in W \mid M, s \models \varphi\}$), thereby reducing the model checking problem to membership checking within the truth set.

The function $Val(M, \varphi)$ terminates in time polynomial relative to the size of the input. This efficiency arises because membership checking is linear in the size of a set. Consequently, solving the model checking problem requires only polynomial time. This result leads us to the following theorem.

Theorem 1. *The model checking problem for our logic is in P.* □

Algorithm 1 Computing the truth set of a formula in a model

Require: $M = (W, E, V)$ is a model, and φ is a formula
1: **function** $Val(M, \varphi)$
2:     **if** $\varphi = p$ **then return** $\{s \in W \mid p \in V(s)\}$
3:     **else if** $\varphi = \neg\psi$ **then return** $W \setminus Val(M, \psi)$
4:     **else if** $\varphi = \psi \to \chi$ **then return** $(W \setminus Val(M, \psi)) \cup Val(M, \chi)$
5:     **else if** $\varphi = \Box^r\psi$ **then**
6:         **initialize** $tmpVal = \emptyset$
7:         **for all** $t \in W$ **do**
8:             **initialize** $n = true$
9:             **for all** $u \in W$ **do**
10:                 **if** $E(t, u) \geq r$ **and** $u \notin Val(M, \psi)$ **then** $n \leftarrow false$
11:             **if** $n = true$ **then** $tmpVal \leftarrow tmpVal \cup \{t\}$
12:         **return** $tmpVal$ ▷ $\{t \in W \mid \forall u \in W : E(t, u) \geq r \Rightarrow u \in Val(M, \psi)\}$

---

3   Frame Definability

In this section, we study the frame definability of the properties listed in Table 1.

We utilize the concept of frame definability to analyze the properties of similarity metrics, S2a', S2b', S2b", S2cl, S2cr, S2c', S2c", S3 and S4'. All of these properties, except for S2b" and S2cr, have been discussed in the introduction. Each property defines a class of frames, thus we treat a frame property as a class of frames. For instance, S3 represents the class of all symmetric frames.

Definition 4 (frame definability). *Let Φ be a set of formulas, and $\mathfrak{F}$ a class of frames. We say that Φ defines (or characterizes) $\mathfrak{F}$, if for all frames F, $F \in \mathfrak{F}$ if and only if, for all $\varphi \in \Phi$, $F \models \varphi$.*

In particular, we aim to verify whether each of the properties is defined by a scheme of formulas that permits the universal substitution of weights. For example, $p \to \Box^r\Diamond^r p$ is a scheme representing the following set of formulas:

Table 1. Frame properties, where (W, E) is a frame and $s, t, u \in W$.

S2a'	$E(s,s) = E(s,t) = E(t,t)$ implies $s = t$	(congruence implies equality)
S2b'	$E(s,s) = E(t,t)$	(equality of self-similarities)
S2b"	$\sup\{E(s,x)|x \in W\} = \sup\{E(t,x)|x \in W\}$	(equality of max similarities)
S2cl	$E(s,s) \geq E(s,t)$	(high self-similarity, left)
S2cr	$E(t,t) \geq E(s,t)$	(high self-similarity, right)
S2c'	$\min\{E(s,s), E(t,t)\} \geq E(s,t)$	(bounded self-similarity, v.1)
S2c"	$E(s,s) + E(t,t) \geq 2E(s,t)$	(bounded self-similarity, v.2)
S3	$E(s,t) = E(t,s)$	(symmetry)
S4'	$E(s,u) \geq E(s,t) + E(t,u) - E(t,t)$	(sharp triangularity)

$$\{p \to \Box^x \Diamond^x p \mid x \in \mathbb{R}\}.$$

For any model M, state s and scheme Γ, we write "$M, s \models \Gamma$" to mean $\forall \varphi \in \Gamma. (M, s \models \varphi)$. Likewise, for a frame F, "$F \models \Gamma$" stands for $\forall \varphi \in \Gamma. (F \models \varphi)$.

3.1 Definable Properties

We state and show the properties that are definable, in the order of S3, S4', S2cl, S2cr, S2c' and S2c", with some relatively easy proofs omitted to save space.

Lemma 1. *S3 is defined by the scheme* $p \to \Box^r \Diamond^r p$.

Proof. This is a weighted variant of the B-axiom in modal logic (i.e., $p \to \Box \Diamond p$). The classical proof for B's definability can be extended to a proof here. $\qquad \Box$

Lemma 2. *S4' is defined by the scheme* $\Diamond^{r_1}(\Diamond^{r_2}q \wedge (p \wedge \Box^r \neg p)) \to \Diamond^{r_1 + r_2 - r}q$.

Proof. Let $F = (W, E)$ be any frame. Suppose $F \in$ S4'. It means that F satisfies sharp triangularity. We show that $F \models \Diamond^{r_1}(\Diamond^{r_2}q \wedge (p \wedge \Box^r \neg p)) \to \Diamond^{r_1 + r_2 - r}q$. Let $M = (W, E, V)$ be any model based on F, and $s \in W$:

$M, s \models \Diamond^{r_1}(\Diamond^{r_2}q \wedge (p \wedge \Box^r \neg p))$
$\Leftrightarrow \exists t \in W, E(s,t) \geq r_1$ and $M, t \models \Diamond^{r_2}q \wedge (p \wedge \Box^r \neg p)$
$\Leftrightarrow \exists t, u \in W, E(s,t) \geq r_1$ and $E(t,u) \geq r_2$ and $M, u \models q$ and $M, t \models p \wedge \Box^r \neg p$
$\Rightarrow \exists t, u \in W, E(s,t) \geq r_1$ and $E(t,u) \geq r_2$ and $M, u \models q$ and $E(t,t) < r$
    $(\text{for} M, t \models \Box^r \neg p \text{and} E(t,t) \geq r \text{imply} M, t \models \neg p)$
$\Rightarrow \exists u \in W, E(s,u) \geq r_1 + r_2 - r$ and $M, u \models q$
    $[r_1 + r_2 - r \leq E(s,t) + E(t,u) - r < E(s,t) + E(t,u) - E(t,t) \leq E(s,u)]$
$\Leftrightarrow M, s \models \Diamond^{r_1 + r_2 - r}q.$

For the converse direction, suppose $F \notin$ S4'. We show that $F \not\models \Diamond^{r_1}(\Diamond^{r_2}q \wedge (p \wedge \Box^r\neg p)) \to \Diamond^{r_1+r_2-r}q$. Since F does not satisfy sharp triangularity, there exist $s, t, u \in W$ and $r_1, r_2, r_3 \in \mathbb{R}$ such that $E(s,t) = r_1$, $E(t,u) = r_2$, $E(t,t) = r_3$ and $E(s,u) < r_1 + r_2 - r_3$. Let V be a valuation on F such that $V(u) = \{q\}$, $V(t) = \{p\}$ and $V(x) = \emptyset$ for any other $x \in W$. Let $M = (W, E, V)$. Let $\epsilon = r_1 + r_2 - r_3 - E(s,u)$, then $\epsilon > 0$. Let $r = r_3 + 0.5\epsilon$. It suffices to show that $M, s \not\models \Diamond^{r_1}(\Diamond^{r_2}q \wedge (p \wedge \Box^r\neg p)) \to \Diamond^{r_1+r_2-r}q$. We show $M, s \models \Diamond^{r_1}(\Diamond^{r_2}q \wedge (p \wedge \Box^r\neg p))$ and $M, s \not\models \Diamond^{r_1+r_2-r}q$:

- For all $x \in W$, $x \neq t$ implies $M, x \models \neg p$, and $E(t,t) = r_3 < r$. It follows that $M, t \models \Box^r\neg p$. Together with $M, t \models p$ we have $M, t \models p \wedge \Box^r\neg p$. Since $E(t,u) \geq r_2$ and $M, u \models q$, we have $M, t \models \Diamond^{r_2}q \wedge (p \wedge \Box^r\neg p)$. Since $E(s,t) \geq r_1$ we have $M, s \models \Diamond^{r_1}(\Diamond^{r_2}q \wedge (p \wedge \Box^r\neg p))$.
- Moreover, since $E(s,u) = r_1 + r_2 - r_3 - \epsilon < r_1 + r_2 - (r_3 + 0.5\epsilon) = r_1 + r_2 - r$, and since $M, w \models \neg q$ whenever $w \neq u$, we have $M, s \not\models \Diamond^{r_1+r_2-r}q$.   □

Lemma 3. *The following hold:*

(1) S2cl is defined by the scheme $\Diamond^r\top \to (\Box^r p \to p)$;
(2) S2cr is defined by the scheme $\Box^r(\Box^r p \to p)$;
(3) S2c' is defined by the scheme $(\Diamond^{r_1}\top \to (\Box^{r_1}p \to p)) \wedge \Box^{r_2}(\Box^{r_2}q \to q)$.

Proof. Let $F = (W, E)$ be any frame. (1) Suppose $F \in$ S2cl. We show that $F \models \Diamond^r\top \to (\Box^r p \to p)$. Let $M = (W, E, V)$ be any model based on F, and $s \in W$: $M, s \models \Diamond^r\top$ and $M, s \models \Box^r p$

$$\Longleftrightarrow M, s \models \Box^r p \text{ and } \exists t \in W, E(s,t) \geq r \text{ and } M, t \models \top$$
$$\Longleftrightarrow M, s \models \Box^r p \text{ and } \exists t \in W, E(s,t) \geq r$$
$$\Longrightarrow M, s \models \Box^r p \text{ and } E(s,s) \geq r \text{ (by S2cl)}$$
$$\Longrightarrow M, s \models p.$$

For the converse direction, suppose $F \notin$ S2cl. We show that $F \not\models \Diamond^r\top \to (\Box^r p \to p)$. Since F does not satisfy S2cl, there exist $s, t \in W$ and $r \in \mathbb{R}$ such that $E(s,s) < E(s,t) = r$. Let V be a valuation on F such that $V(s) = \emptyset$ and $V(x) = \{p\}$ for any other $x \in W$. Let $M = (W, E, V)$. It suffices to show that $M, s \not\models \Diamond^r\top \to (\Box^r p \to p)$: $M, s \models \Diamond^r\top$ holds since $E(s,t) = r$ and $M, t \models \top$, and $M, s \not\models \Box^r p \to p$: since $E(s,s) < r$, and since $M, w \models p$ whenever $w \neq s$, we have $M, s \models \Box^r p$, also $M, s \not\models p$.

(2) Suppose $F \in$ S2cr, namely F satisfies the property $E(y,y) \geq E(x,y)$ for any $x, y \in W$. We show that $F \models \Box^r(\Box^r p \to p)$. Consider any model $M = (W, E, V)$ based on F, and any states $s, t \in W$ such that $E(s,t) \geq r$. It suffices to show that $M, t \models \Box^r p \to p$, which is equivalent to proving that if $M, t \models \Box^r p$, then $M, t \models p$. Assume $M, t \models \Box^r p$. It follows that $E(t,t) \geq r$ implies $M, t \models p$. By $E(s,t) \geq r$ and S2cr, we have $E(t,t) \geq r$. Thus, $M, t \models p$.

For the converse direction, suppose $F \notin$ S2cr. We show that $F \not\models \Box^r(\Box^r p \to p)$. Since F does not satisfy the property, there exist $s, t \in W$ and $r \in \mathbb{R}$ such that $E(t,t) < E(s,t) = r$. Let V be a valuation on F such that $V(t) = \emptyset$ and

$V(x) = \{p\}$ for any other $x \in W$. Let $M = (W, E, V)$. Since $E(s, t) = r$, it suffices to show that $M, t \not\models \Box^r p \to p$: By $E(t, t) < r$, and since $M, w \models p$ whenever $w \neq t$, we have $M, t \models \Box^r p$. Moreover, $M, t \not\models p$.

(3) Notice that a frame satisfies S2c' iff it satisfies both S2cl and S2cr.   □

Lemma 4. *S2c" is defined by the scheme* $\Diamond^{r_1}(p \wedge \Box^{r_2} \neg p) \to (\Box^{2r_1 - r_2} q \to q)$.

Proof. A proof can be given in a similar fashion to Lemma 2.   □

3.2   Undefinable Properties

In this section, we show that the frame properties S2a' and S2b' are not definable. First, we extend the classical notions of *bisimulation* and *bounded morphism* to the weighted epistemic logic we have proposed, showing that they are invariance relations for the logic. We then apply these concepts to prove that there exist two frames, one satisfies S2a' (respectively, S2b') and the other does not, such that any set of formulas valid on the first frame is also valid on the second. Consequently, the undefinability follows.

Definition 5 (bisimulation). *Let* $M = (W, E, V)$ *and* $M' = (W', E', V')$ *be two models, and let* $s \in W$ *and* $s' \in W'$. *We say* (M, s) *and* (M', s') *are* bisimilar, *denoted* $(M, s) \rightleftarrows (M', s')$, *if there exists a relation* $Z \subseteq W \times W'$ *such that* sZs' *and for all* $x \in W$ *and* $x' \in W'$, *if* xZx' *then:* ***Atom*** $V(x) = V'(x')$, *and*

Forth $\forall y \in W. \, \forall r \in \mathbb{R}. \, [E(x, y) = r \Rightarrow \exists y' \in W'.(yZy' \, \& \, E(x', y') \geq r)]$;
Back $\forall y' \in W'. \forall r \in \mathbb{R}. \, [E'(x', y') = r \Rightarrow \exists y \in W.(yZy' \, \& \, E(x, y) \geq r)]$.

Lemma 5 (bisimulation invariance). *Bisimulation preserves truth. I.e., if* $(M, s) \rightleftarrows (M', s')$, *then for any formula* φ, $M, s \models \varphi \Leftrightarrow M', s' \models \varphi$.

Proof. By induction on φ. Let $M = (W, R, V)$ and $M' = (W', R', V')$. Let Z be the bisimulation between (M, s) and (M', s').

$M, s \not\models \Box^r \psi \Leftrightarrow \exists t \in W, E(s, t) \geq r$ and $M, t \not\models \psi$
$ \Rightarrow \exists t \in W, \exists t' \in W', tZt'$ and $E(s', t') \geq r$ and $M, t \not\models \psi$ (Forth)
$ \Rightarrow \exists t' \in W', E(s', t') \geq r$ and $M', t' \not\models \psi$ (induction hypothesis)
$ \Leftrightarrow M', s' \not\models \Box^r \psi$.

The other direction can be shown similarly using Back.   □

Definition 6 (bounded morphism). *Let* $M = (W, E, V)$ *and* $M' = (W', E', V')$ *be two models. A function* $\beta : W \to W'$ *is called a* bounded morphism *from* M *to* M', *if for any* $x, y \in W$: ***Atom*** $V(x) = V'(\beta(x))$, *and*

Forth *If* $E(x, y) = r$ *for some* $r \in \mathbb{R}$, *then* $E'(\beta(x), \beta(y)) \geq r$;
Back $\forall y' \in W'. \forall r \in \mathbb{R}. \, [E'(\beta(x), y') = r \Rightarrow \exists t \in W.(y' = \beta(y) \, \& \, E(x, y) \geq r)]$.

Lemma 6. *Bounded morphism preserves truth and frame validity. That is, if* β *is a bounded morphism from model* $M = (W, E, V)$ *to* $M' = (W', E', V')$,

1. *For all $s \in W$ and all formulas φ, $M, s \models \varphi$ iff $M', \beta(s) \models \varphi$;*
2. *If β is surjective, then for all formulas φ, $(W, E) \models \varphi$ implies $(W', E') \models \varphi$.*

Proof. 1. To see the first claim, it suffices to see that β is in fact a bisimulation between (M, s) and $(M', \beta(s))$, and the claim follows from Lemma 5.
2. Assume that $(W, E) \models \varphi$ and $(W', E') \not\models \varphi$. Then there must be a valuation V' on (W', E'), and state $s' \in W'$, such that $(W', E', V'), s' \not\models \varphi$. Let V be a valuation on (W, E) such that $V(x) = V'(\beta(x))$ for all atoms x. This ensures that β is a bisimulation between $((W, E, V), x)$ and $((W', E', V'), \beta(x))$. Since β is surjective, there exists $s \in W$ such that $\beta(s) = s'$. It follows from Lemma 5 that $(W, E, V), s \not\models \varphi$, contradicting to the assumption. $\square$

Theorem 2. *For any set Γ of formulas,*

1. *Γ does not define S2a'; i.e., for any frame F, it is not: $F \models \Gamma$ iff $F \in$ S2a';*
2. *Γ does not define S2b'; i.e., for any frame F, it is not: $F \models \Gamma$ iff $F \in$ S2b'.*

Proof. 1. Consider two frames $F = (W, E)$ and $F' = (W', E')$. Let $W = \{s, t, u\}$, $W' = \{s', t'\}$. Let each of E and E' be the symmetric closure that satisfies:

- $E(t, t) = E(u, u) = 0$ and $E(s, s) = E(s, t) = E(s, u) = E(t, u) = 1$;
- $E'(s', s') = E'(s', t') = E'(t', t') = 1$.

These two frames are illustrated as follows.

It is easy to see that $F \in$ S2a', while $F' \notin$ S2a'. On the other hand, consider the mapping $\beta = \{(s, s'), (t, t'), (u, t')\}$. If we introduce valuations V on F and V' on F' are such that $V(x) = V'(\beta(x))$ for all states x, it is not hard to verify that β is a surjective bounded morphism from $((W, E, V), x)$ to $((W', E', V'), \beta(x))$. By Lemma 6, for any set Γ of formulas, we have $F \models \Gamma$ implies $F' \models \Gamma$. Assume towards a contradiction that Γ defines S2a'. Since $F' \notin$ S2a', we have $F' \not\models \Gamma$. It follows that $F \not\models \Gamma$, and hence $F \notin$ S2a', leading to a contradiction.
2. Consider two frames F and F' illustrated below:

$$F \quad \bullet_t \overset{-2-}{\underset{1}{\rightleftharpoons}} \bullet_u \underset{2}{—} \circ_s \qquad F' \quad \bullet_{t'} \underset{2}{————} \circ_{s'}$$

$$\begin{pmatrix}0\end{pmatrix} \quad \begin{pmatrix}0\end{pmatrix} \quad \begin{pmatrix}0\end{pmatrix} \qquad\qquad \begin{pmatrix}1\end{pmatrix} \qquad \begin{pmatrix}0\end{pmatrix}$$

It is easy to see that F satisfies S2b', while F' does not. We can then use a similar proof from the above to show that no Γ can define S2b'. $\square$

3.3   Restoring Definability

In the previous section, we showed that no formulas define S2a' or S2b'. We now introduce a property, S2b", previously included in Table 1 without elaboration, and provide necessary details. S2b" states that the supremum (i.e., the least upper bound, which can be any real number or $+\infty$) of the weights of all edges from state s equals the supremum of the weights of all edges from state t. In ordinary cases, the supremum is simply the maximum, but an infinite set of states here may not have a maximum. It can be verified that S2b" combined with S2cl is equivalent to S2b' combined with S2cl: with S2cl, $\sup\{E(s,x) \mid x \in W\} = E(s,s)$, and similarly, $\sup\{E(t,x) \mid x \in W\} = E(t,t)$. This means the similarity metric remains the same when we replace S2b' with S2b". The following theorem illustrates the advantage of S2b".

Lemma 7. *S2b" is defined by the scheme $\Box^{r_1}\bot \to \Box^r\Box^{r_2}\bot$ where $r_2 > r_1$.*

Proof. Let $F = (W,E)$ be a frame. Assume $F \not\models \Box^{r_1}\bot \to \Box^r\Box^{r_2}\bot$ where $r_2 > r_1$. We show that $F \notin$ S2b". By the assumption, there exists a model $M = (W,E,V)$ based on F, and $s \in W$ such that $M,s \not\models \Box^{r_1}\bot \to \Box^r\Box^{r_2}\bot$. Hence $M,s \models \Box^{r_1}\bot$ and $M,s \not\models \Box^r\Box^{r_2}\bot$. From $M,s \models \Box^{r_1}\bot$ we have $E(s,x) < r_1$ for any $x \in W$ (otherwise we have $M,x \models \bot$, which is impossible). Thus $\sup\{E(s,x) \mid x \in W\} \le r_1$. Since $M,s \not\models \Box^r\Box^{r_2}\bot$, there exist $t,u \in W$ such that $E(s,t) \ge r$ and $E(t,u) \ge r_2$. So $\sup\{E(t,x) \mid x \in W\} \ge r_2 > r_1 \ge \sup\{E(s,x) \mid x \in W\}$, which means that $F \notin$ S2b".

For the converse direction, suppose F does not satisfy S2b". We show that $F \not\models \Box^{r_1}\bot \to \Box^r\Box^{r_2}\bot$. Since $F \notin$ S2b", there exist $s,t \in W$ such that $\sup\{E(s,x) \mid u \in W\} < \sup\{E(t,x) \mid x \in W\}$ (where the bigger supremum can be a real number or $+\infty$). Let $E(s,t) = r$ and choose real numbers r_1 and r_2 that satisfy $\sup\{E(s,x) \mid u \in W\} < r_1 < r_2 < \sup\{E(t,x) \mid x \in W\}$. Let $M = (W,E,V)$ be any model based on F. It suffices to show that $M,s \not\models \Box^{r_1}\bot \to \Box^r\Box^{r_2}\bot$. From $\sup\{E(s,x) \mid x \in W\} < r_1$, it follows that $M,s \models \Box^{r_1}\bot$. Since $\sup\{E(t,x) \mid x \in W\} > r_2$, there exists $u \in W$ such that $E(t,u) \ge r_2$. Hence $M,t \not\models \Box^{r_2}\bot$. By $E(s,t) = r$ we get $M,s \not\models \Box^r\Box^{r_2}\bot$.   □

An alternative approach to enhance definability involves extending the language. Allowing the superscript of $\Box^r$ to be an interval rather than a singular real number increases the language's expressive power. For instance, $\Box^{(3,+\infty)}\varphi$ can denote that φ is true in all states with a similarity degree greater than 3 relative to the current state. This expansion from $\mathcal{L}$ to $\mathcal{L}^+$ is made clear by the following grammar of $\mathcal{L}^+$:

$$\varphi := p \mid \neg\varphi \mid (\varphi \to \varphi) \mid \Box^I\varphi$$

where I denotes any open or closed interval on the real line. The interpretation of this new operator for any model $M = (W,E,V)$ and state $s \in W$ is:

$$M,s \models \Box^I\psi \iff \text{for all } t \in W, \text{if } E(s,t) \in I \text{ then } M,t \models \psi.$$

$\mathcal{L}^+$ is demonstrably at least as expressive as $\mathcal{L}$: the $\mathcal{L}^+$-formula $\Box^{[r,+\infty)}\varphi$ is equivalent to the $\mathcal{L}$-formula $\Box^r\varphi$. Consequently, all frame properties definable in $\mathcal{L}$ are also definable in $\mathcal{L}^+$. Furthermore, $\mathcal{L}^+$ exhibits strictly greater expressivity, as it can define both S2a' and S2b'.

Lemma 8 *(proofs omitted for brevity but available upon request).*

1. $(\Box^{(r,+\infty)}p \wedge \Box^{(-\infty,r)}p \wedge \neg p) \to \Box^{[r,r]}((\Box^{(r,+\infty)}q \wedge \Box^{(-\infty,r)}q \wedge \neg q) \to \neg p)$ *defines S2a'*;
2. $(\Box^{(r,+\infty)}p \wedge \Box^{(-\infty,r)}p \wedge \neg p) \to \Box^{(-\infty,+\infty)}(\Box^{[r,r]}q \to q)$ *defines S2b'*.

4   Discussion

We have introduced a theoretical framework for characterizing similarity metrics, providing a new perspective on their properties and implications within the realm of weighted epistemic logic. Table 2 summarizes the (un)definable properties of $\mathcal{L}$.

Table 2. Frame definability of $\mathcal{L}$, where (W, E) is a frame and $s, t, u \in W$.

Name	Property	Characterization $\mathcal{L}$–formula
S2a'	$E(s,s) = E(s,t) = E(t,t) \implies s = t$	(undefinable; probably use $\mathcal{L}^+$)
S2b'	$E(s,s) = E(t,t)$	(undefinable; replaceable by S2b'')
S2b''	$\sup\{E(s,x)|x{\in}W\} = \sup\{E(t,x)|x{\in}W\}$	$\Box^{r_1}\bot \to \Box^r\Box^{r_2}\bot$ where $r_2 > r_1$
S2cl	$E(s,s) \geq E(s,t)$	$\Diamond^r\top \to (\Box^r p \to p)$
S2cr	$E(t,t) \geq E(s,t)$	$\Box^r(\Box^r p \to p)$
S2c'	$\min\{E(s,s), E(t,t)\} \geq E(s,t)$	$(\Diamond^{r_1}\top{\to}(\Box^{r_1}p{\to}p)) \wedge \Box^{r_2}(\Box^{r_2}q{\to}q)$
S2c''	$E(s,s) + E(t,t) \geq 2E(s,t)$	$\Diamond^{r_1}(p \wedge \Box^{r_2}\neg p) \to (\Box^{2r_1-r_2}q \to q)$
S3	$E(s,t) = E(t,s)$	$p \to \Box^r\Diamond^r p$
S4'	$E(s,u) \geq E(s,t){+}E(t,u){-}E(t,t)$	$\Diamond^{r_1}(\Diamond^{r_2}q \wedge (p{\wedge}\Box^r\neg p)) \to \Diamond^{r_1+r_2-r}q$

We have shown that S2a' and S2b' are undefinable in $\mathcal{L}$. However, S2b' can be replaced with the definable S2b'' without altering the similarity metric (S2cl + S2b' = S2cl + S2b''). The property S2a' presents a greater challenge, as no suitable replacement has been identified. A potential solution involves employing the expanded language $\mathcal{L}^+$, which can define all the listed properties.

The relevance of this characterization and the potential benefits of using only definable properties for similarity metric definition warrant consideration. While a comprehensive answer remains elusive, this approach yields valuable insights. Definability in $\mathcal{L}$ effectively compares it with a first-order language (as illustrated in Table 2's "Property" column). Classical modal logic offers a parallel: every modal formula corresponds to a first-order formula that cannot differentiate between bisimilar models (cf. [1]). This analogy raises a natural question: Can a similar correspondence between $\mathcal{L}$ and first-order language be established? If $\mathcal{L}$ indeed represents a fragment, it likely constitutes a highly computable one, akin to classical modal logic. Computational complexity thus provides a compelling rationale for pursuing definable properties. Although space constraints preclude a detailed characterization of distance and partial metric properties (see Sect. 1.1), we can show that D2a is definable (in the dual logic based on $\mathcal{L}$) while P2a' is not (mirroring S2a'). Future research include examining the implications of the distinction between D2a and S2a'/P2a', and deepening our understanding of similarity and dissimilarity concepts.

References

1. Blackburn, P., de Rijke, M., Venema, Y.: Modal Logic. Cambridge (2001)
2. Bukatin, M., Kopperman, R., Matthews, S., Pajoohesh, H.: Partial metric spaces. Am. Math. Mon. **116**(8), 708–718 (2009)
3. Chen, S., Ma, B., Zhang, K.: On the similarity metric and the distance metric. Theoret. Comput. Sci. **410**(24–25), 2365–2376 (2009)
4. Deza, M.M., Deza, E.: Encyclopedia of Distances. Springer, Heidelberg (2009). https://doi.org/10.1007/978-3-642-00234-2
5. Dong, H., Li, X., Wáng, Y.N.: Weighted modal logic in epistemic and deontic contexts. In: Ghosh, S., Icard, T. (eds.) LORI 2021. LNCS, vol. 13039, pp. 73–87. Springer, Cham (2021). https://doi.org/10.1007/978-3-030-88708-7_6
6. Elzinga, C.H., Studer, M.: Normalization of distance and similarity in sequence analysis. Sociol. Meth. Res. **48**(4), 877–904 (2019)
7. Everitt, B.S., Landau, S., Leese, M., Stahl, D.: Cluster Analysis. Wiley (2011)
8. Fagin, R., Halpern, J.Y., Moses, Y., Vardi, M.Y.: Reasoning About Knowledge. The MIT Press, Cambridge (1995)
9. Han, J., Pei, J., Tong, H.: Data Mining: Concepts and Techniques. Morgan Kaufmann, 4 edn. (2022)
10. Hintikka, J.: Knowledge and Belief: An Introduction to the Logic of Two Notions. Cornell University Press, Ithaca, New York (1962)
11. Larsen, K.G., Mardare, R.: Complete proof systems for weighted modal logic. Theoret. Comput. Sci. **546**(12), 164–175 (2014)
12. Liang, X., Wáng, Y.N.: Epistemic logic via distance and similarity. In: Khanna, S., Cao, J., Bai, Q., Xu, G. (eds.) PRICAI 2022. LNCS, vol. 13629, pp. 32–45. Springer, Cham (2022). https://doi.org/10.1007/978-3-031-20862-1_3
13. Matthews, S.G.: Partial metric spaces. In: 8th British Colloquium for Theoretical Computer Science (1992). Research Report 212, University of Warwick
14. Matthews, S.G.: Partial metric topology. Ann. N. Y. Acad. Sci. **728**(1), 183–197 (1994)
15. Meyer, J.J.C., van der Hoek, W.: Epistemic Logic for AI and Computer Science. Cambridge University Press, Cambridge (1995)
16. Naumov, P., Tao, J.: Logic of confidence. Synthese **192**, 1821–1838 (2015)
17. Rozinek, O., Mareš, J.: The duality of similarity and metric spaces. Appl. Sci. **11**(4) (2021)
18. Tan, P.N., Steinbach, M., Karpatne, A., Kumar, V.: Introduction to Data Mining, 2 edn. Pearson (2019)
19. Wierzchoń, S.T., Kłopotek, M.A.: Modern Algorithms of Cluster Analysis. Springer, Cham (2018). https://doi.org/10.1007/978-3-319-69308-8

A Relaxed Symmetric Non-negative Matrix Factorization Approach for Community Discovery

Zhigang Liu, Hao Yan, Yurong Zhong$^{(\boxtimes)}$, and Weiling Li$^{(\boxtimes)}$

School of Computer Science and Technology, Dongguan University of Technology,
Dongguan 523808, China
weilinglicq@outlook.com

Abstract. Community discovery is a crucial issue in the realm of complex network analysis. A Symmetric Non-negative Matrix Factorization (SNMF)-based method is widely used to address this problem. It utilizes a single feature matrix to capture network symmetry, which limits its ability to learn node representations. To break this limitation, this study introduces a novel Relaxed Symmetric Non-negative Matrix Factorization (RSN) approach to enhance an SNMF-based community detector. It works by a) expanding the representational space and its degrees of freedom relying on multiple feature matrices; b) integrating the well-designed equality constraints to enable the model to perceive the network's intrinsic symmetry better; c) employing graph regularization to maintain the local geometric invariance of the network structure; and d) separating constraints from decision variables for efficient optimization via the alternating-direction-method of multipliers (ADMM) principle. The RSN model's effectiveness is demonstrated through empirical research on six social networks, showcasing superior precision in community discovery over existing models and baselines.

Keywords: Undirected Network · Network Representation Learning · Community Discovery · Symmetric Non-negative Matrix Factorization

1 Introduction

Complex networks are pervasive across a multitude of real scenarios [1], e.g., social relationships in social platforms [2], comorbidity patterns in disease networks [3], and protein interactions in bioinformatics [4]. Community stands as a quintessential attribute of a complex network, serving as a window into the underlying organizational architecture of the network. Regarded as a graph clustering problem, community discovery becomes a crucial auxiliary for practical applications, e.g., predicting epidemic transmission trends and identifying biological modules. It has entrenched itself as a longstanding and formidable challenge in complex network analysis, prompting the development of many methods categorized into traditional and learning-based ones.

Traditional approaches such as graph segmentation [5], spectrum analysis [6], and intelligent optimization [7] operate on straightforward principles but often yield suboptimal accuracy and efficiency. Learning-based methods treat community discovery as a

© The Author(s), under exclusive license to Springer Nature Singapore Pte Ltd. 2025
R. Hadfi et al. (Eds.): PRICAI 2024, LNAI 15281, pp. 119–133, 2025.
https://doi.org/10.1007/978-981-96-0116-5_10

network representation learning (NRL) task. These methods offer the merits of flexible modeling and high precision, making them a favored choice in current research. Among them, Non-negative Matrix Factorization (NMF) exhibits notable suitability for graph clustering due to two distinct merits [8], i.e., a) it possesses inherent clustering capabilities—previous work [9] has demonstrated that NMF and its variants are equivalent to advanced clustering techniques such as k-means; and b) it offers excellent interpretability for cluster structures, owing to their linear expression abilities. Hence, they are frequently employed in community discovery [8].

Existing NMF-based community discovery methods aim to enhance their representation learning capabilities. For instance, Wang et al. [10] introduce a non-negative matrix tri-factorization model specifically for community discovery. Pompili et al. [11] demonstrate that incorporating orthogonality constraints can effectively improve the clustering performance of an NMF model. Sun et al. [12] introduce a novel encoder-decoder-based NMF approach for community discovery. Leng et al. [13] present a graph-regularized NMF model with Lp-smoothness constraints, which captures inherent geometric features and ensures a smooth and stable solution. Ma et al. [14] integrate prior information into the factorization process of an NMF model with a multi-layered network to enhance its performance. However, these methods do not fully exploit the inherent symmetry property of undirected networks.

In contrast, a Symmetric Non-negative Matrix Factorization (SNMF) model learns a single feature matrix X to approximate an undirected network's adjacency matrix A, i.e., $\hat{A} = XX^T$. Notably, [9] establishes the equivalence between SNMF and spectral clustering, ensuring well-interpretable clustering properties. Building upon the flexible SNMF, several SNMF-based community detectors have emerged [8]. Yang et al. [15] present a unified interpretation of SNMF-based community detectors and propose a semi-supervised detector incorporating prior knowledge and topology. Shi et al. [16] leverage the prior pairwise constraints to propose a pairwisely constrained SNMF model for community discovery. Ye et al. [17] develop a homophily-preserved SNMF model that captures community structure better by enhancing the intrinsic connection-related constraints. Luo et al. [18] explore linear and nonlinear adjustments to a non-negative multiplicative update (NMU) scheme, achieving high-accuracy SNMF-based community discovery models. While these methods obtain state-of-the-art (SOTA) performance, their representational capacity may be constrained due to the reliance on a single factor for representing a network.

Enhancing the representational capacity of an SNMF model presents a significant challenge. Kuang et al. [19] introduce a non-symmetric variant for graph clustering by incorporating a constraint term to reduce the discrepancy between the feature matrices of a standard NMF model. Li et al. [20] and Liu et al. [21] extend this work by transforming standard SNMF into penalized non-symmetric NMF. Their approach enforces the equality of the two feature matrices, capturing the inherent symmetry of the target network. To achieve this, they introduce an equality-regularization term into the objective function. However, a critical challenge remains: balancing representation learning capacity and symmetry. A small regularization coefficient may inadequately represent symmetry, while a large coefficient can overly emphasize regularization, compromising the fitting of overall loss and representation learning.

Motivated by these observations, this study aims to design an NMF-based community discovery model that strikes a balance between symmetry awareness and representation learning. Hence, a novel Relaxed Symmetric Non-negative Matrix Factorization (RSN) approach is proposed for community discovery with four-fold ideas:

- *Enlarged feature space.* Multiple feature matrices are leveraged to represent an undirected network, thereby enlarging its representational capacity.
- *Symmetry constraint.* By introducing symmetry constraints into the learning objective, our model becomes well aware of the inherent symmetry of the network.
- *Geometry constraint.* We incorporate graph regularization that captures the local topological characteristics, thus maintaining the network's intrinsic geometry.
- *ADMM-based optimization.* We separate the constraints from decision parameters and adopt the ADMM principle to solve the RSN model efficiently. By doing so, such decomposition facilitates the independent learning of decision parameters.

This work makes the following contributions:

a) A highly accurate community discovery model. RSN leverages the well-designed symmetry constraint to enlarge the feature space while ensuring its representational capacity. Meanwhile, graph regularization preserves the network's intrinsic geometry, thus guaranteeing RSN's high representation learning ability.

b) An efficient learning scheme. An ADMM-based learning scheme efficiently solves the RSN model, addressing the symmetry and non-negativity constraints. We also provide algorithmic details and complexity analysis for implementing the model.

Empirical evaluations conducted on six authentic and openly accessible networks demonstrate that the RSN-based community detector substantially outperforms existing baseline and SOTA methods in terms of detection accuracy.

Section 2 gives the foundational concepts and problem formulation. Section 3 presents the RSN-based model for community discovery. Section 4 elucidates the experimental results. Finally, Section 5 concludes the paper.

2 Preliminaries

2.1 Problem Statement

For a network $G = (V, E)$ consisting of a set of n nodes $V = \{v_1, v_2, ..., v_n\}$ and a set of m edges $E = \{e_{ij} \mid i, j \in \{1, 2, ..., n\}\}$, its topology can be described by an adjacency matrix $A = [a_{ij}] \in \mathbb{R}^{n \times n}$. Hence, A is a symmetric and binary matrix for an undirected and unweighted network concerned in this work, and its entry a_{ij} is assigned to one if $e_{ij} \in E$ and zero otherwise. Given G with K communities known as the prior information, a community detector aims to identify the community set that contains K communities as $C = \{C_k \mid C_k \neq \emptyset, \cup k = 1\ K = V, C_k \neq C_t, 1 \leq k \leq K, 1 \leq t \leq K\}$, where C_k is the k-th community in C, and $\cup$ denotes the union set [22].

2.2 NMF-Based Community Discovery

An NMF-based community discovery model assumes that the approximation of each entry a_{ij}, i.e., $\hat{a}_{ij}$, is affected by K communities in a network. Hence, we suppose a non-negative feature matrix for community assignment $X \in \mathbb{R}^{n \times K}$ and the one for basis $U \in \mathbb{R}^{n \times K}$. Given G and A, it learns an approximation $\hat{A}$ to A with feature matrices U and X, yielding $\hat{A} = UX^T$ [23]. To estimate the local optimal solutions for U and X, a non-convex loss function based on the Euclidean distance between A and $\hat{A}$, i.e.,

$$\mathcal{O}_{NMF}(U, X) = \left\| A - UX^T \right\|_F^2, \ s.t. \ U \geq, X \geq 0, \tag{1}$$

where $\|\cdot\|$ calculates a matrix's Frobenius norm.

It is worth mentioning that an NMF model does not take into account the description of network symmetry. To preserve A's symmetry, SNMF leverages a single factor to learn its approximation [18]. The loss function is given as

$$\mathcal{O}_{SNMF}(X) = \left\| A - XX^T \right\|_F^2, \ s.t. \ X \geq 0. \tag{2}$$

An NMF-based method implements community discovery via taking X as a membership soft indicator [21, 22]: $\forall u \in \{1, 2, ..., n\}$ and $k \in \{1, 2, ..., K\}$, x_{uk} can be considered as the probability that node v_u belongs to community C_k, i.e.,

$$\forall v_u \in C_p, \text{ if } p = \arg \max_q x_{uq}, q = \{1, 2, ..., K\}. \tag{3}$$

3 Methods

3.1 Optimization Objective

To capture the symmetry inherent in a target network, we introduce an equality-constraint term, specifically $X = Y$, into the learning objective of RSN, i.e.,

$$\mathcal{O}_{RSN}(X, Y) = \min \frac{1}{2} \left\| A - XY^T \right\|_F^2, \ s.t. \ X = Y, X, Y \geq 0, \tag{4}$$

where A is an adjacency matrix, decision parameters X and Y are desired feature matrices for forming a low-dimensional approximation $\hat{A}$ to A, i.e., XY^T.

In (4), by setting a trade-off coefficient to balance the generalized loss and the constraint term, the equality-like symmetry constraint term "$X = Y$" enforces the two feature matrices to be identical during the training process, thus effectively capturing the symmetry of the target network. However, in practical applications, achieving a balance between representational capacity and symmetry is challenging, because the solutions of the two feature matrices either become too similar thus making the model reduce to an SNMF one, or fail to capture the symmetry effectively.

Hence, to overcome this issue, we introduce two auxiliary parameters P and Q to separate the involved constraints such as symmetry and non-negativity from the decision parameters, thus achieving.

$$\mathcal{O}_{RSN}(X, Y, P, Q) = \frac{1}{2} \min \left\| A - XY^T \right\|_F^2, \; s.t. \, X = P, \, Y = Q, P = Q; P, Q \geq 0. \; (5)$$

To make the model well aware of the local topological geometry of an input network, we introduce a graph-regularization term into (5) and extend it as

$$\mathcal{O}_{RSN}(X, Y, P, Q) = \min \frac{1}{2} \left(\left\| A - XY^T \right\|_F^2 + \lambda \mathrm{Tr}\left(Q^T L Q \right) \right),$$
$$s.t. \, X = P, \, Y = Q, P = Q; P, Q \geq 0, \tag{6}$$

where $\mathrm{Tr}(\cdot)$ denotes the matrix trace operation. $\lambda > 0$ is a tunable coefficient that adjusts the effect of graph regularization. $L = D - A$ denotes A's Laplacian matrix, and D is the degree matrix whose each entry is calculated as $d_{ii} = \sum_l a_{il}$. Note that the learning objective of RSN in (6) exhibits several merits:

- It employs an asymmetric factorization approach, avoiding the reduction of feature space through two distinct feature matrices.
- By transforming the equality-like symmetry constraints on decision parameters into auxiliary constraints, the model relaxes the strong assumption of equality between matrices X and Y, which enhances the feature space and degrees of freedom.
- The introduction of graph regularization ensures that the model preserves the intrinsic local topology, enhancing its awareness of the local community structure.
- While imposing non-negative constraints on auxiliary parameters, a generalized loss is constructed based on decision parameters. This decoupling of non-negative constraints from decision parameters facilitates the optimization of the generalized loss.
- The representation of matrix A's symmetry is guaranteed by the relation $\hat{A} = PQ^T$.

3.2 ADMM-Based Learning Rules

To resolve (6), we employ the ADMM principle to design an efficient learning scheme for RSN. Thus, we begin by formulating an augmented Lagrangian function

$$\mathcal{L}(X, Y, P, Q, K, \Gamma, \Phi) = \frac{1}{2} \left(\left\| A - XY^T \right\|_F^2 + \lambda \mathrm{Tr}\left(Q^T L Q \right) \right) +$$
$$K \circ (X - P) + \Gamma \circ (Y - Q) + \Phi \circ (P - Q) + \frac{\alpha}{2} \|X - P\|_F^2 + \frac{\beta}{2} \|Y - Q\|_F^2$$
$$+ \frac{\theta}{2} \|P - Q\|_F^2, \tag{7}$$

where $\circ$ denotes the Hadamard product. $K^{n \times K}$, $\Gamma^{n \times K}$ and $\Phi^{n \times K}$ are three Lagrangian multipliers related to the equality constraints, i.e., $X - P$, $Y - Q$ and $P - Q$. The effects of augmentation terms, i.e., $\alpha/2\|X - P\|_F^2$, $\beta/2\|Y - Q\|_F^2$ and $\theta/2\|P - Q\|_F^2$, are adjusted with three coefficients, i.e., α, β and θ. The non-negative constraints can be implemented by projecting P and Q onto the non-negative field of real numbers.

With the ADMM framework [24, 25], let t and $t+1$ represent the current and updating iteration status of parameters, and we obtain the following learning sequences:

$$
\begin{cases}
X^{t+1} = \arg\min_X \mathcal{L}(X, Y^t, P^t, Q^t, K^t, \Gamma^t, \Phi^t), \\
Y^{t+1} = \arg\min_Y \mathcal{L}(X^{t+1}, Y, P^t, Q^t, K^t, \Gamma^t, \Phi^t), \\
P^{t+1} = \arg\min_P \mathcal{L}(X^{t+1}, Y^{t+1}, P, Q^t, K^t, \Gamma^t, \Phi^t), \\
Q^{t+1} = \arg\min_Q \mathcal{L}(X^{t+1}, Y^{t+1}, P^{t+1}, Q, K^t, \Gamma^t, \Phi^t), \\
K^{t+1} = K^t + \eta\nabla_K \mathcal{L}(X^{t+1}, Y^{t+1}, P^{t+1}, Q^{t+1}, K, \Gamma^t, \Phi^t), \\
\Gamma^{t+1} = \Gamma^t + \eta\nabla_\Gamma \mathcal{L}(X^{t+1}, Y^{t+1}, P^{t+1}, Q^{t+1}, K^{t+1}, \Gamma, \Phi^t), \\
\Phi^{t+1} = \Phi^t + \eta\nabla_\Phi \mathcal{L}(X^{t+1}, Y^{t+1}, P^{t+1}, Q^{t+1}, K^{t+1}, \Gamma^{t+1}, \Phi),
\end{cases}
\tag{8}
$$

where ∇ denotes the gradient, and η is the learning rate of gradient ascent. Next, we present the detailed derivation of the solutions of X, Y, P, Q, K, Γ and Φ one by one.

1) *Solution of X*

According to the ADMM principle, X can be iteratively optimized by fixing the other variables. Consequently, the Lagrangian function is rendered convex for X, thus facilitating an analytical resolution. This process leads to the subsequent deductions:

$$
\frac{\partial \mathcal{L}(X, Y^t, P^t, Q^t, K^t, \Gamma^t, \Phi^t)}{\partial X} = X(Y^t)^\mathsf{T} Y^t - A^\mathsf{T} Y^t + K^t - \alpha P^t + \alpha X^t = 0. \tag{9}
$$

With (9), the solution of X can be achieved as

$$
X^{t+1} = (AY^t - K^t + \alpha P^t)\left((Y^t)^\mathsf{T} Y^t + \alpha I\right)^{-1}, \tag{10}
$$

2) *Solution of Y*

By fixing the other variables, the solution of Y is achieved by optimizing it independently. Thus, we have

$$
\frac{\partial \mathcal{L}(X^{t+1}, Y, P^t, Q^t, K^t, \Gamma^t, \Phi^t)}{\partial Y} = Y(X^{t+1})^\mathsf{T} X^{t+1} - AX^{t+1} + \Gamma^t + \beta Y - \beta Q^t = 0. \tag{11}
$$

With (11), we achieve the solution of Y, i.e.,

$$
Y^{t+1} = (AX^{t+1} - \Gamma^t + \beta P^t)\left((X^{t+1})^\mathsf{T} X^{t+1} + \beta I\right)^{-1}. \tag{12}
$$

3) *Solution of P*

Similarly, the solution of P is obtained by fixing all the other parameters to optimize itself alternatively. Thus, we achieve

$$\frac{\partial \mathcal{L}\left(X^{t+1}, Y^{t+1}, P, Q^t, K^t, \Gamma^t, \Phi^t\right)}{\partial P} = -K^t + \Phi^t - \alpha X^{t+1} + \alpha P + \theta P - \theta Q^t = 0,$$

$$(13)$$

yielding the solution of P, i.e.,

$$P^{t+1} = \max\left\{\left(K^t - \Phi^t + \alpha X^{t+1} + \theta Q^t\right)\Big/ (\alpha + \theta), 0\right\}, \qquad (14)$$

which is projected onto the non-negative range to fulfill the non-negative constraint.

4) *Solution of Q*

Similarly, by fixing the other variables except for Q, we have

$$\frac{\partial \mathcal{L}\left(X^{t+1}, Y^{t+1}, P^{t+1}, Q, K^t, \Gamma^t, \Phi^t\right)}{\partial Q}$$

$$= \lambda L Q - \Gamma^t - \Phi^t - \beta Y^{t+1} + \beta Q - \theta P^{t+1} + \theta Q = 0, \qquad (15)$$

yielding the solution of Q, i.e.,

$$Q^{t+1} = \max\left\{(\lambda L + (\beta + \theta)I)^{-1}\left(\Gamma^t + \Phi^t + \beta Y^{t+1} + \theta P^{t+1}\right), 0\right\}, \qquad (16)$$

where the value is projected onto the non-negative range to fulfill its non-negativity.

5) *Solution of Lagrangian multipliers*

Based on the principle of ADMM, Lagrangian multipliers, i.e., K, Γ, and Φ, can be optimized via the dual gradient ascent algorithm. Thus, we achieve

$$\begin{cases} K^{t+1} = K^t + \eta\left(X^{t+1} - P^{t+1}\right), \\ \Gamma^{t+1} = \Gamma^t + \eta\left(Y^{t+1} - Q^{t+1}\right), \\ \Phi^{t+1} = \Phi^t + \eta\left(P^{t+1} - Q^{t+1}\right). \end{cases} \qquad (17)$$

Based on the above analysis, an RSN model is achieved.

3.3 Algorithm Design

The implementation of an RSN-based community discovery model on a target undirected network is provided in Algorithm 1, which consists of three phases, i.e., *Initialization*, *Model training* and *Community division*. Their costs are recorded as $T_1 = \Theta(n^2)$, $T_2 = \Theta((n^2 K + n^3)r_{max})$ and $T_3 = \Theta(nK)$, respectively. Thus, the entire computational complexity is summarized as

$$T_{RSN} = T_1 + T_2 + T_3 = \Theta\left(n^2\right) + \Theta\left(\left(n^3 + n^2 K\right)r_{max}\right) + \Theta(nK) \approx \Theta\left(n^3\right). \quad (18)$$

Considering that K is far less than n for a real-world network, some lower-order terms in (18) have been omitted. Since r_{max} (the maximum number of iterations) and K are both positive and small constants, the computational burden of RSN is approximately cubic with the number of nodes, which is higher than most existing NMF-based methods [8]. This is because the inversion operation regarding the Laplacian matrix L (an $n \times n$ matrix) is needed in the learning rule (16).

Nonetheless, owing to the ADMM framework, the learning algorithm has a high convergence speed, which makes the model training finish within a few iterations. Hence, the RSN-based community detector's overall computational burden is comparable with most current NMF models. Moreover, the computational burden could be reduced greatly with the help of GPU.

Algorithm 1: RSN-based Community Discovery Model

Input: A, K, α, β, θ, λ, η, r_{max}, ξ

1.	**Initialize** $D^{n \times n}=0$, $X^{n \times K}$, $Y^{n \times K}$, $P^{n \times K}$, $Q^{n \times K}$, $K^{n \times K}$, $\Gamma^{n \times K}$, $\Phi^{n \times K}$, $C=\{C_1, C_2, ..., C_K\}=\varnothing$, $r=0$, $diff=0$
2.	**for** $i=1$ to n
3.	**for** $l=1$ to n
4.	$d_{ii}=d_{ii}+a_{il}$
5.	**end for**
6.	**end for**
7.	**repeat**
8.	$r=r+1$
9.	Update X with (10)
10.	Update Y with (12)
11.	Update P with (14)
12.	Update Q with (16)
13.	Update K, Γ and Φ with (17)
14.	**if** $r>1$
15.	$diff=\mathcal{O}_{r+1}-\mathcal{O}_r$
16.	**end if**
17.	**until** $diff \leq \xi$ or $r>r_{max}$
18.	**for** all $v_i \in V$
19.	Assign community affiliation based on (1) by taking Q as a membership indicator
20.	**end for**

Output: C

Table 1. Details of datasets adopted in experiments.

Networks	n	m	K	Sources
DBLP	3,572	10,961	3	DBLP collaboration [26]
Amazon	5,112	16,517	143	Amazon product [26]
Flickr	8,051	188,687	193	Flickr social network [26]
Karate	34	78	2	Karate social network [27]
Cornell	195	304	5	WebKB [28]
Wisconsin	265	530	5	WebKB [28]

4 Experiments

4.1 General Settings

A ground-truth-irrelevant metric, i.e., modularity (Q), is first adopted [29] as the validation metric for hyperparameter tuning to achieve fair experimental results. Two evaluation metrics, i.e., normalized mutual information (NMI) [29] and accuracy (AC) [29] are then adopted to assess all tested methods' performance. Six social networks from real applications are used for performance evaluation, as summarized in Table 1.

To verify the effectiveness of RSN, it is compared with nine baseline and SOTA methods, i.e., NMF [30], SNMF [31], NSED [12], ANLS [19], GNMF [15], GSNMF [15], HPNMF [17], L_pNMF [13] and HALS [20]. To eliminate initialization biases, arrays generated with the same random mechanism falling in the scale of [0, 0.5] are adopted to initialize all models. All hyperparameters of tested methods are set with their optimum values. The graph-regularization coefficient is manually tuned in the set $\{10^{-2}, 10^{-1}, 10^0, 10^1, 10^2, 10^3\}$. For RSN, the augmentation coefficients, i.e., α, β and θ in RSN, are tuned in the set $\{2^{-10}, 2^{-8}, 2^{-6}, 2^{-4}, 2^{-2}, 2^0\}$.

To ensure objective outcomes, each final result is derived by averaging the results from ten separate experiments conducted with different initial hypotheses.

4.2 Sensitivity Analysis

Three kinds of hyperparameters, i.e., λ, $\alpha/\beta/\theta$ (we set $\alpha = \beta = \theta$ to speed up the study) and η, are involved in RSN, which are commonly significant to its performance. Thus, in this part, we aim to test their effects on RSN's community discovery performance.

We use *Modularity* as an evaluation metric for tuning to avoid label leakage. We first tune λ on a candidate set $\{0.01, 0.1, 1.0, 10, 100, 1000\}$ by randomly fixing $\alpha/\beta/\theta$ at 2^{-8} and η at 0.005; and then tune $\alpha/\beta/\theta$ on a candidate set $\{2^{-10}, 2^{-8}, 2^{-6}, 2^{-4}, 2^{-2}, 2^0\}$ by randomly fixing η at 0.005 and setting λ at its optimum value; and finally tune η on a candidate set $\{0.001, 0.005, 0.008, 0.01, 0.02, 0.05\}$ by randomly fixing $\alpha/\beta/\theta$ at 2^{-8} and setting λ at its optimum value. Figure 1 depicts hyperparameter sensitivity test results on the DBLP network. Table 2 records the optimum values of these hyperparameters on all networks.

From them, we observe that RSN's precision is highly sensitive to hyperparameters, with optimal values varying depending on the dataset. It is important to note that the self-adaptive selection of these hyperparameters remains a complex and unresolved issue, necessitating further research and effort in our future work.

4.3 Comparison Results

We compare RSN with several baseline and SOTA methods to verify its superiority in community discovery. The average NMI and AC scores of all tested methods on six testing datasets are recorded in Tables 3 and 4. To understand the comparison results well, we calculate the statistical test results in each table, e.g., average Friedman ranks and p-values with a significance level of $\alpha = 0.05$. From them, we conclude that:

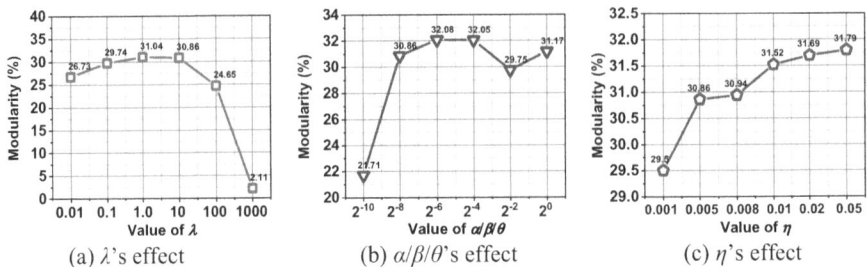

Fig. 1. Results of hyperparameter sensitivity tests on the DBLP network.

Table 2. Hyperparameter settings of the RSN-based community detector on each network.

	DBLP	Amazon	Flickr	Karate	Cornell	Wisconsin
λ	10	100	1	0.1	10	10
$\alpha/\beta/\theta$	2^{-6}	2^{-4}	2^{-4}	2^{-8}	2^{-8}	2^{-4}
η	0.05	0.005	0.02	0.001	0.001	0.05

a) **The relaxed symmetry constraints are effective.** Compared with GNMF, RSN considers the proposed relaxed symmetry constraints that enable RSN to be well aware of symmetry without degradation of its representational capacity. The results in Tables 3 and 4 show that RSN outperforms GNMF on five out of six networks, obtaining higher precision across NMI and AC values, except that they both get full marks on the Karate network. The experimental phenomena tell us that accounting for the inherent symmetry allows RSN to obtain more accurate discovery results. In other words, the relaxed symmetry constraints prove to be effective.

b) **RSN achieves superior accuracy in community detection.** Higher representation learning ability leads to RSN's better performance on community discovery. Results in Tables 3 and 4 demonstrate that RSN outperforms its peers in most testing cases, and achieves the highest precision in community discovery across two evaluation metrics. Moreover, RSN's average Friedman rank is always the lowest among all tested methods, which indicates its significant superiority in obtaining community discovery accuracy gain. In addition, from the statistical results of the Wilcoxon signed-rank tests recorded in Tables 3 and 4, we conclude that RSN obtains significantly higher community discovery accuracy than baseline and SOTA methods on most testing cases with a confidence level of 95%.

4.4   Symmetry Study

In this part, we aim to evaluate RSN's representation learning ability regarding structural symmetry. To do this, we show the distributions of learned approximations for the Flickr and Karate networks in Fig. 2, with the x and y axes respectively representing the values of $\hat{a}_{ij}$ and $\hat{a}_{ji}$. Naturally, if RSN is aware of the target network's symmetry, the corresponding distribution should be symmetric, with data points with data points aligning along the

Table 3. Community discovery results (NMI% ± STD%) of tested models.

NMI	DBLP	Amazon	Flickr	Karate	Cornell	Wisconsin	Ranks[1]	p-value[2]
NMF	22.03 ± 14.19	43.27 ± 2.64	0.45 ± 0.12	100.00 ± 0.00	2.00 ± 0.30	2.52 ± 0.63	7.83	**0.0313**
SNMF	29.25 ± 15.52	45.22 ± 2.29	0.37 ± 0.00	100.00 ± 0.00	1.59 ± 0.21	2.52 ± 1.35	7.33	**0.0313**
NSED	15.98 ± 7.20	40.30 ± 2.10	0.34 ± 0.00	69.15 ± 43.63	2.07 ± 1.41	1.45 ± 0.38	9.50	**0.0156**
ANLS	24.30 ± 2.24	48.73 ± 0.52	0.46 ± 0.12	100.00 ± 0.00	1.05 ± 0.02	3.51 ± 0.26	7.08	**0.0313**
GNMF	26.37 ± 11.69	63.21 ± 9.09	33.55 ± 22.93	100.00 ± 0.00	3.14 ± 0.31	3.87 ± 0.34	4.75	**0.0313**
GSNMF	45.36 ± 1.84	63.15 ± 0.50	23.29 ± 0.81	100.00 ± 0.00	17.74 ± 4.91	4.25 ± 4.38	3.75	**0.0313**
HPNMF	39.36 ± 5.74	74.84 ± 1.13	39.96 ± 0.54	100.00 ± 0.00	13.14 ± 0.96	9.66 ± 4.83	3.08	**0.0313**
LpNMF	25.74 ± 14.10	63.02 ± 8.59	41.12 ± 10.70	100.00 ± 0.00	4.90 ± 4.46	3.16 ± 0.72	5.08	**0.0313**
HALS	50.27 ± 2.35	48.79 ± 1.87	16.87 ± 1.41	89.14 ± 7.68	8.62 ± 3.14	4.52 ± 0.49	5.00	**0.0156**
RSNMF	**55.95 ± 1.62**	**84.90 ± 0.23**	**46.72 ± 1.96**	**100.00 ± 0.00**	**18.03 ± 4.93**	**14.76 ± 4.14**	**1.58**	--

[1] A lower Friedman rank value signifies greater accuracy in community discovery.
[2] Hypotheses that are accepted at a significance level of 0.05 are highlighted.

Table 4. Community discovery results (AC% ± STD%) of tested models.

AC	DBLP	Amazon	Flickr	Karate	Cornell	Wisconsin	Ranks	p-value
NMF	55.50 ± 11.14	69.61 ± 1.77	5.81 ± 0.97	100.00 ± 0.00	39.66 ± 0.87	39.25 ± 1.34	8.08	**0.0313**
SNMF	60.13 ± 11.99	73.53 ± 1.07	7.05 ± 0.24	100.00 ± 0.00	37.78 ± 0.48	38.99 ± 1.08	7.58	**0.0313**
NSED	52.50 ± 5.91	68.26 ± 1.12	7.40 ± 0.63	87.25 ± 18.02	40.85 ± 0.87	40.63 ± 2.05	8.00	**0.0156**
ANLS	62.67 ± 3.07	77.19 ± 1.63	7.53 ± 0.17	100.00 ± 0.00	40.85 ± 0.87	43.90 ± 1.08	5.00	**0.0313**
GNMF	60.60 ± 8.59	75.77 ± 3.02	11.52 ± 3.63	100.00 ± 0.00	40.17 ± 1.28	45.41 ± 0.94	5.42	**0.0313**
GSNMF	74.50 ± 0.71	77.88 ± 1.39	5.49 ± 6.53	100.00 ± 0.00	44.79 ± 0.24	46.29 ± 0.18	4.17	0.0625
HPNMF	72.40 ± 2.11	79.73 ± 3.34	6.31 ± 4.30	100.00 ± 0.00	**46.67 ± 1.83**	46.04 ± 4.44	3.75	0.0938
LpNMF	59.34 ± 10.00	79.51 ± 3.54	10.89 ± 3.91	100.00 ± 0.00	41.88 ± 2.72	40.63 ± 0.78	5.00	**0.0313**
HALS	75.72 ± 2.61	76.14 ± 2.73	4.94 ± 2.07	98.04 ± 1.39	40.68 ± 2.69	46.16 ± 1.17	6.17	**0.0156**
RSNMF	**87.39 ± 0.60**	**83.27 ± 1.26**	**14.64 ± 0.29**	**100.00 ± 0.00**	44.79 ± 0.48	**47.04 ± 0.47**	**1.83**	--

line $y = x$. As shown in Fig. 2, RSN can approximately capture the symmetry of a target undirected network, suggesting that the relaxed symmetry constraints are effective. This ability allows an RSN-based community discovery model to accurately identify symmetry structure characteristics. Similar results are also observed for other networks.

4.5 Convergence Study

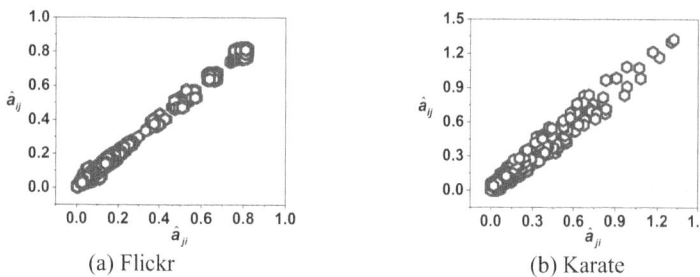

(a) Flickr   (b) Karate

Fig. 2. Data distribution of learned low-rank approximations for the Flickr and Karate networks, with x and y axes representing the values of $\hat{a}_{ij}$ and $\hat{a}_{ji}$, respectively.

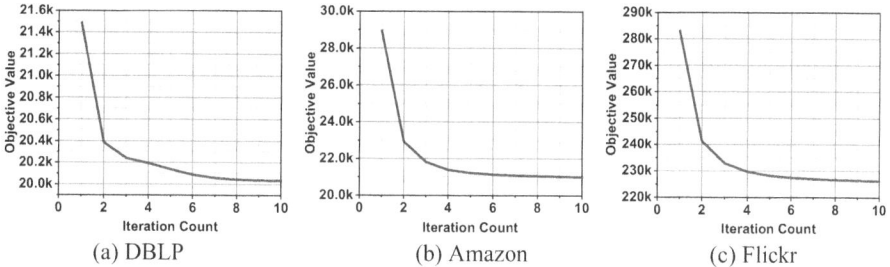

(a) DBLP   (b) Amazon   (c) Flickr

Fig. 3. Convergence curves of RSN on DBLP, Amazon, and Flickr networks.

Figure 3 plots the convergence curves of RSN on DBLP, Amazon, and Flickr networks. From it, we see that the training curve of RSN converges very fast and arrives at a stationary state within ten iterations. Hence, the experimental results support the theoretical conclusion that owing to the help of the ADMM principle that decomposes the learning task into tiny subtasks and alternatively trains the involved parameters, the developed learning scheme can efficiently solve the proposed RSN model.

5 Conclusion

A novel Relaxed Symmetric Non-negative Matrix Factorization (RSN) approach is proposed in this paper to boost an NMF-based community detector's representation learning ability by incorporating the relaxed symmetry constraints to capture the inherent network symmetry characteristics, thus enlarging the feature space. It adopts graph regularization to maintain the local geometric characteristics. An efficient learning scheme based on the ADMM principle is developed to solve the model efficiently. Experimental results across six real-world networks show that the RSN-based community detector outperforms the baseline and SOTA methods. Future work plans to investigate the adaptation of hyperparameters via the Bayesian optimization techniques [32].

Acknowledgments. This work is supported partly by the Guangdong Basic and Applied Basic Research Foundation under Grants 2023A1515110689 and 2022A1515110579, partly by the National Natural Science Foundation of China under Grant 62102086, and partly by the Guangdong Province Universities and College Pearl River Scholar Funded Scheme (2019).

References

1. Boccaletti, S., Bianconi, G., Griado, R., et al.: The structure and dynamics of multilayer networks. Phys. Rep. **544**(1), 1–122 (2014)
2. Liu, P., Xu, Y., Jiang, Q., et al.: Local differential privacy for social network publishing. Neurocomputing **391**, 273–279 (2020)
3. Ghosh, D., Cabrera, J., Adam, T., et al.: Comorbidity patterns and its impact on health outcomes: two-way clustering analysis. IEEE Trans. Big Data **6**(2), 359–368 (2020)
4. Manipur, I., Giordano, M., Piccirillo, M., et al.: Community detection in protein-protein interaction networks and applications. IEEE/ACM Trans. Comput. Bi. **20**(1), 217–237 (2023)
5. Wang, J., Zhang, M., Zhang, J., et al.: Graph-theoretic post-processing of segmentation with application to dense biofilms. IEEE Trans. Image Process. **30**, 8580–8594 (2022)
6. Huang, D., Wang, C., Wu, J., et al.: Ultra-scalable spectral clustering and ensemble clustering. IEEE Trans. Knowl. Data Eng. **32**(6), 1212–1226 (2020)
7. Yang, H., Li, B., Cheng, F., et al.: A node classification-based multiobjective evolutionary algorithm for community detection in complex networks. IEEE Trans. Comput. Social Syst. **11**(1), 292–306 (2024)
8. He, C., Fei, X., Cheng, Q., et al.: A survey of community detection in complex networks using nonnegative matrix factorization. IEEE Trans. Comput. Social Syst. **9**(2), 440–457 (2022)
9. Ding, C., He, X., Simon, H.D.: On the equivalence of nonnegative matrix factorization and spectral clustering. Proc. SIAM Int. Conf. Data Min., pp. 606–610 (2005)
10. Wang, F., Li, T., Wang, X., et al.: Community discovery using nonnegative matrix factorization. Data Min. Knowl. Disc. **22**(3), 493–521 (2011)
11. Pompili, F., Gillis, N., Absil, P.A.: Two algorithms for orthogonal nonnegative matrix factorization with application to clustering. Neurocomputing **141**, 15–25 (2014)
12. Sun, B.J., Shen, H.W., Gao, J.H., et al.: A non-negative symmetric encoder-decoder approach for community detection. In: Proc. ACM Conf. Inf. Knowl. Manage., pp. 597–606 (2017)
13. Zhang, C., Zhang, H., Cai, G., et al.: Graph regularized Lp smooth non-negative matrix factorization for data representation. IEEE/CAA J. Automatica Sin. **6**(2), 584–595 (2019)
14. Ma, X., Dong, D., Wang, Q.: Community detection in multi-layer networks using joint nonnegative matrix factorization. IEEE Trans. Knowl. Data Eng. **31**(2), 273–286 (2019)
15. Yang, L., Cao, X.C., Jin, D., et al.: A unified semi-supervised community detection framework using latent space graph-regularization. IEEE Trans. Cybern. **45**(11), 2585–2598 (2015)
16. Shi, X., Hu, H., He, Y., He, S.: Community detection in social network with pairwisely constrained symmetric non-negative matrix factorization. In: Proc. IEEE/ACM Int. Conf. Adv. Social Netw. Anal. Min., pp. 541–546 (2015)

17. Ye, F., Chen, C., Wen, Z., et al.: Homophily preserving community detection. IEEE Trans. Neural Netw. Learn. Syst. **31**(8), 2903–2915 (2020)
18. Luo, X., Liu, Z., Jin, L., Zhou, Y., Zhou, M.: Symmetric nonnegative matrix factorization-based community detection models and their convergence analysis. IEEE Trans. Neural Netw. Learn. Syst. **33**(3), 1203–1215 (2022)
19. Kuang, D., Yun, S., Park, H.: SymNMF: Nonnegative low-rank approximation of a similarity matrix for graph clustering. J. Glob. Optim. **62**(3), 545–574 (2015)
20. Li, X., Zhu, Z., Li, Q., Liu, K.: A provable splitting approach for symmetric nonnegative matrix factorization. IEEE Trans. Knowl. Data Eng. **35**(3), 2206–2219 (2023)
21. Liu, Z., Luo, X., Zhou, M.: Symmetry and graph bi-regularized non-negative matrix factorization for precise community detection. IEEE Trans. Autom. Sci. Eng. **21**(2), 1406–1420 (2024)
22. Liu, Z., Yi, Y., Luo, X.: A high-order proximity-incorporated nonnegative matrix factorization-based community detector. IEEE Trans. Emerg. Topics Comput. Intell. **7**(3), 700–714 (2023)
23. Wang, J., Li, W., Luo, X.: A distributed adaptive second-order latent factor analysis model. IEEE/CAA J. Automatica Sin. (2023). https://doi.org/10.1109/JAS.2024.124371
24. Luo, X., Zhou, M., Wang, Z., et al.: An effective scheme for QoS estimation via alternating direction method-based matrix factorization. IEEE Trans. Serv. Comput. **12**(4), 503–518 (2019)
25. Luo, X., Zhong, Y., Wang, Z., Li., M.: An alternating-direction-method of multipliers-incorporated approach to symmetric non-negative latent factor analysis. IEEE Trans. Neural Netw. Learn. Syst. **34**(8), 4826–4840 (2023)
26. Leskovec, J., Sosic, R.: SNAP: a general-purpose network analysis and graph-mining library. ACM Trans. Intel. Syst. Tec. **8**(1), 1–20 (2016)
27. Havens, T., Bezdek, J., Leckie, C., et al.: A soft modularity function for detecting fuzzy communities in social networks. IEEE Trans. Fuzzy Syst. **21**(6), 1170–1175 (2013)
28. Wang, X., Cui, P., Wang, J., et al.: Community preserving network embedding. Proc. AAAI Conf. Artif. Intell., pp. 203–209 (2017)
29. Chakraborty, T., Dalmia, A., Mukherjee, A., Ganguly, N.: Metrics for community analysis: a survey. ACM Comput. Surveys **50**(4), 1–37 (2017)
30. Lee, D.D., Seung, H.S.: Algorithms for non-negative matrix factorization. Proc. Adv. Neural Inf. Process. Syst., pp. 556–562 (2000)
31. Wang, D., Li, T., Zhu, S., Ding, C.: Multi-document summarization via sentence-level semantic analysis and symmetric matrix factorization. In: Proc. Int. ACM SIGIR Conf. Res. Dev. Inf. Ret., pp. 307–314 (2008)
32. Pu, L., Zhang, X., Shi, J., et al.: Precise RCS extrapolation via nearfield 3-D imaging with adaptive parameter optimization Bayesian learning. IEEE Trans. Antennas Propag. **70**(5), 3656–3671 (2022)

Enhanced Cognitive Distortions Detection and Classification Through Data Augmentation Techniques

Mohamad Rasmy[1(✉)], Caroline Sabty[2] ⓘ, Nourhan Sakr[3] ⓘ,
and Alia El Bolock[3] ⓘ

[1] Ain Shams University, Cairo, Egypt
`2021170671@cis.asu.edu.eg`
[2] German International University, Cairo, Egypt
`caroline.sabty@giu-uni.de`
[3] American University in Cairo, Cairo, Egypt
`n.sakr@columbia.edu`, `alia.elboloc@aucegypt.edu`

Abstract. Cognitive distortions detrimentally affect mental health by distorting reality and influencing emotions and behavior. While the detection and classification of such irrational thinking patterns grow in significance, limited data resources (and thereby limited work) exist for such task. In this study, we are motivated by the work in [5], where a CNN model using BERT embeddings is selected to detect and classify cognitive distortions. We explore various data augmentation techniques, such as Easy Data Augmentation, word embedding substitution, and back-translation to enhance the quality of the training dataset and fine-tune additional embeddings from RoBERTa and GPT-2 to improve the performance of these tasks. Our experimental results demonstrate a significant increase in the F-score by 1.88% for detection and 5.9% for classification. These enhancements increase the potential for building a supportive tool for individuals and mental health professionals.

Keywords: Cognitive Distortions · Data Augmentation · Deep Learning · Natural Language Processing · Text Classification

1 Introduction and Related Work

Cognitive distortions are irrational and biased thinking patterns that adversely affect mental health and well-being, often leading to conditions such as anxiety, depression, and other psychological disorders [3,23]. Beck's cognitive theory explains that these emotional disturbances result from dysfunctional information processing, characterized by self-statements that are either slightly misconstrued or entirely incorrect [24]. Examples include selectively focusing on negative information while devaluing positive information, interpreting situations in extreme terms, predicting disastrous outcomes without justification, assuming responsibility for events beyond one's control, and equating emotions with factual evidence while disregarding objective reality. Identifying and understanding cognitive distortions are essential for developing effective psychological interventions.

Cognitive Behavioral Therapy (CBT) emphasizes training patients to recognize and correct their cognitive distortions to improve overall mental health and well-being. Recently, online therapy programs have supplemented or replaced traditional CBT, offering convenient access to resources for identifying and addressing biased thinking and negative thought patterns [8,19].

The literature is rich with interesting directions that aim at supporting mental health professionals and patients. For instance, Elsharawi et al. [5] propose an online application that automatically detects and classifies cognitive distortions. The detection and classification of cognitive distortions present a text classification challenge that is similar to emotion classification, sentiment analysis, and mental health diagnostics. The main challenge with such tasks is to avail large volumes of training data to improve the performance and generalizability of machine learning models that process them. The authors publish the first open-source dataset containing annotated journal entries reflecting 14 different types of cognitive distortions. Building on their foundational work, we extend their dataset to enhance cognitive distortion detection and classification models. *In this paper, the scope of our work is to explore data augmentation (DA) techniques, which are widely used in various detection and classification tasks with the goal of extending and diversifying the existing dataset and thus enhancing the model performance.*

The collection and annotation of large datasets are resource-intensive and time-consuming. To mitigate these challenges, the literature investigates a spectrum of DA techniques, where new data is generated from existing samples. DA has demonstrated its efficacy in image classification and shows significant promise in NLP tasks through methods such as paraphrasing, noising, and sampling [6,10,16]. Easy Data Augmentation (EDA) [25] includes Synonym Replacement (SR), Random Insertion (RI) of synonyms, Random Swapping (RS) and Random Deletion (RD) of words. These rule-based techniques have proven simple yet effective for improving text classification results [2,13,18].

Lexical substitution (LS) replaces words in a sentence without altering its semantic meaning. Additionally, model-based approaches use non-contextual word embeddings such as `word2vec` [14] and contextual embeddings like BERT [9], which provides different word representations for the same words in various contexts. The authors in [5] show that a CNN model using BERT embeddings achieves the best performance on the published dataset. Conditional BERT (C-BERT) further enhances this process by predicting tokens based on both the sentence context and its label, increasing accuracy in text classification tasks [26]. Although C-BERT has been effectively used for depression detection [1], we choose standard BERT for our work due to the imbalanced nature of the cognitive distortions dataset. Back-Translation (BT) is another DA technique that involves translating a sentence from the source language to one or more intermediate languages and then back to the original language. This method introduces lexical, syntactic, and structural variations while preserving the overall semantic meaning. It has proven effective in various domains, e.g. toxic comment classification [18], mental health classification [2], and general text classification tasks [12,21].

Our Contribution. In this work, our goal is to extend the dataset published in [5] as a means to provide better quality data to be used for the task of cognitive distortions detection and classification. The impact of this work has potential to support mental health professionals and patients. Our baselines is the CNN model with BERT embeddings from [5]. We examine EDA, LS with BERT embeddings and BT, as these methods are known for capturing complex word relationships and were deemed effective in other similar tasks. To ensure the robustness of our approach, evaluate our experiments in various setups. Additionally, we propose contextual embeddings from RoBERTa and GPT-2. Our results show significant performance improvements over the baseline, with the F-score increasing by 1.88% for distortion detection and by 5.9% for distortion classification.

2   Methodology

We propose two main approaches to enhance the performance of the cognitive distortions classification model. The first approach involves data augmentation to expand the size and diversity of the dataset, using three techniques: EDA, word embedding substitution (WE_Sub), and BT. The second approach improves the classification model itself by testing two additional embedding methods, and comparing the results with fine-tuned GPT-2 and RoBERTa models.

2.1   Cognitive Distortions Dataset

The authors in [5] contributed to the collection and annotation of the first open-source cognitive distortions dataset. The data, in English, was collected from existing social media emotion datasets, namely the Facebook Empathetic Data and Twitter's Sentiment Analysis dataset. The dataset consists of 34,370 sentences, with 59.3% being neutral and 40.7% distorted, facilitating the detection and classification of cognitive distortions. The distorted data is categorized into 14 different types as follows: Shoulds (24.1%), Overgeneralization (23.3%), Emotional Reasoning (16.7%), Blaming (10.3%), Personalization (9.6%), Catastrophizing (7.3%), Jumping to Conclusions (4.3%), Polarization (1.1%), Fallacy of Fairness (0.8%), Global Labeling (0.8%), Mental Filtering (0.7%), Always Being Right (0.3%), Control of Fallacies (0.3%), and Fallacy of Change (0.3%).

2.2   Data Augmentation on Cognitive Distortions Dataset

To overcome the scarcity of cognitive distortions data and expand the training data to improve the model's generalizability, we investigate three DA techniques commonly used for text classification tasks. The first technique is Easy Data Augmentation (EDA), a rule-based method that introduces lexical variation through synonym replacement, random insertion, swapping, and deletion. The second technique involves word embedding substitution, where we explore an improved model-based approach using contextualized embeddings from BERT for word substitution. The third technique is Back Translation (BT), another model-based approach that introduces both lexical and syntactic variation while preserving the semantics of the text. The augmented sentences generated by these methods are assigned the same labels as their respective original sentences.

Easy Data Augmentation. EDA [25] has shown significant improvement in text classification and other NLP tasks such as Named Entity Recognition [20]. As previously mentioned, EDA consists of four operations: SR, RI, RS, and RD. SR involves selecting n random words in a sentence and replacing them with their synonyms. RI involves choosing a random word and inserting one of its synonyms at a random position in the sentence. RS exchanges the positions of two random words in the sentence. RD randomly removes words from the sentence based on probabilities. To expand our training data with more lexical variations, we focus solely on SR and RI, as RS and RD primarily introduce structural changes. For both SR and RI, the number of random words selected (n) is determined based on the sentence length (l), using the formula $n = \alpha \times l$ [25], where α represents the percentage of words to be changed.

We incorporate WordNet [15], a lexical database for English, to search for sets of synonyms (synsets) for any given word. In the SR operation, after extracting synonyms, we combine all the returned synonym lists. To determine the most suitable synonym for replacement, we use a word similarity method based on the cosine similarity of their word embeddings. This method calculates similarity values for each synonym in comparison to the original word, and the synonym with the highest similarity is selected for replacement. In cases where a word is chosen multiple times for SR within the same sentence, we ensure variety by selecting a synonym with slightly lower similarity each subsequent time. For the RI operation, a random word from the sentence is chosen, and its synonyms are identified using the same extraction method. A synonym is then randomly selected and inserted at a randomly generated index within the original sentence. A distorted sentence from the cognitive distortions dataset and its augmentation using SR and RI are presented in Table 1.

Word Embedding Substitution. Word embedding is a type of word representation that maps every word in a sentence to a numerical vector in multi-dimensional space, placing semantically similar words near each other. As an alternative to the previous rule-based replacement, which has limited synonym-based augmentation, word embedding substitution provides greater flexibility and variation, producing more diverse patterns from the original text.

To illustrate the motivation behind its usage, consider an example from the cognitive distortions dataset. The sentence, *"female relatives are trouble-*

some," is labeled as *distorted*. When the EDA augmentation is applied to the word *"female"*, SR methods might replace it with synonyms from WordNet like *distaff* and *femaleperson*, which is limited. In fact, the word *"female"* can also be replaced with non-synonym words like *male, family, close, young*, etc., while still maintaining the distorted label and naturalness of the sentence. This broader range of replacements can help generalize the model by exposing it to a wider variety of patterns, thereby boosting its performance.

To implement this word embedding substitution [9], we utilize the pre-trained contextual embedding model BERT for its capability to model polysemous words effectively and its effectiveness in predicting a certain word based on the left and right context of it. Considering varying sentence lengths, we determine the number of words to be substituted, using the same previous formula $n = \alpha \times l$. Table 1 includes a distorted sentence augmented using word embedding substitution.

Back-Translation. The third DA technique we implement is BT, a method used to paraphrase text while retaining its original meaning. This technique involves translating text into a different language and then back to the original language, preserving semantics while introducing syntactic variations. We use translation models from the Opus-MT project [22], based on MarianMT, an efficient neural machine translation framework supporting multiple language pairs. We translate sentences from English to German, then German to French, and finally back to English. This multi-step translation process is chosen to introduce greater syntactic variation, enhancing the diversity of the augmented dataset. Outlined in Table 1 is a distorted sentence along with its back-translation augmentation.

Table 1. A sample of the generated text using SR, RI, WE_Sub, and BT.

Original Sentence (w/o DA)	I have so many times "what if I fall" "what if a plane falls out the sky" "what if I look too ugly"
SR	consume soh many meter "what if fall" "what if groupa plane drop forbidden the sky" "what if takecare aswell ugly"
RI	I flat have angstrom so many times "what if I fall" "what if airplane a hence plane unity falls consume takecare out the sky" "what if I time look too prohibited ugly"
WE_Sub	I have so important these wonders what if I went down suppose what if a plane falls out the sky "what if I feel too good"
BT	I have so many times what I do when I fall, and when a plane falls from the sky, and when I'm too ugly

2.3   Improving the Cognitive Distortions Classification Model

Based on the work done in [5], the best performing model on their dataset is a CNN model, as shown in Fig. 1. It features three parallel convolutional layers with 512 filters and filter windows of 3 to 5, followed by max-pooling, concatenation, flattening, dropout, and a fully connected layer. This architecture yielded the best performance among the tested models, particularly when trained on contextual embeddings from BERT. The embeddings showed significant improvements over non-contextual embeddings like GloVe and other vectorization methods such as TF-IDF and Count Vectorizer. Building on these findings, our current study explores and compares two additional types of contextual embeddings:

- **RoBERTa (Robustly Optimized BERT Pretraining Approach)**: RoBERTa, like BERT, is designed to understand the context of words within sentences by reconstructing masked parts of the input [11]. RoBERTa improves upon BERT by eliminating the next sentence prediction objective, which the authors in [11] showed to have an equal or slightly higher performance on downstream tasks. Unlike the static masking used in BERT, they employed dynamic masking to generate different masking patterns every time the sequence is fed to the model, yielding a comparable or slightly better performance. RoBERTa was pre-trained using 10 times more data than the original BERT, using longer training times and larger batch sizes. This allowed the model to see four times as many sequences during pretraining compared to BERT, enabling it to gain a better understanding of the text.
- **GPT-2 (Generative Pre-Trained Transformer-2)**: Unlike BERT, GPT-2 is an auto-regressive model that generates text by predicting the next word in a sequence based on the preceding words. GPT-2 is first pre-trained in an unsupervised stage and processes text sequences unidirectionally from left to right, allowing to capture a different aspect of contextual understanding compared to bidirectional models like BERT [17]. In a study comparing their word embeddings and fine-tuning performance on classification tasks [7], GPT-2 demonstrated a higher F-score in fine-tuning than BERT.

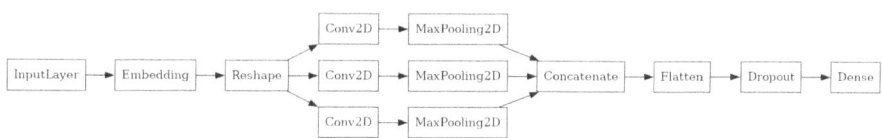

Fig. 1. Architecture of the CNN-BERT baseline classifier model for cognitive distortions

In addition to comparing these embeddings, we test the sequence classification capabilities of models built on these transformers. We use the CNN-BERT model from [5] as our baseline and compare its results with those obtained from other CNN models trained on RoBERTa and GPT-2 embeddings. We evaluate the performance of sequence classification models using transformer-based models from Hugging Face, fine-tuning the entire model along with the classification head added on top. By assessing these models, we aim to determine the most effective approach for detecting and classifying cognitive distortions, leveraging the strengths of both auto-encoding and auto-regressive transformer models.

3   Experiments and Results

Data Augmentation. We test our baseline CNN-BERT with α values in {0.1, 0.2, 0.3, 0.4, 0.5}, as in [25], and obtain the highest F-score at $\alpha = 0.4$ for the combined EDA (SR, RI). For EDA, we generate two augmented sentences per original sentence ($N = 2$), one for SR and one for RI. These methods introduce new variations, enriching the dataset with different lexical and syntactic patterns. We exclude other EDA techniques (RS and RD), as they primarily modify sentence structure without introducing new content. Our focus is on techniques that inject novel variations into the data, broadening the model's exposure to linguistic diversity. Due to data imbalance and the small sample sizes of some classes, conditional BERT [26] is not suitable for word embedding substitution. We opt for the pre-trained BERT approach, substituting 30% of the words (tokenized by BERT) to ensure general embedding-based word substitution.

Data Preproceessing. For the preprocessing, our approach involves standard techniques such as lower-casing text, removing punctuation, unrecognized symbols and tags, and dropping duplicates. We investigate the impact of stemming using PorterStemmer and removing stopwords, following the authors' approach in [5]. However, these techniques are found to be yielding comparable results, and occasionally slightly worse due to contextual embeddings. Therefore, we ultimately opt for a simpler preprocessing pipeline without stemming or stopword removal.

Hyper-Parameters Tuning. We adopt the same hyper-parameters for the CNN architecture as in [5], including the number of filters, filter size, and dropout rate, with Adamax optimizer and Softmax activation. For the sequence classification models of RoBERTa and GPT-2, we fine-tune the learning rate and batch sizes as in [4]. We test various learning rates and batch sizes, setting the optimal rate before tuning the batch size. The best learning rates are 5e-5 for GPT-2 and 4e-5 for RoBERTa, with optimal results achieved using a batch size of 20.

Classification Strategies. The dataset contains 14 distinct distortion types, in addition to a neutral class. Our classification approach addresses 3 distinct tasks:

– **Binary Classification** aims to identify whether a given sample is distorted or not, effectively distinguishing between distorted and neutral data.
– **Multi-Class Classification** focuses on classifying distorted samples into one of the fourteen specific cognitive distortion types.
– **Semantic Grouping Classification** addresses class imbalance among the fourteen distortion types, by grouping them into five broader semantic categories. This strategy, informed by the confusion matrix results, semantic similarities and the psychiatric diagnosis proximity between distortion types, aims to reduce the number of classes while creating balanced categories, thereby simplifying the classification task. The five groups, with their respective size percentages of the total distorted data, are as follows:
  • **Group 1 (16.5%)**: "Blaming", "Always Being Right", "Fallacy of Fairness", "Global Labelling", "Jumping to Conclusions"

- **Group 2 (31.7%)**: "Overgeneralization", "Catastrophizing", "Polarization"
- **Group 3 (18.1%)**: "Emotional Reasoning", "Control of Fallacies", "Fallacy of Change", "Mental Filtering"
- **Group 4 (9.6%)**: "Polarization"
- **Group 5 (24.1%)**: "Shoulds"

Final Training Pipeline Our training pipeline follows a similar approach to [2], using stratified splitting of the dataset into training, validation, and test sets with ratios of 70:10:20, along with early stopping during training. This is to avoid over-fitting, ensure anonymity of test data, and maintain consistent class percentages across stages. Each entry in the training set is augmented once with each technique discussed, except for EDA, where we produce two augments: one for SR and one for RI. To investigate different DA combinations, we test all possible combinations of the three techniques, following $\sum_{i=1}^{n} \binom{n}{i}$, where n = 3 (number of DA techniques). This ensures evaluation from single-technique setups to the combination of all three. The chosen models are then trained on the final training set using the three classification strategies in Sect. 3. Figure 2 shows the above-mentioned pipeline. The interested reader is refered to our implementation[1] for more details.

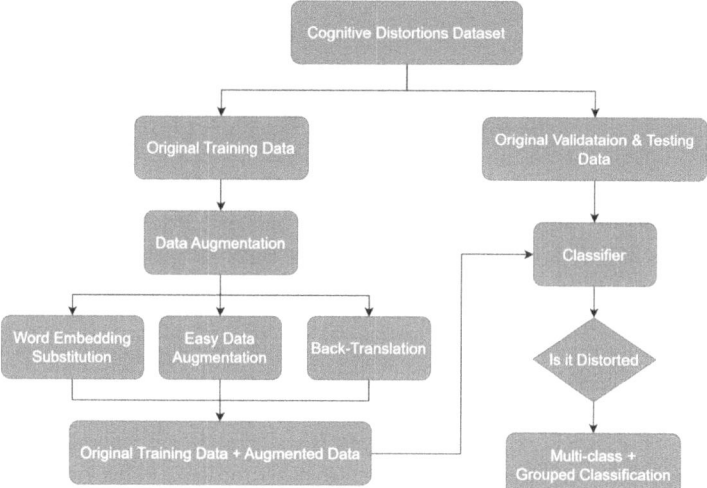

Fig. 2. Data Augmentation and Classification Pipeline. The original dataset is split into training and validation/testing sets. The training data is augmented using three techniques: Word Embedding Substitution, EDA, and BT. Classifier models are trained on all possible combinations of the augmented datasets with the original training data. The classifiers determine if the data is distorted, then classify the distorted data into 14 specific classes and also into 5 broader classes.

---

[1] https://github.com/MHRasmy/CogDistortions-Augmentation-Classification.

3.1   Results and Discussion

This section analyzes the impact of different DA techniques and embedding choices on the performance of our proposed model across binary, multi-class, and grouped classification tasks. For binary classification, using both neutral and distorted data, the datasets comprised 24,717 training samples, 3,531 for validation, and 7,063 for testing. For distortions classification, the datasets included 10,068 training samples, 1,438 for validation, and 2,878 for testing. These datasets maintained the same class distribution percentages due to stratified splitting.

Each DA technique (SR, RI, WE_Sub, and BT) is applied once to the training data, resulting in a single augmentation per technique. Addressing the dataset's imbalance solely through augmentation is challenging, as small classes would require 20–70 times augmentation to balance, leading to models trained on minimal original data. To mitigate bias towards larger classes and evaluate the DA techniques' effectiveness, we use the previously mentioned semantic grouped classification. This approach ensures nearly balanced data by grouping similar classes into broader categories.

Data Augmentation. Among single DA techniques, our results show BT to be yielding the highest F-score gain due to its paraphrasing technique, generating semantically similar sentences with structural and vocabulary changes. RI and SR follow, adding noise and vocabulary changes, enhancing model robustness. The combination of EDA (SR, RI) improves the F-score by 1.87% in binary classification, 2.56% in multi-class classification, and 1.62% in grouped classification. Both precision and recall increase, with a higher rise in precision, which is crucial for detecting cognitive distortions. In mental health contexts, ensuring accurate identification of distorted data (higher precision) is more important than detecting all correct instances (recall). Further performance gains are observed when combining multiple augmented datasets. The highest improvement comes from combining all three DA techniques, adding diversity and expanding the training data, leading to additional F-score increases of 0.07% and 0.19% for binary and multi-class classification tasks, respectively.

Following a similar approach as in [2], we measure the diversity of the augmented data using the Bilingual Evaluation Understudy (BLEU) score. Originally used to evaluate machine translation by comparing it to human reference translations, the BLEU score ranges from 0 to 1, with higher values indicating better translation quality. For DA, we use it to indicate data diversity, where lower values suggest greater diversity. The BLEU score is computed by comparing n-grams of the original and augmented data; in our case, we set $n = 2$, adopting the value from [2]. The BLEU scores for the augmented data are 0.39, 0.56, 0.44 and 0.56 for the SR, RI, WE_Sub, and BT. Accordingly, The most diverse data is generated by SR and word embedding substitution (WE_Sub), as we substitute 40% and 30% of the words in the sentences, respectively. The least diverse data is generated by RI, as we does not remove or substitute any parts of the sentences.

Table 2. F1-Scores for Selected DA Techniques and Models

DA Techniques and Models	Binary F1	Multi-class F1	Semantic Grouping F1
Original Data Without DA (Baseline)$_{\text{CNN-BERT}}$	77.61	45.30	51.58
Original Data Without DA$_{\text{GPT-2 for sequence classification}}$	77.52	46.71	51.42
Original Data Without DA$_{\text{RoBERTa for sequence classification}}$	79.48	50.95	55.70
WE_Sub$_{\text{CNN-BERT}}$	77.62	45.86	51.26
WE_Sub$_{\text{RoBERTa for sequence classification}}$	79.09	48.22	15.22
EDA(SR, RI)$_{\text{CNN-BERT}}$	78.46	47.86	53.20
EDA(SR, RI)$_{\text{RoBERTa for sequence classification}}$	79.49	51.20	53.16
BT$_{\text{CNN-BERT}}$	78.38	46.94	51.79
BT$_{\text{RoBERTa for sequence classification}}$	78.69	49.74	15.22
WE_Sub+EDA(SR, RI)$_{\text{CNN-BERT}}$	78.12	46.24	49.50
WE_Sub+EDA(SR, RI)$_{\text{CNN-RoBERTa}}$	76.98	46.26	51.90
WE_Sub+EDA(SR, RI)$_{\text{RoBERTa for sequence classification}}$	77.64	49.14	15.22
WE_Sub+BT$_{\text{CNN-BERT}}$	78.02	46.80	51.06
WE_Sub+BT$_{\text{CNN-GPT-2}}$	77.90	43.96	49.61
WE_Sub+BT$_{\text{CNN-RoBERTa}}$	77.90	48.13	51.24
WE_Sub+BT$_{\text{RoBERTa for sequence classification}}$	77.84	49.27	15.22
EDA(SR, RI)+BT$_{\text{RoBERTa for sequence classification}}$	79.42	48.79	55.52
WE_Sub+EDA(SR, RI)+BT$_{\text{GPT-2 for sequence classification}}$	78.74	48.78	52.59
WE_Sub+EDA(SR, RI)+BT$_{\text{RoBERTa for sequence classification}}$	79.01	48.99	15.22

Embedding Choice. Our experiments demonstrate the superiority of auto-encoder-based embeddings (BERT, RoBERTa) over the auto-regressive GPT-2 embedding. This can be attributed to the unique nature of the auto-encoders' embeddings, which are designed to output an embedding for every token in the tokenized input sentence and an additional embedding representation for a special [CLS] token, capturing the embedding representation of the entire sequence [4,11]. This comprehensive representation provides the CNN model with a richer understanding of the input.

Furthermore, RoBERTa embeddings consistently outperform BERT embeddings, showcasing F-score improvements of 0.67% and 0.95% in binary and multiclass classifications, respectively. This enhancement stems from RoBERTa's larger model size and pre-training on a larger dataset than BERT's [11]. Fine-tuning the entire RoBERTaForSequenceClassification model yields the most substantial performance boost, achieving F-score increases of 1.88%, 5.65%, and 4.12% across the three classification tasks. This highlights the benefits of adapting the pre-trained model to the specific nuances of the dataset and task.

Overall Performance. The RoBERTaForSequenceClassification model, combined with EDA (SR and RI) augmentation, achieves the highest overall results. This configuration surpasses the baseline CNN-BERT model by 1.88% in F-score for binary classification and 5.9% for multi-class classification. Selected detailed results are presented in Table 2, filtered for the best performing models.

4   Conclusion and Future Work

The paper proposes several approaches for improving the detection and classification of cognitive distortions: applying three different DA techniques, changing the embeddings of the text passages, and fine-tuning transformer models. The proposed and tested DA techniques, both individually and in combination, enhance our multi-class CNN classifier model by 2.75% in the F-score. Testing with RoBERTa's embeddings surpassed the previous existing work that used BERT embeddings with the CNN by 1.41% in the F-score. The best results are obtained by fine-tuning RoBERTaForSequenceClassification on the combined augmented training set generated by all the discussed DA techniques, yielding an increase in the F-score by 1.88% for distortion detection and by 5.9% for distortion classification. Future works invite more investigation on ways to expand the open-source cognitive dataset, possibly using LLMs to automate the annotation process.

References

1. Ali, J., Ngo, D.Q., Bhattacharjee, A., Maiti, T., Singh, T., Mei, J.: Depression detection: text augmentation for robustness to label noise in self-reports. In: Bertolaso, M., Capone, L., Rodríguez-Lluesma, C. (eds.) Digital Humanism: A Human-Centric Approach to Digital Technologies, pp. 81–103. Springer, Cham (2022). https://doi.org/10.1007/978-3-030-97054-3_6

2. Ansari, G., Garg, M., Saxena, C.: Data augmentation for mental health classification on social media. In: Proceedings of the 18th International Conference on Natural Language Processing (ICON), pp. 152–161. NLP Association of India (NLPAI), National Institute of Technology Silchar, Silchar, India (2021)

3. Beck, J.S.: Cognitive Behavior Therapy: Basics & Beyond. Guilford Publications (2020)

4. Devlin, J., Chang, M.W., Lee, K., Toutanova, K.: Bert: pre-training of deep bidirectional transformers for language understanding. arXiv:1810.04805 (2018)

5. Elsharawi, N., El Bolock, A.: C-journal: a journaling application for detecting and classifying cognitive distortions using deep-learning based on a crowd-sourced dataset. In: Proceedings of the 2024 Joint International Conference on Computational Linguistics, Language Resources and Evaluation (LREC-COLING) (2024)

6. Feng, S.Y., et al.: A survey of data augmentation approaches for NLP. In: Findings of the Association for Computational Linguistics: ACL-IJCNLP 2021, pp. 968–988. Association for Computational Linguistics (2021)

7. Gomez-Perez, J.M., Denaux, R., Garcia-Silva, A., Gomez-Perez, J.M., Denaux, R., Garcia-Silva, A.: Understanding word embeddings and language models. A Practical Guide to Hybrid Natural Language Processing: Combining Neural Models and Knowledge Graphs for NLP, pp. 17–31 (2020)

8. Hofmann, S.G., Asnaani, A., Vonk, I.J., Sawyer, A.T., Fang, A.: The efficacy of cognitive behavioral therapy: a review of meta-analyses. Cogn. Ther. Res. **36**, 427–440 (2012)

9. Kobayashi, S.: Contextual augmentation: data augmentation by words with paradigmatic relations. In: Proceedings of the 2018 Conference of the North American Chapter of the Association for Computational Linguistics: Human Language Technologies, Volume 2 (Short Papers), pp. 452–457. Association for Computational Linguistics (2018)

10. Li, B., Hou, Y., Che, W.: Data augmentation approaches in natural language processing: a survey. AI Open **3**, 71–90 (2022)

11. Liu, Y., et al.: Roberta: a robustly optimized bert pretraining approach. arXiv:1907.11692 (2019)
12. Ma, J., Li, L.: Data augmentation for Chinese text classification using back-translation. In: Journal of Physics: Conference Series, vol. 1651, p. 012039. IOP Publishing (2020)
13. Maslej-Krešňáková, V., Sarnovskỳ, M., Jacková, J.: Use of data augmentation techniques in detection of antisocial behavior using deep learning methods. Future Internet **14**(9), 260 (2022)
14. Melamud, O., Levy, O., Dagan, I.: A simple word embedding model for lexical substitution. In: Proceedings of the 1st Workshop on Vector Space Modeling for Natural Language Processing, pp. 1–7 (2015)
15. Miller, G.A.: Wordnet: a lexical database for english. Commun. ACM **38**(11), 39–41 (1995)
16. Perez, L., Wang, J.: The effectiveness of data augmentation in image classification using deep learning. arXiv:1712.04621 (2017)
17. Radford, A., Wu, J., Child, R., Luan, D., Amodei, D., Sutskever, I., et al.: Language models are unsupervised multitask learners. OpenAI Blog **1**(8), 9 (2019)
18. Rastogi, C., Mofid, N., Hsiao, F.I.: Can we achieve more with less? exploring data augmentation for toxic comment classification. arXiv:2007.00875 (2020)
19. Ruwaard, J., Lange, A., Schrieken, B., Dolan, C.V., Emmelkamp, P.: The effectiveness of online cognitive behavioral treatment in routine clinical practice. PLoS ONE **7**(7), e40089 (2012)
20. Sabty, C., Omar, I., Wasfalla, F., Islam, M., Abdennadher, S.: Data augmentation techniques on Arabic data for named entity recognition. Procedia Comput. Sci. **189**, 292–299 (2021)
21. Song, J., Zan, H., Liu, T., Zhang, K., Ji, X., Cui, T.: Text classification based on multilingual back-translation and model ensemble. In: Xu, H., et al. (eds.) CHIP 2023. CCIS, vol. 2080, pp. 231–241. Springer, Singapore (2023). https://doi.org/10.1007/978-981-97-1717-0_21
22. Tiedemann, J., Thottingal, S.: OPUS-MT – building open translation services for the world. In: Proceedings of the 22nd Annual Conference of the European Association for Machine Translation, pp. 479–480. European Association for Machine Translation (2020)
23. Wang, B., Zhao, Y., Lu, X., Qin, B.: Cognitive distortion based explainable depression detection and analysis technologies for the adolescent internet users on social media. Front. Public Health **10**, 1045777 (2023)
24. Weeland, M.M., Nijhof, K.S., Otten, R., Vermaes, I.P., Buitelaar, J.K.: Beck's cognitive theory and the response style theory of depression in adolescents with and without mild to borderline intellectual disability. Res. Dev. Disabil. **69**, 39–48 (2017)
25. Wei, J., Zou, K.: EDA: Easy data augmentation techniques for boosting performance on text classification tasks. In: EMNLP-IJCNLP, pp. 6382–6388. Association for Computational Linguistics, Hong Kong, China (2019)
26. Wu, X., Lv, S., Zang, L., Han, J., Hu, S.: Conditional BERT contextual augmentation. In: Rodrigues, J.M.F., et al. (eds.) ICCS 2019. LNCS, vol. 11539, pp. 84–95. Springer, Cham (2019). https://doi.org/10.1007/978-3-030-22747-0_7

Enhancing Music Genre Classification Using Augmented Features Ensemble Learning Technique

Raad Shariat[ID] and John Z. Zhang[✉][ID]

Department of Math and Computer Science, University of Lethbridge, Lethbridge,
AB T1K 3M2, Canada
raad.shariat@uleth.ca, john.zhang@uleth.ca

Abstract. In *Music Information Retrieval*, classification of music genres is a core task and has been gaining increasing interest by adopting automated classification methods. Among these approaches, ensemble learning techniques have emerged as a promising solution by demonstrating their ability to enhance classification performance across diverse domains. However, traditional ensemble learning techniques may not deliver the desired accuracy improvements when applied to music datasets characterized by highly correlated low-level features associated with music genres. This study presents an innovative ensemble learning technique to address this challenge. The effectiveness of this approach is evaluated alongside established ensemble learning techniques by utilizing three publicly available music datasets, with two containing high-level sentiment-related features and one comprising low-level features extracted from music signals. The empirical experiments indicate that the proposed ensemble learning technique constantly outperforms conventional techniques in terms of classification accuracy. Notably, the proposed technique demonstrates remarkable performance enhancements when processing low-level features, whereas the traditional techniques failed to do so. This research highlights the substantial potential of advanced ensemble learning techniques in music genre classification and provides valuable insights into the strengths and limitations of various ensemble learning techniques when confronted with complex heterogeneous music datasets.

1 Introduction

A dynamic and interdisciplinary field, *Music Information Retrieval* (MIR) focuses on extracting and organizing meaningful information from music-related data [9]. Among the core tasks in MIR, music genre classification plays a crucial role in automatically categorizing musical pieces into predefined genre categories where precise classification is required for various applications, such as content-based music recommendations, playlist generation, and music library organization [2,7,24]. However, the intricate, ambiguous, and subjective nature of music

© The Author(s), under exclusive license to Springer Nature Singapore Pte Ltd. 2025
R. Hadfi et al. (Eds.): PRICAI 2024, LNAI 15281, pp. 146–157, 2025.
https://doi.org/10.1007/978-981-96-0116-5_12

genres and the inherent variability within their categories can make this task significantly challenging [10].

Over the years, a large number of classification techniques have been employed for categorizing music genres, including supervised, unsupervised, and semi-supervised methods. In addition, ensemble learning techniques have shown their popularity for improving classification performance by integrating multiple base models to create a single classifier that is more robust and accurate. Traditional ensemble learning techniques, such as stacking [27], bagging [3], boosting [23], and voting, improve classification accuracy in many MIR tasks, including music genre classification. Despite these advancements, there is still significant potential in ensemble learning techniques for further enhancements. In particular, as illustrated in this study, conventional ensemble learning techniques may not effectively improve music genre classification accuracy in music datasets that comprise highly correlated low-level features related to music genres. To address this challenge, this study proposes an enhanced ensemble learning technique called *Augmented Features Ensemble Learning* (AFEL). This approach combines the strengths of base models by averaging their prediction probabilities, obtained through cross-validation, and incorporating them as additional features to the original feature set. Therefore, the AFEL technique creates a more expressive feature representation that captures the complementary strengths of the base models. Three publicly available music datasets with distinct characteristics, two featuring low correlation among sentimental features and one containing highly correlated acoustic features, were employed in the empirical experiments.

The results suggest that the proposed technique can effectively enhance genre classification performance in terms of accuracy compared to traditional ensemble learning techniques and is particularly beneficial when dealing with music datasets containing highly correlated low-level music features.

2   Previous Works

In recent years, numerous studies have suggested traditional and novel ensemble techniques to boost the genre classification performance in music in MIR. For instance, Silla *et al.* [26] utilized the *Latin Music Dataset* and introduced a novel automatic music genre classification method that employed multiple feature vectors and an ensemble learning technique. The study first divided the music signal into three segments, beginning, middle, and ending parts of the music, extracting features from each piece separately. Then, it merged binary classifiers to produce the final music genre label. This innovative ensemble approach led to improved performance in the majority of cases.

Chathuranga and Jayaratne [5] presented an ensemble approach using two feature vectors and a *Support Vector Machine* (SVM) classifier with a polynomial kernel function and aimed to improve classification accuracy by combining domain-based features from the frequency, temporal, cepstral, and modulation frequency domains. The ensemble technique in their study utilized fusion methods, including late fusion methods, which proved more robust than early fusion approaches. The study by Leartpantulak and Kitjaidure [15] aimed to classify songs into different music genres using feature extraction from audio signals, focusing on timbral texture, rhythmic content, and pitch content. They employed the *Particle Swarm Optimization* (PSO) algorithm for feature selection and utilized the stacking ensemble learning technique to improve prediction accuracy. First, using a music dataset with six genres, they extracted beat, timbral texture, and pitch-related features, resulting in a 43-dimensional feature vector. Then, PSO was applied to select the most important features, resulting in seven chosen features. The study findings suggested that the stacking ensemble learning technique and feature selection helped improve prediction accuracy, demonstrating its effectiveness in genre classification.

Sanden and Zhang [22] underscored the need for further efforts into ensemble techniques for multi-label genre classification tasks. They proposed a set of ensemble techniques, including *Bipartition-based* and *Score-based* ensembles, to address this gap and utilized the *Mulan* open-source library for multi-label learning. The experiments were conducted on three different datasets, revealing that the proposed heterogeneous ensemble techniques improved classification performance across all datasets. The work in [25] proposed a novel automatic approach for classifying genres by stacking SVM, *Relevance Vector Machine* and *Decision Trees*. First, each model was trained individually as *Error-Correcting Output Code Classifiers* (ECOC), transforming the multi-class classification problem into multiple binary classification problems. The results obtained from each binary classifier were then fused using the sum rule, where the classification decision is based on the sum of the posterior probabilities, to evaluate the outcome of the combined model. Finally, the proposed hybrid model was assessed and compared with the individual performances of the models used in the combination. The results indicated that the proposed approach outperformed the other models. Nani *et al.* [18] introduced a novel and efficient ensemble technique for automatic music genre classification by combining various acoustic and visual features from audio files. This approach initially extracted visual characteristics from images created through multiple audio-to-image representation methods, such as spectrogram, harmonic and percussion images, and scattergram. Next, these images were partitioned into sub-windows, from which a collection of local texture descriptors was obtained. Each texture descriptor was then employed to train a separate SVM, with the SVMs ultimately combined for the final output. The experiments in this study demonstrated that merging different texture features led to enhanced performance. In another study, De Almeida *et al.* [8] proposed a dynamic ensemble selection approach for music genre classification by utilizing two distinct pools of classifiers. The *k-Nearest Oracles* (KNORA) method was applied to select classifier ensembles for every test pattern dynamically. The work compared the performance of multiple selection strategies with the best single classifier and the combination of all classifiers in the pool. The experiments showed that the oracle performance of both classifier pools achieved high classification accuracy.

It should be noted that, due to space limitations and the ever-evolving nature of the field, the above literature may not encompass all relevant works but only highlight the effectiveness of ensemble learning techniques in music genre classification tasks. Nevertheless, traditional ensemble learning techniques can exhibit certain limitations. A primary drawback is their focus on merely combining base models without enhancing the representation of feature sets, potentially leading to suboptimal performance. This challenge becomes particularly problematic when dealing with music datasets containing highly correlated features, where base models can achieve satisfactory results without requiring ensemble learning techniques. Therefore, it is essential to develop improved approaches that address these limitations, especially for complex music datasets. Our efforts in this work are directed towards this end.

3   Augmented Features Ensemble Learning

The *Augmented Features Ensemble Learning* (AFEL) technique proposed in this work aims to enhance classification accuracy by effectively utilizing base models' prediction capabilities. Different from the traditional ensemble techniques, such as stacking and blending, AFEL's meta-model is trained on an expanded input feature set by considering the averaged prediction probabilities obtained from base models and using them further. It renders a more sophisticated representation of the input data and allows itself to capitalize on the original features and predictions from the base models. Equation 1 describes the mathematical representation of the AFEL technique in its general form.

$$\hat{y}_i = f_M \left(\text{concat} \left[\overrightarrow{x_i} \, , \, \frac{1}{N} \sum_{j=1}^{N} \overrightarrow{P_j^i}(y_i|\overrightarrow{x_i}, B_j) \right] \right) \tag{1}$$

where $\overrightarrow{x_i}$ is the original feature vector for the input sample i, $\overrightarrow{P_j^i}(y_i|\overrightarrow{x_i}, B_j)$ is the vector of predicted probabilities derived from base model B_j for $\overrightarrow{x_i}$, N is the number of base models involved, $f_M()$ is our meta-model proposed, and $\hat{y}_i$ is the final genre predicted on the augmented input sample i by our model.

In a nutshell, in our proposed AFEL technique, each base model B_j computes a prediction probability vector $\overrightarrow{P_j^i}(y_i|\overrightarrow{x_i}, B_j)$ for the target genre y_i. Such a vector consists of the probabilities of predictions for each possible genre, given $\overrightarrow{x_i}$ and B_j. The prediction vectors from all base models are summed up to form a vector, which is then divided by N, the number of base models, to generate an average prediction vector for $\overrightarrow{x_i}$. We then concatenate this average prediction vector with $\overrightarrow{x_i}$ to create an additional feature for each target genre label. This augmented feature set provides the meta-model $f_M()$ with more information for its classification task. It is expected that these additional pieces of information, in conjunction with the original features, would ultimately lead to an improved final genre prediction $\hat{y}_i$. Algorithm 1 shows the implementation of the AFEL technique for the music genre classification task in this study.

Algorithm 1. Conducting AFEL for genre classification

1: Divide (X, y) (i.e., (music features, genres)) into training and test sets
2: Initialize the set of base models
3: **for** each model in the set of base models **do**
4:     Predict genres using cross-validation on X_{train}
5: **end for**
6: Average the prediction probabilities across all models
7: Concatenate the averaged probabilities with the original features for training and Create X_{meta_train}
8: Initialize $f_M()$ (our proposed meta-model)
9: Train $f_M()$ on X_{meta_train} and y_{train}
10: **for** each model in the set of base models **do**
11:     Train the model on X_{train} and y_{train}
12:     Predict genres on X_{test}
13: **end for**
14: Calculate the average of the prediction probabilities from all base models
15: Concatenate the averaged probabilities with the original features for testing and Create X_{meta_test}
16: Call $f_M()$ to make final classifications on X_{meta_test}

This study utilized five base models representing diverse algorithm families for the AFEL technique and traditional ensemble learning techniques, including stacking, blending, and voting. The base models, with their default hyperparameters, are *Multi-layer Perceptron* (MLP) [17], *Random Forest* (RF) [4], *XGBoost* [6], *LightGBM* [11], and *k-Nearest Neighbors* (k-NN) [20]. Additionally, RF was selected as the meta-model due to its robust performance and capacity to handle linear and non-linear relationships effectively [4].

4   Datasets and Experiment Preparation

Three distinct datasets, *Spotify* [12], *TCC_CED* [16], and *GTZAN* [19], have been selected to assess the effectiveness of the traditional ensemble learning techniques and compare their performance with our proposed AFEL technique. These datasets vary in size and content, with the Spotify dataset comprising 232,725 music pieces, TCC_CED 28,372 pieces, and GTZAN 1,000 pieces.

4.1   Spotify Dataset

As shown in Fig. 1, the correlation analysis results obtained from the *Spearman Correlation* [13] method, which captures the monotonic relationships, reveal that there is generally a low correlation in the Spotify dataset between the features and with the music genres. The highest positive correlation with the genre is observed for acousticness (0.11), and the most negative correlation is for loudness (-0.14). Additionally, most features exhibit weak correlations with each other, with a few notable exceptions, such as energy and loudness (0.81) and acousticness and energy (-0.70).

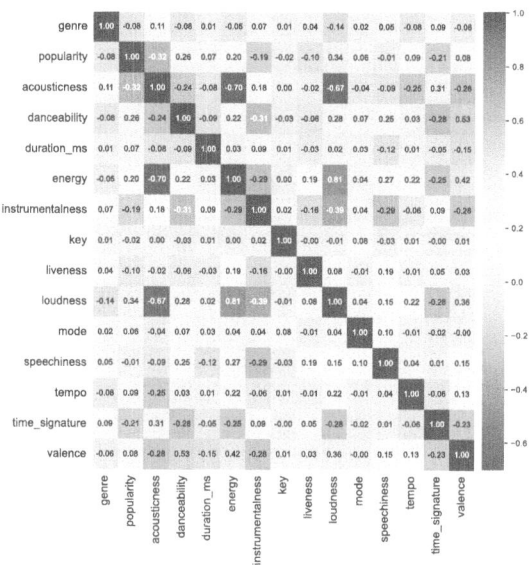

Fig. 1. The correlations among features in the Spotify dataset.

In the Spotify dataset, the high-level features are defined, rather than the acoustic features obtained directly from music signals. This could be a reason for the observed low correlations. Music genres are often distinguished by specific acoustic properties and patterns that are inherently present in the audio signals, such as timbre and harmony. The features in the Spotify dataset mainly represent its music pieces' attributes in sentiment and mood.

4.2   TCC_CED Dataset

Similar to the Spotify dataset, the correlation analysis for the TCC_CED, as shown in Fig. 2, demonstrates that most features exhibit a low correlation with each other and the music genre, with most values remaining near zero, indicating a weak relationship. The strongest negative correlation can be observed between energy and acousticness (-0.72), while the strongest positive correlation is between loudness and energy (0.77). Like the music pieces in Spotify, TCC_CED also mostly includes features associated with sentiment and mood, which may explain the low correlations observed.

4.3   GTZAN Dataset

The GTZAN dataset comprises some standard features in MIR, providing a fundamental indication of each track's sound and timbre, such as *Chroma Short-Time Fourier Transform* (Chroma STFT), *Spectral Rolloff*, *Spectral Centroid*, *Spectral Bandwidth*, *Zero Crossing Rate* (ZCR), and *Mel-Frequency Cepstral*

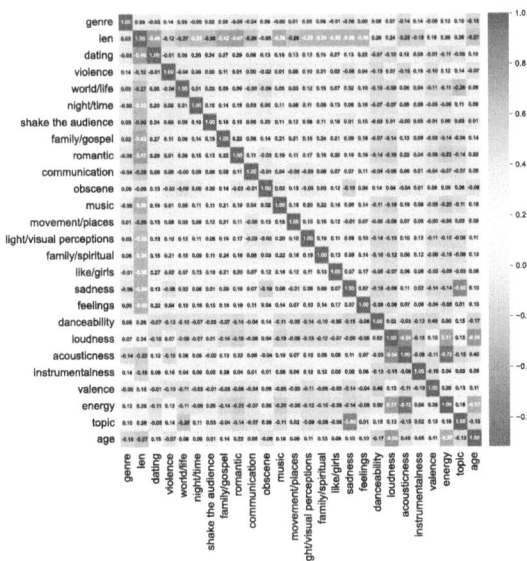

Fig. 2. The correlations among features in the TCC_CED dataset.

Coefficients (MFCCs). As shown in Fig. 3, the results obtained from the GTZAN music dataset reveal significant correlations between several features and the music genre. For instance, Chroma_stft (0.67), spectral_centroid (0.61), spectral_bandwidth (0.61), rolloff (0.60), and mfcc1 (0.46) show strong positive correlations with the music genre, while mfcc2 (−0.57) exhibits a significant negative correlation. In addition, there are frequent high correlations amongst the features themselves, such as spectral_centroid and rolloff (0.99), and between MFCCs. These high correlations could be attributed to the ingrained relationships between these features in music signals since they capture different aspects of the audio signal's structure and characteristics, often reflecting similar patterns or underlying components.

4.4 Data Preprocessing

The most frequent music genres from each dataset were selected to limit target variables and eliminate minority classes, as demonstrated in Table 1. Subsequently, the music genres were encoded, and the non-numeric music feature values were converted into numeric values and standardized using Z-score scaling to ensure compatibility with the research objectives.

4.5 Performance Validation

In this study, a 5-fold cross-validation procedure with an accuracy metric is utilized to evaluate the performance of the models. Cross-validation [21] is a

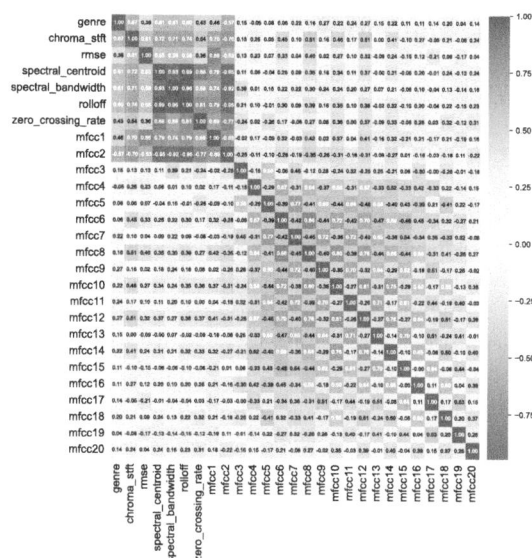

Fig. 3. The correlations among features in the GTZAN dataset.

Table 1. The top five music genres in each dataset.

Datasets	Genres
Spotify	Indie, Soundtrack, Comedy, Pop, Jazz
TCC_CED	Country, Blues, Rock, Pop, Jazz
GTZAN	Classical, Country, Disco, Hip Hop, Blues

technique that splits the data into multiple subsets, or "folds," to train and test the model multiple times [14], thus preventing overfitting and providing a reliable estimate of our model's performance. In particular, the cross-validation procedure with the accuracy metric (shown in Eq. 2) divides the data into five equal parts. The model is trained and tested five times, with one part serving as for testing once and the remaining parts for training. The accuracies of the testing results are then merged and averaged to estimate our model's overall final classification performance.

$$\overline{\text{Acc}} = \frac{1}{5}\sum_{k=1}^{5} \frac{\sum\limits_{i=1}^{C}(TP_{i,k} + TN_{i,k})}{\sum\limits_{i=1}^{C}(TP_{i,k} + TN_{i,k} + FP_{i,k} + FN_{i,k})} \qquad (2)$$

where C represents the number of genres in our experiment, $TP_{i,k}$, $TN_{i,k}$, $FP_{i,k}$, and $FN_{i,k}$ are the number of true positive, true negative, false positive and false negative instances for genre i in fold k, respectively.

5   Results and Discussions

The results from Fig. 4(a) indicate that in the Spotify dataset, ensemble learning techniques, specifically AFEL, stacking, and blending, demonstrated superior performance compared to individual models by leveraging the strengths of multiple models and compensating for individual model limitations. As indicated, AFEL emerged as the best-performing technique, with an average accuracy of 86.5%. Stacking and blending techniques exhibited comparable performance, with stacking slightly outperforming blending by 0.1%. Among individual models, MLP achieved the highest performance (80.8%) due to its ability to learn intricate, non-linear relationships despite low feature correlations. In contrast, k-NN had the poorest results (78.6%), likely due to its sensitivity to noisy features and its difficulty in finding meaningful neighbors in datasets with low feature correlations.

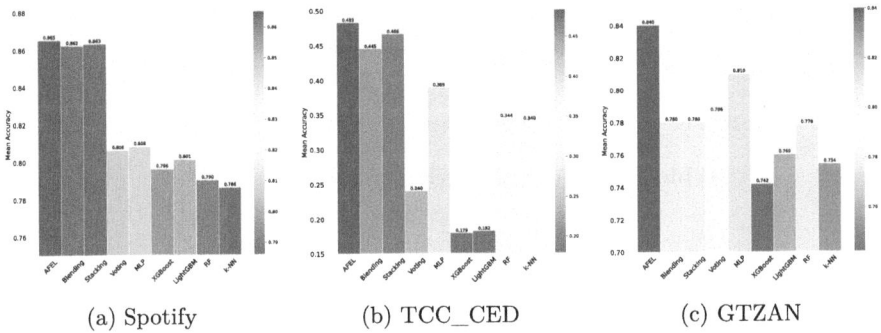

(a) Spotify   (b) TCC_CED   (c) GTZAN

Fig. 4. Performance comparison of models

These findings indicate that ensemble learning techniques that utilize a meta-model, such as stacking and blending, can be effective when handling datasets with low correlations, as they need the predictions from the base models to get the meta-model trained. While our AFEL technique demonstrates a marginal improvement in classification accuracy, it comes with increased computational costs due to the augmented feature set. Given the small differences in accuracy between AFEL, stacking, and blending, it is crucial to weigh these computational factors alongside with the model complexity when aiming to increase classification accuracy for the music pieces from the Spotify dataset.

As for the TCC_CED dataset, as shown in Fig. 4(b), the AFEL technique is ranked as the top-performing method with an average accuracy of 48.3%, followed by stacking at 46.6% and blending at 44.5%. The superior performance of ensemble learning techniques over individual models again highlights their advantages when dealing with datasets exhibiting low feature correlations.

Among the individual models, MLP outperformed the others with an average accuracy of 38.9%. In contrast, XGBoost and LightGBM demonstrated the lowest performance at 17.9% and 18.2%, respectively. The performance of XGBoost and LightGBM can rely significantly on optimizing the hyperparameters. Therefore, employing default hyperparameters in this study could have contributed to their inferior performance. The performance variation of individual models in the TCC_CED dataset, compared to the more consistent performance observed in the Spotify dataset, indicates that the effectiveness of different models might depend not only on the correlation between features but also on the unique characteristics of each dataset. Furthermore, the performance of ensemble learning techniques in both Spotify and TCC_CED datasets demonstrates their capacity to tackle the challenges posed by these datasets. AFEL, in particular, stands out by augmenting the original feature set, providing the meta-model with additional information for improved predictions. The GTZAN dataset, which includes high-level features derived from music signals, presents contrasting results compared to the previous datasets with low feature correlations. As demonstrated in Fig. 4(c), traditional ensemble techniques could not significantly improve performance and even fell short of the average accuracy of MLP (81%). These findings suggest that conventional ensemble techniques may have limited effectiveness when dealing with datasets containing acoustic features highly correlated to the music genre and where the base models already achieve satisfactory results.

Nevertheless, the AFEL technique overcomes this limitation, achieving the highest mean accuracy of 84.0%, outperforming the other ensemble techniques and individual models. This improvement can be attributed to AFEL's unique approach of augmenting the original feature set with averaged probabilities from the base models. Specifically, AFEL has the potential to grasp and catch more complex relationships between features and music genres by utilizing the original highly correlated features while providing the meta-model with additional information. This strategy sets AFEL apart from other ensemble techniques that only rely on base model predictions to train the meta-model. In addition, the advantages of our AFEL technique may lie in the fact that the additional prediction probabilities from base models provide another angle to look at the original data in a dataset. Essentially, their combination reveals more insights into the inherent relationships between features and music genres, strengthening the meta-model's confidence when classifying a new music piece.

It is also important to note that as the number of genres increases, the AFEL technique generates more augmented features, leading to a higher-dimensional feature space, which can result in overfitting due to the *Curse of Dimensionality* [1]. Our initial experiments showed that including all available genres led to performance decline due to this. Therefore, in each dataset, the analysis was limited to the top five genres, to maintain the robustness of our AFEL technique and reduce the negative impact of excessive dimensionality.

6   Conclusion and Future Work

This study introduced the fundamentals of *Augmented Features Ensemble Learning* (AFEL), a novel ensemble learning technique that improves genre classification performance, especially when dealing with music datasets incorporating features highly correlated. AFEL augments the original feature set with prediction capabilities from the base models, providing the meta-model with additional information to conduct better genre predictions. The experimental results on three distinct music datasets (Spotify, TCC_CED, and GTZAN) demonstrated AFEL's enhanced classification performance. The results also underscored AFEL's capability to handle diverse music datasets with varying feature characteristics and overcome the limitations of traditional ensemble techniques and individual models in MIR tasks. Another merit of AFEL lies in its adaptability, as both the base models and the meta-model can be substituted with alternative models to suit the classification task being tackled. However, it is essential to note that adopting ensemble learning techniques may come at the cost of increased computational time and resource requirements. Moreover, AFEL can potentially introduce noise in classification when dealing with a large set of genres, as it augments the original feature set based on the number of existing genres. According to the *Curse of Dimensionality* phenomenon, this increased dimensionality might make it harder for a meta-model to learn the underlying relationships in the data, resulting in decreased performance.

Future work would also focus on employing feature selection and dimensionality reduction techniques to decrease the dimensionality of the augmented feature space and further optimize the performance of the proposed method. Additionally, alternative approaches, including weighted and unweighted averages, would be explored to incorporate the prediction probabilities of base models and evaluate their impact on AFEL's performance. By addressing these challenges and refining the AFEL technique, it is anticipated that even more significant improvements in music genre classification performance can be achieved. In addition, the strategy in the AFEL technique can potentially apply to other data content, such as images, etc.

References

1. Bellman, R.E.: Dynamic Programming. Princeton University Press, New Jersey (2010)
2. Bonnin, G., Jannach, D.: Automated generation of music playlists: survey and experiments. ACM Comput. Surv. (CSUR) **47**(2), 1–35 (2014)
3. Breiman, L.: Bagging predictors. Mach. Learn. **24**, 123–140 (1996)
4. Breiman, L.: Random forests. Mach. Learn. **45**(1), 5–32 (2001)
5. Chathuranga, D., Jayaratne, L.: Musical genre classification using ensemble of classifiers. In: 2012 Fourth International Conference on Computational Intelligence, Modelling and Simulation, pp. 237–242. IEEE (2012)
6. Chen, T., et al.: Xgboost: extreme gradient boosting. R Package Version 0.4-2, vol. 1, no. 4, pp. 1–4 (2015)
7. Cunningham, S.J., Jones, M., Jones, S.: Organizing digital music for use: an examination of personal music collections. In: International Society for Music Information Retrieval Conference. ISMIR (2004)
8. de Almeida, P.R.L., da Silva Júnior, E.J., Celinski, T.M., de Souza Britto, A., de Oliveira, L.E.S., Koerich, A.L.: Music genre classification using dynamic selection of ensemble of classifiers. In: 2012 IEEE International Conference on Systems, Man, and Cybernetics (SMC), pp. 2700–2705. IEEE (2012)

9. Downie, J.S.: Music information retrieval. Ann. Rev. Inf. Sci. Technol. **37**(1), 295–340 (2003)
10. Fu, Z., Lu, G., Ting, K.M., Zhang, D.: A survey of audio-based music classification and annotation. IEEE Trans. Multimedia **13**(2), 303–319 (2010)
11. GuolinKe, Q.M., et al.: Lightgbm: a highly efficient gradient boosting decision tree. Adv. Neural Inf. Process. Syst. **30**, 52 (2017)
12. Hamidani, Z.: Ultimate spotify tracks db. Kaggle (2021)
13. Hauke, J., Kossowski, T.: Comparison of values of Pearson's and spearman's correlation coefficients on the same sets of data. Quaestiones Geographicae **30**(2), 87–93 (2011)
14. King, R.D., Orhobor, O.I., Taylor, C.C.: Cross-validation is safe to use. Nat. Mach. Intell. **3**(4), 276 (2021)
15. Leartpantulak, K., Kitjaidure, Y.: Music genre classification of audio signals using particle swarm optimization and stacking ensemble. In: 2019 7th International Electrical Engineering Congress (iEECON), pp. 1–4. IEEE (2019)
16. Moura, L., Fontelles, E., Sampaio, V., França, M.: Music topics and metadata. Mendeley Data, V1 (2020)
17. Murtagh, F.: Multilayer perceptrons for classification and regression. Neurocomputing **2**(5–6), 183–197 (1991)
18. Nanni, L., Costa, Y.M.G., Aguiar, R.L., Silla Jr, C.N., Brahnam, S.: Ensemble of deep learning, visual and acoustic features for music genre classification. J. New Music Res. **47**(4), 383–397 (2018)
19. Olteanu, A.: Gtzan dataset - music genre classification. Kaggle (2021)
20. Peterson, L.E.: K-nearest neighbor. Scholarpedia **4**(2), 1883 (2009)
21. Refaeilzadeh, P., Tang, L., Liu, H.: Cross-validation. Encycl. Database Syst. **5**, 532–538 (2009)
22. Sanden, C., Zhang, J.Z.: Enhancing multi-label music genre classification through ensemble techniques. In: Proceedings of the 34th International ACM SIGIR Conference on Research and Development in Information Retrieval, pp. 705–714 (2011)
23. Schapire, R.E.: The strength of weak learnability. Mach. Learn. **5**, 197–227 (1990)
24. Schedl, M., Gómez, E., Urbano, J., et al.: Music information retrieval: recent developments and applications. Found. Trends® Inf. Retrieval **8**(2–3), 127–261 (2014)
25. Sharma, S., Fulzele, P., Sreedevi, I.: Novel hybrid model for music genre classification based on support vector machine. In: 2018 IEEE Symposium on Computer Applications & Industrial Electronics, pp. 395–400. IEEE (2018)
26. Silla, C.N., Koerich, A.L., Kaestner, C.A.A.: A machine learning approach to automatic music genre classification. J. Braz. Comput. Soc. **14**, 7–18 (2008)
27. Wolpert, D.H.: Stacked generalization. Neural Netw. **5**(2), 241–259 (1992)

A Multi-layer Network Community Detection Method via Network Feature Augmentation and Contrastive Learning

Min Teng[1], Chao Gao[2(✉)], Zhen Wang[1], and Tanimoto Jun[3]

[1] School of Cybersecurity, Northwestern Polytechnical University,
Xi'an 710072, China
ttengmin@mail.nwpu.edu.cn

[2] School of Artificial Intelligence, OPtics and ElectroNics, Northwestern
Polytechnical University, Xi'an 710072, China
cgao@nwpu.edu.cn

[3] Interdisciplinary Graduate School of Engineering Sciences, Kyushu University,
Fukuoka, Japan
tanimoto@cm.kyushu-u.ac.jp

Abstract. Detecting the community structures of multi-layer networks is important for exploring the node functions and revealing the potential network structures. However, the existing methods mainly rely on the intra-layer features and manual labels, which leads to the high computational overhead and cannot ensure the robustness and accuracy in networks with complex community structures. To solve the above problems, this paper proposes a network feature-augmentation contrastive constraint method (named as NFACC), which achieves the high accuracy and robustness by contrasting the feature-augmented and original multi-layer networks. Specifically, NFACC consists of two main models, i.e., a feature-augmented network generation model and a contrastive learning-based node representation model. Firstly, NFACC integrates the intra-layer and inter-layer features of multi-layer networks to form an optimizable feature-augmented network based on the generation model. Then, it obtains the low-dimensional representations of both the augmented network and each layer of the multi-layer network based on the node representation model. By training these two models, NFACC further merges the intra-layer and inter-layer features and improves the robustness against complex network structures. Finally, NFACC achieves accurate community detection through the trained node representations. Extensive experiments demonstrate that the proposed NFACC method outperforms the state-of-the-art methods in detecting the community structure of multi-layer networks.

Keywords: Multi-layer network · Feature augmentation · Contrastive learning · Community detection

© The Author(s), under exclusive license to Springer Nature Singapore Pte Ltd. 2025
R. Hadfi et al. (Eds.): PRICAI 2024, LNAI 15281, pp. 158–169, 2025.
https://doi.org/10.1007/978-981-96-0116-5_13

1   Introduction

In the real world, entities interact through multiple relationships, forming complex systems. Complex networks are essential for studying these systems as they abstract complex interactions into nodes and edges, representing entities and their relationships, respectively [1]. Community structure, a fundamental aspect of networks, plays a crucial role in revealing the underlying functions of complex systems [2]. Community detection, a central task in network science, aims to accurately identify these structures, which is crucial for understanding node functions and uncovering the potential network topologies. Traditional methods for community detection in single-layer networks are limited to identifying the community structures based on a single type of relationship between entities [3]. In reality, entities are typically involved in multiple types of relationships [4]. Therefore, it is essential to develop multi-layer community detection methods, which can more accurately capture the functions of complex systems by accounting for various types of relationships [5].

Many methods have been proposed to extend the single-layer community detection methods to multi-layer networks. For example, Marko et al. compress a multi-layer network into a single-layer network and then use the traditional single-layer network community detection method to solve the problem of multi-layer network community detection [6]. However, these methods do not consider the connection between layers, which leads to the information loss [4]. Given these problems, researchers have proposed many community detection methods for the special structure of multi-layer networks, including unsupervised and semi-supervised methods. These two types of methods solve the consensus community dividing problem by simultaneously optimizing the topology of each network layer, and making full use of the topological information of multi-layer networks to ensure the high accuracy of community detection [7,8]. However, these methods mainly rely on the intra-layer features or manual labels. In networks with complex topologies and numerous layers, complex structural information or substantial manual labels will hinder the performance of community detection, making it challenging to detect the consensus communities [4].

To address the aforementioned limitations, we propose a multi-layer network community detection method based on the network feature augmentation and contrastive learning, named NFACC. NFACC leverages the rich information contained in datasets to detect the consensus community structures in multi-layer networks. Specifically, NFACC first fuses the intra-layer and inter-layer features and generates an optimizable feature-augmented network, thereby getting rid of the limitations imposed by manual labels. Then, it obtains the low-dimensional representations of both the augmented network and multi-layer network based on the node representation model. Meanwhile, it trains the low-dimensional node representations by contrastive learning, effectively addressing the challenge of accurate community detection in multi-layer networks. The main contributions can be summarized as follows:

- A new feature-augmented network generation model is proposed to generate a feature-augmented network, which is used as a positive example for contrastive learning and eliminates the dependence on manual labels.
- A new contrastive learning-based node representation model is introduced to address the fusion of the intra-layer and inter-layer features. Meanwhile, the node representation is trained by contrastive learning to closely align the outputs of the augmented network and the multi-layer network in the low-dimensional space. By training the above two models, NFACC achieves the high accuracy and robustness without the guidance of manual labels.

The rest of this paper is organized as follows. Section 2 summarizes the related works of multi-layer community detection. Section 3 show the proposed NFACC method. Section 4 shows the extensive experiments. Section 5 gives the conclusion of the paper.

2 Related Work

2.1 Unsupervised Learning-Based Methods

Unsupervised learning-based community detection methods are mainly based on the topology of a multi-layer network and obtain the optimal community divisions based on different methods. For instance, Pizzuti et al. introduced MLMaOP, a many-objective optimization method for community detection. MLMaOP treats each layer as an optimization objective, optimizing all objectives simultaneously to derive a consensus community division [9]. Extensive results underscore the high competitiveness of MLMaOP compared to alternative methods. In addition, Dong et al. introduced the SC-ML method, leveraging the Grassmannian manifold for fusing multi-layer network features. This method initially computes the low-dimensional subspace spanned by the principal eigenvectors of the Laplacian matrix corresponding to each layer [10]. By considering each subspace as a point on the Grassmann manifold, it aggregates all subspaces into a consensus subspace and extracts the consensus community division of the multi-layer network using K-means clustering. Extensive experiments in several artificial and real-world networks verified the effectiveness of the SC-ML. However, although researchers have proposed many methods and each method has its own advantages, existing unsupervised methods face challenges in accurately detecting the community structure in networks with complex structure [11].

2.2 Semi-supervised Learning-Based Methods

To mitigate the excessive reliance on the network structure and improve the accuracy of community detection, some researchers integrated the concept of semi-supervised learning. They proposed semi-supervised learning-based community detection methods specifically designed for multi-layer networks. For example, Gao et al. introduced a new multi-objective evolutionary method, MOEA-CPI, based on the consensus prior information. MOEA-CPI extracts the graph-level and node-level information using Node2vec and Jaccard similarity as prior knowledge to guide the topology, initialization, and optimization processes of MOEA, achieving accurate community structure identification [12]. However, the semi-supervised learning-based community detection methods rely on manual labels or consensus prior information mining, incurring significant time and computational overhead.

In conclusion, we propose a self-supervised method that leverages the rich information inherent in the dataset to generate a feature-augmented network, thereby getting rid of the limitations of manual labels. Moreover, by employing the contrastive learning, we train the node representations of the feature-augmented network and the original network, effectively addressing the challenge of insufficient community detection accuracy in complex structures.

3   The Proposed NFACC Method

3.1   Problem Definition

This paper focuses on multi-layer networks, where each layer contains an identical set of nodes. Specifically, a multi-layer network is defined as $G = (V, E_l)$, with $|V| = N$ and $l = \{1, 2, \ldots, L\}$. Here, G denotes the multi-layer network. V is the node set (with nodes corresponding one-to-one across layers). E_l is the edge set of the l_{th} layer, representing a distinct type of relationship. N is the number of nodes. The aim of multi-layer community detection is to identify a consensus community structure across layers, while considering the complex interactions between the various types of relationships.

3.2   Proposed Method

NFACC mainly consists of three main parts, i.e., the feature-augmented network generation model, contrastive learning-based node representation model, and identification of the consensus communities.

The Feature-Augmented Network Generation Model. Network feature augmentation is a technique designed to enhance model performance by artificially increasing the diversity of training datasets. This technique is particularly useful for datasets with sparse data or limited labeled samples. The primary objective of network feature augmentation is to modify the existing data to generate new, enriched datasets or to create augmented features. Additionally, studies have demonstrated that dual-layer GCNs and MLPs are important tools for network feature augmentation [13]. Therefore, we propose a feature-augmented network generation model based on dual-layer GCN and MLP to efficiently get rid of the manual labels and learn the augmented features of G.

To integrate both inter-layer and intra-layer features of G, we construct an optimizable feature-augmented network $G_F = \{V, E_F\}$. Here, the node set V is the same as in G, and E_F is the union of E_l for $l \in \{1, 2, \ldots, L\}$. G_F integrates features from all layers of G and provides the augmented feature.

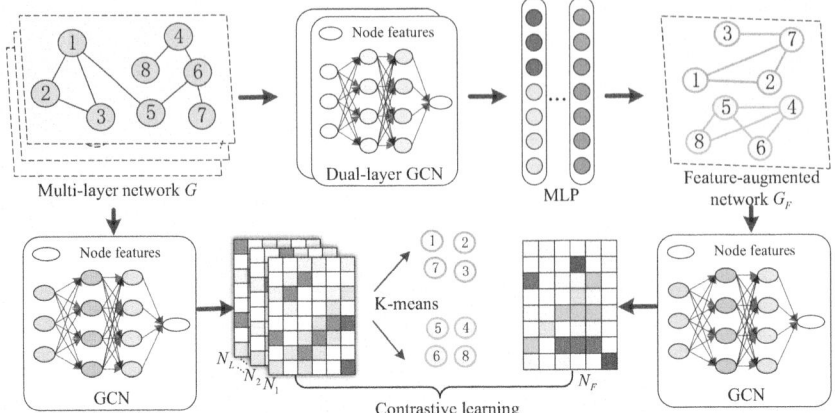

Fig. 1. The framework of the proposed NFACC method. The proposed method comprises three main components, i.e., a feature-augmented network generation model via dual-layer GCN and MLP, a contrastive learning-based node representation model via GCN, and the identification of consensus communities via the K-means method.

Specifically, we first extract and integrate the node features from each layer by aggregating information from its neighbor nodes. This paper uses a dual-layer GCN to accurately aggregate the information from neighbor nodes and generate the node representation H_l for each layer.

$$H_l = PReLU\left(\hat{A}_l PReLU\left(\hat{A}_l X_l W_{(l_0)}\right) W_{(l_1)}\right) \tag{1}$$

where H_l denotes the node representation matrix of the l_{th} layer, A_l is the adjacency matrix, $\widetilde{A}_l = A_l + I$, where I is the identity matrix. $\widetilde{A}_l$ represents the symmetrically normalized A^l, and $\hat{A}_l = D_l^{-1/2}\widetilde{A}_l D_l^{-1/2}$, where D is the degree matrix. X_l is the one-hot feature. $W_{(l_0)}$ and $W_{(l_1)}$ are the learnable weight matrices, and $PReLU$ is the activation function.

To integrate the information from each layer into G_F, NFACC calculates the consensus node representation H_c by averaging the H_l across all layers.

$$H_c = \sum_{l=1}^{L} H_l / L \tag{2}$$

Finally, H_c is used as the input to an MLP to obtain the weight matrix Y for the nodes of G_F.

$$Y = MLP(H_c) \tag{3}$$

The Contrastive Learning-Based Node Representation Model. To constrain and train the node representations of each layer of G, we use the node representations of G_F as anchors, while the corresponding node representations of layers in G serve as positive samples. By minimizing the divergence between the anchors and the positive samples, NFACC ensures that node representations across different layers are mutually informative, thereby effectively capturing the consensus features within the network.

Firstly, using the G_F as input, the feature-augmented node representation H_F is generated by the node representation model (GCN in Fig. 1), and subsequently normalized to obtain N_F.

$$N_F = Normalize(PReLU\left(\hat{A}_F Y W_F\right)) \tag{4}$$

where A_F denotes the adjacency matrix of G_F, Y represents the matrix generated by the MLP, and W_F is the learnable weight matrix.

Then, the original topology and one-hot features of each layer are used as inputs to get the node representation H_l for each layer, which is then normalized to obtain N_l.

$$N_l = Normalize(PReLU\left(\hat{A}_l X_l W_l\right)) \tag{5}$$

where A_l denotes the adjacency matrix of the l_{th} layer of G, X_l represents the one-hot feature, and W_l is the learnable weight matrix.

Finally, to ensure that the node representation of each layer can learn the features from other layers, we design a loss function to minimize the difference between N_l and N_F. Specifically, $N_F(i)$ for each node v_i in G_F serves as the anchor, while $N_l(i)$ for corresponding nodes in G serves as positive samples. By minimizing the difference between $N_F(i)$ and $N_l(i)$, $N_l(i)$ can effectively learn features across different layers.

$$\text{loss} = -\sum_{l=1}^{L} \text{mean}\left(\log\left(\text{diag}\left(s\left(N_F N_l^T / \tau\right)\right)\right)\right) \tag{6}$$

where L denotes the number of network layers, $\text{diag}\left(s\left(N_F N_l^T / \tau\right)\right)$ denotes the diagonal matrix of the softmax operation on the vectors N_l, $\text{mean}(*)$ denotes averaging $*$, $s(*)$ denotes a softmax operation on the vectors, and τ is a constant. The loss calculates the similarity between N_F and N_l by $\text{diag}()$. By optimizing the loss, the difference between the node representations of G_F and the corresponding node in each layer of G is minimized.

Identification of the Consensus Communities. To enhance the integration of intra-layer and inter-layer features and achieve the accurate community detection, this paper averages the trained N_l across layers to obtain the consensus node representation H.

$$H = \frac{1}{L}\sum_{l=1}^{L} N_l \tag{7}$$

The consensus community division ω is obtained based on the H and K-means method:

$$\omega = \{c_1, c_2, ..., c_q\} \tag{8}$$

where q is the community number. The pseudo-code is shown in Algorithm 1.

Algorithm 1 NFACC.

Input: A multi-layer network, G;
Output: The consensus community structure, ω;
1: Initialize parameters;
2: **for** $epoch=1$ to $Epoch$ **do**
3:    **for** $l=1$ to L **do**
4:       Calculate the representation H_l of each layer based on the Eq. (1);
5:    **end for**
6:    Calculate the consensus representation H_c based on the Eq. (2);
7:    Generate the features Y of G_F by MLP based on the Eq. (3);
8:    Calculate the normalized representation N_F of G_F based on the Eq. (4);
9:    **for** $l=1$ to $Layer$ **do**
10:       Calculate the normalized representation N_l of each layer based on the Eq. (5);
11:    **end for**
12:    Calculate the loss between N_l and N_F based on the Eq. (6);
13:    Backward and update the two GCNs and MLP;
14: **end for**
15: Merge the trained N_l and generate the consensus community structure ω by K-means based on the Eqs. (7) and (8).

---

4   Experiments

4.1   Experimental Setup

Comparison Methods and Parameter Settings. Six comparison methods, MOEA-MultiNet [14], COMCLUS [15], S2-jNMF [4], SC-ML [10], GMC [16], and GEAM [17], are selected for comparison. Moreover, the $Epoch$ is set as 90, and τ is set as 1.5 in this paper. Additionally, the parameter settings of comparison methods are consistent with their original papers.

Datasets. The datasets consist of four real-world datasets and two sets of artificial datasets. The basic information of datasets is shown in Table 1. Among them, WTN [18], WBN [19], CoRA [20], and Citeseer [20] are real-world datasets. A-data1 and A-data2 are artificial datasets constructed by mLFR [21].

Table 1. Basic information of datasets.

Dataset	Layers	Nodes	Communities	Edges
WTN	14	183	5	3343
WBN	5	279	10	5307
CoRA	3	1662	3	9235
Citeseer	2	3312	3	24790
A-data1	3	128	4-8	1523
A-data2	9	128	4-8	14785

Metrics. Two common metrics namely Normalized Mutual Information (NMI) and Adjusted Rand Index (ARI) are used in this paper to verify the performance of the methods.

NMI, a widely used metric in community detection [22], effectively measures the dissimilarity between the detected community division and the ground truth community division, providing a measure of community detection accuracy. The NMI is defined in Eq. (9).

$$NMI = \frac{I(\omega;C)}{|H(\omega) + H(C)|/2} \tag{9}$$

where ω denotes the detected community division, C denotes the ground truth community division, $I(\omega;C)$ is the mutual information, and $H(\omega)$ denotes the entropy of ω. The value of NMI ranges from 0 to 1. The closer the NMI value is to 1, the ω is more similar to C.

ARI provides an effective assessment of the accuracy rate by measuring the proportion of correct community divisions [23]. The ARI is defined in Eq. (10).

$$ARI = \frac{RI - E(RI)}{\max(RI) - E(RI)} \tag{10}$$

where $E(RI)$ and $\max(RI)$ denote the expectation of RI and the maximum value of RI, respectively. The RI is defined in Eq. (11).

$$RI = \frac{TP + TN}{TF + FP + FN + TN} \tag{11}$$

where TP and TN denote the correct decisions, FP and FN denote the incorrect decisions. Specifically, TP denotes the number of node pairs that are divided into the same communities in both C and ω. TN denotes the number of node pairs that are divided into different communities in both C and ω. FP denotes the number of node pairs that are divided into different communities in C but into the same communities in ω. FN denotes the number of node pairs that are divided into the same communities in C but into different communities in ω. Based on the above four decisions, a higher value of ARI indicates a higher proportion of correct decisions, which in turn indicates a higher accuracy of community detection.

4.2   Results and Analysis

Results in Real-World Datasets. Table 2 illustrates the superiority of the proposed NFACC method across four different real-world datasets. Specifically, the S2-jNMF method, which employs the semi-supervised learning to extract consensus-dense subgraphs as prior information, performs well in datasets with clear structures like CoRA. However, it underperforms in the WTN and WBN datasets, which consist of more layers, due to its insufficient utilization of inter-layer information. The MOEA-MultiNet method optimizes community detection in multi-layer networks by maximizing modularity and minimizing shared costs through the integration of genetic operations and local search. While it performs adequately in the WBN dataset, it demonstrates average performance in the CoRA dataset and fails to detect community structures in the Citeseer and WTN datasets. This suboptimal performance may stem from the method's inability to fully capture the complex intra-layer features and fuse the features between different network layers during the optimization process. Similarly, GMC also underperforms in the Citeseer and WTN datasets. This can be attributed to GMC's approach of aggregating graph matrices from all views and fusing them into a single unified matrix, which may dilute critical inter-layer information. Both COMCLUS and SC-ML exhibit average performance across all four datasets. Surprisingly, GEAM, which is based on contrastive learning, also shows average performance, indicating its inadequacy in effectively integrating inter-layer and intra-layer features. In contrast, NFACC achieves high accuracy and robustness across all datasets by leveraging contrastive learning to guide model optimization. This approach effectively integrates both intra-layer and inter-layer information, enabling NFACC to perform exceptionally well across datasets of varying scales.

Table 2. The results in real-world datasets. "-" represents that the method cannot successfully detect the community structures and the bold represents that the method has the best performance.

Dataset	Metrics	NFACC	MOEA-MultiNet	COMCLUS	S2-jNMF	SC-ML	GMC	GEAM
WTN	NMI	**0.235**	0.140	0.183	0.157	0.231	0.203	0.227
	ARI	**0.154**	0.052	0.105	0.069	0.129	0.015	0.152
WBN	NMI	**0.403**	0.401	0.328	0.072	0.327	0.223	0.342
	ARI	0.192	0.189	0.176	0.076	**0.276**	0.005	0.157
CoRA	NMI	**0.892**	0.317	0.471	0.769	0.480	0.519	0.171
	ARI	**0.901**	0.243	0.447	0.813	0.485	0.426	0.086
Citeseer	NMI	**0.377**	-	0.182	0.149	0.191	0.042	0.057
	ARI	**0.381**	-	0.119	0.147	0.169	0.012	0.051

Results in Artificial Datasets. To further validate the robustness of the proposed method across different dataset topologies, we employed the mLFR method to generate various artificial datasets. Specifically, two datasets, A-data1 and A-data2, were created, comprising 3 and 9 layers, respectively, with parameters set to $\mu = \{0.5, 0.6\}$ and $D_c = \{0.2 - 0.8\}$. Specifically, increasing μ leads to denser inter-community connections and more complex structures. This trend is evident when comparing Figs. 2(a) and (c) with Figs. 2(b) and (d), where the algorithm's performance declines and shows greater fluctuations. Similarly, as D_c increases, structural differences between nodes across layers become more pronounced. This is reflected in the comparison of Figs. 2(a) and (b) with Figs. 2(c) and (d), where performance decreases and exhibits more significant variations with the increase in D_c. As illustrated in Fig. 2, NFACC consistently demonstrates superior performance, exhibiting smoother fluctuations compared to other methods as D_c varies. In Figs. 2(a) and (c), NFACC shows minimal fluctuation, underscoring its robustness. As shown in Figs. 2(b) and (d), where the network structure is more complex, NFACC still maintains high accuracy and outperforms the other methods. Notely, its effectiveness declines in datasets with $D_c = 0.8$, likely due to increased degree differences among nodes across layers, leading to significant variations. Despite this, NFACC consistently outperforms the comparison methods across most D_c values. In summary, these results highlight the superior robustness of the proposed NFACC across diverse datasets, even in networks with complex structures and ambiguous community boundaries ($\mu = 0.6$).

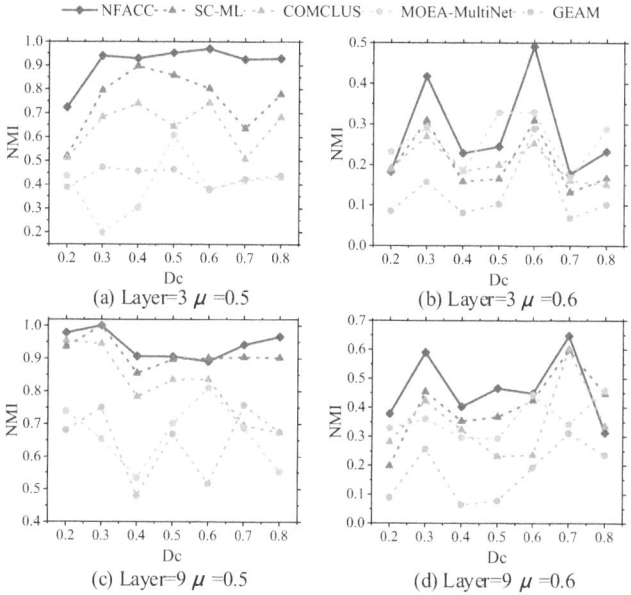

Fig. 2. The results in artificial datasets. (a) and (b) belong to the A-data1 dataset. (c) and (d) belong to the A-data2 dataset.

Overall, these findings suggest that the proposed NFACC method maintains the high accuracy across datasets with diverse topologies, demonstrating its robustness in accurately detecting network communities when guided by an optimizable feature-enhanced network.

5   Conclusion

To address the heavy reliance on intra-layer features and manual labels, and the lack of robustness and high accuracy in networks with complex community structures, this paper proposes a new self-supervised community detection method for multi-layer networks. Specifically, the method mainly consists of two main models, i.e., a feature-augmented network generation model and a contrastive learning-based node representation model. The former is used to fuse the features of the multi-layer network to generate an optimizable feature-augmented network, thereby getting rid of the limitations imposed by manual labels. The latter leverages the feature-augmented network and the original multi-layer network to obtain and train low-dimensional node representations, effectively addressing the challenge of community detection in networks with complex structures. The extensive experiments in four real-world datasets and two artificial datasets verify the performance of the proposed NFACC, demonstrating its robustness in practical applications.

Acknowledgments. This work was supported by the National Key R&D Program of China (No. 2022YFE0112300), the National Natural Science Foundation of China (Nos. U22B2036, 11931015, 61976181), Fok Ying-Tong Education Foundation China (No. 171105), Technology Innovation Leading Program of Shaanxi (No. 2023GXLH-086), the Fundamental Research Funds for the Central Universities (No. G2024WD0151), and the XPLORER PRIZE.

References

1. Berenhaut, K.S., Moore, K.E., Melvin, R.L.: A social perspective on perceived distances reveals deep community structure. Proc. Natl. Acad. Sci. **119**(4), e2003634119 (2022)
2. Kong, L., Gao, C., Peng, S.: Clustering-based network inference with submodular maximization. In: Khanna, S., Cao, J., Bai, Q., Xu, G. (eds.) PRICAI 2022. LNCS, vol. 13629, pp. 118–131. Springer, Cham (2022). https://doi.org/10.1007/978-3-031-20862-1_9
3. Wang, Z., Xia, C., Chen, Z., Chen, G.: Epidemic propagation with positive and negative preventive information in multiplex networks. IEEE Trans. Cybern. **51**(3), 14541462 (2020)
4. Ma, X., Dong, D., Wang, Q.: Community detection in multi-layer networks using joint nonnegative matrix factorization. IEEE Trans. Knowl. Data Eng. **31**(2), 273286 (2018)
5. Yuvaraj, M., Dey, A.K., Lyubchich, V., Gel, Y.R., Poor, H.V.: Topological clustering of multilayer networks. Proc. Natl. Acad. Sci. **118**(21), e2019994118 (2021)
6. Rodriguez, M.A., Shinavier, J.: Exposing multi-relational networks to single-relational network analysis algorithms. J. Informetrics **4**(1), 29–41 (2010)
7. Huang, X., Chen, D., Ren, T., Wang, D.: A survey of community detection methods in multilayer networks. Data Min. Knowl. Disc. **35**(1), 145 (2021)
8. Gao, X., et al.: Multi-view clustering with self-representation and structural constraint. IEEE Trans. Big Data **8**(4), 882893 (2021)
9. Pizzuti, C., Socievole, A.: Many-objective optimization for community detection in multi-layer networks. In: Proceedings of the 2017 IEEE Congress on Evolutionary Computation, pp. 411–418 (2017)
10. Dong, X., Frossard, P., Vandergheynst, P., Nefedov, N.: Clustering on multi-layer graphs via subspace analysis on grassmann manifolds. IEEE Trans. Signal Process. **62**(4), 905918 (2013)

11. Yang, L., Cao, X., Jin, D., Wang, X., Meng, D.: A unified semi-supervised community detection framework using latent space graph regularization. IEEE Trans. Cybern. **45**(11), 25852598 (2014)
12. Gao, C., Yin, Z., Wang, Z., Li, X., Li, X.: Multilayer network community detection: a novel multi-objective evolutionary algorithm based on consensus prior information [feature]. IEEE Comput. Intell. Mag. **18**(2), 4659 (2023)
13. Gao, F., et al.: Soft contextual data augmentation for neural machine translation. In: Proceedings of the 57th Annual Meeting of the Association for Computational Linguistics, pp. 5539–5544 (2019)
14. Liu, W., Wang, S., Gong, M., Zhang, M.: An improved multiobjective evolutionary approach for community detection in multilayer networks. In: Proceedings of the 2017 IEEE Congress on Evolutionary Computation, pp. 443–449 (2017)
15. Ni, J., Cheng, W., Fan, W., Zhang, X.: Comclus: a self-grouping framework for multi-network clustering. IEEE Trans. Knowl. Data Eng. **30**(3), 435448 (2017)
16. Wang, H., Yang, Y., Liu, B.: GMC: graph-based multi-view clustering. IEEE Trans. Knowl. Data Eng. **32**(6), 11161129 (2019)
17. Wang, B., Cai, X., Xu, M.H., Xiang, W.: A graph-enhanced attention model for community detection in multiplex networks. Expert Syst. Appl. **230**, 120552 (2023)
18. Dong, X., Frossard, P., Vandergheynst, P., Nefedov, N.: Clustering with multilayer graphs: a spectral perspective. IEEE Trans. Signal Process. **60**(11), 58205831 (2012)
19. De Domenico, M., Nicosia, V., Arenas, A., Latora, V.: Structural reducibility of multilayer networks. Nat. Commun. **6**(1), 19 (2015)
20. Sen, P., Namata, G., Bilgic, M., Getoor, L., Galligher, B., Eliassi-Rad, T.: Collective classification in network data. AI Mag. **29**(3), 93–93 (2008)
21. Bródka, P.: A method for group extraction and analysis in multilayer social networks. arXiv preprint arXiv:1612.02377 (2016)
22. Amelio, A., Pizzuti, C.: Community detection in multidimensional networks. In: Proceedings of the 26th IEEE International Conference on Tools with Artificial Intelligence, pp. 352–359 (2014)
23. Gligorijević, V., Panagakis, Y., Zafeiriou, S.: Non-negative matrix factorizations for multiplex network analysis. IEEE Trans. Pattern Anal. Mach. Intell. **41**(4), 928940 (2018)

Scene Text Recognition Based on Corner Point and Attention Mechanism

Hui Wang, Tao Hu, Xiaoke Geng, and Kai Li[✉]

School of Computer Science and Technology, Huazhong University of Science and Technology,
Wuhan 430074, China
kli@hust.edu.cn

Abstract. The irregular distribution of text is a significant challenge for current scene text recognizers. Rectification methods based on Thin-Plate Spline (TPS) are adopted by various recognizers due to their plug-and-play nature. However, since the TPS transformation parameters are determined based on text boundaries regressed, it struggles to focus on the position of text areas relative to the image and fails to suppress background interference. Although the rectified images retain the geometric structure of the text, this leads to unnatural character deformation and characters exceeding the image boundaries. To address these issues, this paper proposes a scene text recognition algorithm based on corner points and attention mechanisms. Firstly, a novel irregular text rectification algorithm named CornerTPS is introduced, which integrates corner features with image features, allowing the TPS transformation to focus on character position information and improving the rectification effect for irregular text. Then, CornerTPS is improved to a feature-level rectification, and the rectified corner feature map is integrated into the encoder, further guiding the encoder to focus on text area features and reducing the interference of non-text area corners. Experiments on public datasets demonstrate that the algorithm proposed in this paper has a significant advantage in irregular text recognition.

Keyword: Scene text recognition · Text rectification · Thin-Plate Spline · Corner point map · Attention mechanism

1 Introduction

Scene Text Recognition (STR) aims to identify text instances cropped from real-world scenes into a sequence of characters, such as text on packaging, billboards, and display screens. Due to the diversity of text variations, including distortion, occlusion, blurriness, cluttered backgrounds, and various fonts, constructing a high-quality scene text recognition system remains a complex task. Despite the challenges, STR has numerous practical applications, such as signboard text recognition in autonomous driving, content-based image retrieval, and understanding of street view images. The mainstream approaches in scene text recognition currently are based on Connectionist Temporal Classification (CTC) [1, 2] and attention mechanism-based encoder-decoder methods [3–5].

© The Author(s), under exclusive license to Springer Nature Singapore Pte Ltd. 2025
R. Hadfi et al. (Eds.): PRICAI 2024, LNAI 15281, pp. 170–181, 2025.
https://doi.org/10.1007/978-981-96-0116-5_14

In the context of irregular scene text recognition, text rectification is an effective method. Typically, text rectification is part of the preprocessing stage, aimed at correcting distorted or skewed text to produce an image with text that is approximately horizontally distributed. Rectifiers based on Thin-Plate Spline (TPS) [7] transformations have shown unsatisfactory performance when dealing with challenging distorted text images. The primary reason is that they determine the TPS transformation parameters based on the text boundaries obtained through regression, which are derived from weakly supervised learning and are not accurate enough for text area localization. Moreover, the existing localization networks within TPS transformations tend to focus more on overall image features, making it difficult to pay attention to the positional information of the text area relative to the image, and they are also unable to suppress background interference. As a result, although the rectified images maintain the geometric structure of the text, they also lead to unnatural character deformation and issues where characters exceed the boundaries.

Based on the analysis of the limitations of current TPS-based rectification methods, this paper proposes an algorithm for Scene Text Recognition Based on Corner Point and Attention Mechanism (CAM-STR). Initially, this paper introduces an irregular text rectification algorithm based on the corner point, referred to as CornerTPS. Subsequently, CornerTPS is enhanced to a feature-level rectification, where the rectified corner point feature map is fed into the encoder. This further guides the encoder to focus on the features of the text area and to reduce the interference from non-text area corner points.

The main contributions of this paper are summarized in the following three aspects:

1. This paper utilizes the corner point as an auxiliary feature of the input image. In irregular text, although the fonts and shapes of characters vary, the relative positions of the corner points of the same character's strokes can be considered invariant. Moreover, since the corner point map is sparse, it can suppress most of the background interference.
2. CornerTPS employs a dynamic fusion block to integrate corner point features with image features, using the positional information carried by the corner point map to highlight the features of the text area in the image. This allows the TPS rectification to focus on the character position information, thereby improving the rectification effect of irregular text.
3. This paper refines CornerTPS to a feature-level rectification by incorporating the rectified corner point features into the encoder. This reduces the interference from non-text area corner points on text recognition, enhancing the accuracy of irregular text recognition.

2 Related Work

Based on the transformation forms of text rectification, methods based on text rectification can be broadly categorized into methods based on affine transformation, methods based on Thin-Plate Spline (TPS), and other methods. Methods based on affine transformation aim to eliminate the tilt of text content caused by the shooting angle through simple operations such as translation, scaling, and rotation, but struggle to address distortions caused by the text content itself, such as fan-shaped text and artistic fonts. The first work in this category was conducted by STN [6], which is primarily used for general object rectification.

Generally, irregular text obtained in real scenes usually exhibits anisotropic distortion, which is difficult to correct using affine transformations. Shi et al. proposed ASTER [8] model, replacing the affine transformation in STN with TPS to achieve more flexible rectification. However, due to the weakly supervised nature of STN, the calculation of TPS parameters for highly distorted text is not accurate enough, so RARE and ASTER may not be able to crop a complete text area from the text image, leading to the loss of text information. To better handle this situation, ESIR [9] developed an iterative rectification scheme, designing a novel linear fitting transformation to model the posture of scene text and correct perspective and curvature distortions, reducing the dependence on the quality of control point regression but increasing time consumption. In addition to these two main methods, MORAN [10] treats the text image as a grid and directly regresses the offset of each intersection point. However, since these offsets are not constrained by any geometric transformations, unnatural distortions may occur. SPIN [11] designed a structure-preserving rectifier to address text instances with color distortion.

Compared to these methods, the CornerTPS proposed in this paper utilizes the corner point map as an auxiliary input, enabling the rectification network to focus on character position information, thereby significantly reducing the unnatural distortions exhibited by rectifiers such as TPS. Additionally, CornerTPS retains the weakly supervised nature of the TPS transformation, requiring only word-level annotation, which facilitates its integration into different recognizer frameworks and reduces the difficulty of subsequent recognition.

3 Methodology

3.1 CornerTPS

The CornerTPS structure proposed in this section is depicted in Fig. 1, which includes a corner point detection module, a feature extraction module, and a Corner-Incorporated Parameter Calculation (CIPC). Given an original text image $X \in \mathbb{R}^{H \times W \times 3}$, a corner point detector is first used to generate a corner point map $M \in \mathbb{R}^{H \times W \times 1}$. Then, both X and M are fed into the same feature extractor to generate the original image features F_X and the corner point features F_M. What differs is that the image features will also pass through Coordinate Attention (CA) [12] to highlight important features. Subsequently, CIPC utilizes the features F_X and F_M to generate the final control points. The subsequent process is identical to the standard TPS transformation.

CornerTPS retains the plug-in nature of TPS and can serve as a preprocessor for most scene text recognizers, reducing the difficulty of subsequent recognition.

3.2 Corner-Incorporated Parameter Calculation

The CIPC module receives the image features $F_X \in \mathbb{R}^{C \times H \times W}$ and the corner point features $F_M \in \mathbb{R}^{C \times H \times W}$ extracted by the feature extraction module, which are used to regress the control points. The structure of the feature extractor is shown in Table 1.

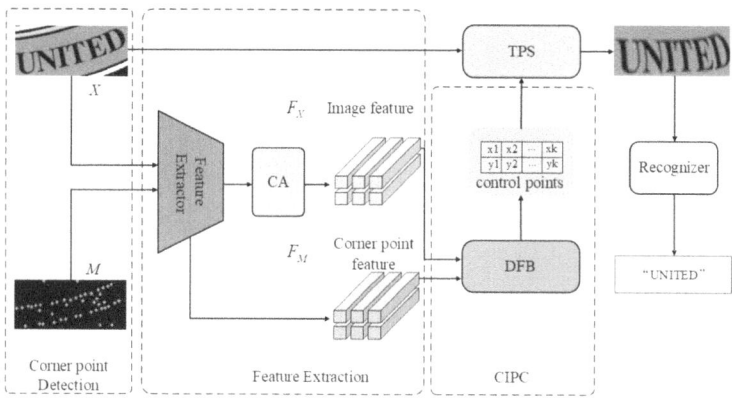

Fig. 1. Architecture of the CornerTPS

In the regression of control points, unlike the traditional TPS that initializes control points along the image boundary, this section adopts the control point initialization method proposed by Zheng et al. [13]. Specifically, the control points $C \in \mathbb{R}^{HW \times 2}$ are uniformly distributed across the image, similar to a grid distribution. As a result, most of the control points are located in the text foreground rather than on the boundary with less information. The number of control points is equal to the spatial resolution of the features F_X and F_M.

After passing through the Dynamic Fusion Block (DFB), the image features are reshaped into a feature sequence $F_X^{''} \in \mathbb{R}^{HW \times C}$ then goes through two linear layers to predict the offset of each control point in the x and y dimensions, combining with the initialized coordinates to obtain the regressed control points $C' \in \mathbb{R}^{HW \times 2}$.

Table 1. Architecture of feature extractor convolution networks

Layers	Configuration	Output
Layer1	Conv(3,64,1*1,1)	32*128
Layer2	Conv(64,64,3*3,2)	16*64
Layer3	Conv(64,128,3*3,2)	8*32
Layer4	Conv(128,256,3*3,2)	4*16

The DFB's structure is shown in Fig. 2, and its core idea is to dynamically weight the image features F_X using the corner point map features F_M to produce character position-aware features F_X', thereby optimizing the control point regression process.

Firstly, two pooling kernels $(H, 1)$ and $(1, W)$ are used to perform one-dimensional average pooling on the corner point map features F_M along the height H and width W dimensions, reducing them to two feature sequences of size $C \times 1 \times W$ and $C \times H \times 1$. After passing through a softmax function, weights along the H and W dimensions are

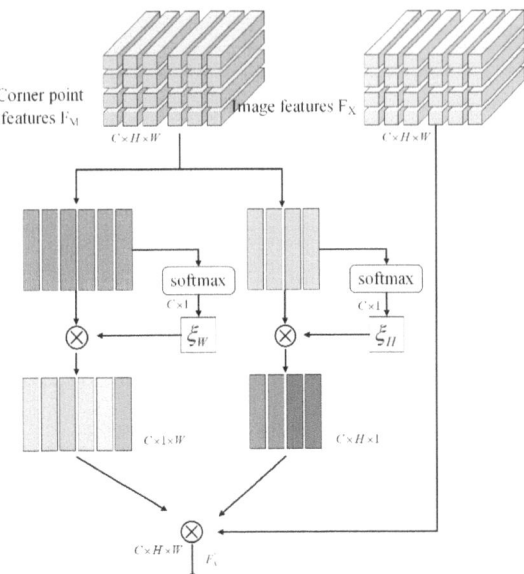

Fig. 2. Architecture of Dynamic Fusion Bolck

calculated, denoted as ξ_H and ξ_W, representing the importance of each row and column, respectively, and reflecting the distribution of corner point features in different directions.

Next, the two obtained feature sequences are multiplied by their corresponding weights ξ_H and ξ_W, thereby enhancing the contribution of important parts within the features. Finally, after passing through a sigmoid function, corner point attention weights ω_H and ω_W are obtained along the height H and width W dimensions.

Lastly, the attention weights ω_H and ω_W are element-wise multiplied with the original text image features F_X to generate the final feature sequence F_X'. By dynamically adjusting the original image features with weights, not only are the key information in the original features retained, but the focus on important areas during the rectification process is also enhanced. F_X' is then fed into a linear layer to predict the offset of each control point on the x-axis and y-axis, thus completing the precise regression of the control points C'.

3.3 CAM-STR

CAM-STR is depicted in Fig. 3, and the structure of the algorithm includes two main modules: feature-level rectification based on CornerTPS and a Transformer encoder that incorporates the corner point. Given the input text image $X \in \mathbb{R}^{H \times W \times 3}$, a shallow CNN composed of two convolutional layers is first applied to obtain the feature representation of the image. Concurrently, a corner point detector is applied to the image to generate the corresponding corner point map $M \in \mathbb{R}^{H \times W \times 1}$, and a shallow CNN is similarly applied to the corner point map to obtain the corner point features.

Next, the image features and corner point features are sent into the CornerTPS for feature-level rectification, resulting in the rectified features $X' \in \mathbb{R}^{\frac{H}{4} \times \frac{W}{4} \times C}$ and

$M' \in \mathbb{R}^{\frac{H}{4} \times \frac{W}{4} \times C}$, where C is the feature dimension. Subsequently, X' and M' are sent into the Transformer encoder that incorporates the corner point map. X' learns the global features of the image X'_d through the multi-head self-attention mechanism and dynamic convolution, while M' is combined with X'_d through the multi-head cross-attention mechanism. Finally, the encoder outputs the features to the Transformer decoder to generate a feature sequence.

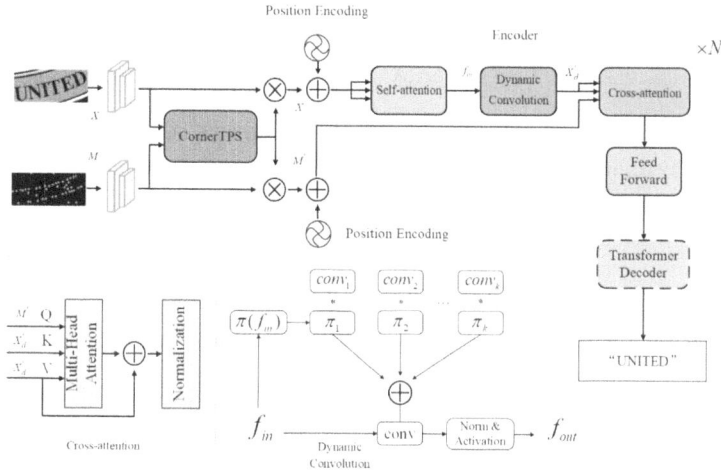

Fig. 3. Architecture of CAM-STR

3.4 Feature-Level Rectification

In the majority of scene text recognition algorithms predicated on text rectification, the text rectifier is configured as a preprocessing step. This approach incurs a significant computational load due to the execution of feature extraction twice. To surmount this limitation, the design of CornerTPS incorporates the sharing of image features with the backbone network of the recognizer, thereby mitigating redundant computations. Specifically, the initial two convolutional layers of the feature extractor within CornerTPS are shared with the shallow CNN of the backbone network. Contrary to initializing control points on the original image, the CornerTPS as depicted in Fig. 3 initiates control points on the feature map output by the shallow CNN. Likewise, the ultimate TPS transformation is also conducted on the feature map.

3.5 Transformer Encoder

Following the acquisition of the rectified text image features and the corner point map features, adaptive 2D positional encoding is initially integrated to incorporate positional information. This section employs the Corner-guided Encoder introduced by Xie et al. [14], with a distinction that the encoder inputs for the CAM-STR have been rectified, thereby effectively mitigating the interference from background elements and corner points in non-textual regions. Additionally, Dynamic Convolution (DC) is introduced to further refine and augment the image feature representation at each stratum of the encoder. To elaborate, within each layer of the encoder, multi-head self-attention is initially deployed to amplify the contextual information of the image features. The multi-head self-attention architecture, analogous to the cross-attention structure delineated in Fig. 3, utilizes the rectified image features as Query (Q), Key (K), and Value (V), with the computation articulated in Eq. (1).

$$f_{in} = SA(Q, K, V) = SA(X', X', X') = softmax(\frac{X'X'^T}{\sigma})X' \tag{1}$$

The Dynamic Convolution (DC) operates in a nonlinear fashion to derive attention maps $\{\pi_k(f_{in})\}$ from the input feature map f_{in}, and dynamically amalgamates a set of K parallel convolutional kernels $\{\tilde{W}_k, \tilde{b}_k\}$, as illustrated in Eqs. (2) and (3).

$$\tilde{W} = \sum_k \pi_k(f_{in})\tilde{W}_k \tag{2}$$

$$\tilde{b} = \sum_k \pi_k(f_{in})\tilde{b}_k \tag{3}$$

The aggregated convolutional kernels $\tilde{W}, \tilde{b}$ are then applied to the input feature map f_{in} to derive the image features X'_d. Post the dynamic convolution, a multi-head cross-attention layer is introduced, leveraging the image features X'_d as both keys and values, and the corner point features M' as queries, to yield an augmented feature representation. The computation of the corner point query in cross-attention is analogous to that of the multi-head self-attention, as delineated in Eq. (4).

$$CCA(Q, K, V) = CCA(M', X'_d, X'_d) = softmax\left(\frac{M'X'^T_d}{\sigma}\right)X'_d \tag{4}$$

Herein, CCA refers to the Corner Cross-Attention mechanism, with σ serving as the scaling coefficient. The corner point map encapsulates the relative spatial information of the characters present in the textual imagery. Employing the corner point map as the querying agent facilitates the pinpointing of salient image features by the corner points. Furthermore, given that the input corner point map has undergone rectification, its corner points are primarily localized within the character domains of the imagery, thereby effectively reducing the disruptive influence of corner points situated in non-textual regions.

4 Experiment

4.1 Dataset and Evaluation Metrics

Following the standard paradigm for experiments in scene text recognition algorithms, the method proposed in this paper is trained on two synthetic datasets and evaluated on six publicly available real-world scene datasets. These datasets are as follows:

MJSynth (MJ) [15] and SynthText (ST) [16] are two synthetic datasets used for training, with 8.91M and 6.95M text instances, respectively.

ICDAR2013 (IC13) [17], Street View Text (SVT) [18], IIIT5k-Words (IIITK) [19], ICDAR2015 (IC15) [20], SVT-Perspective (SVTP) [21], and CUTE80 (CUTE) [22] are the six test sets commonly used to evaluate scene text recognition algorithms. The first three mainly contain regular text, while the last three are primarily composed of irregular text.

4.2 Implementation Details

In the preprocessing phase of the images, the dimensions of all input images are standardized to 32×128 for training as well as evaluation purposes, with a batch processing size of 256. These images undergo various random data augmentation techniques, including minor affine transformations and the introduction of Gaussian noise. The training spans over 6 epochs, utilizing the Adam optimization algorithm and relying solely on word-level annotations. The initial learning rate is established at 3×10^{-4}, which is subsequently reduced to 3×10^{-5} at the commencement of the 4th epoch. A Warm-up strategy is implemented during the initial epoch to mitigate the training gradient volatility, with the initial Warm-up ratio configured at 0.001.

4.3 Ablation Study on Text Rectification

In order to ascertain the efficacy of the individual constituents of CornerTPS, this section employs ASTER as the reference model, substituting its TPS transformation module for the CornerTPS in the context of an ablation study. With the aim of curtailing the duration of training, the ablation experiments are confined to the ST dataset, and assessments are executed on three real-world datasets characterized by irregular text (IC15, SVTP, CUTE). The experimental parameters adhere to the protocols delineated in the preceding sections.

(1) Validating the Effectiveness of the Corner Point Map

In the CornerTPS rectification algorithm, a Dynamic Fusion Block is introduced to leverage the corner point map for more accurate control point regression, thereby optimizing the rectification process for irregular text images. However, the introduction of the corner point map as an additional input raises the question of whether the improvement in rectification effect is primarily due to the increase in input information, rather than the contribution of the corner point map itself. To explore this issue, the corner point map was replaced with other types of images, and multiple ablation experiments were conducted to assess the effectiveness of the corner point map in improving the rectification effect. The experimental results are shown in Table 2.

Initially, the corner point map input within the Dynamic Fusion Block was replaced with the original image, forming an experimental configuration termed "Image + Image." Compared to the baseline model, there was a slight degradation in recognition performance under this configuration. This outcome suggests that the noise and redundant information contained within the original image may lead to incorrect guidance during the rectification process, thereby reducing the rectification effect.

Subsequently, considering that projection segmentation images can also convey the structure and positional information of characters, the corner point map input was replaced with projection segmentation images, creating an experimental setup known as "Image + Seg." Compared to the baseline model, this configuration showed some improvement in rectification effect, indicating that projection segmentation images can assist in text rectification to a certain extent. However, the performance was still lower than that of "Image + Corner," suggesting that projection segmentation images might also contain misleading information with a limited positive contribution to the rectification effect.

In summary, the experimental results lead to the conclusion that the corner point map plays an essential role in enhancing the rectification effect in the CornerTPS algorithm.

Table 2. The effectiveness of corner map

Input	IC15	SVTP	CUTE
Baseline	74.8	76.2	76.8
Image + Corner	**75.5**	**77.4**	**78.5**
Image + Image	74.5	76.0	76.4
Image + Seg	75.3	77.2	78.3

(2) Validating the Effectiveness of the Dynamic Fusion Block

In CornerTPS, the effective fusion of corner point map features with image features is crucial for enhancing the rectification effect. This process determines whether the model can fully leverage the positional information in the corner point map to highlight the features of the text area in the image. To explore the impact of different feature fusion methods on rectification performance, in addition to employing the DFB method, several feature fusion strategies such as addition (Add), multiplication (Multiply), and cross-attention (Cross-attention) were also compared. The experimental results are shown in Table 3.

The additive operation directly sums the corner point features and image features element-wise. Compared to the Baseline, the additive operation leads to a decline in rectification performance. This is primarily because the additive operation may directly introduce noise into the image features and also makes it difficult to differentiate between noise and positional information in the corner point features, thereby reducing the rectification effect.

The multiplicative operation enhances the image features in valuable areas of the corner point map by element-wise multiplication, which to some extent filters out irrelevant background information and makes the model more focused on the location of the text. Compared to the Baseline, the improvement brought by the multiplicative operation is not significant. The cross-attention operation, on the other hand, integrates corner point features and image features through a more complex method, using the attention mechanism to dynamically focus on features that are effective for rectification. However, due to the weakly supervised nature of the TPS rectification process, the cross-attention mechanism struggles to leverage its advantages, resulting in limited performance improvement.

In summary, by comparing different feature fusion strategies, the DFB method has been validated as an efficient strategy for integrating corner point features and image features.

Table 3. The effectiveness of different fusion strategies

fusion strategies	IC15	SVTP	CUTE
Baseline	74.8	76.2	76.8
DFB	**75.5**	**77.4**	**78.5**
Add	74.6	76.0	76.5
Multiply	75.2	76.6	77.4
Cross-attention	75.3	76.8	78.1

4.4 Experimental Results on Text Recognition

Table 4. Comparison results on six standard test datasets

Methods	Regular			Irregular		
	IIIT5K	SVT	IC13	IC15	SVTP	CUTE
CRNN [1]	78.2	80.8	86.7	-	-	-
SATRN [3]	92.8	91.3	94.1	79.0	86.5	87.8
ABINet-LV [5]	**96.2**	93.5	**97.4**	**86.0**	<u>89.3</u>	89.2
GTR [23]	<u>95.8</u>	<u>94.1</u>	<u>96.8</u>	84.6	87.9	**92.3**
SGBANet [24]	95.4	89.1	95.1	78.4	83.1	88.2
ASTER [8]	93.4	89.5	91.8	76.1	78.5	79.5
ESIR [9]	93.3	90.2	91.3	76.9	79.6	83.3
MORAN [10]	91.2	88.3	92.4	68.8	76.1	77.4
SPIN [11]	95.2	90.9	94.8	79.5	83.2	87.5
ASTER + CornerTPS	93.7	90.3	93.7	78.4	81.7	86.3
CAM-STR	95.6	**94.2**	96.2	<u>85.8</u>	**90.6**	<u>91.6</u>

Table 4 presents the comparative experimental results on six standard test datasets. Compared with text rectification-based methods, CAM-STR outperforms all the text rectification recognition algorithms listed in the table. Under the same training conditions, CAM-STR achieved the highest recognition accuracy on two test datasets (SVT, SVTP), and on other test datasets, CAM-STR also approached the accuracy of the current best methods. It is worth mentioning that in the irregular text test set, CAM-STR's overall recognition performance is the best in the table, indicating that CornerTPS can effectively rectify irregular text and reduce the difficulty of subsequent recognition. Compared with ASTER, the accuracy of ASTER + CornerTPS for irregular text improved by about 4%, thus proving the plug-and-play nature of CornerTPS, which can be embedded into most mainstream recognizers to enhance performance and achieve superior recognition results.

5   Conclusion

This paper addresses the issue that current TPS rectification methods struggle to focus on character position information, leading to suboptimal rectification effects, by proposing a scene text recognition algorithm called CAM-STR based on the corner point map and attention mechanism. Initially, an irregular text rectification algorithm called CornerTPS, which incorporates the corner point map, is introduced. The corner point map carries positional information to highlight the features of the text area in the image, enabling TPS rectification to focus on character position information and thus improving the rectification effect of irregular text. Subsequently, CornerTPS is refined to a feature-level rectification, which, while reducing redundant computations, incorporates the rectified corner point feature map into the corner-guided encoder, diminishing the interference of non-text area corner points on text recognition. Comparative and ablation experiments demonstrate that the proposed method in this paper has a distinct advantage in the recognition of irregular text.

References

1. Shi, B., Bai, X., Yao, C.: An end-to-end trainable neural network for image-based sequence recognition and its application to scene text recognition. IEEE Trans. Pattern Anal. Mach. Intell. **39**(11), 2298–2304 (2016)
2. Du, Y., Chen, Z., Jia, C., et al.: SVTR: scene text recognition with a single visual model. In: International Joint Conference on Artificial Intelligence, pp. 884–890 (2022)
3. Lee, J., Park, S., Baek, J., et al.: On recognizing texts arbitrary shapes with 2D self attention. In: IEEE/CVF Conference on Computer Vision and Pattern Recognition Workshops, pp. 2326–2335 (2020)
4. Zhang, B., Xie, H., Wang, Y., et al.: Linguistic more: taking a further step toward efficient and accurate scene text recognition. In: International Joint Conference on Artificial Intelligence, pp. 1704–1712 (2023)
5. Fang, S., Xie, H., Wang, Y., et al.: Read like humans: autonomous, bidirectional and iterative language modeling for scene text recognition. In: IEEE/CVF Conference on Computer Vision and Pattern Recognition, pp. 7094–7103 (2021)
6. Jaderberg, M., Simonyan, K., Zisserman, A., et al.: Spatial Transformer Networks. In: Neural Information Processing Systems (2015)
7. Bookstein, F.: Principal warps: thin-plate splines and the decomposition of deformations. IEEE Trans. Pattern Anal. Mach. Intell. **11**(6), 567–585 (1989)
8. Shi, B., Yang, M., Wang, X., et al.: ASTER: an attentional scene text recognizer with flexible rectification. IEEE Trans. Pattern Anal. Mach. Intell. **41**(9), 2035–2048 (2019)

9. Zhan, F., Lu, S.: ESIR: end-to-end scene text recognition via iterative image rectification. In: IEEE/CVF Conference on Computer Vision and Pattern Recognition, pp. 2054–2063 (2019)
10. Luo, C., Jin, L., Sun, Z.: MORAN: A Multi-Object Rectified Attention Network for scene text recognition. Pattern Recogn. **90**, 109–118 (2019)
11. Zhang, C., Xu, Y., Cheng, Z., et al.: SPIN: structure-preserving inner offset network for scene text recognition. In: AAAI Conference on Artificial Intelligence, pp. 3305–3314 (2021)
12. Hou, Q., Zhou, D., Feng, J.: Coordinate attention for efficient mobile network design. In: IEEE/CVF Conference on Computer Vision and Pattern Recognition, pp. 13708–13717 (2021)
13. Zheng, T., Chen, Z., Bai, J., et al.: TPS++: attention-enhanced thin-plate spline for scene text recognition. In: International Joint Conference on Artificial Intelligence, pp. 1777–1985 (2023)
14. Xie, X, Fu, L., Zhang, Z., et al.: Toward understanding WordArt: corner-guided transformer for scene text recognition. In: European Conference on Computer Vision, pp. 303–321 (2022)
15. Jaderberg, M., Simonyan, K., Vedaldi, A., et al.: Synthetic data and artificial neural networks for natural scene text recognition. arXiv Preprint (2014). arXiv:1406.2227
16. Gupta, A., Vedaldi, A., Zisserman, A.: Synthetic data for text localisation in natural images. In: IEEE Conference on Computer Vision and Pattern Recognition, pp. 2315–2324 (2016)
17. Karatzas, D., Shafait, F., Uchida, S., et al.: ICDAR 2013 robust reading competition. In: International Conference on Document Analysis and Recognition, pp. 1484–1493 (2013)
18. Wang, K., Babenko, B., Belongie, S.: End-to-end scene text recognition. In: IEEE International Conference on Computer Vision, pp. 1457–1464 (2011)
19. Mishra, A., Alahari, K., Jawahar, C.: Scene text recognition using higher order language priors. British Machine Vision Conference, pp. 1–12 (2012)
20. Karatzas, D., Gomezbigorda, L., Nicolaou, A., et al.: ICDAR 2015 competition on Robust Reading. In: International Conference on Document Analysis and Recognition, pp. 1156–1160 (2015)
21. Phan, T., Shivakumara, P., Tian, S., et al.: Recognizing text with perspective distortion in natural scenes. In: IEEE International Conference on Computer Vision, pp. 569–576 (2013)
22. Risnumawan, A., Shivakumara, P., Chan, C., et al.: A robust arbitrary text detection system for natural scene images. Expert Syst. Appl. **41**(18), 8027–8048 (2014)
23. He, Y., Chen, C., Zhang, J., et al.: Visual semantics allow for textual reasoning better in scene text recognition. In: AAAI Conference on Artificial Intelligence, pp. 1210–1218 (2022)
24. Zhong, D., Lyu, S., Shivakumara, P., et al.: SGBANet: semantic GAN and balanced attention network for arbitrarily oriented scene text recognition. In: European Conference on Computer Vision, pp. 464–480 (2022)

A Comprehensive Framework
for Debiased Sample Selection Across All
Noise Types

Naihao Wang and Ruirui Li[✉]

Beijing University of Chemical Technology, Beijing, China
{wangnaihao,liruirui}@mail.buct.edu.cn

Abstract. Label noise poses a challenging task, impacting the model's generalization when trained with noisy labels. Existing noise is primarily categorized as symmetric/asymmetric noise, instance-dependent noise, and real-world noise. Most current methods are effective under specific assumptions, limiting their ability to handle all types of noise. To address this issue, we propose a debiased sample selection method. Initially, we ensure noise sparsity in each training iteration through sample correction. Subsequently, to achieve accurate sample partitioning, we employ implicit regularization and debiasing techniques to obtain more robust representations. Additionally, we use feature-based K-nearest neighbors (KNN) for clean sample selection during training. To enhance generalization, we incorporate common consistency regularization techniques. Extensive experiments demonstrate the effectiveness of our approach.

Keywords: noisy label learning · implicit regularization · debias · semi-supervised learning · sample selection

1 Introduction

Deep learning has achieved remarkable advancements in recent years, leading to breakthroughs in various domains such as computer vision, natural language processing, and speech recognition. Nonetheless, procuring a model with robust generalization capabilities often necessitates meticulously curated datasets for supervised training, which in turn demands high-quality annotations. In practical scenarios, a substantial portion of data is frequently devoid of high-quality labels, or any labels, rendering labeled data annotation both costly and time-consuming.

Current strategies for acquiring annotations include crowdsourcing and web scraping, significantly diminishing the duration and expense associated with sample labeling. However, these approaches inherently introduce low-quality, noisy labels into the datasets, detrimentally affecting model performance. Consequently, the challenge of effectively mitigating the adverse impact of noisy labels

This work was supported in part by National Natural Science Foundation of China under Grant No. 62101021.

on model training has emerged as a prominent and dynamic area of research within deep learning. Researchers are actively exploring novel methodologies to enhance the reliability of models trained on imperfect datasets, aiming to bolster their robustness and generalization skills despite noise in the training data.

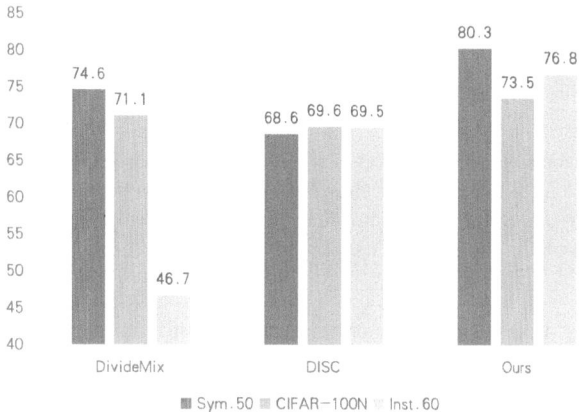

Fig. 1. Performance Comparison of Models Under Various Noise Types: DivideMix excels on symmetric noise but performs averagely on real-world noise and IDN. DISC excels on IDN and real-world noise but performs averagely on symmetric noise. Our model demonstrates good performance across all noise types.

In recent developments in imperfect information learning, sample selection methods such as DivideMix [8] have garnered attention for their approach in bifurcating data into clean and noisy samples. Clean samples are treated as labeled data, while noisy samples are treated as unlabeled data, facilitating learning through semi-supervised methods. However, methods based on sample selection are heavily dependent on the model and the selection strategy utilized. If the chosen data contains mislabeling errors or lacks balance, the model trained on this data will likely exhibit bias. This bias, in turn, can exacerbate labeling errors and data imbalance. Current research has explored a variety of sample selection strategies, such as small-loss sample selection, Co-teaching [4] mutual selection and instance-dependent selections like DISC [10]. Nevertheless, no single sample selection strategy has proven to be generally applicable across varying noise types, diverse training stages, and disparate data distribution conditions. Figure 1 illustrates the performance of models under various noise conditions. This limitation significantly hampers the practical applicability of these robust methods in real-world scenarios.

We propose a novel approach that combines explicit feature voting selection with implicit sparse selection. Additionally, we introduce a large margin loss to mitigate bias and optimize the model's representation during training. Our contributions can be summarized as follows:

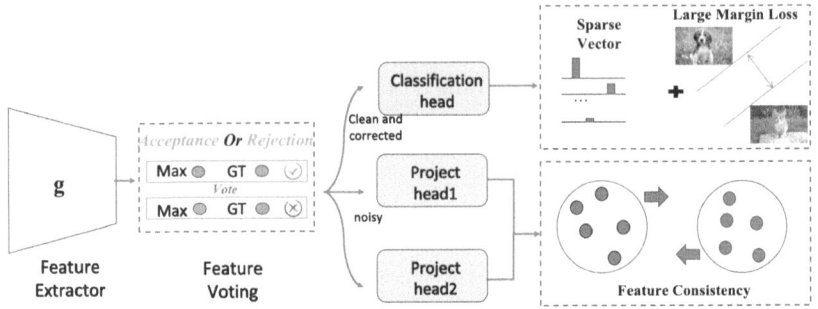

Fig. 2. The Architecture of Our Proposed Method: Clean samples selected through explicit feature voting and corrected samples are fed into a supervised training head with sparse regularization for further implicit clean sample learning. Uncorrected noisy samples undergo feature consistency constraint training.

- We introduce a dual selection mechanism that combines explicit feature voting and implicit sparse selection.
- We propose a new large margin loss to enhance model representation.
- We develop a general framework that achieves optimal classification accuracy without requiring parameter adjustment, applicable to both synthetic and real datasets with varying types and ratios of noise.

2   Related Work

Many early studies focused on developing robust loss functions, proposing methods such as the Mean Absolute Error (MAE) [2], Generalized Cross Entropy [18] and Symmetric Cross Entropy (SCE) [14]. These powerful loss functions provide a certain degree of protection against overfitting noise in the model. However, they often underperform when confronted with complex label noise.

In the context of class-dependent noise, numerous studies have attempted to estimate the noise transition matrix [3,11]. The Dual T method [16] mitigates the reliance on posterior probability by decomposing the transition matrix into two matrices that are easier to estimate. The Cycle T method [1] views the transition matrix as a small learnable network and estimates it through forward-backward cycle consistency regularization. Although these methods theoretically maintain statistical consistency, they struggle to adapt to different types and levels of noise due to the inherent difficulty in accurately estimating the transition matrix.

Currently, popular approaches for learning with noisy labels are based on sample selection methods. Some techniques aim to mitigate confirmation bias by designing better sample selection strategies. For example, UniCon [20] proposes a unified sample selection strategy based on the Jensen-Shannon divergence. DISC [10] leverages dual-view training and devises an instance-dependent dynamic threshold to divide the dataset into three subsets-clean, hard, and noisy-and processes them separately. Other methods attempt to optimize the representation space using self-supervised learning techniques. For instance, CC [19] employs maximum-minimum consistency regularization to obtain more robust latent space representations, preventing the model from overfitting to noise. The latest trend involves combining representation learning and prediction probabilities during the training process for sample selection.

3   Method

We propose a versatile framework to address all current types of noise, termed Debiased Sample Selection (DSS), as illustrated in Fig. 2. Our algorithm is remarkably straightforward, delivering optimal results through dual selection mechanisms: explicit feature voting and implicit sparse selection, coupled with a debiasing technique embedded within the representation. The specific details of the proposed methodology will be elaborated on in subsequent sections.

We initially cast this problem as a classification task for convenience and clarity, with the number of classes denoted by C. We define the dataset as $D = \{(x_i, y_i)\}_{i=1}^{N}$, where x_i and y_i represent the i-th sample and its associated noisy label, respectively. The variable θ denotes the parameters of the network, and N indicates the dataset size. The function $f()$ is the network prediction, and $L()$ represents the Cross-Entropy (CE) loss.

3.1   Explicit Feature Voting

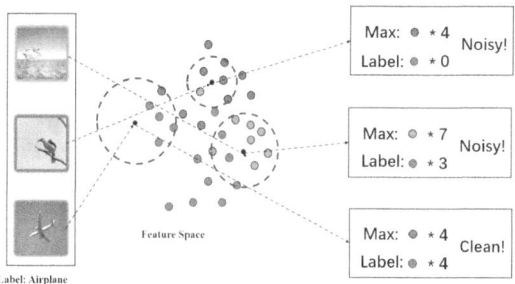

Fig. 3. Sample Selection Based on Normalized Feature Similarity with Top-K Voting for Clean Sample Identification

Explicit sample selection is conducted at the feature level, which can be considered a relatively crude method for sample selection. The initial sample features are derived from representations learned during the pre-training phase or the warm-up stage. Subsequently, these features are updated and refined from representations that the model learns and modifies throughout the training process (Fig. 3).

With these sample features in hand, we measure the similarity between two samples by computing the cosine similarity between their respective feature vectors. This similarity metric helps us determine how closely related two samples are within the locality of their feature space. We then sort the samples by their similarity scores in ascending order and select the top-K nearest neighbors to form a smaller subset, denoted as N_i. Using the labels of these K nearest samples, we perform a weighted smoothing of the current label. We posit that the current label is accurate if and only if most samples within the set N_i have labels similar to the smoothed label.

Consider a current sample x_i with feature representation s_i, and a neighboring sample x_j with feature representation s_j. The cosine similarity between these two samples can be mathematically expressed as:

$$s_{ij} \triangleq \frac{s_i^T s_j}{\|s_i\|_2 \|s_j\|_2} \tag{1}$$

where $\|s_i\|_2$ and $\|s_j\|_2$ denote their $L2$ norms. This formulation enables us to assess the similarity quantitatively, facilitating the selection and validation of sample labels in the training process.

Subsequently, we utilize s_{ij} as the weighting factor to smooth the label of sample x_i using the sample labels from the set N_i. Let the updated label be denoted as l_i', and the original label as l. The updated label l_i' can be computed using the following equation:

$$l_i' = \frac{1}{K} \sum_{x_j \in N_i} s_{ij} \cdot l_j \tag{2}$$

In the final step, we vote between l_i' and the original label l_j. If the number of samples in N_i for which l_i' matches their respective labels l_j exceeds half the size of the set N_i, the sample x_i is considered to have the correct label. Consequently, we select it as a valid data point.

3.2   Implicit Sparse Regularization

We selectively isolate clean samples, while utilizing an instance-level adaptive sample correction algorithm, as proposed in the DISC work [10], to amend noisy samples. This correction algorithm evaluates the confidence in predictions by comparing the discrepancy between current predictions and EMA-smoothed predictions. Based on this confidence level, the sample labels are automatically modified. The adjusted sample labels ensure a more sparsely distributed correction, maintaining a level of data diversity. Although the corrected data are not entirely accurate, we introduce an implicit sparse regularization method as a supplementary measure.

This method allocates an additional set of sparse vectors to each sample, used explicitly to estimate the probability of sample noise. Consequently, the original optimization problem is recast into a risk minimization problem as follows:

$$\min_{\boldsymbol{\theta},\{u_i\}_{i=1}^{N}} \sum_{i=1}^{N} L\left(f(x_i,\boldsymbol{\theta}) + u_i, y_i'\right) \tag{3}$$

Let $\boldsymbol{u}$ be the aforementioned set of positive sparse data vectors, and y_i' be the corrected label. Our design is motivated by prior research, which indicates that deep neural networks characterized by over-parameterization tend to prefer solutions with low-rank and sparse intrinsic properties. Another study demonstrates that if the noise is sparse, it can be effectively modeled through a low-rank framework. Hence, we train $\boldsymbol{u}$ concurrently with $\boldsymbol{\theta}$. These sparse vectors can be viewed as an implicit regularizer that autonomously selects clean samples for learning.

In summary, by integrating both low-rank modeling and adaptive correction methods, our approach leverages the inherent tendencies of deep neural networks to improve the robustness and accuracy of predictions amidst noisy data, thereby facilitating a more reliable dataset for training.

3.3   Debiased Large Margin Loss

Even when data is meticulously curated and labels are rigorously corrected, models during training inherently tend to predict some simpler categories. If left unaddressed, this tendency can amplify existing biases within the model. To mitigate overconfidence, inspired by debiasPL, we apply the following formula to adjust the predicted probabilitie, we defined it as $\hat{p}$:

$$\tilde{f}_i = f\left(x_i; \theta\right) - \alpha \log \hat{p} \tag{4}$$

where $\hat{p} \leftarrow m\hat{p} + (1-m)\frac{1}{\mu B}\sum_{k=1}^{\mu B} p_k$. Here, μB represents the batch size, and m and α are constant hyper-parameters equal to 0.99 and 0.5, respectively. The corrected logits are then processed using the softmax function to generate the final model predictions.

Additionally, we maximize entropy in the feature space to enhance inter-class fairness while enforcing specific boundaries between classes. For this purpose, we designed and implemented a Debiased Large Margin Loss, defined as follows:

$$L_{\text{debias}} = -\sum_{i=1}^{N}\sum_{j=1}^{C} y'_i \log \frac{e^{\tilde{f}_i^j}}{\sum_{k=1}^{C} e^{\tilde{f}_i^k}} \tag{5}$$

where y'_i represents the current label of the i-th sample, f_i represents the i-th prediction in Eq. (4) and e represents the base of the natural logarithm.

3.4   Model Training

During the warm-up phase, we apply the implicit regularization method introduced in Sect. 3.2 to prevent potential noise fitting caused by the epoch settings.

This approach ensures a robust initialization for subsequent sample selection. Specifically, we utilize the entire training dataset during the warm-up phase and update the model using the following loss function:

$$L_{warm} = \frac{1}{N} \sum_{i=1}^{N} L\left(f\left(x_i; \theta\right) + u_i, y_i\right) \tag{6}$$

During the training phase, as opposed to the warm-up phase, we update the model exclusively using the clean dataset identified in Sect. 3.1 and the corrected data from Sect. 3.2. Additionally, we employ the implicit regularization method introduced in Sect. 3.2 to mitigate noise fitting.

$$L_{train} = \frac{1}{N} \sum_{i=1}^{N} L\left(f\left(x_i; \theta\right) + u_i, y_i\right) \tag{7}$$

Following the approach in DivideMix, we perform mixup operations on samples selected via feature voting, defining the loss as L_{mix}, to further enhance the model's performance. Additionally, to fully leverage training samples outside the clean set, we introduce two trainable feature projection heads, proj1 and proj2, which map high-dimensional features to lower-dimensional spaces, promoting feature consistency. Crucially, this feature consistency method does not update our classification head, thus avoiding the accumulation of confirmation bias. For a sample x_i with its strongly and weakly augmented views x_1 and x_2, this method can be defined as:

$$L_{pc} = -\frac{\boldsymbol{p}_1^\top \boldsymbol{p}_2}{\|\boldsymbol{p}_1\|_2 \|\boldsymbol{p}_2\|_2} \tag{8}$$

where $\boldsymbol{p}_1 \triangleq h_{\text{proj1}}\left(h_{\text{proj2}}\left(f\left(\boldsymbol{x}_1\right)\right)\right)$ and $\boldsymbol{p}_2 \triangleq h_{\text{proj2}}\left(f\left(\boldsymbol{x}_1\right)\right)$.

4   Experiment

We validate the effectiveness of our method on synthesized noise (CIFAR-10, CIFAR-100 with symmetric, instance-dependent noise) and real-world noise (CIFAR-10N/100N, Clothing-1M and Webvision). Subsequently, we conducted ablation experiments to verify the effectiveness of each individual component. All our experiments were implemented based on a single GeForce RTX3090 GPU and PyTorch 1.8.0.

4.1   Synthetic Noise

DataSet. CIFAR-10 and CIFAR-100 [7] are commonly used image classification datasets, widely employed in computer vision for training and evaluating image classification algorithms and models. Existing synthetic label noise can be categorized into two types based on the dependence relationship between data features and class labels: symmetric noise (comprising symmetric and asymmetric noise) and instance-dependent noise (IDN). IDN is generated by assigning random noise rates to each instance, sampled from a truncated Gaussian distribution. Symmetric noise is obtained by randomly flipping labels with equal probabilities. Asymmetric noise is generated by flipping a pair of specified classes or confusing category labels with a fixed probability. Following prior research, we conducted experiments on CIFAR-10 and CIFAR-100 with symmetrical noise levels (20%, 50%, 80%), as well as CIFAR-10 with asymmetrical noise at 45% and IDN levels (20%, 40%, 60%).

Experimental Setup. We employed PreResNet18 [6] as the backbone network and trained it for 300 epochs on CIFAR-10 and CIFAR-100. For fair comparisons, we utilized SGD as the optimizer with a batch size of 128. The learning rate was set to 0.02 and decayed to 0.002 over the course of 300 epochs. For CIFAR-10, we set the learning rate of the parameter $\mathbf{u}$ to 100; for CIFAR-100, the learning rate of $\mathbf{u}$ was set to 1.

Compare With SOTA Methods. Table 1 and Table 2 present the results on IDN and symmetric noise for CIFAR-10 and CIFAR-100. Table 1 showcases the performance of our method against IDN in CIFAR-10 and CIFAR-100. On CIFAR-100, we outperform the current SOTA, DISC[], by 2.18%, 2.34%, and 7.25% at different noise rates. On CIFAR-10, we surpass the current SOTA by 0.83%, 0.96% and 0.40% at 20%, 40% and 60% noise.

Table 2 illustrates our outstanding performance in both symmetric and asymmetric noise. We achieve remarkable accuracy on CIFAR-10, surpassing 97% accuracy at 20% symmetric noise and reaching 94.1% accuracy at 90% symmetric noise. When dealing with CIFAR-100, we also demonstrate excellent performance, outperforming the latest work, RobustLR, by 3.6%, 5%, 7.8%, and 11.2% at 20%, 50%, 80%, and 90% symmetric noise, respectively.

4.2 Real-World Noise

Dataset. CIFAR-10N and CIFAR-100N are real-world datasets annotated with noise. CIFAR-10N includes five levels of noisy data: Aggrerate, Random1, Random2, Random3, and Worst. For testing purposes, we selected Aggrerate, Random1, and Worst, with noise rates of 9.03%, 17.23%, and 40.21%, respectively. Each image in CIFAR-100N contains a coarse label and a fine label, with noise rates of 25.60% and 40.20%, respectively. We use fine labels. WebVision 1.0 [9] is composed of data from two sources: Google and Flickr. It consists of 1000 classes and 2.4 million images. Following the [12], we utilized the first 50 classes of WebVision 1.0 as training data and subsequently tested our model on the validation sets of both WebVision and ILSVRC2012. The Clothing1M [15] dataset has a noise rate of approximately 38.5%. It is collected from online shopping websites and comprises 1 million training images and 10,000 test images.

Table 1. Comparison with the SOTA methods on CIFAR-10 and CIFAR-100 with IDN.

DataSet	CIFAR-10			CIFAR-100		
Method	Inst.20%	Inst.40%	Inst.60%	Inst.20%	Inst.40%	Inst.60%
CE	83.93 ±0.15	67.64 ±0.26	43.83 ±0.33	57.35 ±0.08	43.17 ± 0.15	24.42 ± 0.16
Co-teaching	88.87 ±0.24	73.00 ±0.24	62.51 ±1.98	43.30 ±0.39	23.21 ±0.57	12.58 ±0.58
Reweight-R	90.04 ±0.46	84.11 ±2.47	72.18 ±2.47	58.00 ±0.36	43.83 ±8.42	36.07 ±9.73
Peer Loss	89.12 ±0.76	83.26 ±0.42	74.53 ±1.22	61.16 ±0.64	47.23 ±1.23	31.71 ±2.06
DivideMix	93.33 ±0.14	95.07 ±0.11	85.50 ±0.71	79.04 ±0.21	76.08 ±0.35	46.72 ±1.32
CORSES2	91.14 ±0.46	83.67 ±1.29	77.68 ±2.24	66.47 ±0.45	58.99 ±1.49	38.55 ±3.25
CAL	92.01 ±0.12	84.96 ±1.25	79.82 ±2.56	69.11 ±0.46	76.58 ±1.40	63.17 ±3.30
CC	93.68 ±0.12	94.97 ±0.09	94.95 ±0.11	79.61 ±0.19	76.58 ±0.25	59.40 ±0.46
DISC	96.48 ±0.04	95.94 ±0.04	95.05 ±0.05	80.12 ±0.13	78.44 ±0.19	69.57 ±0.14
Ours	**97.31** ±0.04	**96.90** ±0.04	**95.45** ±0.05	**82.30** ±0.13	**80.78** ±0.19	**76.82** ±0.14

Table 2. Comparison with the SOTA methods on CIFAR-10 and CIFAR-100 with Sym. All the results are directly from their original papers.

DataSet		CIFAR-10					CIFAR-100			
Noise Type		Sym.				Asym.	Sym.			
Method		20%	50%	80%	90%	40%	20%	50%	80%	90%
CE	Best	86.8	79.4	62.9	42.7	85.0	59.0	43.1	19.2	10.1
	Last	82.7	57.9	26.1	16.8	72.3	58.7	42.8	18.1	3.5
DivideMix	Best	96.1	94.6	93.2	76.0	93.4	77.3	74.6	60.2	31.5
	Last	95.7	94.4	92.9	75.4	92.1	76.9	74.2	59.6	31.0
ELR+	Best	92.4	90.8	81.1	78.7	93.0	74.9	63.8	60.8	33.4
	Last	91.8	90.3	80.1	-	-	74.6	63.4	30.2	-
PGDF	Best	96.7	96.3	94.7	84.0	94.8	81.3	78.0	66.7	42.3
	Last	96.6	96.2	94.6	83.1	94.5	81.2	77.6	65.9	41.7
SOP+	Best	96.3	95.5	94.0	60.3	93.8	78.9	75.7	63.3	11.7
	Last	96.1	95.2	93.7	59.7	-	78.4	75.4	63.2	5.3
RobustLR	Best	96.5	95.8	94.3	92.8	94.4	79.1	75.3	66.7	37.5
	Last	96.4	95.7	94.2	92.8	93.7	78.6	74.6	66.2	37.3
Ours	Best	**97.3**	**97.0**	**95.9**	**94.1**	**95.6**	**82.7**	**80.3**	**74.5**	**48.7**
	Last	**97.3**	**96.9**	**95.8**	**93.8**	**95.4**	**82.5**	**80.2**	**74.5**	**48.7**

Table 3. Comparison on CIFAR-10N and CIFAR-100N.

DataSet	CIFAR-10N					CIFAR-100N
Method	Aggregate	Random1	Random2	Random3	Worst	Noise fine
Co-teaching	91.20	90.33	90.30	90.15	83.83	60.37
	±0.13	±0.13	±0.17	±0.18	±0.13	±0.27
ELR+	94.83	94.43	94.20	94.34	91.09	66.72
	±0.10	±0.41	±0.24	±0.22	±1.60	±0.07
DivideMix	95.01	95.16	94.89	95.03	92.56	71.13
	±0.71	±0.19	±0.23	±0.20	±0.42	±0.48
SOP+	95.61	95.28	95.31	95.39	93.24	67.81
	±0.13	±0.13	±0.10	±0.11	±0.21	±0.23
PGDF	95.35	94.95	94.78	94.92	94.22	67.76
	±0.12	±0.21	±0.34	±0.28	±0.29	±0.35
CC	95.63	95.11	94.93	95.09	94.24	71.21
	±0.21	±0.31	±0.37	±0.21	±0.40	±0.22
Ours	**97.12**	**96.75**	**96.60**	**96.68**	**94.88**	**73.23**
	±0.08	±0.12	±0.09	±0.15	±0.19	±0.31

Experimental Setup. For CIFAR-10N and CIFAR-100N, we utilized PreRes-Net18 as the backbone network and trained for 300 epochs. To ensure a fair comparison, we employed SGD as the optimizer with a batch size of 128 and initialized the learning rate to 0.02. For CIFAR-10N, the learning rate of $\mathbf{u}$ is set to 10, and for CIFAR-100N is set to 1. For WebVision, following [12], we employed Inception-ResNetV2 [13] (not pre-trained) as the backbone network, set the batch size to 32, initialized the learning rate to 0.01, and configured the learning rate for $\mathbf{u}$ as 1. For Clothing1M, following the guidelines in [17], we utilized ResNet50 [5] (pre-trained) as the backbone network, set the batch size to 64, initialized the learning rate to 0.002, and set the learning rate for $\mathbf{u}$ to 0.1.

Compare With SOTA Methods. The results on real datasets are presented in Table 3 and Table 4. Table 3 presents our results on CIFAR-10N and CIFAR-100N. We outperformed CC by 1.49%, 1.64%, 1.63%, 1.59%, and 0.64% on CIFAR-10N, demonstrating the excellent performance of our method. On CIFAR-100N, we exceeded CC by 2.02%. This indicates that our approach effectively handles various complex real-world datasets, especially when dealing with an increased number of categories, leading to higher learning challenges. When compared to the current state-of-the-art (SOTA) in Table 4, we consistently achieved the best performance. On Clothing1M, we attained a performance of 75.31%, surpassing PGDF by 0.12%. Notably, our model does not rely on extravagant assumptions and requires minimal hyperparameter tuning. Given that Clothing1M is a long-tail dataset, our adopted oversampling and bias elimination methods effectively mitigate biased learning induced by long-tail issues. Our approach also demonstrated superior performance on WebVision and ILSVRC12, further emphasizing its effectiveness in handling synthetic noise and delivering outstanding results on real datasets.

Table 4. Comparison on Clothing1M and WebVision.

Dataset	Clothing 1M	WebVision top1	top5	ILSVRC12 top1	top5
CE	69.21	-	-	-	-
ELR+	74.81	77.78	91.68	70.29	89.76
DivideMix	74.76	77.32	91.64	75.20	90.84
PGDF	75.19	81.47	94.03	75.45	93.11
CC	74.54	79.36	93.64	76.08	93.86
SSR	74.83	80.92	92.8	75.76	91.76
RobustLR	-	81.84	94.12	75.48	93.76
DISC	73.72	80.28	92.28	77.44	92.28
Ours	**75.31**	**81.95**	**94.28**	**77.67**	**94.08**

Table 5. Ablation study of ourmethod. ISR represents Implicit Sparse Regularization, and DLML corresponds to the debiased large margin loss mentioned in Sect. 3.3.

DataSet	CIFAR-10		CIFAR-100	
Noise Type	Inst.40	Sym.50	Inst.40	Sym.50
Ours	**96.90**	**97.00**	**80.78**	**80.30**
w/o Warm-up	96.12	96.41	80.10	79.65
w/o IR	95.82	96.14	79.98	79.26
w/o DLML	96.33	96.42	80.04	79.81

4.3   Ablation Study

To validate the effectiveness of our method, we conducted ablation experiments by removing different modules. The experimental results are shown in Table 5. We tested various types of noise and found that implicit regularization contributes the most to the model's performance. Additionally, warm-up helps us obtain a well-initialized pretraining representation, which is equally crucial for the model's final results. Through experimentation, we have demonstrated that all our modules enhance the model's robustness.

5   Conclusion

This paper presents a comprehensive network framework suitable for different types of noise learning. The framework achieves more robust representations by utilizing implicit regularization and debiasing techniques, thereby facilitating balanced and accurate sample selection. Additionally, it incorporates instance-level dynamic thresholds to correct samples during training, maintaining noise sparsity throughout the learning process. Extensive experiments demonstrate the effectiveness of the proposed modules and methods.

References

1. Cheng, D., et al.: Class-dependent label-noise learning with cycle-consistency regularization. Adv. Neural. Inf. Process. Syst. **35**, 11104–11116 (2022)
2. Ghosh, A., Kumar, H., Sastry, P.S.: Robust loss functions under label noise for deep neural networks. In: Proceedings of the AAAI Conference on Artificial Intelligence, vol. 31 (2017)
3. Goldberger, J., Ben-Reuven, E.: Training deep neural-networks using a noise adaptation layer. In: International Conference on Learning Representations (2016)
4. Han, B., et al.: Co-teaching: robust training of deep neural networks with extremely noisy labels. In: Advances in Neural Information Processing Systems, vol. 31 (2018)

5. He, K., Zhang, X., Ren, S., Sun, J.: Deep residual learning for image recognition. In: Proceedings of the IEEE Conference on Computer Vision and Pattern Recognition, pp. 770–778 (2016)

6. He, K., Zhang, X., Ren, S., Sun, J.: Identity mappings in deep residual networks. In: Leibe, B., Matas, J., Sebe, N., Welling, M. (eds.) ECCV 2016. LNCS, vol. 9908, pp. 630–645. Springer, Cham (2016). https://doi.org/10.1007/978-3-319-46493-0_38

7. Krizhevsky, A., Hinton, G., et al.: Learning multiple layers of features from tiny images (2009)

8. Li, J., Socher, R., Hoi, S.C.: Dividemix: learning with noisy labels as semi-supervised learning. arXiv preprint arXiv:2002.07394 (2020)

9. Li, W., Wang, L., Li, W., Agustsson, E., Van Gool, L.: Webvision database: visual learning and understanding from web data. arXiv preprint arXiv:1708.02862 (2017)

10. Li, Y., Han, H., Shan, S., Chen, X.: Disc: learning from noisy labels via dynamic instance-specific selection and correction. In: Proceedings of the IEEE/CVF Conference on Computer Vision and Pattern Recognition, pp. 24070–24079 (2023)

11. Patrini, G., Rozza, A., Krishna Menon, A., Nock, R., Qu, L.: Making deep neural networks robust to label noise: a loss correction approach. In: Proceedings of the IEEE Conference on Computer Vision and Pattern Recognition, pp. 1944–1952 (2017)

12. Song, H., Kim, M., Lee, J.G.: Selfie: refurbishing unclean samples for robust deep learning. In: International Conference on Machine Learning, pp. 5907–5915. PMLR (2019)

13. Szegedy, C., Ioffe, S., Vanhoucke, V., Alemi, A.: Inception-v4, inception-resnet and the impact of residual connections on learning. In: Proceedings of the AAAI Conference on Artificial Intelligence, vol. 31 (2017)

14. Wang, Y., Ma, X., Chen, Z., Luo, Y., Yi, J., Bailey, J.: Symmetric cross entropy for robust learning with noisy labels. In: Proceedings of the IEEE/CVF International Conference on Computer Vision, pp. 322–330 (2019)

15. Xiao, T., Xia, T., Yang, Y., Huang, C., Wang, X.: Learning from massive noisy labeled data for image classification. In: Proceedings of the IEEE Conference on Computer Vision and Pattern Recognition, pp. 2691–2699 (2015)

16. Yao, Y., et al.: Dual T: reducing estimation error for transition matrix in label-noise learning. Adv. Neural. Inf. Process. Syst. **33**, 7260–7271 (2020)

17. Zhang, Y., Zheng, S., Wu, P., Goswami, M., Chen, C.: Learning with feature-dependent label noise: a progressive approach. arXiv preprint arXiv:2103.07756 (2021)

18. Zhang, Z., Sabuncu, M.: Generalized cross entropy loss for training deep neural networks with noisy labels. In: Advances in Neural Information Processing Systems, vol. 31 (2018)

19. Zhao, G., Li, G., Qin, Y., Liu, F., Yu, Y.: Centrality and consistency: two-stage clean samples identification for learning with instance-dependent noisy labels. In: Avidan, S., Brostow, G., Cissé, M., Farinella, G.M., Hassner, T. (eds.) ECCV 2022. LNCS, vol. 13685, pp. 21–37. Springer, Cham (2022). https://doi.org/10.1007/978-3-031-19806-9_2

A Traffic Flow Prediction Model Integrating Dynamic Implicit Graph Information

You Wu[1,2(✉)], Jingfeng Guo[1,2(✉)], Xiao Chen[3], Xiao Pan[4],
and Bin Liu[5]

1 College of Information Science and Engineering, Yanshan University,
Qinhuangdao 066004, Hebei, China
youwu@stumail.ysu.edu.cn, jfguo@ysu.edu.cn
2 The Key Laboratory for Computer Virtual Technology and System Integration of
Hebei Province, Qinhuangdao 066004, Hebei, China
3 Research Center for Marine Science, Hebei Normal University of Science and
Technology, Qinhuangdao 066004, China
4 School of Information Science and Technology, Shijiazhuang Tiedao University,
Shijiazhuang 0500198, Hebei, China
smallpx@stdu.edu.cn
5 Big Data and Social Computing Research Center, Hebei University of
Science and Technology, Shijiazhuang 0500198, Hebei, China
liubin@hebust.edu.cn

Abstract. Traffic flow prediction based on road network is of great significance in logistics transportation planning and traffic management dispatch. Under the dual influence of spatial and temporal dependency factors, how to improve the accuracy of traffic flow prediction has become a current research hotspot. However, existing studies mostly use static graph structures to capture spatial dependency, ignoring the dynamic implicit graph information contained in traffic flow, resulting in insufficient spatial information learned by graph models and ignoring the temporal dependency impact of traffic flow. Therefore, this paper proposes a new traffic flow prediction model (IDIGI) that integrates dynamic implicit graph information. First, the model constructs a dynamic implicit graph based on time-segmented sensor traffic flow embedding representation, which is then integrated with topological graph to form a dynamic fusion graph; Secondly, it extracts the temporal dependency of traffic flow using down-sampling sequences; Finally, it compares favorably with six baseline models on four real datasets, significantly outperforming existing graph prediction models.

Keywords: Traffic flow prediction · Dynamic graph · Graph convolutional network · Recurrent neural network · Attention network

1 Introduction

Spatiotemporal data prediction refers to forecasting variables at a specific time and location, and it has been widely applied in fields such as intelligent transportation, climate change, and disease spread [3]. In the classic prediction tasks

© The Author(s), under exclusive license to Springer Nature Singapore Pte Ltd. 2025
R. Hadfi et al. (Eds.): PRICAI 2024, LNAI 15281, pp. 194–208, 2025.
https://doi.org/10.1007/978-981-96-0116-5_16

within the transportation domain, traffic flow data in urban road networks exhibit significant spatiotemporal characteristics. For instance, traffic flow shows temporal variations throughout the day and spatial differences between city centers and suburbs. In recent years, with the acceleration of urbanization, the existing road capacity can no longer meet the rapid growth in the number of vehicles, resulting in significant issues such as urban traffic congestion, environmental pollution, and energy waste. Therefore, timely and accurate traffic flow prediction is significant for personal travel planning, logistics transport planning, and traffic management and dispatching.

Traditional traffic flow prediction methods usually employ statistical models or machine learning approaches [16]. However, with the development of deep learning techniques and graph neural networks, traffic flow prediction based on spatiotemporal graph structures has demonstrated excellent performance in terms of prediction accuracy, becoming a hot topic in current research. For instance, the STGCN model [6] uses a fixed graph structure built with expert knowledge to capture the relationships in traffic flow between sensors. The FOGS model [11] uses Node2vactor [5] to obtain features for each sensor and employs these features to derive the spatial graph of traffic flow between sensors. Currently, traffic flow prediction models that integrate implicit information are still in their infancy, and several pressing issues still need to be addressed: (1) Existing studies have not fully considered the dynamic characteristics of traffic flow. Most of these studies construct static graphs using historical data to represent the spatial correlation between sensors. However, traffic flow is dynamically changing, and static graphs cannot reflect the differences in correlation at different times. (2) The information in current graph models must be more comprehensive. These studies primarily consider the topological dependencies between sensors or fuse simple implicit graphs through Beta distributions, still overlooking other implicit correlation factors and weights that affect traffic flow prediction, such as traffic flow's temporal or functional correlation. (3) Current research neglects the temporal dependency of traffic flow. These studies only extract spatial dependencies by calculating the correlation of traffic flow between sensors, but both spatial and temporal dependency factors influence traffic flow prediction. Therefore, how to extract the dynamic features of traffic flow, integrate the topological dependencies and implicit information between sensors to extract the spatial dependencies of traffic flow, and how to extract the temporal dependencies of traffic flow to build accurate prediction models are the focus of this research.

To address the above issues, we propose a novel traffic flow prediction model based on graph and recurrent neural network architectures called IDIGI (Integrating Dynamic Implicit Graph Information). This model obtains the functional and temporal graphs of traffic flow between sensors by calculating the correlations of traffic flow on the road and enriches the graph information by integrating these graphs with the sensor topology graph provided by the dataset. The main contributions of this paper are as follows:

1. A dynamic graph module is proposed based on sensor traffic flow embedding representation. This module constructs embedding representations of

time-segmented traffic flows, better reflecting the temporal variation characteristics of traffic flow. It constructs implicit graphs based on the functional and temporal characteristics of the road network and further integrates them with the topology graph to establish a dynamic fusion graph. This dynamic fusion graph contains more road network information and effectively extracts the spatial dependencies of traffic flow.

2. A temporal dependency module is proposed. This module down-samples the traffic flow into two sub-sequences. It extracts the features of the two sub-sequences separately and merges them in their original order. The merged features contain more temporal information about the traffic flow.

3. Experiments were conducted on four real-world road traffic datasets. Compared with six baseline models, the results show that the IDIGI model has better predictive performance.

2 Related Work

Traffic flow prediction has been widely studied, with recent advancements focusing more on graph neural networks. Constructing graphs is crucial for accurate prediction. Current methods for constructing graphs in traffic flow prediction include sensor topology-based graphs and data-adaptive sensor correlation graphs.

In research that utilizes sensor topology graphs, the road traffic network is generally represented as a graph, applying graph convolution to understand spatial dependencies. The DCRNN [9] represents the changes in traffic flow over time as a diffusion process, suggesting a diffusion convolution method to seize spatial dependencies while incorporating Gated Recurrent Units [4] (GRU) for addressing temporal dynamics. Meanwhile, the ASTGCN [17] uses spatial and temporal attention techniques to identify dynamic spatial and temporal relationships in traffic flow, respectively. Nevertheless, depending exclusively on sensor topology graphs presents difficulties in capturing the inherent or long-term dependencies associated with traffic flow.

Due to the significant impact of graph structure quality on time series prediction performance, many recent studies have integrated data-adaptive sensor correlation graphs into the traffic road network. AGCRN [1] employs separate weights and biases to learn embedding vectors for each sensor, enabling the learning of an adjacency matrix without being constrained by the prior road network structure. STFGNN [8] utilizes the Dynamic Time Warping [2] (DTW) algorithm to construct a temporal graph, merging it with a given spatial graph to form a new spatiotemporal fusion graph. RGSL [15] builds functional correlation graphs (implicit graphs) among sensors in a data-adaptive manner using traffic flow data and proposes a Laplacian module to integrate both explicit and implicit graphs. However, while these methods consider learning inherent graph structures from time series patterns, they overlook the dynamic relationships between traffic flows of sensors.

3 Prerequisite Knowledge

In traffic flow-based networks, sensors on roads are considered nodes, and the connectivity between road segments where the sensors are located is used as edges to construct a sensor topology graph. An implicit graph is also constructed using the correlation of traffic flow data obtained from the sensors, facilitating traffic flow prediction.

To aid in understanding, relevant symbols (Table 1) and concepts are introduced as follows:

Table 1. Symbol Description.

Symbol	Annotation
$\mathcal{G}_S$	Sensor Topology Graph
$\mathcal{G}_I$	Implicit Graph
V	Set of Nodes
E_S	The Collection of Edges in a Sensor Topology Graph
E_I	The Collection of Edges Learned by Function L
$\mathcal{G}_{IF}$	The Functional Dependency Graph of Traffic Flow Between Sensors
$\mathcal{G}_{IT}$	The Temporal Dependency Graph of Traffic Flow Between Sensors
X	Traffic Flow Dataset

Definition 1. The sensor topology graph is defined as a tuple $\mathcal{G}_S = (V, E_S)$; where V represents the set of nodes, $N = |V|$ represents the number of nodes (number of sensors), and E_S represents the set of edges.

Definition 2. Given the sensor topology graph $\mathcal{G}_S = (V, E_S)$, $X_I^{(wt)}$ represents the traffic flow of the t-th sliding window, and the implicit graph corresponding to the t-th sliding window is denoted as $\mathcal{G}_I(\text{t}) = (V, E_I^{(t)})$. V is the set of nodes in $\mathcal{G}_S$, and $E_I^{(t)} = L(V, X_I^{(wt)})$ represents the edges learned by function L based on the traffic flow data between sensors in the t-th sliding window.

Moreover, in the sensor topology $\mathcal{G}_S$, $A_I^{(t)} = Fun(V, X_I^{(wt)})$ represents the weight matrix of the edges, as shown in Eq. (1): $\forall v_i, v_j \in V$, if $(v_i, v_j) \in E_S$, then $\text{Dis}(v_i, v_j)$ represents the distance between the sensors; if $(v_i, v_j) \notin E_S$, then $A_S(v_i, v_j) = 0$.

$$A_S(v_i, v_j) = \begin{cases} \text{Dis}(v_i, v_j) & (v_i, v_j) \in E_S \\ 0 & (v_i, v_j) \notin E_S \end{cases} \tag{1}$$

Similarly, in the implicit graph $\mathcal{G}_I$, $A_I^{(t)} = Fun(V, X_I^{(wt)})$ represents the implicit correlation matrix of traffic flow between sensors in the t-th sliding window. For example, in the t-th sliding window, the temporal and functional correlation graphs of traffic flow between sensors are $\mathcal{G}_{IT}^{(t)}$ and $\mathcal{G}_{IF}^{(t)}$, respectively, and the corresponding temporal and functional correlation matrices are $A_{IT}^{(t)}$ and $A_{IF}^{(t)}$. $A_{IT}^{(t)}(i\ ,j)$ denotes the temporal correlation matrix of traffic flow between sensor i and sensor j, and $A_{IF}^{(t)}(i\ ,j)$ denotes the functional correlation matrix of traffic flow between sensor i and sensor j.

Problem Definition of Traffic Flow Prediction. Given a traffic flow dataset $X = \{X(1), \cdots\cdots, X(t) \cdots\cdots, X(M)\} \in \mathbb{R}^{N \times M}$, where N is the number of sensors and M is the total amount of traffic flow data, $X(t) \in \mathbb{R}^{N \times 1}$ represents the traffic flow data collected by N sensors at time t. The problem of traffic flow prediction involves learning a function (f) based on the historical data of (T) time steps, which predicts the traffic flow data for the next (K) time steps by integrating the sensor topology graph $\mathcal{G}_S$ and the implicit graph $\mathcal{G}_I$, as shown in Eq. (2).

$$[X(t - T + 1), ..., X(t)] \xrightarrow{f} [X(t + 1), ..., X(t + K)] \tag{2}$$

4   IDIGI: Integrating Dynamic Implicit Graph Information

In traffic flow prediction tasks, it is essential to consider the static topology of sensor structures and the impact of some implicit dynamic information on traffic flow. To better learn the other implicit correlation factors, dynamic variation features, and temporal dependencies that affect traffic flow prediction, we propose a new traffic flow prediction model, IDIGI (Integrating Dynamic Implicit Graph Information), as shown in Fig. 1. Based on the dynamic correlations between traffic flow data, the model constructs a Dynamic Graph Module (DGM) to learn the spatial features of traffic flow. An LSTM-based Time Dependent Module (TDM) is used to extract the temporal features of traffic flow, and the Spatio Temporal Fusion Module (STFM) integrates spatial and temporal features to achieve traffic flow prediction.

4.1   Dynamic Graph Module

Existing studies typically learn a static implicit graph based on historical traffic flow data to represent the correlations between sensors. However, in reality, the correlations in traffic flow between sensors vary over time. For instance, considering the traffic flow of 20 sensors, as shown in Fig. 2(a), the correlations between sensors are derived from the traffic flow correlations over the entire period. In contrast, Fig. 2(b) illustrates the time-segmented traffic flow correlations between sensors within four hours, revealing significant differences in correlations. For example, the first sensor has weak correlations with other sensors at the second time point, while it shows strong correlations with other sensors at the fourth time. Hence, a single static implicit graph cannot capture the temporal variation characteristics. To more accurately reflect the temporal variations in traffic flow, it is necessary to construct dynamic graphs by considering the time-segmented

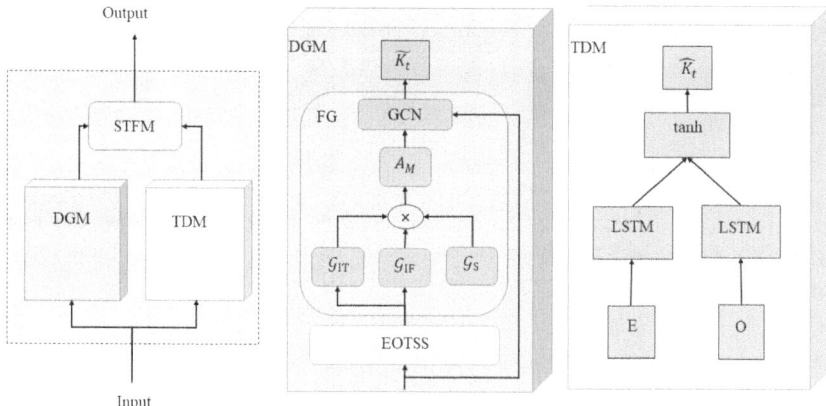

Fig. 1. The traffic flow prediction model integrating dynamic implicit graph information (IDIGI). This framework consists of a DGM (Dynamic Graph Module) and a TDM (Time Dependent Module). In this model, DGM extracts embeddings of traffic flow based on Embeddings of Time-Segmented Sensor Traffic Flow (EOTSS) and constructs an implicit graph based on the FG (Fusion Graph). This implicit graph is then integrated with the topology graph to extract the spatial features of the traffic flow. In the DGM, $\widetilde{K}_t$ represents spatial features of the traffic flow. In the TDM, $\widehat{K}_t$ represents temporal features of the traffic flow, E represents even sequences and O represents odd sequences.

correlations between sensors, thereby improving the effectiveness of traffic flow prediction.

The dynamic graph comprises a topological graph (provided by the dataset) and an implicit graph. The construction process of the dynamic graph is primarily divided into two steps: 1) embedding representation of traffic flow by time-segmented sensors, and 2) integrating the implicit graph constructed based on this embedding representation with the topological graph of the sensors to form the dynamic graph. Detailed explanations of each step are provided below.

The Embedding Representation of Traffic Flow by Time-Segmented Sensors. A sliding window divides the given traffic flow dataset $X \in \mathbb{R}^{N \times M}$ into different time periods in the sensor embedding process. If the size of the sliding window is w and the stride is L, the dataset can be divided into $\lfloor \frac{M-w}{L} \rfloor + 1$ windows, denoted as $(K_1, K_2, \cdots, K_{\lfloor \frac{M-w}{L} \rfloor + 1})$. For each time window data $K_t \in \mathbb{R}^{N \times w}$, a fully connected layer is constructed to extract the traffic flow features of each sensor within the time window, resulting in d-dimensional embedding representations for N sensors, denoted as $H(t) \in \mathbb{R}^{N \times d}$, as shown in Eq. (3). The sliding window $K_t = \{X(t), \ldots, X(t + w - 1)\}$, $\sigma()$ represents the Tanh function, and W_1 and b_1 represent the learnable parameter matrices.

$$H(t) = \sigma\left([X(t), \ldots, X(t + w - 1)] \times W_1 + b_1\right) \tag{3}$$

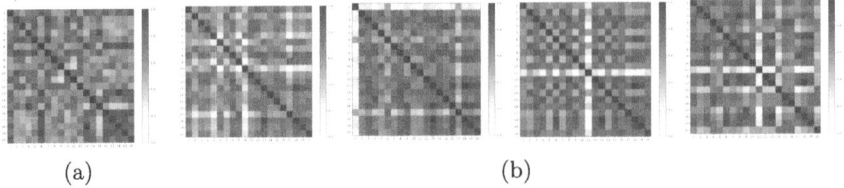

(a)   (b)

Fig. 2. Example of traffic flow correlation between sensors. Each row and column represents a sensor, and the shade of color in the (i)th row and (j)th column indicates the degree of correlation between the (i)th and (j)th sensors.

Each sliding window yields a vector representation $H(t)$ for a set of sensors, which can be used to construct a static graph based on each vector representation $H(t)$, as shown in Fig. 3. Since the sliding window changes over time, the dynamic implicit graph is composed of a series of static graphs that change over time.

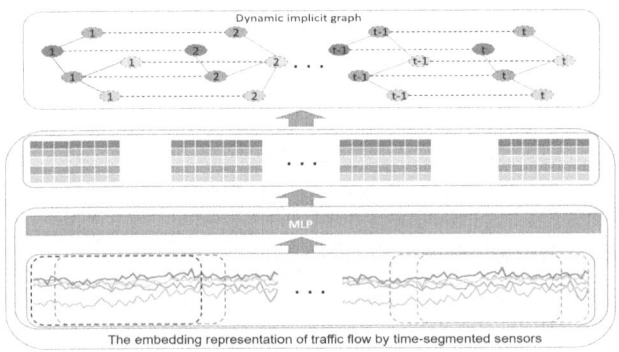

Fig. 3. The process of dynamic implicit graph formation (The relationship between the sensors changes over time). The MLP is a feedforward neural network with a multi-layer structure composed of multiple neurons.

Fusion Graph. When constructing a graph based on traffic flow, it is essential to consider both the topological dependencies among sensors and the dynamic implicit information in the traffic flow. However, existing research primarily focuses on topological dependencies between sensors or integrates simple implicit graphs through Beta distribution for traffic flow prediction. This approach presents several issues: (1) It overlooks other implicit correlation factors affecting traffic flow prediction, such as temporal or functional correlations of the traffic flow; (2) Beta distribution values are empirical and may be subject to cognitive bias; (3) Different datasets may have different characteristics, and using empirical values to set the weights of topological and implicit graphs lacks generality. Therefore, constructing implicit graphs based on traffic flow correlations and allocating weights between topological and implicit graphs are crucial for improving traffic flow prediction. These are the two critical issues addressed in this section.

Two roads may have similar traffic flows simultaneously, reflecting the temporal similarity of the road network. If both roads have commercial areas or schools, the traffic flow on these roads may exhibit similar variation patterns. This similarity is related to time and the functionality of the buildings on the roads, reflecting the functional similarity of the road network. Therefore, it is necessary to construct an implicit graph that captures the functional and temporal correlations of traffic flow in the road network, formally defined as follows.

The implicit graph based on the temporal correlation of traffic flow embeddings between sensors is denoted as $\mathcal{G}_{\text{IT}}(t) = (V, \text{E}_{\text{IT}}^{(t)})$. In the t-th sliding window, the temporal correlation matrix of traffic flows among all sensors (V) is denoted as $A_{IT}^{(t)}$. Given two sensors i and j, $H^i(t)$ and $H^j(t)$ represent the traffic flow embeddings of sensors i and j in the t-th sliding window, respectively. Euclidean distance is typically used to represent the temporal correlation $A_{IT}^{(t)}(i,j)$ of traffic flow between sensors. If the traffic flows are similar at the same time, the $A_{IT}^{(t)}(i,j)$ value is smaller, indicating a substantial similarity between i and j; otherwise, the similarity is weak [8], as shown in Eq. (4).

$$A_{IT}^{(t)}(i,j) = \sqrt{\sum \left(H^i(t) - H^j(t)\right)^2} \tag{4}$$

The implicit graph based on the functional correlation of traffic flow embeddings between sensors is denoted as $\mathcal{G}_{\text{IF}}(t) = (V, E_{IF}^{(t)})$. In the t-th sliding window, the functional correlation matrix of traffic flows among all sensors (V) is denoted as $A_{IF}^{(t)}$. Given two sensors i and j, the $cos\theta$ is typically used to represent the similarity between two functional areas. The larger the cosine value, the more substantial the similarity between i and j; otherwise, the similarity is weak [15], as shown in Eq. (5).

$$A_{IF}^{(t)}(i,j) = \frac{H^i(t)^T H^j(t)}{\| H^i(t) \| \cdot \| H^j(t) \|} \tag{5}$$

$A_{IF}^{(t)}$ and $A_{IT}^{(t)}$ are obtained by calculating the embeddings through functions, and the values in the matrices represent the degree of correlation between sensors. However, some smaller values might be due to data errors rather than actual correlations between sensors. To address this issue, Gumble Softmax [12] is used to learn the extreme value distribution in $A_{IF}^{(t)}$ and $A_{IT}^{(t)}$, preserving the maxima in $A_{IF}^{(t)}$ and the minima in $A_{IT}^{(t)}$ to achieve the sparsification of $A_{IF}^{(t)}$ and $A_{IT}^{(t)}$.

The sensor topology graph, functional correlation implicit graph, and temporal correlation implicit graph each reflect different traffic flow characteristics between sensors from different perspectives. To obtain richer graph information, these three graphs are fused. However, the information in these graphs varies, and their impact on traffic flow also differs. Therefore, it is crucial to determine how to allocate weights and merge the three graphs. Unlike traditional methods of sampling weighted coefficients from a beta distribution, this module calculates weights using attention mechanisms, allowing for weight allocation based on the impact of each graph on traffic flow. Let $A_M^{(t)}$ be the dynamic correlation matrix after fusion, f_a denote the self-attention network [14], and θ_a, θ_b, and θ_c be the parameters of the attention network. The three graphs are combined using the attention network, as shown in Eq. (6).

$$A_M^{(t)} = f_a(A_S; \theta_a) + f_a\left(A_{IF}^{(t)}; \theta_b\right) + f_a\left(A_{IT}^{(t)}; \theta_c\right) \tag{6}$$

Let $K_t \in \mathbb{R}^{N \times w}$ be the input data, $A_M^{(t)}$ be the dynamic correlation matrix after fusion, W_M and b_M be the learnable parameters, and D be the degree matrix. The spatial features $\widetilde{K_t}$ of the t-th window are extracted through graph convolution, as shown in Eq. (7).

$$\widetilde{K_t} = \left(D^{-\frac{1}{2}} A_M^{(t)} D^{-\frac{1}{2}}\right) K_t W_M + b_M \tag{7}$$

4.2   Temporal Dependency Module

Spatial and temporal dependency factors influence traffic flow prediction. Existing research only extracts spatial dependency by calculating the correlation of traffic flow between sensors, ignoring the temporal dependency of traffic flow. Therefore, how to extract the temporal dependency of traffic flow is the problem this section aims to address.

Due to differences in sampling rates and the number of sensors, traffic flow data exhibits temporal redundancy. Temporal redundancy, as shown in Fig. 4, refers to viewing the collected traffic flow data as $K_t \in \mathbb{R}^{N \times w}$, where N is the dimension and w represents the length. Usually, there exists rank $(K_t) <$ min(N, w), indicating that K_t generally has a low-rank property, which implies the existence of redundancy in traffic flow data [10]. Therefore, when extracting the temporal dependency of traffic flow, it is necessary to consider the problem of temporal redundancy.

By leveraging the low-rank characteristics of existing traffic flow data, the initial time series is downsampled into odd and even sequences. Considering that LSTM has advantages in handling long-term sequence dependencies and can effectively capture long-distance dependencies, it is selected as the time extractor. Finally, these temporal features are merged in their original order to obtain the temporal features $\widehat{K_t}$ of the t-th window, as shown in Eq. (8).

$$\begin{aligned} K_{t,1}, K_{t,2} &- sampled(K_t) \\ \widehat{K}_{t,l} &= lstm(K_{t,i}) \quad i \in [1,2] \\ \widehat{K_t} &= merge(\widehat{K_{t,1}}, \widehat{K_{t,2}}) \end{aligned} \tag{8}$$

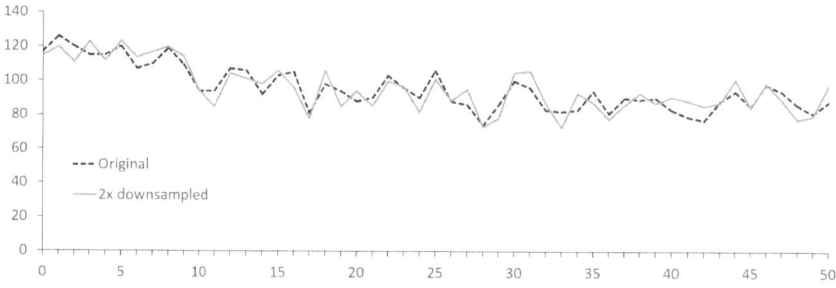

Fig. 4. The redundancy of temporal information.

4.3   Spatio Temporal Fusion Module

As shown in Fig. 1, the traffic flow data of the t-th window is input, and the spatial features of the traffic flow are extracted through the DGM, while the temporal features are extracted through the TDM. To more accurately predict the traffic flow data for the next window, it is necessary to fuse the spatial and temporal features. This is achieved through a constructed fully connected layer (STFM), thus obtaining the traffic flow $K_{t+1}^{\cdots}$ for the (t+1)-th window. As shown in Eq. (9), $\widetilde{K_t}$ and $\widehat{K_t}$ respectively represent the spatial and temporal features of the t-th window, $\sigma()$ denotes the Tanh function, and W_2 and b_2 denote the learnable parameter matrix.

$$K_{t+1}^{\cdots} = \sigma\big((\widetilde{K_t} + \widehat{K_t}) \times W_2 + b_2\big) \tag{9}$$

To effectively measure the average deviation between the predicted and actual values, the mean absolute error (MAE) is introduced as the model's loss function, as shown in Eq. (10). $\tau = \lfloor \frac{M-w}{L} \rfloor + 1$ and W_θ represent all the learnable parameters in the IDIGI model.

$$\mathcal{L}(W_\theta) = \frac{1}{\tau}\Sigma_{t=1}^{\tau}|K_{t+1}^{\cdots} - K_{t+1}| \tag{10}$$

5   Analysis of Experimental Results

5.1   Datasets

The detailed information of the four public datasets is shown in Table 2. The Performance Measurement System (PEMS) of the California Department of

Table 2. Data set description

Data Set	Sensors	Edges	Dataset Size	Time Range	Time Interval (in minutes)
PEMS03	358	547	26208	2018/9/1–2018/11/30	5
PEMS04	307	340	16992	2018/1/1–2018/2/28	5
PEMS07	883	866	28224	2017/5/1–2017/8/31	5
PEMS08	170	295	17856	2016/7/1–2016/8/31	5

Transportation collects these traffic flow datasets from California and aggregates them into 5-min intervals, yielding 288 time steps per day.

5.2 Baseline

This study adopts the following six methods as baselines for the experiment:

LSTM [7]: Long Short-Term Memory network, which effectively captures the temporal dependencies of traffic flow.

STGCN [6]: Spatio-Temporal Graph Convolutional Network uses convolution structures in the spatiotemporal domain to extract spatiotemporal features.

ASTGCN [17]: Attention-based Spatio-Temporal Graph Convolutional Network uses attention mechanisms to model spatial and temporal correlations.

STSGCN [13]: Spatio-temporal synchronous Graph Convolutional Network constructs a local spatiotemporal graph to capture spatiotemporal correlations.

STFGNN [8]: Spatio-temporal fusion graph neural network, designed with a spatiotemporal fusion graph, combines fusion graph neural modules and gated convolution modules to model spatiotemporal correlations.

RGSL [15]: Regularized Graph Structure Learning based on Semantic Knowledge adaptively generates an implicit graph from the data and merges it with an explicit graph to learn spatiotemporal correlations.

5.3 Experimental Setup

In order to ensure alignment with previous research [8,13], the data is divided into three subsets: training, validation, and testing, following a ratio of 6:2:2. A sequence of twelve consecutive time steps (equivalent to 1 h) of past data is utilized to forecast the subsequent twelve time steps (also 1 h).

The experiments are conducted on a server with a GeForce RTX 4090 24G GPU, operating within a Pytorch deep learning framework. Training of the models employs the Adam optimizer, which is configured with a learning rate of 0.003. The batch size is set at 64, while the training process spans 100 epochs.

Evaluation Metrics: The effectiveness of the models is assessed through Mean Absolute Error (MAE), Root Mean Square Error (RMSE), and Mean Absolute Percentage Error (MAPE).

Table 3. Performance Comparison Against Baselines

Methods		LSTM	STGCN	ASTGCN	STSGCN	STFGNN	RGSL	IDIGI
PEMS03	MAE	21.33	17.49	17.69	17.48	16.77	15.55	15.53
	RMSE	35.11	30.12	29.66	29.21	28.34	27.94	27.86
	MAPE	22.83%	17.15%	19.40%	16.78%	16.30%	15.80%	15.90%
PEMS04	MAE	25.37	21.93	22.93	21.19	19.83	19.48	19.20
	RMSE	39.35	35.19	35.22	33.65	31.88	32.06	31.22
	MAPE	17.18%	14.21%	16.56%	13.90%	13.02%	12.89%	12.69%
PEMS07	MAE	29.97	25.38	28.05	24.26	22.07	21.76	21.85
	RMSE	44.94	38.78	42.57	39.03	35.80	35.40	35.28
	MAPE	13.77%	11.08%	13.92%	10.21%	9.21%	9.77%	9.41%
PEMS08	MAE	21.74	17.76	18.43	17.13	16.64	15.92	15.82
	RMSE	32.97	27.46	28.11	26.80	26.22	25.64	25.27
	MAPE	13.96%	11.34%	12.36%	10.96%	10.60%	10.19%	10.09%

5.4 Comparative Experiment And Analysis

The experimental outcomes for the four publicly available datasets are presented from Table 3. From these results, several key observations can be drawn, along with corresponding analyses (with lower values indicating improved performance): The proposed method significantly outperforms all other state-of-the-art baselines by analyzing the results on the four datasets. Specifically, in terms of the MAE metric on the PEMS04 dataset, IDIGI achieves improvements of 24.32%, 12.44%, 16.27%, 9.4%, 3.18%, and 1.44% over LSTM, STGCN, ASTGCN, STSGCN, STFGNN, and RGSL, respectively. This demonstrates the superiority of the framework to some extent.

IDIGI outperforms STFGNN by 2.07% in RMSE on PEMS04 and approximately 3.62% in RMSE on PEMS08. In IDIGI, a traffic flow function graph is constructed between sensors, which is then fused with the traffic flow time graph using an attention mechanism. This fused graph captures more comprehensive information.

IDIGI outperforms RGSL by 2.62% in RMSE on PEMS04 and by approximately 1.44% in RMSE on PEMS08. In RGSL, historical data is constructed into a static graph to represent the correlation between sensors, which overlooks the dynamic correlation between them. However, IDIGI uses a dynamic graph to represent the time-segmented correlations between sensors, allowing for the extraction of differences in correlation across different time periods.

Table 4. Comparison of per epoch training time (in seconds).

Methods	DCRNN	STGCN	ASTGCN	STSGCN	STFGNN	RGSL	IDIGI
PEMS04	62	97	85	112	129	108	147
PEMS08	21	43	38	50	53	45	56

From Table 4, on the PEMS08 dataset, compared to models like STGCN, ASTGCN, STSGCN, STFGNN, and RGSL that also utilize GCN, the IDIGI model comprehensively considers both the spatial and temporal dependencies of traffic flow data, It can accurately capture the dynamic relationships between traffic flows. Not only is its time efficiency on the same order of magnitude as the baseline models, but it also improves the RMSE metric by 1.44%-10.10%. Compared to simpler models like LSTM, although its time efficiency is lower, it achieves a 6.71%–23.35% improvement in RMSE.

5.5   Ablation Experiments

In this framework, there are three main components: (1) the EOTSS module (2) the FG modul (3) the TDM module. To illustrate the impact of these modules, we conducted ablation experiments on IDIGI, with results shown in Table 5.

Table 5. IDIGI Ablation Experiments

EOTSS	FG	TDM	PEMS04 Dataset			PEMS08 Dataset		
			MAE	RMSE	MAPE	MAE	RMSE	MAPE
			19.48	32.06	12.89%	15.92	25.64	10.19%
√			19.38	31.96	12.75%	15.74	25.17	10.11%
√	√		19.28	31.23	12.78%	15.82	25.12	10.22%
√	√	√	19.2	31.22	12.69%	15.82	25.27	10.09%

From Table 5, the following conclusions and analyses can be drawn: Adding the EOTSS module improves the MAE, RMSE, and MAPE metrics on the PEMS04 dataset by 0.51%, 0.31%, and 1.08%, respectively. This improvement is due to the dynamic nature of inter-sensor traffic flow relationships, and the dynamic graphs constructed using embeddings extracted by EOTSS can better capture these dynamic relationships.

Adding the EOTSS and FG modules improves MAE, RMSE, and MAPE by 1.02%, 2.58%, and 0.85% on the PEMS04 dataset. This is due to incorporating semantic factors that assess sensor interrelationships. By combining the sensor topology graph with temporal and functional traffic correlations, the model gains richer information, leading to more accurate predictions.

Adding the EOTSS, FG, and TDM modules improves the MAE, RMSE, and MAPE metrics on the PEMS04 dataset by 1.44%, 2.62%, and 1.55%, respectively. This is because both spatial and temporal dependencies influence traffic flow prediction. Adding the TDM module enhances IDIGI's capability to learn temporal features, improving its performance.

6   Conclusion

Based on the sensor embedding representations, a dynamic implicit graph was constructed, and an LSTM model based on a down-sampling method was employed to propose a novel traffic flow prediction model, IDIGI. This model fully considers the spatial and temporal dependencies of traffic flow data, accurately reflecting the dynamic relationships of traffic flows and effectively addressing the information limitations in graph models. By comparing IDIGI with six baseline models across four real datasets, which show that approaches significantly outperform the existing baselines.

Acknowledgments. This study was funded by National Natural Science Foundation of China (No. 62172352), National Natural Science Foundation of China (No. 42306218), S&T Program of Hebei (No. 226Z0102G), Hebei Natural Science Foundation (No. F2023407003), Hebei Natural Science Foundation (No. F2023407003), Hebei Provincial Department of Education Youth Elite Project (No. BJ2021085).

Disclosure of Interests. The authors have no competing interests to declare that are relevant to the content of this article.

References

1. Bai, L., Yao, L., Li, C., Wang, X., Wang, C.: Adaptive graph convolutional recurrent network for traffic forecasting. In: NIPS 2020 (2020)
2. Berndt, D.J., Clifford, J.: Using dynamic time warping to find patterns in time series, pp. 359–370. AAAI Press (1994)
3. Chang, Z., Zhang, X., Wang, S., Ma, S., Gao, W.: STRPM: a spatiotemporal residual predictive model for high-resolution video prediction, pp. 13926–13935 (2022)
4. Dey, R., Salem, F.M.: Gate-variants of gated recurrent unit (GRU) neural networks, pp. 1597–1600 (2017)
5. Grover, A., Leskovec, J.: node2vec: scalable feature learning for networks, pp. 855–864. Association for Computing Machinery, New York (2016)
6. Han, H., Zhang, M., Hou, M.: STGCN: a spatial-temporal aware graph learning method for poi recommendation. In: 2020 IEEE International Conference on Data Mining (ICDM), pp. 1052–1057 (2020)
7. Hochreiter, S., Schmidhuber, J.: Long short-term memory. Neural Comput. **9**(8), 1735–1780 (1997)
8. Li, M., Zhu, Z.: Spatial-temporal fusion graph neural networks for traffic flow forecasting. CoRR abs/2012.09641 (2020)
9. Li, Y., Yu, R., Shahabi, C., Liu, Y.: Graph convolutional recurrent neural network: data-driven traffic forecasting. CoRR abs/1707.01926 (2017)
10. Li, Z., Rao, Z., Pan, L., Xu, Z.: MTS-mixers: multivariate time series forecasting via factorized temporal and channel mixing (2023)
11. Rao, X., Wang, H., Zhang, L.: Fogs: first-order gradient supervision with learning-based graph for traffic flow forecasting, pp. 3926–3932. International Joint Conferences on Artificial Intelligence Organization (2022)
12. Shang, C., Chen, J., Bi, J.: Discrete graph structure learning for forecasting multiple time series. CoRR abs/2101.06861 (2021)
13. Song, C., Lin, Y., Guo, S.: Spatial-temporal synchronous graph convolutional networks: a new framework for spatial-temporal network data forecasting (2020)
14. Xu, M., Dai, W., Liu, C., Gao, X., Lin, W.: Spatial-temporal transformer networks for traffic flow forecasting (2021)

15. Yu, H., Li, T., Yu, W., Li, J.: Regularized graph structure learning with semantic knowledge for multi-variates time-series forecasting, pp. 2362–2368. International Joint Conferences on Artificial Intelligence Organization (2022)
16. Zhang, J., Xu, X., Xiao, F.: STBGRN: a traffic prediction model based on spatiotemporal bidirectional gated recurrent units and graph convolutional residual networks. Int. J. Comput. Intell. Syst. **17**(1), 125 (2024)
17. Zhu, J., Wang, Q., Tao, C., Deng, H.: AST-GCN: attribute-augmented spatiotemporal graph convolutional network for traffic forecasting. IEEE Access **9** (2021)

A Recursive Learning Algorithm for the Least Squares SVM

Xiao-Lei Xia$^{(\boxtimes)}$ (ID) and Mingxing Ouyang

Guangdong Songshan Polytechnic College, Shaoguan, People's Republic of China
xxia01@gdsspt.edu.cn

Abstract. The decision function of the LS-SVM is often spanned by all the training samples, which is known as the issue of non-sparsity. This paper proposes a new recursive learning algorithm, selecting one training sample into the decision function at one time. The proposed algorithm first selects the training sample which minimizes the sum of squared loss for the linear regression model associated with the LS-SVM. At each of the subsequent iterations, the algorithm identifies and selects the training sample yielding a classifier which performs the best on those unselected training samples. For the update of the parameter vector of the LS-SVM due to addition of an extra training sample into the solution, it is demonstrated that the parameter vector can be derived without explicit inversion of the coefficient matrix of the linear system associated with the LS-SVM. This approach greatly reduces the computational complexity of the proposed algorithm. Experimental results on the checkerboard dataset demonstrated the proposed LS-SVM, parameterized by a smaller number of training samples than the standard LS-SVM, can recognize the checkerboard pattern accurately. The proposed LS-SVM model also demonstrated generalization performances superior to other sparse models on five datasets from the UCI repository.

Keywords: least-squares support vector machine · sparsity · recursive learning

1 Introduction

Over the last two decades, the least-squares support vector machine (LS-SVM) has attracted considerable research interest [6]. Falling into the category of supervised learning algorithms, the LS-SVM is an extension of the SVM which has been one of the most popular machine learning techniques. Empirically, the LS-SVM is comparable to the SVM in terms of the generalization performance.

Training the LS-SVM is a quadratic programming (QP) problem subject to equality constraints, which yields a hyperplane separating samples of two opposing classes. The training samples making actual contributions to the separating hyperplane are referred to as the support vectors (SV). A major bottleneck in the LS-SVM learning is that a majority, or all in most cases, of its training

© The Author(s), under exclusive license to Springer Nature Singapore Pte Ltd. 2025
R. Hadfi et al. (Eds.): PRICAI 2024, LNAI 15281, pp. 209–220, 2025.
https://doi.org/10.1007/978-981-96-0116-5_17

samples end up SVs. It is known as the "non-sparsity" problem of the LS-SVM. Because the time complexity of classifying a testing sample comes down to the number of SVs, non-sparsity of the solution can cause the testing phase to be too computationally expensive.

A number of methods have been proposed to combat the nonsparisty problems, which can be categorized into two groups—"post-processing methods" and "pre-processing methods". The post-processing methods approximate the normal vector for the optimal separating hyperplane identified by the LS-SVM with a reduced number of SVs. They are often referred to as "pruning methods" and differ in the rules they use to discover trivial SVs. For example, Suykens et al. proposed to evaluate the SVs by the magnitude of their associated Lagrange multipliers [14]. The larger the magnitude was, the less likely the SV was to be pruned. de Kruif and de Vries recommended to remove the SV whose absence introduced the least approximation error [3]. Without explicitly implementing the training procedure, they derived analytically the model upon exclusion of a sample. Xia et al. reckoned that the training sample leading to the slightest fluctuation of the dual objective function be removed [9]. They provided an analytical derivation of the parameter vector of the model upon omission of a training sample, which eased the computational overhead. Geebelen et al. proposed to transform a non-separable classification problem to a separable one in the feature space, which reduced the number of support vectors [15]. Burges et al. approximated the weight vector by a reduced set of support vectors [16]. Downs et al. selected a number of support vectors so that each of the remaining support vectors can be expressed as their linear combination [17].

In contrast to "post-processing methods", "pre-processing methods" seek to generate sparse LS-SVMs directly. An example was the fixed-size LS-SVM in which the full kernel matrix was approximated by a low-rank one through use of the Nystrom method [18]. The technique of Sparse Conjugate Directions Pursuit iteratively constructs a conjugate set of vectors of increasing cardinality, and produces a sparse solution of the linear system to be solved. Karsmakers et al. applied the technique to the fixed-size LS-SVM [20]. Mall et al. proposed to impose a constraint of minimizing the L_0 norm of the normal vector [4]. Cawley et al. assumed that the normal vector of the optimal hyperplane can be spanned by a limited number of the training samples [1]. Samples that led to the minimal leave-one-out cross-validation error were selected into the solution. Liu et al. proposed a weighted L_q adaptive LS-SVM model in which the parameter q was adaptively chosen to fit the data structure [19]. Jiao et al. proposed to identify and select iteratively the SV whose addition made the most outstanding contribution to the dual of the LS-SVM [2]. The kernel matching pursuit (KMP) algorithm has also been used to suppress the number of SVs in the LS-SVM. The KMP algorithm performs in a greedy manner and selects a single basis function achieving the steepest decrease in the sum of squared error [5,7]. Advantageously, application of the KMP algorithm can eliminate redundancies among selected basis functions by ensuring their linear independence between each other [8]. Zhou et al. proposed to perform pivoted Cholesky decomposition on the kernel matrix to find its low rank representation, which eventually led to a sparse LS-SVM classifier [10].

In this paper, a recursive learning algorithm is proposed to build a sparse LS-SVM classifier. The proposed algorithm identifies the first SV as the training sample which minimizes the sum of squared loss for the linear regression model associated with the LS-SVM. At each of the subsequent iterations, the algorithm identifies and selects the training sample yielding a classifier which performs the best on those unselected training samples. Addition of an extra sample into the solution necessitates the update of the parameter vector of the LS-SVM. Fortunately, it is demonstrated that the parameter vector can be derived without explicit inversion of the coefficient matrix, which reduced the computational complexity of the proposed algorithm.

The formulation and the training algorithm of the LS-SVM are reviewed in Sect. 2. Section 3 introduces the proposed recursive LS-SVM algorithm, preceded by a new metric that evaluates the prediction error made by the model constructed from the selected training samples on those unselected training samples. It is then shown that the prediction error of a model can be evaluated without explicit inversion of the coefficient matrix of the linear system associated with the LS-SVM. In Sect. 4, the proposed learning algorithm is compared against the standard LS-SVM in terms of their generalization performances on the checkerboard dataset. It is followed by experiments on five datasets from the UCI repository and comparison with multiple sparse LS-SVM models. The concluding remarks are given in Sect. 5.

2   Training the Least-Squares Support Vector Machine

Consider the binary classification problem presented by the dataset consisting of ℓ samples $\mathbf{x}_1, \ldots, \mathbf{x}_\ell$, where $\mathbf{x}_i \in \mathbb{R}^d$. The class label for $\mathbf{x}_i$ is given by y_i which is either -1 or $+1$.

After mapping the data into the feature space by a function Φ where they become separable, a separating hyperplane in the form of

$$f(x) = \mathbf{w}^\top \Phi(\mathbf{x}_i) + b \tag{1}$$

can be learnt. The LS-SVM algorithm learns the separating hyperplane with the maximum margin and the minimum training cost. The search is mathematically expressed as a quadratic programming problem:

$$\min_{\mathbf{w},b,\xi} \quad \frac{1}{2}\mathbf{w}^\top \mathbf{w} + \frac{\gamma}{2}\sum_{i=1}^{\ell}\xi_i^2$$

$$\text{s.t.} \quad \mathbf{w}^\top \Phi(\mathbf{x}_i) + b = y_i - \xi_i \tag{2}$$

where ξ_i $(i = 1, \ldots, \ell)$ are the "slack variables" which allow for classification errors on certain training samples. The parameter γ controls the degree to which $\sum_{i=1}^{\ell}\xi_i$ is penalized.

The Lagrangian for Equation (2), with Lagrange multipliers α_i, is:

$$\mathcal{L} = \frac{1}{2}\mathbf{w}^\top\mathbf{w} + \frac{\gamma}{2}\sum_{i=1}^{\ell}\xi_i^2 - \sum_{i=1}^{\ell}\alpha_i[\mathbf{w}^\top\Phi(\mathbf{x}_i) + b - y_i + \xi_i] \tag{3}$$

Setting $\frac{\partial\mathcal{L}}{\partial\mathbf{w}} = 0$, $\frac{\partial\mathcal{L}}{\partial b} = 0$ and $\frac{\partial\mathcal{L}}{\partial\xi_i} = 0$, it gives the optimality conditions:

$$\mathbf{w} = \sum_{i=1}^{\ell}\alpha_i\Phi(\mathbf{x}_i) \tag{4}$$

$$\sum_{i=1}^{\ell}\alpha_i = 0 \tag{5}$$

$$\alpha_i = \gamma\xi_i, \quad i = 1,\ldots,\ell \tag{6}$$

Making use of the above optimal conditions, the dual Lagrangian can be derived:

$$\min_{\alpha} \frac{1}{2}\sum_{i=1}^{\ell}\sum_{j=1}^{\ell}\alpha_i\alpha_j k(\mathbf{x}_i,\mathbf{x}_j) + \frac{\gamma}{2}\sum_{i=1}^{\ell}\alpha_i^2 - \sum_{i=1}^{\ell}y_i\alpha_i$$

$$\text{s.t.} \quad \sum_{i=1}^{\ell}\alpha_i = 0 \tag{7}$$

where $k(\mathbf{x}_i,\mathbf{x}_j) = \Phi(\mathbf{x}_i)^\top\Phi(\mathbf{x}_j)$ is known as the "kernel function".

Introducing a Lagrangian multiplier, denoted as b, the equality constraint, can be moved into the objective function [12]:

$$\min_{\alpha,b} \frac{1}{2}\sum_{i=1}^{\ell}\sum_{j=1}^{\ell}\alpha_i\alpha_j k(\mathbf{x}_i,\mathbf{x}_j) + \frac{\gamma}{2}\sum_{i=1}^{\ell}\alpha_i^2 - \sum_{i=1}^{\ell}y_i\alpha_i + b\sum_{i=1}^{\ell}\alpha_i \tag{8}$$

Setting the partial derivatives of the objective function with respect to α and b to zero, gives

$$\sum_{i=1}^{\ell}\alpha_i = 0 \tag{9}$$

and

$$\sum_{j=1}^{\ell}\alpha_j k(\mathbf{x}_i,\mathbf{x}_j) + \gamma\alpha_i + b = y_i \tag{10}$$

for $\forall i \in \{1,2,\ldots,\ell\}$.

These $(\ell+1)$ equations can be expressed as a linear system of:

$$\begin{bmatrix} 0 & \vec{\mathbf{1}}^\top \\ \vec{\mathbf{1}} & \mathbf{K} + \gamma\mathbf{I} \end{bmatrix}\begin{bmatrix} b \\ \alpha \end{bmatrix} = \begin{bmatrix} 0 \\ \mathbf{y} \end{bmatrix} \tag{11}$$

where the (i, j) element of the matrix $\mathbf{K}$ is $k(\mathbf{x}_i, \mathbf{x}_j)$, $\mathbf{I}$ is the $\ell \times \ell$ identity matrix and the column vector $\overrightarrow{\mathbf{1}}$ is comprised of ℓ ones.

By representing the vector of model parameters as $\mathbf{p} = [b, \boldsymbol{\alpha}^\top]^\top$ and defining the matrices $\mathbf{Q}$ and $\mathbf{t}$ as:

$$\mathbf{Q} = \begin{bmatrix} 0 & \overrightarrow{\mathbf{1}}^\top \\ \overrightarrow{\mathbf{1}} & \mathbf{K} + \gamma\mathbf{I} \end{bmatrix}, \quad \mathbf{t} = \begin{bmatrix} 0 \\ \mathbf{y} \end{bmatrix}$$

Equation (11) can be rewritten as:

$$\mathbf{Q}\mathbf{p} = \mathbf{t} \tag{12}$$

Many techniques including Conjugate-Gradient method and Gauss elimination can be applied to the linear system. However, the resultant $\mathbf{p}$ has very few non-zero elements, which is referred to non-sparseness problem of the LS-SVM.

3   A Recursive Learning Algorithm for the Least-Squares SVM

The proposed algorithm selects one training sample at one iteration into the solution. At each iteration, the set of training samples is practically split into two subsets represented by $\boldsymbol{\theta}$ and $\boldsymbol{\tau}$ respectively, where $\boldsymbol{\theta}$ is composed of indices of the selected samples and $\boldsymbol{\tau}$ consists of indices of the unselected samples.

The search for the sample to be selected at an iteration can be mathematically expressed as the following minimization problem:

$$\min_j \sum_{i \in \tau, i \neq j} e(i, j) \tag{13}$$

where $j \in \tau$. The function $e(i, j)$ evaluates, upon selection of the sample $\mathbf{x}_j$ as the new SV, the prediction error of the resultant classifier on an unselected sample $\mathbf{x}_i$ $(i \neq j)$. Letting $f_j(\mathbf{x}_i)$ be the decision value that $\mathbf{x}_i$ obtains from the model associated with $\mathbf{x}_j$, $e(i)$ is defined as:

$$e(i, j) = \begin{cases} 0 & \text{if } y_i f_j(\mathbf{x}_i) > 0 \text{ and } |f_j(\mathbf{x}_i)| \geq 1 \\ 1 - |f_j(\mathbf{x}_i)| & \text{if } y_i f_j(\mathbf{x}_i) > 0 \text{ and } |f_j(\mathbf{x}_i)| < 1 \\ 1 & \text{if } y_i f_j(\mathbf{x}_i) \leq 0 \end{cases}$$

In non-mathematical terms, the selected sample at each iteration is the one yielding the classifier which commits the minimal classification errors on the unselected samples.

3.1   Efficient Computation of $f_j(x_i)$

The computational load of our algorithm comes down primarily to computation of $f_j(x_i)$. Luckily, $f_j(x_i)$ can be computed without explicitly evaluating the model parameters at each iteration, which is described in this section.

At the j-th iteration, the vector of model parameters, $\mathbf{p}_j$, is given by the solution of a set of linear equations:

$$\mathbf{Q}_j \mathbf{p}_j = \mathbf{t}_j \tag{14}$$

where $\mathbf{Q}_j$ represents the coefficient matrix associated with the current set of SVs represented by $\mathbf{X}_S$. $\mathbf{t}_j$ denotes the current target vector.

Assuming that a sample $\mathbf{x}_k$ where $k \in \tau$ is being selected into the solution. The coefficient matrix grows into $\mathbf{Q}_{j+1}$ accordingly:

$$\mathbf{Q}_{j+1} = \left[\begin{array}{c|c} \mathbf{Q}_j & \mathbf{k}_{Sk} \\ \hline \mathbf{k}_{Sk}^T & c \end{array} \right] \tag{15}$$

where the vector $\mathbf{k}_{Sk} = [1 \quad \mathbf{K}(\mathbf{X}_S, \mathbf{x}_k)^T]^T$ and the constant $c = \mathbf{K}(\mathbf{x}_k, \mathbf{x}_k) + \frac{1}{\gamma}$.

It can be verified that [11]:

$$\mathbf{Q}_{j+1}^{-1} = \left[\begin{array}{c|c} \mathbf{Q}_j^{-1} & \mathbf{0} \\ \hline \mathbf{0} & 0 \end{array} \right] + \frac{\mathbf{u}\mathbf{u}^T}{c - \mathbf{k}_{Sk}^T \mathbf{Q}_j^{-1} \mathbf{k}_{Sk}}, \tag{16}$$

where the vector $\mathbf{u} = \left[\begin{array}{c} \mathbf{Q}_j^{-1} \mathbf{k}_{Sk} \\ -1 \end{array} \right]$. Equation (16) facilitates the efficient computation of $\mathbf{Q}_{j+1}^{-1}$ without explicit inversion.

Meanwhile, the LS-SVM model $\mathbf{p}_{j+1}$ at the $(j+1)$-th iteration can be evaluated as:

$$\mathbf{p}_{j+1} = \mathbf{Q}_{j+1}^{-1} \left[\begin{array}{c} \mathbf{t} \\ y_k \end{array} \right] \tag{17}$$

$$= \left[\begin{array}{c} \mathbf{Q}_j^{-1} \mathbf{t} \\ 0 \end{array} \right] + \frac{[\mathbf{t}^T \quad y_k]\mathbf{u}}{c - \mathbf{k}_{Sk}^T \mathbf{Q}_j^{-1} \mathbf{k}_{Sk}} \mathbf{u} \tag{18}$$

$$= \left[\begin{array}{c} \mathbf{p}_j \\ 0 \end{array} \right] + \frac{\mathbf{t}^T \mathbf{Q}_j^{-1} \mathbf{k}_{Sk} - y_k}{c - \mathbf{k}_{Sk}^T \mathbf{Q}_j^{-1} \mathbf{k}_{Sk}} \left[\begin{array}{c} \mathbf{Q}_j^{-1} \mathbf{k}_{Sk} \\ -1 \end{array} \right] \tag{19}$$

$$= \left[\begin{array}{c} \mathbf{p}_j \\ 0 \end{array} \right] + \beta \left[\begin{array}{c} \mathbf{Q}_j^{-1} \mathbf{k}_{Sk} \\ -1 \end{array} \right] \tag{20}$$

where y_k is the class label for $\mathbf{x}_k$ and $\beta = \frac{\mathbf{t}^T \mathbf{Q}_j^{-1} \mathbf{k}_{Sk} - y_k}{c - \mathbf{k}_{Sk}^T \mathbf{Q}_j^{-1} \mathbf{k}_{Sk}}$.

For an unselected sample represented by $\mathbf{x}_i$ where $i \in \tau$ and $i \neq k$, the decision value it obtains from the LS-SVM model $\mathbf{p}_{j+1}$ is:

$$f_{j+1}(\mathbf{x}_i) = \mathbf{p}_{j+1}^T \left[\begin{array}{c} \mathbf{v} \\ \mathbf{K}(\mathbf{x}_k, \mathbf{x}_i) \end{array} \right] \tag{21}$$

where $\mathbf{v} = [1 \quad \mathbf{K}(\mathbf{X}_S, \mathbf{x}_i)^T]^T$.

Substituting Eq. (20) into Eq. (21), it follows that:

$$f_{j+1}(\mathbf{x}_i) = \left([\mathbf{p}_j^T \ 0] + \beta[\mathbf{k}_{Sk}^T \mathbf{Q}_j^{-1} - 1] \right) \begin{bmatrix} \mathbf{v} \\ \mathbf{K}(\mathbf{x}_k, \mathbf{x}_i) \end{bmatrix} \tag{22}$$

$$= \mathbf{p}_j^T \mathbf{v} + \beta \mathbf{k}_{Sk}^T \mathbf{Q}_j^{-1} \mathbf{v} - \mathbf{K}(\mathbf{x}_k, \mathbf{x}_i) \tag{23}$$

$$= f_j(\mathbf{x}_i) + \beta \mathbf{v}^T \mathbf{Q}_j^{-1} \mathbf{k}_{Sk} - \mathbf{K}(\mathbf{x}_k, \mathbf{x}_i) \tag{24}$$

where $f_j(\mathbf{x}_i) = \mathbf{p}_j^T \mathbf{v}$ is the decision value the LS-SVM model parameterized by $\mathbf{p}_j$ assigns $\mathbf{x}_i$.

Equation (24) suggests that, by keeping $f_j(\mathbf{x}_i)$ in the memory, $f_{j+1}(\mathbf{x}_i)$ can be efficiently updated without explicitly calculating $\mathbf{p}_{j+1}$.

3.2   Initialization

The algorithm starts with a set of two SVs of opposing class labels. This section describes the selection strategy of these two SVs.

Initially, the matrix $\mathbf{Q}$ consists of $(\ell + 1)$ columns, i.e., $\mathbf{Q} = (\boldsymbol{\phi}_0, \boldsymbol{\phi}_1, \ldots, \boldsymbol{\phi}_\ell)$. $\boldsymbol{\phi}_i$, where $(i = 1, \ldots, \ell)$, corresponds to a "basis function" $\mathbf{k}(\cdot, \mathbf{x}_i)$ which is parameterized by $\mathbf{x}_i$. In fact, $\boldsymbol{\phi}_i$ consists of the evaluation of $\mathbf{k}(\cdot, \mathbf{x}_i)$ on the training samples. For the linear regression problem presented by Equation (14), the contribution of $\boldsymbol{\phi}_i$ to the sum of squared loss, denoted as δE_i, can be proven to be:

$$\delta E_i = \frac{(\mathbf{t}^T \boldsymbol{\phi}_i)^2}{\boldsymbol{\phi}_i^T \boldsymbol{\phi}_i} \tag{25}$$

Proof of Eq. (25) is available in [8].

The first SV is selected by solving the optimization problem of:

$$\max_i \quad \delta E_i \tag{26}$$

where i is its index.

The second SV is selected by solving Eq. (13), subject to an additional constraint that it comes from the class opposed to the one the first SV belongs to.

4   Experimental Evaluation

Experiments were performed on a number of well-known public datasets. The proposed algorithm was compared against the standardard LS-SVM, as well as multiple sparse LS-SVM models including the fixed-sized LS-SVM, the L_0 norm LS-SVM [4], the FSA-LSSVM and the PFSA-LSSVM developed by Jiao et al. [2].

The proposed LS-SVM learning algorithm was coded in Matlab. The kernel function was chosen to be the Radial Basis Function:

$$K(\mathbf{x}, \mathbf{x}_i) = \exp(-\sigma \parallel \mathbf{x} - \mathbf{x}_i \parallel^2) \tag{27}$$

10-fold cross validation was performed to optimize the parameter σ of the RBF kernel, as well as the regularization parameter γ of the LS-SVM. For both parameters, the values that were evaluated were $\{2^i\}$ where the integer i grew sequentially from -10 to $+10$.

4.1   Results on the Checkerboard Dataset

The checkerboard dataset has 1000 data points from the XY-plane, with 486 points belonging to one class and 514 points the other class. The data points form a pattern of "checkerboard", which is illustrated in Fig. 1(a). Prior to training the SVM, the data points are scaled to $[-1, +1]$.

With the standard LS-SVM, the optimal parameter setting is $\gamma = 2^6$ and $\sigma = 2^{-4}$, leading to the maximal 10-fold cross validation accuracy of 95.0%. The generalization performance of the LS-SVM is illustrated by Fig. 1(b), where the classifier recognizes the checkerboard pattern in the XY plane. The normal vector of the classifier is constructed by 1000 support vectors.

Figure 1(c) and Fig. 1(d) depict the performance of the classifiers generated from the proposed learning algorithm which are parameterized by 400 and 200 SVs respectively. The two classifiers exhibited fair generalization ability and generally recognized the checkerboard pattern. The graphs demonstrate that our proposed learning algorithm has great potential in building a sparse LS-SVM classifier with satisfactory generalization ability.

4.2   The UCI Datasets

Experiments were also performed on five datasets from the UCI repository which were Flare Solar, Breast Cancer, Ringnorm, Banana and Waveform, available at http://theoval.cmp.uea.ac.uk/matlab/#benchmarks. Each of the UCI datasets was randomly split into a training set and a testing set 100 times. For each split, the number of samples for training and testing has been listed in Table 1. Following the practice of Wu et al. [13], the first 20 partitions was used to evaluate the performance of various algorithms. The test accuracy averaged across the 20 partitions was reported.

The proposed algorithm was compared against the fixed-sized LS-SVM, the L_0 norm LS-SVM [4], the FSA-LSSVM and the PFSA-LSSVM [2].

Table 1. The training/testing splits of the datasets

Dataset	Train (#)	Test (#)	Total (#)
Banana	400	4900	5300
Breast cancer	200	77	263
Ringnorm	400	7000	7400
Waveform	400	4600	5000
Flare Solar	666	400	144

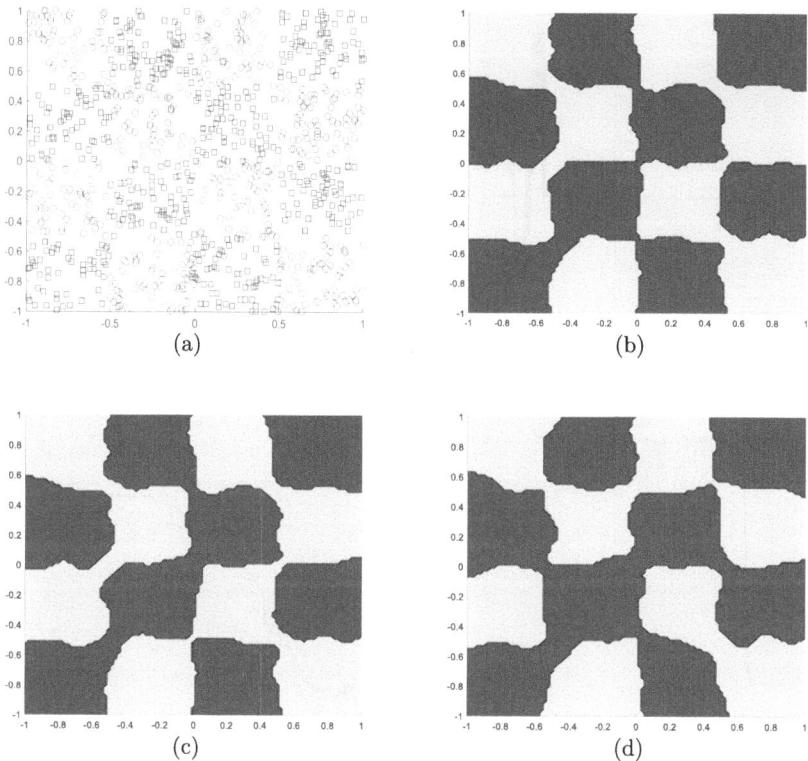

Fig. 1. (a) The checkerboard dataset; (b) The standard LS-SVM spanned by all the training samples; (c) The proposed sparse LS-SVM spanned by 400 SVs; (d) The proposed sparse LS-SVM spanned by 200 SVs.

4.3   Results on the UCI Datasets

Figure 2(a) to Fig. 2(e) present the performance of various algorithms on the datasets of Flare Solar, Breast Cancer, Ringnorm, Banana and Waveform respectively. For each graph, the x-axis indicates the number of SVs and the y-axis gives the average test accuracy. The performance of a specific algorithm was illustrated by a curve, describing how the test accuracy changes as the number of SVs grows from 0 to the total number of training samples. The curve representing proposed training algorithm was colored in dashed blue. The methods of the FSA-LSSVM and the PFSA-LSSVM, the fixed-sized (FS) LS-SVM and the L_0 norm LS-SVM were represented by curves in red, black, green and magenta respectively.

Figure 2(a) indicates that, the proposed algorithm performed better than both the FS-LSSVM and the L_0 norm LS-SVM on the Flare Solar dataset, particularly when the number of SVs was less than 100 or greater than 500. Comparatively, the performance of both the FSA-LSSVM and pFSA-LSSVM

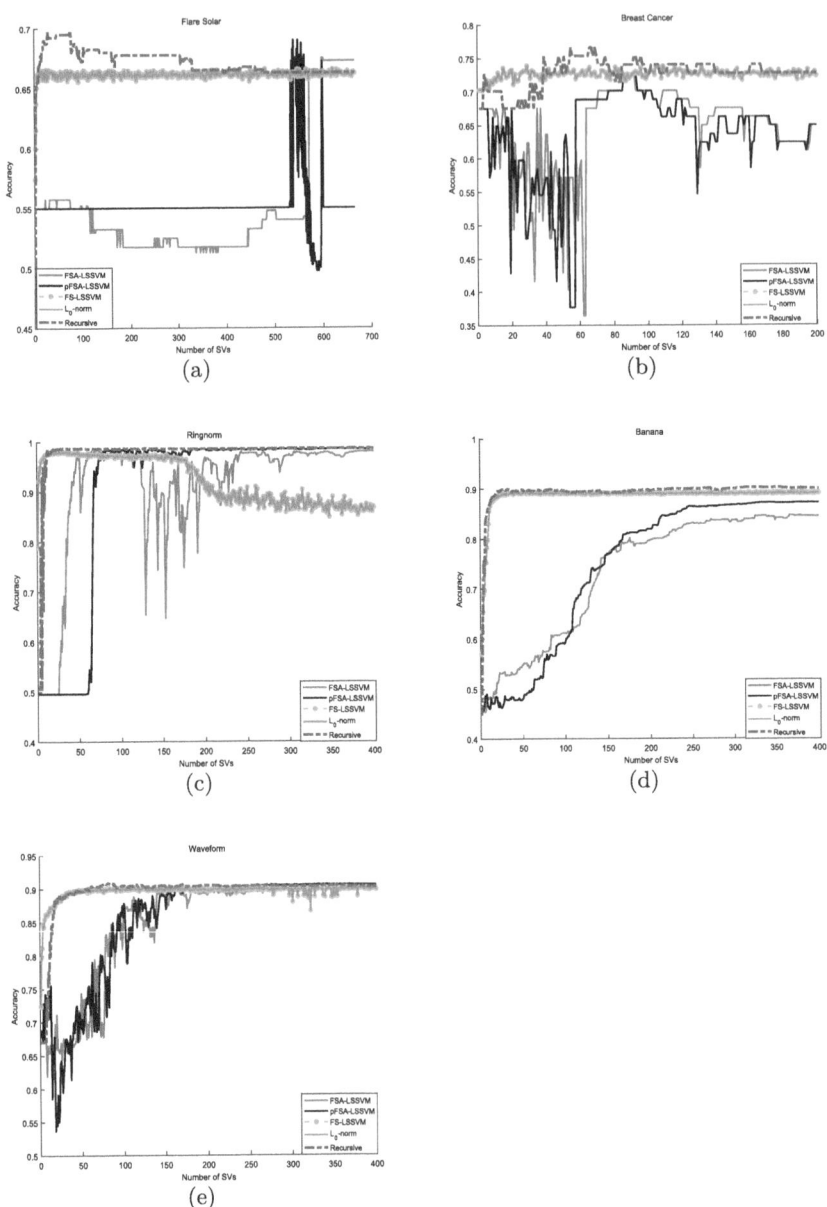

Fig. 2. Results on: (a) the Flare Solar dataset; (b) the Breast Cancer dataset; (c) the Ringnorm dataset; (d) the Banana dataset; (e) the Waveform dataset. (Color figure online)

was the worst when the number of SVs was small. Figure 2(b) shows that, when the number of SVs reached approximately 60, the proposed algorithm achieved the highest accuracy than the rest methods on the Breast Cancer dataset. Furthermore, the proposed algorithm continued to outperform the other methods as the number of SVs grew larger. Figure 2(c) shows that, the proposed algorithm excelled the other methods in terms of the test accuracy on the Ringnorm dataset. Figure 2(d) shows that, the proposed performed slightly better than the FS-LSSVM and the L_0 norm LS-SVM and maintained higher accuracy compared to the FSA-LSSVM and pFSA-LSSVM on the Banana dataset. The superiority of the proposed algorithm was evident when the number of SVs was less than 200. Figure 2(e) shows that, on the Waveform dataset, the proposed performed slightly better than the other approaches and achieved the highest accuracy when the number of SVs was roughly 100.

Overall, generalization performance of the proposed algorithm was demonstrated to be comparable to that of the FS-LSSVM and the L_0 norm LS-SVM and noticeably superior to that of the FSA-LSSVM and pFSA-LSSVM methods.

5   Conclusions

The proposed learning algorithm has demonstrated to possess enhanced sparsity compared to the standard LS-SVM. Furthermore, compared to other sparse LS-SVM models, the proposed algorithm has exhibited very competitive generalization performance. Future work includes application of the proposed algorithm to large datasets and evaluation of its scalability.

Acknowledgments. This work was funded by the Department of Education, Guangdong Province, P.R.China under Grant 2021KCXTD072 and Shaoguan Municipal Science and Technology Bureau, P.R.China under Grant 210730164532226.

Disclosure of Interests. The authors have no competing interests to declare that are relevant to the content of this article.

References

1. Cawley, G.C., Talbot, N.L.: Fast exact leave-one-out cross-validation of sparse least-squares support vector machines. Neural Netw. **17**(10), 1467–1475 (2004)
2. Jiao, L., Bo, L., Wang, L.: Fast sparse approximation for least squares support vector machine. IEEE Trans. Neural Netw. **18**(3), 685–697 (2007)
3. de Kruif, B., de Vries, T.: Pruning error minimization in least squares support vector machines. IEEE Trans. Neural Netw. **14**(3), 696–702 (2003)
4. Mall, R., Suykens, J.A.: Very sparse lssvm reductions for large-scale data. IEEE Trans. Neural Netw. Learn. Syst. **26**(5), 1086–1097 (2015)
5. Popovici, V., Bengio, S., Thiran, J.P.: Kernel matching pursuit for large datasets. Pattern Recogn. **38**(12), 2385–2390 (2005)
6. Vapnik, V.: The Nature of Statistical Learning Theory. Springer, New York (1995). https://doi.org/10.1007/978-1-4757-3264-1

7. Vincent, P., Bengio, Y.: Kernel matching pursuit. Mach. Learn. **48**(1), 165–187 (2002)
8. Xia, X.L.: Training sparse least squares support vector machines by the QR decomposition. Neural Netw. **106**, 175–184 (2018)
9. Xia, X.L., Zhou, S.M., Ouyang, M., Xiang, D., Zhang, Z., Zhou, Z.: A dual-based pruning method for the least-squares support vector machine. IFAC-PapersOnLine **56**(2), 10377–10383 (2023)
10. Zhou, S.: Sparse lssvm in primal using cholesky factorization for large-scale problems. IEEE Trans. Neural Netw. Learn. Syst. **27**(4), 783–795 (2016)
11. Kuh, A., De Wilde, P.: Comments on pruning error minimization in least squares support vector machines. IEEE Trans. Neural Netw. **18**(2), 606–609 (2007)
12. Cauwenberghs, G., Poggio, T.: Incremental and decremental support vector machine learning. Adv. Neural Inf. Process. Syst. **13** (2000)
13. Wu, M., Schölkopf, B., Bakır, G., Cristianini, N.: A direct method for building sparse kernel learning algorithms. J. Mach. Learn. Res. **7**(4) (2006)
14. Suykens, J.A., De Brabanter, J., Lukas, L., Vandewalle, J.: Weighted least squares support vector machines: robustness and sparse approximation. Neurocomputing **48**(1–4), 85–105 (2002)
15. Geebelen, D., Suykens, J.A., Vandewalle, J.: Reducing the number of support vectors of svm classifiers using the smoothed separable case approximation. IEEE Trans. Neural Netw. Learn. Syst. **23**(4), 682–688 (2012)
16. Burges, C.J.: Simplified support vector decision rules. In: Proceedings of the Thirteenth International Conference on International Conference on Machine Learning, pp. 71–77 (1996)
17. Downs, T., Gates, K.E., Masters, A.: Exact simplification of support vector solutions. J. Mach. Learn. Res. **2**(Dec), 293–297 (2001)
18. De Brabanter, K., De Brabanter, J., Suykens, J.A., De Moor, B.: Optimized fixed-size kernel models for large data sets. Comput. Stat. Data Anal. **54**(6), 1484–1504 (2010)
19. Liu, J., Li, J., Xu, W., Shi, Y.: A weighted lq adaptive least squares support vector machine classifiers-robust and sparse approximation. Expert Syst. Appl. **38**(3), 2253–2259 (2011)
20. Karsmakers, P., Pelckmans, K., De Brabanter, K., Van Hamme, H., Suykens, J.A.: Sparse conjugate directions pursuit with application to fixed-size kernel models. Mach. Learn. **85**, 109–148 (2011)

BDEL: A Backdoor Attack Defense Method Based on Ensemble Learning

Zhihuan Xing[1], Yuqing Lan[2(✉)], Yin Yu[3], Yong Cao[2,4], Xiaoyi Yang[2(✉)],
Yichun Yu[1,2,3,4], and Dan Yu[4]

[1] School of Computer Science and Engineering, Beihang University, Beijing 100191,
China
[2] School of Software, Beihang University, Beijing 100191, China
{lanyuqing,xyyang001}@buaa.edu.cn
[3] School of Cyberspace Science and Technology, Bejing Institute of Technology,
Beijing 100081, China
[4] China Standard Intelligent Security Co., Ltd., Beijing 100097, China

Abstract. Deep neural networks (DNNs) are susceptible to backdoor
attacks. Previous researches have demonstrated the challenges in both
removing poisoned samples from compromised datasets and repairing
contaminated models. These difficulties arise as attackers employ adaptive strategies, enhancing the stealthiness of their attacks and thereby
evading detection by defenders. To address these challenges, we propose
BDEL, a defense method based on ensemble learning, aimed at enhancing
the model intrinsic robustness against backdoor attacks. BDEL focuses
on strengthening the model directly, thus avoiding the need for assumptions about the attackers. In addition, BDEL does not require the retention of a clean dataset and is compatible with any existing DNN. Specifically, we construct random subsets from the original dataset and train
individual base classifiers on these subsets, each equipped with a different
network architecture. During the training process of these base classifiers,
a self-ensembling strategy is employed to enhance the intrinsic robustness
of the model. To the best of our knowledge, we are the first to propose a
method to enhance model robustness against backdoor attacks through
self-ensembling. We evaluated BDEL against various types of backdoor
attacks. The results demonstrate that BDEL is effective in defending
against these attacks and achieves state-of-the-art performance.

Keywords: Security of deep learning · Backdoor attacks · Ensemble
learning

1 Introduction

DNNs have demonstrated remarkable success in numerous critical applications
such as face recognition [5], object detection [3], and autonomous driving [1],
illustrating their advantages over conventional computing methods. However,
deep learning models used in these sectors are susceptible to backdoor attacks

R. Hadfi et al. (Eds.): PRICAI 2024, LNAI 15281, pp. 221–235, 2025.
https://doi.org/10.1007/978-981-96-0116-5_18

[25,48]. Attackers leverage the advanced learning capabilities of DNNs to forge a strong link between triggers and target labels, thereby effectively embedding a hidden vulnerability.Once a backdoor is implanted, the model will misclassify poisoned samples containing triggers as the target category designated by attackers, causing by malicious features overriding its benign ones during prediction. The backdoor in the model activates only when predicting poisoned samples with triggers and does not affect the ability of the model to predict clean samples.

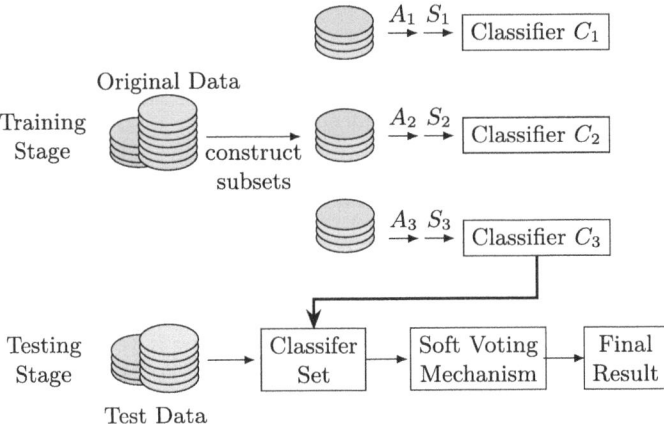

Fig. 1. Overall architecture diagram. A denotes different algorithms using different network architectures. S denotes different self-ensembling methods.

Previous researchs have shown that defense methods such as poisoning sample detection and detoxifying poisoned models are highly challenging, as attackers can implement backdoor attacks by finding more concealed triggers. Neural Cleanse [41] conducts poisoning detection on models and prunes poisoned neurons to detoxify the model. This technique requires a large number of input samples for detection and performs well only with small triggers. The attack methods proposed by Shokri et al. [35] and the N-to-One and One-to-N attack methods by Xue et al. [46] successfully bypassed Neural Cleanse [41], and the method by Shokri et al. [35] could deceive Neural Cleanse [41] into pruning benign neurons during the defense process. FinePruning [27] and Neural Attention [23] both require retaining 10% of absolutely clean samples from the training data for defense; Wang et al. [42] proposed a backdoor attack defense using the honeypot concept, which also requires preserving 5% of absolutely clean data for defense. Although ANP [45] and ABL [22] significantly reduce the success rate of attacks, they lead to a substantial decrease in the model's accuracy for benign tasks. Jia et al. [17] proposed Bootstrap Aggregating (bagging) [4] for intrinsic robustness against backdoor attacks, achieving 91.1% certified accuracy on the MNIST [20] dataset with any 100 samples altered. Despite [17] proving the robustness of Bagging against data poisoning attacks, the effectiveness of

Bagging alone in defending against backdoor attacks in practical applications is not satisfactory.

To address the limitation of existing defense methods, we propose BDEL, a backdoor attack defense method based on ensemble learning that introduces diversity into the model. To address the limitations of existing defense methods, we propose BDEL,a backdoor defense via ensemble learning. By enhancing the model's intrinsic robustness, BDEL defends against backdoor attacks without directly confronting the attacker. BDEL effectively defends against previously hard-to-detect data poisoning backdoor attacks. In simple terms, BDEL first constructs multiple random subsets from the original dataset. Then, using different network architectures, we train multiple base classifiers on these subsets. Each base classifier is trained using self-ensembling. Finally, we aggregate these base classifiers to obtain the ultimate classifier. BDEL does not require the retention of clean training samples and is not dependent on any specific network architecture.

To construct a superior ensemble learning system, the key lies in integrating multiple base classifiers that are not only high-performing but also diverse from one another. BDEL is rooted in this principle, as illustrated in Fig. 1. We employ the Bagging technique to introduce diversity into the dataset by creating random subsets through sampling with replacement, where the size of each random subset is smaller than that of the original dataset. Each base classifier is then trained on one of these random subsets. We provide a simple example to explain why Bagging can, to some extent, defend against backdoor attacks, as shown in Fig. 2. To incorporate diversity among neural networks, we train a variety of deep neural networks. To enhance the performance of the base classifiers, we use self-ensembling to improve their robustness. During the training of individual base classifiers, we record their optimization trajectories and aggregate these trajectories using self-ensembling to produce the final classifier. We assign a lower aggregation weight to the most recent weights, increasing the model's reliance on historical weights and reducing sensitivity to recent changes in model weights. This makes the final model obtained through self-ensembling more stable and less susceptible to partial poisoning optimization trajectories. To introduce diversity in self-ensembling, we adjust the self-ensembling algorithm parameters during training to derive different aggregation formulas, which are then applied to various base classifiers. Once all base classifiers are obtained, during the deployment phase, we use all base classifiers to make parallel predictions on test samples. Each base classifier outputs a probability distribution vector, and we aggregate these outputs using a soft voting mechanism to produce the final result. Our experiments confirm that the results obtained through soft voting are superior to those obtained through hard voting.

Our contributions are summarized as follows:

- We introduce a novel multi-level diversity approach for ensemble learning in the defense against backdoor attacks, characterized by diversification across datasets, model architectures, and self-ensembling mechanisms. Our strategy enhances the robustness of individual base classifiers through a

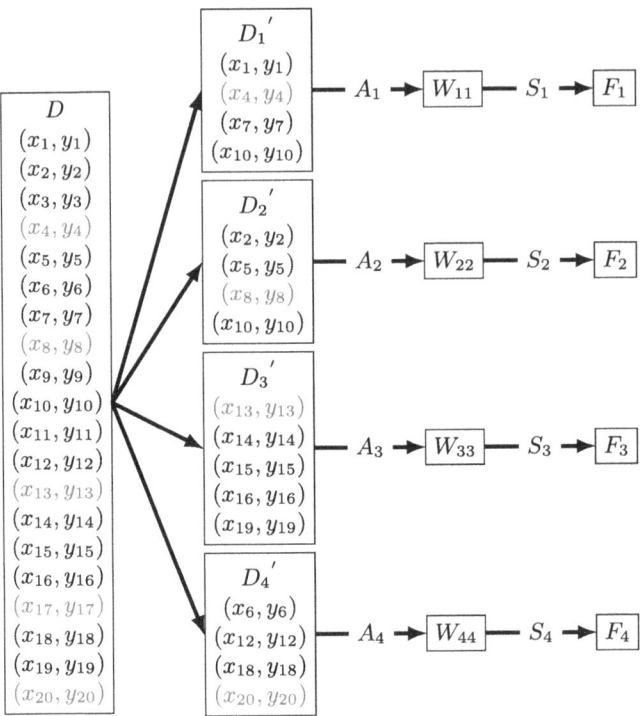

Fig. 2. D is consist of many samples (x_n, y_n), where the red samples are poisoned. After constructing random subsets $(D_n{}')$ for the training data, the base classifiers are trained using these random subsets (and using algorithm A), obtaining the optimization weight trajectories (W) during the training process. Subsequently, ensemble methods (S) are applied to aggregate the optimization weight trajectories into the base classifier (F). Only four base classifiers, instead of much more classifiers in practice, are listed here. (Color figure online)

self-ensembling algorithm. This approach mitigates model overfitting to backdoor features through ensemble learning, thereby elevating model robustness against backdoor attacks.

- To the best of our knowledge, we are the first to apply self-ensembling techniques for defending against backdoor attacks. BDEL significantly enhances defense mechanisms against such attacks, empirically demonstrating superior performance over existing methodologies through improved detection accuracy and reduced vulnerability.
- We conducted extensive evaluations of BDEL on a widely recognized public dataset: CIFAR-10 [18]. The empirical results reveal that BDEL effectively counters various attack strategies, outperforming existing methods in average defense effectiveness and achieving state-of-the-art performance.

2   Related Work

This section provides a concise overview of the current advancements in both backdoor attack strategies and defense mechanisms. Subsequently, it introduces the recently proposed ensemble learning techniques.

2.1   Backdoor Attacks

Backdoor attacks are a type of attack in the training process of DNNs, characterized by the model performing normally on clean data but generating incorrect outputs once the attack is triggered. BadNets [13] represents a backdoor attack methodology, where attackers embed specific patterns within training data to maliciously manipulate deep neural network behavior. Current research on backdoor attacks has focused on creating more stealthy and effective poisoned samples through innovative trigger designs. Some attack strategies [21,51] achieve stealth by minimizing the pixel differences between the original and triggered images. Additionally, numerous attacks [10,34] embed backdoors by manipulating the training loss function, enhancing the consistency between the latent representations of clean and triggered images for increased stealth. Some other effective strategies use natural triggers [8,28,29], employing naturally occurring features or patterns in regular input data as triggers. Nevertheless, these methods primarily emphasize stealth while neglecting the robustness demands of backdoors. Therefore, numerous studies have focused on exploring robust backdoor attacks. For instance, Zhang *et al.* introduced a method [49] involving data augmentation for poisoned samples. However, this approach increases the complexity and difficulty of implanting backdoors, thereby requiring a higher poisoning rate for effectiveness. Furthermore, Xu *et al.* employed feature-consistency training during the training process [47], minimizing the distance in the feature space between triggered samples and their compressed versions. Backdoor attacks can be categorized into dirty-label attacks [15,31] and clean-label attacks [2,12], with the distinction based on whether the labels of poisoned training samples are modified. Clean-label attacks present a higher challenge for detection mechanisms due to the absence of overt discrepancies between the images and their corresponding labels.

2.2   Backdoor Defenses

Existing backdoor defense mechanisms primarily focus on preventing the learning of backdoors during the training process or eliminating them after the training process is complete. Some methods aim to eliminate backdoors by reconstructing or fine-tuning the infected models. For example, Fine-Pruning [27] strategically eliminates neurons that are potentially compromised by backdoor attacks by assessing their activation patterns. Zhao *et al.* [50] introduced the concept of model connectivity technique to systematically clear out backdoors embedded in infected models. Li *et al.* [23] proposed to employ the model distillation technique to effectively remove backdoors from infected models. Additionally, some other approaches aim to disrupt backdoor triggers by pre-processing the model inputs. For instance, Neural Cleanse [40] detects backdoor samples by identifying a trigger for each class that can misclassify clean images. It indicates a model might be compromised if a significantly smaller trigger is required for one class compared to others. Despite its effectiveness in detecting backdoor samples, the method is computationally intensive due to unknown target labels at runtime. Furthermore, Li et al. *et al.* [26] used a method of reducing sample size and then applying flipping and padding to invalidate triggers in inference samples. Moreover, some methods aim to determine whether an inference sample contains a malicious trigger and thereby identify samples that could compromise model integrity. For example, STRIP [11] assumes backdoor triggers remain effective under clean image overlays. By overlaying clean images onto the target and analyzing predictions, if overlaid images yield consistently low entropy, the model is identified as infected.

2.3   Ensemble Learning

In traditional studies, ensemble learning methods have been extensively investigated to enhance model performance, improve generalization, and manage uncertainty for out-of-distribution data. Following initial successes in enhancing performance through neural network ensembles [14], bagging [4], and boosting [9], Kuncheva *et al.* [19] conducted an extensive evaluation of the relationship between sub-model diversity and ensemble accuracy. They discovered that a greater diversity typically leads to higher ensemble accuracy, indicating the necessity for specifically designed diversity metrics and training algorithms. Sinha *et al.* [36] proposed diversifying the sub-models with variational information bottleneck and diversity-inducing adversarial loss to further improve the ensemble accuracy. Wen *et al.* [43] proposed resolving the scalability issue of deep ensembles or Bayesian neural networks by reducing the memory and computation cost with shared-weight across sub-models and rank-1 parameterization. Pang *et al.* [32] introduced the ADP regularization approach to promote enhanced diversity in non-maximal predictions of sub-models with the aim of improving ensemble model accuracy and generalization.

3   Method

This section starts with an overview of the threat model. We subsequently detail BDEL in Sect. 3.1.

3.1   Threat Model

In the context of our study, the adversary's objective is to return a poisoned dataset. When models are trained on this dataset, the resulting poisoned models achieve a level of predictive accuracy for regular samples that is comparable to that of benign models. However, when the input contains a trigger pre-set by an attacker, the poisoned model will classify the result into the target label designated by the attacker.

3.2   Proposed Method

To construct an efficient ensemble learning model, it is crucial to integrate multiple base learners that are not only outstanding but also varied. This implies that each base learner should not only demonstrate high predictive accuracy but also contribute significant diversity among the learners. Embracing this concept, we have introduced diversity in datasets, model structures, and through self-ensembling strategies, while also enhancing the robustness of base classifiers with a self-ensembling algorithm. Adopting this strategy has led to the development of a suite of powerful and diverse base classifiers, which has markedly enhanced the accuracy of the model in predicting benign samples. Furthermore, this approach has substantially strengthened the resilience of the model against poisoned samples.

Dataset Diversity. To achieve dataset diversity, we employed a bagging method for random subset partitioning of dataset D. Initially, we define the total dataset D as a collection comprising n samples, each consisting of a feature vector x_i and its corresponding label y_i:

$$D = \{(x_i, y_i) \mid x_i \in \mathbb{R}^d, y_i = f(x_i), f : \mathbb{R}^d \to \mathcal{Y}, \forall i \in \{1, 2, \ldots, n\}\} \qquad (1)$$

Here, x_i represents the ith sample located in the d-dimensional real space $\mathbb{R}^d$, y_i is the corresponding label belonging to the label set $\mathcal{Y}$. The function f denotes the mapping relationship from the feature space to the label set. Through bootstrapping, m samples are randomly drawn from D to form a random subset D'_s. By repeating this process c times, we obtain c random subsets, creating a collection of random subsets: $D' = \{D'_1, D'_2, \ldots, D'_c\}$. This method introduces dataset diversity, yielding multiple distinct random subsets D'.

Model Structural Diversity. To achieve diversity in model structures, we selected h different deep learning algorithms for training. Let us consider a set of deep learning algorithms $A = \{A_1, A_2, \ldots, A_h\}$. For each algorithm A_j in the set, we apply it to a previously generated random subset D'_s:

$$A_j(D'_s) \text{ for each } D'_s \in D' \qquad (2)$$

Through this method, we introduce diversity in the model structures, which enhances the generalization ability of the entire ensemble system and its robustness to backdoor attacks.

Self-Ensembling. We construct more robust base classifiers through a self-ensembling method. To further enhance the diversity among sub-classifiers, we employ various self-ensembling algorithms to train different sub-classifiers. Specifically, for each sub-dataset D'_s, we use algorithm A_j to perform l training epochs. At the end of each training epoch, we record the model weight updates of algorithm A_j, thereby obtaining its trajectory of weight optimization:

$$W_{sj} = A_j(D'_s) = \{W_{sj}^{(1)}, W_{sj}^{(2)}, \ldots, W_{sj}^{(l)}\} \tag{3}$$

Here, W_{sj} represents the trajectory of weight optimization by algorithm A_j over the training process for subset D'_s, covering all weight updates from the first epoch to the lth epoch. The model weight updating strategy follows the formula:

$$W_{sj}^{(t)} = W_{sj}^{(t-1)} - \eta \nabla L(W_{sj}^{(t-1)}, D'_s) \tag{4}$$

where t represents the current training epoch, η is the learning rate, and ∇L is the gradient of the loss function L with respect to weights $W_{sj}^{(t-1)}$.

In the self-ensembling of a single base classifier, we utilize the exponential moving average (EMA) method, implemented as follows:

$$\text{EMA}_t = \alpha W_{sj}^{(t)} + (1 - \alpha)\text{EMA}_{t-1} \tag{5}$$

The smoothing factor α is calculated by the formula:

$$\alpha = \frac{k}{t + k} \tag{6}$$

Here, α adjusts the influence of new weights in the calculation. By selecting different constant k values, we can adjust the value of α, thereby producing a variety of EMA aggregation strategies. The weight trajectory W_{sj} of each dataset D'_s corresponding to algorithm A_j will be aggregated according to the respective EMA formula. Ultimately, we obtain a collection of base classifiers $F = \{f_1, f_2, \ldots, f_n\}$, each distinct yet effective, matching the number of random subsets.

Model Fusion. During prediction, we input a test sample into F, where for any given test sample x, each classifier $f_i \in F$ outputs a probability distribution vector r_i, indicating the probabilities that the sample belongs to each possible category. Hence, for c classifiers, the result set R can be represented as $R = \{r_1, r_2, \ldots, r_c\}$. We then employ a soft voting mechanism to average these probability distributions, with the final prediction being the category with the highest average probability. Specifically, each element $\bar{r}_j$ of the post-soft-voting probability vector $\bar{r}$ can be calculated using the following equation:

$$\bar{r}_j = \frac{1}{c} \sum_{i=1}^{c} r_{ij} \tag{7}$$

Here, r_{ij} represents the predicted probability by the ith classifier that the test sample belongs to class j. The final predicted category C is:

$$C = \arg\max_j(\bar{r}_j) \tag{8}$$

In this context, $\arg\max_j$ signifies identifying the class j that maximizes $\bar{r}_j$. Through soft voting, we achieve the fusion of models, enhancing the overall model's accuracy in predicting benign samples and its robustness against poisoned samples.

4   Evaluation

4.1   Settings

Dataset and Model. Experiments were carried out on the CIFAR-10 dataset [18]. When constructing random subsets, each subset contained 20% of the samples from the original dataset. An ensemble approach was employed using three models: GoogLeNet [37], InceptionV3 [38], and DenseNet121 [16], with each model training five base classifiers, totaling 15 base classifiers. For predictions, the 15 base classifiers operated in parallel, and their outcomes were aggregated into a final result through a soft voting mechanism.

Backdoor Attacks. We evaluated the effectiveness of BDEL against eight different backdoor attacks. Specifically, BDEL was tested with BadNet employing a white square pattern (referred to as BadNet-S) and BadNet using a six-pixel grid pattern (BadNet-Grid), both introduced in [13]. Moreover, we assessed BDEL against the employment of square and HelloKitty patterned Blend attacks [7] (referred to as Blend-S and Blend-H, respectively), where Blend-S exhibits a higher degree of concealment compared to Blend-H when subjected to human inspection, making it less detectable. We also tested the defense effectiveness of BDEL against WaNet [30]. BDEL also successfully defended N-to-One attack, a feat not achieved by either Neural Cleanse or Activation Clustering.

During the poisoning phase, the poisoning rate adheres to the original settings of each attack method. Specifically, for N-to-One [46], we set the number of poisoned samples to 400, and for both A-Blend and A-Patch, the poisoning rate was set to 0.3%. For all other attacks, the poisoning rate was set to 10%.

Baseline Methods. We compared BDEL with commonly used backdoor attack defense mechanisms, including normal training (referred to as "No Defense"), Neural Cleanse (NC) [41], Activation Clustering (AC) [6], Spectral Signature (SS) [39], Reconstructive Neuron Pruning (RNP) [24], and Anti-backdoor Learning (ABL) [22]. The configurations for these methods were all in accordance with the setups described in [44]. For the configuration of attack method parameters, all defense methods except for RNP followed the settings outlined in [44]. The settings for RNP were in accordance with the original paper [24].

Evaluation Metrics. The overall performance of the framework is assessed using two metrics: accuracy of benign tasks (ACC) and attack success rate (ASR).

(1) ACC refers to the model's accuracy when predicting benign samples.

(2) ASR represents the percentage of poisoned test samples successfully misled by the model into being classified as the attacker's target label samples.

In essence, ACC signifies the performance of benign tasks, while ASR indicates the defense capability against backdoor attacks. A higher ACC and a lower ASR denote a more effective defense.

4.2   Main Results

The main results of BDEL on the CIFAR-10 dataset under eight attack methods are shown in Table 1 and Table 2. Firstly, we evaluated the ASR and ACC of models under a no defense setting, specifically on GoogLeNet, InceptionV3, and DenseNet121. It was observed that, when subjected to the same attack, there was a significant variation in ASR among these models, while the differences in ACC were minimal. These findings are detailed in Table 1. Subsequently, we compared the defensive efficacy of BDEL with that of five state-of-the-art defense methods under eight backdoor attacks. Our defense mechanism consistently maintained an ACC of over 93% across all attacks, closely aligning with the ACC observed in these models under the no defense setting. Notably, only in the case of defending against the A-blend attack did the ASR slightly exceed 1%. To the best of our knowledge, we are the pioneers in devising a defense against N-to-One attack strategies, achieving a mere 0.11% ASR in such scenarios. The results underscore that BDEL's overall performance is superior to that of the other five defense methods, as elaborated in Table 2.

4.3   Ablation Studies

The Importance of Self-Ensembling. In this section, we demonstrate the importance of self-ensembling. Omitting the self-ensembling operation during the construction of individual base classifiers leads to rapid poisoning of these classifiers, consequently poisoning the final ensemble model as well. We conducted experiments with an ensemble of three models: GoogLeNet, InceptionV3, and DenseNet121, training five base classifiers for each model, totaling 15 base classifiers. For predictions, the 15 base classifiers operated in parallel, and their results were aggregated into a final outcome through soft voting. The experimental results, shown in Table 3 and compared with BDEL in Table 2, indicate an increase in the ASR against BadNets-S [13] to 95.36%, against BadNets-Grid [13] to 96.61%, against Blend-H [7] to 5.31%, against WaNet [30] to 35.25%, against N-to-One [46] to 97.66%, and against A-Blend [33] to 31.6%, while maintaining a relatively low ASR against Blend-S [7] and A-Patch [33]. This experiment validates the effectiveness of our self-ensembling method.

Table 1. The ASR and ACC for the CIFAR-10 dataset against eight backdoor attack methods under the no defense setting, separately for GoogLeNet, InceptionV3, and DenseNet121.

Backdoor Attacks	GoogLeNet		InceptionV3		DenseNet121	
	ASR	ACC	ASR	ACC	ASR	ACC
BadNets-S	96.90	93.15	98.21	92.93	97.46	95.19
BadNets-Grid	97.16	95.00	98.87	93.88	98.65	95.37
Blend-H	65.57	92.05	99.90	93.46	99.27	93.50
Blend-S	82.49	93.67	91.05	92.95	92.46	93.72
WaNet	88.77	92.45	93.89	93.20	94.91	94.55
A-Blend	75.35	94.28	83.64	93.97	97.96	95.36
A-Patch	44.23	94.53	69.26	94.75	99.89	94.48
N-to-One	99.82	94.44	99.36	94.47	99.93	95.55

Table 2. The ASR and ACC of BDEL on the CIFAR-10 dataset under 8 different backdoor attack methods are compared with the ASR and ACC of other defense methods.

Backdoor Attacks	NC		AC		SS		RNP		ABL		BDEL (Ours)	
	ASR	ACC	ASR	ACC	ASR	ACC	ASR	ACC	ASR	ACC	ASR	ACC
BadNets-S	1.27	89.05	86.23	88.8	92.41	89.98	–	–	**0.00**	83.32	0.03	**93.94**
BadNets-Grid	–	–	–	–	–	–	0.20	92.22	–	–	**0.18**	**93.55**
Blend-H	99.92	93.47	99.72	88.52	99.84	90.35	**0.33**	92.62	0.73	77.30	0.84	**93.80**
Blend-S	–	–	–	–	–	–	–	–	–	–	**0.00**	**93.87**
WaNet	7.53	91.80	96.80	91.93	90.17	91.94	10.98	92.83	**0.00**	83.19	0.41	**93.76**
A-Blend	–	–	76.00	91.60	62.00	91.50	**1.09**	90.38	–	–	1.26	**93.06**
A-Patch	–	–	97.50	91.50	93.10	91.50	–	–	–	–	**0.30**	**93.70**
N-to-One	–	–	–	–	–	–	–	–	–	–	**0.11**	**93.83**

Table 3. The ASR and ACC for the CIFAR-10 dataset against eight backdoor attack methods showed substantial improvements when the self-ensembling step is used (after), compared with the step was omitted (before). S-E represents Self-Ensembling.

		BadNets-S	BadNets-Grid	Blend-H	Blend-S	WaNet	N-to-One	A-Blend	A-Patch
w/o S-E	ASR	95.36	96.61	5.31	0.14	35.25	97.55	31.60	0.45
	ACC	94.41	94.43	94.26	94.47	93.51	94.42	94.44	94.41
w/ S-E	ASR	0.03	0.18	0.84	0.00	0.41	0.11	1.26	0.30
	ACC	93.94	93.55	93.80	93.87	93.76	93.83	93.06	93.70

Hard Voting is Less Effective than Soft Voting. In this section, we evaluated the effectiveness of aggregating the results of 15 base classifiers using hard

Table 4. The ASR and ACC for the CIFAR-10 dataset against eight backdoor attack methods when employing hard voting during the decision-making process.

		BadNets-S	BadNets-Grid	Blend-H	Blend-S	WaNet	N-to-One	A-Blend	A-Patch
Hard Voting	**ASR**	0.05	0.21	0.91	0.02	0.52	0.11	1.71	0.33
	ACC	93.62	93.35	93.55	93.55	93.44	93.65	93.52	93.51
Soft Voting	**ASR**	0.03	0.18	0.84	0.00	0.41	0.11	1.26	0.30
	ACC	93.94	93.55	93.80	93.87	93.76	93.83	93.06	93.70

voting. The comparison highlights the superiority of soft voting over hard voting. The results, as presented in the table, demonstrate that soft voting outperforms hard voting in both ACC and ASR (Table 4).

5   Conclusion

In this paper, we propose BDEL, a defense method against backdoor attacks based on ensemble learning. BDEL is not only effective in defending against known attacks but also enhances the model's robustness against unknown threats, thereby significantly improving the model's security and stability. Moreover, we propose a method for self-ensemble enhancement of the model's robustness against backdoor attacks within the ensemble learning framework. Extensive experiments validate the efficacy of the proposed defense methods.

References

1. Ando, A., Gidaris, S., Bursuc, A., Puy, G., Boulch, A., Marlet, R.: Rangevit: towards vision transformers for 3d semantic segmentation in autonomous driving. In: CVPR 2023, Vancouver, BC, Canada, 17–24 June 2023, pp. 5240–5250 (2023)
2. Barni, M., Kallas, K., Tondi, B.: A new backdoor attack in CNNS by training set corruption without label poisoning. In: ICIP 2019, pp. 101–105 (2019)
3. Bejnordi, B.E., Habibian, A., Porikli, F., Ghodrati, A.: SALISA: saliency-based input sampling for efficient video object detection. In: ECCV 2022. vol. 13670, pp. 300–316. Springer, Heidelberg (2022). https://doi.org/10.1007/978-3-031-20080-9_18
4. Breiman, L.: Bagging predictors. Mach. Learn. **24**, 123–140 (1996)
5. Chai, J.C.L., Ng, T., Low, C., Park, J., Teoh, A.B.J.: Recognizability embedding enhancement for very low-resolution face recognition and quality estimation. In: CVPR 2023, pp. 9957–9967 (2023)
6. Chen, B., et al.: Detecting backdoor attacks on deep neural networks by activation clustering. arXiv preprint arXiv:1811.03728 (2018)
7. Chen, X., Liu, C., Li, B., Lu, K., Song, D.: Targeted backdoor attacks on deep learning systems using data poisoning. arXiv preprint arXiv:1712.05526 (2017)
8. Cheng, S., Liu, Y., Ma, S., Zhang, X.: Deep feature space trojan attack of neural networks by controlled detoxification. In: AAAI 2021, pp. 1148–1156 (2021)

9. Dietterich, T.G.: Ensemble methods in machine learning. In: Kittler, J., Roli, F. (eds.) MCS 2000. LNCS, vol. 1857, pp. 1–15. Springer, Heidelberg (2000). https://doi.org/10.1007/3-540-45014-9_1

10. Doan, K.D., Lao, Y., Li, P.: Backdoor attack with imperceptible input and latent modification. In: Advances in Neural Information Processing Systems 34: Annual Conference on Neural Information Processing Systems 2021, NeurIPS 2021, 6–14 December 2021, virtual, pp. 18944–18957 (2021)

11. Gao, Y., Xu, C., Wang, D., Chen, S., Ranasinghe, D.C., Nepal, S.: STRIP: a defence against trojan attacks on deep neural networks. In: Proceedings of the 35th Annual Computer Security Applications Conference, ACSAC 2019, San Juan, PR, USA, 09–13 December 2019, pp. 113–125. ACM

12. Gao, Y., Li, Y., Zhu, L., Wu, D., Jiang, Y., Xia, S.: Not all samples are born equal: towards effective clean-label backdoor attacks. Pattern Recogn. **139**, 109512 (2023)

13. Gu, T., Liu, K., Dolan-Gavitt, B., Garg, S.: Badnets: evaluating backdooring attacks on deep neural networks. IEEE Access **7**, 47230–47244 (2019)

14. Hansen, L.K., Salamon, P.: Neural network ensembles. IEEE Trans. Pattern Anal. Mach. Intell. **12**(10), 993–1001 (1990)

15. Hu, X., et al.: Practical attacks on deep neural networks by memory trojaning. IEEE Trans. Comput. Aided Des. Integr. Circuits Syst. **40**(6), 1230–1243 (2021)

16. Huang, G., Liu, Z., Van Der Maaten, L., Weinberger, K.Q.: Densely connected convolutional networks. In: Proceedings of the IEEE Conference on Computer Vision and Pattern Recognition, pp. 4700–4708 (2017)

17. Jia, J., Cao, X., Gong, N.Z.: Intrinsic certified robustness of bagging against data poisoning attacks. In: AAAI 2021, vol. 35, pp. 7961–7969 (2021)

18. Krizhevsky, A., Hinton, G., et al.: Learning multiple layers of features from tiny images (2009)

19. Kuncheva, L.I., Whitaker, C.J.: Measures of diversity in classifier ensembles and their relationship with the ensemble accuracy. Mach. Learn. **51**(2), 181–207 (2003)

20. LeCun, Y., Bottou, L., Bengio, Y., Haffner, P.: Gradient-based learning applied to document recognition. Proc. IEEE **86**(11), 2278–2324 (1998)

21. Li, S., Xue, M., Zhao, B.Z.H., Zhu, H., Zhang, X.: Invisible backdoor attacks on deep neural networks via steganography and regularization. IEEE Trans. Dependable Secur. Comput. **18**(5), 2088–2105 (2021)

22. Li, Y., Lyu, X., Koren, N., Lyu, L., Li, B., Ma, X.: Anti-backdoor learning: training clean models on poisoned data. Adv. Neural. Inf. Process. Syst. **34**, 14900–14912 (2021)

23. Li, Y., Lyu, X., Koren, N., Lyu, L., Li, B., Ma, X.: Neural attention distillation: erasing backdoor triggers from deep neural networks. arXiv preprint arXiv:2101.05930 (2021)

24. Li, Y., et al.: Reconstructive neuron pruning for backdoor defense. In: ICML, pp. 19837–19854 (2023)

25. Li, Y.: Poisoning-based backdoor attacks in computer vision. In: AAAI (2023)

26. Li, Y., Zhai, T., Wu, B., Jiang, Y., Li, Z., Xia, S.: Rethinking the trigger of backdoor attack. CoRR arxiv:2004.04692 (2020)

27. Liu, K., Dolan-Gavitt, B., Garg, S.: Fine-pruning: defending against backdooring attacks on deep neural networks. In: Bailey, M., Holz, T., Stamatogiannakis, M., Ioannidis, S. (eds.) RAID 2018. LNCS, vol. 11050, pp. 273–294. Springer, Cham (2018). https://doi.org/10.1007/978-3-030-00470-5_13

28. Liu, Y., Lee, W., Tao, G., Ma, S., Aafer, Y., Zhang, X.: ABS: scanning neural networks for back-doors by artificial brain stimulation. In: CCS 2019, pp. 1265–1282 (2019)

29. Liu, Y., Ma, X., Bailey, J., Lu, F.: Reflection backdoor: a natural backdoor attack on deep neural networks. In: ECCV 2020, vol. 12355, pp. 182–199. Springer, Heidelberg (2020). https://doi.org/10.1007/978-3-030-58607-2_11

30. Nguyen, A., Tran, A.: Wanet–imperceptible warping-based backdoor attack. arXiv preprint arXiv:2102.10369 (2021)

31. Nguyen, T.A., Tran, A.T.: Input-aware dynamic backdoor attack. In: Advances in Neural Information Processing Systems 33: Annual Conference on Neural Information Processing Systems 2020, NeurIPS 2020, 6–12 December 2020, virtual (2020)

32. Pang, T., Xu, K., Du, C., Chen, N., Zhu, J.: Improving adversarial robustness via promoting ensemble diversity. In: ICML, pp. 4970–4979 (2019)

33. Qi, X., Xie, T., Li, Y., Mahloujifar, S., Mittal, P.: Circumventing backdoor defenses that are based on latent separability. arXiv preprint arXiv:2205.13613 (2022)

34. Ren, Y., Li, L., Zhou, J.: Simtrojan: stealthy backdoor attack. In: ICIP 2021, pp. 819–823 (2021)

35. Shokri, R., et al.: Bypassing backdoor detection algorithms in deep learning. In: 2020 IEEE European Symposium on Security and Privacy (EuroS&P), pp. 175–183. IEEE (2020)

36. Sinha, S., Bharadhwaj, H., Goyal, A., Larochelle, H., Garg, A., Shkurti, F.: Dibs: diversity inducing information bottleneck in model ensembles. In: Proceedings of the AAAI Conference on Artificial Intelligence, vol. 35, pp. 9666–9674 (2021)

37. Szegedy, C., et al.: Going deeper with convolutions. In: CVPR 2015, pp. 1–9 (2015)

38. Szegedy, C., Vanhoucke, V., Ioffe, S., Shlens, J., Wojna, Z.: Rethinking the inception architecture for computer vision. In: Proceedings of the IEEE Conference on Computer Vision and Pattern Recognition, pp. 2818–2826 (2016)

39. Tran, B., Li, J., Madry, A.: Spectral signatures in backdoor attacks. Adv. Neural Inf. Process. Syst. **31** (2018)

40. Wang, B., et al.: Neural cleanse: identifying and mitigating backdoor attacks in neural networks. In: 2019 IEEE Symposium on Security and Privacy, SP 2019, San Francisco, CA, USA, 19–23 May 2019, pp. 707–723 (2019)

41. Wang, B., et al.: Neural cleanse: identifying and mitigating backdoor attacks in neural networks. In: 2019 IEEE Symposium on Security and Privacy (SP), pp. 707–723. IEEE (2019)

42. Wang, H., Hong, J., Zhang, A., Zhou, J., Wang, Z.: Trap and replace: defending backdoor attacks by trapping them into an easy-to-replace subnetwork. Adv. Neural. Inf. Process. Syst. **35**, 36026–36039 (2022)

43. Wen, Y., Tran, D., Ba, J.: Batchensemble: an alternative approach to efficient ensemble and lifelong learning. In: 8th International Conference on Learning Representations, ICLR 2020, Addis Ababa, Ethiopia, 26–30 April 2020. OpenReview.net (2020)

44. Wu, B., et al.: Backdoorbench: a comprehensive benchmark of backdoor learning. Adv. Neural. Inf. Process. Syst. **35**, 10546–10559 (2022)

45. Wu, D., Wang, Y.: Adversarial neuron pruning purifies backdoored deep models. Adv. Neural. Inf. Process. Syst. **34**, 16913–16925 (2021)

46. Xue, M., He, C., Wang, J., Liu, W.: One-to-n & n-to-one: two advanced backdoor attacks against deep learning models. IEEE Trans. Dependable Secure Comput. **19**(3), 1562–1578 (2020)

47. Xue, M., Wang, X., Sun, S., Zhang, Y., Wang, J., Liu, W.: Compression-resistant backdoor attack against deep neural networks. Appl. Intell. **53**(17), 20402–20417 (2023)

48. Yu, Y., Wang, Y., Yang, W., Lu, S., Tan, Y., Kot, A.C.: Backdoor attacks against deep image compression via adaptive frequency trigger. In: CVPR 2023, pp. 12250–12259 (2023)
49. Zhang, J., et al.: Poison ink: robust and invisible backdoor attack. IEEE Trans. Image Process. **31**, 5691–5705 (2022)
50. Zhao, P., Chen, P., Das, P., Ramamurthy, K.N., Lin, X.: Bridging mode connectivity in loss landscapes and adversarial robustness. In: 8th International Conference on Learning Representations, ICLR 2020, Addis Ababa, Ethiopia 26–30 April 2020. OpenReview.net (2020)
51. Zhong, H., Liao, C., Squicciarini, A.C., Zhu, S., Miller, D.J.: Backdoor embedding in convolutional neural network models via invisible perturbation. In: CODASPY '20: Tenth ACM Conference on Data and Application Security and Privacy, New Orleans, LA, USA, 16–18 March 2020, pp. 97–108 (2020)

Customizing Spatial-Temporal Graph Mamba Networks for Pandemic Forecasting

Haowei Xu[1], Chao Gao[1(✉)], Xianghua Li[1], Zhen Wang[2], and Tanimoto Jun[3]

[1] School of Artificial Intelligence, Optics and Electronics (iOPEN), Northwestern Polytechnical University, Xi'an, People's Republic of China
hwxu@mail.nwpu.edu.cn, {cgao,li_xianghua}@nwpu.edu.cn
[2] School of Cybersecurity, Northwestern Polytechnical University, Xi'an, People's Republic of China
ttengmin@mail.nwpu.edu.cn, w-zhen@nwpu.edu.cn
[3] Interdisciplinary Graduate school of Engineering Sciences, Kyushu University, Fukuoka, Japan
tanimoto@cm.kyushu-u.ac.jp

Abstract. The global spread of COVID-19 has emphasized the need for accurate pandemic prediction. While previous studies used spatiotemporal and graph-structured mobility data for outbreak forecasts, these models often suffer from long training times and high computational demands, limiting their effectiveness in dynamic scenarios. Additionally, varying regional mobility patterns add complexity, making manual model adjustments difficult. This paper presents AutoGMN, an automated architecture search framework utilizing bidirectional Graph Mamba Networks. We construct a graph where nodes represent regions, with historical COVID-19 data and human mobility as edge weights. The model forecasts future case numbers, integrating transmission control strategies. To reduce manual intervention, we employ differentiable neural architecture search. Our approach, validated against benchmarks in three European countries, shows superior performance in epidemiological forecasting.

Keywords: Pandemic forecasting · Spatial-temporal graph representation learning · Mamba · Neural architecture search

1 Introduction

The sudden onset of COVID-19 has led to numerous fatalities and a significant global economic impact. Due to the pandemic's severity and the need for accurate disease spread forecasting, deep learning has become a promising tool to combat COVID-19. In many fields, data naturally lends itself to graph representations. For predicting COVID-19 spread, social network data could provide insights into interactions, but in its absence, mass mobility data can serve as a proxy. Increased movement within and between regions correlates with higher transmission risk. Representing this mobility data as a graph allows for the use of advanced techniques such as spatio-temporal graph (STG) models.

R. Hadfi et al. (Eds.): PRICAI 2024, LNAI 15281, pp. 236–242, 2025.
https://doi.org/10.1007/978-981-96-0116-5_19

Attention-based methods like the Spatial-Temporal Transformer are widely used in spatio-temporal graph (STG) learning due to their ability to capture dynamic temporal and spatial features. However, a key challenge (CH1) exists: **while Transformer-based methods enhance STG relationship learning, their effectiveness in long-term forecasting is hindered by the quadratic computational complexity, $O(n^2)$, of the attention mechanism**. Moreover, encoding all contextual features through attention is often unnecessary for long-term dependency modeling [4]. This has led to increased interest in alternatives. Recent approaches, such as Mamba and its variants, termed Selective State Space Models (SSSM), have gained attention in areas like computer vision and natural language processing [1]. Mamba, a deep learning-based SSSM, bypasses attention scores by learning context via recurrent hidden states, using a selection mechanism to prioritize key input data [2]. However, another challenge (CH2) is that **developing an STG Mamba for downstream tasks remains difficult due to the labor-intensive process of manual design**, often leading to suboptimal results [3].

To determine if the model can capture the complex dynamics of COVID-19, it is evaluated on recent data to predict the number of new cases. The results indicate that STG-Mamba, when applied to mobility data, shows significant potential in forecasting the spread of the disease. In sum, the significant contributions of this research are delineated as follows:

- **Pandemic Graph Construction.** The spread of COVID-19 across different regions within a country is explored, utilizing the representational power of graph learning to encode the epidemic's fundamental dynamics.
- **Automated STG Mamba.** A structured approach for designing STG Mambas is presented, comprising three steps: (1) Positional and Structural Encodings, (2) Local Encoding, and (3) Selective SSM Encoder. Building on this, AutoGMN is introduced as a differentiable neural architecture search framework designed to automate the construction of Spatial-Temporal Graph Mamba Networks. This framework effectively captures the complex heterogeneous dependencies within STG networks and accurately models the dynamic evolution of the STG system over time, making it highly suitable for STG learning.
- The proposed approach is evaluated using data from four countries: France, Italy, Spain, and England. The results indicate that this method surpasses benchmark models and generates valuable predictions.

2 Methodology

2.1 Graph Construction

In Fig. 1, each country is represented as a graph $G = (V, E)$, where $n = |V|$ is the number of nodes. Over time, a series of graphs $G^{(1)}, \ldots, G^{(T)}$ is generated, with each graph corresponding to a specific date. Mobility data forms a

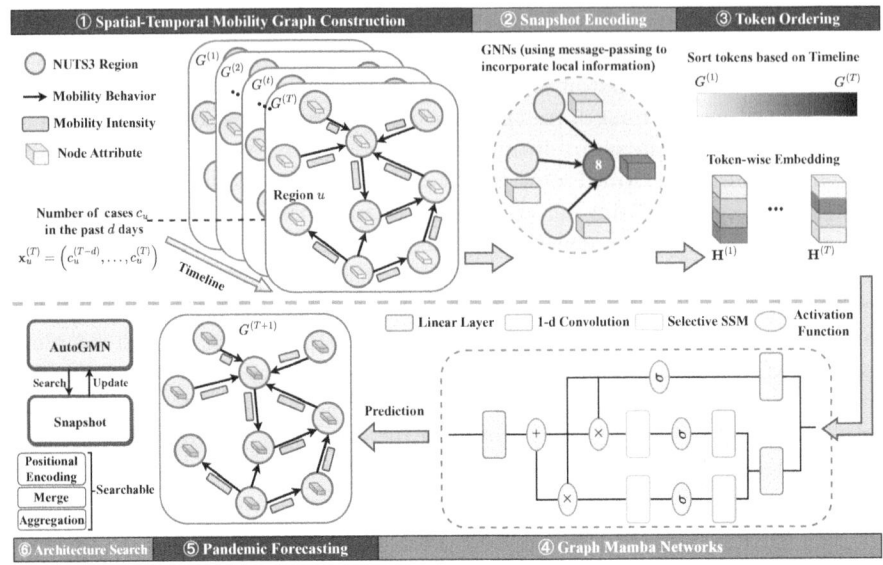

Fig. 1. Overview of our framework.

weighted, directed graph, with vertices as NUTS3 regions and edges representing movement patterns. The weight $A_{v,u}^{(t)}$ on edge (v, u) reflects the number of people moving between regions at time t, including self-loops for internal movement. By multiplying the mobility between regions with the number of cases $c_u^{(t)}$, a relative score of potential infected movement is derived. For each region, the vector $\mathbf{x}_u^{(t)} = \left(c_u^{(t-d)}, \ldots, c_u^{(t)} \right)^{\top} \in \mathbb{R}^d$ captures case counts over the past d days. Message passing on this network generates feature vectors by integrating scores from all regions.

2.2   Spatial-Temporal Graph Mamba Networks

Local Encoding. Given a node $v \in V$ and its sequence of tokens (subgraphs), the subgraph undergoes encoding through the encoder $\phi(\cdot)$. This process generates $\mathbf{x}_v^1, \mathbf{x}_v^2, \ldots, \mathbf{x}_v^{ms-1}, \mathbf{x}_v^{ms} \in \mathbb{R}^d$ according to the following equation:

$$\mathbf{x}_v^{((i-1)s+j)} = \phi\left(G\left[T_i^j(v) \right], \mathbf{X}_{T_i^j(v)} \right), \tag{1}$$

where $1 \le i \le m$ and $1 \le j \le s$. The encoder, such as a GNN, encodes nodes relative to a sampled set of walks into feature vectors.

Bidirectional Mamba. SSMs, as recurrent models, require ordered input, whereas graph-structured data lacks order, necessitating permutation-equivariant encoders. The Mamba architecture adapts with two recurrent scan modules to process data bidirectionally. For tokens t_i and t_j $(i > j)$, in the forward scan, t_i follows t_j, passing information about t_j, which can flow into hidden states or be filtered. In the backward scan, t_j follows t_i, carrying t_i's information. This is crucial when $m = 0$ (node tokenization). Formally, in the forward pass, let $\boldsymbol{\Phi}$ be the input sequence and A the relative positional encoding. We have:

$$
\begin{aligned}
\boldsymbol{\Phi}_{\text{input}} &= \sigma\left(\text{Conv}\left(\mathbf{W}_{\text{input LayerNorm}}(\boldsymbol{\Phi})\right)\right), \\
\mathbf{B} &= \mathbf{W}_{\mathbf{B}}\boldsymbol{\Phi}_{\text{input}}, \quad \mathbf{C} = \mathbf{W}_{\mathbf{C}}\boldsymbol{\Phi}_{\text{input}}, \quad \boldsymbol{\Delta} = \text{Softplus}\left(\mathbf{W}_{\boldsymbol{\Delta}}\boldsymbol{\Phi}_{\text{input}}\right), \\
\overline{\mathbf{A}} &= \text{Discrete}_{\mathbf{A}}(\mathbf{A}, \boldsymbol{\Delta}), \\
\overline{\mathbf{B}} &= \text{Discrete}_{\mathbf{B}}(\mathbf{B}, \boldsymbol{\Delta}), \\
\boldsymbol{H} &= \text{SSM}_{\overline{\mathbf{A}},\overline{\mathbf{B}},\mathbf{C}}\left(\boldsymbol{\Phi}_{\text{input}}\right), \\
\boldsymbol{H}_{\text{forward}} &= \mathbf{W}_{\text{forward, 1}}\left(\boldsymbol{H} \odot \sigma\left(\mathbf{W}_{\text{forward, 2}}\,\text{LayerNorm}(\boldsymbol{\Phi})\right)\right),
\end{aligned}
\tag{2}
$$

where $\mathbf{W}$, $\mathbf{W}_\mathbf{B}$, $\mathbf{W}_\mathbf{C}$, $\mathbf{W}_{\boldsymbol{\Delta}}$, $\mathbf{W}_{\text{forward, 1}}$, and $\mathbf{W}_{\text{forward, 2}}$ are learnable parameters, $\sigma(\cdot)$ is a nonlinear function (e.g., SiLU), LayerNorm$(\cdot)$ is layer normalization, and SSM$(\cdot)$ is the state space model. The backward pass uses $\boldsymbol{\Phi}_{\text{inverse}}$ as input (a matrix with rows $\mathbf{x}_v^1, \mathbf{x}_v^2, \ldots, \mathbf{x}v^{sm}$) and produces $\boldsymbol{H}_{\text{backward}}$. The final encodings are obtained as:

$$
\boldsymbol{H} = \mathbf{W}_{\text{out}}\left(\boldsymbol{H}_{\text{forward}} + \boldsymbol{H}_{\text{backward}}\right).
\tag{3}
$$

Pandemic Forecasting. After capturing spatial dependencies and temporal dynamics from county-level mobility graphs, a ReLU function is applied through a fully connected layer to predict future COVID-19 case and death counts:

$$
\left\{\hat{\mathbf{Y}}^{(t)} \mid t = T+1, \ldots, T+h\right\} = \text{ReLU}\left(\mathbf{W}\mathbf{H}^{(T)} + \mathbf{b}\right),
\tag{4}
$$

where ReLU$(\cdot)$ represents the ReLU activation function, ensuring nonnegative case counts. The parameters $\mathbf{W} \in \mathbb{R}^{d \times h}$ and $\mathbf{b} \in \mathbb{R}^{n_c \times h}$ are learnable. The mean squared error is selected as the loss function:

$$
\mathcal{L} = \frac{1}{nT} \sum_{t=1}^{T} \sum_{v \in V} \left(y_v^{(t+1)} - \hat{y}_v^{(t+1)}\right)^2
\tag{5}
$$

where $y_v^{(t+1)}$ denotes the reported number of cases for region v at day $t+1$ and $\hat{y}_v^{(t+1)}$ denotes the predicted number of cases.

2.3 Neural Architecture Search

Patterns of virus transmission across regions vary due to multiple factors. NAS automates the search for optimal STGMN architectures, avoiding manual design. Section 2.2 demonstrates that the message-passing layer and PE/SE are searchable. **PE module** uses positional encoding methods such as random walk, Laplacian eigenvector, SVD-based, and centrality encoding. **Aggregation module** enhances node representation through five GNNs: GCN, GAT, SAGE, GIN, and an MLP. **Merge module** synthesizes graph representations using LSTM, concatenation, maximum, mean, summation, and optional skip-connections (Table 1).

Table 1. The operations for the search space of AutoGMN.

Module	Operation	Candidate
PE	α_e	RandomWalk, Laplacian, SVD, Centrality
Aggregation	α_n	GCN, GAT, SAGE, GIN
Merge	α_l	M_LSTM, M_CONCAT, M_MAX, M_MEAN, M_SUM
	α_s	IDENTITY, ZERO

3   Experiments

3.1   Experimental Settings

Datasets, Baselines and Metrics. Table 2 presents an overview of the preprocessed data. The start date marks the earliest availability of both mobility and case data. Some regions are excluded due to the absence of COVID-19 cases or the inability to map them with Facebook mobility data. We compare our proposed models with several baselines and methods used in COVID-19 forecasting, including a two-layer LSTM, CovidGNN, and spatio-temporal networks combining GNN with LSTM or Transformer. Additionally, we assess NAS techniques such as random search, Bayesian search, and GraphNAS. The performance is evaluated by comparing predicted total cases in each region with the ground truth over the test set:

$$\text{error} = \frac{1}{ndt} \sum_{t=T+1}^{T+dt} \sum_{v \in V} \left| \hat{y}_v^{(t)} - y_v^{(t)} \right| \tag{6}$$

Table 2. Summary of the available data for the 3 considered countries.

Country	Time	Regions	Average New Cases
Italy	$24/2 - 12/5$	105	25.65
England	$13/3 - 12/5$	129	16.7
Spain	$12/3 - 12/5$	35	61
France	$10/3 - 12/5$	81	7.5

3.2   Performance Comparisons

As shown in Table 3, the GNN+LSTM model captures spatial relationships via the graph structure and manages time series data using LSTM, enhancing predictive accuracy. Our Mamba model, with a bidirectional scanning module, processes temporal data in both directions, improving robustness and accuracy. Additionally, Mamba achieves high-performance predictions with less training time and more efficient use of computational resources.

Table 3. Performance comparison across different models and forecast periods.

Model	Up to next 3 Days			Up to next 7 Days			Training Time (hours)
	England	France	Italy	England	France	Italy	
LSTM	9.11	8.08	22.94	8.97	8.13	23.17	2.3
CovidGNN	10.58	10.34	24.86	12.25	11.56	27.39	4.1
GNN+LSTM	7.20	6.95	18.45	7.35	7.10	19.05	4.1
GNN+Transformer	6.85	6.65	17.90	7.00	6.80	18.50	5.3
Random	8.50	8.20	21.10	8.60	8.30	21.50	3.7
Bayesian	8.00	7.80	20.30	8.10	7.90	20.70	3.3
GraphNAS	7.50	7.30	19.10	7.60	7.40	19.50	4.5
AutoGMN	**6.05**	**5.83**	**14.08**	**6.33**	**5.90**	**14.61**	**2.5**

4   Conclusion

This paper presents AutoGMN, an automated architecture search framework using bidirectional Graph Mamba Networks. By leveraging mobility graphs, the bidirectional Mamba model, and neural architecture search, AutoGMN enhances pandemic forecasting accuracy while minimizing dependence on manual model design. Results show AutoGMN's superior performance in pandemic forecasting, underscoring its potential for future public health applications.

Acknowledgements. This work was supported by the National Key R&D Program of China (No. 2022YFE0112300), the National Natural Science Foundation of China (Nos. U22A2098, 61976181, 11931015), Fok Ying-Tong Education Foundation, China (No. 171105), Technology Innovation Leading Program of Shaanxi (No. 2023GXLH-086), the Fundamental Research Funds for the Central Universities (No. G2024WD0151), and the XPLORER PRIZE.

References

1. Gu, A., Dao, T.: Mamba: linear-time sequence modeling with selective state spaces. arXiv preprint arXiv:2312.00752 (2023)
2. Gu, A., et al.: Combining recurrent, convolutional, and continuous-time models with linear state space layers. Adv. Neural. Inf. Process. Syst. **34**, 572–585 (2021)

3. Liu, Y., Sun, Y., Xue, B., Zhang, M., Yen, G.G., Tan, K.C.: A survey on evolutionary neural architecture search. IEEE Trans. Neural Netw. Learn. Syst. **34**(2), 550–570 (2023)
4. Patro, B.N., Agneeswaran, V.S.: Mamba-360: survey of state space models as transformer alternative for long sequence modelling: methods, applications, and challenges. arXiv preprint arXiv:2404.16112 (2024)

Distribution-Aligned Sequential Counterfactual Explanation with Local Outlier Factor

Shoki Yamao[1], Ken Kobayashi[1]([✉])(ID), Kentaro Kanamori[2]([✉]),
Takuya Takagi[2]([✉])(ID), Yuichi Ike[3]([✉])(ID), and Kazuhide Nakata[1]([✉])(ID)

[1] Tokyo Institute of Technology, Ookayama, Meguro-ku, Tokyo 152-8552, Japan
`{yamao.s.aa,kobayashi.k.ar,nakata.k.ac}@m.titech.ac.jp`
[2] Fujitsu Limited, Kamikodanaka, Kawasaki, Kanagawa 211-8588, Japan
`{k.kanamori,takagi.takuya}@fujitsu.com`
[3] Kyushu University, Motooka, Nishi-ku, Fukuoka 819-0395, Japan
`ike@imi.kyushu-u.ac.jp`

Abstract. Sequential counterfactual explanation is one of the counterfactual explanation methods suggesting how to sequentially change the input feature vector to obtain the desired prediction result from a trained classifier. To show realistic sequential change, existing methods construct a neighborhood graph and obtain a path from the original feature vector to reach a sample for which the model outputs the desired result. However, constructing an appropriate neighborhood graph is challenging and time-consuming in practice. This study proposes a new sequential counterfactual explanation method that generates a realistic path without constructing a neighborhood graph. To evaluate the reality of the suggested path, we first define a cost function based on the Local Outlier Factor (LOF) that assesses how much each vector in the path deviates from the underlying data distribution. Then, we propose an algorithm for generating a path by iteratively decreasing our cost function. Since our cost function is non-differentiable due to LOF, we use a local linear approximation to obtain a local descent direction. Our numerical experiments demonstrated that our method could generate a realistic path that aligns with the data distribution, and its computational time was more stable than the existing method.

Keywords: Counterfactual Explanation · Local Outlier Factor · Explainable Machine Learning

1 Introduction

In recent years, due to the advancement of machine learning, complex machine learning models have been applied to various decision-making processes in the real world, such as medical diagnoses, loan approvals, and judicial decisions. To improve trustworthiness and explainability in such decision-making, there has

R. Hadfi et al. (Eds.): PRICAI 2024, LNAI 15281, pp. 243–256, 2025.
https://doi.org/10.1007/978-981-96-0116-5_20

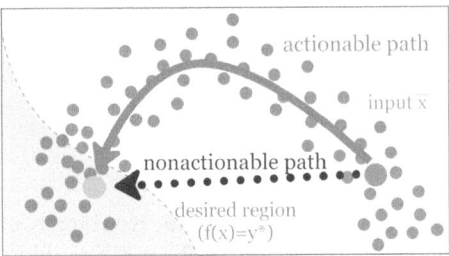

Fig. 1. Examples of actionable counterfactual explanation.

been a growing societal demand for the interpretability of machine learning models. In this study, we focus on counterfactual explanation (CE) [20], which is one of the post-hoc methods for extracting explanations from individual prediction results.

CE methods show a perturbed feature vector to obtain a desired prediction result when a user receives an unfavorable prediction result. For an input $\bar{x}$ of a user who receives an unfavorable prediction result from a prediction model f, CE methods show a perturbed feature vector x^* to obtain a desired prediction result y^*, i.e., $f(x^*) = y^*$. Let us consider an example case of loan approval: a prediction model f outputs "reject" to a user $\bar{x}$. In this case, CE methods suggest how the user's feature vector $\bar{x}$ should be changed to get the loan approved. The suggested change of the feature vector $a = x^* - \bar{x}$ can be seen as an action that the user should take to obtain the desired prediction result. Since CE methods offer such constructive insights to users, they have attracted increasing attention in recent years [9].

While most existing CE methods focus on showing such a perturbed feature vector x^* [19], it is often insufficient in practical situations [16]. For example, when samples are distributed on a curved manifold as shown in Fig. 1, linearly changing the original input $\bar{x}$ towards x^* may be unrealistic. In such cases, it is preferable for CE methods to present a "path" from $\bar{x}$ to x^* in addition to the perturbed feature vector. We refer to a *path* as a sequence of feature vectors $\{x^{(t)}\}_{t=1}^T$, where $x^{(1)} = \bar{x}$ and $x^{(T)} = x^*$, and following the path corresponds to sequentially changing the feature vectors. From such a path, users can understand what sequential changes are needed to obtain the desired prediction result.

To provide a path for users, Poyiadzi et al. [16] proposed the *Feasible and Actionable Counterfactual Explanation (FACE)*. There the following requirements for a path were introduced:

Feasibility. The terminal $x^{(T)}$ is close to samples whose prediction results are the desired label;
Actionablity. Each vector $x^{(t)}$ $(t = 1, \ldots, T)$ in the path does not deviate from the data distribution.

To find a feasible and actionable path, FACE constructs a neighborhood graph of given samples in the feature space as a preprocessing. Then, for a given instance $\bar{x}$, FACE finds a path $\{x^{(t)}\}_{t=1}^{T}$ on the neighborhood graph to reach a sample whose prediction result is desired.

However, constructing an appropriate neighborhood graph for FACE is challenging in practice. FACE constructs a neighborhood graph on the basis of a radius threshold, where two samples are connected if their distance is lower than the threshold. Setting the threshold too small may lead to a disconnected neighborhood graph, making it impossible for FACE to output a path. Furthermore, in high-dimensional cases where the neighborhood graph is likely to be complete, FACE tends to output a trivial path consisting only of the original input $\bar{x}$ and the terminal x. Additionally, generating a path by FACE is sometimes time-consuming, which we will demonstrate in our experiments. To avoid these issues, we aim to develop a new sequential CE method suggesting a feasible and actionable path without a neighborhood graph.

1.1 Our Contributions

This study proposes a sequential CE method that presents a feasible and actionable path considering the data distribution without constructing a neighborhood graph. To assess the feasibility and actionability of paths, we employ the Local Outlier Factor (LOF) [3], which evaluates how anomalous a given vector is. We define an LOF-based cost function for perturbed vectors and propose an algorithm to generate a path of feature vectors by iteratively decreasing the cost function.

The contributions of this study can be summarized as follows.

- We introduce a cost function based on the LOF to assess the feasibility and actionability of paths. Specifically, our cost function consists of two LOF values: one uses all samples to evaluate actionability, and the other uses samples for which the desired label is predicted to assess feasibility.
- We propose an algorithm to generate a path by iteratively updating the feature vector to decrease the cost function. Since the proposed cost function is non-differentiable due to the LOF, we use local linear regression [10] to obtain a descent direction for the cost function.
- We demonstrate the effectiveness of our method on two real datasets. Our experimental results showed that our method produces paths that align with the data distribution. Additionally, while the computation times of FACE were not stable depending on input instances, our method achieved stable and comparable computation times.

Figure 2a and 2b respectively shows a running example of FACE and our method for a two-dimensional feature space. The gray points represent samples with undesired labels, and the orange points represent those with the desired label. The pink point represents the original feature vector, the blue points represent the suggested path, and the red point is the terminal of the path. In Fig. 2a, we see that the suggested path by FACE was zigzagging. Such an unnecessary zigzagging path makes it difficult for users to understand and execute

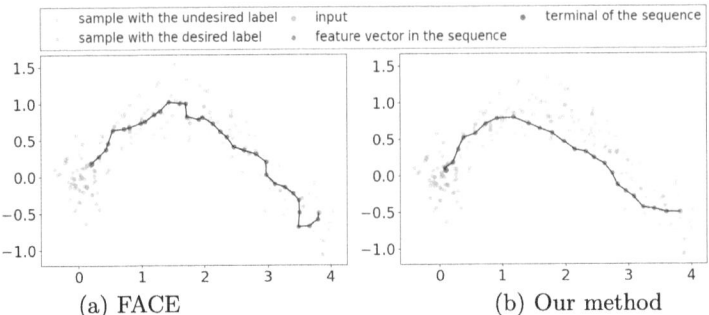

Fig. 2. Illustrations of the paths generated by FACE and our method for a two-dimensional synthetic dataset.

sequential changes of feature vectors to get the desired output. On the other hand, Fig. 2b shows that our method succeeded in outputting a path that avoids unnecessary zigzagging while aligning data distribution.

1.2 Related Work

While few studies have focused on both feasibility and actionability, several methods have focused on realizing feasibility in CE. One of the similar studies to our method is DACE [11]. To obtain a feasible perturbed vector, DACE introduces a cost function that considers feature correlations and LOF. Its cost minimization problem is solved as a mixed-integer linear optimization problem. In addition to DACE, Tsiourvas et al. [17] used LOF to consider data distribution for feasible counterfactual explanations. Another feasibility-focused CE method is MOC [6], which gives a formulation of a multi-objective optimization problem to obtain a perturbed vector that satisfies multiple requirements, including feasibility. Furthermore, autoencoder-based CE methods [7,15,18] have been proposed to consider data distribution for feasibility. Similar to our method, there are approaches that use density functions to consider data distribution [8,14,21]. While various CE methods have been proposed to consider feasibility, these methods only output a perturbed vector and do not provide an actionable path.

To the best of our knowledge, FACE [16] is the only CE method that provides an actionable path. For a given labeled sample set, FACE first creates a neighborhood graph using a defined radius $\epsilon > 0$. In this graph, two samples are connected if their weighted distance is less than ϵ. Then, FACE finds the shortest path connecting the original feature vector and a sample predicted to be the desired label. Since FACE outputs a path consisting of samples, it cannot be distant from the data distribution, which ensures actionability. However, the outputs of FACE highly depend on the structure of the neighborhood graph, and setting an appropriate radius ϵ is sometimes difficult, especially in high-dimensional cases. For example, if we set a small ϵ, the neighborhood graph may be disconnected, and FACE fails to find a path to obtain the prediction result. On the other hand, if ϵ is large, the neighborhood graph can be complete, and FACE tends to output a meaningless path that directly connects the original feature vector and the perturbed vector. Also, this increases computation time exponentially to generate a neighborhood graph, making it impractical for real-world use.

2   Preliminaries

2.1   Notation

Let a positive integer n be the number of features, and $\boldsymbol{x} \in \mathbb{R}^n$ be the input feature vector. A classifier $f\colon \mathbb{R}^n \to \{-1, +1\}$ outputs the prediction result, where $+1$ is the desired label and -1 is the undesired label. We also assume a metric space $(\mathbb{R}^n, d)$, where $d\colon \mathbb{R}^n \times \mathbb{R}^n \to \mathbb{R}_{\geq 0}$ is a distance function such as the Euclidean distance.

2.2   Local Outlier Factor

Local Outlier Factor (LOF) [3] is a popular outlier score based on the local densities of a set of samples. Given an input vector $\boldsymbol{x} \in \mathbb{R}^n$, it evaluates how much $\boldsymbol{x}$ is an outlier by comparing the local density of $\boldsymbol{x}$ to those of its neighborhood samples.

Let $\mathcal{X} \subseteq \mathbb{R}^n$ be a given sample set. For a vector $\boldsymbol{x} \in \mathbb{R}^n$, let the set of its k-nearest neighbors be $N_k(\boldsymbol{x}) \subseteq \mathcal{X}$, and let k-distance$(\boldsymbol{x})$ denote the distance between the k-th nearest samples to $\boldsymbol{x}$. For two vectors $\boldsymbol{x}, \boldsymbol{x}' \in \mathbb{R}^n$, the reachability distance is defined as follows:

$$\text{reach-dist}_k(\boldsymbol{x}, \boldsymbol{x}') = \max\{k\text{-distance}(\boldsymbol{x}'), d(\boldsymbol{x}, \boldsymbol{x}')\}. \tag{1}$$

Then, the k-local reachability density is defined as follows:

$$\text{lrd}_k(\boldsymbol{x}) = \frac{|N_k(\boldsymbol{x})|}{\displaystyle\sum_{\boldsymbol{x}' \in N_k(\boldsymbol{x})} \text{reach-dist}_k(\boldsymbol{x}, \boldsymbol{x}')}, \tag{2}$$

where $|N_k(\boldsymbol{x})|$ is the number of samples included in $N_k(\boldsymbol{x})$.

For a vector $\boldsymbol{x} \in \mathbb{R}^n$, k-LOF is defined as the average of the ratios of the k-local reachability densities between $\boldsymbol{x}$ and the samples in $N_k(\boldsymbol{x})$:

$$q_k(\boldsymbol{x} \mid \mathcal{X}) = \frac{1}{|N_k(\boldsymbol{x})|} \sum_{\boldsymbol{x}' \in N_k(\boldsymbol{x})} \frac{\text{lrd}_k(\boldsymbol{x}')}{\text{lrd}_k(\boldsymbol{x})}. \tag{3}$$

When $q_k(\boldsymbol{x} \mid \mathcal{X})$ is close to one, the local density around $\boldsymbol{x}$ is similar to those of the samples in $N_k(\boldsymbol{x})$, indicating that $\boldsymbol{x}$ is not an outlier. Conversely, when $q_k(\boldsymbol{x} \mid \mathcal{X})$ is large, the local density around $\boldsymbol{x}$ is smaller compared to its neighbors, suggesting that $\boldsymbol{x}$ is likely an outlier.

3 Proposed Method

3.1 Problem Setting and Requirements

We consider a situation where a trained classifier $f \colon \mathbb{R}^n \to \{-1, +1\}$ and a set of samples $\mathcal{X} \subseteq \mathbb{R}^n$ are given. Let us define $\mathcal{X}_+ := \{x \in \mathcal{X} \mid f(x) = +1\}$, which we refer to as the desired sample set. For a given instance $\bar{x} \in \mathbb{R}^n$ with $f(\bar{x}) = -1$, we aim to find a sequence of feature vectors $P := \{x^{(t)}\}_{t=1}^T \subseteq \mathbb{R}^n$ that satisfies the following requirements:

- *Validity*: the terminal vector $x^{(T)}$ is predicted as the desired label by the classifier, i.e., $f(x^{(T)}) = +1$;
- *Feasibility*: the terminal vector $x^{(T)}$ is close to the desired sample set $\mathcal{X}_+$;
- *Actionability*: each feature vector $x^{(t)} \in P$ $(t = 1, 2, \ldots, T)$ is close to the sample set $\mathcal{X}$.

Additionally, we focus on a model-agnostic situation, where we can only access the output of f and not use any other information about f when constructing a path P.

3.2 Cost Function

The objective of our method is to generate a path that aligns with $\mathcal{X}$ and whose terminal is close to $\mathcal{X}_+$. To this end, we introduce a cost function that consists of a distance and LOF as follows. For a distance function $d \colon \mathbb{R}^n \times \mathbb{R}^n \to \mathbb{R}_{\geq 0}$ and an instance $\bar{x} \in \mathbb{R}^n$, we define our cost function of the perturbed vector as

$$C(x \mid \bar{x}) := d(x, \bar{x}) + \gamma q_k(x \mid \mathcal{X}_+) + \eta q_{k'}(x \mid \mathcal{X}), \qquad (4)$$

where k, k' are the parameters for LOF and $\gamma, \eta \geq 0$ are the trade-off parameters. The first term assesses the closeness of the perturbed vector x to the original input $\bar{x}$. The second and third terms are LOF of x with respect to $\mathcal{X}_+$ and $\mathcal{X}$, which assess the feasibility and actionability of the perturbed vector, respectively. Since LOF takes large values for outliers, minimizing $q_k(x \mid \mathcal{X}_+)$ and $q_{k'}(x \mid \mathcal{X})$ ensures that the optimal solutions are expected to be close to $\mathcal{X}_+$ and $\mathcal{X}$.

3.3 Algorithm

We describe our proposed algorithm to generate a feasible and actionable path by iteratively updating the feature vector to decrease the cost function (4). Since the proposed cost function is non-differentiable due to LOF, we use local linear regression [10] to obtain a descent direction for the cost function.

First, we initialize the algorithm by setting $t \leftarrow 1$, the initial vector $x^{(1)} \leftarrow \bar{x}$, and initial path $P^{(1)} \leftarrow \{x^{(1)}\}$. At the t-th iteration $(t \geq 1)$ with the current vector $x^{(t)}$, we apply local linear regression [10] with the l-nearest neighbors $N_l(x^{(t)}) \subseteq \mathcal{X}$. Let x_i be the i-th sample in $\mathcal{X}$ $(i = 1, \ldots, |\mathcal{X}|)$ and $c_i = C(x_i \mid \bar{x})$. The index set of samples included in $N_l(x^{(t)})$ is denoted by $I^{(t)} \subseteq \{1, \ldots, |\mathcal{X}|\}$.

Algorithm 1. Distribution-aligned Sequential Counterfactual Explanation
***

Input: The original instance $\bar{\boldsymbol{x}} \in \mathbb{R}^n$, the cost function parameters $\gamma, \eta \geq 0$, the regularization parameter $\lambda \geq 0$, the step-size $\beta \in [0, 1]$, and the maximum number of iterations T.

Output: The sequence of feature vectors $P^{(T)}$.

1: Set $t \leftarrow 1$, $\boldsymbol{x}^{(1)} \leftarrow \bar{\boldsymbol{x}}$, $P^{(1)} \leftarrow \{\boldsymbol{x}^{(1)}\}$.
2: **for** $t = 1, \ldots, T - 1$ **do**
3:     Construct the set of the l-neighborhoods $N_l(\boldsymbol{x}^{(t)})$.
4:     For each feature vector $\boldsymbol{x}_i \in N_l(\boldsymbol{x}^{(t)})$, evaluate its cost as $c_i \leftarrow C(\boldsymbol{x}_i \mid \bar{\boldsymbol{x}})$ ($i = 1, \ldots, l$).
5:     Construct a linear approximation of the cost function C at $\bar{\boldsymbol{x}}$ by local linear regression:

$$\left(\boldsymbol{\theta}^{(t)}, \theta_0^{(t)}\right) \in \underset{(\boldsymbol{\theta}, \theta_0) \in \mathbb{R}^n \times \mathbb{R}}{\arg\min} \sum_{i \in I^{(t)}} (c_i - \boldsymbol{\theta}^\top \boldsymbol{x}_i - \theta_0)^2 + \lambda \left(\|\boldsymbol{\theta}\|_2^2 + \theta_0^2\right).$$

6:     Update the feature vector as $\boldsymbol{x}^{(t+1)} \leftarrow \boldsymbol{x}^{(t)} - \beta \boldsymbol{\theta}^{(t)}$.
7:     Update the pass as $P^{(t+1)} \leftarrow P^{(t)} \cup \{\boldsymbol{x}^{(t+1)}\}$
8: **end for**
9: **return** $P^{(T)}$
***

To find a descent direction of the cost function C at $\boldsymbol{x}^{(t)}$, we solve the following the ℓ_2-regularized least squares problem:

$$\left(\boldsymbol{\theta}^{(t)}, \theta_0^{(t)}\right) \in \underset{(\boldsymbol{\theta}, \theta_0) \in \mathbb{R}^n \times \mathbb{R}}{\arg\min} \sum_{i \in I^{(t)}} (c_i - \boldsymbol{\theta}^\top \boldsymbol{x}_i - \theta_0)^2 + \lambda \left(\|\boldsymbol{\theta}\|_2^2 + \theta_0^2\right), \quad (5)$$

where $(\boldsymbol{\theta}, \theta_0) \in \mathbb{R}^n \times \mathbb{R}$ is a parameter to be estimated, and $\lambda \geq 0$ is the regularization parameter. Since the estimated linear function $\boldsymbol{\theta}^{(t)\top} \boldsymbol{x} + \theta_0^{(t)}$ is a linear approximation of the cost function C at $\boldsymbol{x}^{(t)}$, the coefficient $\boldsymbol{\theta}^{(t)}$ is expected to be a local ascent direction of C at $\boldsymbol{x}^{(t)}$. Thus, we update the current vector as

$$\boldsymbol{x}^{(t+1)} \leftarrow \boldsymbol{x}^{(t)} - \beta \boldsymbol{\theta}^{(t)},$$

where $\beta \in [0, 1]$ is a given parameter for the step size. Then, we update the pass as $P^{(t+1)} \leftarrow P^{(t)} \cup \{\boldsymbol{x}^{(t+1)}\}$ and increment t by one. We repeat this procedure until t reaches $T - 1$ and then output the resulting path $P^{(T)}$. We summarize our algorithm in Algorithm 1.

Remark 1. The reason for incorporating the ℓ_2 regularization term in the objective function (5) is to ensure the uniqueness of the optimal solution even when the neighborhood size l is small.

Remark 2. We can use our approach to generate a path when we already have a terminal vector. Suppose that we use a certain CE method and obtain a perturbed feature vector $\boldsymbol{x}_{\mathrm{CE}}$ with $f(\boldsymbol{x}_{\mathrm{CE}}) = +1$. Then, we can generate a path from $\bar{\boldsymbol{x}}$ to $\boldsymbol{x}_{\mathrm{CE}}$ in a similar way. Specifically, we define the cost function as

$$C(\boldsymbol{x} \mid \bar{\boldsymbol{x}}) := q_k(\boldsymbol{x} \mid \{\boldsymbol{x}_{\mathrm{CE}}\}) + \eta q_{k'}(\boldsymbol{x} \mid \mathcal{X}). \quad (6)$$

Then, we generate a path from $\bar{x}$ to x_{CE} by iteratively updating the feature vector with decreasing the cost function (6) as Algorithm 1.

4   Experiments

We conducted numerical experiments on real datasets to investigate the effectiveness of our method by comparing the performance with existing CE methods. Our experiments were implemented with Python 3.6.5 and performed on an Nvidia Tesla P100 GPU (60 GB, 5.3 TFlops). All codes and datasets used in the experiments are available at https://github.com/isct-nakatalab/dist-alignedCE.

4.1   Experimental Setup

We used two datasets: `Adult` [2] and `Bank Marketing` [13], where we converted all categorical features to one-hot vectors. After the conversion, the total number of features for `Adult` and `Bank Marketing` were 108 and 48, respectively. `Adult` contains 8,842 samples, while `Bank Marketing` includes 45,211 samples. Our experiments used logistic regression and XGBoost [5] for the classifier f.

  We set the parameters of our method as follows: For the cost function (4), we employed the scaled Euclidean distance as the distance function d to align its scale with the LOF, where the Euclidean distance was multiplied by a factor of 5×10^{-4}. We also set the number of neighbors $(k, k') = (10, 5)$ in Equation (4) and the regularization parameter $\lambda = 10^{-4}$ in Equation (5). For `Bank Marketing`, we set the parameters of LOF as $(\gamma, \eta) = (0.5, 0.08)$ for logistic regression and $(0.5, 0.05)$ for XGBoost. For `Adult`, on the other hand, we set the parameters of LOF as $(\gamma, \eta) = (1, 0.5)$ for logistic regression and $(1, 0.1)$ for XGBoost. These values were determined by our preliminary experiments, where we first tuned the ratio of γ to η to ensure that the path reached the desired label set $\mathcal{X}_+$. Then, γ was adjusted according to the dimension of the feature vector, noting that paths in high-dimensional data often failed to reach $\mathcal{X}_+$ for a small γ. For the parameters of Algorithm 1, we set the number of neighbors used in local linear regression $l = 10$, the step size $\beta = 0.2$, and the maximum number of iterations $T = 1000$ for both datasets.

  We compared our method to two existing CE methods. The first baseline was FACE [16]. For the parameters of the radius used in FACE, we set $\epsilon = 3.0$ for `Adult` and $\epsilon = 3.2$ for `Bank Marketing`. We used a Gaussian kernel density function for the density function. These parameters were set as large as possible, ensuring that the constructed neighborhood graphs would likely remain connected and the construction of a neighborhood graph would be completed within 24 h. We also used NICE [4] as the second baseline. This method obtains a perturbed feature vector for which the given classifier outputs the desired label. Since this method does not output a path by itself, we constructed a path by equally dividing line segments connecting the input vector and the perturbed vector.

Table 1. Results for `Adult` ($|\mathcal{X}| = 48842$, $n = 108$)

	Logistic Regression		XGBoost	
	A-LOF	F-LOF	A-LOF	F-LOF
FACE	1.931±0.629	1.544±0.593	1.712±0.688	1.540±0.987
NICE	1.945±0.747	1.668±0.671	1.908±1.092	1.545±1.016
Our Method	**1.605±0.976**	**1.471±0.486**	**1.304±0.588**	**1.497±0.987**

To evaluate the feasibility and actionability of the suggested path P given by each method, we used two types of metrics:

- **Feasibility LOF Score (F-LOF).** Let $\boldsymbol{x}_{\mathrm{end}} \in P$ be its terminal vector, we calculated $q_k(\boldsymbol{x}_{\mathrm{end}} \mid \mathcal{X}_+)$ to assess the feasibility of P.
- **Actionability LOF Score (A-LOF).** To assess the actionability of P, we calculated $\max_{\boldsymbol{x} \in P} q_{k'}(\boldsymbol{x} \mid \mathcal{X})$, which is the worst LOF among the vectors on the path for $\mathcal{X}$.

It is important to note that the number of vectors included in P can be different for each method in our experiments. To ensure consistent evaluations for A-LOF among all the methods, we either sampled or divided the obtained path P into 20 vectors at equal intervals when calculating A-LOF.

Since FACE sometimes failed to output a path, we conducted FACE multiple times to ensure that FACE successfully outputs a path at least 30 times. Specifically, we performed 100 trials for `Bank Marketing`, 300 trials for `Adult` with logistic regression, and 150 trials for `Adult` with XGBoost. Then, for each setting, we ran our method and NICE as many times as FACE successfully output a path and compared their results.

4.2 Results and Discussion

Tables 1 and 2 summarize the experimental results of each method. We see that our method achieved the lowest A-LOF among all methods regardless of the dataset and classification model. These results demonstrated that our method obtained paths that were closer to the samples than those obtained by the other methods. In terms of F-LOF, FACE was the best for `Bank Marketing` in Table 2 for both logistic regression and XGBoost. However, it should be noted that the difference in F-LOF between our method and FACE was small. In addition, for the results for `Adult` in Table 1, our method obtained lower F-LOF than the other methods for both logistic regression and XGBoost. We can, therefore, conclude that the terminal vector of the path given by our method did not deviate from $\mathcal{X}_+$ compared to FACE. Comparing F-LOF of our method to that of NICE, we found that our method outperformed NICE except for `Bank Marketing` with the logistic regression. Overall, our method effectively provided paths with good actionability and feasibility.

Table 2. Results for `Bank Marketing` ($|\mathcal{X}| = 45211$, $n = 48$)

	Logistic Regression		XGBoost	
	A-LOF	F-LOF	A-LOF	F-LOF
FACE	1.629±0.398	**1.017±0.054**	1.838±0.537	**1.024±0.054**
NICE	1.526±0.385	1.035±0.060	1.577±0.432	1.054±0.052
Our Method	**1.499±0.366**	1.033±0.070	**1.336±0.320**	1.043±0.059

Figures 3 and 4 show box plots of the computation times for constructing a path by each method, where a green triangle and an orange horizontal line represent the mean and median, respectively. From these figures, NICE was much faster than the others. Unlike FACE and our method, this result is because NICE only focuses on finding a single perturbed vector. Comparing our method with FACE, the median computation time of FACE was smaller than our method for all data and all models. However, we can see that the computation time of FACE was highly volatile, and it sometimes took a long time to output a path. As FACE finds a path on a neighborhood graph, its computation can be strongly influenced by the graph structure, which is one of the reasons for the instability in the computation time. Therefore, when a reliable output within a certain time is critical, our method may be preferable to FACE.

Next, we compare the preprocessing time of our method and FACE. For a given sample set $\mathcal{X}$, the two methods are required to construct the desired sample set $\mathcal{X}_+$ as a preprocessing. Also, FACE needs the construction of a neighborhood graph from $\mathcal{X}$. To compare the entire preprocessing time for these methods, we randomly divided 48,842 samples of `Adult` into five groups and executed the preprocessing to subsets of the groups. Figure 5 shows the transition of the preprocessing time of each method for `Adult` with varying numbers of samples to be preprocessed. In Fig. 5, the horizontal and vertical axes represent the number of samples and the log-transformed preprocessing time in seconds, respectively. The results show that the preprocessing time of both methods increased as the number of samples grew. However, the preprocessing time of our method was consistently shorter than that of FACE, and the difference was larger as the number of samples increased. In contrast to FACE, our method does not require the construction of a neighborhood graph in the preprocessing step, contributing to reducing the preprocessing time significantly.

4.3   Example of a Path

To discuss whether our method can provide realistic paths for users, we show an example of a path given by our method to an instance for `Adult`. The prediction task of `Adult` is to determine whether an individual's annual income exceeds $ 50K or not.

We show an example of a user predicted not to exceed $ 50K in Table 3, and Table 4 shows the three feature vectors in the suggested path to the user.

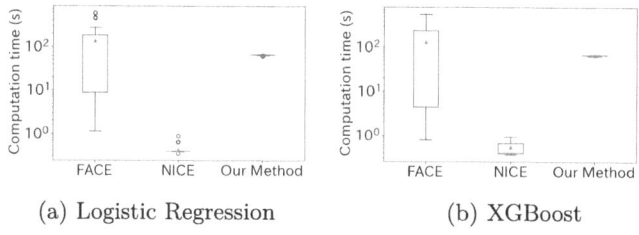

Fig. 3. Computation time for `Bank Marketing`.

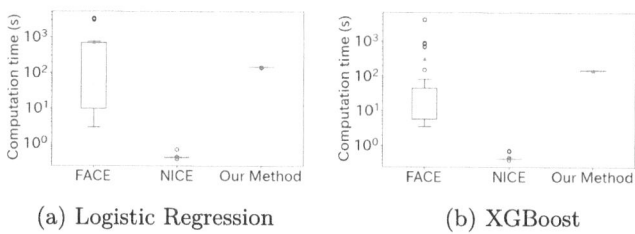

Fig. 4. Computation time for `Adult`.

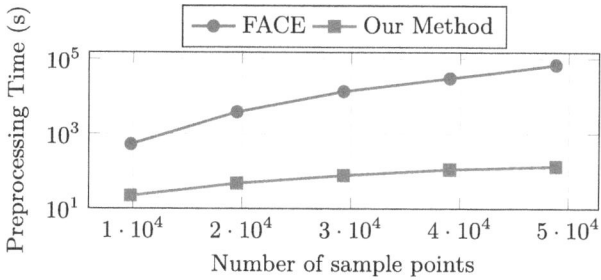

Fig. 5. Preprocessing time of FACE and our method.

The path in Table 4 recommends reducing "capital-loss" and increasing "hours-per-week" from the origin to the intermediate. From the intermediate to the terminal, the path suggests continuing to reduce "capital-loss" while keeping "hours-per-week" at 51. This suggested path means that the user should first focus on increasing "hours-per-week", and after that, as long as keeping "hours-per-week" is at least 51, the user can continue to reduce "capital-loss" from 127, which can give insight into how to act to reach the terminal vector.

5 Conclusion and Future Work

We proposed an actionable counterfactual explanation method for machine learning models that shows both the destination of a feature vector and a distribution-aligned path to reach it. We introduced a cost function based on the Local Outlier

Table 3. Example feature vector predicted to "<50K" in `Adult`.

age	workclass	flnwgt	education	education-num	marital-status	occupation
38	Private	154410	HS-grad	9	Married-civ-spouse	Craft-repair
relationship	race	sex	capital-gain	capital-loss	hours-per-week	native-country
Husband	White	Male	0	2051	40	Poland

Table 4. Example of a path generated by our method for `Adult`.

Feature	Origin	Intermediate	Terminal
capital-loss	2051 $\longrightarrow$	1277$\longrightarrow$	11
hours-per-week	40 $\longrightarrow$	57 $\longrightarrow$	51

Factor (LOF) for all the sample points and those with the desired label into the cost function. Our method generates a sequence of feature vectors according to the direction of decreasing the cost function with a local linear regression. Our numerical experiments demonstrated that our method succeeded in generating sequences that are along with the data distribution.

One of the possible future work is to ensure the validity of the terminal of the path given by our method. Since our path generation process relies only on LOF, the prediction model can fail to output the desired output for the terminal. Therefore, we need to extend our method to ensure that the prediction model outputs the desired label for the terminal. Also, it should be noted that since our method minimizes the cost function, including LOF, the evaluation with LOF-based metrics may sometimes overestimate its performance. Since there have been several metrics to evaluate whether the suggested actions are acceptable to the users [1,12], we are interested in investigating whether our method yields preferable paths in terms of these metrics.

Acknowledgments. This work was supported by JSPS KAKENHI Grant Number 24K17465.

Disclosure of Interests. The authors have no competing interests to declare that are relevant to the content of this article.

References

1. Alotaibi, H., Singh, R.: Metrics for evaluating actionability in explainable AI. In: Proceedings of the 20th Pacific Rim International Conference on Artificial Intelligence, pp. 481–487 (2023)
2. Becker, B., Kohavi, R.: Adult (1996). https://doi.org/10.24432/C5XW20

3. Breunig, M.M., Kriegel, H.P., Ng, R.T., Sander, J.: LOF: identifying density-based local outliers. ACM SIGMOD Rec. **29**(2), 93–104 (2000)
4. Brughmans, D., Leyman, P., Martens, D.: NICE: an algorithm for nearest instance counterfactual explanations. Data Min. Knowl. Disc. (2023). https://doi.org/10.1007/s10618-023-00930-y
5. Chen, T., Guestrin, C.: XGBoost: a scalable tree boosting system. In: Proceedings of the 22nd International Conference on Knowledge Discovery and Data Mining, pp. 785–794. ACM (2016)
6. Dandl, S., Molnar, C., Binder, M., Bischl, B.: Multi-objective counterfactual explanations. In: Proceedings of the 16th International Conference on Parallel Problem Solving from Nature, pp. 448–469 (2020)
7. Dhurandhar, A., et al.: Explanations based on the missing: towards contrastive explanations with pertinent negatives. In: Proceedings of the 32nd International Conference on Neural Information Processing Systems, pp. 590–601 (2018)
8. Dhurandhar, A., Pedapati, T., Balakrishnan, A., Chen, P.Y., Shanmugam, K., Puri, R.: Model agnostic contrastive explanations for structured data. arXiv preprint (2019). https://doi.org/10.48550/arxiv.1906.00117
9. Guidotti, R.: Counterfactual explanations and how to find them: literature review and benchmarking. Data Min. Knowl. Disc. (2022). https://doi.org/10.1007/s10618-022-00831-6
10. Hastie, T., Tibshirani, R., Friedman, J.: The Elements of Statistical Learning Data Mining, Inference, and Prediction, 2nd edn. Springer, New York (2009). https://doi.org/10.1007/978-0-387-84858-7
11. Kanamori, K., Takagi, T., Kobayashi, K., Arimura, H.: DACE: distribution-aware counterfactual explanation by mixed-integer linear optimization. In: Proceedings of the 29th International Joint Conference on Artificial Intelligence, pp. 2855–2862 (2020)
12. Kshetry, N., Kantardzic, M.: What-if XAI framework (WiXAI): from counterfactuals towards causal understanding. J. Comput. Commun. **12**(06), 169–198 (2024)
13. Moro, S., Cortez, P., Rita, P.: A data-driven approach to predict the success of bank telemarketing. Decis. Supp. Syst. **62**, 22–31 (2014)
14. Nguyen, T.D.H., Bui, N., Nguyen, D., Yue, M.C., Nguyen, V.A.: Robust Bayesian recourse. In: Proceedings of the 38th Conference on Uncertainty in Artificial Intelligence (PMLR), vol. 180, pp. 1498–1508 (2022)
15. Pawelczyk, M., Broelemann, K., Kasneci, G.: Learning model-agnostic counterfactual explanations for tabular data. In: Proceedings of the Web Conference 2020, pp. 3126–3132 (2020)
16. Poyiadzi, R., Sokol, K., Santos-Rodriguez, R., De Bie, T., Flach, P.: Face: feasible and actionable counterfactual explanations. In: Proceedings of the AAAI/ACM Conference on AI, Ethics, and Society, pp. 344–350 (2020)
17. Tsiourvas, A., Sun, W., Perakis, G.: Manifold-aligned counterfactual explanations for neural networks. In: Proceedings of the International Conference on Artificial Intelligence and Statistics (PMLR), vol. 238, pp. 3763–3771 (2024)
18. Van Looveren, A., Klaise, J.: Interpretable counterfactual explanations guided by prototypes. In: Machine Learning and Knowledge Discovery in Databases, Research Track, pp. 650–665 (2021)
19. Verma, S., Boonsanong, V., Hoang, M., Hines, K.E., Dickerson, J.P., Shah, C.: Counterfactual explanations and algorithmic recourses for machine learning: a review. arXiv preprint (2020). https://doi.org/10.48550/arxiv.2010.10596

20. Wachter, S., Mittelstadt, B., Russell, C.: Counterfactual explanations without opening the black box: automated decisions and the GDPR. Harvard J. Law Technol. **31**(2), 841–887 (2018)
21. Zhang, S., Chen, X., Wen, S., Li, Z.: Density-based reliable and robust explainer for counterfactual explanation. Expert Syst. Appl. **226**, 120214 (2023)

T-FIA: Temporal-Frequency Interactive Attention Network for Long-Term Time Series Forecasting

Haoning Yang[1], Yimin Wang[2], Yixi Wang[3], and Jun Chen[1(✉)]

[1] National Engineering Research Center for Multimedia Software (NERCMS), School of Computer Science, Wuhan University, Wuhan, China
`chenj@whu.edu.cn`
[2] Zhongnan University of Economics and Lawomics and Law, Wuhan, China
[3] State grid Hubei Electric Power Co., Ltd., Information and Communication Branch, Wuhan, China

Abstract. Long-term time series forecasting is crucial in various domains, including weather, traffic, and energy. In a time series, the time domain contains intuitive time-varying characteristics, affording valuable insights into predicting trends and details, while the frequency domain harbors underlying periodic patterns, identifying pivotal elements within historical data essential for forecasting. However, prior methodologies often fixated exclusively on either the temporal or frequency domain, falling short in capturing the information within historical data in a holistic view for forecasting. To address the issue mentioned above, we propose a **T**emporal-**F**requency **I**nteractive **A**ttention Network (**T-FIA**) to refine the modeling of time series by concurrently harnessing insights from both the temporal and frequency domains. In T-FIA, we formulate a temporal-frequency interactive encoder to capture domain-specific information from the dual perspectives of temporal and frequency domains. Subsequently, we facilitate information interaction between them, enhancing a more comprehensive understanding of time series and enabling precise time series forecasting. Experimental evaluations on seven datasets demonstrate the effectiveness of our proposed T-FIA.

Keywords: Time Series Forecasting · Temporal-Frequency · Attention

1 Introduction

Long-term time series forecasting, involving the prediction of multiple future steps by considering a substantial historical context, stands as one of the most fundamental problems in time series analysis and is widely applied in many real-world scenarios, including weather [1], transportation [3] and energy [5].

Recently, With the rapid development of deep learning, numerous models based on deep learning have been explored for forecasting [10], yielding promising results. These models can be broadly divided into two categories:

R. Hadfi et al. (Eds.): PRICAI 2024, LNAI 15281, pp. 257–268, 2025.
https://doi.org/10.1007/978-981-96-0116-5_21

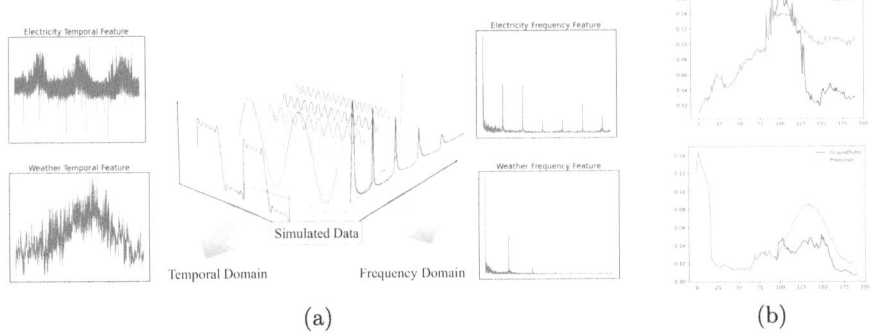

Fig. 1. Analysis of time series in temporal and frequency domains. The temporal domain predominantly captures more intuitive temporal variations, while the frequency domain harbors potential global periodic information, both of which hold significant implications for time series forecasting.

One focuses on capturing temporal dependencies in the time domain. For example, PatchTST [11] employs patching techniques to convert time series, initially consisting of individual timestamps, into a sequence of temporal segments, significantly enriching the semantic information within the time series. The other concentrates on the frequency domain characteristics of time series. FEDformer [17] integrates frequency-enhanced attention to model time series features in the frequency domain. FiLM [16] maintains historical information while mitigating noisy signals' impact by utilizing Fourier analysis. However, the majority of methods emphasize either the time or frequency domain, rendering them incapable of capturing both the time-varying characteristics in the time domain and the underlying periodic patterns in the frequency domain, thereby lacking a comprehensive understanding of time series.

Through investigation of both simulated and real-world data, as illustrated in Fig. 1a, we can discern trends and fluctuations of variables in the time domain, offering a more intuitive view of temporal changes. Simultaneously, in the frequency domain, we observe a series of peaks that reflect the underlying periodicity of the time series, offering insight into the underlying patterns. Both types of information are crucial for forecasting. The first and second rows of Fig. 1b show the forecasting results using time or frequency domain information alone, respectively. It can be seen that using time domain information alone makes it difficult to capture cyclical variations, while using frequency domain information alone fails to capture the fluctuating characteristics of time, leading to overly smooth forecasting results.

Motivated by this rationale, we propose T-FIA for Long-term time series forecasting, where the fundamental component, T-FIA Encoder, comprises multiple blocks. In each block, the Fourier transform is initially applied to generate features in the frequency domain. Subsequently, encoding is employed separately for the obtained time and frequency domain features. Finally, an attention mechanism facilitates interaction between these features. Through this methodology, the model demonstrates proficiency in capturing both the temporal variations within the time domain and the underlying patterns within the frequency domain. Experimental evaluations on seven datasets, compared with six benchmark methods, demonstrate the effectiveness of our proposed T-FIA.

The main contributions of this work are as follows:

- We investigate the temporal and frequency domains of time series, analyzing the significance of the information embedded in them for time series forecasting.
- We introduce the Temporal-Frequency Interactive Attention Network, leveraging the interaction of temporal and frequency domain features to effectively enhance long-term time series forecasting.
- We conduct extensive experiments on seven datasets from diverse domains, demonstrating the effectiveness of our approach.

2 Related Work

Researchers have proposed numerous time series forecasting methods, ranging from traditional statistical approaches [7] to machine learning methods [4], and currently, deep learning techniques with promising results. In the following section, we describe existing research based on the domain of information utilized, including the time domain and frequency domain

2.1 Time Series Forecasting in Time Domain

The time-varying characteristics are essential in time series forecasting. Many solutions [11,13,15] have been proposed to capture the temporal domain dependencies. PatchTST [11] introduces the concept of channel-independence and utilizes patching techniques to convert time steps into temporal segments, thereby significantly enriching the semantic information. DLinear [15] employs a simple one-layer linear model to process each channel of the time series individually, achieving commendable prediction results. TimesNet [13] converts the time series into the 2D space by extracting a series of periods and analyzes the time-domain variations through convolution. In contrast to our approach, the aforementioned time-domain methods have difficulties in capturing the complete underlying periodic patterns, owing to the absence of frequency-domain information.

2.2 Time Series Forecasting in Frequency Domain

The periodic variations hold significance in time series forecasting. Therefore, several methods [14,16,17] have extracted insights from the frequency domain to enhance forecasting. For example, Autoformer [14] replaces self-attention by introducing the auto-correlation mechanism implemented with Fourier transforms. FEDformer [17] utilizes a Fourier-enhanced structure to encode features, calculating attention score directly within the frequency domain. FiLM [16] employs Legendre Polynomials projections to approximate historical information with Fourier projection to eliminate noise. Unlike our methodology, the frequency-domain methods mentioned above present challenges in modeling detailed temporal variations, given the absence of time-domain information.

3   Method

3.1   Preliminary

In the long-term time series forecasting, the objective is to utilize historical data $X = \{x_{t-L+1} \ldots x_t\}$ within a look-back window of size L to predict the values $\hat{X} = \{x_{t+1} \ldots x_{t+T}\}$ over the next T future time steps. Here, x_t denotes the multivariate time vector with C features at time step t.

Following the previous works [11], we also model time series from the perspective of channel independence. Regarding the aforementioned multivariate time series $X \in \mathbb{R}^{C \times L}$ with C features, we decompose it into C univariate sequences $X^i \in \mathbb{R}^{1 \times L}$, where $i = 1, 2, ..., C$. T-FIA independently models and predicts these univariate sequences, ultimately combining the individual univariate predictions to obtain multivariate forecasting results. Due to the absence of multivariate sequences in the model and for ease of subsequent descriptions, the symbol X will be used to represent X^i in the following sections of the paper.

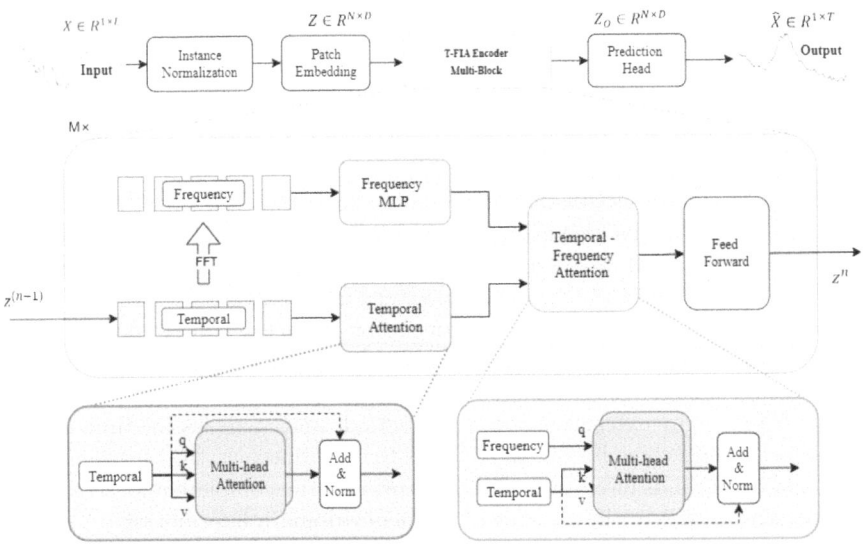

Fig. 2. T-FIA Network Architecture. The core component of the T-FIA network is the T-FIA encoder, which consists of multiple blocks. Within each block, temporal domain and frequency domain features are initially acquired, followed by encoding through Frequency MLP and Temporal Attention, respectively, and finally, the interaction of these features is accomplished by Temporal-Frequency Interactive Attention.

3.2   T-FIA Network

The overall architecture of the T-FIA Network is illustrated in Fig. 2 and the entire process can be divided into three phases. In the first phase, we preprocess the univariate time series for subsequent feature extraction through the T-FIA encoder in both temporal and frequency domains. We apply instance normalization historical data to reduce the impact of distribution shifts between the training and testing sets. As demonstrated by PatchTST [11], temporal patches formed by multiple consecutive timestamps contain richer semantic information, which is essential for learning representations that contribute to forecasting. Therefore, We employ a patching technique after instance normalization, where N denotes the number of patches. After patching, embedding is performed with a trainable linear projection at patch level for further processing by the encoder, where D is the dimension of embedded space. Simultaneously, to preserve the positional relationships between patches, a positional encoding is also introduced.

In the second phase, we use the proposed T-FIA for encoding and interaction of features within the temporal and frequency domains. The T-FIA encoder is structured with M blocks. Within each block, the temporal domain is initially processed by Fourier transform to obtain corresponding frequency domain features. Following this, it encodes the obtained features from both domains, capturing inherent dependencies, including temporal variations and frequency patterns. Finally, the interaction between the temporal domain and the frequency domain features occurs. After M-block of processing, the resulting features encapsulate information from both domains.

In the final phase, predictions for the time series values at T future time steps are made based on the features derived from the T-FIA encoder. More precisely, the features with high dimensionality are projected onto the length of T with a linear projection. Subsequently, Instance denormalization [8] is applied to ensure consistency in the distribution between the predicted and historical data, ultimately yielding the conclusive predicted values.

3.3   Temporal-Frequency Interactive Attention

To better illustrate the M-block T-FIA Encoder structure, we'll focus on the n-th block of the T-FIA encoder. Taking the output $z^{n-1} \in \mathbb{R}^{D \times N}$ from the preceding block as input, this block produces the processed features denoted as $z^n \in \mathbb{R}^{D \times N}$. As a consequence, we derive $z^0 = Z$, serving as the input for the entire encoder, while $z^M = Z_o$ represents its output.

Frequency Process. The whole structure takes features in the temporal domain as input. To establish interaction between the temporal and frequency domains, it is essential to acquire corresponding frequency features. For the input $z^{n-1} \in \mathbb{R}^{D \times N}$, we execute the Fast Fourier Transform (FFT) on dimension D to extract the frequency features at the patch level within dimension N. The obtained features are in the complex number domain and are denoted as $z^n_{FFT} \in \mathbb{C}^{D \times N}$. However, as the temporal domain features exist solely in the real number domain, a conversion of the Fourier transform result is carried out by calculating its amplitude, allowing for subsequent temporal-frequency interaction.

To further capture meaningful frequency information, we utilize an MLP to encode the initial frequency features derived from the preceding process. The processed frequency domain features are denoted as $z_f^n \in \mathbb{R}^{D \times N}$.

Temporal Attention. Temporal domain features often involve a combination of time-varying attributes, such as trends or short-term fluctuations, which require substantial effort to capture. Here, the multi-head attention mechanism is employed to model temporal domain features. The adeptness of attention in capturing long-range dependencies enables us to acquire a more robust representation of the time domain, serving as a solid basis for subsequent interactions.

In particular, we model the relationships between patches of the input features $z^{(n-1)}$. In each head of the multi-head attention mechanism, temporal domain features are transformed into query (Q_t), key (K_t), and value (V_t) matrices through linear projection, where $Q_t, K_t, V_t \in \mathbb{R}^{N \times D}$. Subsequently, attention output is computed using the following formula:

$$\text{Attention}(Q_t, K_t, V_t) = \text{Softmax}(\frac{Q_t K_t^T}{\sqrt{D}})V_t. \tag{1}$$

Following the acquisition of the attention output, encoded time domain features denoted as $z_t^n \in \mathbb{R}^{N \times D}$ are derived through additional residual connections [6] and layer normalization [2].

Temporal-Frequency Attention. The multi-head attention mechanism is utilized here to establish interaction between the temporal and frequency domain features obtained earlier. As the final output of time series forecasting is represented in the time domain, achieving feature interaction goals in both temporal and frequency domains while preserving the consistency of the obtained time domain information becomes essential. Taking this factor into account, we carry out linear projection for time-domain features, converting them into key (K_t) and value (V_t) matrices, while the frequency-domain features are projected as query (Q_f) matrices in each attention head, where $Q_f, K_t, V_t \in \mathbb{R}^{N \times D}$. The interaction between the two domain features is achieved through matrix operations applied to the query and key. This ensures that the resulting attention output captures the time-varying properties in the temporal domain and can effectively incorporate potential periodic information in the frequency domain. The interaction process is mathematically expressed as follows:

$$\text{Attention}(Q_f, K_t, V_t) = \text{Softmax}(\frac{Q_f K_t^T}{\sqrt{D}})V_t. \tag{2}$$

The features resulting from interaction, labeled as $z_{tf}^n \in \mathbb{R}^{D \times N}$, are acquired by introducing extra residual connections and layer normalization. Like other attention-based frameworks, the current T-FIA block utilizes a Feed Forward Network (FFN) to process the interacted features and generate the output $z^n \in \mathbb{R}^{N \times D}$, denoted by $z^n = \text{FFN}(z_{tf}^n)$.

Loss Function. We combine L1 loss and L2 loss to mitigate the impact of the frequent outliers on forecasting, enhancing the robustness of our model. The loss function is defined as Eq. 3.

$$\mathcal{L} = \frac{1}{T} \sum_{i=1}^{T} ((\hat{x}_i - x_i)^2 + |\hat{x}_i - x_i|). \tag{3}$$

Discussion. The time domain of the time series contains intuitive time-varying characteristics that yield valuable insights into predicting trends and intricate fluctuations, while the frequency domain harbors underlying periodic patterns identifying crucial elements in historical data essential for forecasting. The absence of either domain prevents the model from comprehensively capturing information for forecasting. Unlike previous methods, we facilitate the interaction between the separately encoded time and frequency domain features, allowing us to leverage time-varying information within the time domain and potential periods in the frequency domain for enhanced predictive capabilities.

4 Experiments

4.1 Experimental Setup

Datasets. We evaluate the performance of our proposed T-FIA on 7 widely used long-term forecasting datasets, including Traffic, Electricity, Weather, and 4 ETT datasets (ETTh1, ETTh2, ETTm1, ETTm2). Table 1 summarizes the detailed statistics of these datasets, including sequence length, number of features, and sampling frequency for each dataset. Following previous protocol [14], we split the datasets into training, validation, and test sets based on a ratio of 6:2:2 for the ETT dataset, and a ratio of 7:1:2 for other datasets.

Table 1. The statistics of datasets in the experiment.

Dataset	Length	Feature	Frequency
ETTh	17420	7	1 h
ETTm	69680	7	15 min
Weather	52696	21	10 min
Electricity	26304	321	1 h
Traffic	17544	862	1 h

Baselines. We select 6 well-acknowledged long-term time series forecasting models as benchmarks. including supervised version of PatchTST [11], TimesNet [13], DLinear [15], FiLM [16], Autoformer [14] and FEDformer [17]. The detailed description of these models can be found in Sect. 2. When opting for these baseline models, our selection involves picking representative methods that correspond to the domain (i.e. temporal or frequency) of time series modeling.

For a fairer comparison, the look-back window L is set at 96 for all datasets, and the prediction horizons T are defined as $\{96, 192, 336, 720\}$. We present the baseline results from TimesNet except for PatchTST and FiLM. For these two, we reproduce their results with $L = 96$ relying on the officially released code.

Setup. As for our model, the number of T-FIA blocks is chosen from $M \in \{1, 2, 3\}$. The dimension of latent representations D is set from $\{256, 512\}$. For smaller datasets such as ETTh, we designate the number of heads in multi-head attention as 4, while 8 for the remaining datasets. The feed-forward network consists of 2 linear layers with GELU activation function. The first layer projects the latent dimension D to $2D$, while the second layer projects it back.

All the deep learning networks are implemented in PyTorch [12] and trained on a single NVIDIA RTX A100 40GB GPU. We utilize the Adam [9] optimizer with an initial learning rate of 10^{-3} and the loss function mentioned above for model optimization. Batch size is set to 32. The default training process is 10 epochs and is early stopped after 3 epochs if there is no loss reduction observed on the validation set. Each experiment is conducted three times. The mean square error (MSE) and mean absolute error (MAE) are employed as evaluation metrics.

4.2 Main Results

Comprehensive multivariate time-series forecasting results are listed in Table 2. Our proposed T-FIA network achieved a total of 50 top-1 and 55 top-2 across all 56 forecasting combinations from all seven datasets. In contrast to PatchTST and FiLM, recognized as the best-performing time-domain and frequency-domain methods in the baseline, our method achieves superior results in all prediction scenarios. This underscores the efficacy of the T-FIA network and emphasizes the significance of executing interactions between time-domain and frequency-domain features for time series forecasting.

4.3 Ablation Study

Effectiveness of Temporal-Frequency Interaction. To further validate the efficiency of our proposed temporal-frequency interactive attention, we carry out an ablation experiment following the same setup as the main experiment. We compare the T-FIA network with two alternative models named *PrueT* and *PrueF*, both of which rely solely on information from a single domain for time series forecasting. Within PrueT, we transform the query's input of TFIA from the frequency domain to the time domain. In other words, the modified model integrates two Temporal Attention modules. Within PrueF, we leverage the concept from [17] to handle features in the frequency domain while obtaining the ultimate prediction results in the temporal domain. In particular, we apply the Fourier transform to convert time-domain features into the frequency domain. Subsequently, we compute the attention score directly in the frequency domain

Table 2. Multivariate long-term time series forecasting results on seven datasets with a fixed input length $I = 96$ and prediction length $O \in \{96, 192, 336, 720\}$. A lower MSE/MAE indicates better forecasting performance. The best results are highlighted in **bold** and the second best are underlined.

Methods		T-FIA (Ours)		PatchTST (2023)		TimesNet (2023)		DLinear (2023)		FiLM (2022)		FEDformer (2022)		Autoformer (2021)	
Metric		MSE	MAE	MSE	MAE	MSE	MAE	MSE	MAE	MSE	MAE	MSE	MAE	MSE	MAE
ETTm1	96	**0.312**	**0.350**	0.326	0.364	0.338	0.375	0.345	0.372	0.352	0.370	0.379	0.419	0.505	0.475
	192	**0.359**	**0.377**	0.367	0.388	0.374	0.387	0.380	0.389	0.388	0.387	0.426	0.441	0.553	0.496
	336	**0.395**	**0.400**	0.396	0.405	0.410	0.411	0.413	0.413	0.420	0.407	0.445	0.459	0.621	0.537
	720	**0.456**	**0.438**	0.463	0.446	0.478	0.450	0.474	0.453	0.478	0.439	0.543	0.490	0.671	0.561
ETTm2	96	**0.174**	**0.253**	0.176	0.259	0.187	0.267	0.193	0.292	0.184	0.267	0.203	0.287	0.255	0.339
	192	**0.240**	**0.299**	0.243	0.303	0.249	0.309	0.284	0.362	0.248	0.307	0.269	0.328	0.281	0.340
	336	**0.303**	**0.339**	0.306	0.342	0.321	0.351	0.369	0.427	0.309	0.344	0.325	0.366	0.339	0.372
	720	**0.400**	**0.398**	0.406	0.401	0.408	0.403	0.554	0.522	0.407	0.399	0.421	0.415	0.433	0.432
ETTh1	96	**0.372**	**0.391**	0.402	0.415	0.384	0.402	0.386	0.400	0.389	0.399	0.376	0.419	0.449	0.459
	192	**0.416**	**0.419**	0.454	0.441	0.436	0.429	0.437	0.432	0.443	0.439	0.420	0.448	0.500	0.482
	336	**0.452**	**0.439**	0.492	0.458	0.491	0.469	0.481	0.459	0.484	0.461	0.459	0.465	0.521	0.496
	720	**0.459**	**0.461**	0.483	0.474	0.521	0.500	0.519	0.516	0.525	0.519	0.506	0.507	0.514	0.512
ETTh2	96	**0.284**	**0.334**	0.294	0.342	0.340	0.374	0.333	0.387	0.292	0.341	0.358	0.397	0.346	0.388
	192	**0.361**	**0.384**	0.366	0.389	0.402	0.414	0.477	0.476	0.392	0.404	0.429	0.439	0.456	0.452
	336	**0.410**	**0.424**	0.411	0.427	0.452	0.452	0.594	0.541	0.426	0.438	0.496	0.487	0.482	0.486
	720	**0.423**	**0.445**	0.428	0.446	0.462	0.468	0.831	0.657	0.443	0.459	0.463	0.474	0.515	0.511
Traffic	96	**0.473**	**0.300**	0.500	0.330	0.593	0.321	0.650	0.396	0.652	0.395	0.587	0.366	0.613	0.388
	192	**0.477**	**0.303**	0.499	0.325	0.617	0.336	0.598	0.370	0.605	0.371	0.604	0.373	0.616	0.382
	336	**0.494**	**0.309**	0.513	0.330	0.629	0.336	0.605	0.373	0.614	0.371	0.621	0.383	0.622	0.337
	720	**0.528**	**0.327**	0.549	0.347	0.640	0.350	0.645	0.394	0.692	0.428	0.626	0.382	0.660	0.408
ECL	96	0.181	**0.269**	0.186	0.276	**0.168**	0.272	0.197	0.282	0.197	0.275	0.193	0.308	0.201	0.317
	192	0.187	**0.276**	0.192	0.282	**0.184**	0.289	0.196	0.285	0.198	0.279	0.201	0.315	0.222	0.334
	336	0.204	**0.292**	0.208	0.297	**0.198**	0.300	0.209	0.301	0.217	0.302	0.214	0.329	0.231	0.338
	720	0.247	0.325	0.249	0.329	**0.220**	**0.320**	0.245	0.333	0.279	0.357	0.246	0.355	0.254	0.361
Weather	96	**0.172**	**0.210**	0.183	0.224	**0.172**	0.220	0.196	0.255	0.195	0.235	0.217	0.296	0.266	0.336
	192	**0.218**	**0.250**	0.231	0.263	0.219	0.261	0.237	0.296	0.238	0.270	0.276	0.336	0.307	0.367
	336	**0.273**	**0.291**	0.283	0.300	0.280	0.306	0.283	0.335	0.289	0.305	0.339	0.380	0.359	0.395
	720	0.351	**0.341**	0.356	0.349	0.365	0.359	**0.345**	0.381	0.358	0.350	0.403	0.428	0.419	0.428
1st Count		**50**		0		7		1		0		0		0	

and revert the processed frequency domain features back to the time domain through the inverse Fourier transform to produce the final prediction results.

As the results shown in Table 3, the T-FIA network, which implements the interaction of the temporal and frequency domains, outperforms PrueT and PrueF on all three datasets. This once again demonstrates the significance of the time and frequency domain interaction for time series forecasting and the effectiveness of the proposed T-FIA network.

4.4 Model Analysis

Analysis of Loss Function. Previous models commonly employed the L2 loss as the loss function. However, the L2 loss exhibits sensitivity to outliers. In the context of real-world time series data, where outliers are frequently present, this sensitivity diminishes the model's robustness. We perform experiments to

Table 3. Ablation of temporal-frequency interaction structure. PrueT and PrueF represent two model variants that exclusively handle time series in the time and frequency domains, respectively. **Bold** indicates the best.

Dataset		ETTh1				Traffic				Electricity			
Prediction Length		96	192	336	720	96	192	336	720	96	192	336	720
T-FIA	MSE	**0.372**	**0.416**	**0.452**	**0.459**	**0.473**	**0.477**	**0.494**	**0.528**	**0.181**	**0.187**	**0.204**	**0.247**
	MAE	**0.391**	**0.419**	**0.439**	**0.461**	**0.300**	**0.303**	**0.309**	**0.327**	**0.269**	**0.276**	**0.292**	**0.325**
PrueT	MSE	0.376	**0.416**	0.459	0.476	0.480	0.483	0.500	0.536	0.183	0.189	0.206	0.252
	MAE	**0.391**	**0.419**	0.441	0.470	0.305	0.306	0.312	0.329	0.271	0.277	0.294	0.328
PrueF	MSE	0.382	0.433	0.478	0.480	0.556	0.536	0.545	0.582	0.191	0.194	0.210	0.251
	MAE	**0.391**	0.421	0.444	0.469	0.342	0.329	0.333	0.351	0.273	0.278	0.294	0.326

Table 4. Analysis of loss function. HL denotes our hybrid loss function, while L2 represents the L2 loss function. **Bold** indicates the best.

Dataset		ETTh1				Weather				Electricity			
Prediction Length		96	192	336	720	96	192	336	720	96	192	336	720
T-FIA(HL)	MSE	**0.372**	**0.416**	**0.452**	**0.459**	**0.172**	**0.218**	**0.273**	**0.351**	0.181	**0.187**	0.204	0.247
	MAE	**0.391**	**0.419**	**0.439**	**0.461**	**0.210**	**0.250**	**0.291**	**0.341**	**0.269**	**0.276**	**0.292**	**0.325**
T-FIA(L2)	MSE	0.376	0.420	0.456	0.470	0.173	**0.218**	0.274	**0.351**	**0.180**	**0.187**	**0.203**	**0.244**
	MAE	0.397	0.425	0.445	0.468	0.214	0.254	0.295	0.345	**0.269**	0.279	0.295	0.327

investigate the impact of our hybrid loss function and the result is shown in Table 4. In contrast to L2 loss, the hybrid loss yields superior MSE results in the majority of cases, along with enhanced MAE results across all scenarios.

Additionally, it is essential to highlight that T-FIA can achieve results surpassing the baselines even when trained with L2 loss. This further underscores the significance of our proposed temporal-frequency interaction mechanism.

Analysis of Model Parameters. To evaluate the sensitivity of T-FIA to diverse model configurations, we experiment by varying model parameters. Specifically, we alter the number of T-FIA encoder blocks, denoted as $M = \{1, 2, 3\}$, and choose the latent representation dimension as $D = \{256, 512\}$. Figure 3 reveals that the MSE metrics of T-FIA across multiple datasets exhibit minimal variation with varying model parameter settings, highlighting the robustness of T-FIA to diverse model configurations.

Varying Look-Back Window size. Previous works [15] have noted that longer input lengths do not always enhance forecasting performance, especially for Transformer-based methods, since time points from an earlier stage may distract attention. As shown in Fig. 4, the performance of our proposed T-FIA consistently improves as the look-back window size increases. This finding suggests that our method is capable of capturing more information from longer input sequences, leading to enhanced performance.

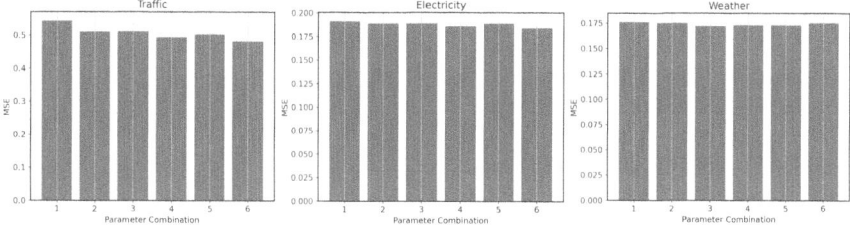

Fig. 3. MSE metrics with varying model parameter settings. Each bar represents the MSE score of a specific parameter combination. The combinations $(M, D) = (1, 256), (1, 512), (2, 256), (2, 512), (3, 256), (3, 512)$ are sequentially labeled from 1 to 6 in the figure. The experiments are conducted under the context where both the input and prediction steps are set to 96.

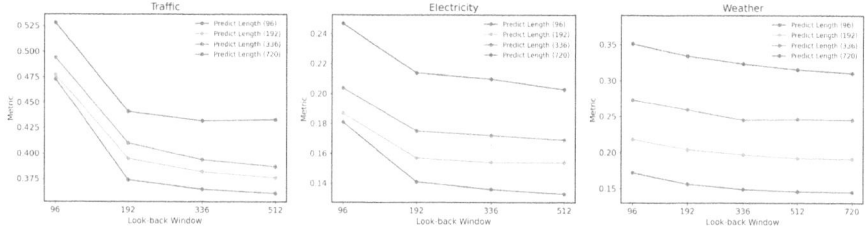

Fig. 4. MSE metrics for varying look-back windows on three datasets. Due to the limitation of CUDA memory, the experiments of ECL and traffic datasets are only conducted on four different look-back windows $\{96, 192, 336, 512\}$.

5   Conclusion

In this paper, we propose a Temporal-Frequency Interactive Attention Network (T-FIA) for long-term time series forecasting. In T-FIA, we devise a temporal-frequency interactive encoder to capture domain-specific information from the dual perspectives of temporal and frequency domains. Subsequently, we facilitate an informative interaction between them, enabling the model to both capture time-varying properties in the time domain and discern the underlying periods in the frequency domain, achieving accurate long-term time series forecasts through such a more comprehensive perspective. Experimental evaluations on seven datasets demonstrate the effectiveness of our proposed T-FIA.

Acknowledgments. This work is supported by an Internet Energy Lab project named "Sensing, transmission and extraction and deterministic network prototype development for two-way transmission of energy Internet source charge". The numerical calculations in this paper have been done on the supercomputing system in the Supercomputing Center of Wuhan University

Disclosure of Interests. The authors have no competing interests to declare that are relevant to the content of this article.

References

1. Angryk, R.A., et al.: Multivariate time series dataset for space weather data analytics. Sci. Data **7**(1), 227 (2020)
2. Ba, J.L., Kiros, J.R., Hinton, G.E.: Layer normalization. arXiv preprint arXiv:1607.06450 (2016)
3. Cai, L., Janowicz, K., Mai, G., Yan, B., Zhu, R.: Traffic transformer: capturing the continuity and periodicity of time series for traffic forecasting. Trans. GIS **24**(3), 736–755 (2020)
4. Chen, T., Guestrin, C.: Xgboost: a scalable tree boosting system. In: Proceedings of the 22nd ACM SIGKDD International Conference on Knowledge Discovery and Data Mining, pp. 785–794 (2016)
5. Deb, C., Zhang, F., Yang, J., Lee, S.E., Shah, K.W.: A review on time series forecasting techniques for building energy consumption. Renew. Sustain. Energy Rev. **74**, 902–924 (2017)
6. He, K., Zhang, X., Ren, S., Sun, J.: Deep residual learning for image recognition. In: Proceedings of the IEEE Conference on Computer Vision and Pattern Recognition, pp. 770–778 (2016)
7. Ho, S.L., Xie, M.: The use of arima models for reliability forecasting and analysis. Comput. Ind. Eng. **35**(1–2), 213–216 (1998)
8. Kim, T., Kim, J., Tae, Y., Park, C., Choi, J.H., Choo, J.: Reversible instance normalization for accurate time-series forecasting against distribution shift. In: International Conference on Learning Representations (2021)
9. Kingma, D.P., Ba, J.: Adam: a method for stochastic optimization. arXiv preprint arXiv:1412.6980 (2014)
10. Lim, B., Zohren, S.: Time-series forecasting with deep learning: a survey. Phil. Trans. R. Soc. A **379**(2194), 20200209 (2021)
11. Nie, Y., Nguyen, N.H., Sinthong, P., Kalagnanam, J.: A time series is worth 64 words: long-term forecasting with transformers. In: The Eleventh International Conference on Learning Representations (2022)
12. Paszke, A., et al.: Pytorch: an imperative style, high-performance deep learning library. In: Advances in Neural Information Processing Systems, vol. 32 (2019)
13. Wu, H., Hu, T., Liu, Y., Zhou, H., Wang, J., Long, M.: Timesnet: temporal 2D-variation modeling for general time series analysis. arXiv preprint arXiv:2210.02186 (2022)
14. Wu, H., Xu, J., Wang, J., Long, M.: Autoformer: decomposition transformers with auto-correlation for long-term series forecasting. Adv. Neural. Inf. Process. Syst. **34**, 22419–22430 (2021)
15. Zeng, A., Chen, M., Zhang, L., Xu, Q.: Are transformers effective for time series forecasting? In: Proceedings of the AAAI Conference on Artificial Intelligence, vol. 37, pp. 11121–11128 (2023)
16. Zhou, T., et al.: Film: frequency improved legendre memory model for long-term time series forecasting. Adv. Neural. Inf. Process. Syst. **35**, 12677–12690 (2022)
17. Zhou, T., Ma, Z., Wen, Q., Wang, X., Sun, L., Jin, R.: Fedformer: frequency enhanced decomposed transformer for long-term series forecasting. In: International Conference on Machine Learning, pp. 27268–27286. PMLR (2022)

Multi-modal Food Recommendation Using Clustering and Self-supervised Learning

Yixin Zhang[1], Xin Zhou[2], Qianwen Meng[1], Fanglin Zhu[1], Yonghui Xu[1],
Zhiqi Shen[3(✉)], and Lizhen Cui[1(✉)]

[1] School of Software and Joint SDU-NTU Centre for Artificial Intelligence
Research (C-FAIR), Shandong University, Jinan, China
{yixinzhang,mqw_sdu,zfl}@mail.sdu.edu.cn, clz@sdu.edu.cn,
xu.yonghui@hotmail.com

[2] Alibaba-NTU Singapore Joint Research Institute, Nanyang Technological
University, Singapore, Singapore
xin.zhou@ntu.edu.sg

[3] College of Computing and Data Science, Nanyang Technological University,
Singapore, Singapore
zqshen@ntu.edu.sg

Abstract. Food recommendation systems serve as pivotal components
in the realm of digital lifestyle services, designed to assist users in discovering recipes and food items that resonate with their unique dietary
predilections. Typically, multi-modal descriptions offer an exhaustive profile for each recipe, thereby ensuring recommendations that are both personalized and accurate. Our preliminary investigation of two datasets
indicates that pre-trained multi-modal dense representations might pre-
cipitate a deterioration in performance compared to ID features when
encapsulating interactive relationships. This observation implies that ID
features possess a relative superiority in modeling interactive collaborative signals. Consequently, contemporary cutting-edge methodologies
augment ID features with multi-modal information as supplementary features, overlooking the latent semantic relations between recipes. To rectify
this, we present CLUSSL, a novel food recommendation framework that
employs CLUstering and Self-Supervised Learning. Specifically, CLUSSL
formulates a modality-specific graph tailored to each modality with dis-
crete/continuous features, thereby transforming semantic features into
structural representations. Furthermore, CLUSSL procures recipe representations pertinent to different modalities via graph convolutional operations. A self-supervised learning objective is proposed to foster independence between recipe representations derived from different unimodal
graphs. Comprehensive experiments on real-world datasets substanti-
ate that CLUSSL consistently surpasses state-of-the-art recommendation
benchmarks in performance.

Keywords: Food Recommendation · Multi-modal · Clustering ·
Self-supervised Learning

1 Introduction

© The Author(s), under exclusive license to Springer Nature Singapore Pte Ltd. 2025
R. Hadfi et al. (Eds.): PRICAI 2024, LNAI 15281, pp. 269–281, 2025.
https://doi.org/10.1007/978-981-96-0116-5_22

Table 1. Performance of different modalities as item embedding w.r.t. LightGCN [6].

LightGCN	Allrecipes		Food.com	
	Recall@20	NDCG@20	Recall@20	NDCG@20
– ID	0.1147	0.0572	0.1365	0.0960
– Ingredient	0.1140	0.0578	0.1466	0.1034
– Image	0.1111	0.0557	0.1377	0.0932
– Text	0.1136	0.0562	0.1365	0.0932

ID means default setting of [6]. For ingredient, we lookup ingredient embedding table and aggregate the corresponding representations as item embeddings. For image and text, we use the pre-trained features as item embeddings via an additional projector.

Dietary intake is a critical determinant of human health and well-being, impacting both physiological and psychological states. Food recommendation systems (FRSs) aim to leverage user interaction data, multi-modal content, and ingredient information to personalize recipe suggestions that align with individual dietary needs. FRSs have seen notable advancements in recent years, driven by increased research interest and a wider range of lifestyle applications [11].

With the pervasive presence of multi-modal data linked to recipes, contemporary advancements have witnessed the assimilation of abundant metadata, encompassing elements such as ingredients and visual attributes, to enhance the precision of recommendations. For example, HAFR [1] jointly models interaction data, ingredients, and visual features. Similarly, SCHGN [12] further considers higher-order relationships and calorie intake preferences. However, these methods predominantly leverage user, recipe, and ingredient IDs to capture collaborative signals, relegating multi-modal information to secondary feature roles. Meanwhile, our preliminary investigation (Table 1) demonstrates that directly utilizing continuous representations (embeddings) derived from multi-modal features (e.g., image and text embeddings) for collaborative filtering (CF) tasks may degrade recommendation performance. In contrast, using discrete features such as IDs yields superior results. Interestingly, employing ingredient information, also a discrete feature, as recipe embeddings leads to competitive performance. These findings suggest that discrete features are more effective in capturing the underlying structure of the data. Consequently, multi-modal models like FREE-DOM [16] propose an item-item graph construction based on similarities between transformed multi-modal features, where item IDs encapsulate the structural relationships derived from these features. While it can represent some level of similarity through item-item graphs, it fails to explicitly model the underlying categorical taxonomy (e.g., desserts, casseroles) that defines a crucial aspect of recipe semantics. This deficiency hinders its capacity to effectively integrate and discriminate between latent thematic categories within the culinary domain.

To this end, this work proposes CLUSSL, a novel multi-modal food recommendation model that employs clustering and self-supervised learning. Specifically, CLUSSL utilizes a novel two-stage approach to exploit multi-modal recipe information for recommendation. In the first stage, unsupervised clustering is applied to unimodal data (e.g., image and text features) with pre-trained continuous representations. These clusters act as "prototype nodes", summarizing the key semantic features within each modality. Subsequently, for each modality, a modality-specific graph is constructed to capture the relationships between these prototype nodes. This graph construction leverages ID features to encode the inherent structure of the data. Graph convolutional networks are then employed to effectively propagate and aggregate these semantic relationships across the graphs, allowing CLUSSL to exploit the rich relational information embedded within each modality. Furthermore, CLUSSL incorporates a distance correlation constraint within a self-supervised learning framework. This constraint ensures that the learned recipe representations from different modalities (e.g., image-based and text-based) maintain a degree of independence. By combining these techniques, CLUSSL leverages the strengths of both unimodal data and multi-modal relationships, leading to demonstrably improved recommendation accuracy compared to existing baselines, as confirmed by extensive evaluations on real-world datasets.

2   Related Work

In this section, we review the most relevant existing methods in food recommendation and multi-modal recommendation.

2.1   Food Recommendation

In response to the diversified needs for food, FRSs are committed to providing accurate and personalized recommendation services for users. Recently, HAFR [1] develops a hierarchical attention mechanism to integrate the metadata (i.e., images and ingredients) with user-recipe interactions for recommendation. Moving beyond general CF methods, FGCN [2] employs graph neural networks to extract high-order connections among users, recipes, and ingredients, yet it omits the integration of visual features. Furthermore, RecipeRec [14] constructs heterogeneous graph to encapsulate the aforementioned relational structures. Finally, SCHGN [12] captures the relations of ingredients and capture the user's preference on food calories. Although these methods have demonstrated efficacy, the potential of leveraging comprehensive multi-modal data remains untapped.

2.2   Multi-modal Recommendation

Multi-modal recommendation systems (MMRSs) strive to enhance items' representations for better performance by incorporating features from different modalities. Early studies, such as VBPR [5], incorporate multi-modal contents with items' ID embeddings to extend the general CF framework. Inspired by the great success of graph-based methods, MMGCN [15] attempts to inject high-order semantics into user/item representations via message passing on modality-specific graphs. From another perspective, FREEDOM [16] constructs an item-item semantic graph from pre-trained multi-modal features to supplement the user-item interactions. BM3 [17] and LGMRec [3] adopt self-supervised learning objectives into MMRSs, showcasing a notable boost. Divergent from extant methods that align cross-modal semantics, CLUSSL proposes to transform uni-modal semantics into structural correlations via the utilization of clustering.

3   Preliminaries

In this section, we formulate the problem of food recommendation with multi-modal information and introduce the construction of the modality-specific graph.

3.1   Problem Formulation

Let $\mathcal{U}$ denote the set of users and $\mathcal{I}$ denote the set of food recipes. The user-recipe binary interaction matrix is denoted by $\mathcal{Y} \in \{0,1\}^{|\mathcal{U}| \times |\mathcal{I}|}$, where $|\mathcal{U}|$ and $|\mathcal{I}|$ represent the cardinalities of users and recipes, respectively. Each entry $\mathcal{Y}_{u,i} = 1$ indicates that user u has interacted with recipe i. Associated with each recipe i is the following modality information: i) modality information with discrete features. We only consider recipe-ingredient relationships, denoted as $\mathcal{M}_{\mathcal{A}_i} \in \{0,1\}^{|\mathcal{A}|}$. The collection of ingredients across all recipes forms the complete ingredient set $\mathcal{A}$, with cardinality $|\mathcal{A}|$. ii) modality information with continuous features. In this work, we focus on visual features $\mathcal{M}_{v_i} \in \mathbb{R}^{d_v}$ and textual features $\mathcal{M}_{t_i} \in \mathbb{R}^{d_t}$. Specifically, $\mathcal{M}_{v_i}$ are obtained from image of recipe i through ResNet [4], while $\mathcal{M}_{t_i}$ are extracted from textual description of recipe i using a pre-trained T-5 model [9].

We formally define the problem as follows. Based on the given notation, our objective is to predict the probability that user u will consume recipe i, taking into account user-recipe interactions and the recipe's multi-modal information.

3.2   Construction of Modality-Specific Graphs

Although heterogeneous graphs can include multiple types of vertices and edges, which helps to alleviate data sparsity and improve recommendation effectiveness [12,14], their complex structure poses significant challenges for model training. In this work, we propose constructing modality-specific bipartite graphs based on the discrete or continuous features for each modality.

Construct Bipartite Graph via Discrete Features. Given the ingredient set $\mathcal{A} = \{a\}$ and the recipe set $\mathcal{I} = \{i\}$, the observed relationships between these sets are captured by the matrix $\mathcal{R}^{\mathcal{A}} \in \{0,1\}^{|\mathcal{A}| \times |\mathcal{I}|}$, where each entry $\mathcal{R}^{\mathcal{A}}_{a,i} = 1$ if ingredient a belongs to item i, otherwise $\mathcal{R}^{\mathcal{A}}_{a,i} = 0$. The i-th column denotes the discrete features $\mathcal{M}_{\mathcal{A}_i}$ of recipe i regarding the ingredient modality. Based on the relationship matrix $\mathcal{R}^{\mathcal{A}}$, we construct a bipartite graph $\mathcal{G}_{\mathcal{A}} = \{(a, \mathcal{R}^{\mathcal{A}}_{a,i}, i) | a \in \mathcal{A}, i \in \mathcal{I}, \mathcal{R}^{\mathcal{A}}_{a,i} = 1)\}$.

Construct Bipartite Graph via Continuous Features. According to [8], closely binding item representations with raw modality features learned by pre-trained model can be detrimental. Thus, instead of using raw features as individual node representations, we introduce modality-specific cluster centres as "prototype nodes". Specifically, taking visual features as an example, we utilize

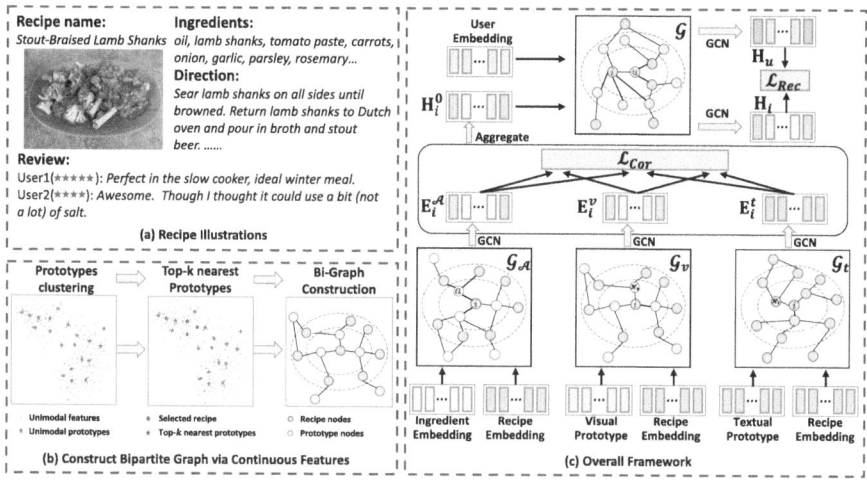

Fig. 1. (a) exemplifies a recipe with its associated modalities, (b) showcases the construction of the modality-specific graph via continuous multi-modal features, and (c) illustrates the overall framework of the proposed CLUSSL.

K-means to cluster the modality feature vectors into $|\mathcal{N}_v|$ cluster centers, i.e., $\mathcal{N}_v$ denotes visual prototype nodes. Then we select the top k nearest prototypes to define the visual-specific relationships for each recipe and form the matrix $\mathcal{R}^v \in \{0,1\}^{|\mathcal{N}_v| \times |\mathcal{I}|}$, where each entry $\mathcal{R}^v_{n,i} = 1$ if prototype node n belongs to top k set of recipe i, otherwise $\mathcal{R}^v_{n,i} = 0$. Based on the relationship matrix $\mathcal{R}^v$, we construct a bipartite graph $\mathcal{G}_v = \{(n, \mathcal{R}^v_{n,i}, i)|n \in \mathcal{N}_v, i \in \mathcal{I}, \mathcal{R}^v_{n,i} = 1)\}$. Similarly, we construct the textual-specific bipartite graph $\mathcal{G}_t = \{(n, \mathcal{R}^t_{n,i}, i)|n \in \mathcal{N}_t, i \in \mathcal{I}, \mathcal{R}^t_{n,i} = 1)\}$.

4 Methodology

This section delves into the individual components of CLUSSL. The overall architecture of the proposed method is illustrated in Fig. 1.

4.1 Graph Collaborative Filtering Backbone

In general, GNN-based CF methods [6] produce informative representations for users and items based on the message propagation and aggregation scheme, which exploit higher-order connectivity in the user-item graph and achieve state-of-the-art performance for recommendation. Following [3,16,17] , we employ an efficient and effective LightGCN [6] as backbone to encode the structure of the user-recipe bipartite graph. Formally, we denote this user-recipe graph as $\mathcal{G} = \{(u, \mathcal{Y}_{u,i}, i)|u \in \mathcal{U}, i \in \mathcal{I}, \mathcal{Y}_{u,i} = 1)\}$ based on user-recipe interaction matrix $\mathcal{Y} \in \mathbb{R}^{|\mathcal{U}| \times |\mathcal{I}|}$. We obtain the adjacency matrix of the user-item graph as follows:

$$\mathbf{A} = \begin{pmatrix} 0 & \mathcal{Y} \\ \mathcal{Y}^T & 0 \end{pmatrix}. \tag{1}$$

Given l-th layer embedding matrix $\mathbf{H}^l$, the simplified message passing process in LightGCN is defined as:

$$\mathbf{H}^{l+1} = (\mathbf{D}^{-1/2}\mathbf{A}\mathbf{D}^{-1/2})\mathbf{H}^l, \tag{2}$$

where $\mathbf{H}^0 \in \mathbb{R}^{(|\mathcal{U}|+|\mathcal{I}|)\times d}$ is the 0-th layer embedding matrix. User embeddings are randomly initialized and recipe embeddings are learned through different modality-specific graphs (introduced in Sect. 4.2). $\mathbf{D}$ is a $(|\mathcal{U}| + |\mathcal{I}|) \times (|\mathcal{U}| + |\mathcal{I}|)$ diagonal matrix, also called the degree matrix, and the node embeddings of the $(l + 1)$-th layer are only linearly aggregated from the l-th layer with a symmetrically normalized matrix $\mathbf{D}^{-1/2}\mathbf{A}\mathbf{D}^{-1/2}$. Lastly, representations from all hidden layers are aggregated through a readout function to obtain the final embedding matrix used for recommendation:

$$\begin{aligned} \mathbf{H}_u &= \mathrm{READOUT}(\mathbf{H}_u^0, \mathbf{H}_u^1, \ldots, \mathbf{H}_u^L), \\ \mathbf{H}_i &= \mathrm{READOUT}(\mathbf{H}_i^0, \mathbf{H}_i^1, \ldots, \mathbf{H}_i^L), \end{aligned} \tag{3}$$

where $\mathbf{H}_u$ and $\mathbf{H}_i$ denote the final representations of user u and recipe i, respectively, the READOUT function can be any differentiable function. Common designs include weighted sum, last-layer only, and others. We use the default mean function [16,17] in practice.

To generate recipe recommendations for user u, we first predict the interaction scores between the user and candidate recipes. Then, we rank candidate recipes based on the predicted scores in descending order and select the top-k recipes as recommendations for the user. The interaction score is calculated as:

$$\hat{y}_{u,i} = \mathbf{H}_u{}^T\mathbf{H}_i, \tag{4}$$

where $\hat{y}_{u,i}$ is the prediction score of user u towards recipe i. A high score suggests that the user prefers the recipe.

To capture the collaborative information from implicit feedback, we adopt Bayesian Personalized Ranking (BPR) loss [10] in model training. Specifically, BPR loss ensures that the prediction score of the observed interactions higher than sampled unobserved ones. Formally:

$$\mathcal{L}_{Rec} = \sum_{(u,i^+,i^-)\in\mathcal{O}} -log\sigma(\hat{y}_{u,i^+} - \hat{y}_{u,i^-}), \tag{5}$$

where σ is the sigmoid function, $\mathcal{O} = \{(u, i^+, i^-)|\mathcal{Y}_{u,i^+} = 1, \mathcal{Y}_{u,i^-} = 0\}$ denotes the pairwise training data, and i^- denotes a sampled recipe that user u has not interacted with.

4.2   Unimodal Graph Representation Learning

Given the modality-specific bipartite graphs $\mathcal{G}_\mathcal{A}$, $\mathcal{G}_v$, and $\mathcal{G}_t$ towards different modalities, we employ graph convolutional networks to perform information propagation and aggregation. Without losing generality, we employ Light-GCN as the graph encoder. The convolutional operations are consistent with equations detailed in Eq. 2 and Eq. 3, which are derived from the corresponding adjacency matrix Eq. 1. We transform these discrete features into dense-valued vectors through embedding lookup tables: recipes ($\mathbf{E}_{\mathcal{I}} \in \mathbb{R}^{|\mathcal{I}| \times d}$), ingredients ($\mathbf{E}_{\mathcal{A}} \in \mathbb{R}^{|\mathcal{A}| \times d}$), image prototypes ($\mathbf{E}_v \in \mathbb{R}^{|\mathcal{N}_v| \times d}$), and text prototypes ($\mathbf{E}_t \in \mathbb{R}^{|\mathcal{N}_t| \times d}$), where d is the embedding space dimensionality. Utilizing these embeddings as the initial representations (0-th layer), we perform graph propagation and aggregation on each modality-specific graph to obtain the final representations of recipe i, denoted as $\mathbf{E}_i^{\mathcal{A}}$, $\mathbf{E}_i^v$, and $\mathbf{E}_i^t$, respectively.

Based on the embeddings mentioned above, we aggregate these embeddings to define the 0-th embedding of recipe i in Eq. 2:

$$\mathbf{H}_i^0 = \text{Aggregate}(\mathbf{E}_i^{\mathcal{A}}, \mathbf{E}_i^v, \mathbf{E}_i^t). \tag{6}$$

In this work, we simply define Aggregate($\cdot$) as vector summation. The embedding $\mathbf{H}_i^0$ encompasses a holistic perspective on recipe's multi-modal profile, which is further used to capture collaborative information from user-recipe interactions.

4.3 Cross-Modal Self-supervised Learning

To ensure the stability of learning recipe representations, we propose a self-supervised regularization to encourage the recipe representations (i.e., $\mathbf{E}_i^{\mathcal{A}}$, $\mathbf{E}_i^v$, and $\mathbf{E}_i^t$) to preserve sufficient independent information and avoid redundancy. Although we learn the representations from different modality-specific graphs, there might still be redundancy due to high-order aggregation. To further promote independence among these, we adopt the distance correlation [13] as a regularization technique. Distance correlation can capture the relationship between representations learned from different modalities while encouraging them to retain informative independence. Formally, we define it as follows:

$$\mathcal{L}_{Cor} = \sum_{m,n \in \{\mathcal{A},v,t\}, m \neq n} \frac{dCov(\mathbf{E}_i^m, \mathbf{E}_i^n)}{\sqrt{dVar(\mathbf{E}_i^m) \cdot dVar(\mathbf{E}_i^n)}}, \tag{7}$$

where $dCov(\cdot)$ is the distance covariance between two matrices, and $dVar(\cdot)$ represents its own distance variance. Distance correlation helps mitigate the representation collapse often induced by other self-supervised constraints by maximizing dependencies between different modality-specific graphs.

4.4 Multi-task Learning

The proposed CLUSSL can be optimized in an end-to-end manner through a unified objective function, defined as follows:

$$\mathcal{L} = \mathcal{L}_{Rec} + \lambda \sum_{i \in (i^+, i^-)} \mathcal{L}_{Cor} + \eta \|\Theta\|_2^2, \tag{8}$$

where λ is trade-off coefficient for balancing self-supervised loss contributions. η and Θ represent L_2 regularization coefficient and model parameters, respectively.

5 Experiments

5.1 Experimental Settings

Dataset. We perform experiments using two datasets gathered from real-world platforms www.allrecipes.com and www.food.com. Each recipe encompasses images, textual descriptions, ingredients, and user-provided ratings, as shown in Fig. 1(a). Within the scope of this study, ratings that lie between 1 and 5 are regarded as implicit feedback indicators. Consistent with prior works [1,12], we reserve the most recent 30% of user interactions for the test set and divide the remaining interactions into training (60%) and validation (10%) sets. A summary of the datasets' characteristics following preprocessing is presented in Table 2.

Table 2. Statistics of the experimental dataset.

Characteristics	Allrecipes	Food.com
#Users	68,768	7,596
#Items	45,630	29,943
#Interactions	1,093,845	323,199
#Ingredients	19,987	5,098
Sparsity (%)	99.96	99.85

Metrics and Evaluation. During the training phase, one negative recipe is sampled for each user-recipe pair within the training set. The performance of various approaches is evaluated utilizing two prevalent metrics: Recall@K and Normalized Discounted Cumulative Gain@K (denoted by NDCG@K), with K being pragmatically determined as 10 and 20. For each metric, we initially calculate the accuracy for individual users, and then report the averaged accuracy for all testing users. Consistent with prior works [1,12], we generate a set of 500 negative recipes, biased towards popularity, for each user and user's associated recipes within the test set.

Baseline Methods. We compare the proposed CLUSSL with the following baseline methods. **General Collaborative Filtering:** BPR [10], NeuMF [7], LightGCN [6]. **Multi-Modal Recommendation:** VBPR [5], MMGCN [15], BM3 [17]. FREEDOM [16], LGMRec [3]. **Food Recommendation:** HAFR[1] [1], FGCN [2], SCHGN[2] [12].

Implementation Details. We implement CLUSSL and baseline methods using PyTorch[3] and conduct evaluations on a NVIDIA TITAN RTX GPU card. To ensure a fair assessment, we choose the hyper-parameters for baseline methods following the original paper, and the optimal settings are identified based on the grid-search and validation set. For the proposed CLUSSL, we empirically set batch size to 512, embedding size to 64, learning rates to 0.002 and 0.001

---

[1] https://github.com/elisagao122/HAFR.

[2] https://github.com/TAEYOUNG-SYG/SCHGN.

[3] https://pytorch.org/.

Table 3. The recommendation performance achieved by different methods. The best results are in **boldface**, and the second best results are underlined.

Method	Allrecipes				Food.com			
	Recall@10	Recall@20	NDCG@10	NDCG@20	Recall@10	Recall@20	NDCG@10	NDCG@20
BPR	0.0637	0.1101	0.0418	0.0555	0.0750	0.1255	0.0726	0.0877
NeuMF	0.0636	0.1106	0.0411	0.0550	0.0741	0.1253	0.0725	0.0879
LightGCN	0.0668	0.1147	0.0430	0.0572	0.0829	0.1365	0.0802	0.0960
VBPR	0.0667	0.1115	0.0453	0.0575	0.0757	0.1315	0.0757	0.0923
MMGCN	0.0669	0.1143	0.0440	0.0580	0.0767	0.1293	0.0744	0.0901
BM3	0.0676	0.1152	0.0442	0.0583	0.0810	0.1313	0.0793	0.0938
FREEDOM	0.0710	0.1191	0.0441	0.0585	0.0843	0.1405	0.0827	0.0996
LGMRec	0.0661	0.1119	0.0452	0.0586	0.0849	0.1409	0.0847	0.1008
HAFR	0.0703	0.1142	0.0480	0.0608	0.0712	0.1248	0.0685	0.0855
FGCN	0.0666	0.1138	0.0426	0.0567	0.0756	0.1284	0.0725	0.0886
SCHGN	0.0720	0.1186	0.0480	0.0617	0.0818	0.1338	0.0744	0.0906
CLUSSL	**0.0880**	**0.1372**	**0.0690**	**0.0822**	**0.0943**	**0.1516**	**0.1144**	**0.1262**

for Allrecipes and Food.com, respectively. Step decay of the learning rate is also adopted. The trade-off coefficient λ tuned in $\{0, 0.001, 0.005, 0.01, 0.05, 0.1, 0.5, 1\}$. The number of prototypes, top-k nearest prototypes in modality-specific graph are also searched in grid. The number of top-k nearest prototypes are set to 6 and 10 for Allrecipes and Food.com, respectively. We repeat the experiments five times and report the average results.

5.2   Performance Comparison

Table 3 summarizes the performance of various food recommendation methods on two real-world datasets. Based on the results, we have the following observations.

Firstly, the Superiority of CLUSSL. The proposed CLUSSL demonstrates significant superiority over general CF models, multi-modal recommendation models and the state-of-the-art food recommendation models across all dataset. This indicates that the proposed CLUSSL is exceptionally well-designed for food recommendation, effectively leveraging both multi-modal information with discrete and continuous features.

Secondly, the Effectiveness of Multi-modal Features. By incorporating multi-modal features reasonably, almost all models have achieved better performance. For instance, VBPR outperforms the backbone BPR. Multi-modal recommenders based on LightGCN (i.e., CLUSSL, BM3, FREEDOM, and LGM-Rec) basically achieve better results than LightGCN alone. Additionally, HAFR and SCHGN take into account not only visual features but also and ingredients information, demonstrating superior performance over other multi-modal models on Allrecipes.

Thirdly, the Variability of Modal Semantics on Performance. Almost all multi-modal models showcase improved recommendation results. However, we observe that the performance of BM3 is inferior to LightGCN on Food.com. Moreover, HAFR and SCHGN are designed to deeply integrate multi-modal features with recipe embeddings for prediction, yet their performance on Food.com is less than satisfactory. One potential reason might be that interactive collaborative signals are more easily captured by deep networks in relatively dense datasets, leading complex multi-modal semantics to contribute adverse effects without well-designed modules. The proposed CLUSSL mitigates this issue by transforming semantic features into structural representation.

Finally, the Effectiveness of Self-supervised Learning. SCHGN achieves better performance than HAFR by employing a self-supervised ingredient prediction objective. BM3 and LGMRec leverage contrastive learning as an auxiliary optimization function, achieving notable success. We also partially attribute significant improvements of CLUSSL to self-supervised learning. More in-depth discussions can be found in ablation study and sensitivity analysis.

5.3 Ablation Study

To study the importance of each component of CLUSSL, we consider the following CLUSSL variants for evaluation: i) w/o $\mathcal{M}_{v_i}$, ii) w/o $\mathcal{M}_{t_i}$, iii) w/o $\mathcal{M}_{\mathcal{A}_i}$. These variants involve removing specific modal features related to recipes, thereby excluding their respective modality-specific graphs. iv) w/o $\mathcal{L}_{Cor}$: we set λ to 0 in Eq. 8 to eliminate the self-supervised learning component.

Table 4. The recommendation performance of CLUSSL and its variants.

Method	Allrecipes		Food.com	
	Recall@20	NDCG@20	Recall@20	NDCG@20
w/o $\mathcal{M}_{v_i}$	0.1214	0.0655	0.1477	0.1176
w/o $\mathcal{M}_{t_i}$	0.1240	0.0677	0.1479	0.1236
w/o $\mathcal{M}_{\mathcal{A}_i}$	0.1268	0.0694	0.1477	0.1196
w/o $\mathcal{L}_{Cor}$	0.1246	0.0621	0.1487	0.1110
CLUSSL	0.1372	0.0822	0.1516	0.1262

Table 4 summarizes the performance of CLUSSL variants on Allrecipes and Food.com datasets. Several observations are noteworthy: CLUSSL consistently outperforms w/o $\mathcal{M}_{v_i}$, w/o $\mathcal{M}_{t_i}$, and w/o $\mathcal{M}_{\mathcal{A}_i}$ across both datasets, indicating that removing any multi-modal information leads to decreased performance. This underscores the utility of all modalities in enhancing recommendation accuracy. Additionally, the effectiveness of these modalities varies. Generally, "a picture is worth a thousand words" – visual features prove more crucial than textual or ingredient features. Textual information often contains redundant data, while ingredient features are confined by predefined sets. In contrast, visual features vividly depict food appearance, color, shape, and composition, crucial for stimulating user interest and appetite, thereby offering significant advantages. Furthermore, experiments w/o $\mathcal{L}_{Cor}$ highlight the role of self-supervised learning in improving recipe representations for food recommendation. By promoting distinctiveness across modalities, CLUSSL ensures independence among multi-modal information, thereby enhancing recommendation effectiveness.

5.4   Parameter Sensitivity Study

We also perform experiments to study the impacts of three hyper-parameters: the trade-off coefficient λ for balancing self-supervised loss, the number of prototypes in graphs $\mathcal{G}_v$ and $\mathcal{G}_t$, and the number of top-k nearest prototypes in graphs $\mathcal{G}_v$ and $\mathcal{G}_t$. Figure 2 shows the performance of CLUSSL with respect to different settings on both datasets.

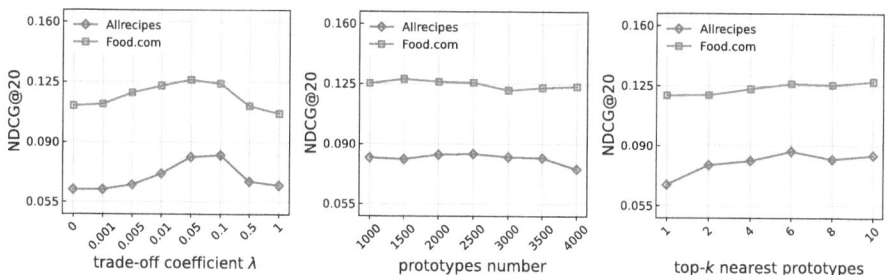

Fig. 2. The performance trends of CLUSSL with respect to different settings of coefficient λ, prototypes number, and top-k nearest on Allrecipes and Food.com datasets.

As depicted in Fig. 2, the results of the coefficient λ on the two datasets show-case a consistent trend: the performance first improves to reach optimal and then declines as λ increases. These results suggest that reasonable self-supervised con-straints enable recipe representations to retain more comprehensive information, thereby enhancing recommendation performance. Regarding the number of pro-totypes, the performance trend appears relatively stable. Additionally, the best performance is achieved by setting top-k to 6 and 10 on Allrecipes and Food.com datasets, respectively.

6   Conclusion

In this paper, we propose a novel multi-modal food recommendation model, namely CLUSSL, which employs clustering to transform modal semantics into modality-specific structures across each modality. Moreover, CLUSSL leverages cross-modal self-supervised learning to encourage that recipe representations induced by different modality-specific graphs preserve sufficiently independent information. The backbone network can further benefit from independent rep-resentations with the self-supervised constraints, which provides superior per-formance. Experimental results on two real-world datasets verify that CLUSSL consistently outperforms state-of-the-art baseline recommendation models.

Acknowledgements. This research is supported, in part, by the Natural Science Foundation of China (No. 92367202, No. 62202279), Outstanding Youth Science Fund

Project (Overseas) of Shandong (No. 2023HWYQ-039), Natural Science Foundation of Shandong Province (No. ZR2022QF018, No. ZR2023LZH006), the Youth Student Fundamental Research Funds of Shandong University, the State Scholarship Fund by the China Scholarship Council (CSC). This research is also supported, in part, by the RIE2025 Industry Alignment Fund - Industry Collaboration Projects (IAF-ICP) (Award I2301E0026), administered by A*STAR, as well as supported by Alibaba-NTU Singapore Joint Research Institute (JRI), Nanyang Technological University, Singapore.

References

1. Gao, X., et al.: Hierarchical attention network for visually-aware food recommendation. IEEE Trans. Multimedia **22**(6), 1647–1659 (2019)
2. Gao, X., Feng, F., Huang, H., Mao, X.L., Lan, T., Chi, Z.: Food recommendation with graph convolutional network. Inf. Sci. **584**, 170–183 (2022)
3. Guo, Z., Li, J., Li, G., Wang, C., Shi, S., Ruan, B.: Lgmrec: local and global graph learning for multimodal recommendation. arXiv preprint arXiv:2312.16400 (2023)
4. He, K., Zhang, X., Ren, S., Sun, J.: Deep residual learning for image recognition. In: Proceedings of the IEEE Conference on Computer Vision and Pattern Recognition, pp. 770–778 (2016)
5. He, R., McAuley, J.: VBPR: visual Bayesian personalized ranking from implicit feedback. In: Proceedings of the AAAI Conference on Artificial Intelligence, vol. 30 (2016)
6. He, X., Deng, K., Wang, X., Li, Y., Zhang, Y., Wang, M.: Lightgcn: simplifying and powering graph convolution network for recommendation. In: Proceedings of the 43rd International ACM SIGIR Conference on Research and Development in Information Retrieval, pp. 639–648 (2020)
7. He, X., Liao, L., Zhang, H., Nie, L., Hu, X., Chua, T.S.: Neural collaborative filtering. In: Proceedings of the 26th International Conference on World Wide Web, pp. 173–182 (2017)
8. Hou, Y., He, Z., McAuley, J., Zhao, W.X.: Learning vector-quantized item representation for transferable sequential recommenders. In: Proceedings of the ACM Web Conference 2023, pp. 1162–1171 (2023)
9. Raffel, C., et al.: Exploring the limits of transfer learning with a unified text-to-text transformer. J. Mach. Learn. Res. **21**(140), 1–67 (2020)
10. Rendle, S., Freudenthaler, C., Gantner, Z., Schmidt-Thieme, L.: BPR: Bayesian personalized ranking from implicit feedback. arXiv preprint arXiv:1205.2618 (2012)
11. Rostami, M., Farrahi, V., Ahmadian, S., Jalali, S.M.J., Oussalah, M.: A novel healthy and time-aware food recommender system using attributed community detection. Expert Syst. Appl. **221**, 119719 (2023)
12. Song, Y., Yang, X., Xu, C.: Self-supervised calorie-aware heterogeneous graph networks for food recommendation. ACM Trans. Multimed. Comput. Commun. Appl. **19**(1s), 1–23 (2023)
13. Székely, G.J., Rizzo, M.L., Bakirov, N.K.: Measuring and testing dependence by correlation of distances (2007)
14. Tian, Y., Zhang, C., Guo, Z., Huang, C., Metoyer, R., Chawla, N.V.: Reciperec: a heterogeneous graph learning model for recipe recommendation. In: Proceedings of the 31st IJCAI Conference on Artificial Intelligence, pp. 3466–3472 (2022)

15. Wei, Y., Wang, X., Nie, L., He, X., Hong, R., Chua, T.S.: MMGCN: multi-modal graph convolution network for personalized recommendation of micro-video. In: Proceedings of the 27th ACM International Conference on Multimedia, pp. 1437–1445 (2019)
16. Zhou, X., Shen, Z.: A tale of two graphs: freezing and denoising graph structures for multimodal recommendation. In: Proceedings of the 31st ACM International Conference on Multimedia, pp. 935–943 (2023)
17. Zhou, X., et al.: Bootstrap latent representations for multi-modal recommendation. In: Proceedings of the ACM Web Conference 2023, pp. 845–854 (2023)

A Quality Assessment Method of Few-Shot Datasets Based on the Fusion of Quantity and Quality

Zhengchao Zhang[1], Lianke Zhou[1(✉)], Junzheng Sun[2], and Nianbin Wang[1]

[1] College of Computer Science and Technology, Harbin Engineering University, Harbin 150001, Heilongjiang, China
zhoulianke@hrbeu.edu.cn
[2] The System Design Institute of Mechanical-Electrical Engineering, Beijing 100854, China

Abstract. The goal of few-shot learning is to learn a better performing model using only a small amount of data. Therefore, the quality of a small amount of data (the few-shot dataset) is a key factor in the effectiveness of model learning. It is especially important to assess the quality of the few-shot datasets before the few-shot learning. Existing data quality assessment methods are more likely to assess the quality of datasets qualitatively from multiple subjective dimensions and indicators, and there are few methods that assess the quality of few-shot datasets from both quantitative and qualitative perspectives together. Therefore, this paper proposes a quality assessment method of few-shot datasets based on the fusion of quantity and quality, which enriches the research on few-shot learning methods. First, from the quantitative perspective, the method introduces two key factors affecting the minimum sample size of few-shot datasets, namely, sample complexity and category diversity. Then, from the qualitative perspective, based on the information entropy theory, it establishes a quality assessment method that integrates multiple objective dimensions, which include intra-class feature consistency, inter-class feature dissimilarity, and task relevance. Finally, experimental analyses are carried out on several popular few-shot datasets under three scenarios to verify the effectiveness of the proposed method.

Keywords: The fusion of quantity and quality · The quality of few-shot datasets · Information entropy · Deep learning · Transfer learning · Meta-learning

1 Introduction

With the development of machine learning, deep learning [1] methods have achieved better results in various fields [2]. The success of data-driven machine learning methods depends heavily on the quality of the datasets used for training. A high quality dataset is essential for realizing the value of the data itself. Gong et al. [3]consider a high quality dataset to be one that accurately represents real-world phenomena in a comprehensive and unbiased way.

R. Hadfi et al. (Eds.): PRICAI 2024, LNAI 15281, pp. 282–293, 2025.
https://doi.org/10.1007/978-981-96-0116-5_23

In the case of big data, the data quality has become a crucial factor affecting the performance of machine learning models. More and more researchers are conducting research on data quality assessment methods. Taleb et al. [4]firstly proposed 5V features for big data, including Volume, Velocity, Variety, Veracity, Value. Gong et al. [3]proposed a comprehensive data quality assessment process in machine learning, which includes an evaluation framework consisting of 8 quality dimensions and 32 evaluation metrics. Furthermore, they discussed the computation of these evaluation metrics. Existing methods assess the quality of datasets from a qualitative point of view, with little consideration of sample size.

In some scenarios, the impact of few-shot datasets on the model learning effect will be more obvious due to the sharp decrease in the number of samples. Different few-shot datasets contain different features, resulting in large differences in the performance of their learned models. However, in few-shot learning [5–7]methods, more improvements are made from methodological and modeling perspectives. Few methods consider the situation of the quality of few-shot datasets, but the quality of few-shot datasets will directly affect the learning effect of the models. Therefore, we study the quality assessment method of few-shot datasets from both quantitative and qualitative perspectives.

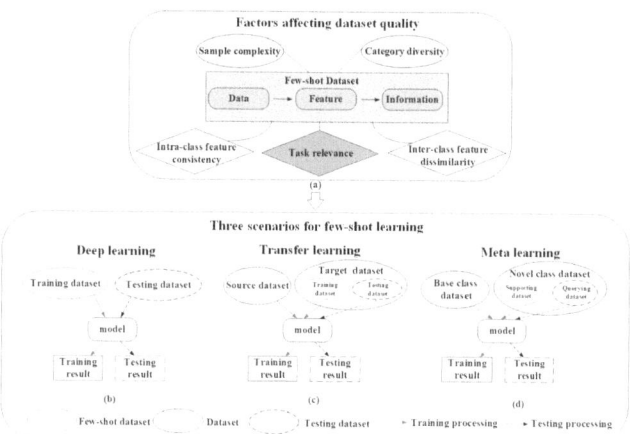

Fig. 1. Illustration of quality assessment method of few-shot datasets in multiple scenarios

Based on the above research motivation, we propose a quality assessment method of few-shot datasets based on the fusion of quantity and quality, as shown in Fig. 1. Our main contributions include the following:

1. From the quantitative perspective, two key factors affecting the minimum sample size of few-shot datasets, namely, sample complexity and category diversity, are introduced and analyzed.
2. From the qualitative perspective, a quality assessment method integrating multiple dimensions is established based on the information entropy theory, which includes intra-class feature consistency, inter-class feature dissimilarity

and task relevance. And the quality calculation methods of few-shot datasets are given in multiple scenarios respectively.

3. We conducted relevant experiments for many different few-shot learning methods in different few-shot learning scenarios (deep learning, transfer learning and meta-learning), and there is a strong correlation between the testing results of the models and the evaluation results of the method, which verifies the effectiveness of the method.

2   Methodology

2.1   Overall

Aiming at the problem of quality assessment of few-shot datasets, this paper proposes a method based on the fusion of quantity and quality, and its main idea is shown in Fig. 2. The core idea of quantity and quality fusion refers to the mechanism of fusing the sample quantity and quality of few-shot datasets from three levels of data, features and information. The quantity of few-shot determines the lower limit of the model learning effect, while the quality of few-shot determines the upper limit of the model learning effect. From the perspective of quantity, two factors affecting the number of few-shot, namely sample complexity and category diversity, are considered. After reaching the minimum sample size, three factors affecting quality, namely intra-class feature consistency, inter-class feature dissimilarity and task relevance, are considered from a qualitative perspective.

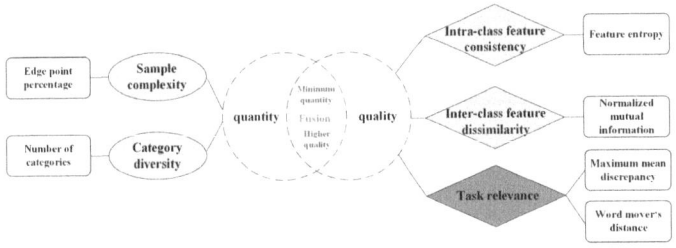

Fig. 2. Schematic diagram of the quality assessment method of few-shot datasets based on the fusion of quantity and quality

2.2   A Quality Assessment Method of Few-Shot Datasets Based on the Fusion of Quantity and Quality

Analysis of the Quantity in the Structure of Few-Shot Datasets
The sample size of few-shot datasets is one of the key factors affecting the effectiveness of training models. It is the small sample size that can directly lead to the risk of the trained network model failing to converge or overfitting. In this subsection, we mainly consider two factors affecting the sample size, which are the sample complexity and the category diversity, as shown in Fig. 3.

- **Sample complexity**

As shown in Fig. 3(a), compared with the handwritten digital images, the target recognized images are complex and difficult to recognize. The minimum sample size required to learn complex images is more than the sample size of simple images under the condition of satisfying model learning.

Complex images usually have complex structural attributes, and structural attributes can be preserved by edges. Therefore, we calculate the complexity of an image by quantifying the percentage of edge points, which can be expressed as:

$$P_{EP} = \frac{\#(edges\_pixels)}{\#(images\_pixels)} \tag{1}$$

where,
$\#(edges\_pixels)$denotes the number of edge pixels and $\#(images\_pixels)$ is the total number of pixels in the image. The number of edge pixels of an image can be calculated by Canny [8] edge detection method.

- **Category diversity**

For this factor of category diversity affecting the sample size of few-shot datasets, it is considered and analyzed from two perspectives.

In deep learning and transfer learning, since the objectives of classification in the training dataset (source domain dataset) and testing dataset (target domain dataset) are the same. The number of categories in the dataset will directly affect the classification effect of the classifier when the total number of samples of a single category is fixed. When the number of categories is small, its classification accuracy is high. As the number of categories increases, its accuracy will decrease, as shown in Fig. 3(b).

In the meta-learning, on the basis of considering the categories of the novel class (few-shot), we should rather consider how to better improve the category diversity in the base class dataset to provide the novel class dataset with more effective prior knowledge, so as to satisfy the fast learning of the novel classes, as shown in Fig. 3(c).

Analysis of the Quality in the Structure of the Few-Shot Dataset

Since the data are in a high-dimensional space, the measurement using the distance between data points has certain limitations, while it cannot reflect the overall distribution of the data in the high-dimensional space. Therefore, the information entropy is used to measure the quality of the few-shot datasets themselves, which includes intra-class feature consistency and inter-class feature dissimilarity. In transfer learning and meta-learning scenarios, task relevance is also considered. We would like to obtain a few-shot dataset with high consistency, high dissimilarity and high correlation.

- **Intra-class feature consistency**

Because of the small sample size of few-shot datasets, it is particularly important that each class represents the typical features that the class possesses through

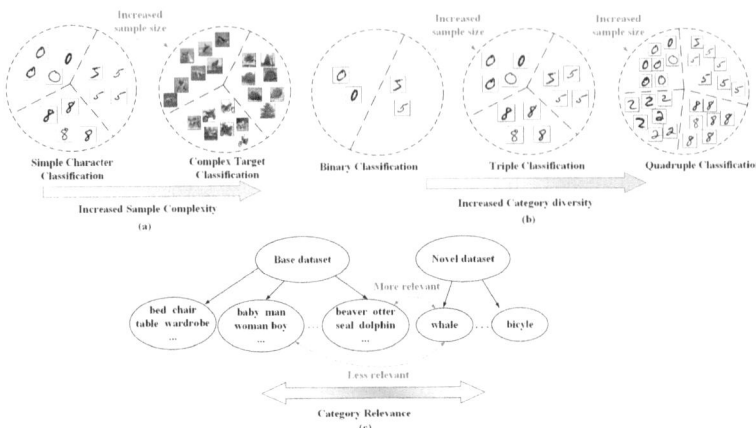

Fig. 3. Factors affecting sample size of few-shot dataset (a) Sample complexity (b)Category diversity (c)Category relevance

only a small number of samples. Therefore, we use information entropy to measure the feature consistency contained in few-shot datasets in each of the same categories.

First, the similarity between samples of the same category in the few-shot dataset is calculated as shown in the following equation.

$$K^{(c)}(x, y) = \left\{ similarity(f(x), f(y)) \mid x, y \in D^{(c)} \right\} \qquad (2)$$

where $K^c(x, y)$ denotes the feature similarity matrix of category c and $f(\cdot)$ is the embedding function. x and y are the samples from the same category, and $similarity(\cdot, \cdot)$ is the similarity metric function.

Then, after obtaining the similarity matrix within the class, the eigenvalues of its matrix are calculated as shown in the following equation.

$$\lambda^{(c)} = eigenvalue \left(K^{(c)} \right) \qquad (3)$$

where $\lambda^{(c)}$ represents the n eigenvalues of the n-order matrix of class c.

Finally, the feature entropy of the few-shot datasets is calculated using $\lambda^{(c)}$ to assess the consistency of the few-shot dataset as shown in the following equation.

$$S_{con} = \frac{1}{C} \sum_{i=1}^{C} \exp \left(- \sum_{j=1}^{n} \lambda_j^{(i)} \log \lambda_j^{(i)} \right) \qquad (4)$$

S_{con} denotes the feature entropy of the few-shot dataset, C is the number of categories, and $\lambda_j^{(i)}$ denotes the j-th eigenvalue of the i-th category feature similarity matrix.

• Inter-class feature dissimilarity

Under the condition of high intra-class feature consistency, we also need to evaluate the dissimilarity of features among classes. When performing a classification task, the more dissimilar the features among classes, the better the model learns the unique features that distinguish them. Therefore, unsupervised clustering can be used to classify samples with similar features into the same group. The greater the dissimilarity of features between classes, the more the clustering results are consistent with the results of true labels.

First, the predicted label information is obtained by grouping similar samples into the same category through unsupervised clustering.

$$pre\_label = \text{KMeans}(f(x), C) \tag{5}$$

where pre_label is the predicted label results, $f(\cdot)$ is the embedding function, and C is the number of clusters.

Then, the normalized mutual information between the clustering results and the true labels is calculated as the dissimilarity of the few-shot dataset. S_{dis} can be expressed as:

$$S_{dis} = \text{NMI}(pre\_label; true\_label) = \frac{2\text{MI}(pre\_label; true\_label)}{\text{H}(pre\_label) + \text{H}(true\_label)} \tag{6}$$

where $\text{NMI}(\cdot; \cdot)$ denotes normalized mutual information. pre_label and $true\_label$ are unsupervised clustering label results and true label results, respectively. $\text{MI}(\cdot; \cdot)$ denotes mutual information, and $\text{H}(\cdot)$ denotes cross entropy.

In summary, intra-class feature consistency and inter-class feature dissimilarity are used to analyze the quality of the few-shot dataset itself. The quality score can be expressed as $\frac{S_{con}}{S_{dis}}$. The smaller its value indicates that the higher quality of the few-shot dataset.

• Task relevance

In the transfer learning and meta-learning scenarios, in addition to the quality situation of the few-shot dataset itself, the relevance between the dataset (source domain dataset and base class dataset) used to assist the few-shot learning and the few-shot dataset also directly affects the learning effect of the models.

In the transfer learning, the label space of the source and target domains is the same. Therefore, the feature distribution relationship between the source and target domains needs to be considered as the relevance of their tasks. The more similar the data distribution of the source domain is to that of the target domain, the more it helps the learning of the target domain. We use the maximum mean discrepancy (MMD) [9] to calculate the relevance between the source domain and the target domain, as shown in the following equation.

$$S_{mmd} = \left\| \frac{1}{|X_S|} \sum_{x_s \in X_S} \emptyset(x_s) - \frac{1}{|X_T|} \sum_{x_t \in X_T} \emptyset(x_t) \right\| \tag{7}$$

where x_s is source domain point and x_t is target domain point. $\emptyset(\cdot)$ denotes the embedding function.

In the meta-learning, the label space of the base class dataset and the novel class dataset is different. Therefore, the relevance between the base class tasks and the novel class tasks needs to be considered. The more relevant the base class tasks is to the novel class tasks, the more they help the learning of the novel class tasks, as shown in Fig. 3(c). We use word mover's distance(WMD) [10] to calculate the relevance between the base class tasks and the novel class tasks. First, the mean vector of all feature vectors in each category in the base class dataset D' is computed, as the center support point c_i' of the category. Then, based on the idea of WMD, the calculation of the relevance between the novel class tasks (few-shot tasks) and the base class tasks can be expressed as:

$$S_{wmd} = \frac{1}{NM} \sum_{i=1}^{N} \sum_{j=1}^{M} wmd\left(c_i', c_j\right) \tag{8}$$

where c_i' is the centroid of each category in the base class tasks, c_j is the center of each category in the novel class tasks, and $wmd(\cdot; \cdot)$ is the metric function, which can be in the form of cosine similarity.

3   Experiments

In this section, in order to evaluate the effectiveness of the proposed method, different scenarios, different methods, different model structures (CNNs, Resnet50, Vgg16), and different datasets (Digital datasets (MNIST and USPS), CIFAR-100 dataset and Office-31 dataset (Amazon, Webcam and Dslr)) are selected as the objects of the evaluation system in this study. Both quantitative and qualitative aspects of the few-shot datasets are systematically analyzed.

3.1   Experiments on Quality Assessment of Few-Shot Datasets Based on Deep Learning

First, for the four datasets used in all experiments, the average complexity of their images was calculated. The image complexity of the MNIST and USPS datasets is 0.0211 and 0.0230 respectively. The image complexity of the CIFAR-100 and Office-31 datasets is 0.2353 and 0.2675. Among them, each image in the simple character datasets contains only one character, and their complexity is around 0.02. The target recognition datasets mostly represent the real world and their complexity is around 0.25, which is significantly higher than that of simple character images.

Then, we conducted quantitative experiments with few-shot datasets on the MNIST and CIFAR-100 datasets. The total number of samples in the training set selected in the MNIST dataset is 2000, and 5000 samples from 10 categories are randomly selected as the training set in the CIFAR-100 dataset. We randomly selected 90% to 10% of the samples from training set as the few-shot datasets (each group performed 10 randomly selected experiments), and the models were tested using the same test set after training. The results are shown in Fig. 4. In

Fig. 4(a), MNIST_best, MNIST_average, and MNIST_worst denote the best, average, and worst results on the same test set for the same training sample size condition, respectively. Similarly, in Fig. 4(b), CIFAR-100_best, CIFAR-100_average and CIFAR-100_worst denote the same meaning on the CIAFR-100 dataset.

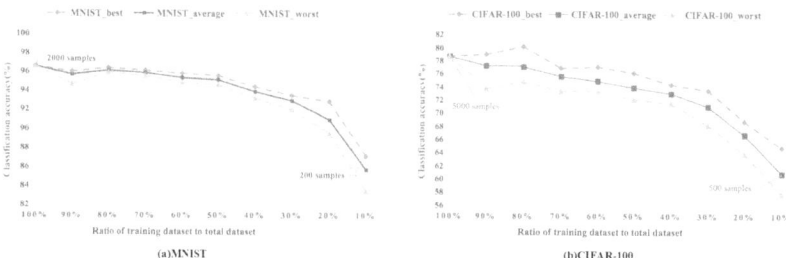

(a)MNIST   (b)CIFAR-100

Fig. 4. Relationship between training set sample size and model classification accuracy in deep learning scenario

Finally, multiple sets of few-shot datasets with different sample sizes were randomly extracted from the MNIST dataset and the CIFAR-100 dataset (20, 40, 60 and 80 per class for the few-shot datasets of MNIST and 100, 150, 200 and 250 per class for the few-shot datasets of CIFAR-100). The intra-class feature entropy and the inter-class feature normalized mutual information were calculated. Compared the quality score differences between $\frac{S_{con}}{S_{dis}}$ and SER-FIQ method [11] in calculating high quality few-shot datasets and low quality few-shot datasets. The network models were trained by the few-shot datasets, and then the performance of the models was tested with the same test dataset. The results are shown in Table 1.

Table 1. The quality score ($\frac{S_{con}}{S_{dis}}$) and test accuracy of different few-shot datasets.

Dataset	MNIST				CIFAR-100			
Sample size per category	20	40	60	80	100	150	200	250
S_{con} of high quality dataset	2.77	2.82	2.88	3.06	2.54	3.00	3.45	3.64
S_{con} of low quality dataset	2.95	3.12	3.13	3.13	2.97	3.75	3.86	3.89
S_{dis} of high quality dataset	0.60	0.65	0.67	0.68	0.70	0.70	0.81	0.74
S_{dis} of low quality dataset	0.50	0.57	0.58	0.61	0.56	0.56	0.74	0.70
$\frac{S_{con}}{S_{dis}}$ of high quality dataset	**4.60**	**4.36**	**4.32**	**4.50**	**3.63**	**4.25**	**4.27**	**4.90**
$\frac{S_{con}}{S_{dis}}$ of low quality dataset	5.94	5.52	5.42	5.13	5.25	6.67	5.20	5.54
Quality score difference of $\frac{S_{con}}{S_{dis}}$	1.26	1.16	1.10	0.63	1.62	2.42	0.93	0.64
Quality score difference of SER-FIQ	0.65	0.43	0.55	0.23	0.45	0.56	0.51	0.48
Test accuracy of high quality dataset	88.54%	92.67%	94.08%	94.50%	69.10%	72.20%	74.40%	75.10%
Test accuracy of low quality dataset	82.85%	89.53%	91.80%	92.90%	62.90%	68.20%	67.40%	70.40%

Experimental analysis:

(1) As shown in Fig. 4, in order to achieve a balance between the sample size of few-shot and the model learning effect, a simple dataset requires about 60 samples per category, while a complex dataset requires nearly 200 samples per category. Reducing the sample size further will lead to a sharp decline in the model learning effect. In deep learning scenario, the minimum number of samples required varies depending on the complexity of the samples, and the more complex the data, the higher the minimum sample size required.

(2) As illustrated in Table 1, the trends of the statistical results on two datasets are almost the same in most cases. With the same sample size, the intra-class feature consistency (S_{con}) of the high quality few-shot dataset is lower than that of the low quality few-shot dataset. On both datasets, the value of intra-class feature consistency increases with increasing sample size. The inter-class feature dissimilarity (S_{dis}) of high quality few-shot datasets is higher than that of low quality few-shot datasets. $\frac{S_{con}}{S_{dis}}$ of high quality datasets is smaller. At the same time, compared with SER-FIQ method, the proposed method distinguishes between high quality and low quality few-shot datasets more clearly.

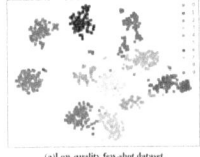 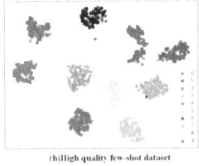

(a)Low quality few-shot dataset   (b)High quality few-shot dataset

Fig. 5. The t-SNE Visualization results for the low quality dataset and high quality dataset in the CIFAR-100 dataset

t-SNE Visualization Experiment: In the ten classification experiment on the CIFAR-100 dataset, we conducted a visualization experiment on two randomly selected few-shot datasets with the same sample size (100 samples per category), as shown in Fig. 5. Figure 5(a) is the low quality few-shot dataset, which trains a model with an accuracy of 62.9%. Figure 5(b) is the high quality few-shot dataset, which trains a model with an accuracy of 69.1%. Comparing Fig. 5(a) and Fig. 5(b), it can be seen that the samples of the same category in Fig. 5(b) are more compact (feature entropy is small), and more sparse between different categories (normalized mutual information is large).

3.2 Experiments on Quality Assessment of Few-Shot Datasets Based on Transfer Learning

In transfer learning, for the OFFICE-31 dataset, we performed two transfer tasks, Amazon→ Webcam and Amazon → Dslr. The sample size of the source domain dataset is 30 or 60, and the sample size of the target domain dataset is 5 or 10. Then, intra-class feature entropy, inter-class normalized mutual informa-tion, maximum mean discrepancy from the source domain dataset, and quality score were calculated for different target domain datasets. Finally, the source and target domain datasets were used to train the network models by DSAN [12] method, and then the models were tested with the same test dataset. The results are shown in Fig. 6.

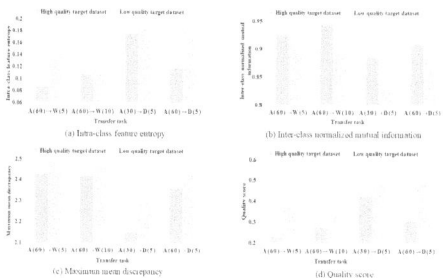

Fig. 6. Comparison of three indicators and quality score for different target domain datasets in the OFFICE-31 dataset transfer tasks

t-SNE Visualization Experiment: In the USPS→MNIST transfer task from digital datasets, we conducted visualization experiments on a randomly selected source domain dataset (30 samples per category) and two target domain datasets (10 samples per category), as shown in Fig. 7. The source and target domain datasets were used to train the network models by DAN [13] method.

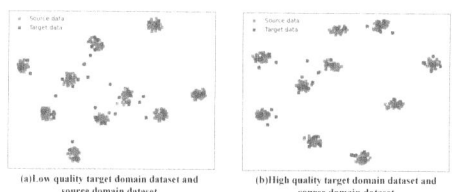

Fig. 7. Visualization results for high quality and low quality datasets in the USPS→MNIST task from digital datasets

Experimental analysis:

(1) As shown in Fig. 6(d), in the transfer learning, $S_{mmd} \times \frac{S_{con}}{S_{dis}}$ is used as a measure of the quality of the target domain datasets. The smaller result of it represents the higher quality of the target dataset.
(2) As shown in Fig. 7(a) and (b), the accuracy of the trained models on the target domain testing dataset is 86.8% and 92.7%, respectively. It can be seen that the high quality target domain data is closer to the source domain data.

3.3 Experiments on Quality Assessment of Few-Shot Datasets Based on Mata-Learning

In meta-learning, for the CIFAR-100 dataset, we conducted 5-way 5-shot and 5-way 10-shot experiments. First, intra-class feature entropy, inter-class normalized mutual information, and word mover's distance were calculated for different few-shot datasets. Then, the network models were trained using different few-shot datasets and base class dataset by MAML [14] method. The performance of the models were tested with the same test dataset, and the results are shown in Fig. 8.

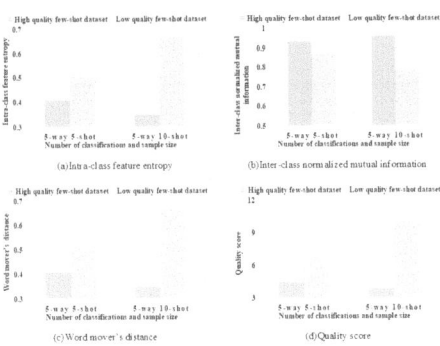

Fig. 8. Comparison of three indicators and quality score for different few-shot datasets in the CIFAR-100 dataset

Experimental analysis:

As shown in Fig. 8(d), in the meta-learning, $S_{wmd} \times \frac{S_{con}}{S_{dis}}$ is used as a measure of the quality of the few-shot datasets. The smaller its result represents the higher quality of the few-shot dataset.

4 Conclusion and Discussion

In few-shot learning, the quality situation of datasets will more directly affect the learning effect of the network models. In this paper, a single-modal quality assessment method of few-shot datasets based on the fusion of quantity and quality is proposed. Quality assessment experiments and comparison experiments were conducted in three scenarios using different few-shot learning methods and network models, and the results of the quality assessment of datasets are highly correlated with the test results of their training models, which verifies the effectiveness of the proposed method. Assessed high quality few-shot datasets are more conducive to few-shot learning. In future work we will consider how domain knowledge can be integrated into existing quality assessment methods for multi-modal learning, enabling more effective to assess the quality of few-shot datasets.

Acknowledgments. This work is supported by the Basic Research Project (JCKY2021206B028).

References

1. LeCun, Y., Bengio, Y., Hinton, G.: Deep learning. Nature **521**(7533), 436–444 (2015)
2. Wei, X.S., et al.: Fine-grained image analysis with deep learning: a survey. IEEE Trans. Pattern Anal. Mach. Intell. **44**(12), 8927–8948 (2021)
3. Gong, Y.D., Liu, G.Z., Xue, Y.Z., Li, R., Meng, L.Z.: A survey on dataset quality in machine learning. Inf. Softw. Technol. **162**, 1–12 (2023)
4. Taleb, I., Serhani, M.A., Dssouli, R.: Big data quality assessment model for unstructured data. In: Proceedings of the 13th International Conference on Innovations in Information, pp. 69–74. UAEU; IEEE; Esri (2018). https://doi.org/10.1109/INNOVATIONS.2018.8605945
5. Song, Y., Wang, T., Mondal, S.K., Sahoo, J.P.: A comprehensive survey of few-shot learning: evolution, applications, challenges, and opportunities. ACM Comput. Surv. **55**, 1–40 (2023)
6. Li, X.X., Sun, Z., Xue, J.H., Ma, Z.Y.: A concise review of recent few-shot meta-learning methods. Neurocomputing **456**(5), 463–468 (2021)
7. Hospedales, T., Antoniou, A., Micaelli, P., Storkey, A.: Meta-learning in neural networks: a survey. IEEE Trans. Pattern Anal. Mach. Intell. **44**(9), 5149–5169 (2022)
8. Canny, J.: A computational approach to edge detection. IEEE Trans. Pattern Anal. Mach. Intell. **8**(6), 679–698 (1986)
9. Gretton, A., Borgwardt, K.M., Raschand, M.J., Schölkopf, B., Smola, A.: A kernel two-sample test. J. Mach. Learn. Res. **13**(1), 723–773 (2012)
10. Kusner, M.J., Sun, Y., Kolkin, N.I., Weinberger, K.Q.: From word embeddings to document distances. In: Bach, F., Blei, D. 32nd International Conference on Machine Learning, Lille, France, vol. 37, pp. 957–966 (2015). arxiv:1811.01713
11. Terhorst, P., Kolf, J.N., Damer, N., Kirchbuchner, F., Kuijper, A.: SER-FIQ: unsupervised estimation of face image quality based on stochastic embedding robustness. In: Proceedings of the IEEE/CVF Conference on Computer Vision and Pattern Recognition (CVPR), pp. 5650–5659. Virtual, United states (2021). https://doi.org/10.1109/CVPR42600.2020.00569
12. Zhu, Y.C., et al.: Deep subdomain adaptation network for image classification. IEEE Trans. Neural Netw. Learn. Syst. **32**(4), 1713–1722 (2020)
13. Long, M.S., Cao, Y., Wang, J.M., Jordan, M.: Learning transferable features with deep adaptation networks. IEEE Trans. Pattern Anal. Mach. Intell. **41**(12), 3071–3085 (2019)
14. Finn, C., Abbeel, P., Levine, S.: Model-agnostic meta-learning for fast adaptation of deep networks. In: Precup, D., Teh, Y.W. (eds.) 34th International Conference on Machine Learning, Sydney, Australia, vol. 70, pp. 1856–1868 (2017). https://doi.org/10.48550/arXiv.1703.03400

Deep Learning

CSDCNet: A Semantic Segmentation Network for Tubular Structures

Feiyang Dong[1,2], Jizhong Jin[1,2], Lei Li[1,2], Heyang Li[1,2],
and Yucheng Zhang[1(✉)]

[1] Institute of Computing Technology, Chinese Academy of Sciences, Beijing 100190,
China
{dongfeiyang22s,jinjizhong22s,zhangyucheng}@ict.ac.cn
[2] University of Chinese Academy of Sciences, Beijing 101408, China

Abstract. Tubular structure segmentation is essential across various domains, including medical imaging, remote sensing, and industrial inspection. While traditional models rely on expert knowledge for feature extraction, deep learning offers a more efficient approach. However, existing deep neural networks still have room for enhancement. This paper introduces an enhanced U-Net with a cascaded shared dilated convolution module, which broadens the receptive field and retains finer image details. Additionally, a cascaded multi-scale dice loss fusion module is incorporated to leverage diverse scales of structural information, enhancing prediction accuracy. Experiments on public datasets and comparisons with mainstream models demonstrate our model's superiority, particularly in perceiving tubular structures. Our model achieves mIoU of 84.3 and 81.4 on the DRIVE dataset and the Massachusetts Roads dataset, respectively. The research advances applications like retinal vessel detection, urban road mapping, and industrial defect identification.

Keywords: Semantic segmentation · U-Net · Dilated convolution · Tubular structure extraction

1 Introduction

Semantic segmentation of tubular structures is crucial for computer vision, enabling automatic extraction of features like blood vessels, roads, and cracks from images. In medical image analysis, semantic segmentation can help doctors diagnose conditions by extracting coronary arteries from cardiac CT scans or retinal vessels from fundus images. In remote sensing image analysis, it can be used to extract tubular road structures or river structures from satellite imagery for urban traffic planning and environmental monitoring, and to identify tubular gully structures for geological disaster detection. In industrial vision inspection, extracting tubular cracks from metal images can be utilized for metal flaw detection. Given the complexity of tubular structures, improving segmentation techniques is imperative.

© The Author(s), under exclusive license to Springer Nature Singapore Pte Ltd. 2025
R. Hadfi et al. (Eds.): PRICAI 2024, LNAI 15281, pp. 297–308, 2025.
https://doi.org/10.1007/978-981-96-0116-5_24

Current approaches to tubular structure extraction and segmentation fall into three main categories: (1) Morphology-based methods [1–3] segment structures using their shape characteristics, modeled as topological graph or tree structures, and rely on graph theory for segmentation, but they are computationally intensive and lack strong generalization capabilities; (2) Traditional machine learning methods [4–6] use handcrafted features like grayscale and wavelet features with classifiers such as SVM, and AdaBoost for tasks like blood vessel segmentation. These methods typically require specific domain knowledge to design suitable feature extractors and have limited generalization capabilities; (3) Deep learning methods [7–11], focusing on designing neural networks for segmentation, have shown promise but often struggle with limited receptive fields due to convolutions and detail loss from pooling operations. Tubular structures have complex topological characteristics, often appearing slender, curved, and even intersecting in images, posing challenges to existing models for semantic segmentation of tubular structures.

In response, our study introduces a U-Net network [7] enhanced with a cascaded shared dilated convolution (CSDC) module we designed. We integrate this module into the U-Net backbone [7], strategically placing it before each max-pooling operation in the encoding layers. This approach broadens the convolutional kernel's receptive field and, through multi-scale feature fusion, retains more image detail, thereby improving predictive accuracy. Additionally, we refine the original U-Net's loss function [7] with a cascaded multi-scale dice loss fusion module that leverages the full spectrum of tubular structure scales, addressing discontinuity issues associated with single-scale losses. Our comparative experiments validate the network's enhanced performance, demonstrating a marked improvement in the perception of tubular structures.

2 Related Work

In this section, we first introduce several methods used for the segmentation of tubular structures. Then, we discuss the advantages of using dilated convolution in computer vision applications.

2.1 Segmentation Methods for Tubular Structures

Researchers have proposed various methods for the extraction and segmentation of tubular structures. In the early stages, morphology-based methods segmented tubular structures by leveraging their distinctive shapes. For example, Staal et al. [1] extracted vascular centerlines using a ridge line algorithm, followed by a k-nearest neighbor (KNN) classifier that relies on local centerline data for segmentation. Zana et al. [2] introduced an algorithm combining mathematical morphology and curvature analysis to capture the tree-like geometry of vessels, refining segmentation with cross-curvature assessment. Türetken et al. [3] utilized a graph theory-based global optimization approach, integrating geometric priors to extract tubular structures from noisy 2D and 3D images. These methodologies model tubular structures as graph topologies or tree structures, employing graph theory algorithms and morphological operations for segmentation and inference.

Traditional machine learning approaches typically relied on handcrafted features, coupled with classifiers for segmenting tubular structures. For instance, Ricci et al. [4] employed orthogonal line detectors and grayscale features for feature vector construction, followed by SVM-based pixel classification to segment retinal blood vessels. Lupascu et al. [5] extracted grayscale features, encoded the local intensity and geometry of tubular structures across scales, and utilized AdaBoost for feature selection and model training. Fraz et al. [6] analyzed feature vectors based on gradient fields and Gabor filters, trained diverse classifiers, and combined their outputs to improve segmentation robustness and precision. While these methods show promise on certain datasets, they often demand domain-specific expertise for feature engineering and may lack broad applicability. As deep learning advances, an increasing number of studies are exploring deep learning-based segmentation methods for tubular structures, aiming to surpass conventional techniques in performance and generalizability.

With the advent of deep learning, deep neural network models including Fully Convolutional Networks (FCN) [12], U-Net [7], etc. have been widely applied to various semantic segmentation tasks, greatly improving the processing efficiency of large-scale image data. In 2015, FCN [12] pioneered the use of convolutional neural networks for semantic segmentation, enabling end-to-end pixel-level predictions. FCN [12] replaces fully connected layers with convolutional ones, accepting arbitrary input sizes and drastically cutting down neural network parameters. It introduces Skip Connections to blend deep and shallow feature maps, enhancing spatial detail recovery and segmentation accuracy. In 2015, U-Net [7] emerged as a deep convolutional neural network tailored for medical image segmentation, adeptly tackling accuracy challenges in scenarios with limited training data. Its symmetric encoder-decoder architecture is U-Net's [7] hallmark, featuring convolutional and max pooling layers in the encoder, complemented by convolutional and upsampling layers in the decoder. Skip Connections link encoder and decoder layers, merging low-level and high-level features. The encoder captures and compresses image features, while the decoder upscales and refines these features to generate precise segmentation outcomes. In 2022, Xin Yang and colleagues proposed the DCU-net [13] for tubular structure analysis, which consists of two U-Nets. The network utilizes deformable convolution for robust feature extraction, adapting to vascular deformations. A residual channel attention module connects the two U-Nets, enhancing the efficiency of information transfer. In 2023, the DSCNet [14] proposed dynamic snake convolution on the basis of deformable convolution to pay attention to the characteristics of tubular structures. Although the aforementioned deep neural networks for semantic segmentation of tubular structures have achieved some good performance, there is still room for improvement. Some models often fail to predict extremely fine tubular structures, while others may exhibit discontinuous predictions when facing continuous tubular structures.

2.2   Dilated Convolution

In 2015, Fisher Yu and colleagues [15] introduced dilated convolution to broaden the receptive field of convolutional kernels. Dilated convolutions capture a wider context at the pixel level without compromising resolution, enhancing predictive accuracy. The dilation rate, a key parameter, dictates the spacing between kernel elements. Standard convolutions have a dilation rate of 1, equating them to a special case of dilated convolutions. By increasing element spacing, dilated convolutions expand the receptive field, as illustrated in Fig. 1: a 3x3 kernel with a dilation rate of 2 matches the field of a 5x5 standard kernel. This expansion is beneficial for dense prediction tasks like semantic segmentation, without adding parameters or computational overhead, thus minimizing model costs. This study leverages the characteristic of dilated convolution by designing the CSDC module to expand the receptive field of the convolutional kernel, reducing the detail loss caused by max pooling operations, allowing the model to capture context information across different scales, and enhancing the model's feature extraction capabilities.

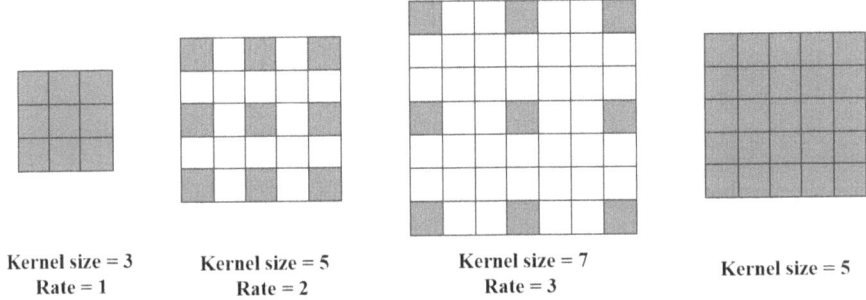

Kernel size = 3   Kernel size = 5   Kernel size = 7   Kernel size = 5
Rate = 1   Rate = 2   Rate = 3

Fig. 1. Dilated Convolutions with Different Dilation Rates.

3   Research Method

3.1   Network Structure

Dilated convolution has been widely applied in segmentation tasks and has achieved good results. DeepLabV1 [16] is the first to harness varying dilation rates for multi-scale context capture in 2014. DeepLabV3+ [17] advances this in 2018 with an encoder-decoder framework that seamlessly blends low-level and high-level features, enhancing segmentation precision. In 2017, PSPNet [18], introduces the Pyramid Pooling Module to capture multi-scale contextual information using pooling operations at different scales.

Tubular structures, known for their elongated and irregularly curved shapes, present challenges for traditional semantic segmentation networks. These networks' limited receptive fields often struggle with noise and shadow interference during segmentation, impairing their effectiveness. To address this, we introduce the cascaded shared dilated convolution module (CSDC), depicted in Fig. 2. The CSDC module combines dilated convolutions of varying dilation rates across layers to expand the receptive field and share feature information. Our approach involves three parallel branches processing the input data. The first branch uses a 3x3 dilated convolution with a dilation rate of 1 to detect fine-scale features. The second branch integrates the input and first branch's output, applying a 3x3 dilated convolution with a dilation rate of 2, followed by a 1x1 dilated convolution, to capture medium-scale features. The third branch merges input data with outputs from the first two branches, utilizing a 3x3 dilated convolution with a dilation rate of 4, then a 1x1 convolution, to extract larger-scale features. The feature maps from all branches are concatenated and fused using a 1x1 convolution, creating an enriched feature map. This cascaded structure amalgamates multi-scale features, retaining more image details, which in turn, boosts the model's predictive accuracy and overall generalization capability.

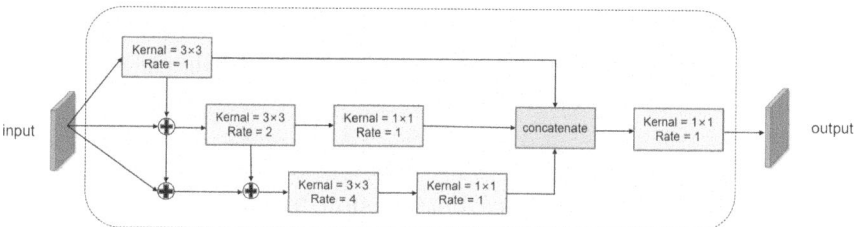

Fig. 2. Cascaded Shared Dilated Convolution Module.

We integrate dilated convolution into our network to boost its tubular structure segmentation capabilities. Our study adopts U-Net [7] as the backbone due to its encoder-decoder architecture and more modest parameter count compared to DeepLabV3+ [17]. U-Net's [7] relative simplicity and use of fewer layers, as opposed to the deeper backbones like ResNet101 [19] or Xception [20] in DeepLabV3+ [17], contribute to its lower complexity and swifter convergence. We opt for U-Net [7] as the backbone of our research, with the aim of further refining its capabilities. The conventional U-Net [7] framework incorporates convolutional and max pooling layers within its encoder. Convolutional layers pinpoint local features, whereas max pooling layers diminish the feature maps' spatial dimensions by extracting salient local features, effectively condensing spatial data and broadening the receptive field. This approach enables the model to seize global context and advanced features while eliminating superfluous details and noise. Nonetheless, max pooling can also erode feature map details. To counteract this, we strategically position the CSDC module ahead of the max pooling phase in each encoder layer of U-Net, as shown in Fig. 3. This preemptive expansion of the receptive field prior to downsampling minimizes the resolution and detail loss in feature maps. Consequently, it softens the impact of max pooling's limitations and augments the model's feature extraction prowess.

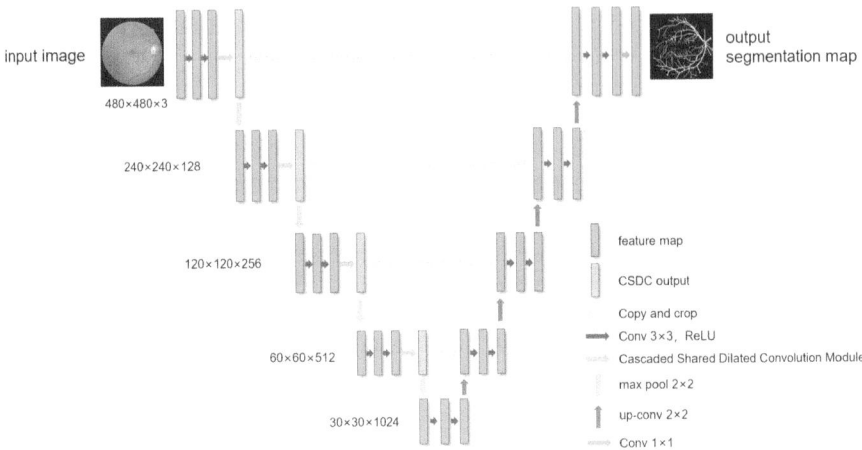

Fig. 3. U-Net Network with Cascaded Shared Dilated Convolution Module.

3.2   Cascaded Multi-scale Dice Loss Fusion Module

In semantic segmentation of tubular structures, tubular pixels constitute a significantly smaller area compared to the background, leading to an imbalance between positive and negative samples. This can skew the model's predictive weighting across categories, impacting overall performance. To address this, we've opted to substitute the standard cross-entropy loss with the Dice loss, which is calculated as follows:

$$L_{\text{Dice}} = 1 - \frac{2\sum_{i=1}^{n} y_i \hat{y}_i}{\sum_{i=1}^{n} y_i + \sum_{i=1}^{n} \widehat{y}_i} \tag{1}$$

In which $\hat{y}_i$ denotes the model's prediction for the ith pixel, and y_i signifies the actual label of that pixel.

To counteract the risk of inadequate tubular structure extraction accuracy from a single-scale loss function, we engineer a cascaded multi-scale dice loss fusion module, as depicted in Fig. 4. This module enhances the model's feature perception by assessing and integrating loss across scales, enabling it to discern both fine details and broader image context, thus boosting its generalization. To be specific, after generating the model's predictions, we downscale the W×H groundtruth by factors of 4 and 16 to achieve smaller groundtruth matrices of

$W/2 \times H/2$ and $W/4 \times H/4$. These are juxtaposed with the side outputs from the uppermost three layers of our network to ascertain losses at three distinct scales. We linearly combine the loss functions from three scales to derive the final loss function, denoted as L_{sum}, the calculation method is as follows:

$$L_{\text{sum}} = \alpha L_{\text{Dice}}^{(1)} + \beta L_{\text{Dice}}^{(2)} + \gamma L_{\text{Dice}}^{(3)} \tag{2}$$

where $L_{\text{Dice}}^{(1)}$, $L_{\text{Dice}}^{(2)}$, and $L_{\text{Dice}}^{(3)}$ represent the losses at each scale, and the linear combination coefficients are α, β, and γ, respectively.

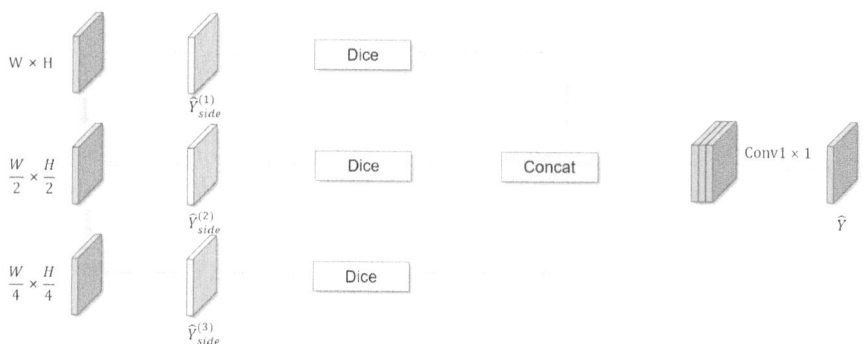

Fig. 4. Cascaded Multi-scale Dice Loss Fusion Module.

4   Research

4.1   Dataset

In this research, we utilized two public datasets for our experiments: the Digital Retinal Images for Vessel Extraction (DRIVE) dataset [1] and the Massachusetts Road dataset. Both datasets contain images with a multitude of tubular structural features. The DRIVE dataset [1], hailing from the Dutch Diabetic Retinopathy Screening Program, comprises 40 color fundus images, split evenly into training and testing sets. Captured with a Canon CR5 non-mydriatic 3CCD camera, these images offer a resolution of 565×584 pixels. The Massachusetts Road dataset, introduced by Mnih et al., is a remote sensing collection for road extraction and segmentation, totaling 1,171 aerial images. It is segmented into 1,108 images for training, 14 for validation, and 49 for testing, each with a 1500×1500-pixel resolution. This dataset encompasses a range of road scenes, from urban streets to rural paths and highways. To ensure the fairness of the experiments, the datasets were divided following conventional methods and proportions.

4.2   Evaluation Metrics

This study quantitatively assesses the performance of the tubular structure semantic segmentation model using metrics like mIoU, recall, and F1 score. The mIoU metric measures the overlap between the model's predictions and the groundtruth for each class, calculated as the ratio of intersection to union. The mean IoU of all classes gives the mIoU. Representing the class count as n, the formulas for IoU and mIoU are as follows:

$$\text{IoU} = \frac{Area\ of\ Overlap}{Area\ of\ Union} \tag{3}$$

$$\text{mIoU} = \frac{1}{n} \sum_{i}^{n} \text{IoU}_i \tag{4}$$

In the semantic segmentation of tubular structures, these structures typically occupy a minimal area of the image, resulting in a dataset with significantly fewer positive samples than negative ones. In these cases, the recall is a key indicator of the model's ability to detect tubular structures. The recall is calculated as follows:

$$\text{Recall} = \frac{TP}{TP + FN} \tag{5}$$

where TP and FN represent true positive and false negative respectively.

We also employed the F1 score in our experiments as a metric for overall model performance, providing a balance between recall and precision. The formulas for precision and F1 score are as follows::

$$\text{Precision} = \frac{TP}{TP + FP} \tag{6}$$

$$\text{F1 Score} = 2 * \frac{Recall * precision}{Recall + precision} \tag{7}$$

4.3   Experimental Setups

This experiment leveraged the PyTorch framework, training on an RTX 4090 GPU. Data augmentation through random scaling, flipping, and cropping was applied to enhance model learning across varied sizes, orientations, and positions. For the DRIVE dataset, training comprised 200 epochs with an SGD optimizer at a 0.01 learning rate, 0.9 momentum, and 1e-4 weight decay. The Massachusetts Road dataset used 60 epochs with matching parameters. A warmup strategy initialized training for stability, followed by learning rate decay across iterations. After extensive experimentation, we ultimately determined that the proportionality coefficients α, β, and γ in the cascaded multi-scale loss fusion module are 1, 0.5, and 0.3, respectively.

4.4   Experimental Results and Analysis

We evaluate the performance of the U-Net [7], Attention U-Net [21], DCU-net [13], DSCNet [14], and CSDCNet on both the DRIVE dataset [1] and Massachusetts Road dataset to assess our CSDC module and the cascaded multi-scale fusion Dice loss. Table 1 displays the segmentation results of CSDCNet and comparative models on the DRIVE dataset and the Massachusetts Road dataset. CSDCNet generally outperforms the others, showing superior segmentation accuracy. Compared to the U-Net network without the addition of the CSDC module and the cascaded multi-scale dice loss fusion module, our model significantly improves mIoU, recall, and F1 score. The results suggest that CSD-CNet enhance the ability to focus on tubular structures.

Table 1. Segmentation results on the DRIVE dataset and the Massachusetts Roads dataset.

Dataset	Model	mIoU	Recall	F1 score
DRIVE	U-Net	78.1	86.1	86.8
	Attention U-Net	81.4	88.5	89.1
	DCU-net	82.0	89.0	89.1
	DSCNet	81.4	90.1	87.1
	CSDCNet	**84.3**	**91.6**	**91.3**
Massachusetts Road	U-Net	74.1	85.5	83.2
	Attention U-Net	77.9	86.6	86.2
	DCU-net	78.7	84.9	86.8
	DSCNet	79.0	86.7	**87.1**
	CSDCNet	**81.4**	**87.6**	86.8

For a more objective assessment of algorithm performance, we performed qualitative analyses on both the DRIVE and Massachusetts Road datasets. Figure 5 and Fig. 6 display a sequence of images for each dataset, showcasing the original image, ground truth, CSDCNet's output, and the segmentation results from classic models like U-Net [7], Attention U-Net [21], DCU-net [13], and DSC-Net [14]. It can be observed that CSDCNet performs the best in extracting vascular structures in fundus images and road structures in remote sensing images, while the other models exhibit more loss in these details. For instance, some shorter roads occupy a very low proportion of pixels in the image, which UNet and Attention U-Net fail to recognize. DCUnet and DSCNet sometimes misidentify other categories in the image background as tubular structures. Thanks to the CSDC module and the cascaded multi-scale dice loss fusion module we designed, even slender and low-contrast tubular structures can be identified by CSDCNet. The results on the DRIVE dataset indicate that our model achieves better detection of subtle tubular structures in the central region of the eye. The

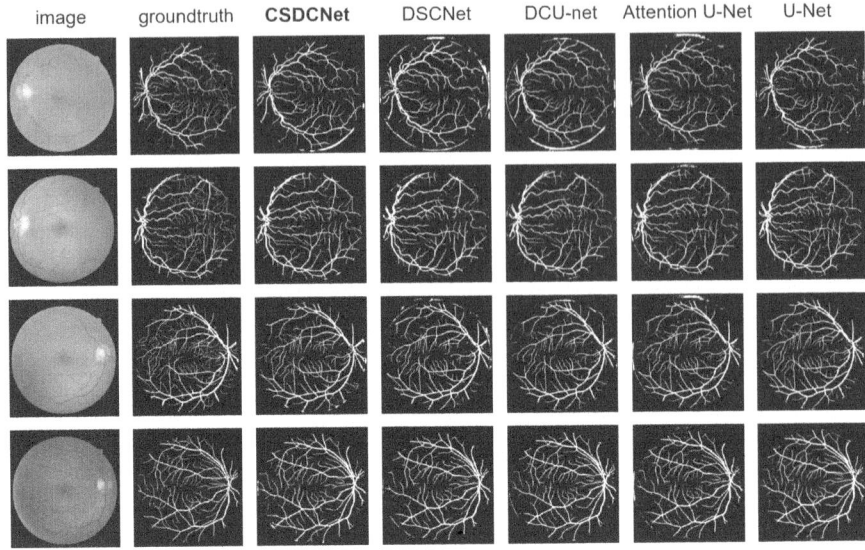

Fig. 5. Examples of segmentation results on the DRIVE dataset.

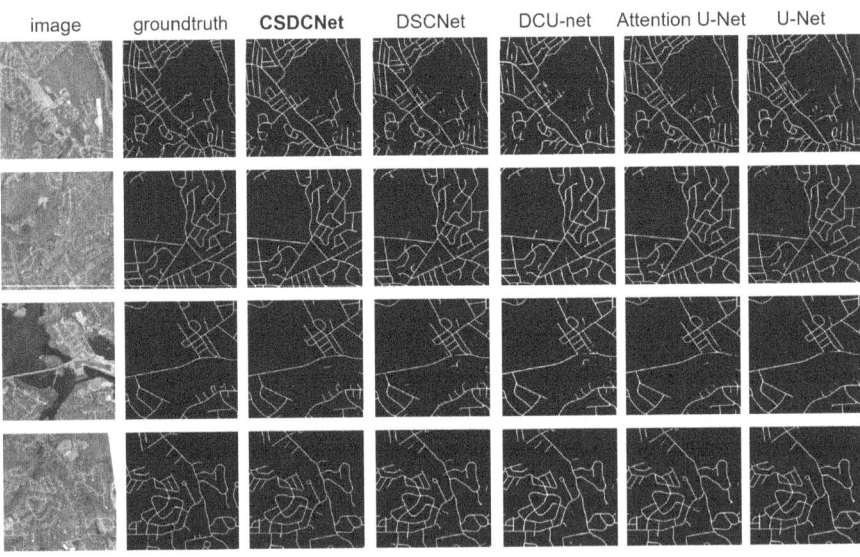

Fig. 6. Examples of segmentation results on the Massachusetts Roads dataset.

results on the Massachusetts Road dataset demonstrate that our model produces less noise, thereby reducing the likelihood of false positives. The results reveal that CSDCNet offers greater accuracy and continuity in segmenting slender, irregularly curved tubular structures.

5   Conclusion and Future Work

Tubular structure extraction and segmentation is a foundational task for various applications. Traditional models, constrained by their reliance on domain-specific knowledge, have limited generalization capabilities. To overcome this, we develope a U-Net network integrated with the CSDC module. Our module expands the convolutional kernel's receptive field and enhances the model's predictive performance by maintaining detailed image information through multi-scale feature fusion. Additionally, our cascaded multi-scale dice loss fusion module addresses the issue of insufficient segmentation accuracy at a single scale, thereby increasing the model's robustness. Our model demonstrates superior performance in tubular structure extraction in comparative experiments on two public datasets, offering significant advantages for medical image analysis, remote sensing, and industrial vision. Looking ahead, we plan to incorporate attention mechanisms into our model to further refine its ability to identify and understand tubular structures.

Acknwledgments. This paper was supported by Innovation Funding of Institute of Computing Technology, Chinese Academy of Sciences under Grant No. E261030.

References

1. Staal, J., Abramoff, M., Niemeijer, M., Viergever, M., van Ginneken, B.: Ridge-based vessel segmentation in color images of the retina. IEEE Trans. Med. Imaging **23**(4), 501–509 (2004). https://doi.org/10.1109/TMI.2004.825627
2. Zana, F., Klein, J.C.: Segmentation of vessel-like patterns using mathematical morphology and curvature evaluation. IEEE Trans. Image Process. **10**(7), 1010–1019 (2001). https://doi.org/10.1109/83.931095
3. Turetken, E., González, G., Blum, C., Fua, P.: Automated reconstruction of dendritic and axonal trees by global optimization with geometric priors. Neuroinformatics **9**, 279–302 (2011). https://doi.org/10.1007/s12021-011-9122-1
4. Ricci, E., Perfetti, R.: Retinal blood vessel segmentation using line operators and support vector classification. IEEE Trans. Med. Imaging **26**, 1357–65 (2007). https://doi.org/10.1109/TMI.2007.898551
5. Lupaşcu, C.A., Tegolo, D., Trucco, E.: FABC: retinal vessel segmentation using adaboost. Trans. Info. Tech. Biomed. **14**(5), 1267–1274 (2010). https://doi.org/10.1109/TITB.2010.2052282
6. Fraz, M., et al.: An ensemble classification-based approach applied to retinal blood vessel segmentation. IEEE Trans. Bio-Med. Eng. **59**, 2538–48 (2012). https://doi.org/10.1109/TBME.2012.2205687
7. Ronneberger, O., Fischer, P., Brox, T.: U-net: convolutional networks for biomedical image segmentation. In: Navab, N., Hornegger, J., Wells, W.M., Frangi, A.F. (eds.) MICCAI 2015. LNCS, vol. 9351, pp. 234–241. Springer, Cham (2015). https://doi.org/10.1007/978-3-319-24574-4_28
8. Guo, C., Szemenyei, M., Yi, Y., Wang, W., Chen, B., Fan, C.: Sa-unet: spatial attention u-net for retinal vessel segmentation (2020)

9. Oktay, O., et al.: Anatomically constrained neural networks (ACNN): application to cardiac image enhancement and segmentation. IEEE Trans. Med. Imaging **37**(2), 384–395 (2017). https://doi.org/10.1109/TMI.2017.2743464

10. Sanchesa, P., Meyer, C., Vigon, V., Naegel, B.: Cerebrovascular network segmentation of MRA images with deep learning, pp. 768–771 (2019). https://doi.org/10.1109/ISBI.2019.8759569

11. Ni, J., et al.: Global channel attention networks for intracranial vessel segmentation. Comput. Biol. Med. **118**, 103639 (2020). https://doi.org/10.1016/j.compbiomed.2020.103639

12. Long, J., Shelhamer, E., Darrell, T.: Fully convolutional networks for semantic segmentation, pp. 3431–3440 (2015). https://doi.org/10.1109/CVPR.2015.7298965

13. Yang, X., Li, Z., Guo, Y., Zhou, D.: DCU-net: a deformable convolutional neural network based on cascade u-net for retinal vessel segmentation. Multimedia Tools Appl. **81** (2022). https://doi.org/10.1007/s11042-022-12418-w

14. Qi, Y., He, Y., Qi, X., Zhang, Y., Yang, G.: Dynamic snake convolution based on topological geometric constraints for tubular structure segmentation. In: Proceedings of the IEEE/CVF International Conference on Computer Vision, pp. 6070–6079 (2023)

15. Yu, F., Koltun, V.: Multi-scale context aggregation by dilated convolutions. arXiv preprint arXiv:1511.07122 (2015). https://doi.org/10.48550/arXiv.1511.07122

16. Chen, L.C., Papandreou, G., Kokkinos, I., Murphy, K., Yuille, A.L.: Semantic image segmentation with deep convolutional nets and fully connected CRFs. arXiv preprint arXiv:1412.7062 (2014). https://doi.org/10.48550/arXiv.1412.7062

17. Chen, L.C., Zhu, Y., Papandreou, G., Schroff, F., Adam, H.: Encoder-decoder with atrous separable convolution for semantic image segmentation (2018)

18. Zhao, H., Shi, J., Qi, X., Wang, X., Jia, J.: Pyramid scene parsing network, pp. 6230–6239 (2017). https://doi.org/10.1109/CVPR.2017.660

19. He, K., Zhang, X., Ren, S., Sun, J.: Deep residual learning for image recognition, pp. 770–778 (2016). https://doi.org/10.1109/CVPR.2016.90

20. Chollet, F.: Xception: deep learning with depthwise separable convolutions, pp. 1800–1807 (2017). https://doi.org/10.1109/CVPR.2017.195

21. Oktay, O., et al.: Attention u-net: learning where to look for the pancreas (2018)

Neural Network Surrogate Based on Binary Classification for Assisting Genetic Programming in Searching Scheduling Heuristic

Ruiqi Chen[ID], Yi Mei[ID], Fangfang Zhang[(✉)][ID], and Mengjie Zhang[ID]

Centre for Data Science and Artificial Intelligence & School of Engineering and Computer Science, Victoria University of Wellington, Wellington 6140, New Zealand
{ruiqi.chen,yi.mei,fangfang.zhang,mengjie.zhang}@ecs.vuw.ac.nz

Abstract. Dynamic job shop scheduling (DJSS) is an NP-hard optimisation problem requiring real-time responses to newly arrived jobs. Scheduling heuristics generated by genetic programming can make high-quality decisions in DJSS, but evaluating these heuristics through simulations is very time-consuming. To speed up evaluations, surrogate models based on machine learning have been developed to predict fitness values. However, existing surrogates are primarily simplistic machine learning models with overly simplified input features, which overlook important characteristics of scheduling heuristics. To enhance prediction accuracy, we propose a new feature representation that comprehensively represents the behaviour of a scheduling heuristic. Additionally, a neural network binary classifier is employed as the surrogate model to learn the complex patterns in the proposed feature representation. Experimental results indicate that the proposed algorithm can find better scheduling heuristics and converge faster compared to the existing algorithms. Further analysis reveals both the new feature representation and the neural network binary classification-based surrogate model enhance the prediction accuracy and contribute to the performance improvement.

Keywords: Dynamic job shop scheduling · Genetic programming · Surrogate · Neural network

1 Introduction

Dynamic job shop scheduling (DJSS) necessitates constant adaptation to frequent job arrivals, requiring immediate dispatch decisions. Genetic Programming (GP) has been widely used for automatically evolving scheduling heuristics for DJSS [4,14,15]. GP treats scheduling rules as individuals that are improved generation by generation through evolutionary principles. The fitness evaluation of these individuals requires time-consuming scheduling simulations. To expedite the evaluation process, various surrogate-assisted GP methods have been developed [6,13]. Instead of running expensive simulations, they use computationally cheaper surrogate models to predict fitness values. Many competitive surrogates are built using machine learning (ML) models [2,8]. However, existing state-of-the-art machine learning surrogates primarily use simplistic models, such as K-Nearest Neighbours (KNN). These models have limited ability to learn the complex relationships in the data. Additionally, the input features are often over-simplified through extensive feature engineering, resulting in the loss of crucial information needed for accurate predictions. Furthermore, existing state-of-the-art surrogates are primarily regression models that directly predict fitness values. Since the GP algorithm changes the scheduling instance each generation (known as instance rotation [8]), the fitness values of individuals across different generations are incomparable. Consequently, incorporating individuals from different generations into the training data is challenging for existing methods, making it difficult to fully utilise all evaluated individuals.

To address the above issues, we propose a new feature representation, the raw-type Phenotypic Characterisation (PC), to comprehensively represent the behaviours of the individual and employ a neural network (NN) as the surrogate model to capture the complex patterns in the raw-type PC. Additionally, the surrogate operates in a binary classification manner by comparing pairs of individuals and predicts the superior one. In this mechanism, evaluated individuals within the same generation are compared to form training data. Training data from different generations are comparable because the relative relationships between pairs of individuals remain stable and are less affected by instance rotation. Consequently, the surrogate model can leverage more training data.

The primary aim of this research is to enhance the effectiveness and efficiency of GP in evolving high-quality scheduling rules through the proposed surrogate. To achieve this aim, the following research objectives are established:

1. Design a new feature representation that comprehensively reflects the behaviour of individuals, thereby assisting surrogate models in making accurate predictions.
2. Develop a surrogate model based on a NN binary classifier to predict the relative relationship between two scheduling rules, which not only effectively learns complex patterns from data but also leverages a larger volume of training data.
3. Conduct experiments to compare the proposed method with both basic GP and existing GP with KNN-based surrogates, analysing prediction accuracy and assessing the impact of data volume on the surrogate model.

2   Literature Review

2.1   Dynamic Job Shop Scheduling

Job shop scheduling is an NP-hard combinatorial optimisation problem that involves determining the processing order of a set of jobs on a set of machines. Each job has a due date and comprises a sequence of operations that must be executed in a predefined order. Each operation is processed on a specific machine for a duration without interruption. A machine can only process one operation at a time. This article focuses on the dynamic scheduling problem, where new

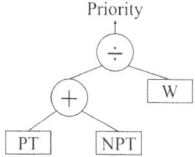

Fig. 1. An example of a scheduling heuristic.

jobs continuously arrive. The information for these jobs is unknown until they arrive [6]. In this paper, we consider minimising three common objectives [3]: mean tardiness (T_{mean}), weighted tardiness (WT_{mean}), and maximum tardiness (T_{max}).

2.2 Genetic Programming for DJSS

Scheduling heuristics enable real-time decision-making for job sequencing in DJSS. GP is a powerful method for evolving high-quality scheduling heuristics, renowned for its flexible representation that accommodates various heuristics within its search space. The tree-based structure is a commonly used representation in GP [6,9]. An example of a tree-based scheduling heuristic is depicted in Fig. 1. This heuristic maps features to priorities, with features gathered at the decision point serving as the terminal nodes (or leaves) of the tree. Functions act as interior nodes, and the priority is returned from the root node. In the example in Fig. 1, the priority of a job is calculated as $(PT+NPT)/W$, where PT and NPT are the processing time of the current operation and the next operation, respectively, and W is the weight of the job. The job with the highest priority is then selected for processing.

For evolving scheduling heuristics, GP follows a standard evolutionary process, and evaluate each candidate scheduling heuristic by applying it to DJSS decision-making simulations and measuring the steady-state scheduling performance. To this end, sufficiently long simulations are required, which is time consuming.

2.3 Surrogate-Assisted GP for DJSS

Surrogate techniques have been successfully utilised in GP to reduce the intense computational costs associated with evaluations. In the context of DJSS, surrogate models fall into two categories [9]: simplified simulation models and ML models.

Nguyen *et al.* [6] introduced surrogates based on simplified simulation models, reducing the scale of problems (i.e., fewer jobs and machines) to facilitate more cost-effective evaluations. This technique can be used to accelerate tasks such as feature selection for job shop scheduling [5]. Zhang *et al.* [12] further advanced this by proposing an adaptive surrogate strategy that dynamically adjusts the fidelity of simulation models across generations. The multifidelity-based surrogate is also employed to facilitate knowledge transfer through a collaborative mechanism [9].

The KNN surrogate with phenotypic characterisation, first introduced by Hildebrandt and Branke [2], is a highly influential ML surrogate model. This method posits that individuals with similar PC vectors likely exhibit analogous behaviours, thus having similar fitness. The similarity between PC vectors is quantified using their Euclidean distance. Zhang *et al.* [10] expanded this approach to multi-tree GP, evolving both routing and sequencing rules simultaneously for dynamic flexible job shop scheduling problems. Subsequent studies have confirmed the efficacy of KNN surrogate in multi-objective optimisations [7] and the knowledge transfer for multi-task learning [11].

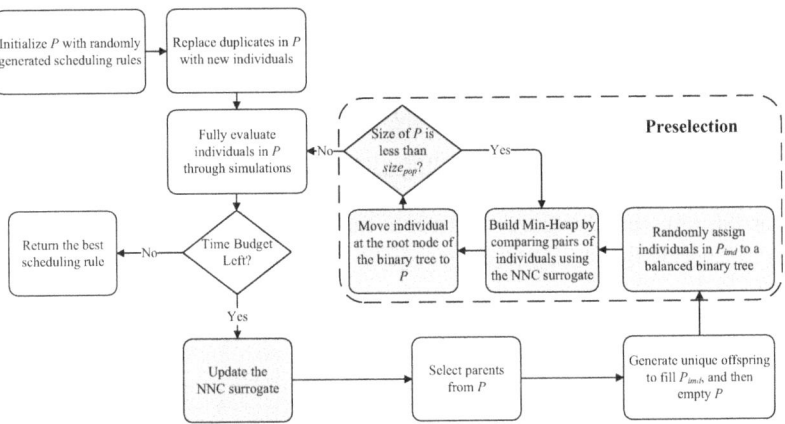

Fig. 2. Flowchart of the SGP-NNC algorithm.

KNN is the most commonly used ML model for building surrogates in the aforementioned studies. However, the KNN surrogate is limited in its ability to capture complex, non-linear relationships within the data, as it relies purely on distance metrics. Additionally, KNN is sensitive to irrelevant or redundant features, requiring extensive feature engineering. The potential of employing more sophisticated ML models to directly learn from raw data remains unexplored.

3   Proposed Method

3.1   Framework

We propose a novel surrogate-assisted GP algorithm based on a NN Classifier, referred to as SGP-NNC. This algorithm features novel preselection and surrogate update processes within its framework (as shown in Fig. 2, where the components distinct from the existing surrogate-assisted GP are highlighted in dark boxes). In this framework, we first generate random scheduling rules to initialise the population P with size $size_{pop}$. Individuals with identical PC vectors are identified as duplicates and replaced with randomly regenerated ones. We evaluate the individuals in P through scheduling simulations to get their real fitness.

		Decision Situation s_1				Decision Situation s_2			
Candidate Jobs		J_1	J_2	J_3	J_4	J_5	J_6	J_7	J_8
Raw-type PC (Priority)	Ind_1	15	9	17	85	44	22	62	84
	Ind_2	54	48	42	56	23	35	79	59
Ref Ranking		3	4	2	1	2	1	4	3
Ranking-type PC	Ind_1	1				3			
	Ind_2	1				4			

Fig. 3. Example of calculating the raw-type and ranking-type PC.

The PC vectors and real fitness of these individuals are used as training data to update the NNC surrogate. Subsequently, we conduct tournament selection to choose parents and produce offspring through crossover, mutation, and elitism (copying top individuals in P). We continue generating new offspring, retaining only those with unique PC vectors, until the intermediate population, which is considerably larger than P, is fully filled. Population P is then emptied, and top individuals in P_{imd} are selected using the min-heap technique. A min-heap is a binary tree data structure where the value of parent nodes is less than or equal to the value of its children. Individuals in P_{imd} are first randomly assigned to a balanced binary tree. We then build the min-heap (detailed in [1]) by comparing pairs of individuals using the NNC surrogate to predict the better individual. The desired individual can be found at the root node of the binary tree. This selection process is repeated until the top $size_{pop}$ individuals are selected.

This preselection approach is markedly distinct from existing surrogates that sort the entire P_{imd} based on the fitness values of individuals. The min-heap offers a time complexity advantage over sorting algorithms when we only need to find the top subset and do not require ordering the remaining elements.

3.2   New Phenotypic Characterisation Representation

The behavioural features of an individual are extracted as the PC vector and serve as the input to the NNC surrogate model. To represent the behaviour of an individual, we apply them to a set of predefined decision situations and concatenate the priority values into the PC vector. Figure 3 presents a simple example with two decision situations, each containing four candidate jobs. After analysing the situation, an individual assigns a priority value to each candidate. We visualise priority values with rectangular bars and highlight the highest priority in each decision situation in orange. Priority values comprehensively reflect the detailed assessment of the candidates, according to which the individual makes scheduling decisions. We propose using priority values as a new PC representation, referred to as the raw-type PC, as priorities are the raw output of an individual. In Fig. 3, the raw-type PC of Ind_1 is an 8-dimensional vector $\langle 15, 9, 17, 85, 44, 22, 62, 84 \rangle$.

The commonly used existing PC representation neglects the detailed information in priority values and directly takes the scheduling decision (candidate

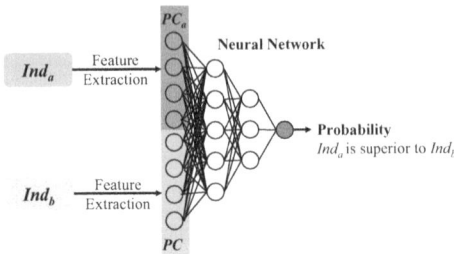

Fig. 4. Architecture of the NNC surrogate.

with the highest priority) as the behaviour of an individual. To quantify differences in decisions among different individuals, a manually designed reference rule is introduced. It provides a ref ranking for each candidate, and the ranking value corresponding to the highest priority is recorded as an element of the PC vector [2]. This PC representation is a vector of ref rankings, so we refer to it as the ranking-type PC. For instance, the ranking-type PC of Ind_1 in Fig. 3 is the vector $\langle 1, 3 \rangle$.

Ranking-type PC utilises domain knowledge to refine the features as low-dimensional vectors. Although it is easy to process by ML models, it has two major flaws. Firstly, it heavily relies on the reference rule, which is a scheduling heuristic. The performance of the reference rule cannot be guaranteed, and features extracted by this method may vary when using different reference rules. However, PC is an inherent property of an individual and should not be influenced by external factors such as the setting of the reference rules. Secondly, ranking-type PC struggles to distinguish subtle differences in individual behaviours. Taking the two individuals in Fig. 3 as an example, ranking-type PC sees their behaviour in decision situation s_1 as identical since they both assign the highest priority to job J_4. However, there are subtle differences in their assessments of the candidates. Ind_1 assigns a considerably higher priority to J_4 than to other candidates, firmly choosing this candidate; by contrast, Ind_2 allocates similar priorities across all four candidates, indicating a lack of strong preference.

The raw-type PC overcomes these flaws because it does not depend on reference rules, eliminates ambiguity in representing individual behaviours, and accurately reflects the nuances in individual behaviours.

3.3   Surrogate Model Based on Neural Network Binary Classifier

The proposed NNC surrogate model is shown in Fig. 4. It compares two individuals by horizontally concatenating their PC vectors (normalised using min-max scaling according to the minimum and maximum values of a PC vector) into a single vector which is then fed into a neural network. The output is a single value representing the probability that Ind_a is superior to Ind_b.

The updating of surrogate models is an online learning process where new data (evaluated individuals) arrives each generation. These updates enable the surrogate to adapt to constantly evolving individuals. Unlike KNN surrogate,

Table 1. Parameter settings for surrogate-assisted GP.

GP Parameter	Value	NNC surrogate parameter	Value
Population size ($size_{pop}$)	1000	Number of hidden layers	3
Intermediate Population size	3000	Number of neurons	64, 64, 32
Crossover / Mutation rate	90% / 10%	Activation	ReLU
Elitism	10	Learning rate	0.001
Parent selection	Tournament (size 7)	Optimiser	Adam
Maximum depth	8		

which must clear previous data and rebuild the surrogate from scratch, SGP-NNC can retain previously learned knowledge as it does not conflict with new data. This capability allows for the neural network parameters in SGP-NNC to be updated through incremental learning. To collect the training data, the evaluated individuals in each generation are compared with each other; if Ind_a has a better real fitness than Ind_b, the label for this pair is set to 0, otherwise, it is set to 1. The NN parameters are updated using stochastic gradient descent to minimise the binary cross-entropy loss.

4   Experimental Design

This paper adopts the widely recognised DJSS simulation configuration [3]. In each simulation scenario, jobs arriving continuously are processed by 10 machines. To ensure the simulation reflects a stable state of the job shop, we initially release 1000 jobs to "warm up" the system. Subsequently, we monitor the next 5000 jobs to evaluate the performance of dispatching rules. Jobs arrive at the job shop following a Poisson process with a rate $\lambda = \mu P_M/p$, where μ represents the average processing time of the machines, and P_M signifies the probability of a job visiting a machine. The utilisation level (p) is employed to control the busyness of the job shop [8]; a higher utilisation level corresponds to a busier job shop. Jobs are assigned varying weights, with 20%, 60%, and 20% of the jobs having weights of 1, 2, and 4, respectively. The number of operations per job follows a uniform discrete distribution ranging from 2 to 10. The processing times for these operations are drawn from a discrete distribution with values between 1 and 99.

Features of the job shop are extracted to support decision-making processes. This study adopts 16 commonly used features in DJSS, as detailed in [3]. We align our parameter settings with the mainstream settings for surrogate-assisted GP in DJSS [2,8,10], which are presented in Table 1. Following previous studies [8,10], we calculate the PC vector based on 40 predefined decision situations, each containing 7 candidate jobs. Consequently, the dimension of the ranking-type PC is 40, while the dimension of the raw-type PC is 280.

Table 2. Test performance of basic GP, SGP-random, SGP-KNNR, and SGP-NNC.

Scenario	Basic GP	SGP-random	SGP-KNNR	SGP-NNC
$\langle WT_{mean}, 0.85 \rangle$	718.3(6.6)	713.6(3.3)($\uparrow$)	710.4(2.9)($\uparrow\uparrow$)	710.2(2.5)($\uparrow\uparrow\approx$)
$\langle WT_{mean}, 0.95 \rangle$	1673.6(23.6)	1663.3(22.1)($\approx$)	1646.2(17.8)($\uparrow\uparrow$)	1635.9(13.2)($\uparrow\uparrow\uparrow$)
$\langle T_{mean}, 0.85 \rangle$	395.5(4.3)	392.0(2.4)($\uparrow$)	389.4(1.4)($\uparrow\uparrow$)	389.0(1.2)($\uparrow\uparrow\approx$)
$\langle T_{mean}, 0.95 \rangle$	979.0(10.7)	973.5(6.6)($\uparrow$)	968.3(6.9)($\uparrow\uparrow$)	964.6(4.7)($\uparrow\uparrow\uparrow$)
$\langle T_{max}, 0.85 \rangle$	1425.9(31.5)	1410.4(33.6)($\approx$)	1375.1(29.9)($\uparrow\uparrow$)	1372.0(25.6)($\uparrow\uparrow\approx$)
$\langle T_{max}, 0.95 \rangle$	3263.4(131.8)	3194.9(97.3)($\approx$)	3107.3(102.4)($\uparrow\uparrow$)	3057.0(94.3)($\uparrow\uparrow\approx$)
Average Rank	3.49	2.94	1.97	1.60

5   Experiment Results

5.1   Test Performance

In the following experiments, we test the proposed SGP-NNC algorithm on six scheduling scenarios: $\langle WT_{mean}, 0.85 \rangle$, $\langle WT_{mean}, 0.95 \rangle$, $\langle T_{mean}, 0.85 \rangle$, $\langle T_{mean}, 0.95 \rangle$, $\langle T_{max}, 0.85 \rangle$, and $\langle T_{max}, 0.95 \rangle$. The scheduling objectives include WT_{mean}, T_{mean}, and T_{max}; and the utilisation levels of the job shop are 0.85 or 0.95. The test set for each scenario consists of 30 scheduling instances unseen by the model. All scenarios are minimisation problems, so lower objective values indicate better performance. In previous studies, basic GP needed to evolve for 51 generations to find high-quality scheduling rules [8,9]. Since the training time varies when using surrogates, we set the average training time of basic GP with 51 generations as the time budget for all the compared algorithms [9].

In existing studies, the state-of-the-art machine learning surrogate employs KNN regression and ranking-type PC to predict fitness values [2]. We refer to the GP algorithm assisted by this surrogate as SGP-KNNR. The performance of the proposed SGP-NNC algorithm is compared with that of Basic GP and SGP-KNNR. Unlike SGP algorithms, basic GP lacks a preselection process that removes duplicate individuals. To assess the net improvement from the prediction accuracy of surrogates, we introduced a comparison algorithm, SGP-random, which follows the same procedures as other SGPs but randomly predicts fitness values. Table 2 shows the mean and standard deviation of objective values for the four algorithms over 30 independent runs, analysed using the Wilcoxon rank-sum test and the Friedman test with a significance level of 5%. "($\uparrow$)" and "($\downarrow$)" denote results significantly better or worse than competitors, respectively, while "($\approx$)" indicates no significant differences. For example, in scenario $\langle WT_{mean}, 0.85 \rangle$, SGP-NNC performs significantly better than Basic GP and SGP-random and performs similarly to SGP-KNNR. Additionally, we present the average rank of each algorithm across all scenarios.

The results show that the proposed SGP-NNC algorithm outperforms all other algorithms, with the best average rank of 1.60. When compared with the state-of-the-art SGP-KNNR algorithm, SGP-NNC exhibits lower mean objective values and smaller standard deviations across all six scenarios. In scenarios $\langle WT_{mean}, 0.95 \rangle$ and $\langle T_{mean}, 0.95 \rangle$, the performance of SGP-NNC is significantly

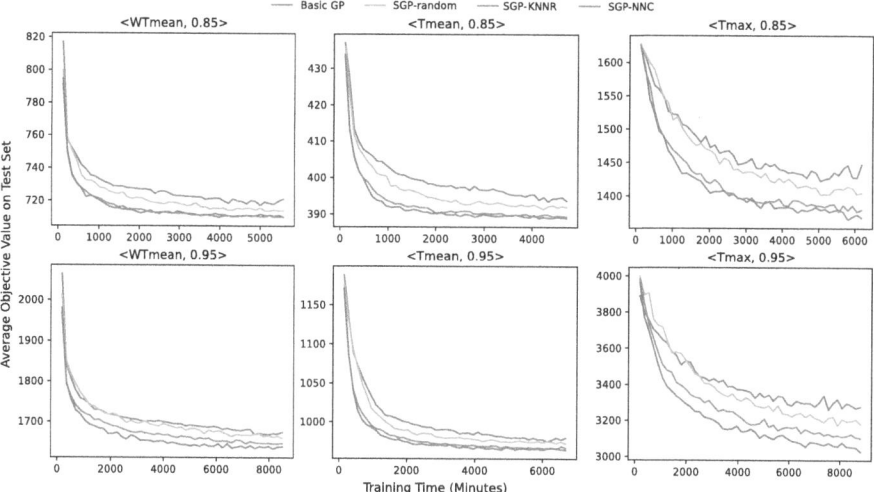

Fig. 5. Average objective value curves of Basic GP, SGP-random, SGP-KNNR, and SGP-NNC on the test set over 30 independent runs.

better than SGP-KNNR. SGP-random shows significant improvement over Basic GP in three of six scenarios, demonstrating that the process of removing duplicates enhances algorithm performance by maintaining population diversity. Both SGP-NNC and SGP-KNNR significantly outperform SGP-random in all six scenarios, indicating that accurate predictions of promising individuals help GP find better scheduling rules.

An effective SGP algorithm is expected to exhibit high convergence speed. To analyse the efficiency of the algorithms in comparison, we recorded their best output (scheduling rule) at each generation and tested them on the test set. The average objective value curves of the four algorithms on the six scheduling scenarios are shown in Fig. 5. According to the figure, SGP-NNC converges much faster than Basic GP and SGP-random in all six scenarios. The SGP-KNNR algorithm shows comparable convergence speed, but the curves of SGP-NNC generally lie beneath those of SGP-KNNR in most scenarios except $\langle WT_{mean}, 0.85\rangle$. Its advantages are particularly evident in scenarios $\langle WT_{mean}, 0.95\rangle$ and $\langle T_{max}, 0.95\rangle$, indicating that, given the same amount of training time, SGP-NNC is most likely to yield the best scheduling rules.

5.2 Ablation Study

SGP-NNC contains two new components: the raw PC type and the NNC surrogate. Although the results demonstrate the superiority of SGP-NNC, it is essential to investigate the effect of the raw-type PC and the NNC surrogate separately. To this end, we pair ranking-type and raw-type PC with KNNR and NNC surrogates to form four variants: Ranking-KNNR, Ranking-NNC, Raw-

Table 3. Test performance of the four variants: Ranking-KNNR, Ranking-NNC, Raw-KNNR, and Raw-NNC.

Scenario	Ranking-KNNR	Ranking-NNC	Raw-KNNR	Raw-NNC
$\langle \text{WT}_{\text{mean}}, 0.85\rangle$	710.4(2.9)	711.0(3.9)($\approx$)	710.7(3.2)($\approx\approx$)	710.2(2.5)($\approx\approx\approx$)
$\langle \text{WT}_{\text{mean}}, 0.95\rangle$	1646.2(17.8)	1645.0(15.0)($\approx$)	1640.0(14.1)($\approx\approx$)	1635.9(13.2)($\uparrow\uparrow\approx$)
$\langle \text{T}_{\text{mean}}, 0.85\rangle$	389.4(1.4)	389.5(1.5)($\approx$)	388.9(1.5)($\approx\approx$)	389.1(1.2)($\approx\approx\approx$)
$\langle \text{T}_{\text{mean}}, 0.95\rangle$	968.3(6.9)	967.4(5.4)($\approx$)	968.3(7.8)($\approx\approx$)	964.6(4.7)($\uparrow\uparrow\approx$)
$\langle \text{T}_{\text{max}}, 0.85\rangle$	1375.1(29.9)	1384.6(23.0)($\approx$)	1377.1(26.5)($\approx\approx$)	1372.0(25.6)($\approx\approx\approx$)
$\langle \text{T}_{\text{max}}, 0.95\rangle$	3107.3(102.4)	3126.4(74.8)($\approx$)	3066.7(82.5)($\approx\uparrow$)	3057.0(94.3)($\approx\uparrow\approx$)
Average Rank	2.61	2.79	2.41	2.20

KNNR, and Raw-NNC. Their test performances on the six scheduling scenarios over 30 independent runs are shown in Table 3.

The p-value of the Friedman test for the four algorithms is 1.1E-4, far less than 0.05, indicating that the performances of the four variants differ and require further pairwise Wilcoxon rank sum tests. Raw-NNC performs best with an average rank of 2.20, suggesting that both raw-type PC and NNC surrogate contribute to the advantage of SGP-NNC. According to the average ranks, the two variants using raw-type PC generally outperform those using ranking-type PC, indicating that raw-type PC leads to the major performance improvement in the proposed algorithm. When comparing Raw-KNNR and Raw-NNC, although the Wilcoxon rank-sum test shows no significant difference between them, Raw-NNC achieves better mean performance in five out of six scenarios.

5.3 Prediction Accuracy Analysis

In this section, we conduct a further analysis on the prediction accuracy of different surrogate models. A clear performance difference among the surrogate models can be seen in scenario $\langle \text{WT}_{\text{mean}}, 0.95\rangle$. It is interesting to investigate if this performance difference is truly due to the prediction abilities of the different surrogates. To this end, we fully evaluate the individuals in P_{imd} across 10 GP runs and check if the good individuals are actually selected.

First, we rank individuals according to their real fitness, with the top 1000 being those desired to be selected. Figure 6(a) shows the proportion of individuals ranked at a specific place that are correctly selected by different surrogate models. From the figure, we observe that the better the individuals are, the higher the proportion they are selected. Raw-NNC exhibits higher prediction accuracy across the whole spectrum, indicating that the superior performance of SGP-NNC is attributed to the accurate predictions made by the surrogate.

Figure 6(b) provides a detailed illustration of the 3000 offspring are selected by the proposed NNC surrogate. Each pixel in this heatmap represents a specific individual in a specific generation and rank, with the colour indicating the count of selections across 10 GP runs. The yellower the colour, the more frequently the individual is selected. From the figure, we observe that a large proportion of top-ranked individuals are selected by the NNC surrogate.

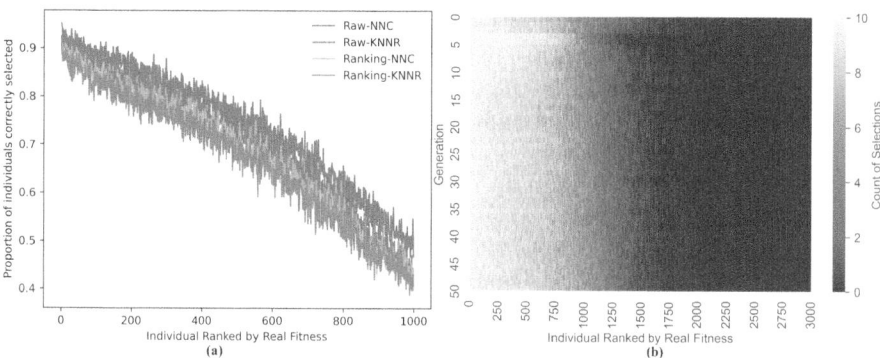

Fig. 6. Prediction accuracy: (a) Comparison of four surrogate variants (b) The heatmap of individual selection counts of the proposed NNC surrogate across 10 GP runs.

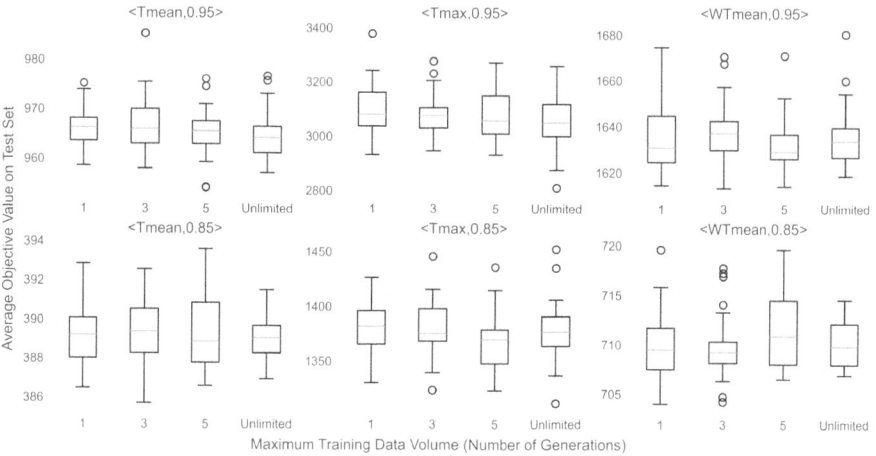

Fig. 7. Test performance of the SGP-NNC algorithm with different volumes of training data for the surrogate.

5.4   Impact of Training Data Volume

A notable characteristic of the proposed SGP-NNC algorithm is its ability to be trained with more data. To investigate the impact of training data volume on SGP-NNC, we conduct an experiment where the surrogate is trained on maximum of 1, 3, or 5 generations of data. When the training times of a NN reached this limit, its parameters are reinitialised. The test performances of SGP-NNC with different volumes of training data are shown in Fig. 7. The x-axis represents the maximum generations of data the surrogate is trained on, while the "Unlimited" serves as a control group where training data contains all the historical data. The y-axis represents the average objective value, with lower values being better.

From the results, we can see that the increase in training data slightly improves algorithm performance only in scenarios $\langle \mathrm{T_{mean}}, 0.95 \rangle$ and $\langle \mathrm{T_{max}}, 0.95 \rangle$. However, there is no apparent pattern in other scenarios, indicating that increasing the training data volume does not significantly benefit the algorithm. Nevertheless, the performance does not degrade when using more than one generation of data, suggesting that the binary classification mechanism effectively makes data from different generations compatible.

There are three possible reasons why increasing the training data does not improve algorithm performance as expected. First, the neural networks may have reached their model capacity during training, so additional data does not enhance their ability to distinguish good individuals. Second, training data from the current generation are most influential because newly generated offspring is most similar to individuals in the current generation. Therefore, even if the surrogate discards previously learned knowledge and trains on only one generation of data, it can still provide competitive performance. Third, not all training data are equally important; individuals from previous generations can be less important or redundant. Therefore, additional training data can introduce noise, hindering the performance of the surrogate.

6   Conclusion

The primary goal of this paper is to design an effective surrogate model that enhances the effectiveness of GP in discovering good scheduling rules. This goal is achieved through the newly proposed SGP-NNC algorithm. By using priority values as raw-type PC and employing a NN binary classifier as the surrogate model, SGP-NNC considerably improves the prediction accuracy of the surrogate. Extensive experiments across six scheduling scenarios show that SGP-NNC finds better heuristics and converges faster than basic GP and SGP-KNNR, though increased training data does not yield notable benefits.

The study addresses previous inadequacies in the PC representation and demonstrates the effectiveness of neural network surrogates. The proposed binary classification mechanism sheds new light on the surrogate design, which was originally dominated by fitness value regression. Further exploration of classification-based surrogates is expected to be promising. Additionally, the proposed surrogate is a general approach for predicting the performance of heuristics based on its behaviour. Similar ideas can be applied to other combinatorial optimisation problems, such as project scheduling and vehicle routing. Our future work will focus on identifying important training samples, better leveraging increased data volume, exploring improved preselection methods, and incorporating statistical models to further assist surrogate predictions.

References

1. Al-Jaloud, E.S., Al-Aqel, H.A., Badr, G.H.: Comparative performance evaluation of heap-sort and quick-sort algorithms. Int. J. Comput. Acad. Res. **3**(2), 39–57 (2014)
2. Hildebrandt, T., Branke, J.: On using surrogates with genetic programming. Evol. Comput. **23**(3), 343–367 (2015)
3. Huang, Z., Mei, Y., Zhang, F., Zhang, M.: Grammar-guided linear genetic programming for dynamic job shop scheduling. In: Proceedings of the Genetic and Evolutionary Computation Conference, pp. 1137–1145. ACM (2023)
4. Jakobović, D., Marasović, K.: Evolving priority scheduling heuristics with genetic programming. Appl. Soft Comput. **12**(9), 2781–2789 (2012)
5. Mei, Y., Nguyen, S., Xue, B., Zhang, M.: An efficient feature selection algorithm for evolving job shop scheduling rules with genetic programming. IEEE Trans. Emerg. Topics Comput. Intell. **1**(5), 339–353 (2017)
6. Nguyen, S., Zhang, M., Tan, K.C.: Surrogate-assisted genetic programming with simplified models for automated design of dispatching rules. IEEE Trans. Cybern. **47**(9), 2951–2965 (2017)
7. Zeiträg, Y., Figueira, J.R., Horta, N., Neves, R.: Surrogate-assisted automatic evolving of dispatching rules for multi-objective dynamic job shop scheduling using genetic programming. Expert Syst. Appl. **209**, 118194 (2022)
8. Zhang, F., Mei, Y., Nguyen, S., Tan, K.C., Zhang, M.: Instance-rotation-based surrogate in genetic programming with brood recombination for dynamic job-shop scheduling. IEEE Trans. Evol. Comput. **27**(5), 1192–1206 (2023)
9. Zhang, F., Mei, Y., Nguyen, S., Zhang, M.: Collaborative multifidelity-based surrogate models for genetic programming in dynamic flexible job shop scheduling. IEEE Trans. Cybern. **52**(8), 8142–8156 (2022)
10. Zhang, F., Mei, Y., Nguyen, S., Zhang, M.: Phenotype based surrogate-assisted multi-objective genetic programming with brood recombination for dynamic flexible job shop scheduling. In: IEEE Symposium Series on Computational Intelligence, pp. 1218–1225 (2022)
11. Zhang, F., Mei, Y., Nguyen, S., Zhang, M., Tan, K.C.: Surrogate-assisted evolutionary multitask genetic programming for dynamic flexible job shop scheduling. IEEE Trans. Evol. Comput. **25**(4), 651–665 (2021)
12. Zhang, F., Mei, Y., Zhang, M.: Surrogate-assisted genetic programming for dynamic flexible job shop scheduling. In: Mitrovic, T., Xue, B., Li, X. (eds.) AI 2018. LNCS (LNAI), vol. 11320, pp. 766–772. Springer, Cham (2018). https://doi.org/10.1007/978-3-030-03991-2_69
13. Zhou, Y., Yang, J.J., Huang, Z.: Automatic design of scheduling policies for dynamic flexible job shop scheduling via surrogate-assisted cooperative co-evolution genetic programming. Int. J. Prod. Res. **58**(9), 2561–2580 (2020)
14. Đurasević, M., Jakobović, D.: Comparison of schedule generation schemes for designing dispatching rules with genetic programming in the unrelated machines environment. Appl. Soft Comput. **96**, 106637 (2020)
15. Đurasević, M., Jakobović, D.: Selection of dispatching rules evolved by genetic programming in dynamic unrelated machines scheduling based on problem characteristics. J. Comput. Sci. **61**, 101649 (2022)

HN-Darts:Hybrid Network Differentiable Architecture Search for Industrial Scenarios

Jie Li, Yuxia Wang, Yifan Wang, Ruiyun Yu, and Xingwei Wang[✉]

Northeastern University, Shenyang, China
{lijie,yury,wangxw}@mail.neu.edu.cn, {2201876,2001252}@stu.neu.edu.cn

Abstract. Neural architecture search is a powerful tool in image processing, automating model construction and reducing human involvement. However, its deployment on edge devices with limited computing resources is often impeded by the size of large models, a concern overlooked by most NAS methods focused solely on accuracy. We propose a hybrid network search approach that integrates the glore_unit, a novel component that replaces traditional cells to optimize model size without sacrificing accuracy. By leveraging the Differentiable Architecture Search (Darts) and a Googlenet-like hypernet, we've redefined the search space to prioritize compactness and precision, enhanced by a temperature factor for more reliable search selections. Our experiments on cifar10 and ImageNet showcase a model with a 2.35% error rate and 2.76M parameters on cifar10, and a Top-1 error rate of 23.75%, Top-5 error rate of 7.13% with 3.9M parameters on ImageNet, demonstrating SOTA accuracy with a significant reduction in model parameters, making it suitable for environments with constrained computational resources.

Keywords: Differentiable architecture search · Hybrid network · Light weight model · Glore_unit · Temperature factor

1 Introduction

In conventional intelligent industries, refining deep neural networks was a meticulous and expert-driven manual process, effective but demanding in terms of time and resources. Neural architecture search (NAS) is propelling industrial scenarios towards greater intelligence. Recent advancements have targeted the architectural search for specific, realistic objectives. For instance, Hot-started NAS[7] leverages evolutionary algorithms with a hot start to expedite the search, acknowledging the task-specific nature of embedded devices, and yields superior models with enhanced search efficiency. Concurrently, AutoMSR[8] employs a tree-structured Parzen estimator to identify optimal hyperparameters within hyperparameter subspaces, constructing an optimal graph neural network model that excels in multi-label classification tasks.

This work is supported by the Fundamental Research Funds for the Central Universities (N2116014), and the New Generation Information Technology Innovation Project of the Ministry of Education (2021ITA10011).

However, much of the existing work[9,10] has focused on optimizing search accuracy and efficiency, overlooking practical deployment challenges in industry. Beyond accuracy and speed, deployment demands also encompass model size and computational needs, which directly relate to resource consumption and latency.

To address these gaps in NAS models, we propose an innovative hybrid NAS of convolutional neural networks(CNN) and graph convolutional networks(GCN) approach tailored for practical industrial applications. This model defines the submodel's resource allocation based on the generated model's parameter count and computational demand, ensuring optimal performance within the constraints of real-world deployment.

2   Proposed Method

2.1   Preliminary: Differentiable Architecture Search (Darts)

We define the overall search space as $O=\{o_1, o_2, o_3\}$, which represents different sub operation types, such as 3*3 convolution and 5*5 convolution. Each edge of the defined network structure $x_{i,j}$ has a set of sub operations, corresponding to each sub operation being assigned a weight $\alpha_o^{(i,j)}$ on the edge. This means that the discrete operation selection problem is defined as a continuous weight optimization problem. By defining the output on each edge as the weighted sum of mixed operations, the specific calculation process can be expressed as follows:

$$\bar{o}^{(i,j)}(x) = \sum_{o \in O} \frac{\exp\left(\alpha_o^{(i,j)}\right)}{\sum_{o' \in O} \exp\left(\alpha_{o'}^{(i,j)}\right)} o(x) \tag{1}$$

2.2   Differentiable Architecture Search for Hybrid Neural Networks

Hybrid Network Search. We've tailored the evaluation model's search unit by setting a smaller block count N compared to standard Darts. During search, we propose a modified space with $4*n$ glore_units, where n denotes the intermediate nodes per unit. The size of the search space is $O_h = {o_h^{(i,j)}}^k * o_g^k$, where $o_h^{(i,j)}$ represents the feature-driven connections between nodes, and o_g represents the distinct sub-operations executed during the dimensionality reduction.

Figure 1 shows the search space structure of the hybrid network. The search edge of glore_unit is added after each intermediate node. Selection favors edges with higher values, and sub-operations on these edges employ a shared weight γ. The final unit output calculated formula is as follows:

$$f_g(x_i) = \sum_{o_g \in O_g} \gamma_{o_g} \cdot o_g(x_i) \tag{2}$$

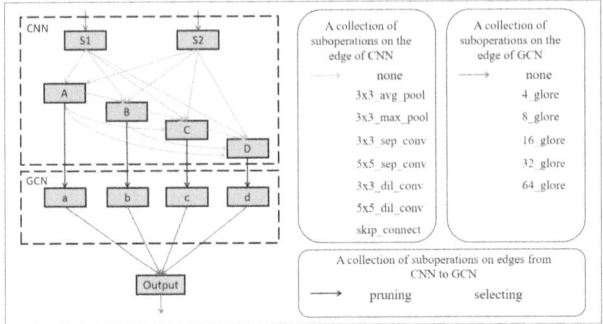

Fig. 1. Hybrid Network DARTS

Application of Temperature Factor. Considering that the purpose is to make weights more distinguishable, we consider the concept of temperature factor T in knowledge distillation, and the specific formula is as follows:

$$\bar{o}_h^{(i,j)}(x) = \sum_{o_h \in O_h} \frac{\exp\left(\alpha_{o_h}^{(i,j)}/T\right)}{\sum_{o_h' \in O_h} \exp\left(\alpha_{o_h'}^{(i,j)}/T\right)} o_h(x) \tag{3}$$

3   Experiments

3.1   DataSet and Metrics

The CIFAR10 dataset comprises 60,000 32×32 resolution images categorized into 10 classes. The ImageNet stands as the world's largest image recognition repository, encompassing 1,000 categories with 1.2 million training images and 50,000 validation images, typically resized to 224×224 for processing. We assess the efficacy of our search algorithms across four key metrics: accuracy, search cost, parameter count, and floating point operations.

3.2   Experimental Results on CIFAR10 and ImageNet

We conducted comprehensive model searches and evaluations on CIFAR10 and ImageNet. Table 1 details our CIFAR10 results, showing a 1.11% error rate reduction over manual designs like DenseNet. On ImageNet, as shown in Table 2, we improved by 2.7% against ShuffleNet. Our accuracy is on par with SOTA networks and, compared to recent NAS methods such as IDARTS and PC-DARTS, our model excels in complexity and size, featuring only 2.76M parameters on CIFAR10 and 3.9M on ImageNet.

Table 1. Comparison with SOTA architectures on CIFAR10.

Architecture	Test Err. (%)	Params (M)	Search Cost (GPU-days)	Search Method
DenseNet-BC[15]	3.46	2.56	~	Manual
AmoebaNet-A[2]	3.34	3.2	3150	evolution
AmoebaNet-B[2]	2.55	2.8	3150	evolution
DARTS (1st order)[4]	3	3.3	0.4	gradient
EfficientNet-B0[17]	1.90	4.0	~	gradient
PC-DARTS[16]	2.57	3.3	0.1	gradient
IDARTS[6]	2.32	4.2	0.1	gradient
HN-Darts	**2.35**	**2.76**	**0.1**	gradient

Table 2. Comparison with SOTA architectures on ImageNet

Architecture	Test Err.(%)		Params(M)	X+(M)	Search Cost(GPU-days)	Search Method
	Top-1	Top-5				
ShuffleNet 2x (v1)[18]	26.4	10.2	-5	524	~	Manual
ShuffleNet 2x (v2)[19]	25.1		-5	591	~	Manual
AmoebaNet-C[2]	24.3	7.6	6.4	570	3150	evolution
DARTS(2nd order)[4]	26.7	8.7	4.7	574	4	gradient
EfficientNet-B0[17]	22.9	6.70	5.3	536	~	gradient
PC-DARTS[16]	25.1	7.8	5.3	586	0.1	gradient
IDARTS[6]	23.8	7.2	5.8	657	0.1	gradient
HN-Darts	**23.75**	**7.13**	**3.9**	**481**	**0.1**	gradient
PC-DARTS(Imagenet)[16]	24.2	7.3	5.3	597	3.8	gradient
IDARTS (Imagenet)[6]	23.5	7	6.2	714	3.8	gradient
HN-Darts(Imagenet)	**23.3**	**6.94**	**4.1**	**537**	**4.1**	gradient

Ablation Experiment. The experimental analysis in Table 3 demonstrates the impact of the glore_unit and temperature factor (TF and GU) on model performance. When the original method's unit stack count is reduced, a notable accuracy drop is occurred due to a direct depth alteration without structural optimization. However, by incorporating a temperature factor and a hybrid structure, the model's accuracy improved by 0.04% and 1.05% respectively. This indicates that while the temperature factor offers a slight boost, the mixed structure is pivotal for significantly enhancing model accuracy.

Table 3. Ablation experiments on CIFAR10 and ImageNet

TF	GU	Test Err.(%)	Search Cost (GPU-days)
x(20 unit)	x(20 unit)	2.57	0.1
x	x	3.81	0.1
✓	x	3.35	0.1
x	✓	2.76	0.1
✓	✓	2.35	0.1

4 Conclusions

We propose HN-Darts, an architecture search method that efficiently generates both large and lightweight models by leveraging GCN to enhance image recognition accuracy through semantic region relationships. The method's temperature factor ensures reliable sub-operation selection, leading to the automated creation of accurate, deployable models at the edge without substantial computational overhead. Our future work will delve into numerical quantization, exploring multibit quantization for non-binary convolutional neural networks to achieve higher accuracy and compression ratios with minimal resource consumption.

Disclosure of Interests. The authors declare that there are no conflicts of interest regarding the publication of this paper.

References

1. Zoph, B., Le, Q.V.: Neural architecture search with reinforcement learning. arXiv preprint arXiv:1611.01578 (2016)
2. Real, E., et al.: Regularized evolution for image classifier architecture search. In: Proceedings of the AAAI Conference on Artificial Intelligence, vol. 33, no. 01 (2019)
3. Nakai, K., Matsubara, T., Uehara, K.: Att-DARTS: differentiable neural architecture search for attention. In: 2020 International Joint Conference on Neural Networks (IJCNN) (2020)
4. Liu, H., Simonyan, K., Yang, Y.: Darts: differentiable architecture search. arXiv preprint arXiv:1806.09055 (2018)
5. Liu, J., Yan, J., Xu, H., Wang, Z., Huang, J., Xu, Y.: Finch: enhancing federated learning with hierarchical Neural Architecture Search. IEEE Trans. Mob. Comput. **23**(5), 6012–6026 (2024)
6. Xue, S., et al.: IDARTS: interactive differentiable architecture search. In: Proceedings of the IEEE/CVF International Conference on Computer Vision (2021)
7. Hendrickx, L., Van Ranst, and W., Goedemé, T.: Hot-started NAS for task-specific embedded applications. In: Proceedings of the IEEE/CVF Conference on Computer Vision and Pattern Recognition (2022)
8. Chen, J., et al.: AutoMSR: auto molecular structure representation learning for multi-label metabolic pathway prediction. IEEE/ACM Trans. Comput. Biol. Bioinf. (2022)
9. Yang, J., Liu, Y., Xu, H.: HOTNAS: hierarchical optimal transport for neural architecture search. In: 2023 IEEE/CVF Conference on Computer Vision and Pattern Recognition (CVPR) (2023)
10. Zhong, Z., et al.: Blockqnn: efficient block-wise neural network architecture generation. IEEE Trans. Pattern Anal. Mach. Intell. **43**(7), 2314–2328 (2020)
11. Wu, F., Gao, J., Hong, L., Wang, X., Zhou, C., Ye, N.: G-NAS: generalizable neural architecture search for single domain generalization object detection. In: Proceedings of the AAAI Conference on Artificial Intelligence (2024)
12. Jiang, B., Zhang, Z., Lin, D., Tang, J., Luo, B.: Semi-supervised learning with graph learning-convolutional networks. In: 2019 IEEE/CVF Conference on Computer Vision and Pattern Recognition (CVPR), Long Beach, CA, USA, pp. 11305–11312 (2019)

13. Cai, Z., Chen, L., Liu, P., Ling, T., Lai, Y.: EG-NAS: neural architecture search with fast evolutionary exploration. In: Proceedings of the AAAI Conference on Artificial Intelligence (2024)
14. Yang, J., Liu, Y., Xu, H.: HOTNAS: hierarchical optimal transport for neural architecture search. In: 2023 IEEE/CVF Conference on Computer Vision and Pattern Recognition (CVPR) (2023)
15. Huang, G., et al.: Densely connected convolutional networks. In: Proceedings of the IEEE Conference on Computer Vision and Pattern Recognition (2017)
16. Xu, Y., et al.: Pc-darts: partial channel connections for memory-efficient architecture search. arXiv preprint arXiv:1907.05737 (2019)
17. Tan, M., Le, Q.V.: EfficientNet: rethinking model scaling for convolutional neural networks. ArXiv arxiv:1905.11946 (2019)
18. Zhang, X., et al.: Shufflenet: an extremely efficient convolutional neural network for mobile devices. In: Proceedings of the IEEE Conference on Computer Vision and Pattern Recognition (2018)
19. Ma, N., et al.: Shufflenet v2: practical guidelines for efficient cnn architecture design. In: Proceedings of the European Conference on Computer Vision (ECCV) (2018)
20. Sheth, P., Xie, P.: Improving differentiable neural architecture search by encouraging transferability. In: International Conference on Learning Representations (2023)
21. Odema, M., Al Faruque, M.A.: PrivyNAS: privacy-aware neural architecture search for split computing in edge-cloud systems. IEEE Internet Things J. **11**(4), 6638–6651 (2024)

High-Order Structure Enhanced Graph Clustering Network

Yangfan Zhang⬛ and Bing Guo$^{(\boxtimes)}$⬛

College of Computer Science, Sichuan University, Chengdu, China
guobing@scu.edu.cn

Abstract. The area of graph clustering has received significant attention due to its diverse applications in various domains such as recommender systems and bioinformatics. However, most of the existing methods (i) lack the effective use of high-order neighbor information due to the message passing mechanism of graph neural networks (GNNs), and (ii) ignore high-order modularity information. To address these shortcomings, we propose a new clustering method named High-Order Structure Enhanced Graph Clustering Network (HSEGC). Specifically, HSEGC integrates a multi-head attention fusion graph convolution module to formulate a weighted adjacency matrix, thereby enriching high-order neighbor information. Moreover, HSEGC incorporates a modularity maximization module to capture high-order modularity information effectively. Comprehensive experiments conducted on four commonly used benchmark datasets demonstrate the efficacy of HSEGC in leveraging high-order information for deep clustering.

Keywords: Graph Neural Network · Deep Clustering · Unsupervised Learning

1 Introduction

Graphs are fundamental data structures which capture complex relationships among objects. In the real world, a myriad of applications can be theoretically modeled as graphs, such as social network analysis [5], traffic flow prediction [7], and bioinformatics [19]. Deep clustering, a prevalent unsupervised learning approach, segments data into distinct groups without pre-assigned labels, revealing intrinsic structures and patterns. For instance, auto-encoder (AE) [8] distills node information by reconstructing attribute features.

However, traditional deep clustering algorithms struggle with graph datasets' intricate topological structures. Graph convolutional networks (GCNs) [9] have emerged as a powerful solution for graph-based clustering tasks. Specifically, the structural deep clustering network (SDCN) [2] introduces an integrated framework which combines the AE-derived representations with GCN to mitigate GCN's over-smoothing issue. Attention-driven Graph Clustering Network (AGCN) [15] employs dual attention-based fusion modules to merge AE and GCN features adaptively. Graph clustering network with structure embedding enhanced (GC-SEE) [3] utilizes graph attention auto-encoder module to bolster clustering accuracy by integrating attributes importance-based structure information.

Predominantly, these methods focus on first-order neighborhood information, thereby neglecting the incorporation of more nuanced higher-order information. Furthermore, they consider only topological and attribute information, overlooking high-order modularity details. To address these limitations, we propose the High-Order Structure Enhanced Graph Clustering Network (HSEGC), a novel methodology adept at assimilating higher-order network information.

Specifically, we introduce a multi-head attention fusion graph convolution (MHAFGC) module, which achieves attribute fusion and harnesses multi-head attention to seize high-order information. And a modularity maximization (MM) module is designed to capture substantive higher-order structure information.

In summary, our primary contributions are as follows.

- We introduce a multi-head attention-based fusion module to adeptly integrate distinct feature sources, enriching high-order neighbor information within the resulting integrated features.
- A dedicated modularity maximization module is designed to augment the high-order modularity information, underpinned by a objective function formulated to optimize clustering outcomes by thoroughly considering varying structure information.
- Extensive experiments conducted on four datasets have demonstrated the superiority of HSEGC over the existing methods.

2   Related Work

Numerous deep clustering methods [14] have recently been introduced, yielding promising outcomes. Graph auto-encoder (GAE) [10] crafted a framework that unites auto-encoders with graph feature extraction. SDCN [2] combined AE and GCN to incorporate the structural information into deep clustering. AGCN [15] leveraged an attention mechanism to fuse node features and topological structure information. DFCN [16] designed a information fusion module to combine AE and GAE. GC-SEE [3] introduce GATE module to integrate different structure information. Transformer has gained much attention due to its ability to improve GNNs' defect related to handling long-range dependencies [4,6,18].

Besides, the utility of high-order information has been substantiated as instrumental for superior clustering outcomes [20]. The concept of modularity (Q) was proposed as a measure of high-order structure information to evaluate the robustness of network structures [13]. Given modularity's importance, numerous researchers have striven to refine its optimization with the aim of augmenting clustering efficiency. For instance, community detection algorithm based on unsupervised attributed network embedding (CDBNE) [21] captured the community structures through modularity maximization. DGCLUSTER [1] leveraged GNNs to optimize the modularity objective without pre-specifying the number of clusters.

3   The Proposed Method

In this section, we introduce the architecture of the HSEGC model designed for graph clustering. The overall framework of our model is illustrated in Fig. 1.

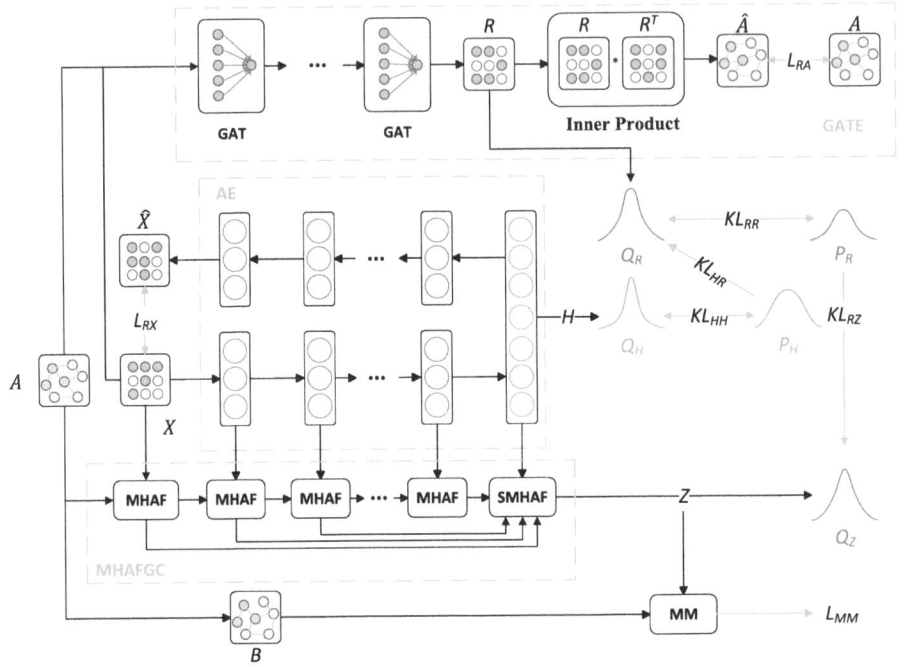

Fig. 1. The overall framework of HSEGC

3.1   Auto-encoder

AE is a fundamental unsupervised learning algorithm that is central to feature extraction. The l-th layer of encoder can be expressed as

$$\mathbf{H}_e^{(l)} = \phi(\mathbf{W}_e^{(l)}\mathbf{H}_e^{(l-1)} + \mathbf{b}_e^{(l)}) \tag{1}$$

where $\mathbf{H}_e^{(l)}$ is the representation learned by the l-th layer in encoder. $\mathbf{W}_e^{(l)}$ and $\mathbf{b}_e^{(l)}$ are the weight matrix and bias of the l-th layer in encoder, respectively. The representation $\mathbf{H}_d^{(l)}$ learned by the decoder can be derived as follows

$$\mathbf{H}_d^{(l)} = \phi(\mathbf{W}_d^{(l)}\mathbf{H}_d^{(l-1)} + \mathbf{b}_d^{(l)}) \tag{2}$$

where $\mathbf{W}_d^{(l)}$ and $\mathbf{b}_d^{(l)}$ are the weight matrix and bias of the l-th layer in decoder, respectively. The reconstruction of raw data $\hat{\mathbf{X}}$ is the output of the decoder part, namely $\hat{\mathbf{X}} = \mathbf{H}_d^{(L)}$. Finally, the reconstruction loss can be defined as

$$\mathcal{L}_{RX} = \frac{1}{N} \left\| \mathbf{X} - \hat{\mathbf{X}} \right\|_2^2 \tag{3}$$

3.2 Graph Attention Auto-encoder

For the encoder, the representation of node i learned by the l-th layer is given by

$$\mathbf{R}_i^{(l)} = \sigma\left(\sum_{j \in N_i} \alpha_{ij}^{(l)} \mathbf{W}^{(l)} \mathbf{R}_j^{(l-1)} \right) \tag{4}$$

where $\mathbf{R}_i^{(l)}$ is the representation of node i and $\mathbf{R}_j^{(l-1)}$ is the representation of j-th neighbor of node i. $\mathbf{W}^{(l)}$ is a weight matrix and $\alpha_{ij}^{(l)}$ denotes an attention coefficient calculated as

$$\alpha_{ij}^{(l)} = \frac{\exp(\mathbf{M}_{ij}(\text{LeakyReLU}(\mathbf{a}^{\mathrm{T}}(\mathbf{W}\mathbf{x}_i \,\|\, \mathbf{W}\mathbf{x}_j))))}{\sum_{j \in N_i} \exp(\mathbf{M}_{ij}(\text{LeakyReLU}(\mathbf{a}^{\mathrm{T}}(\mathbf{W}\mathbf{x}_i \,\|\, \mathbf{W}\mathbf{x}_j))))} \tag{5}$$

where $\mathbf{M}_{ij}$ is a proximity matrix reflecting the topological relevance of node i and node j which is given by

$$\mathbf{M} = (\mathbf{S} + \mathbf{S}^2 + \cdots + \mathbf{S}^t)/t \tag{6}$$

where $\mathbf{S}$ denotes the transition matrix, and $\mathbf{S}_{ij} = 1/d_i$ if there is an edge between node i and node j and $\mathbf{S}_{ij} = 0$ otherwise. The decoder reconstructs the topological structure of the graph through the inner product of $\mathbf{R}$ and $\mathbf{R}^{\mathrm{T}}$

$$\hat{\mathbf{A}} = \phi(\mathbf{R}\mathbf{R}^{\mathrm{T}}) \tag{7}$$

Subsequently, the reconstruction loss of the adjacency matrix is defined as

$$\mathcal{L}_{RA} = -\frac{1}{N^2} \sum_{i=1}^{N^2} [\mathbf{A}_i \log(\hat{\mathbf{A}}_i) + (1 - \mathbf{A}_i)\log(1 - \hat{\mathbf{A}}_i)] \tag{8}$$

3.3 Multi-head Attention Fusion Graph Convolution

Multi-head Attention Fusion Module. Initially, $\mathbf{Z}^{(l)}$ and $\mathbf{H}^{(l)}$ are concatenated, subsequently transformed by a full-connected layer for dimension adjustment. Then, a tanh activation is applied, followed by normalization through softmax and ℓ_2 regularization. The corresponding expression is given by

$$\mathbf{M}^{(l)} = \ell_2(\text{softmax}(\tanh([\mathbf{H}^{(l)} \,\|\, \mathbf{Z}^{(l)}]\mathbf{W}^{(l)}))) \tag{9}$$

$\mathbf{W}^{(l)}$ is the weight matrix of the l-th layer. The fused features are computed by

$$\mathbf{Z}'^{(l)} = \mathbf{M}_1^{(l)} \odot \mathbf{H}^{(l)} + \mathbf{M}_2^{(l)} \odot \mathbf{Z}^{(l)} \tag{10}$$

where $\mathbf{M}_1^{(l)}$ and $\mathbf{M}_2^{(l)}$ are the weight vectors of $\mathbf{H}^{(l)}$ and $\mathbf{Z}^{(l)}$, respectively. $\odot$ denotes the Hadamard product. To capture the higher-order information, the multi-head attention mechanism is utilized

$$\mathbf{e}_{ij}^{k,(l)} = \exp(\frac{(\mathbf{Q}^{k,(l)}\mathbf{Z}_i^{\prime k,(l)})(\mathbf{K}^{k,(l)}\mathbf{Z}_j^{\prime k,(l)})^{\mathrm{T}}}{\sqrt{d}}), \mathbf{E}_{ij}^{k,(l)} = \frac{\mathbf{e}_{ij}^{k,(l)}\widetilde{\mathbf{L}}_{ij}^{k,(l)}}{\sum_{w=1}^{N}\mathbf{e}_{iw}^{k,(l)}\widetilde{\mathbf{L}}_{iw}^{k,(l)}} \quad (11)$$

where $\mathbf{E}^{k,(l)}$ is the adaptive adjacency matrix of l-th layer. $\mathbf{Q}^{k,(l)}$ and $\mathbf{K}^{k,(l)}$ are learnable parameters in l-th layer. d and k denote the feature dimension and the k-th attention head. $\widetilde{\mathbf{L}} = \widetilde{\mathbf{D}}^{-\frac{1}{2}}\widetilde{\mathbf{A}}\widetilde{\mathbf{D}}^{-\frac{1}{2}}$ is the normalized adjacency matrix.

Finally, the output of MHAF module can be obtained by

$$\mathbf{Z}^{k,(l+1)} = \widetilde{\mathbf{L}}\mathbf{E}^{k,(l)}\mathbf{V}^{k,(l)}\mathbf{Z}^{\prime k,(l)}, \mathbf{Z}^{(l+1)} = \sum_{k=1}^{H}\frac{\mathbf{Z}^{k,(l+1)}}{H} \quad (12)$$

where $\mathbf{V}^{k,(l)}$ is a learnable parameter, and H is the total number of attention heads.

Scale-Wise Multi-head Attention Fusion Module. The SMHAF module is designed to encapsulate multi-scale information through the embedded representations obtained from different layers

$$\widetilde{\mathbf{Z}} = [\mathbf{Z}^{(1)} \,||\, \mathbf{Z}^{(2)} \,||\cdots||\, \mathbf{Z}^{(L)} \,||\, \mathbf{H}_e^{(L)}], \mathbf{M}^{(L)} = \ell_2(\mathrm{softmax}(\tanh(\widetilde{\mathbf{Z}}\mathbf{W}))) \quad (13)$$

Differing from MHAF, weighted representations from all layers are concatenated

$$\mathbf{Z}^{\prime(L)} = [\mathbf{M}_1^{(L)} \odot \mathbf{Z}^{(1)} \,||\cdots||\, \mathbf{M}_L^{(L)} \odot \mathbf{Z}^{(L)} \,||\, \mathbf{M}_{L+1}^{(L)} \odot \mathbf{H}_e^{(L)}] \quad (14)$$

The subsequent processing, mirroring the approach in MHAF, employs the multi-head attention mechanism to generate scale-wise aggregated output

$$\mathbf{e}_{ij}^{k,(L)} = \exp(\frac{(\mathbf{Q}^{k,(L)}\mathbf{Z}_i^{\prime k,(L)})(\mathbf{K}^{k,(L)}\mathbf{Z}_j^{\prime k,(L)})^{\mathrm{T}}}{\sqrt{d}}),$$

$$\mathbf{E}_{ij}^{k,(L)} = \frac{\mathbf{e}_{ij}^{k,(L)}\widetilde{\mathbf{L}}_{ij}^{k,(L)}}{\sum_{w=1}^{N}\mathbf{e}_{iw}^{k,(L)}\widetilde{\mathbf{L}}_{iw}^{k,(L)}} \quad (15)$$

$$\mathbf{Z}^{k,(L)} = \widetilde{\mathbf{L}}\mathbf{E}^{k,(L)}\mathbf{V}^{k,(L)}\mathbf{Z}^{\prime k,(L)}, \mathbf{Z}^{(L)} = \sum_{k=1}^{H}\frac{\mathbf{Z}^{k,(L)}}{H}$$

The final model output undergoes softmax function to prepare the probability distribution for clustering results

$$\mathbf{Q}_Z = \mathrm{softmax}(\mathbf{Z}^{(L)}), s.t. \sum_{j=1}^{k}Q_{Zij} = 1, Q_{Zij} > 0 \quad (16)$$

where Q_{Zij} is the probability of node i belonging to cluster j. Then we can obtain the predicted cluster label by

$$y_i = \arg\max_{j} Q_{Zij} \quad (17)$$

3.4 Modularity Maximization

Modularity is calculated by comparing the actual connectivity of edges in the graph with their expected conditions, which is defined as follows .

$$Q = \frac{1}{2m} Tr(\mathbf{U}^\mathsf{T} \mathbf{B} \mathbf{U}) \tag{18}$$

where $\mathbf{B}_{ij} = A_{ij} - \frac{d_i d_j}{2m}$. m is the total number of edges in the network. $Tr(\cdot)$ denotes the trace of the matrix. $\mathbf{U}$ denotes the cluster assignment matrix and can be defined as

$$\mathbf{U}_{ij} = \begin{cases} 1, & i \in C_j \\ 0, & \text{otherwise} \end{cases} \tag{19}$$

where C_j and i denote the j-th cluster and the node i, respectively. Since modularity maximization is an NP-hard problem, we utilize a relax concept of the modularity to optimize it, i.e., $Tr(\mathbf{U}^\mathsf{T}\mathbf{U}) = N$. To obtain $\mathbf{U}$, we design the MM module. Specifically, we first regularized $\mathbf{Z}^{(L)}$ from SMHAF

$$\mathbf{U} = \tanh(\ell_2(\mathbf{Z}^{(L)})) \tag{20}$$

Then, we square the results to ensure the output is transformed into a positive coordinate space and apply ℓ_2 regularization to the results

$$\mathbf{U} = \ell_2(\mathbf{U}^2) \tag{21}$$

The final modularity maximization loss function can be expressed as

$$\mathcal{L}_{MM} = -\frac{1}{2m} Tr(\mathbf{B}\mathbf{U}\mathbf{U}^\mathsf{T}) \tag{22}$$

3.5 Self-learning Clustering

We employ the Student's t-distribution [12] to measure the similarity between representation and centroid, and refine the outcomes through an auxiliary target distribution. The formulations of the Student's t-distribution are given by

$$Q_{Hij} = \frac{(1 + \|\mathbf{h}_i - \boldsymbol{\mu}_j\|^2)^{-1}}{\sum_{j'}(1 + \|\mathbf{h}_i - \boldsymbol{\mu}_{j'}\|^2)^{-1}}, Q_{Rij} = \frac{(1 + \|\mathbf{r}_i - \boldsymbol{\nu}_j\|^2)^{-1}}{\sum_{j'}(1 + \|\mathbf{r}_i - \boldsymbol{\nu}_{j'}\|^2)^{-1}} \tag{23}$$

where $\mathbf{h}_i$ and $\mathbf{r}_i$ correspond to the i-th row of $\mathbf{H}^{(L)}$ and $\mathbf{R}^{(L')}$, respectively. $\boldsymbol{\mu}_j$ and $\boldsymbol{\nu}_j$ represent the j-th cluster centroids. Subsequently, the auxiliary target distribution is used to refine the outcomes

$$P_{Hij} = \frac{Q_{Hij}^2/\sum_i Q_{Hij}}{\sum_{j'} Q_{Hij'}^2/\sum_i Q_{Hij'}}, P_{Rij} = \frac{Q_{Rij}^2/\sum_i Q_{Rij}}{\sum_{j'} Q_{Rij'}^2/\sum_i Q_{Rij'}} \tag{24}$$

Table 1. The details of the datasets

Dataset	Samples	Dimension	Edges	Classes
CORA	2708	1433	5278	7
DBLP	4057	334	3528	4
CITE	3327	3703	4552	6
UAT	1190	239	13599	4

Consequently, $\mathbf{Q}_H$ and $\mathbf{Q}_R$ can be optimized through the minimization of the KL divergence between $\mathbf{P}_H$ and them.

$$\mathcal{L}_H = \sum_i \sum_j P_{Hij} \log \frac{P_{Hij}}{Q_{Hij}} + \sum_i \sum_j P_{Hij} \log \frac{P_{Hij}}{Q_{Rij}} \tag{25}$$

Then, $\mathbf{P}_R$ is utilized to refine the distribution $\mathbf{Q}_R$ and clustering results $\mathbf{Q}_Z$

$$\mathcal{L}_R = \sum_i \sum_j P_{Rij} \log \frac{P_{Rij}}{Q_{Rij}} + \sum_i \sum_j P_{Rij} \log \frac{P_{Rij}}{Q_{Zij}} \tag{26}$$

Finally, the total loss of our model can be formulated as follows

$$\mathcal{L} = \lambda_1 * \mathcal{L}_{RA} + \lambda_2 * \mathcal{L}_{RX} + \lambda_3 * \mathcal{L}_H + \lambda_4 * \mathcal{L}_R + \lambda_5 * \mathcal{L}_{MM} \tag{27}$$

where $\lambda_1, \lambda_2, \lambda_3, \lambda_4$ and λ_5 are hyper-parameters.

4   Experiments

4.1   Datasets

We conducted the experiments on four widely used datasets. Details regarding these datasets are summarized in Table 1.

4.2   Baselines

Our method was compared with several types of clustering algorithms, including GCN-based methods, GAT-based methods, mixed methods, contrastive learning based methods and modularity maximization based method:

- **GAE** [10]: A method that employs GCN for learning graph representations in the context of clustering.
- **DAEGC** [17]: This method integrates an attention mechanism in representation learning.
- **SDCN** [2]: Merging AE and GCN, SDCN is a method that combines representations from both models for graph clustering
- **AGCN** [15]: Utilizing an attention mechanism, AGCN adaptively integrates features learned by AE and GCN for clustering tasks.

Table 2. Parameters settings for different datasets.

Dataset	Pre-training		Training				
	lr	epoch	lr	epoch	λ_3	λ_4	λ_5
CORA	$2e^{-4}$	50	$6e^{-4}$	50	$1e^{-3}$	$1e^{-3}$	$1e^{-3}$
DBLP	$1e^{-3}$	50	$1e^{-3}$	50	1	10	10
CITE	$1e^{-3}$	50	$1e^{-3}$	50	1000	1000	1000
UAT	1e–4	50	1e–3	200	1	1	0.1

- **DFCN** [16]: The DFCN model leverages a triple self-supervised strategy to enhance the aggregated representations learned from AE and GAE.
- **DCRN** [11]: Incorporating a dual information correlation reduction strategy, DCRN aims to minimize information correlation for clustering.
- **GC-SEE** [3]: Building upon the AGCN framework, GC-SEE emphasizes the importance of attributes for increased clustering accuracy.
- **CDBNE** [21]: This method incorporates the topology structure and node attributes of a network, followed by capturing the mesoscopic community structure via modularity maximization.

Metrics. We utilize four widely used metrics: Accuracy (ACC), Normalized Mutual Information (NMI), Adjusted Rand Index (ARI) and macro F1-score (F1). Higher values across these metrics signify improved clustering performance.

4.3   Implementation Details

Parameter Settings. To ensure comparability, our network's parameters align with those specified by [3]. Our training process is structured into two phases. Initially, we separately pre-train the AE and GATE modules. Following this, the model undergoes further training with 50 iterations on the CORA, DBLP, and CITE datasets, and 200 iterations on the UAT dataset. For the parameters in Eq. (27), λ_1 and λ_2 are uniformly set to 10 and 1 across all datasets. Variability is introduced in the values of λ_3, λ_4, λ_5 and the learning rate with specific settings tailored to each dataset as detailed in Table 2. Consistency in our experimental procedure is maintained by conducting each experiment 10 times, with the mean results reported in alignment with the methods of the compared studies. Our training procedure was executed with PyTorch and a GPU (GeForce RTX 4060).

4.4   Analysis of Clustering Results

The experimental results on four datasets are shown in Table 3. The values in bold and the underlined ones represent the best and second-best clustering performances, respectively. From these results, we draw the following conclusions:

Table 3. Clustering results on four datasets (mean±std)

Method	CORA				DBLP			
	ACC	NMI	ARI	F1	ACC	NMI	ARI	F1
GAE	63.80±1.29	47.64±0.37	38.00±1.19	65.86±0.69	61.21±1.22	30.80±0.91	22.02±1.40	61.41±2.23
DAEGC	67.21±0.59	50.63±0.71	47.33±0.62	60.82±0.64	62.05±0.48	32.49±0.45	21.03±0.52	61.75±0.67
SDCN	50.70±0.09	33.78±0.07	25.76±0.07	44.13±0.07	68.05±1.81	39.50±1.34	39.15±2.01	67.71±1.51
AGCN	53.70±2.44	33.97±3.19	24.72±2.50	46.27±2.54	73.26±0.37	39.68±0.42	42.49±0.31	72.80±0.56
DFCN	56.87±0.05	38.81±0.04	29.79±0.04	55.92±0.06	76.00±0.80	43.70±1.00	47.00±1.50	75.00±0.80
DCRN	61.93±0.47	45.13±1.57	33.15±0.14	49.50±0.42	<u>79.66±0.25</u>	<u>48.95±0.44</u>	<u>53.60±0.46</u>	<u>79.28±0.26</u>
GC-SEE	<u>73.58±0.74</u>	53.02±0.41	<u>51.22±0.88</u>	<u>71.48±0.79</u>	79.23±0.96	48.04±1.46	53.51±1.82	78.55±0.99
CDBNE	71.04±1.05	<u>53.32±0.12</u>	50.72±0.46	68.93±1.27	79.08±0.68	48.52±0.41	53.23±0.45	78.86±0.93
Our	**75.42±0.77**	**55.27±0.72**	**54.43±0.97**	**73.14±0.86**	**80.24±0.71**	**49.85±1.03**	**55.45±1.41**	**79.70±0.72**

	CITE				UAT			
	ACC	NMI	ARI	F1	ACC	NMI	ARI	F1
GAE	61.35±0.80	34.63±0.65	33.55±1.18	57.36±0.82	48.97±1.52	20.69±0.98	18.33±1.79	47.95±1.52
DAEGC	64.54±1.39	36.41±0.86	37.78±1.24	62.20±1.32	52.29±0.49	21.33±0.44	20.50±0.51	50.33±0.64
SDCN	65.96±0.31	38.71±0.32	40.17±0.43	63.62±0.24	52.25±1.91	21.61±1.26	21.63±1.49	45.59±3.54
AGCN	68.79±0.23	41.54±0.30	43.79±0.31	62.37±0.21	53.63±0.18	21.82±0.24	20.98±0.24	52.14±0.17
DFCN	69.50±0.20	43.90±0.20	45.50±0.30	64.30±0.20	33.61±0.09	**26.49±0.41**	11.87±0.23	25.79±0.29
DCRN	70.86±0.18	**45.86±0.35**	<u>47.64±0.30</u>	**65.83±0.21**	49.92±1.25	24.09±0.53	17.17±0.69	44.81±0.87
GC-SEE	<u>70.90±0.56</u>	44.00±0.64	46.47±0.76	63.12±0.66	<u>55.68±0.36</u>	23.00±0.22	<u>22.36±0.35</u>	<u>54.85±0.52</u>
CDBNE	69.51±0.34	43.74±0.23	44.36±2.85	<u>64.67±0.34</u>	52.44±0.65	20.77±0.67	20.38±0.71	51.18±0.86
Our	**71.84±0.25**	<u>45.45±0.51</u>	**47.80±0.41**	63.41±0.57	**57.25±0.38**	<u>25.08±0.39</u>	**24.46±0.47**	**56.71±0.42**

- Our method demonstrates the superior clustering outcomes on CORA and DBLP datasets, rivaling the best results on CITE and UAT datasets. For instance, our approach improves ACC by 2.50%, NMI by 3.66%, ARI by 6.27%, and F1 by 2.32% on the CORA dataset compared to the top-performing baseline method. This success can be attributed to HSEGC's effective use of high-order information to enrich structural details.
- Methods like SDCN, which combine node features and topological structure information, surpass GNN-based methods and inspire subsequent research. Building on SDCN, AGCN employs an attention mechanism to adaptively fuse the information learned by AE and GCN, achieving better outcomes. DFCN fine-tunes the results employing a triplet self-supervision strategy. Compared with AGCN, GC-SEE introduces a GATE module to learn structure information based on the importance of nodes, thereby improving performance. CDBNE captures mesoscopic community structure through modularity maximization. Leveraging high-order structure information effectively, our method performs better than these methods. DCRN performs better on CITE dataset, possibly because this dataset contains many feature and graph structure redundancies, which need to be reduced to improve performance.

4.5   Analysis of Ablation Studies

To assess the impact of our designed modules, we conducted ablation studies on four datasets. The outcomes of these ablation studies are shown in Table 4.

Table 4. The ablation studies on four datasets

Dataset	Metrics	HSEGC	w/o MHAFGC	w/o MM	w/o MM + F	w/o MM + S
CORA	ACC	**75.42±0.77**	73.93±0.70	74.97±0.69	74.36±0.78	74.70±0.50
	NMI	**55.27±0.72**	52.99±0.27	54.71±0.79	53.52±0.72	54.54±0.56
	ARI	**54.43±0.97**	51.39±1.11	53.79±1.73	52.19±1.45	53.76±0.89
	F1	**73.14±0.86**	71.66±0.84	72.58±0.77	72.33±0.77	72.11±0.73
DBLP	ACC	**80.24±0.71**	79.89±0.74	79.86±0.90	79.29±1.07	79.84±0.74
	NMI	**49.85±1.03**	49.14±0.89	49.49±1.05	48.41±1.31	49.34±0.98
	ARI	**55.45±1.41**	54.78±1.14	54.70±1.50	53.59±2.10	54.71±1.43
	F1	**79.70±0.72**	79.28±0.84	79.37±0.96	78.74±1.05	79.34±0.74
CITE	ACC	**71.84±0.25**	71.44±0.37	71.72±0.27	70.96±0.39	71.46±0.27
	NMI	**45.45±0.51**	44.81±0.55	45.34±0.48	44.29±0.49	44.92±0.43
	ARI	**47.80±0.41**	47.27±0.55	47.63±0.51	46.43±0.70	47.12±0.47
	F1	**63.41±0.57**	63.16±0.42	62.93±0.63	62.39±0.64	62.72±0.58
UAT	ACC	**57.25±0.38**	56.45±0.27	56.92±0.47	56.45±0.59	56.83±0.56
	NMI	**25.08±0.39**	23.57±0.30	24.47±0.49	23.62±0.47	24.42±0.65
	ARI	**24.46±0.47**	23.28±0.33	23.88±0.45	23.02±0.54	23.78±0.75
	F1	**56.71±0.42**	56.08±0.32	56.35±0.68	55.56±0.76	56.20±0.63

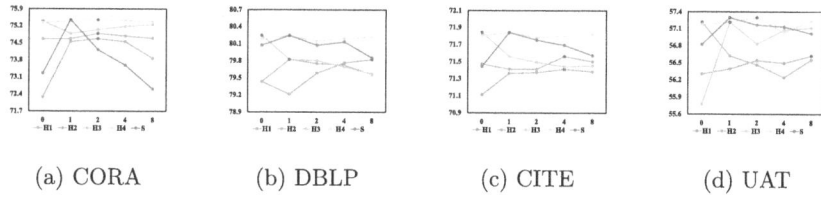

(a) CORA   (b) DBLP   (c) CITE   (d) UAT

Fig. 2. ACC with different head numbers of MHAF and SMHAF on four datasets

Analysis of MM: The exclusion of the MM module led to a retraining of our model, revealing a decline in performance across varying extents. This outcome underscores the value of high-order modularity information imparted by the MM module in bolstering clustering efficiency.

Analysis of MHAFGC: A detailed assessment of the MHAFGC module's impact was conducted by initially analyzing the module in entirety, followed by separate evaluations of the MHAF and SMHAF components.

– The removal of the entire MHAFGC module resulted in a significant performance dip compared to the HSEGC model, highlighting the indispensable role of high-order neighbor information learned by MHAFGC. A comparative analysis revealed that models without MHAFGC fared worse than those lacking MM, illustrating the relatively greater significance of high-order neighbor information over modularity information within our framework.

– Comparatively removing the MHAF and SMHAF modules, against the backdrop of an MM-absent model, showcased a universal decline in clustering outcomes. Moreover, the performance of models without MHAF in addition to MM was notably inferior to those lacking SMHAF and MM. This observation denotes the pivotal contribution of single-layer high-order neighbor information within the MHAFGC architecture. An inferred rationale for this trend could be the inefficiency in capturing high-order information in shallow layers without MHAF, culminating in the impediment of deep layer information extraction and the exacerbation of long-range dependency issues.

Analysis of Different Head Numbers of MHAF and SMHAF: We carried out the experiment to evaluate the effectiveness of multi-head attention mechanism within our model and identify relatively suitable hyper-parameter for each layer. As shown in Fig. 2, Hi (i = 1, 2, 3, 4) denotes the i-th layer of MHAF, and S denotes SMHAF. The best values are highlighted in red. We took head numbers through $\{0, 1, 2, 4, 8\}$ and Hi = 0 denotes the GCN devoid of the multi-head attention mechanism. For our datasets, we discovered that the results were superior when the head number of a certain MHAF layer was set to 0. The primary explanation for this outcome is likely the deep GCN structure of our model, which leads to an over-smoothing issue.

5   Conclusion

In this paper, we proposed the High-Order Structure Enhanced Graph Clustering Network (HSEGC), a novel approach aimed at harnessing high-order structure information within graphs. Incorporating a multi-head attention fusion graph convolution (MHAFGC) module and a modularity maximization (MM) module, HSEGC is adept at capturing detailed neighbor and modularity characteristics. Extensive experiments on four commonly used datasets demonstrated that our method optimizes clustering performance through efficient utilization of high-order information. Ablation studies further corroborated the significance of both high-order neighbor information and modularity information to our model's precision and robustness.

Acknowledgments. This work was supported in part by the National Natural Science Foundation of China under Grant No. U2268204 and 62172061; National Key R&D Program of China under Grant No.2023YFB3308300; the Science and Technology Project of Sichuan Province under Grant No.2023ZHCG0014, 2023ZHCG0011, 2022YFG0155, 2022YFG0157, 2021GFW019, 2021YFG0152, 2021YFG0025, 2020YFG0322; the Science and Technology Project of Chengdu City under Grant No.2023-XT00-00005-GX.

References

1. Bhowmick, A., Kosan, M., Huang, Z., Singh, A., Medya, S.: Dgcluster: a neural framework for attributed graph clustering via modularity maximization. In: Proceedings of the AAAI Conference on Artificial Intelligence, vol. 38, no. 10, pp. 11069–11077 (2024)
2. Bo, D., Wang, X., Shi, C., Zhu, M., Lu, E., Cui, P.: Structural deep clustering network. In: Proceedings of the Web Conference 2020, pp. 1400–1410 (2020)
3. Ding, S., Wu, B., Xu, X., Guo, L., Ding, L.: Graph clustering network with structure embedding enhanced. Pattern Recogn. **144**, 109833 (2023)
4. Dwivedi, V.P., Bresson, X.: A generalization of transformer networks to graphs. arXiv preprint arXiv:2012.09699 (2020)
5. Gao, Y., Yu, X., Zhang, H.: Overlapping community detection by constrained personalized pagerank. Expert Syst. Appl. **173**, 114682 (2021)
6. Gong, L., Tu, W., Zhou, S., Zhao, L., Liu, Z., Liu, X.: Deep fusion clustering network with reliable structure preservation. IEEE Trans. Neural Netw. Learn. Syst., 1–12 (2022)
7. Guo, S., Lin, Y., Wan, H., Li, X., Cong, G.: Learning dynamics and heterogeneity of spatial-temporal graph data for traffic forecasting. IEEE Trans. Knowl. Data Eng. **34**(11), 5415–5428 (2022)
8. Hinton, G.E., Salakhutdinov, R.R.: Reducing the dimensionality of data with neural networks. Science **313**(5786), 504–507 (2006)
9. Kipf, T.N., Welling, M.: Semi-supervised classification with graph convolutional networks. arXiv preprint arXiv:1609.02907 (2016)
10. Kipf, T.N., Welling, M.: Variational graph auto-encoders. arXiv preprint arXiv:1611.07308 (2016)
11. Liu, Y., et al.: Deep graph clustering via dual correlation reduction. In: Proceedings of the AAAI Conference on Artificial Intelligence, vol. 36, no. 7, pp. 7603–7611 (2022)
12. Van der Maaten, L., Hinton, G.: Visualizing data using t-sne. J. Mach. Learn. Res. **9**(11) (2008)
13. Newman, M.E.J.: Modularity and community structure in networks. Proc. Natl. Acad. Sci. **103**(23), 8577–8582 (2006)
14. Peng, Z., Jia, Y., Liu, H., Hou, J., Zhang, Q.: Maximum entropy subspace clustering network. IEEE Trans. Circuits Syst. Video Technol. **32**(4), 2199–2210 (2022)
15. Peng, Z., Liu, H., Jia, Y., Hou, J.: Attention-driven graph clustering network. In: Proceedings of the 29th ACM International Conference on Multimedia, pp. 935–943 (2021)
16. Tu, W., et al.: Deep fusion clustering network. In: Proceedings of the AAAI Conference on Artificial Intelligence, vol. 35, no. 11, pp. 9978–9987 (2021)
17. Wang, C., Pan, S., Hu, R., Long, G., Jiang, J., Zhang, C.: Attributed graph clustering: a deep attentional embedding approach. arXiv preprint arXiv:1906.06532 (2019)
18. Wu, Q., Zhao, W., Li, Z., Wipf, D.P., Yan, J.: Nodeformer: a scalable graph structure learning transformer for node classification. Adv. Neural Inf. Process. Syst. **35**, 27387–27401 (2022)
19. Yu, Z., Lu, Y., Wang, Y., Tang, F., Wong, K.C., Li, X.: Zinb-based graph embedding autoencoder for single-cell rna-seq interpretations. In: Proceedings of the AAAI Conference on Artificial Intelligence, vol. 36, pp. 4671–4679 (2022)

20. Zhou, D., et al.: High-order structure exploration on massive graphs: a local graph clustering perspective. ACM Trans. Knowl. Disc. Data **15**(2) (2021)
21. Zhou, X., Su, L., Li, X., Zhao, Z., Li, C.: Community detection based on unsupervised attributed network embedding. Expert Syst. Appl. **213**, 118937 (2023)

CAFGO: Confidence-Adaptive Factor Graph Optimization Algorithm for Fusion Localization

Fan Wu[1] , Zineng Zhou[2,3] , Haiyong Luo[2,3](✉) , Fang Zhao[1](✉) ,
and Bo Zhou[4]

[1] Beijing University of Posts and Telecommunications, No. 10, Xitucheng Road,
Haidian District, Beijing, China
{wufan98326,zfsse}@bupt.edu.cn
[2] University of Chinese Academy of Sciences, Beijing, China
[3] Institute of Computing Technology Chinese Academy of Sciences, No. 6 Kexueyuan
South Road, Haidian District, Beijing, China
{zhouzineng22s,yhluo}@ict.ac.cn
[4] Science and Innovation Center, Guoxing Avenue, Lingang Economic Development
Zone, Yibin, Sichuan, China
Bo.zhou@tinno.com

Abstract. Accurate positioning algorithms are crucial for autonomous
vehicle navigation and robotics. The fusion of data from GNSS, INS, and
odometers can provide comprehensive positioning results across various
environments. However, effectively integrating data from sources with
varying reliability levels remains a significant challenge. To address this
challenge, we propose a fusion positioning framework that dynamically
optimizes the weights of navigation sources. This framework leverages
a plug-and-play factor graph algorithm and utilizes a padding mask to
flexibly extract features from opportunistically acquired sensor data. It
learns the relative fusion weights of different navigation systems based
on these data features, thus offering more robust and accurate positioning results in complex and dynamic urban environments. Comprehensive
experiments and evaluations demonstrate the effectiveness and superiority of our algorithm.

Keywords: Factor Graphs · Deep Learning · Sensor Fusion · Adaptive
Weight Estimation · Autonomous Navigation · Robust Positioning

1 Introduction

The growing demand for precise and reliable localization systems, driven by the
proliferation of applications such as autonomous navigation and smart cities, has
underscored the limitations of traditional single-navigation methods like GNSS
and INS. To address these issues, multi-sensor fusion localization has emerged

---

F. Wu and Z. Zhou—Equal contribution.

R. Hadfi et al. (Eds.): PRICAI 2024, LNAI 15281, pp. 341–347, 2025.
https://doi.org/10.1007/978-981-96-0116-5_28

as a promising solution that combines data from various sensors to enhance overall positioning performance [1]. Extended Kalman Filters (EKF) are widely employed to fuse data from GNSS and INS [2]. However, these methods face challenges in addressing nonlinear and non-Gaussian positioning problems [3]. To mitigate these issues, particle filters have been utilized for multi-source fusion, but their effectiveness diminishes in complex urban environments [4]. To improve the fusion process, a dynamic weight optimization method based on residual error has been proposed [5], aiming to refine fusion outcomes. However, this app-roach requires strong knowledge assumptions and extensive domain expertise, which may not always align with the realities of changing application environ-ments [6]. Some deep Kalman filtering methods have been proposed to improve the localization performance, but they are still constrained by the nonlinear and non-Gaussian characteristics of the KF [7]. Factor graph optimization (FGO) methods have gained attention due to their ability to utilize more historical observation information [4], But these methods require strong knowledge-based assumptions. With the rapid development of deep learning [8], some studies have begun combining these techniques with FGO algorithms to improve positioning accuracy [9]. However, these approaches often fail to fully exploit the synergistic potential of combining deep learning with FGO and overlook the correlations between weights in multi-source fusion systems.

This paper introduces the Confidence-Adaptive Factor Graph Optimization (CAFGO) algorithm, a deep FGO framework for multi-sensor fusion localiza-tion. The CAFGO framework uses a data-driven approach to extract features from measurement and observation data, dynamically estimating sensor confi-dence and adjusting fusion in real-time. This reduces reliance on prior domain knowledge while enhancing adaptability, precision, and reliability in complex and dynamic environments. A specialized network architecture was developed to optimize sensor feature extraction, and experiments with real-world GNSS and INS data validate the algorithm's superior performance in precise and resilient localization.

2   Methods

This paper proposes a deep FGO framework that integrates deep learning meth-ods with an FGO-based multi-source fusion positioning algorithm. This section provides a detailed description of the proposed algorithm's specifics. The algo-rithmic framework is illustrated in Fig. 1.

In the context of the GNSS/INS positioning problem, considering the inde-pendence of GNSS observations and INS measurements, the positioning problem can be articulated using Bayesian rules as follows:

$$\hat{\mathbf{x}} = \operatorname{argmax} P\left(\mathbf{x}_t \mid \mathbf{G}_t, \mathbf{I}_t\right) = \operatorname{argmax} P\left(\mathbf{G}_t \mid \mathbf{x}_t\right) \cdot P\left(\mathbf{x}_t \mid \mathbf{x}_{t-1}, \mathbf{I}_t\right) \qquad (1)$$

where $\hat{\mathbf{x}}$ is the optimal system state set, $\mathbf{G}_t$ represents the GNSS measurement performed at epoch t, and $\mathbf{I}_t$ denotes the motion information from INS. Here, $\mathbf{x}_t$ and $\mathbf{x}_{t-1}$ indicate the system state at time t and t-1, respectively.

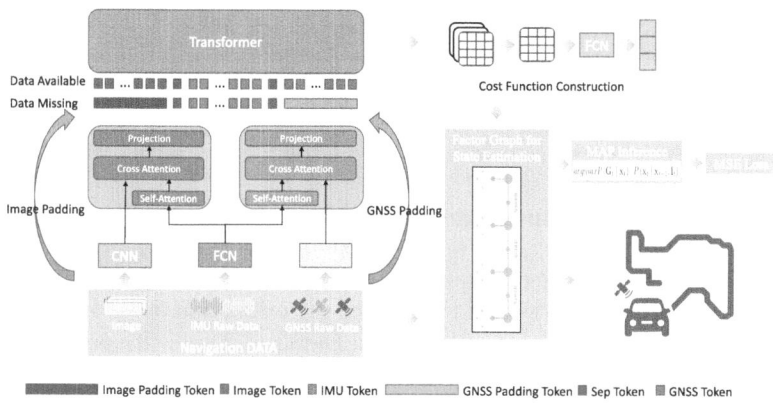

Fig. 1. An overview of CAFGO algorithm.

Conventional factor graph error calculation methods typically assign fixed weights to each error function. However, as previously noted, the reliability of navigation data is differentially impacted by varying environments. To enhance navigation and localization performance further, this study introduces the CAFGO algorithmic framework for adaptive weight estimation, which facilitates optimized fusion for localization. A novel error formulation has also been developed, as illustrated below.

$$\hat{X} = \arg\min \sum_t \alpha \left\| e_{\text{ins}}^t \right\|^2 + \beta \left\| e_{\text{GNSS}}^t \right\|^2 + \gamma \left\| e_{\text{image}}^t \right\|^2 \tag{2}$$

where α, β, and γ are parameters in the vector θ, and θ is the parameter vector obtained from network training, which is utilized to weigh and fuse the components of each error vector. The proposed CAFGO framework outputs additional weight parameters and integrates them into the θ vector to make more flexible use of opportunistic data and maintain good scalability of the factor graph. When data from a positioning system are obtained, the corresponding weight is dynamically adjusted.

This study examines the end-to-end optimization of the error between the ground truth positioning results, denoted by $\hat{X}_{gt}$, and the MAP estimate $\hat{X}_{MAP}$ derived from the factor graph.

$$L(\theta) = \sum_t \left\| X_{\text{gt}}^t \ominus X_{\text{MAP},\theta}^t \right\|^2 \tag{3}$$

where $\ominus$ represents a generalized subtraction operation used to calculate the difference between the true position values and the estimated positions obtained from the FGO. This calculated difference provides critical feedback for further optimization of the model parameters.

The input dataset $\mathbf{z}$ is defined as follows:

$$\mathbf{z} = (z_{GNSS}, z_{INS}, z_{image}) \tag{4}$$

where $z_{GNSS} = (S_{num}, S_{pse}, s_{cn0}, s_{pos})$ represents the number of observed satellites at time t, the pseudo-range residual for each observed satellite, the carrier-to-noise ratio (C/N0) for each observed satellite, and the position of the satellites at time t, respectively. $z_{INS} = (m_{acc}, m_{gyro})$ means the outputs of accelerometer and gyroscope, respectively. $z_{image} = (image_{t-1}, image_t)$ represents the obtained images at time t and t-1.

Considering the opportunistic nature of data acquisition, The model structure employed in this study first applies a padding mask to preprocess the raw observational data, ensuring data alignment. This paper proposes a novel network model architecture designed to enhance the extraction of features from the measurement data and the observation data. Data processed with padding masks first undergo feature extraction. Considering the spatial structure of image data and GNSS raw observation data, this paper employs a CNN to extract features from image and GNSS raw observation data. At the same time, an FCN is used to extract features from INS time-series data. The extracted feature data are fed into a cross-attention layer for feature learning in high-dimensional space. This model structure is designed to ensure that the features of each navigation data source are fully represented, thereby avoiding the potential information mixing and loss that may occur with direct fusion.

3   Experimental Evaluation

3.1   Data Preparation and Implementation Details

We utilized the KITTI dataset and the UrbanNavDataset. For effective model training, we preprocessed the datasets by segmenting the lengthy trajectory data into smaller units, each comprising 100 data points. The experimental simulations were executed on a high-performance computing cluster equipped with four NVIDIA GeForce RTX 3090 Ti GPUs. Model training was conducted with a learning rate of 2e–5 and a batch size of 16, spanning 30 epochs. The average duration for training was approximately 8 h. For inference tasks, a single NVIDIA GeForce RTX 3090 Ti GPU was utilized. The model was implemented using the jaxfg framework[1]. The experimental setup involves evaluating 10 different trajectories, each consisting of 100 data points, to ensure statistical significance. The results are averaged to provide a clear comparison. To evaluate the navigation model's precision and reliability, we have employed the following metrics to furnish a comprehensive overview of the system's performance in terms of both the precision of positioning estimates and the consistency there of: Root Mean Squared Error (RMSE)(m), 1 σ error (m) and 2 σ error(m).

3.2   Comparative Analysis

The comparative analysis of the proposed CAFGO method against several prevalent temporal data optimization models and several benchmark algorithms as

---

[1] https://github.com/brentyi/jaxfg.

delineated in Table 1. Experimental results show that compared with the EKF baseline, the RMSE of the proposed model is reduced by 60.49%. Compared to the LSTM network, the model achieves a 66.84% RMSE reduction in KITTI. The negative effect of the LSTM model on this task is that it is difficult to extract the features of multi-sensors effectively, and simply fusing data features without considering their structure will introduce more noise. For the fixed weight method, initial values were set based on domain knowledge, achieving meter-level positioning error. Traditional methods, such as Gaussian approaches, perform well under ideal Gaussian noise conditions but often fail to adapt to real-world scenarios' more complex non-Gaussian noise. The Huber method, known for its robustness to outliers, exhibits better performance but does not achieve the adaptability required for optimal sensor fusion. In contrast, the CAFGO method consistently outperforms these methods, quickly responding to environmental changes and optimizing the weights of multi-source sensor data in real-time, providing more accurate weight estimation.

Table 1. Positioning accuracy of different fusion models.

Dataset	Metrics	EKF	UKF	LSTM	Fixed	Gaussian	Huber	**CAFGO**
KITTI	RMSE (m)	1.62	1.31	1.93	1.13	0.92	0.87	**0.64**
	1 σ Error	1.98	1.49	2.37	1.39	1.28	1.13	**0.83**
	2 σ Error	2.42	1.76	2.61	1.75	1.57	1.46	**1.15**
UrbanNavDataset	RMSE (m)	1.63	1.21	2.53	1.26	1.04	1.18	**0.78**
	1 σ Error	1.85	1.33	2.67	1.54	1.32	1.37	**0.79**
	2 σ Error	2.36	1.95	3.73	2.88	2.65	2.71	**2.23**

In Fig. 2, we analyze using the GNSS factor as an example, where the red curve represents the error between the GNSS positioning results and the true values, and the green curve indicates the corresponding changes in the weight of the GNSS factor. It can be observed that as the error increases, the network correspondingly reduces the weight assigned to the GNSS factor. Conversely, when the error decreases, the corresponding weight is increased. This variation demonstrates that the method can accurately evaluate and assign appropriate weights to the information from various sensors, thereby obtaining a more precise estimate.

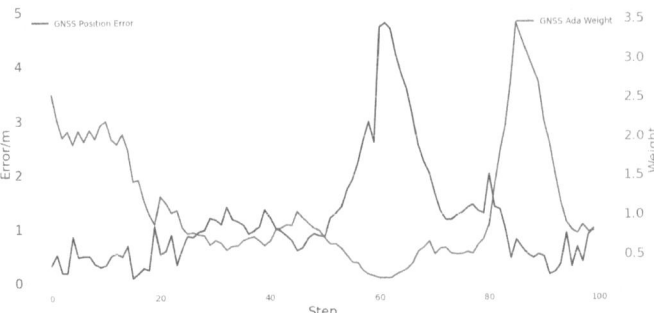

Fig. 2. Comparison of GNSS Positional Track Error Trends

4   Conclusion

This paper introduces a novel multi-component navigation and localization system that combines deep learning with factor graph optimization through an end-to-end approach, offering superior flexibility and performance over traditional post-optimization fusion methods. The CAFGO algorithm significantly improves multi-sensor fusion localization, especially in complex urban environments, by enhancing robustness and accuracy while addressing challenges related to data availability and variability. Experimental results demonstrate that CAFGO outperforms traditional methods like EKF, UKF, and LSTM networks on datasets such as KITTI and UrbanNav. Its adaptive weighting mechanism, which dynamically adjusts sensor confidence levels based on real-time data, outperforms conventional adaptive methods (Gaussian, Huber, and Baseline), significantly reducing RMSE and error bounds in challenging environments like urban canyons. Future work will focus on refining the integration of diverse data sources, exploring advanced network architectures for better interpretability and scalability, and incorporating additional sensor modalities, such as LiDAR, magnetometer, and barometric pressure sensors, to further enhance system robustness and accuracy.

Acknowledgements. This work was supported in part by the Strategic Priority Research Program of Chinese Academy of Sciences under Grant XDA28040500, the National Natural Science Foundation of China under Grant 62261042, the Key Research Projects of the Joint Research Fund for Beijing Natural Science Foundation and the Fengtai Rail Transit Frontier Research Joint Fund under Grant L221003, the Beijing Natural Science Foundation under Grant 4232035 and 4222034, and the BUPT Excellent Ph.D. Students Foundation CX2022131.

References

1. Niu, X., Tang, H., Zhang, T., Fan, J., Liu, J.: Ic-gvins: a robust, real-time, ins-centric gnss-visual-inertial navigation system. IEEE Rob. Autom. Lett. **8**(1), 216–223 (2022)
2. Boguspayev, N., Akhmedov, D., Raskaliyev, A., Kim, A., Sukhenko, A.: A comprehensive review of gnss/ins integration techniques for land and air vehicle applications. Appl. Sci. **13**(8), 4819 (2023)
3. Dong, Y., Wang, D., Zhang, L., Li, Q., Jie, W.: Tightly coupled gnss/ins integration with robust sequential kalman filter for accurate vehicular navigation. Sensors **20**(2), 561 (2020)
4. Wen, W., Pfeifer, T., Bai, X., Hsu, L.T.: Factor graph optimization for gnss/ins integration: a comparison with the extended kalman filter. NAVIGATION: J. Inst. Navig. **68**(2), 315–331 (2021)
5. Clark, R., Wang, S., Wen, H., Markham, A., Trigoni, N.: Vinet: visual-inertial odometry as a sequence-to-sequence learning problem. In: Proceedings of the AAAI Conference on Artificial Intelligence, vol. 31 (2017)
6. Liu, Y., Luo, Q., Zhou, Y.: Deep learning-enabled fusion to bridge gps outages for ins/gps integrated navigation. IEEE Sens. J. **22**(9), 8974–8985 (2022)
7. Fan, W., et al.: Predicting the noise covariance with a multitask learning model for kalman filter-based gnss/ins integrated navigation. IEEE Trans. Instrum. Meas. **70**, 1–13 (2020)
8. Liu, N., Hui, Z., Zhong, S., Qiao, L., Dong, Y.: Integrated navigation on vehicle based on low-cost sins/gnss using deep learning. Wireless Pers. Commun. **126**(3), 2043–2064 (2022)
9. Zhu, R., Yang, M., Liu, W., Song, R., Yan, B., Xiao, Z.: Deepavo: efficient pose refining with feature distilling for deep visual odometry. Neurocomputing **467**, 22–35 (2022)

MFNAS: Multi-fidelity Exploration in Neural Architecture Search with Stable Zero-Shot Proxy

Wei Fu, Wenqi Lou$^{(\boxtimes)}$, Yunji Qin, Lei Gong, Chao Wang, and Xuehai Zhou

University of Science and Technology of China, Hefei, China
{fw1219,qinyunji_21}@mail.ustc.edu.cn,
{louwenqi,leigong0203,cswang,xhzhou}@ustc.edu.cn

Abstract. Neural architecture search (NAS) automates the design of neural networks for specific tasks. Recently, zero-shot NAS has attracted much attention. Unlike traditional NAS, which relies on training to rank architectures, zero-shot NAS uses gradients or activation information to evaluate architecture performance. However, existing zero-shot NAS methods are limited by their inconsistent architecture ranking and the evaluation bias of their search algorithm, making it challenging to discover networks with high accuracy efficiently. To address this dilemma, this paper proposes an efficient and stable search framework for zero-shot NAS. Firstly, we design a stable zero-shot proxy, which achieves good consistency with network accuracy by utilizing filtered gradient information. On this basis, we employ a multi-fidelity evolutionary algorithm for efficient exploration. This algorithm utilizes multi-fidelity proxies to correct the bias towards certain types of networks and enhances the ability to distinguish high-performing architectures, achieving rapid convergence through performance-directed multi-point crossover and mutation. Experimental results conducted on NATS-Bench demonstrate that our framework can discover high-performance architectures within minutes of GPU time, outperforming existing training-free and training-based NAS methods. The code is available at https://github.com/mine7777/MFNAS.

Keywords: Neural Architecture Search · Evolution Algorithm · Zero-Shot

1 Introduction

In the past few years, deep neural networks (DNNs) have been widely used in fields such as computer vision and natural language processing [3,9]. However, the pursuit of high network accuracy has resulted in an increase in network size and network complexity. Manual neural network design requires expert knowledge and repeated trials, making the time cost and demand for computing resources increase. To this end, researchers proposed neural architecture search

(NAS), which reduces labor costs by automatically exploring optimal architectures [2,7].

The design space of network architecture grows exponentially with the topologies and sizes of network layer operators (10^{18} in DARTS [16]), so NAS focuses on finding high-performance neural networks efficiently. Based on how network architectures are ranked and evaluated, NAS methods can be categorized into three types: N-shot, one-shot, and zero-shot [24]. N-shot NAS, the earliest method, trains all sampled networks from scratch and ranks them based on test accuracies. While accurate, this approach is time-consuming and resource-intensive [2]. To strike a balance between network architecture ranking consistency and training overhead, one-shot NAS integrates all possible networks into a supernet and uses weight-sharing techniques to evaluate each subnet, significantly reducing training overhead [6,16]. However, this method still faces a heavy burden of network training, requiring several GPU days. Zero-shot NAS, a recent approach that completely avoids training overhead and can discover high-quality solutions within a few GPU hours, has received widespread attention [13,15,19].

The process of zero-shot NAS begins with the search algorithm providing the networks to be evaluated in each iteration. Then, the zero-shot proxy assesses the network and ranks architectures accordingly. Guided by the ranking of network architectures, the search algorithm selects the next networks for evaluation until a stopping condition is met, e.g., a certain number of iterations. Ultimately, the algorithm outputs the network with the highest score. The proxy can score the network based on the number of parameters/FLOPS or use network weights or gradients through a small amount of forward and backward propagation to avoid network training entirely [12].

We find that the existing zero-shot NAS still has problems with ranking consistency and search efficiency. Firstly, their proxies often incorporate noise gradients from the network that have excessively high or low values and result in a disparity between proxy-based rankings and actual accuracy rankings. Moreover, their search processes use random sampling or simple evolutionary algorithms, so their evolution of the architectures is inevitably influenced by evaluation bias or fails to capture the traits of superior architectures, resulting in relatively low search efficiency and search results [13,15].

To solve these problems, we propose a multi-fidelity evolutionary search framework for zero-shot NAS. We design a stable zero-shot proxy, filter gradient information according to the degree of gradient aggregation, and then use gradient consistency to score network architectures. Besides, we adopt a multi-fidelity evolutionary algorithm using low-fidelity and high-fidelity proxies to screen the current optimal architecture, thereby balancing bias in the early searching process. With multi-point crossover and mutation, it can complete the exploration of the design space. Integrating the proxy and the search algorithm, our framework can quickly converge to high-accuracy architectures. Overall, the main contributions of this paper are:

- We propose a stable zero-shot proxy that uses gradient information as input. The proxy first filters noisy gradient information and then utilizes the gradient consistency of the network to score the architecture.
- We propose an evolutionary search algorithm based on zero-shot proxy, enhancing its ability to identify excellent networks through a multi-fidelity approach. By combining evaluation feedback, we conduct multi-point crossover and mutation of the network architecture, thereby achieving fast convergence of the search algorithm.
- Experimental results on two benchmarks(NATS-Bench-TSS and NATS-Bench-SSS) show that scores of the network given by our zero-shot proxy are highly correlated with the actual accuracies. Using the proxy, our multi-fidelity evolutionary algorithm effectively improves the convergence speed of the search algorithm. The accuracy of the resulting optimal network architecture surpasses that of previous training-based and training-free methods.

2   Related Work

Training-based Neural Architecture Search: Neural Architecture Search (NAS) was introduced to minimize the trial and error involved in manual architecture design and was further used for joint search of software and hardware [17,18]. Early NAS approaches trained candidate architectures and used the resulting accuracy as a proxy. Baker et al. [2] utilized reinforcement learning to guide architecture exploration, requiring 10 GPUs for 8–10 days. To alleviate the time cost, One-shot NAS [4,16] reduced the number of trained networks to one by integrating all candidates into a supernet, ranking subnets through weight-sharing. Methods like DARTS and its variants [4,16] optimized the supernet using differentiable strategies and selected the final architecture.

Training-free NAS: To address the heavy training burden of traditional NAS methods, researchers have turned to focus on training-free NAS, also known as zero-shot NAS. Zero-shot NAS alleviates the bottleneck problem of the NAS algorithm by proposing proxies to evaluate the network. Some zero-shot proxies are based on network weights' importance [11,21,23], while others rely on intermediate results of network forward propagation [15,19]. Recently, ZiCo [13] introduced the gradient coefficient of variation as a ranking metric, outperforming the number of the parameters. Although ZiCo has a high correlation, it is affected by noisy gradients that have excessively high or low values and shows bias towards networks with more parameters. Furthermore, these training-free NAS methods rely on basic evolutionary algorithms or random selection for exploring the design space, which either cannot obtain the characteristics of excellent architecture or fall into the preferences of certain types of networks, thereby limiting search efficiency and search results.

Multi-fidelity Strategy: Multi-fidelity optimization typically uses multiple evaluators with different confidence levels, which have different characteristics and preferences. This method is initially used for hyperparameter optimization (HPO) in networks, with well-known examples being successive halving [10] and Hyperband [14]. Successive halving fixes resource quantity to evaluate each individual and decreases the individuals in each iteration. Hyperband combines multiple successive halving processes with different initializations. However, these methods are applied in training-based searches to consider the computational resources costs and final network accuracy. In zero-shot NAS, the bottleneck of the algorithm is no longer the huge training cost, but the accurate ranking and evaluation bias of the network.

3   Method

In this Section, we propose our zero-shot NAS framework. Compared with previous work, we optimize the process from two aspects: zero-shot proxy design and search algorithm. The framework overview is shown in Fig. 1.

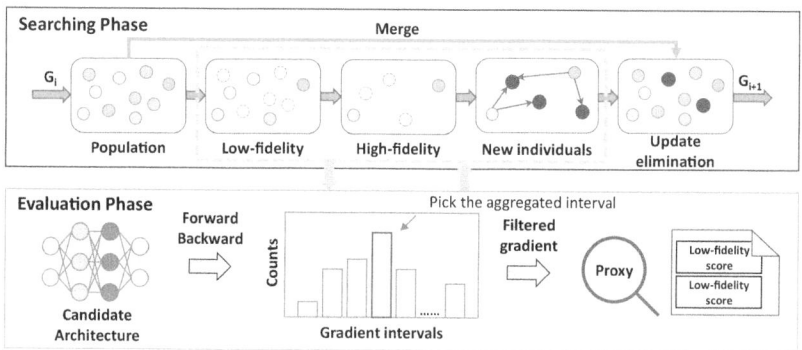

Fig. 1. The overview of our zero-shot NAS framework.

The evaluation phase reads an architecture as input and collects its gradients. Using the gradient filtering strategy, the low-fidelity and high-fidelity scores are obtained and sent to the search algorithm. During the search phase, we maintain a network architecture population, and the multi-fidelity search algorithm will invoke the evaluation phase to select current optimal individuals. Then we use the optimal ones to generate new individuals. After population update and elimination, we get the next generation. Iterating by the search algorithm, the multi-fidelity strategy will finally be performed on all explored architectures and output the optimal one.

3.1   Zero-Shot Proxy

We will introduce the design of the zero-shot proxy first. Our proxy uses gradient information as input. Gradients are used for the update of weight parameters in the neural network training process. Let $f(x, \theta)$ represent the neural network to be evaluated, where θ is the parameters of the neural network and x is the input of the neural network. We use $B = \{(x_1, y_1), (x_2, y_2)...(x_b, y_b)\}$ to denote the data in a batch. x_i and y_i is the i-th input and label respectively and θ_j is the j-th weight. The calculation of the gradients can be expressed as Eq. 1.

For a good network, we hope that the gradients of different training data for a single parameter are similar, because higher consistency of the gradient among a batch means a smaller probability of network parameter update oscillations, and can lead to higher accuracy. To this end, we propose a basic version of the zero-shot proxy GCO_{base} to represent the gradient consistency. First, we use data from several mini-batches to calculate gradients. Then we compute the consistency of the gradients obtained from different batches to represent the oscillation probability of network weight updates. We use $B_k = \{(x_1, y_1), (x_2, y_2), ...(x_b, y_b)\}, k \in [1, n]$ to denote one of the n training batches with a batch size of b. Then our basic gradient consistency proxy is expressed as Eq. 2.

$$grad(\theta_j, B) = \frac{1}{b} \sum_{i=1}^{b} \frac{\partial Loss(y_i, f(x, \theta))}{\partial \theta_j} \tag{1}$$

$$GCO_{base}(grad(\Theta, \mathbf{B})) = \sum_{i=1}^{L} log(\sum_{\theta_j \in \Theta_i} \frac{|E_{B_k} grad(\theta_j, B_k)|}{\sqrt{Var_{B_k} grad(\theta_j, B_k)}}) \tag{2}$$

where L is the number of network layers and Θ, Θ_i is all parameters of the network and the i-th layer, respectively. The higher the value of this score, the more stable the gradients of different batches are, and the faster the training loss of the corresponding network architecture is reduced. Note that we preserve the sign of the gradient when summing it up. The sign of the gradient indicates the direction of the gradient update and can be used to capture the oscillation of weight parameters caused by gradients in the opposite direction.

Evaluation Bias Correction: Our GCO_{base} can effectively represent the consistency of the gradient, but it is obviously affected by the number of network parameters and is easily biased towards networks with more parameters like existing zero-shot proxies. However, the increase in the number of parameters does not always bring significant network performance gains. Instead, layers without network parameters such as residual connections can effectively improve network performance, which cannot be captured by GCO_{base}. To correct our zero-shot proxy's preference for the number of parameters, we propose a gradient consistency correction term, called GCO_{mean}, which weakens the impact of the number of parameters in a single network layer by dividing the number of parameters. The calculation formula of GCO_{mean} is shown as Eq. 3.

$$GCO_{mean}(grad(\Theta, \mathbf{B})) = \sum_{i=1}^{L} log(\frac{1}{|\Theta_i|} \sum_{\theta_j \in \Theta_i} \frac{|E_{B_k} grad(\theta_j, B_k)|}{\sqrt{Var_{B_k} grad(\theta_j, B_k)}}) \tag{3}$$

Gradient Filter: Past zero-shot methods use all gradient information to evaluate network performance. However, gradients that are too large or too small are not conducive to the convergence of the network, and blindly utilizing all information may lead to evaluation bias [25]. For gradients that are too large or too small, we call them gradient noise. In order to determine the noise range of each network architecture, we use fine-grained gradient preprocessing to filter the noise information before calculating the zero-shot proxy. Specifically, for each network, we collect all gradients and divide them into different intervals according to their absolute values. Then, we select the interval with the highest gradient density for the calculation of the proxy, while the gradients in other intervals will be filtered out, as shown in Fig. 1. Assuming that Θ' is the filtered gradient, the proxy expression of filtered-grad consistency is as follows:

$$\text{FGCO}_{base}(grad(\Theta, \mathbf{B})) = \text{GCO}_{base}(grad(\Theta', \mathbf{B})) \tag{4}$$

$$\text{FGCO}_{mean}(grad(\Theta, \mathbf{B})) = \text{GCO}_{mean}(grad(\Theta', \mathbf{B})) \tag{5}$$

3.2   Multi-fidelity Evolution Algorithm

In the multi-fidelity evolutionary algorithm, we maintain a population and explore the search space through population update and elimination. Different from previous approaches [13,15] where architectures for mutation are directly selected by proxy or chosen randomly, we employ a multi-fidelity strategy to select several high-quality architectures to balance the evaluation bias. Selected architectures serve as parents to generate new individuals, preserving the architectural traits of superior networks. The new individuals are merged with the previous generation and eliminated based on the low-fidelity proxy. We will discuss the multi-fidelity mechanism, crossover and mutation processes respectively.

Multi-fidelity Strategy: The multi-fidelity mechanism of this paper aims to reduce the bias of the search process. It is divided into two parts.

The low-fidelity proxy uses the FGCO_{base} and the correction items FGCO_{mean} to distinguish network architectures and filter out the top-k network architectures. The fused two proxies prevent some potential architectures from being ignored in the early search. Our low-fidelity proxy is calculated by Eq. 6. The max in the equation means the maximum scores of all evaluated networks.

$$\text{Proxy}_{lowf} = \frac{\text{FGCO}_{base}}{max\,\text{FGCO}_{base}} + \frac{\text{FGCO}_{mean}}{max\,\text{FGCO}_{mean}} \tag{6}$$

The high-fidelity proxy is used to select the top architecture among the selected top-k. We use FGCO_{base} as our high-fidelity proxy because it is highly correlated with network accuracy, which is shown as Eq. 7.

$$\text{Proxy}_{highf} = \text{FGCO}_{base} \tag{7}$$

Crossover and Mutation: The population update depends on the crossover and mutation of individuals in the population. In our framework, we adopt a performance-directed crossover and mutation process. First, we use a multi-fidelity strategy to select outstanding individuals in the current population as parents. Subsequently, we designed multi-point crossover and mutation methods for the network architecture. In the search space of operator topology, the crossover child requires two parents' structures and inherits the parent operators randomly at the position of the changeable operator; mutation child can be completed by a single parent individual, with several mutation operators randomly selected and other positions retained. In the size search space, the changeable genes are the layer width. The variation in two types of search spaces is shown in Fig. 2.

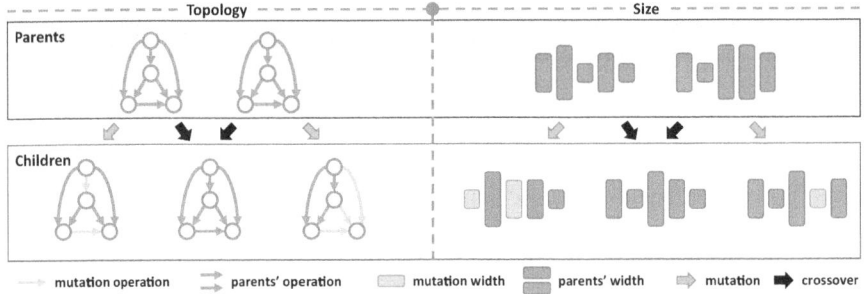

Fig. 2. Children individuals generated by multi-point mutation and crossover in topology and size search space.

4   Experiments

In this section, we show the effectiveness of the proposed proxy and our search results. We conduct the experiment in the same way as the previous zero-shot NAS works [13,15]. First, we verify the correlation between the ranking given by the zero-shot proxy and the actual accuracy ranking on two benchmarks. Subsequently, we present the search results obtained by our search framework on two popular benchmarks. Finally, we conduct ablation experiments to verify the effectiveness of the gradient noise filtering strategy and the multi-fidelity strategy.

Benchmark: We selects NATS-Bench [5] as the search benchmark. NATS-Bench is a popular NAS benchmark that can measure NAS algorithms in terms of network topology and network size. It contains two sub-search spaces: (1) **NATS-Bench-TSS**, also known as NASBench-201, contains 15625 different network architectures, and differences between networks are reflected in the topology. (2) **NATS-Bench-SSS** contains 32768 different network architectures, and the differences between these networks are reflected in the width of each network layer. Both benchmarks provide the accuracy of all architectures on CIFAR-10, CIFAR-100, and ImageNet-16–120 datasets. For the sake of brevity, we refer to these two datasets as TSS and SSS respectively.

4.1 Proxy Correlation Analysis

We used our proxy to rank network architectures on three datasets of two benchmarks, TSS and SSS, and calculated the correlation with the real rankings. We use Spearman's ρ(SPR) and Kendall's τ(KT) to represent the correlation coefficient. The range of both coefficients is $[-1,1]$. A larger coefficient (closer to 1) means the ranking is closer to the real accuracy ranking.

Baselines: We compare our proxy with existing zero-shot NAS proxies, including SNIP [11], GRASP [23], SynFlow [21], Fisher [22], GradNorm [1], NASWOT [19], ZenScore [15], GradSign [26], ZiCo [13]. In addition, as the parameters and FLOPs of the network are very effective estimators for network evaluation [12], we also add these two proxies to the baseline.

Table 1. Spearman's ρ(SPR) and Kendall's τ(KT) of different zero-shot proxies on NATS-Bench-TSS and NATS-Bench-SSS. CF10, CF100 and Img16 represent CIFAR-10, CIFAR-100, and ImageNet16-120, respectively.

Benchmark	TSS						SSS					
Dataset	CF10		CF100		Img16		CF10		CF100		Img16	
Coefficient	KT	SPR	KT	SPR	KT	SPR	KT	SPR	KT	SPR	KT	SPR
SNIP [11]	0.46	0.63	0.46	0.63	0.43	0.58	0.42	0.59	0.46	0.62	0.57	0.76
GraSP [23]	0.37	0.54	0.36	0.51	0.40	0.56	-0.09	-0.13	0.01	0.01	0.29	0.42
SynFlow [21]	0.54	0.73	0.57	0.76	0.56	0.75	0.61	0.81	**0.60**	**0.80**	0.39	0.57
Fisher [22]	0.40	0.55	0.41	0.55	0.37	0.50	0.30	0.44	0.41	0.55	0.33	0.47
GradNorm [1]	0.46	0.63	0.47	0.63	0.43	0.58	0.35	0.51	0.34	0.49	0.49	0.67
NASWOT [19]	0.57	0.77	0.62	0.80	0.60	0.78	0.45	0.63	0.43	0.59	0.42	0.59
ZenScore [15]	0.29	0.38	0.28	0.36	0.29	0.40	0.50	0.69	0.52	0.71	0.69	0.87
ZiCo [13]	0.61	0.80	0.61	0.81	0.60	0.79	0.54	0.73	0.55	0.75	0.70	0.88
GradSign [26]	0.58	0.77	0.59	0.79	0.59	0.78	0.21	0.30	0.16	0.27	0.04	0.05
Param	0.57	0.75	0.55	0.73	0.52	0.69	0.53	0.72	0.54	0.73	0.65	0.84
FLOPs	0.54	0.73	0.51	0.71	0.49	0.67	0.19	0.28	0.21	0.30	0.38	0.53
$FGCO_{base}$	**0.65**	**0.84**	**0.66**	**0.84**	**0.63**	**0.84**	**0.72**	**0.90**	0.53	0.72	**0.72**	**0.89**

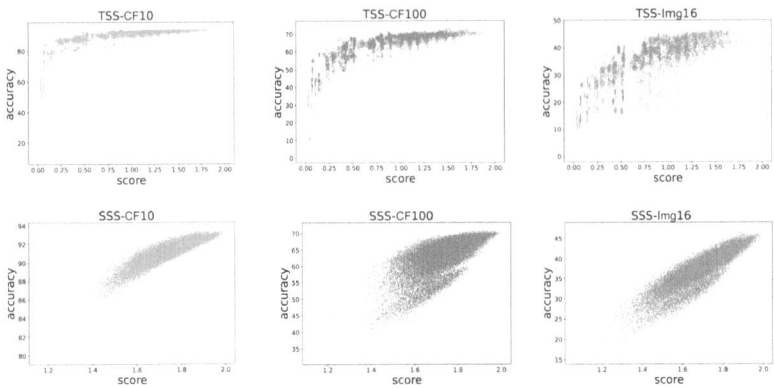

Fig. 3. Visualization of test accuracy versus GCO_{base} score on CIFAR-10, CIFAR-100, ImageNet16-120 of NATS-Bench-TSS and NATS-Bench-SSS

Results: As shown in Table 1, our proxy is not only highly correlated with accuracy, but also outperforms existing zero-shot proxies in most scenarios. Especially on CIFAR-10 of SSS, the Spearman's ρ of our proxy reaches 0.9 ($[-1,1]$), which is 11.1% higher than the highest among previous proxies. For ZiCo [13] proposed by the latest zero-shot work, we maintain a higher consistency in most cases. Due to the differences in various application scenarios, no zero-shot proxies can be completely applicable to all datasets [12]. Although the correlation doesn't beat all baselines on the CIFAR-100 dataset of SSS, we found that the results we searched were still the best in further experimental verification.

Moreover, the positive correlation between test accuracy and the proxy score is visualized in Fig. 3. The overall upward trend means that the higher the score given by our proxy, the higher the actual accuracy of the network. We can see that architectures with higher scores are likely to achieve higher accuracy.

4.2   Search Result Comparision

To evaluate the performance of the search framework proposed in this paper, we conduct search experiments on two benchmarks, NATS-Bench-TSS and NATS-Bench-SSS. With proposed metrics and multi-fidelity search algorithms, our framework explores the network architecture space with 50 populations, 75 iterations, and no restrictions on resources.

Results on TSS: We select existing training-based NAS methods and training-free NAS methods as baselines. The results in Table 2 show that our method outperforms all benchmarks. Compared with the training-based method, our method not only searches for architectures with higher accuracy but also reduces the search GPU second from 2e4 to 300, which means that the search efficiency has been improved by 66.7x. Compared with the training-free method, our framework keeps the search time in minutes of GPU time and brings a promoted accuracy in all datasets.

Table 2. Mean ± std accuracies and time cost on NATS-Bench-TSS with different NAS methods. Time of training-based methods are taken from [12]. Time of zero-shot methods is recorded on 1 NVIDIA A100.

	GPU Sec.	CIFAR-10	CIFAR-100	ImageNert16-120	Method
REA [20]	2e4	93.92 ± 0.30	71.84 ± 0.99	45.54 ± 1.03	N-shot
BOHB [8]	2e4	93.61 ± 0.52	70.85 ± 1.28	44.42 ± 1.49	N-shot
Darts- [4]	11520	93.80 ± 0.40	71.53 ± 1.51	45.12 ± 0.82	One-shot
Naswot [19]	306	92.96 ± 0.81	69.98 ± 1.22	44.44 ± 2.10	Zero-shot
Gradsign [26]	167	93.31 ± 0.47	70.33 ± 1.28	42.42 ± 2.81	Zero-shot
ZiCo [13]	334	94.0 ± 0.4	71.1 ± 0.3	41.8 ± 0.3	Zero-shot
Ours	**225**	**94.21 ± 0.19**	**72.91 ± 0.88**	**46.34 ± 0**	Zero-shot
Resnet [9]	-	93.37	70.86	43.63	Manual
optimal	-	94.37	73.51	47.31	-

Results on SSS: We compare our framework with previous zero-shot NAS work on the SSS dataset. Results from previous work are taken from [12]. The search results are shown in Table 3. It can be seen that the actual test accuracy of the optimal architecture given by our zero-shot framework is very close to the optimal accuracy in the dataset. Besides, our search result is higher than previous proxies, showing our framework's keen identification of the optimal architecture.

Table 3. Test accuracy (%) of searched architectures on NATS-Bench-SSS with different zero-shot proxies.

	optimal	SNIP [11]	Synflow [21]	Zenscore [15]	GradSign [26]	#Param	Ours
CF100	70.92	68.36	66.84	69.92	57.40	70.28	**70.36**
Img16	46.73	45.63	35.37	46.27	33.97	44.73	**46.33**

4.3 Ablation Study

Our ablation experiments are conducted on TSS. We evaluate the impact of gradient filtering strategies and multi-fidelity strategies.

Impact of Gradient Filtering Strategy: We randomly select 1000 architectures for experiments on CIFAR-10, CIFAR-100, and ImageNet16-120 on TSS, and calculate the correlation between scores given by proxy and accuracy before and after the gradient filtering strategy. The results in Table 4 show that after adopting the gradient filtering strategy, Spearman's ρ and Kendall's τ between proxy scores and actual network accuracy have been improved, indicating that this strategy can effectively improve the consistency of ranking of network architecture by proxy.

Table 4. The ablation study of gradient filtering strategy on proxy design.

	CIFAR-10		CIFAR-100		ImageNet16-120	
	KT	SPR	KT	SPR	KT	SPR
w/o grad filter	0.61	0.81	0.62	0.81	0.61	0.80
Ours	**0.66**	**0.84**	**0.67**	**0.85**	**0.63**	**0.82**

Impact of Multi-fidelity Strategies: We visualize our search process of CIFAR-10, CIFAR-100 and ImageNet16-120 on TSS. Figure 4 shows the changes in the optimal accuracy given by the algorithm as the search algorithm iterates. To conduct comparative experiments on multi-fidelity strategies, we evaluate the results of using only correction term $FGCO_{mean}$, high-fidelity proxy $Proxy_{highf}$, low-fidelity proxy $Proxy_{lowf}$ and multi-fidelity strategies respectively. Figure 4 shows that the multi-fidelity strategy can converge quickly and select excellent architectures, leading to less search time. In addition, the variability of our multi-fidelity algorithm is minimized, showing that the strategy enhanced the stability of the search process.

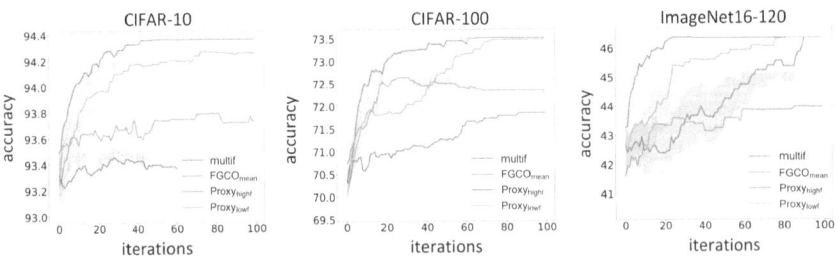

Fig. 4. The ablation study of multi-fidelity strategy on NATS-Bench-TSS. Standard deviations are scaled down by a factor of 3 for visualization purposes. The multif represents using the multi-fidelity strategy as fitness.

5   Conclusion

In this paper, we introduce a search framework for zero-shot NAS that utilizes filtered gradient information to enhance ranking consistency through a stable zero-shot proxy. We propose an evolutionary algorithm incorporating a multi-fidelity strategy, performance-directed crossover, and mutation for zero-shot NAS. Experimental results on the NATS-Bench benchmarks demonstrate that our framework rapidly converges to high-performance architectures. Moreover, our metrics exhibit a strong correlation with accuracy, enabling searches within minutes and outperforming both training-free and training-based network architectures.

Our future work will focus on expanding our framework to a broader range of NAS scenarios. We also plan to integrate our search framework with hardware design space to optimize the performance across different platforms.

Acknowledgments. This work is partially supported by the National Key R&D Program of China (under Grant 2017YFA0700900, 2017YFA0700903), the USTC Research Funds of the Double First-Class Initiative (under Grant YD2150002011), and the National Natural Science Foundation of China (under Grants 62102383 and 62172380).

References

1. Abdelfattah, M.S., et al.: Zero-cost proxies for lightweight NAS. In: 9th International Conference on Learning Representations, ICLR (2021)
2. Baker, B., et al.: Designing neural network architectures using reinforcement learning. In: International Conference on Learning Representations (2016)
3. Brown, T., et al.: Language models are few-shot learners. In: Advances in Neural Information Processing Systems (2020)
4. Chu, X., Wang, X., Zhang, B., Lu, S., Wei, X., Yan, J.: Darts-: robustly stepping out of performance collapse without indicators. In: International Conference on Learning Representations (2020)
5. Dong, X., Liu, L., Musial, K., Gabrys, B.: Nats-bench: benchmarking nas algorithms for architecture topology and size. IEEE Trans. Pattern Anal. Mach. Intell. **44**(7), 3634–3646 (2021)
6. Dong, X., Yang, Y.: Searching for a robust neural architecture in four gpu hours. In: Proceedings of the IEEE/CVF Conference On Computer Vision and Pattern Recognition (2019)
7. Elsken, T., Metzen, J.H., Hutter, F.: Neural architecture search: a survey. J. Mach. Learn. Res. **20**(55), 1–21 (2019)
8. Falkner, S., et al.: Bohb: robust and efficient hyperparameter optimization at scale. In: International Conference on Machine Learning (2018)
9. He, K., et al.: Deep residual learning for image recognition. In: Proceedings of the IEEE Conference on Computer Vision and Pattern Recognition (2016)
10. Jamieson, K., Talwalkar, A.: Non-stochastic best arm identification and hyperparameter optimization. In: Artificial intelligence and statistics (2016)
11. Lee, N., Ajanthan, T., Torr, P.: Snip: single-shot network pruning based on connection sensitivity. In: International Conference on Learning Representations (2018)

12. Li, G., Hoang, D., Bhardwaj, K., Lin, M., Wang, Z., Marculescu, R.: Zero-shot neural architecture search: Challenges, solutions, and opportunities. IEEE Transactions on Pattern Analysis and Machine Intelligence (2024)

13. Li, G., Yang, Y., Bhardwaj, K., Marculescu, R.: Zico: zero-shot NAS via inverse coefficient of variation on gradients. In: The Eleventh International Conference on Learning Representations, ICLR (2023)

14. Li, L., et al.: Hyperband: a novel bandit-based approach to hyperparameter optimization. J. Mach. Learn. Res. **18**(185), 1–52 (2018)

15. Lin, M., et al.: Zen-nas: a zero-shot nas for high-performance image recognition. In: Proceedings of the IEEE/CVF International Conference on Computer Vision (2021)

16. Liu, H., et al.: DARTS: differentiable architecture search. In: 7th International Conference on Learning Representations, ICLR (2019)

17. Lou, W., et al.: Unleashing network/accelerator co-exploration potential on fpgas: a deeper joint search. IEEE Transactions on Computer-Aided Design of Integrated Circuits and Systems (2024)

18. Lou, W., et al.: Octcnn: a high throughput fpga accelerator for cnns using octave convolution algorithm. IEEE Trans. Comput. **71**(8), 1847–1859 (2021)

19. Mellor, J., et al.: Neural architecture search without training. In: International Conference on Machine Learning (2021)

20. Real, E., et al.: Regularized evolution for image classifier architecture search. In: Proceedings of the AAAI Conference on Artificial Intelligence (2019)

21. Tanaka, H., Kunin, D., Yamins, D.L., Ganguli, S.: Pruning neural networks without any data by iteratively conserving synaptic flow. In: Advances in Neural Information Processing Systems (2020)

22. Turner, J., et al.: Blockswap: fisher-guided block substitution for network compression on a budget. In: 8th International Conference on Learning Representations, ICLR (2020)

23. Wang, C., et al.: Picking winning tickets before training by preserving gradient flow. In: 8th International Conference on Learning Representations, ICLR (2020)

24. Xie, X., Song, X., Lv, Z., Yen, G.G., Ding, W., Sun, Y.: Efficient evaluation methods for neural architecture search: a survey. arXiv e-prints, pp. arXiv–2301 (2023)

25. Yang, L., et al.: Sweet gradient matters: Designing consistent and efficient estimator for zero-shot architecture search. Neural Netw. **168**, 237–255 (2023)

26. Zhang, Z., Jia, Z.: Gradsign: model performance inference with theoretical insights. In: The Tenth International Conference on Learning Representations, ICLR (2022)

DyAGL: A Dynamic-Aware Adaptive Graph Learning Network for Next POI Recommendation

Tianci Wang[1,2], Yantong Lai[1,2(✉)], Yiyuan Wang[3], and Ji Xiang[1]

[1] Institute of Information Engineering, Chinese Academy of Sciences, Beijing, China
{wangtianci,xiangji}@iie.ac.cn
[2] School of Cyber Security, University of Chinese Academy of Sciences, Beijing, China
laiyantong.ucas@gmail.com
[3] Harbin Institute of Technology, Harbin, China

Abstract. Next point-of-interest (POI) recommendation is a flourishing task within location-based services, where user check-in behaviors are influenced not only by their personal preferences and current intents but also by the intricate geographical dependencies among POIs. Existing methods generally construct pre-defined POI graphs and learn unified static representations. However, the pre-defined graphs heavily depend on domain knowledge and data quality. Few studies have explored the feasibility of adaptive graph learning to replace manually designed graphs, but they ignore the important dynamic dependencies among POIs in spatial-temporal scenarios. To tackle these challenges, we propose a novel framework **Dy**namic-aware **A**daptive **G**raph **L**earning (DyAGL) for next POI recommendation. Specifically, to capture dynamic and intricate dependencies among POIs, we first design a spatial-temporal enhanced adaptive graph learning module, which mines fine-grained geographical dependencies automatically via similarity learning of POI embeddings. Moreover, we propose a dynamic personalized intent-aware module that incorporates the learned fine-grained representations of POIs and personalized spatial-temporal information to further capture user dynamic behavioral intents and preferences. Extensive experiments on three real-world public datasets demonstrate the superior performance of DyAGL.

Keywords: Next POI recommendation · Graph structure learning · Graph convolutional networks · Attention mechanism

1 Introduction

Next Point-of-interest (POI) recommender systems assist users in discovering attractive places from massive activity service providers, which have become a crucial task to address 'where to go next' concerns in location-based social network (LBSN) services. Considering users' historical trajectories with rich spatial-temporal information, next POI recommendation aims to capture their personal preferences, current intents and provide suitable destinations [2,3].

© The Author(s), under exclusive license to Springer Nature Singapore Pte Ltd. 2025
R. Hadfi et al. (Eds.): PRICAI 2024, LNAI 15281, pp. 361–374, 2025.
https://doi.org/10.1007/978-981-96-0116-5_30

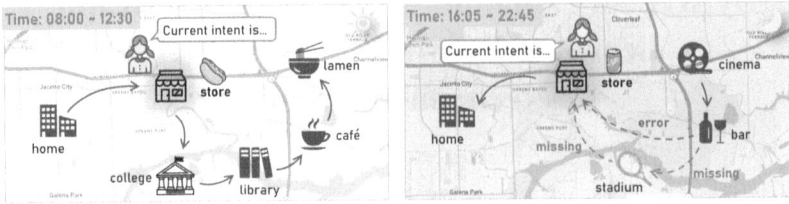

Fig. 1. A motivating example of the dynamic information in Jessica's trajectories

To benefit from the inherent spatial-temporal dependencies in human mobility patterns, next POI recommendation is typically characterized by modeling sequential, periodicity, and geographical correlation to depict user personalized interests [11]. Earlier sequence-based studies generally incorporate spatial-temporal interval information between successive check-ins to explore the user transition patterns from a local view, ranging from Markov Chains, Recurrent Neural Networks (RNNs) [9] to self-attention mechanisms [7]. Recently, representation learning based on flexible Graph Neural Networks (GNNs) has been explored to capture high-order collaborative signals of POIs from a global view, alleviating the filter bubble effects [1] and enhancing the expressiveness of POI embeddings. For instance, Graph-Flashback [8] constructs a spatial-temporal knowledge graph for POI representation learning and integrates the learned graph into existing sequential models to better capture transition patterns. Zone-enhanced method ToP [10] pre-defines graphs based on the geographical distance and transition patterns among POIs, as well as the transition frequency of categories.

Although prior GNN-based methods have achieved considerable performance, there are still some notable limitations. **First, most prior methods mainly rely on pre-defined graphs, which heavily depend on domain knowledge and data quality.** The correlations of POIs in real-world are complex and diverse, constructing POI-POI relation graphs under the guidance of empirical knowledge (e.g., transition similarity assumption [13]) may not capture the potential dependencies effectively. Furthermore, pre-defined graphs are also influenced by the dataset quality. In Fig. 1, the absence of check-in record '*stadium*' leads to the creation of missing and erroneous edges, which would introduce noise into the graph topology and result in low-quality POI representations. **Second, few studies have explored adaptive graph learning for next POI recommendation, but they limited to static topologies, ignoring important dynamic dependencies in spatial-temporal scenarios.** For example, we observe that Jessica enjoys stopping by the store in the morning to buy something for breakfast. After hearty exercise at night, she tends to visit the store to purchase a drink. It can be found that the '*store*' offers services like '*breakfast restaurant*' in the morning, and has a closer dependency with $\{college, library, café\}$. At night, the services of '*store*' are more like '*drink shops*' and the relation is closer to $\{stadium, bar, cinema\}$. Static graphs fail to portray dynamic relations adequately, and the learned low-quality representations could further limit the capture of users' preferences and current behavioral intentions.

To address above limitations, we propose a novel method Dynamic-aware Adaptive Graph Learning Network (DyAGL). Specifically, we design a fine-grained spatial-temporal enhanced adaptive graph learning module to explore the dynamic dependencies among POIs in different contexts via graph structure learning. Instead of manually designing complicated graph construction rules, the module learns graph topologies by applying node similarity metrics on POI embeddings. Subsequently, we devise a dynamic personalized intent-aware module under the guidelines of periodicity, sequential and dynamic geographical dependencies. The module integrates a well-designed personalized intent self-attention layer and a trajectory spatial-temporal attention layer, incorporating fine-grained POI representations learned from the adaptive graphs to model user preferences and current behavioral intentions. Finally, we design a multi-task prediction and optimization module to jointly iterate and optimize adaptive graph structures as well as node embeddings. In summary, our main contributions are as follows:

- We propose a novel method DyAGL for next POI recommendation, which leverages fine-grained graph structure learning to alleviate the limitations of traditional static pre-defined graphs, and fully explore the dynamic dependencies among POIs influenced by spatial-temporal factors.
- We develop a dynamic personalized intent-aware module that leverages a well-designed personalized intent self-attention layer and a trajectory attention layer to capture user preferences and dynamic intents in different spatial-temporal scenarios.
- Extensive experiments on three real-world LBSN datasets demonstrate that DyAGL significantly outperforms existing state-of-the-art recommendation methods.

2   Related Work

Sequential-Based POI Recommendation. With the flourishing of deep learning techniques, sequential-based neural networks including RNNs and attention mechanisms dominate the next POI recommendation tasks. Considering the pivotal role of spatial-temporal factors in capturing user preferences, a surge of studies attempt to incorporate these information into sequential-based models. LSTPM [9] extends several LSTM units with a context-aware non-local network to learn long and short term user preferences. Flashback [14] equips RNN with spatial-temporal intervals and computes an aggregated hidden state from past multi-level periodicity patterns. CHA [18] uses a spatial-temporal decay LSTM and explores the category hierarchy with attention mechanism to enhance the robustness of POI representations. STAN [7] extends attention mechanism by spatial-temporal interval matrices to intensify the relation between non-consecutive POIs in check-in sequences. However, the sequential-based methods exhibit some inherent drawbacks and lead to low-quality node representations, i.e., oversimplifying the impact of complex spatial-temporal factors on user mobility behavior, and relying solely on local view to learn embeddings.

GNN-Based POI Recommendation. Inspired by the great success of GNNs, recent efforts attempt to characterize relations among POIs from global view and improve the expressiveness of POI embeddings by graph representation learning. SGRec [4] adopts the graph attention network to extract user trajectory patterns from the global view for learning POI representations and user preferences. HMT-GRN [5] designs a graph recurrent network to learn sequential dependencies and POI embeddings by pre-defined spatial-temporal graphs. GETNext [16] encodes user transition patterns by conducting graph convolution on a well-designed user-agnostic global trajectory flow map. AGRAN [12] explores latent static geographical dependencies among POIs creatively by graph structure learning and learns more expressive representations. In general, existing GNN-based approaches rely on sub-optimal pre-defined or static graph structures, which fail to capture the latent dynamic dependencies among POIs influenced by temporal factors, thus significantly degrading the performance of representation learning.

3   Problem Formulation

Let $\mathcal{U} = \{u_1, u_2, ..., u_{|\mathcal{U}|}\}$ denotes a set of $|\mathcal{U}|$ users and $\mathcal{P} = \{p_1, p_2, ..., p_{|\mathcal{P}|}\}$ denotes a set of $|\mathcal{P}|$ POIs. Each POI $p_i \in \mathcal{P}$ is a real-world place and is represented by a unique geographical coordinate tuple (lon_i, lat_i). A check-in record $l_k^{u_i} = (u_i, p_k, t_k)$ indicates that user u_i has visited POI p_k at timestamp t_k. The trajectory of user u_i is a sequence $\mathcal{S}^{u_i} = \{l_1^{u_i}, l_2^{u_i}, ..., l_{|\mathcal{S}^{u_i}|}^{u_i}\}$ that consists of all his/her check-in records sorted by chronological order. All users trajectories can be described as $\mathcal{S} = \{\mathcal{S}^{u_1}, \mathcal{S}^{u_2}, ..., \mathcal{S}^{u_{|\mathcal{U}|}}\}$.

Problem: (Next POI Recommendation). Based on users' historical trajectories $\mathcal{S}$, for each user u_i, when u_i sends a recommendation request at the next time t_{k+1}, our goal is to recommend a top-K POI list that best satisfies his/her current behavioral intent.

4   Method

4.1   Fine-Grained Spatial-Temporal Enhanced Adaptive Graph Learning

Fine-Grained Adaptive Graph Construction. For graph representation learning methods like Graph Convolutional Networks (GCNs), the effectiveness of learned embeddings is primarily determined by adjacency matrix. Based on empirical knowledge or self-formulated rules, prior researchers have explored the utilization of various pre-defined adjacency matrices. However, the relations of POIs are not static.

To increase the expressivity of POI representations, as shown in Fig. 2, the week is initially divided into $\mathcal{T} = \{1, 2, ..., |\mathcal{T}|\}$ time slots. For each time slot $\tau \in \mathcal{T}$, we initialize a d-dimensional trainable embedding matrix $H_\tau = \{p_1^\tau, p_2^\tau, ..., p_{|\mathcal{P}|}^\tau\} \in \mathbb{R}^{|\mathcal{P}| \times d}$ for all POIs, and obtain the set $H = \{H_\tau | \tau = 1, 2, ..., |\mathcal{T}|\} \in \mathbb{R}^{|\mathcal{T}| \times |\mathcal{P}| \times d}$ for all time slots. Inspired by work [12], we utilize embedding similarity to infer the dynamic dependencies among POIs in different temporal contexts automatically. To be specific, for each pair of POIs $< p_i, p_j >$, we assess their dependencies at τ by computing the latent vector similarity with the following weighted cosine function:

$$A_{i,j}^\tau = cos\left(p_i^\tau W_{sim}^\tau, p_j^\tau W_{sim}^\tau\right), \tag{1}$$

where $A_{i,j}^\tau \in [-1, 1]$ represents an entry of adjacency matrix A^τ, and $W_{sim}^\tau \in \mathbb{R}^{d \times d}$ is a trainable matrix for embedding projection in time slot τ. During the training, as the optimization of POI embeddings progresses, the adjacency matrix A^τ would also be updated adaptively, gradually approaching an optimal graph topology.

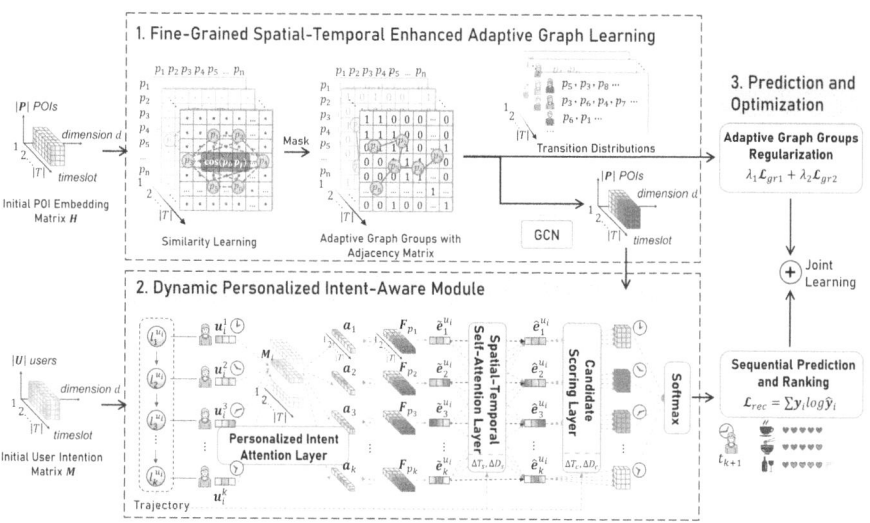

Fig. 2. The overall architecture of DyAGL

Fine-Grained Adaptive Graph Sparsification. From the preceding steps, we derive a collection of fully connected adjacency matrices $A = \{A^\tau | \tau = 1, 2, ..., |\mathcal{T}|\}$. Then, we sparsify each matrix to reduce computational costs:

$$\hat{A}^\tau_{i,j} = \begin{cases} 1, & A^\tau_{i,j} \geq \delta \\ 0, & otherwise \end{cases} \tag{2}$$

where threshold δ influences the sparsity of graph adjacency matrices and we set $\delta = 0.4$ in this paper. $\hat{A}^\tau_{i,j} \in \{0, 1\}$ is the entry of matrix $\hat{A}^\tau$.

Fine-Grained Adaptive Graph Convolution. By leveraging neighbors information and employing propagation-aggregation operations with spectral GCN on adaptive graph $\hat{A}^\tau$, we enhance the expressivity of learned POI representations to better capture their roles and characteristics within the overarching graph structure. For each time slot τ, we have:

$$H^{l+1}_\tau = \sigma(\hat{D}^{-\frac{1}{2}}_\tau \hat{A}^\tau \hat{D}^{-\frac{1}{2}}_\tau H^l_\tau W^l_\tau), \tag{3}$$

where $\hat{D}_\tau$ is the degree matrix and H^l_τ represents the message of POIs at l-th layer. W^l_τ denotes a trainable matrix and $\sigma(\cdot)$ is the sigmoid function. $H^{l+1}_\tau \in \mathbb{R}^{|\mathcal{P}| \times d}$ denotes the updated representations. Due to leveraging cosine similarity in adaptive graph construction, the self-similarity of each POI is numerically equal to 1. Therefore, there is no need an additional self-connection operation $\hat{A}_\tau = \hat{A}_\tau + I$ for ego information aggregation.

4.2 Dynamic Personalized Intent-Aware Module

Previous studies have found that human mobility trajectories exhibit pronounced temporal periodicity, sequential and geographical dependencies. Therefore, we first design a personalized intent attention layer to fully explore the periodic patterns in check-in behaviors. Then, a spatial-temporal self-attention layer is devised to model the influence of spatial-temporal factors on user dynamic intents.

Personalized Intention Attention Layer. We initialize a set of $|\mathcal{T}|$ latent vectors $M_i = \{u_i^1, u_i^2, ..., u_i^{|\mathcal{T}|}\} \in \mathbb{R}^{|\mathcal{T}| \times d}$ for each user $u_i \in \mathcal{U}$, where $u_i^\tau \in M_i$ represents the primary intent representation of user u_i in time slot τ. The fine-grained trainable intent matrix of all users can be denoted as $M = \{M_i | i = 1, 2, ..., |\mathcal{U}|\} \in \mathbb{R}^{|\mathcal{T}| \times |\mathcal{U}| \times d}$. To facilitate training, given a trajectory sequence $\mathcal{S}^{u_i}$, we set a maximum length L and fetch a fixed-length session $s^{u_i} = \{l_1^{u_i}, l_2^{u_i}, ..., l_L^{u_i}\}$ by truncating the whole check-in sequence $\mathcal{S}^{u_i}$ if $|\mathcal{S}^{u_i}| \geq L$ or padding to the left otherwise without affecting the experimental outcomes. Each record $l_k^{u_i} = (u_i, p_k, t_k)$ has three features: user id u_i, location id p_k and specific check-in timestamp t_k. We project t_k to its corresponding time slot τ_k, yielding a new triplet (u_i, p_k, τ_k). From the fine-grained intent matrix M_i, we extract the corresponding intent embedding $u_i^{\tau_k}$ and perform intent attention operation:

$$a_k = \text{softmax}\left(\frac{u_i^{\tau_k} W^Q \cdot (M_i W^K)^\top}{\sqrt{d}}\right), \tag{4}$$

where the attention coefficient $a_k \in \mathbb{R}^{|\mathcal{T}|}$ quantifies the correlation of the behavioral intent of user u_i in τ_k with other time periods. $W^Q, W^K \in \mathbb{R}^{d \times d}$ are weight matrices. Then, we extract the vectors at all time slots from matrix H by check-in POI id p_k and form a new matrix $F_{p_k} = \{p_k^1, p_k^2, ..., p_k^{|\mathcal{T}|}\} \in \mathbb{R}^{|\mathcal{T}| \times d}$. Finally, we transform the fetched sequence s^{u_i} into a latent embedding sequence $\tilde{E}_{(hist)}^{u_i} = \{\tilde{e}_1^{u_i}, \tilde{e}_2^{u_i}, ..., \tilde{e}_L^{u_i}\} \in \mathbb{R}^{L \times d}$ with:

$$\tilde{e}_k = \sum_{i=1}^{|\mathcal{T}|} a_k^i \cdot p_k^i \cdot W^V, \tag{5}$$

where $W^V \in \mathbb{R}^{d \times d}$, a_k^i is an entry of a_k and $p_k^i \in F_{p_k}$ denotes the activity connotation of POI p_k in time slot i. $\tilde{e}_k \in \tilde{E}_{(hist)}^{u_i}$ is the representation of check-in record $l_k^{u_i}$.

Spatial-Temporal Self-attention Layer. Explicitly modeling spatial-temporal context has been proven to be advantageous in understanding user preferences. We leverage the spatial-temporal interval between m-th and n-th check-ins to depict personalized fine-grained dependencies. First, the spatial-temporal relation matrices is defined as:

$$\begin{cases} T_{m,n}^{(hist)} = \psi(\Delta t_{m,n}^{u_i}) \\ D_{m,n}^{(hist)} = \psi(\Delta d_{m,n}^{u_i}), \end{cases} \tag{6}$$

here $\Delta t_{m,n}^{u_i} = |t_m - t_n| \in \mathbb{N}$, and $\Delta d_{m,n}^{u_i} = \text{Haversine}^1(lon_m, lat_m, lon_n, lat_n) \in \mathbb{N}$ is used to calculate the distance between two POIs. $\psi(x) = 1/log(e + x)$ is a decay function. $T_{m,n}^{(hist)}$ and $D_{m,n}^{(hist)}$ are entries of the history temporal and spatial matrix $T^{(hist)}, D^{(hist)} \in \mathbb{R}^{L \times L}$ respectively. Then, we merge two weight matrix by:

$$\Delta_{TD}^{(hist)} = \rho \cdot T^{(hist)} + (1 - \rho) \cdot D^{(hist)}, \tag{7}$$

where $\Delta_{TD}^{(hist)} \in \mathbb{R}^{L \times L}$ and ρ is a balance parameter.

Subsequently, to equip our DyAGL with the effective capability of capturing multiple dependencies within trajectories, we design an extension to self-attention that integrates spatial-temporal information for dynamic personalized preference modeling:

$$\hat{E}_{(hist)}^{u_i} = \text{softmax}\left(\frac{\tilde{E}_{(hist)}^{u_i} W^Q \cdot (\tilde{E}_{(hist)}^{u_i} W^K)^\top + \Delta_{TD}^{(hist)}}{\sqrt{d}} \right) \cdot \tilde{E}_{(hist)}^{u_i} W^V, \tag{8}$$

where $W^Q, W^K, W^V \in \mathbb{R}^{d \times d}$. Then, each $\tilde{e}_k \in \tilde{E}_{(hist)}^{u_i}$ is transformed to a new representation $\hat{e}_k$ and the updated representation of sequence s^{u_i} is $\hat{E}_{(hist)}^{u_i} = \{\hat{e}_1^{u_i}, \hat{e}_2^{u_i}, ..., \hat{e}_L^{u_i}\}$.

Candidate Scoring Layer. Similarly, we calculate distance between candidate POIs and history check-ins to construct candidate spatial matrix $D^{(cand)} \in \mathbb{R}^{|\mathcal{P}| \times L}$. In constructing candidate temporal matrix, we calculate the time difference between the next recommendation request send and each history check-in occurrence, deriving $T^{(cand)} \in \mathbb{R}^L$. Then we expand $T^{(cand)}$ to match the dimensions of $D^{(cand)}$ and obtain the candidate spatial-temporal matrix $\Delta_{TD}^{(cand)}$. The score of each candidate POI is calculate as follows:

$$\hat{y}^{u_i} = \text{Sum}\left(\text{softmax}\left(\frac{E_{(cand)}^{u_i} \cdot [\hat{E}_{(hist)}^{u_i}]^\top + \Delta_{TD}^{(cand)}}{\sqrt{d}} \right) \right), \tag{9}$$

where $E_{(cand)}^{u_i} = \{p_1^{\tau_{k+1}}, p_2^{\tau_{k+1}}, \cdots, p_{|\mathcal{P}|}^{\tau_{k+1}}\} \in \mathbb{R}^{|\mathcal{P}| \times d}$ is all candidate POI embeddings at time slot τ_{k+1} fetched from matrix H. Sum$(\cdot)$ denotes summation across the last dimension. The preference assessment vector $\hat{y}^{u_i} = \{\hat{y}_1^{u_i}, \hat{y}_2^{u_i}, ..., \hat{y}_{|\mathcal{P}|}^{u_i}\} \in \mathbb{R}^{|\mathcal{P}|}$, where the entry $\hat{y}_j^{u_i}$ indicates the extent that user u_i would like to visit POI p_j at time t_{k+1}.

4.3 Prediction and Optimization

We leverage a multi-task learning strategy to jointly optimize the fine-grained adaptive graph structures, nodes dynamic embeddings and next POI recommendation task.

---

^{1} https://pypi.org/project/haversine/.

Fine-Grained Adaptive Graph Regularization. In experiments, we observe that early convergence of the model is challenging. This is primarily due to the quality of the early adjacency matrices heavily relies on the initialization of POI embeddings, which may lead to sub-optimal solutions and difficulty in model convergence.

To solve this problem, we make a reasonable assumption that the real geographical dependencies does not deviate excessively from the transition patterns among POIs exhibited in trajectories. In this case, we attempt to directly conduct the parameter regularization towards the optimal graph topology. We construct an approximate distribution matrix $G = \{G^1, G^2, ..., G^{|\mathcal{T}|}\} \in \mathbb{R}^{|\mathcal{T}| \times |\mathcal{P}| \times |\mathcal{P}|}$ by transition patterns and utilize it as supervision to optimize the adaptive graph. Each entry $G_{i,j}^{\tau} \in G^{\tau}$ is denoted as the frequency that users have visited both POI p_i and p_j during the same period τ. The discrepancy between two discrete distributions is measured by KL divergence:

$$\mathcal{J}_{gr1} = \frac{1}{|\mathcal{P}| \cdot |\mathcal{T}|} \sum_{\tau=1}^{|\mathcal{T}|} \sum_{i=1}^{|\mathcal{P}|} KL(\text{softmax}(G_i^{\tau}) || \text{softmax}(\hat{A}_i^{\tau})), \qquad (10)$$

where G_i^{τ} and $\hat{A}_i^{\tau}$ represent the i-th row of G^{τ} and $\hat{A}^{\tau}$ respectively. $KL(\cdot||\cdot)$ denotes the KL divergence formula. Additionally, to alleviate the problem of node embedding collapse, we introduce an unsupervised loss function based on negative sampling:

$$\mathcal{J}_{gr2} = -\sum_{\tau=1}^{|\mathcal{T}|} \sum_{i=1}^{|\mathcal{P}|} \left[\frac{1}{|Pos_i^{\tau}|} \sum_{m \in Pos_i^{\tau}} \log \sigma \left(p_i^{\tau} p_m^{\tau \mathrm{T}} \right) + \frac{1}{|Neg_i^{\tau}|} \sum_{n \in Neg_i^{\tau}} \log \sigma \left(-p_i^{\tau} p_n^{\tau \mathrm{T}} \right) \right] \qquad (11)$$

where Pos_i^{τ} denotes the neighbors of node p_i in time slot τ, and Neg_i^{τ} represents the set of randomly selected negative samples.

Sequential Prediction and Ranking. The dynamic personalized intent awareness module can be broadly regarded as a sequence prediction process, so we formulate the learning objective as a cross-entropy loss function:

$$\mathcal{J}_{rec} = -\sum_{u_i \in \mathcal{U}} \sum_{s^{u_i} \in \mathcal{S}^{u_i}} \sum_{j=1}^{|\mathcal{P}|} \left[y_j^{s^{u_i}} \log(\hat{y}_j^{s^{u_i}}) + (1 - y_j^{s^{u_i}}) \log(1 - \hat{y}_j^{s^{u_i}}) \right], \qquad (12)$$

where $\hat{y}_j^{s^{u_i}}$ is an entry of $\hat{y}^{s^{u_i}}$, and $y_j^{s^{u_i}}$ equals to 1 if p_j is the real visit of user u_i at next time in session s^{u_i} and 0 otherwise. Finally, we obtain the hybrid learning objective $\mathcal{J}$:

$$\mathcal{J} = \mathcal{J}_{rec} + \lambda_1 \mathcal{J}_{gr1} + \lambda_2 \mathcal{J}_{gr2} + \mu ||\Theta||_2, \qquad (13)$$

where λ_1, λ_2 control the weight of supervised graph regularization and unsupervised graph learning, respectively. $||\Theta||_2$ denotes the $L2$ regularization under the influence of the parameter μ.

5   Experiments

5.1   Experimental Setup

We conduct experiments on three real-world datasets of Foursquare [15,17]: NYC, TKY[2] and SIN[3]. In line with earlier studies, we first filter out POIs with less than 10 visits, sort the check-ins by time. Then divide them into non-overlapping sets, allocating the first 70% of check-ins for training and the rest for testing. The statistical overview of each dataset after pre-processing is shown in Table 1.

Table 1. Statistical information of three datasets.

Dataset	#Users	#POIs	#Check-ins	#Sessions	#Sparsity
NTC	1,083	5,135	147,938	5,689	99.35%
TKY	2,293	7,873	447,570	16,407	99.32%
SIN	2,320	3,600	170,119	7,104	98.94%

5.2   Baseline Models

We contrast DyAGL with several representative methods and briefly introduce them. (1) **ST-RNN** [6]: The first model to consider spatial-temporal factors in sequential neural networks. (2) **LSTPM** [9]: A novel LSTM-based method that captures long- and short-term preferences with a non-local and geo-dilated network. (3) **STAN** [7]: An attention-based method that incorporates non-contiguous visits and non-adjacent locations. (4) **SGRec** [4]: A GNN-based method using a Seq2Graph mechanism to extract collaborative signals among POIs from global check-in trajectories. (5) **HMT-GRN** [5]: A novel GNN-based method that uses graph neural network and multi-granularity region matrices to alleviate data sparsity. (6) **GETNext** [16]: A GCN-based model that captures common visiting-order transitions on a customized global trajectory flow map. (7) **AGRAN** [12]: A novel GCN-based method exploring graph structure learning to model complex geographical dependencies among POIs.

5.3   Evaluation Metrics and Parameter Settings

The model produces a personalized list for each user, with the top-K POIs that the user is most likely to visit. We employ standard evaluation metrics, Recall@K for assessing recommendation accuracy and NDCG@K for evaluating the quality of the ranked list. Specifically, we report the metrics for $K \in \{5, 10, 20\}$, calculating each metric 5 times and taking the average.

---

[2] http://www-public.imtbs-tsp.eu/~zhang_da/pub/dataset_tsmc2014.zip.

[3] https://personal.ntu.edu.sg/gaocong/data/poidata.zip.

We maintain the parameter settings from the original papers for the baselines. For our DyAGL, we pad each pre-processed session to a maximum length of $L = 30$ and divide a week into $|\mathcal{T}| = 21$ time slots. The balance parameter ρ is set to 0.5. We adopt Adam as optimizer with the learning rate $1e^{-3}$, λ_1 of 0.25 and $\lambda_2 = 1 - \lambda_1$. The coefficient μ of $L2$ regularization is set to $1e^{-4}$ and dropout rate of 0.3. The hidden dimension d is established at 64 with a batch size of 30 and 50 negative samples.

5.4 Performance Comparisons

The recommendation performance of our DyAGL and the baselines on three datasets is summarized in Table 2, with relative improvement calculated against the best baselines. The results reveal the following insights:

Table 2. Performance comparison of next POI recommendation on three datasets

Dataset	Metrics	ItemPop	ST-RNN	LSTPM	STAN	SGRec	HMT-GRN	GETNext	AGRAN	DyAGL	%Improv.
NYC	R@5	0.0428	0.2536	0.2668	0.2578	0.2619	0.2670	<u>0.2744</u>	0.2467	**0.3108**	13.27%
	R@10	0.0497	0.2840	0.3193	0.3317	0.3338	0.3382	<u>0.3580</u>	0.3379	**0.3704**	3.46%
	R@20	0.0656	0.3027	0.3711	0.4077	0.3967	0.4146	<u>0.4209</u>	0.4022	**0.4357**	3.52%
	N@5	0.0232	0.1904	0.2001	0.1880	0.1799	<u>0.2014</u>	0.1853	0.1683	**0.2162**	7.35%
	N@10	0.0254	0.2113	0.2135	0.2122	0.2028	<u>0.2172</u>	0.2126	0.1981	**0.2376**	9.39%
	N@20	0.0294	0.2160	0.2303	0.2315	0.2185	<u>0.2403</u>	0.2287	0.2145	**0.2674**	11.28%
TKY	R@5	0.0991	0.2372	0.2467	0.2462	0.2218	0.2516	<u>0.2778</u>	0.2439	**0.2840**	2.23%
	R@10	0.1288	0.2826	0.3089	0.3151	0.2951	<u>0.3364</u>	0.3359	0.3241	**0.3545**	5.38%
	R@20	0.1581	0.3208	0.3594	0.3870	0.3794	<u>0.4031</u>	0.3898	0.3863	**0.4062**	3.03%
	N@5	0.0642	0.1825	0.1834	0.1671	0.1517	0.1801	<u>0.2035</u>	0.1647	**0.2110**	0.77%
	N@10	0.0737	0.1972	0.2036	0.1893	0.1757	<u>0.2235</u>	0.2223	0.1911	**0.2339**	3.69%
	N@20	0.0811	0.2069	0.2166	0.2075	0.1974	0.2336	<u>0.2361</u>	0.2071	**0.2456**	4.02%
SIN	R@5	0.0393	0.1146	0.1092	<u>0.1638</u>	0.1479	0.1588	0.1637	0.1610	**0.1801**	9.95%
	R@10	0.0643	0.1370	0.1479	<u>0.2129</u>	0.1888	0.1905	0.2063	0.1949	**0.2271**	6.67%
	R@20	0.0972	0.1687	0.1880	<u>0.2680</u>	0.2347	0.2364	0.2538	0.2440	**0.2837**	5.86%
	N@5	0.0213	0.0868	0.0770	0.1243	0.1128	0.1223	<u>0.1302</u>	0.1253	**0.1381**	6.64%
	N@10	0.0292	0.0941	0.0897	0.1399	0.1260	0.1323	<u>0.1428</u>	0.1365	**0.1532**	6.07%
	N@20	0.0374	0.1020	0.0998	0.1540	0.1378	0.1439	<u>0.1548</u>	0.1489	**0.1649**	6.52%

- Our DyAGL surpasses all baseline models across each metric. For instance, on the NYC dataset, it outperforms the best baselines by 3.52% – 13.27%. We attribute the improvements to several key factors: (1) DyAGL captures dynamic and intricate geographical dependencies among POIs using fine-grained adaptive graph structure learning in diverse spatio-temporal scenarios. (2) DyAGL smoothly incorporates fine-grained POI representations into a dynamic intent-aware recommendation framework, enabling the capture of user preferences and evolving behavioral intentions. (3) By employing the multi-task learning strategy, DyAGL continuously optimizes the graph topology and boosts recommendation performance.

- Attention-based methods are more competitive than statistical and RNN-based methods due to the ability of capturing complex relations between non-adjacent check-ins. The success of STAN demonstrates the significance of modeling spatial-temporal information in next POI recommendation. However, these methods are still restricted to local views and fail to consider the higher-order dependencies.
- GNN-based methods distil higher-order collaborative signals from the global POI relation graphs and achieve more impressive performance than other baselines, but they are still constrained by sub-optimal pre-defined graph topologies.
- AGRAN innovatively explores the significance of leveraging graph structure learning to model the complex dependencies among POIs. However, from a certain perspective, the graph learned by AGRAN is still static and sub-optimal because it ignores important dynamic dependencies among POIs in spatial-temporal scenarios.

5.5 Ablation Study

We create four variants to assess DyAGL's component effectiveness. $DyAGL_{w/o\ Graph}$ skips constructing and training fine-grained adaptive graphs, instead randomly initializing embedding vectors for all POIs. $DyAGL_{w/o\ Intent}$ removes the personalized intent attention layer and generates the trajectory representation sequences directly with POI embeddings. $DyAGL_{w/o\ ST-hist}$ and $DyAGL_{w/o\ ST-cand}$ remove the historical and candidate spatio-temporal weight matrices, $\Delta_{TD}^{(hist)}$ and $\Delta_{TD}^{(cand)}$, respectively.

Figure 3 displays the ablation results, and we have some findings: (1) $DyAGL_{w/o\ Graph}$ only leverages local information to optimize fine-grained POI representations, leading to obvious performance degradation. This reconfirms the effectiveness of our adaptive graph representation learning in capturing dynamic spatio-temporal dependencies among POIs. (2) $DyAGL_{w/o\ Intent}$ highlights the importance of capturing users' personalized dynamic intents, which exhibit periodic relations across different time slots. Our personalized intent attention layer mines these correlations, reducing discrepancies in similar user intent representations across different spatio-temporal contexts. (3) $DyAGL_{w/o\ ST-hist}$ and $DyAGL_{w/o\ ST-cand}$ show that explicitly modeling spatial-temporal factors play an important role in capturing complex user transition patterns.

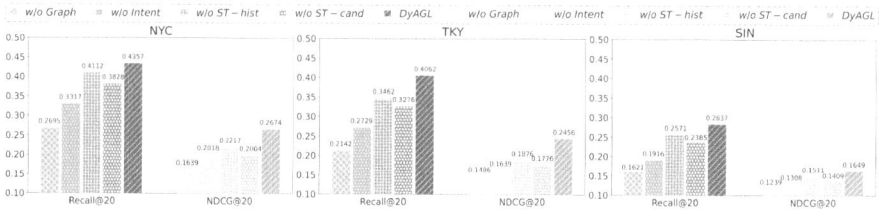

Fig. 3. Performance comparison for variants of DyAGL on three datasets

5.6   Hyperparameter Analysis

In Fig. 4, we further analyze the impact of key hyperparameters by controlling variables. (1) It is evident that the model's performance is limited when the dimension is less than 64. This suggests that low-dimensional embeddings struggle to represent extensive fine-grained information. (2) We vary the negative sample number $|Neg_i^\tau|$ in from 0 to 100 and find that performance stabilizes when the number reaches 50. (3) Performance drop noticeably when the number of time slots $|\mathcal{T}|$ exceed 21. We hypothesize that this increase intensifies graph sparsity, leading to poorer node embeddings. (4) We observe that overly small δ values often result in the adjacency matrix $\boldsymbol{A}$ being filled with ones, making model convergence challenging. (5) Proper supervised signals enhance graph structure learning efficiency. However, when λ_1 approaches 1, the fine-grained adaptive graphs are compelled into a fixed topology structure. Moreover, as λ_2 nears 0, the absence of graph contrastive constraints leads to overly smoothed node embeddings. (6) The spatio-temporal balance parameter has little effect on model performance.

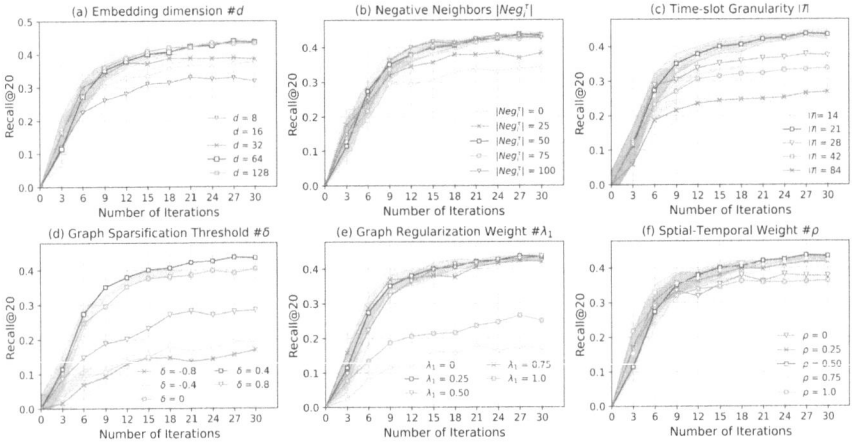

Fig. 4. Analysis of key hyperparameters on NYC dataset

6   Conclusion and Future Work

This paper propose a novel network DyAGL for next POI recommendation. We initially adopt node similarity learning to capture intricate POI dependencies in spatial-temporal scenarios, followed by a dynamic personalized intent-aware module. Comprehensive experiments validate the effectiveness of DyAGL. For future work, we will investigate instant graph representation learning methods to alleviate the issue of high training costs towards large-scale streaming data.

References

1. Kitchens, B., Johnson, S.L., Gray, P.: Understanding echo chambers and filter bubbles: the impact of social media on diversification and partisan shifts in news consumption. MIS Q. **44**(4), 1619–1649 (2020)
2. Lai, Y., et al.: Disentangled contrastive hypergraph learning for next poi recommendation. In: Proceedings of the 47th International ACM SIGIR Conference on Research and Development in Information Retrieval, pp. 1452–1462 (2024)
3. Lai, Y., Su, Y., Wei, L., Wang, T., Zha, D., Wang, X.: Adaptive spatial-temporal hypergraph fusion learning for next poi recommendation. In: ICASSP 2024-2024 IEEE International Conference on Acoustics, Speech and Signal Processing, pp. 7320–7324. IEEE (2024)
4. Li, Y., Chen, T., Luo, Y., Yin, H., Huang, Z.: Discovering collaborative signals for next POI recommendation with iterative Seq2Graph augmentation. In: IJCAI International Joint Conference on Artificial Intelligence, pp. 1491–1497. AAAI Press (2021)
5. Lim, N., Hooi, B., Ng, S.K., Goh, Y.L., Weng, R., Tan, R.: Hierarchical multi-task graph recurrent network for next poi recommendation. In: Proceedings of the 45th International ACM SIGIR Conference on Research and Development in Information Retrieval, pp. 1133–1143 (2022)
6. Liu, Q., Wu, S., Wang, L., Tan, T.: Predicting the next location: a recurrent model with spatial and temporal contexts. In: Proceedings of the AAAI Conference on Artificial Intelligence, vol. 30, no. 1 (2016)
7. Luo, Y., Liu, Q., Liu, Z.: STAN: spatio-temporal attention network for next location recommendation. In: Proceedings of the Web Conference 2021, pp. 2177–2185 (2021)
8. Rao, X., Chen, L., Liu, Y., Shang, S., Yao, B., Han, P.: Graph-flashback network for next location recommendation. In: Proceedings of the 28th ACM SIGKDD Conference on Knowledge Discovery and Data Mining, pp. 1463–1471 (2022)
9. Sun, K., Qian, T., Chen, T., Liang, Y., Nguyen, Q.V.H., Yin, H.: Where to go next: modeling long-and short-term user preferences for point-of-interest recommendation. In: Proceedings of the AAAI Conference on Artificial Intelligence, vol. 34, no. 1, pp. 214–221 (2020)
10. Wang, E., Xu, Y., Yang, Y., Jiang, Y., Yang, F., Wu, J.: Zone-enhanced spatio-temporal representation learning for urban poi recommendation. IEEE Trans. Knowl. Data Eng. **35**, 9628–9641 (2023)
11. Wang, T., Lai, Y., Chen, G., Wang, R., Shen, J., Xiang, J.: A dynamic-aware heterogeneous graph neural network for next poi recommendation. In: Liu, F., Sadanandan, A.A., Pham, D.N., Mursanto, P., Lukose, D. (eds.) Pacific Rim International Conference on Artificial Intelligence, vol. 14325, pp. 313–326. Springer, Singapore (2023). https://doi.org/10.1007/978-981-99-7019-3_30
12. Wang, Z., Zhu, Y., Wang, C., Ma, W., Li, B., Yu, J.: Adaptive graph representation learning for next poi recommendation. In: Proceedings of the 46th International ACM SIGIR Conference on Research and Development in Information Retrieval, pp. 393–402 (2023)
13. Wang, Z., Zhu, Y., Zhang, Q., Liu, H., Wang, C., Liu, T.: Graph-enhanced spatial-temporal network for next poi recommendation. ACM Trans. Know. Discov. Data (TKDD) **16**(6), 1–21 (2022)
14. Yang, D., Fankhauser, B., Rosso, P., Cudre-Mauroux, P.: Location prediction over sparse user mobility traces using RNNs. In: Proceedings of The Twenty-Ninth International Joint Conference on Artificial Intelligence, pp. 2184–2190 (2020)
15. Yang, D., Zhang, D., Zheng, V.W., Yu, Z.: Modeling user activity preference by leveraging user spatial temporal characteristics in LBSNs. IEEE Trans. Syst. Man Cybern. Syst. **45**(1), 129–142 (2014)

16. Yang, S., Liu, J., Zhao, K.: GETNext: trajectory flow map enhanced transformer for next poi recommendation. In: Proceedings of the 45th International ACM SIGIR Conference on Research and Development in Information Retrieval, pp. 1144–1153 (2022)
17. Yuan, Q., Cong, G., Ma, Z., Sun, A., Thalmann, N.M.: Time-aware point-of-interest recommendation. In: Proceedings of the 36th International ACM SIGIR Conference on Research and Development in Information Retrieval, pp. 363–372 (2013)
18. Zang, H., Han, D., Li, X., Wan, Z., Wang, M.: CHA: categorical hierarchy-based attention for next poi recommendation. ACM Trans. Inf. Syst. (TOIS) 40(1), 1–22 (2021)

Acoustic Classification of Bird Species Using Improved Pre-trained Models

Jie Xie[1,2(✉)], Mingying Zhu[3,4], and Juan Gabriel Colonna[5]

[1] School of Computer and Electronic Information and School of Artificial Intelligence, Nanjing Normal University, Nanjing, China
xiej8734@gmail.com
[2] Key Laboratory of Modern Acoustics, MOE, Nanjing University, Nanjing, China
[3] School of Economics, Nanjing University, 22 Hankou Road, Nanjing 210093, Jiangsu, China
[4] Johns Hopkins University - Hopkins-Nanjing Center for Chinese and American Studies 162 Shanghai Road Nanjing University, Nanjing 210093, Jiangsu, China
[5] Federal University of Amazonas, Manaus, Amazonas, Brazil

Abstract. Acoustic classification of bird species plays an important role in accurately monitoring bird diversity. Traditional methods of bird species identification, such as visual observation and manual recording, can be time-consuming and require specialized expertise. Acoustic classification, which leverages the unique vocalizations of birds, offers a promising alternative for efficient and automated species identification. Previous studies have explored various pre-trained ImageNet models for acoustic classification of bird species. However, applying pre-trained ImageNet models directly to audio classification tasks presents a challenge due to the domain mismatch between visual and auditory data. In this study, we present a novel classification framework based on a pre-trained AudioNet model. In order to improve the performance of bird sound classification, the attention mechanism is used to generate important features and gated recurrent unit is used to capture temporal information. The experimental outcomes verify the effectiveness of our proposed system in the classification of bird audio segments, achieving impressive metrics: an accuracy of 97.88%, a precision of 97.95%, a recall of 97.29%, and an F1-score of 97.58%. These figures reflect the system's remarkable performance in distinguishing among 20 distinct bird species.

Keywords: Bird sound classification · Pre-trained model · Attention · GRU

1 Introduction

Acoustic classification of bird species plays an important role in accurately monitoring bird diversity. Traditional methods of bird species identification, such as visual observation and manual recording, can be time-consuming and require specialized expertise. Recent development of acoustic sensor networks provides

R. Hadfi et al. (Eds.): PRICAI 2024, LNAI 15281, pp. 375–382, 2025.
https://doi.org/10.1007/978-981-96-0116-5_31

a novel way to classify bird species using the unique vocalizations of birds [12]. Using an acoustic sensor per day, several gigabytes of compressed data can be generated which makes it necessary to develop automating species identification in acoustic data sets [11].

In recent years, the application of Convolutional Neural Networks (CNNs) has gained popularity in audio classification tasks. In this approach, audio signals are frequently transformed into two-dimensional representations, such as spectrograms, and subsequently processed by CNNs as if they were visual images. Constructing a CNN-based classification system often involves leveraging pre-trained models that have been extensively trained on large-scale visual datasets, such as ImageNet [5]. This approach has become a prevalent strategy due to its effectiveness and efficiency, which can offer a robust starting point for these classification tasks. However, applying pre-trained ImageNet models directly to audio classification tasks presents a challenge due to the domain mismatch between visual and auditory data.

To address the above issues, we present a novel classification framework based on a pre-trained AudioNet model. Here, the used CNN architecture is the pre-trained CNN14 from Pre-trained Audio Neural Networks [6]. In order to improve the performance of bird sound classification, the attention mechanism is used to generate important features and gated recurrent unit (GRU) is used to capture temporal information.

The remainder of this paper is organized as follows: Section 2 summarizes the related work on bird sound classification. Section 3 describes the methods. Section 3 describes the composition of audio datasets for the experiments, the CNN architectures used for bird sound classification. Section 4 describes the experiments conducted and evaluates the performance of different CNN architectures. Finally, Sect. 5 concludes the paper.

2   Related Work

In recent years, numerous studies have harnessed the power of pre-trained models for the classification of bird sounds. Zhong et al. [13] conducted a comparative analysis of three models for identifying 24 bird and amphibian species. They evaluated VGG-16 and ResNet-50, both equipped with custom loss functions and pseudo-labeling techniques. For the pre-trained model, they utilized the pre-trained weights of ResNet50 and fine-tuned the model by introducing a fully connected layer, a dropout layer, and an output layer. Sun et al. [9] leveraged the parameters of the Keras VGG-19 model for classifying animal sounds, where they explored the benefits of data augmentation and transfer learning, demonstrating improvements in performance. Dias et al. [3] employed a ResNet-50 model pre-trained on ImageNet [1] for classifying 12 bird and anuran species, also incorporating data augmentation to enhance performance. However, their findings indicated that a more compact network could outperform ResNet-50 pre-trained on ImageNet, particularly in fine-grained scenarios involving bird and anuran species. All the aforementioned models were pre-trained on ImageNet. Beyond ImageNet pre-trained models, models pre-trained on AudioNet have also been explored. Qiu et al. [8] utilized the VGGish transfer learning network, pre-trained by AudioSet [4], to classify 38 types of bird species associated with power grid faults, achieving better results than CNN models using spectrograms and Mel-spectrograms. In conclusion, pre-trained models have become a staple in the field of bird sound classification.

Despite the proven efficacy of these methods in classifying bird species using audio data, they often overlook the inherent domain discrepancies between visual and auditory data. Furthermore, to enhance the performance of bird sound classification, it is crucial to incorporate the selection of salient features and the capture of temporal information.

3 Methods

In Fig. 1, we illustrate the general structure of the proposed framework in this study. Here, the learnable parameters of PANNs are passed to our proposed models with inserted attention and GRU modules.

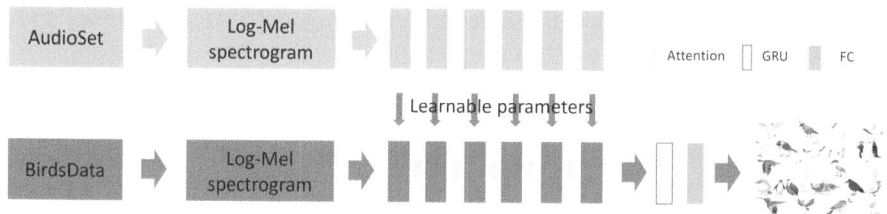

Fig. 1. The architecture of the proposed bird sound classification system. Here, GRU denotes gated recurrent unit and FC denotes fully connected layer.

3.1 Data Description

The data used is Birdsdata[1], which is curated and collected through a collaboration between the Beijing Zhiyuan Institute of Artificial Intelligence and Hundred Birds Data. The dataset comprises recordings of 20 prevalent bird species. All bird sound clips underwent rigorous noise reduction and were trimmed to uniform lengths. The Birdsdata includes 14,311 bird sound clips, whose duration is 2 s. However, the sampling rate of those recordings is non-uniform (Fig. 2).

3.2 Log-Mel Spectrogram

The bird sounds are converted into log-Mels spectrogram time-frequency representation, which is used as the input to the pretrained CNN. To be specific, we

---

[1] https://data.baai.ac.cn/details/Birdsdata, accessed on 20 October 2023.

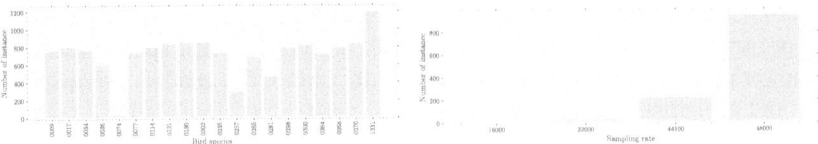

Fig. 2. Number of instances for all bird species of Birdsdata and Number of instances of different sampling rates.

first convert the audio data from stereo to mono by averaging both right and left channels. Then, the audio data is resampled to 48 kHz for standardizing the sampling rate (Fig. 2). Next, the data is normalized ranging between −1 and 1. Finally, we represent audio data through log-Mel spectrograms, utilizing a Hann window of 1024 samples and a hop length of 320 samples. The Mel-spectrogram is configured with 64 frequency bands, spanning from 50 Hz to 20 kHz, and employs a Fast Fourier Transform size of 1024. Finally, different from the original batch normalization used in CNN14, we apply Min-Max normalization to the obtained log-Mel-spectrogram. In addition, the generated log-Mel spectrogram is resized to [224, 224] when using the pre-trained ImageNet models and converted to a three-channel feature representation by simply repeating the spectrogram. For the CNN14, the spectrogram size is 64×301 with one channel.

3.3 Pre-trained Audio Neural Networks with CBAM and GRU

Kong et al. [6] introduced Pre-trained Audio Neural Networks (PANNs), a suite of models developed using the extensive AudioSet dataset [4]. This dataset encompasses 5000 h of audio content, categorized under 527 distinct sound labels. The PANNs project has released 15 pre-trained models to the public, including CNN10, CNN14, ResNet38, and ResNet54. These models were trained on audio snippets extracted from YouTube videos, forming a comprehensive repository of over 2 million audio recordings. The AudioSet dataset is meticulously curated, featuring a balanced training set comprising 22,160 audio files, with a minimum of 50 instances per sound class. Additionally, an evaluation set of 20,371 audio files is included, with each file being 10 s in length or padded with zeros to meet this duration requirement. These pre-trained models, particularly CNN10, CNN14, and ResNet54, have demonstrated exceptional performance in classification tasks across the 527 sound classes, setting new benchmarks in the field.

In our research, we have chosen to employ the CNN14 model as an encoder for characterizing bird sounds. This decision is informed by the model's proven capability to capture intricate audio features, which is crucial for accurate sound classification and analysis. To further improve the classification performance, Convolutional Block Attention Module (CBAM) and GRU are used. CBAM is an attention mechanism designed to enhance the feature representation capabilities of CNNs [10]. CBAM is particularly effective in improving the performance of CNNs on tasks such as image classification, object detection, and segmentation by allowing the network to focus on the most informative features and suppress less relevant ones. Here, we insert CBAM into CNN14 to improve the performance. GRU is a type of recurrent neural network (RNN) architecture used in deep learning, which helps the network to capture information from previous time steps more effectively than traditional RNNs [2].

In this study, we use CBAM to improve the spatial feature representation and use GRU's ability to capture long-term dependencies. Two strategies are explored for inserting CBAM and GRU into CNN14: *CBAM+GRU v1* adds CBAM between the convolultional blocks, while *CBAM+GRU v2* adds CBAM inside the convolutional block. As for the GRU, it is applied to the feature embedding of CNN14.

4   Experiments

4.1   Experimental Setup

For the training process, we employ a batch size of 32 and set the learning rate to 0.0001. The Adam optimizer is utilized to facilitate efficient convergence. The training is conducted over 200 epochs, ensuring thorough learning of the model parameters. In addition, SpecAugment [7] is used to improve the final classification performance. Here, the number of time and frequency steps for ResNet50 and EfficientNetB3 are 80, while they are set to 100 and 20, respectively for CNN14. As for the results, we implement a five-fold cross-validation methodology to assess the model's performance comprehensively. The aggregated outcomes are presented in terms of accuracy, precision, recall, and F1-score.

4.2   Experimental Results

Table 1 shows the classification performance of pre-trained ImageNet and AudioNet models. We can find that the pre-trained AudioNet model (CNN14) using SpecAugment achieves the highest accuracy, precision, recall, and F1-score amounting to 97.83%, 97.7%, 97.27%, and 97.43%, respectively. Without SpecAugment, CNN14 is also the best performing model, while EffcientNetB3 is the worst. Here, the pretrained CNN14 used Mel-spectrogram for obtaining the original weights, while both ResNet50 and EfficientNetB3 used nature image for getting the weights. Therefore, domain mismatch exists when using those models pre-trained on nature images (such as ImageNet) for classifying Mel-spectrogram. In addition, SpecAugment is proved to be an effective way to boost the performance for all pre-trained models. For CNN14, the accuracy, precision, recall, and F1-score is improved by 1.63%, 1.82%, 1.59%, and 1.71%, respectively.

Compared to the original CNN14, we apply Min-Max normalization to log-Mel-spectrogram rather than batch normalization. Figure 3 shows the effect of normalization, where batch normalization and Min-Max normalization are compared. We can observe that Min-Max normalization can obtain better performance than batch normalization.

Table 1. Classification performance of three pre-trained models with and without SpecAugment. Bold font indicates best result obtained

Model	Accuracy	Precision	Recall	F1-score
ResNet50 w/o specaug	0.9606	0.9567	0.9491	0.9524
EfficientNetB3 w/o specaug	0.9554	0.9542	0.9441	0.9478
CNN14 w/o specaug	0.9620	0.9588	0.9568	0.9572
ResNet50 w/ specaug	0.9667	0.9686	0.9585	0.9626
EfficientNetB3 w/ specaug	0.9762	0.9745	0.9685	0.9710
CNN14 w/ specaug	**0.9783**	**0.9770**	**0.9727**	**0.9743**

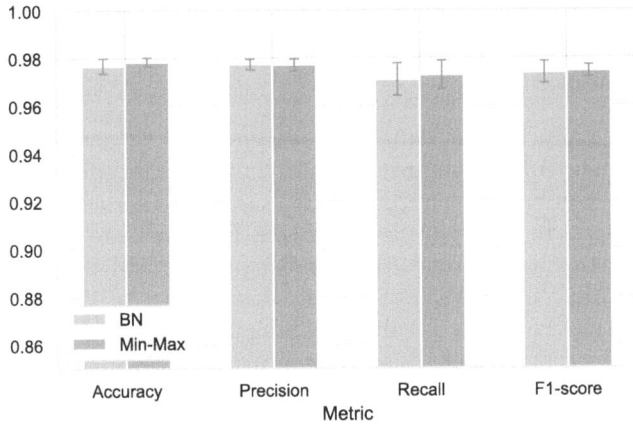

Fig. 3. Performance comparison between batch normalization and Min-Max normalization.

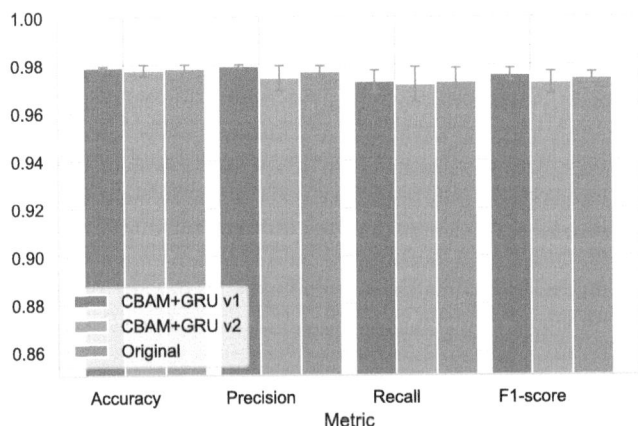

Fig. 4. Performance comparison of CNN14+CBAM+GRU and CNN14.

To further improve the classification performance, we add CBAM and GRU to CNN14. Figure 4 compares the performance of pre-trained AudioNet models in terms of CBAM and GRU. It is observed that *CABM+GRU v1* can further improve the classification performance of CNN14, where the final accuracy, precision, recall, and F1-score are 97.88%, 97.95%, 97.29%, and 97.58%. However, *CABM+GRU v2* leads to the reduced performance.

5 Conclusion

In this study, we propose a novel classification framework based on a pre-trained AudioNet model integrating CBAM and GRU. Our comparison experiments show that the pre-trained AudioNet model presented is promising for acoustic classification of bird species, which obtains better performance than those pre-trained ImageNet models. The use of CBAM and GRU provides better classification performance than using the original model. Additionally, SpecAugment can improve the performance for all pre-trained models. Future research will explore the classification performance of more bird species and classify bird species in contentious long-duration recordings.

Acknowledgments. This work is supported by National Natural Science Foundation of China (Grant No: 32371556, 61902154 and 72004092). This work is also supported by the Fundamental Research Funds for the Central Universities (grants No. 020414380195).

References

1. Deng, J., Dong, W., Socher, R., Li, L.J., Li, K., Fei-Fei, L.: ImageNet: a large-scale hierarchical image database. In: 2009 IEEE Conference on Computer Vision and Pattern Recognition, pp. 248–255. IEEE (2009)
2. Dey, R., Salem, F.M.: Gate-variants of gated recurrent unit (GRU) neural networks. In: 2017 IEEE 60th International Midwest Symposium on Circuits and Systems (MWSCAS), pp. 1597–1600. IEEE (2017)
3. Dias, F.F., Ponti, M.A., Minghim, R.: A classification and quantification approach to generate features in soundscape ecology using neural networks. Neural Comput. Appl., 1–15 (2021). https://doi.org/10.1007/s00521-021-06501-w
4. Gemmeke, J.F., et al.: Audio set: an ontology and human-labeled dataset for audio events. In: 2017 IEEE International Conference on Acoustics, Speech and Signal Processing (ICASSP), pp. 776–780. IEEE (2017)
5. Han, X., et al.: Pre-trained models: past, present and future. AI Open **2**, 225–250 (2021)
6. Kong, Q., Cao, Y., Iqbal, T., Wang, Y., Wang, W., Plumbley, M.D.: PANNs: large-scale pretrained audio neural networks for audio pattern recognition. IEEE/ACM Trans. Audio Speech Lang. Process. **28**, 2880–2894 (2020)
7. Park, D.S., et al.: SpecAugment: a simple data augmentation method for automatic speech recognition. arXiv preprint arXiv:1904.08779 (2019)

8. Qiu, Z., Wang, H., Liao, C., Lu, Z., Kuang, Y.: Sound recognition of harmful bird species related to power grid faults based on VGGish transfer learning. J. Electr. Eng. Technol. **18**(3), 2447–2456 (2023). https://doi.org/10.1007/s42835-022-01284-z

9. Sun, Y., Maeda, T.M., Solís-Lemus, C., Pimentel-Alarcón, D., Buřivalová, Z.: Classification of animal sounds in a hyperdiverse rainforest using convolutional neural networks with data augmentation. Ecol. Ind. **145**, 109621 (2022)

10. Woo, S., Park, J., Lee, J.Y., Kweon, I.S.: CBAM: convolutional block attention module. In: Proceedings of the European Conference on Computer Vision (ECCV), pp. 3–19 (2018)

11. Xie, J., Towsey, M., Zhang, J., Roe, P.: Adaptive frequency scaled wavelet packet decomposition for frog call classification. Eco. Inform. **32**, 134–144 (2016)

12. Zhang, L., Towsey, M., Xie, J., Zhang, J., Roe, P.: Using multi-label classification for acoustic pattern detection and assisting bird species surveys. Appl. Acoust. **110**, 91–98 (2016)

13. Zhong, M., et al.: Multispecies bioacoustic classification using transfer learning of deep convolutional neural networks with pseudo-labeling. Appl. Acoust. **166**, 107375 (2020)

Aspect Term Extraction via Dynamic Attention and a Densely Connected Graph Convolutional Network

Xin Sun[1]([✉]), Yongqing Mi[1], Jia Liu[2,3], and Hongao Li[1]

[1] School of Computer Science and Technology, Beijing Institute of Technology, Beijing 100081, China
`{sunxin,3220231245,3120191012}@bit.edu.cn`
[2] Center for Educational Technology and Resource Development, Ministry of Education, Beijing, P.R. China
[3] National Center for Educational Technology, NCET, Beijing 100031, China
`liujia@moe.edu.cn`

Abstract. Aspect term extraction is a crucial step in aspect-level sentiment analysis, significantly affecting the accuracy of sentiment classification. Therefore, improving the precision of aspect term extraction is vital for enhancing the performance of sentiment analysis. The limitations of existing methods include inadequate consideration of syntactic information and inter-word dependencies, as well as the challenge of mitigating weight noise during dependency tree conversion. To address these issues, we propose an aspect term extraction approach that leverages dynamic attention and graph convolutional network. Our method utilizes a densely connected graph convolutional network to capture dependency information between distant terms, thereby enriching vector semantics. Furthermore, it integrates a dynamic attention mechanism informed by dependency parsing to highlight critical dependencies and mitigate noise interference. We benchmark our model against state-of-the-art approaches on four widely used public datasets. The results indicate that our proposed method significantly enhances the performance of aspect term extraction. Specifically, our model improves upon baseline models on the Lap14 and Rest15 datasets, with increases in macro-F1 scores of 0.45, and 0.04, respectively.

Keywords: Aspect term extraction · Graph convolutional network · Dynamic attention mechanism

1 Introduction

Aspect-level sentiment analysis, also known as opinion mining at the aspect level, is a sub-field of natural language processing. Unlike document-level sentiment analysis, which provides an overall sentiment score for an entire document, aspect-level sentiment analysis aims to determine the sentiment associated with

© The Author(s), under exclusive license to Springer Nature Singapore Pte Ltd. 2025
R. Hadfi et al. (Eds.): PRICAI 2024, LNAI 15281, pp. 383–395, 2025.
https://doi.org/10.1007/978-981-96-0116-5_32

particular attributes, such as product reviews, social media posts, or customer feedback. Aspect-level sentiment analysis is a more fine-grained type of sentiment analysis, which consists of two sub-tasks: aspect term extraction and sentiment classification. As shown in Fig. 1, "battery capacity" and "power cord" are two aspects of the entity "phone". The purpose of aspect term extraction is to extract structured information from opinionated sentences, identifying "battery capacity" and "power cord" as the sentiment targets within the sentence.

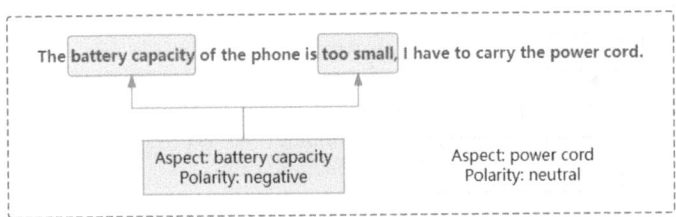

Fig. 1. Example of aspect-level sentiment analysis based on aspect term extraction.

Aspect term extraction methods typically include sequence labeling approaches, various data augmentation techniques, as well as deep learning models such as conditional random fields (CRF), recurrent neural networks (RNN), and Transformer. With the advancement of deep learning techniques, current approaches involve the deployment of graph convolutional networks [1, 16] and attention mechanisms [4, 18] to effectively process and weigh the importance of various words or phrases in the text. These approaches have improved the performance of aspect term extraction. However, the direct use of an adjacency matrix derived from the dependency tree can result in equal weighting of syntactic dependencies, potentially propagating irrelevant noise. Methods based on attention mechanism do not account for how previous predictions can constrain the error margin for subsequent predictions.

To tackle the aforementioned challenges, we introduce a novel aspect term extraction model that leverages dynamic attention and a densely connected graph convolutional network (DA-DCGCN). Initially, we utilize the bidirectional language model BERT to derive sentence vector representations, which are then fed into the network layers. Subsequently, we employ a densely connected graph convolutional network (DC-GCN) to bolster the learning capacity of our model, thereby improving the capture of dependency information for terms separated by distance within complex sentences. Following this, we incorporate a dynamic attention mechanism grounded in dependency syntax analysis to minimize noise within the network layers. Ultimately, we concatenate the hidden vector representations from all layers of the DC-GCN to form input vectors for the conditional random field (CRF), which identifies the optimal path among hidden vectors and label dependencies. Our experiments on public datasets have yielded competitive outcomes.

Our key contributions are as follows:

- We implement a dense connection strategy that thoroughly integrates hidden vector information across all graph levels, thereby capturing inter-term dependencies in complex sentences and mitigating the problem of over-smoothing.
- Our dynamic attention mechanism, grounded in dependency syntax analysis, fully leverages the relationships between hidden nodes in the graph, thereby refining the calibration of inter-word dependency weights and reducing noise in the syntactic analysis.
- Experimental results on public datasets demonstrate that our model significantly enhances the precision of aspect term extraction.

2 Related Works

2.1 Sequence Labeling-Based Methods

Sequence labeling involves identifying the most suitable sequence of tags for a given sequence. Liu et al. [7] pioneered the use of Bi-LSTM on sentiment-annotated data, converting the extraction of evaluation objects in fine-grained sentiment analysis into a BIO tagging problem. Xu et al. [20] introduced a dual-embedding-based convolutional neural network that integrates general-purpose and domain-specific embeddings into a novel, simple CNN structure for extracting evaluation objects. Ma et al. [8] investigated treating aspect term extraction as a Seq2Seq problem to leverage the full sentence's meaning and to overcome challenges in handling label dependencies. These methods effectively harness label dependency information, however, they primarily focus on noun phrases near the evaluation object, often overlooking the broader sentence context. Additionally, these approaches necessitate a considerable volume of high-quality training data, which is scarce due to the constraints of time and labor.

2.2 Graph Convolutional Network-Based Methods

Graph convolutional networks (GCNs) demonstrate superior performance in processing graph-structured data, particularly dependency trees. Owing to their robust performance and interpretability, GCNs efficiently aggregate information from dependency trees, facilitating the extraction of meaningful information pertinent to the targets. Marcheggiani and Titov [9] were the first to apply GCNs to sequences of word tokens for semantic role labeling. Sun et al. [15] introduced a method that integrates semantic dependency trees with GCNs to enrich vector representations and establish decision criteria for extraction tasks. Liang et al. [6] proposed an interactive architecture fortified with dependency syntax knowledge, developing a GCN that captures relational dependencies to enrich syntactic information. Nonetheless, many GCN-based methods naively use the adjacency matrix from dependency trees, resulting in equal weighting of syntactic dependencies and potentially introducing irrelevant information. This redundancy can introduce noise and detract from the extraction performance.

2.3   Attention-Based Methods

In recent years, several researchers have explored the integration of attention mechanisms to enhance extraction performance. Wang et al. [19] developed a multi-task learning framework that harnesses attention mechanisms to learn integrated representations of aspect terms and sentiment relationships. Phan et al. [10] employed word-based, dependency-based, and contextual embeddings for information representation and utilized self-attention mechanisms to learn syntactic features, thereby mitigating the impact of irrelevant terms. Xu et al. [21] proposed an attention-based convolution neural network which could adaptively capture the previous meanings of words to assign different importance to the respective embeddings. Although these methods incorporate attention mechanisms, they overlook the potential of previous predictions to constrain the error space for current predictions, and they do not dynamically adjust attention to mitigate error propagation effectively.

3   The Methodology of DA-DCGCN

In this section, we proposes our DA-DCGCN model and the overall framework is shown in Fig. 2. Firstly, we introduce BERT encoding layer for sentence encoding to enhance the vector representation. Secondly, DC-GCN is proposed to capture dependency information of distant terms, enriching vector semantics and mitigating the issue of over-smoothing. Subsequently, a dynamic attention mechanism based on dependency syntax analysis is added to distinguish the dependency relationships. Finally, CRF is utilized to find the optimal path between hidden vectors and dependency relationships.

3.1   BERT Encoding Layer

Compared to some previous word encoding models, BERT possesses more precise capturing ability and stronger encoding capabilities. Using the BERT model to encode the word vector of user reviews helps to achieve better aspect term extraction results.

The DA-DCGCN model preprocesses the input sentence $X = [x_1, x_2, \ldots, x_n]$ into [CLS] sentence [SEP], where n represents the number of words in the sentence. After encoding by the BERT layer, the text representation sequence $H^{(0)} = [h_1^{(0)}, h_2^{(0)}, \ldots, h_n^{(0)}], H^{(0)} \in \mathbb{R}^{n \times d}$ is obtained, d represents the vector dimension output by the BERT model, and the calculation is as follows:

$$H^{(0)} = BERT(x_1, x_2, ..., x_n) \tag{1}$$

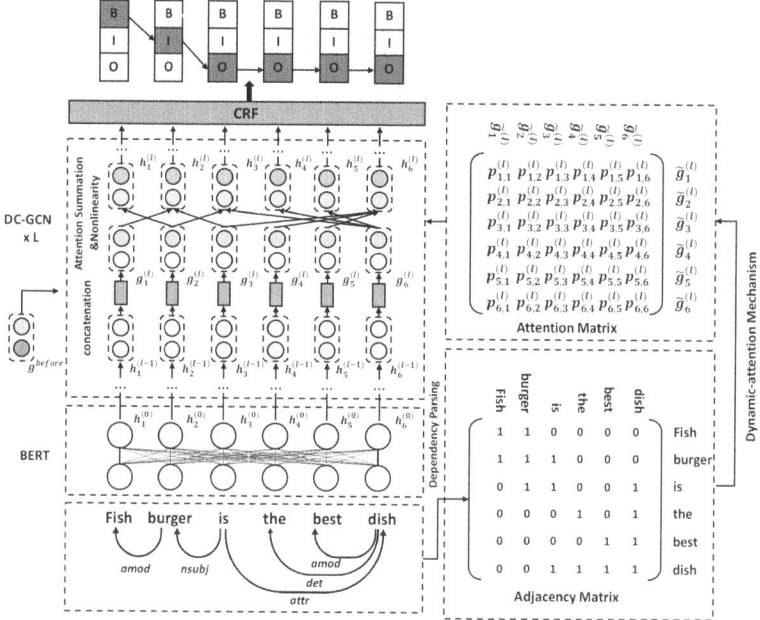

Fig. 2. The overall structure of the dynamic attention and densely connected graph convolutional networks.

3.2   Densely Connected Graph Convolutional Network

Dense connections allow for the concatenation of hidden vectors output by each layer of the graph convolutional network. This identifies dependency information among distant terms in complex user reviews, mitigating the issue of over-smoothing.

On an undirected graph $G = (V, E)$, the calculation at node v in layer l for the input vector $h^{(l-1)}$ is as follows:

$$h_v^{(l)} = \rho\left(\sum_{u \in N(v)} W^{(l)} h_u^{(l-1)} + b^{(l)} \right) \tag{2}$$

where $h_v^{(l)}$ denotes the output vector, $W^{(l)}$ represents the weight matrix, $b^{(l)}$ is the bias vector, $N^{(v)}$ refers to the neighboring nodes of node v, and ρ stands for an activation function, such as RELU.

Dense connection is the core concept of the DC-GCN network. With the dense connection, node v in layer l not only receives input from $h^{(l-1)}$ but also gathers information from all previous layers. We define $g_u^{(l)}$ as the concatenation of the initial node vector and the vectors produced from all previous layers:

$$g_u^{(l)} = \left\{ H^{(0)}; H^{(1)}; ...; H^{(l-1)} \right\} \tag{3}$$

Although the dense connection can deeply capture the deep-level dependency of distant terms, to improve the efficiency of training, the size of each hidden layer is set to be very small. Therefore, the convolution calculation in the last layer needs to be adjusted to:

$$h_v^{(l)} = \rho\left(\sum_{u \in N(v)} W^{(l)} g_u^{(l)} + b^{(l)}\right) \tag{4}$$

The dimensions of these hidden layers are determined by the number of layers L and the input feature dimension d. Here, d_{hidden} is defined as d/L, implying that the column dimension of the weight matrix increases by d_{hidden} for each layer, so $W^{(l)} \in \mathbb{R}^{d_{hidden} \times d^{(l)}}$. Therefore, we can deduce that $d^{(l)} = d + d_{hidden} \times (l-1)$.

Finally, the DC-GCN aggregates the hidden layer vectors obtained from the graph convolutions as follows:

$$H^{out} = \left\{H^{(1)}; H^{(1)}; ...; H^{(L)}\right\} \tag{5}$$

$$H^{(l)} = \left\{h_1^{(l)}; h_2^{(l)}; ...; h_n^{(l)}\right\} \tag{6}$$

3.3   Dynamic Attention Based on Dependency Syntax Analysis

DA-DCGCN introduces dynamic attention based on dependency syntax analysis trees, which provides more enriched weight information for inter-word relationships, and distinguishes between strong and weak dependencies, thereby enhancing performance.

The model employs a multi-layer perceptron to map relationships between different nodes in the graph. The calculation of self-attention based on dependency syntax analysis is as follows:

$$p'_{i,j} = \frac{a_{i,j} \cdot exp(S)}{\sum_{j=1}^{n} a_{i,j} \cdot exp(S)} \tag{7}$$

$$S = \rho(s^T[W_a h_i^{(0)}; W_a h_j^{(0)}]) \tag{8}$$

where ρ stands for LeakyReLU.

Furthermore, to obtain deeper inter-word information in the graph, the DA-DCGCN model establishes a dynamic attention mechanism. It performs self-attention calculations for each layer of the DC-GCN based on dependency syntax analysis, as follows:

$$p_{i,j}^{(l)} = \frac{a_{i,j} \cdot exp(S')}{\sum_{j=1}^{n} a_{i,j} \cdot exp(S')} \tag{9}$$

$$S' = \rho(s^T[W_a \widetilde{g}_i^{(l)}; W_a \widetilde{g}_j^{(l)}]) \tag{10}$$

$$\widetilde{g}_u^{(l)} = W_{(l)} g_u^{(l)} \tag{11}$$

where $\widetilde{g}^{(l)} = \left\{ \widetilde{g_1}^{(l)}; \widetilde{g_2}^{(l)}; ...; \widetilde{g_n}^{(l)} \right\}$ represents the input vector, W_a and s^T are the weight matrix and $a_{i,j}$ denotes the adjacency matrix resulting from dependency syntax analysis.

Finally, the convolution calculation is modified to obtain the final result:

$$h_i^{(l)} = RELU(\sum_{j=1}^{n} p_{i,j}^{(l)} W^{(l)} g_j^l + b^{(l)}) \tag{12}$$

where $p_{i,j}^{(l)}$ denotes the normalized weight coefficients obtained from the attention calculation of layer l.

3.4 CRF Sequence Labeling Layer

Conditional Random Field can leverage rich sequence features to find the optimal sequence labeling across the entire sequence, significantly reducing the issue of label bias.

The model performs sequence labeling calculations as follows:

$$p(y|H^{out}; W, b) = \frac{\prod_{i=1}^{n} S}{\sum_{y' \in \mathbb{C}(H^{out})} \prod_{i=1}^{n} S'} \tag{13}$$

$$S = exp(W_{y_{i-1}, y_i}^T H^{out} + b_{y_{i-1}, y_i}) \tag{14}$$

$$S' = exp(W_{y'_{i-1}, y'_i}^T H^{out} + b_{y'_{i-1}, y'_i}) \tag{15}$$

where H^{out} represents the sequence of hidden states output by the dense connected graph convolutional layer, W is the weight matrix, b is the bias vector, and the subscripts denote the label pairs.

To train the CRF layer, the DA-DCGCN model employs the maximum conditional likelihood estimation method. Therefore, the final log-likelihood of the weight matrix is:

$$L(W, b) = \sum_{(h_i, y_i)} \log p(y_i | h_i^{out}; W, b) \tag{16}$$

Finally, the CRF layer is trained using the Viterbi algorithm to obtain the optimal sequence $y = (y_1, y_2, ..., y_n)$, where y_i is chosen from a set of possible labels, which includes the elements "B", "I", and "O".

4 Experiments

4.1 Datasets and Parameter Settings

The experiments validate the performance of the model using four SemEval datasets: SemEval2014 Task4 [13], SemEval2015 Task12 [11], and SemEval2016

Table 1. Statistical information of SemEval datasets.

	Lap14		Rest14		Rest15		Rest16	
	Train	Test	Train	Test	Train	Test	Train	Test
#Sent.	3045	800	3041	800	1315	685	2000	676
#Aspect	2342	650	3686	1134	1209	547	1757	622

Task5 [12]. Among them, SemEval2014 Task4 includes two datasets: Lap14 and Rest14. The SemEval datasets primarily consist of reviews related to laptops and restaurants.

Table 1 summarizes the number of sentences and aspect terms in the training and test sets for each dataset. #Sent. denotes the count of sentences, while #Aspect indicates the number of aspect terms. The experiments utilize the F1 score to evaluate the performance of each model.

The DA-DCGCN employs the BERT model for encoding, and the dimension of the output hidden layer vector is 768, the maximum text length is set to 85, the initial learning rate is 0.00001, the Batch size is 16, and the dropout value is 0.5. The syntax parsing utilizes the LAL Parser as the syntax parsing tool. The training employs the Adam optimizer for optimization, with the number of densely connected graph convolutional layers set to 3 and the dropout set to 0.4 to prevent overfitting.

4.2   Experimental Results and Analysis

To validate the effectiveness of the DA-DCGCN, the following ten models are selected as baseline models for comparison:

1) **MIN** [5] proposes a novel LSTM-based deep multi-task learning framework, which includes two LSTMs equipped with extended memories and neural memory operations and also incorporates sentimental sentence constraints. 2) **HAST** [4] utilizes historical information, sentence structure, and contexts to improve the aspect term extraction from user reviews. 3) **Seq2Seq4ATE** [8] treats aspect term extraction as a sequence-to-sequence task, employing an attention mechanism to focus on neighboring words within each phrase. 4) **DECNN** [20] treats aspect term extraction as a sequence labeling task, feeding general and domain-specific vectors into a simple multi-layer convolutional neural network. 5) **CDA** [3] utilizes a masked sequence-to-sequence model to generate enhanced data in a controllable manner, thereby improving the extraction performance. 6) **BeeAE** [14] proposes an effective framework by integrating both contextual and linguistic features with the artificial bee colony-based feature selection method. 7) **RAL Model-2** [17] introduces reinforcement learning which extracts an optimal sample from the entire unlabelled training data and hence optimizes data annotation by reducing the time and effort linked to the labeling process. 8) **SoftProtoE** [2] proposes a framework that can correlate words with each other through soft prototypes., addressing the issue of long-tail distributions. 9). **Xu et al.** [22] leveraged back translation to augment the

training data for aspect term extraction, providing diverse pragmatic modes for learning when semantics remains unchanged. 10). **SJCL** [23] utilized a span-based joint extraction framework with contrastive learning to enhance both term extraction and pairing in pair-wise aspect and opinion term extraction.

Table 2. Comparative experiments with baseline models.

Model	Lap14	Rest14	Rest15	Rest16
MIN	77.58	–	–	73.44
HAST	79.52	85.61	71.46	73.61
Seq2Seq4ATE	79.02	84.08	69.89	72.82
DECNN	81.39	86.04	71.18	74.39
CDA	81.58	–	–	75.19
RAL Model-2	78.67	85.63	67.52	73.61
BeeAE	80.70	84.70	72.20	74.80
SoftProtoE	<u>83.19</u>	**87.39**	<u>73.27</u>	76.98
Xu et al.	80.10	<u>86.71</u>	70.17	75.31
SJCL	72.55	78.43	73.14	**80.12**
DA-DCGCN	**83.64**	86.21	**73.31**	<u>77.41</u>

The experimental results for the four datasets are shown in Table 2. The best results are bolded in the table, while the second-best results are underlined. In terms of F1 score, the DA-DCGCN demonstrates enhancements of 0.45, 0.04, respectively, over the second-best performance in the Lap14 and Rest15. In the Rest14 dataset, SoftProtoE surpasses the DA-DCGCN, which may be attributed to the dataset's inherent long-tail distribution. SoftProtoE leverages global knowledge to enhance the extraction task, thereby effectively mitigating the challenges posed by the long-tailed distribution. In the REST16 dataset, SJCL achieved a higher score, which due to its advantage for pair-wise aspect and opinion term extraction. For sentences without explicit opinions, extraction of aspects becomes challenging, thus our method achieves higher scores on all the other datasets. Overall, our DA-DCGCN exhibits superior performance compared to most baseline models.

4.3   Ablation Study

To evaluate the performance of each component in the DA-DCGCN, we separately designed four ablation baseline models:

DA-DCGCN-w/o-dynamic: Replace the dynamic attention with a single attention calculation performed on the input vectors.

DA-DCGCN-w/o-dynamic-attention: Remove the dynamic attention to validate the role of the dynamic attention mechanism within the DC-GCN.

DA-DCGCN-w/o-DCGCN: Replace the multi-layer DC-GCN with a single-layer basic graph convolutional network to validate the critical utility of the DC-GCN in aspect term extraction.

DA-DCGCN-w/o-CRF: Replace the CRF with a Softmax decoding layer to validate the effectiveness of the CRF sequence labeling layer.

Table 3. Results of ablation experiments.

Model	Lap14	Rest14	Rest15	Rest16
DA-DCGCN-w/o-dynamic	83.18	86.04	72.67	77.01
DA-DCGCN-w/o-dynamic-attention	82.92	85.73	71.60	76.29
DA-DCGCN-w/o-DCGCN	83.21	85.89	72.64	77.05
DA-DCGCN-w/o-CRF	83.17	85.90	73.07	76.98
DA-DCGCN	**83.64**	**86.21**	**73.31**	**77.41**

Table 3 analysis several significant insights: (1) The dynamic aspect enhances the model's capability to filter out extraneous information and delve into more profound semantic features; (2) The dynamic attention mechanism empowers the model to acquire a deeper understanding of semantic information and to discern inter-word dependencies with greater clarity; (3) Dense connections and graph convolutional networks enables the robust capture of syntactic details from dependency trees, enriches the semantics of the vectors, uncovers dependencies between distant terms, and mitigates over-smoothing; (4) CRF sequence labeling identifies the most suitable path between hidden vectors and dependency relationships, thereby enhancing the model's performance.

4.4   Effect of Different Dependency Parsers

Aspect term extraction based on syntactic information typically relies on dependency parsers to construct dependency trees. To assess the influence of various dependency parsers on the model's extraction efficacy, we compared the performance of three parsers: Stanford Parser, BiAffine Parser, and LAL Parser, using the English Penn Treebank dataset. The evaluation metrics employed are UAS and LAS, with UAS denoting the F1 score for unlabeled data and LAS representing the F1 score for labeled data. The results are presented in Table 4.

Additionally, we also compared the performance of our model using different dependency parsers. As can be seen from the experimental results in Table 5, LAL Parser achieves the best performance on the Lap14, Rest14, and Rest16 datasets. This indicates that the improvement in the performance of the dependency parser contributes to enhancing the effectiveness of aspect term extraction. Therefore, this model selects the LAL Parser as the dependency parser.

Table 4. Comparison of different dependency parsers.

Dependency Parser	UAS	LAS
Stanford Parser	94.10	91.49
BiAffine Parser	95.90	94.25
LAL Parser	**97.42**	**96.26**

Table 5. The impact of different dependency parsers on model performance.

Dependency Parser	Lap14	Rest14	Rest15	Rest16
Stanford Parser	83.38	85.87	72.92	77.10
BiAffine Parser	83.17	86.09	**73.45**	77.37
LAL Parser	**83.64**	**86.21**	73.31	**77.41**

5 Conclusion

This paper investigates the aspect term extraction task. In response to existing methods that do not fully consider syntactic information and inter-word dependency relationships, and issues such as the generation of weight noise, we propose an aspect term extraction method, DA-DCGCN. Our model enriches vector semantics through a densely connected graph convolutional network and incorporates dynamic attention based on dependency syntax analysis to distinguish inter-word dependencies. These improvement addresses the issue of over-smoothing and mitigates noise interference. Experiments on public datasets demonstrate that our model can effectively improve the performance of aspect term extraction.

Acknowledgments. This paper is supported by the National Key Research and Development Program of China (2022YFC3303501) and Monitoring and Early Warning Service Platform Project (2023-275-1-1).

References

1. Cetoli, A., Bragaglia, S., O'Harney, A.D., Sloan, M.: Graph convolutional networks for named entity recognition. arXiv preprint arXiv:1709.10053 (2017)
2. Chen, Z., Qian, T.: Enhancing aspect term extraction with soft prototypes. In: Proceedings of the 2020 Conference on Empirical Methods in Natural Language Processing (EMNLP), pp. 2107–2117 (2020)
3. Li, K., Chen, C., Quan, X., Ling, Q., Song, Y.: Conditional augmentation for aspect term extraction via masked sequence-to-sequence generation. arXiv preprint arXiv:2004.14769 (2020)
4. Li, X., Bing, L., Li, P., Lam, W., Yang, Z.: Aspect term extraction with history attention and selective transformation. arXiv preprint arXiv:1805.00760 (2018)

5. Li, X., Lam, W.: Deep multi-task learning for aspect term extraction with memory interaction. In: Proceedings of the 2017 Conference on Empirical Methods in Natural Language Processing, pp. 2886–2892 (2017)
6. Liang, Y., Meng, F., Zhang, J., Chen, Y., Xu, J., Zhou, J.: A dependency syntactic knowledge augmented interactive architecture for end-to-end aspect-based sentiment analysis. Neurocomputing **454**, 291–302 (2021)
7. Liu, P., Joty, S., Meng, H.: Fine-grained opinion mining with recurrent neural networks and word embeddings. In: Proceedings of the 2015 Conference on Empirical Methods in Natural Language Processing, pp. 1433–1443 (2015)
8. Ma, D., Li, S., Wu, F., Xie, X., Wang, H.: Exploring sequence-to-sequence learning in aspect term extraction. In: Proceedings of the 57th Annual Meeting of the Association for Computational Linguistics, pp. 3538–3547 (2019)
9. Marcheggiani, D., Titov, I.: Encoding sentences with graph convolutional networks for semantic role labeling. arXiv preprint arXiv:1703.04826 (2017)
10. Phan, M.H., Ogunbona, P.O.: Modelling context and syntactical features for aspect-based sentiment analysis. In: Proceedings of the 58th Annual Meeting of the Association for Computational Linguistics, pp. 3211–3220 (2020)
11. Pontiki, M., Galanis, D., Papageorgiou, H., Manandhar, S., Androutsopoulos, I.: Semeval-2015 task 12: aspect based sentiment analysis. In: Proceedings of the 9th International Workshop on Semantic Evaluation (SemEval 2015), pp. 486–495 (2015)
12. Pontiki, M., et al.: Semeval-2016 task 5: aspect based sentiment analysis. In: ProWorkshop on Semantic Evaluation (SemEval-2016), pp. 19–30. Association for Computational Linguistics (2016)
13. Pontiki, M., Galanis, D., Pavlopoulos, J., Papageorgiou, H., Androutsopoulos, I., Manandhar, S.: Semeval-2014 task 4: aspect based sentiment analysis. In: Proceedings of the 8th International Workshop on Semantic Evaluation, SemEval@COLING 2014, Dublin, Ireland, 23-24 August 2014, pp. 27–35 (2014)
14. Shi, J., Li, W., Bai, Q., Ito, T.: BeeAE: effective aspect term extraction with artificial bee colony. J. Supercomput. **78**(16), 17969–17991 (2022)
15. Sun, C., Huang, L., Qiu, X.: Utilizing BERT for aspect-based sentiment analysis via constructing auxiliary sentence. arXiv preprint arXiv:1903.09588 (2019)
16. Sun, K., Zhang, R., Mensah, S., Mao, Y., Liu, X.: Aspect-level sentiment analysis via convolution over dependency tree. In: Proceedings of the 2019 Conference on Empirical Methods in Natural Language Processing and the 9th International Joint Conference on Natural Language Processing (EMNLP-IJCNLP), pp. 5679–5688 (2019)
17. Venugopalan, M., Gupta, D.: A reinforced active learning approach for optimal sampling in aspect term extraction for sentiment analysis. Expert Syst. Appl. **209**, 118228 (2022)
18. Wang, B., Lu, W.: Learning latent opinions for aspect-level sentiment classification. In: Proceedings of the AAAI Conference on Artificial Intelligence, vol. 32 (2018)
19. Wang, F., Lan, M., Wang, W.: Towards a one-stop solution to both aspect extraction and sentiment analysis tasks with neural multi-task learning. In: 2018 International Joint Conference on Neural Networks (IJCNN), pp. 1–8. IEEE (2018)
20. Xu, H., Liu, B., Shu, L., Yu, P.S.: Double embeddings and CNN-based sequence labeling for aspect extraction. arXiv preprint arXiv:1805.04601 (2018)
21. Xu, J., et al.: Context-aware dynamic word embeddings for aspect term extraction. IEEE Trans. Affect. Comput. **15**(1), 144–156 (2024)

22. Xu, Q., Hong, Y., Chen, J., Yao, J., Zhou, G.: Data augmentation via back-translation for aspect term extraction. In: 2023 International Joint Conference on Neural Networks (IJCNN), pp. 1–8. IEEE (2023)
23. Yang, J., Dai, F., Li, F., Xue, Y.: Span-based pair-wise aspect and opinion term joint extraction with contrastive learning. In: Liu, F., Duan, N., Xu, Q., Hong, Y. (eds.) CCF International Conference on Natural Language Processing and Chinese Computing, vol. 14303, pp. 17–29. Springer, Cham (2023). https://doi.org/10.1007/978-3-031-44696-2_2

NLDF: Neural Light Dynamic Fields for 3D Talking Head Generation

Guanchen Niu⬤, Songsong Cheng⬤, and Teng Li$^{(\boxtimes)}$⬤

Anhui University, Hefei, China
z22301091@stu.ahu.edu.cn, {sscheng,liteng}@ahu.edu.cn

Abstract. Talking head generation based on the neural radiation fields (NeRF) model has shown promising visual effects. However, the slow rendering speed of NeRF seriously limits its application. In this work, a novel Neural Light Dynamic Fields (NLDF) model is proposed aiming to achieve generating high quality 3D talking face with significant speedup. The NLDF represents light fields based on light segments, and a deep network is used to learn the entire light beam's information at once. In learning the knowledge distillation is applied and the NeRF based synthesized result is used to guide the correct coloration of light segments in NLDF. The propose method effectively represents the facial light dynamics in 3D talking video generation, and it achieves approximately 30 times faster speed compared to state-of-the-art NeRF based method, with comparable generation visual quality.

Keywords: talking face · NeRF · deep learning

1 Introduction

Learning from short video sequences, audio-driven talking head synthesis is a promising research topic with wide-ranging applications such as film production, video conferencing, human-computer interaction, and digital human creation.

Conventional approaches utilized GAN networks, as well as VAE to generate the 2D face. These methods effect with less consideration of 3D head motion.

In recent years, NeRF [3] is excellent 3D rendering capabilities have driven the development of 3D talking head generation. Approaches like ADNeRF [2] and DFRF [6] can generate high-quality talking videos with simple input training videos. LipNeRF [1] synchronized lip movements with speech more effectively by combining NeRF with GAN techniques.GENEFACE [8] uses a deformation-based approach to generate high-quality results. Despite of the promising visual quality, the slow rendering speed limits their applications seriously. For example, to generate a 512×512 resolution 30-second video takes about 7 h using a V100 GPU with ADNeRF.

This work is supported by The University Synergy Innovation Program of Anhui Province (No: GXXT-2022-037).

In the field of 3D reconstruction, Instant-NGP [4] uses hash encoding with a small MLP network, significantly improving rendering speed. RADNeRF [7] extends this method to accelerate the rendering process. However, this approach requires additional networks to explicitly handle eye features.

This paper presents Neural Light Dynamic Fields (NLDF), a method that accelerates 3D talking head generation while preserving high visual quality. NLDF renders pixels in a single pass with light segments, avoiding the extensive computations of NeRF. It also uses knowledge distillation from a teacher NeRF model to improve dynamic scene quality. The NLDF achieves a rendering speed that is ∼30 times faster than ADNeRF [2] and ∼70 times faster than DFRF [6]. It also surpasses previous methods regarding generation quality in 3D talking video synthesis. In summary, this paper makes the following contributions:

- We propose a novel NLDF model that efficiently generates high quality 3D talking videos driven by audio features. By using light segments for rendering, NLDF greatly improves both rendering speed and visual quality compared to NeRF based methods.
- We propose a knowledge distillation method that guides the NLDF model using the density and color outputs of neural radiation fields.
- We propose a novel active pool training strategy that focuses on high-frequency movements, accelerating the model's convergence.

2 Method

2.1 NLDF Network

The proposed NLDF talking video generation framework, depicted in Fig. 1, leverages pose parameters estimated from each frame in the video to derive light beam information. This information includes light beam origin (x_o, y_o, z_o) and direction (x_d, y_d, z_d). These raw light beams can be encoded with K sampling points, resulting in features with 3K dimension. We feed the light beam features processed by the beam encoder module and audio features $\mathbf{a}$ into the NLDF model, which comprises a deep residual MLP network.

Considering that the total color value of a light beam can be viewed as the sum of all photons along the light beam, we roughly segment the spatial positions of photons along the light beam direction into M categories. The network formula is as follows:

$$F_\phi : (x_o, y_o, z_o, x_d, y_d, z_d, \mathbf{a}) \rightarrow \{c_{\varphi i}\}_{i=1,...M} \qquad (1)$$

where ϕ represents the trained NLDF model, $\mathbf{a}$ represents the inputted audio feature, and $c_{\varphi i}$ represents the color value of the i-th segment of the light beam. M represents the number of segments for a single light beam, serving as a hyperparameter, set to 4 in this study. The network produces color values for M light beam segments, which are subsequently accumulated through a rendering process to compute pixel values. In Fig. 1, we utilize an 88-layer ResMLP network, as our color prediction network.

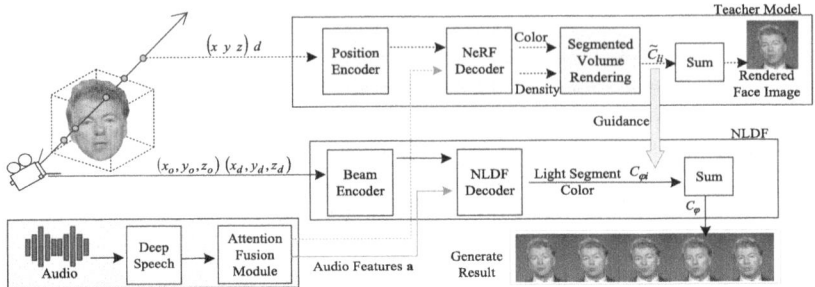

Fig. 1. NLDF framework.

2.2   NeRF-Based Teacher Network

The teacher speaker radiance fields network generates color values using voxel rendering. Following is the network calculation formula for the speaker NeRF, where audio a serves as one driving feature for generating talking videos:

$$F_\theta' : (\mathbf{a}, d, p) \to (c, \sigma) \tag{2}$$

Here, θ represents the network parameters of the speaker radiance fields, $\mathbf{a}$ denotes the audio features, d is the direction of the ray, and p represents the spatial coordinates of the sampling points in the scene. The network outputs color values c and σ density along the ray. We followed the network training methodology of ADNeRF [2], employing the MSE loss function to train the teacher speaker radiation fields network until convergence and subsequently freezing its network parameters.

2.3   Voxel Rendering for NLDF

We partition the sampling points along the ray direction in the speaker's radiation fields teacher network into M (4 in this study) sets, each containing N/M sampling points (the total number of sampling points in the radiation fields N is four times N/M). We apply the voxel rendering formula (Eq. 3 below) to calculate the color value $\tilde{c}_{li}$ of this light segment for each set of sampling points.

$$\tilde{c}_{li} = \sum_{k=1+(i-1)\times N/M}^{i \times N/M} \exp\left(-\sum_{j=1}^{k-1} \sigma_j \delta_j\right) (1 - \exp(-\sigma_j \delta_j)) c_k \tag{3}$$

Here, i represents the subset index of sampling points on the light beam. $\tilde{c}_{li}$ represents the color value of the i-th light segment calculated by the teacher speaker radiance fields through voxel rendering. σ is the radiance fields sampling point density, and δ is the sampling depth interval. c_k represents the color predicted by the network for the k-th sampling point.

We use the 4 sets of light segment color values obtained from the teacher network to guide the learning of the light segment representation in the student network. In other words, a loss function $loss_{rs}$ is established using $\tilde{c}_{li}$ and $c_{\varphi i}$ of the light segments output by the radiance fields $\tilde{c}_{li}$ to guide the output of the speaker NLDF:

$$loss_{rs} = \sum_{r \in N_l} \sum_{i=1}^{M} \|c_{\varphi i} - \tilde{c}_{li}\|_2^2 \tag{4}$$

where N_l represents the total number of sampled light beams in a training batch. $c_{\varphi i}$ represents the color value of the i-th light segment output by the NLDF network.

By aggregating the $c_{\varphi i}$ values for each light beam to obtain the pixel value c_φ, $loss_r$ is calculated by comparing it against the ground truth pixel values c_g.

We calculate the Mean Squared Error (MSE) loss between c_φ and the real pixel value c_g from the image. The final loss is defined as follows:

$$loss = loss_r + \lambda loss_{rs}, \quad where \quad loss_r = \sum_{r \in N_l} \|c_\varphi - c_g\|_2^2 \tag{5}$$

λ is a hyperparameter, and in our experiments, it is set to 0.2.

2.4   Active Light Beam Training Strategy

For each training iteration, 4096 randomly sampled pixels are chosen from an image in the training set, where 90% of these pixels correspond to facial regions. The NLDF network predicts these pixels, sorts the loss in ascending order, and selects the top j beams to add or replace in the active beam pool.

3   Experiments

3.1   Experimental Setup

Dataset. We used high-resolution YouTube videos from the HDTF dataset [9], which contains 362 videos, selecting 10 videos and cropping the facial regions.

Table 1. Comparison of other methods. "GT" is real videos. It's preferable for the SyncNet scores offset↓ to be close to the GT scores.

Method	Test set A						Test set B			
	PSNR↑	SSIM↑	LPIPS↓	SyncNet↓↑	Flops Speedup		PSNR↑	SSIM↑	LPIPS↓	SyncNet↓↑
GT				$-6/2.471$						$-5/8.967$
Makeittalk	21.24	**0.986**	0.1649	$-15/0.088$			16.13	0.9552	0.2272	$-11/0.0311$
Wav2lip	29.86	0.960	0.1190	$-3/2.934$			28.19	0.9553	0.1286	$-3/8.842$
ADNeRF	27.91	0.960	0.1255	$-15/0.466$	1×		24.75	0.9557	0.1462	$-10/0.776$
DFRF	31.94	0.954	0.0897	$-6/1.516$	~0.4×		29.39	0.9522	**0.0858**	$-5/5.544$
Ours	**32.59**	0.955	**0.0852**	$-6/1.416$	~30×		**29.95**	**0.9557**	0.0926	$-5/4.267$

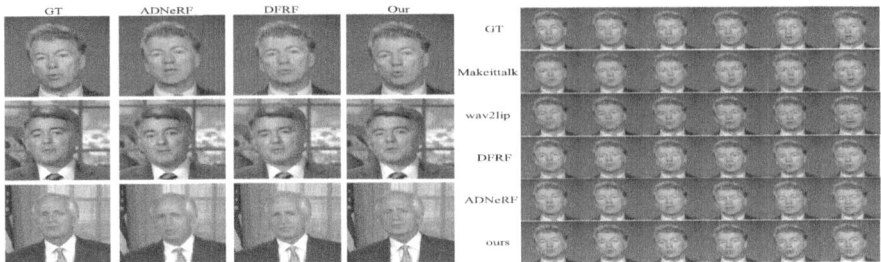

Fig. 2. The left graph shows the results of different data generation, and the right graph shows the results of continuously generated frames.

The videos were resampled to 25 FPS, with 80 % used for training and the rest for testing, ensuring no overlap between the sets.

Evaluation Metrics. Our method selects PSNR↑, SSIM↑, LPIPS↓, and Sync scores (offset↓/confidence↑) as evaluation metrics to effectively assess the fidelity, structural similarity, perceptual realism, and lip-sync accuracy of the generated videos. Since this paper does not involve facial expression features, we did not use landmark similarity metrics such as LMD.

3.2 Comparison of Methods and Ablation Experiments

Comparison With the Existing Methods. In this section, we compare our method with existing 2D and 3D methods on two target speaker datasets (A and B). The evaluation results in Table 1 are based on approximately 600k training iterations, ensuring model convergence. Although Wav2lip [5] achieves higher Sync scores using SyncNet as a discriminator, it produces mouth shapes that differ from natural ones. Figure 2 shows that 2D methods like Wav2lip [5] and Makeittalk [10] generate generic mouth shapes, while our method creates shapes specific to the individuals used in training, making them more realistic. As shown in Table 1, our NLDF scores higher in PSNR↑, SSIM↑ and LPIPS↓ than most existing methods and is comparable to DFRF [6]. Additionally, our method is 30 times faster than ADNeRF [2] and 70 times faster than DFRF [6].

Table 2. Knowledge distillation ablation experiment.

	PSNR↑	SSIM↑	LPIPS↓
Ours (400k)	**32.59**	**0.9653**	**0.0837**
Ours (100k)	30.02	0.9621	0.1065
w/o Knowledge distillation (400k)	32.38	0.9539	0.0852
w/o Active strategy (100k)	30.22	0.9640	0.1145
28 layer (400k)	30.23	0.9618	0.1076
50 layer (400k)	30.06	0.9592	0.0996

Ablation Experiment. In this section, we perform ablation experiments from different perspectives. Table 2 shows the results of the knowledge distillation ablation study with the model converged at 400k iterations. While the improvements in metrics are modest, they help correct frames with blurry artifacts. The active strategy ablation, also shown in Table 2, indicates that the model trained with this strategy achieves a significant improvement in the LPIPS↓ metric at 100k iterations, demonstrating the effectiveness of this strategy in speeding up convergence, saving an average of 30 % training time across multiple datasets. Additionally, we conducted experiments at different network depths with 400k training iterations, as shown in Table 2. It is observed that increasing the number of layers does not significantly change the PSNR↑ and SSIM↑ scores, but it does significantly improve the LPIPS↓ score, enhancing the model's ability to describe facial movements.

4 Conclusion

Our proposed NLDF method achieves a rendering speed approximately 30 times faster than radiation field methods while still generating high-fidelity talking head animations and allowing free manipulation of head poses.

References

1. Chatziagapi, A., Athar, S., Jain, A., Rohith, M., Bhat, V., Samaras, D.: LipNeRF: what is the right feature space to lip-sync a NeRF? In: 2023 IEEE 17th International Conference on Automatic Face and Gesture Recognition, pp. 1–8. IEEE (2023)
2. Guo, Y., Chen, K., Liang, S., Liu, Y.J., Bao, H., Zhang, J.: AD-NeRF: audio driven neural radiance fields for talking head synthesis. In: Proceedings of the IEEE/CVF International Conference on Computer Vision, pp. 5784–5794 (2021)
3. Mildenhall, B., Srinivasan, P.P., Tancik, M., Barron, J.T., Ramamoorthi, R., Ng, R.: NeRF: representing scenes as neural radiance fields for view synthesis. Commun. ACM **65**(1), 99–106 (2021)
4. Müller, T., Evans, A., Schied, C., Keller, A.: Instant neural graphics primitives with a multiresolution hash encoding. ACM Trans. Graph. **41**(4), 1–15 (2022)
5. Prajwal, K., Mukhopadhyay, R., Namboodiri, V.P., Jawahar, C.: A lip sync expert is all you need for speech to lip generation in the wild. In: Proceedings of the 28th ACM International Conference on Multimedia, pp. 484–492 (2020)
6. Shen, S., Li, W., Zhu, Z., Duan, Y., Zhou, J., Lu, J.: Learning dynamic facial radiance fields for few-shot talking head synthesis. In: Avidan, S., Brostow, G., Cissé, M., Farinella, G.M., Hassner, T. (eds.) European Conference on Computer Vision, vol. 13672, pp. 666–682. Springer, Cham (2022). https://doi.org/10.1007/978-3-031-19775-8_39
7. Tang, J., et al.: RAD-NeRF: real-time neural radiance talking portrait synthesis via audio-spatial decomposition. arXiv preprint arXiv:2211.12368 (2022)
8. Ye, Z., Jiang, Z., Ren, Y., Liu, J., He, J., Zhao, Z.: GeneFace: generalized and high-fidelity audio-driven 3D talking face synthesis. arXiv preprint arXiv:2301.13430 (2023)

9. Zhang, Z., Li, L., Ding, Y., Fan, C.: Flow-guided one-shot talking face generation with a high-resolution audio-visual dataset. In: Proceedings of the IEEE/CVF Conference on Computer Vision and Pattern Recognition, pp. 3661–3670 (2021)
10. Zhou, Y., Han, X., Shechtman, E., Echevarria, J., Kalogerakis, E., Li, D.: MakeltTalk: speaker-aware talking-head animation. ACM Trans. Graph. **39**(6), 1–15 (2020)

Enhanced Knowledge Tracing via Frequency Integration and Order Sensitivity

Songtao Cai📍 and Li Li[✉]

College of Computer and Information Science, School of Software,
Southwest University, Chongqing, China
lily@swu.edu.cn

Abstract. Knowledge tracing (KT) is a pivotal component of online education systems, aiming to assess and predict students' knowledge states based on their learning history. Existing knowledge tracing models have achieved considerable success, yet they have neglected the frequency of interactions between students and knowledge points. Frequency information can aid in more stable modeling of students' knowledge states. In this study, we incorporate frequency data into our model's question embeddings, enabling it to consider the frequency of student-knowledge concept interactions. Moreover, the order within students' learning sequences is crucial, but knowledge tracing models based on the transformer architecture, with their attention mechanisms, are insensitive to the sequence order. We propose the N-transformer structure that combines transformer with order-sensitive RNNs, effectively enhancing the model's sensitivity to the order in students' learning sequences. Subsequently, we employ a simpler and more effective method for prior knowledge modeling, directly extracting prior knowledge related to the current exercise from the model's predicted knowledge state at the previous time step. Finally, we have designed a decay function for the attention mechanism based on the Ebbinghaus forgetting curve to simulate the students' forgetting behavior. Ultimately, we conducted experiments on four datasets, Our model has achieved up to a 3% increase in AUC compared to the baseline on some datasets.

Keywords: Knowledge tracing · Deep learning · Intelligent tutoring systems

1 Introduction

With the development of online learning platforms, the question of how to leverage the vast amount of data generated by these platforms for more effective educational assistance has become a crucial issue [6]. Knowledge tracing involves assessing a student's current knowledge status based on their historical learning sequences. With knowledge tracing, we can provide efficient and practical learning recommendations for students. Therefore, knowledge tracing is considered a fundamental aspect of educational support.

Prior knowledge is closely intertwined with the updating of the student's knowledge state [7]. On the same problem, different students possess varying levels of prior knowledge, leading to distinct changes in their knowledge states. However, previous research may lack specificity and interpretability in terms of prior knowledge and student personality. Furthermore, students' learning rates may differ for different Knowledge concept(KCs) and at different times for the same KC. Therefore, a dynamic approach is necessary to capture the evolving personalities of students during the learning process.We propose that by specifically designing the model that predicts the student's knowledge state, the knowledge state obtained can serve as the prior knowledge for the student at the next time-step.Through this approach, we are better equipped to capture the personalized features of students and the dynamic changes in their knowledge states without overly complicating the model.

Calculating the learning rate for each KC is complex and depends on various factors, including the student's prior exposure to similar KCs, which eases the learning of new ones. Identifying such prior encounters requires analyzing the student's learning history and understanding the inter-KC relationships, typically guided by domain experts. This process is intricate and data on KC difficulty is scarce, complicating the task further, as higher difficulty KCs tend to have slower learning rates.To overcome these challenges, we propose a hypothesis that the number of interactions a student has with the same KC can provide rich information. If a student can master a KC with relatively few practice attempts, it can be inferred that the learning rate for that KC is high for the student. Conversely, if a student continues to engage in practice for a specific KC, it suggests that the learning rate for that KC is low for the student.By employing this method, we can infer a student's learning rate for a KC based on the number of interactions with the same KC, thereby compensating for the lack of data on learning rate.This approach, based on the number of student interactions with the same KC, offers a means to understand individual learning rates without an excessive reliance on manual input from domain experts.Additionally, we have observed that our model provides more stable predictions of students' knowledge states, which may also be a result of incorporating the frequency of interactions between students and knowledge concepts.

In addition, some studies have argued that transformers are not very sensitive to order problems in time series [14], but these orders have an important role in knowledge tracing. Therefore, we have designed an N-transformer structure that is more sensitive to sequence order, making it more suitable for our knowledge tracing tasks.

To more accurately simulate the forgetting behavior in the learning process, we have optimized the attention mechanism within the Transformer model. The attention mechanism plays a vital role in the Transformer, capturing the associative information between different positions in the input sequence. By refining the attention mechanism, we have enabled it to better simulate human forgetting behavior.

Finally, we conducted experiments on four real-world datasets, demonstrating that our model can more accurately predict student responses. In addition, we validated the contribution of each module of our model through ablation studies.

2   Knowledge Tracing Problem Set Up

Knowledge tracing involves predicting a student's future responses to questions based on their previous learning interactions. Specifically, the response sequence is composed of the questions $q_t^i \in \mathbb{N}^+$ answered by the student at all prior times, the knowledge points $c_t^i \in \mathbb{N}^+$ contained within those questions, and the student's answers $r_t^i \in \{0, 1\}$, In which i denotes the student's identifier number. Since our subsequent discussions pertain to the learning sequence of the same student, we omit the superscript i here. t represents the time at which the student answers the questions.For the response r_t, 0 indicates that the student failed to answer the question correctly, while 1 represents that the student answered the question correctly.

Problem Definition. Providing the students' learning interaction up to time $t - 1$ $\{(q_1, c_1, r_1), ..., (q_{t-1}, c_{t-1}, r_{t-1})\}$,the task of KT aims to predict the student's response r_t at time t.

3   Proposed Framework

Our model TPKT can be divided into three main modules: Temporal-Aware Question Encoder, Knowledge-Adaptive Response Encoder, and Knowledge-State Estimate Network (Fig. 1).

3.1   Temporal-Aware Question Encoder

In our study, we employed the Rasch model-based embeddings [2], a concise and highly interpretable Item Response Theory (IRT) model [11], to construct embedding representations for questions and questions-responses. Specifically, each question's embedding vector is designed to consist of two parts. Firstly, the question's embedding vector $x_t \in \mathbb{R}^D$ (D denotes the dimension of these embeddings)includes the embedding representation $q_{c_t} \in \mathbb{R}^D$ of the KC it pertains to. Secondly, the question's embedding vector also includes a variation vector $v_{c_t} \in \mathbb{R}^D$, which summarizes the patterns of variation among different questions under the same KC. This enables the model to better understand the differences and similarities between questions.Furthermore, we introduced a difficulty parameter $u_{q_t} \in \mathbb{R}$ to control the deviation between each question and the KC it covers.

For each question-response pair, we employed a similar approach to extend the embedding representation $y_t \in \mathbb{R}^D$. Specifically, we used the KC-response

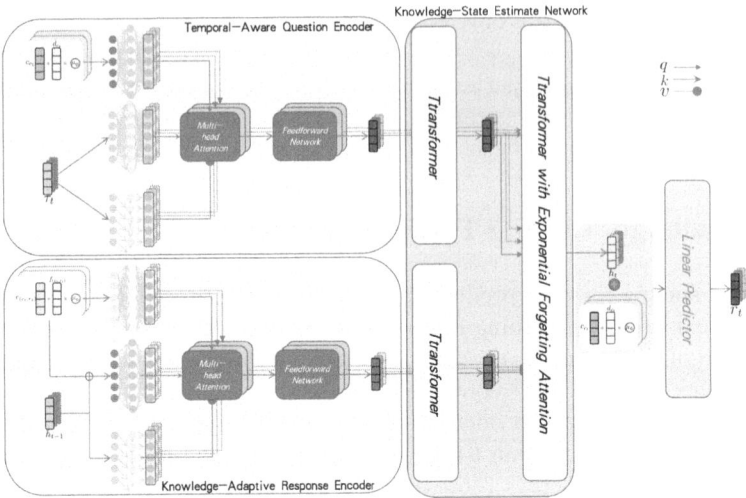

Fig. 1. Overview of our method.

embedding vector $a_{(c_t,r_t)} \in \mathbb{R}^D$ and the variation vector $w_{(c_t,r_t)} \in \mathbb{R}^D$ to represent the characteristics of the question-response pair. This design allows us to comprehensively analyze the relationship between questions, KCs, and student responses.

Moreover, to reduce the number of parameters and improve the model's efficiency, we shared a set of difficulty parameters between questions and question-response embeddings:

$$x_t = q_{c_t} + v_{c_t} \otimes u_{q_t} \tag{1}$$

$$y_t = a_{(c_t,r_t)} + w_{(c_t,r_t)} \otimes u_{q_t} \tag{2}$$

We propose a hypothesis that **the frequency of interactions between students and knowledge points contains rich information**. For instance, for highly difficult questions, a low and consistently incorrect interaction frequency may indicate that the question exceeds the student's ability range. In order to enable the model to learn rich information contained in the number of interactions between student and individual KCs, we designed the Temporal-Aware Question Encoder module. Firstly, we counted the number of interactions between students and KCs, and recorded the sequence of interactions for each student with a specific KC. For example, if the interaction sequence between a student and a KC is $(c_1, c_1, c_2, c_3, c_2, c_2, c_4, c_5, \dots)$, the corresponding frequency sequence would be $(1, 2, 1, 1, 2, 3, 1, 1, \dots)$. We then truncated the frequencies greater than 50 to 50, which helps control the influence of outliers or excessively large data on subsequent analysis. Next, we transformed the discrete frequency sequence into continuous vector representations $\tau_t \in \mathbb{R}^D$ through an embedding layer. To enable the model to better capture the complex relationship between the difficulty of different questions and the frequency of interactions between students and knowledge concepts, we have introduced the cross-attention mechanism, commonly used in multimodal tasks, into knowledge tracing.Specifically, we have replaced the self-attention mechanism in the transformer with a cross-attention mechanism, using both the question embedding x_t and the frequency embedding τ_t as inputs to the transformer, rather than just the question embedding alone.

As is well known, attention mechanisms primarily focus on pairwise relationships between elements in an input sequence, calculating the relevance between each pair of elements (question embeddings) in the sequence to generate static representations. consequently, it is insensitive to the order of students' learning sequences, while the ignored order in the sequence may contain important information. For example, if a student answers a difficult question correctly but then answers an easy question incorrectly, we can infer that the student may have guessed the previous difficult question. On the other hand, RNNs are specifically designed to handle sequence data. They can effectively capture the sequential relationships in learning sequences. Thus, we have designed the N-transformer structure, where specifically, the question embedding x_t and frequency embedding τ_t are processed through an RNN before being used as inputs for the cross-attention mechanism. Our N-transformer structure significantly enhances the model's sensitivity to sequence order.:

$$X_t = (w_{l_0} \cdot \tau_t + b_{l_o}) \cdot \alpha_0 \tag{3}$$

$$\alpha_0 = Softmax(\frac{x_{rt}^\top \cdot \tau_{rt}}{\sqrt{D_k}}) \in [0, 1] \tag{4}$$

$$x_{rt} = RNN(x_t) \tag{5}$$

$$\tau_{rt} = RNN(\tau_t) \tag{6}$$

Here in, $X_t \in \mathbb{R}^D$ denotes the question embedding that incorporates frequency information. The parameters w_{l_0} and b_{l_o} are learnable parameters.

3.2   Knowledge-Adaptive Response Encoder

Students' knowledge state transitions after answering the same question vary under different knowledge states. For students who have already mastered the KC, their mastery level will not change much after answering the question; while for novices, their mastery level of the KC will be greatly improved after answering the question. In order to accurately capture students' prior knowledge, we extract prior knowledge related to the current KC from the predicted student knowledge state in the previous time step.

Specifically, we first multiply the student's knowledge state at the previous time step by a parameter α, and add the result to the question-response embedding to get the vector β_t. The parameter α is used to scale the knowledge state to balance the influence between prior knowledge and the current question representation, so as to better adapt to different situations and questions. By adjusting the value of parameter α, we can control the relative importance of prior knowledge. When the value of parameter α is large, the weight of prior knowledge increases, and the model is more dependent on the previous knowledge state. In this case, the model will pay more attention to the student's past learning performance, regard prior knowledge as an important clue, and tend to rely on this knowledge for prediction. Vice verse.

Similarly, we also employ our N-transformer structure here, where β_t, after processing by an RNN, serves as the key , and β_t, after processing by a linear layer, serves as the value, and the question-response embedding after RNN processing is used as the query:

$$Yt = (w_{l_1} \cdot \beta_t + b_{l_1}) \cdot \alpha_1 \tag{7}$$

$$\alpha_1 = Softmax(\frac{y_{rt}^\top \cdot \beta_{rt}}{\sqrt{D_k}}) \in [0,1] \tag{8}$$

$$y_{rt} = RNN(y_t) \tag{9}$$

$$\beta_{rt} = RNN(\beta_t) \tag{10}$$

$$\beta_t = y_t + \alpha \cdot h_{t-1} \tag{11}$$

Herein, $Y_t \in \mathbb{R}^D$ represents the interaction embedding that incorporates prior knowledge.The parameters w_{l_1} and b_{l_1} are learnable parameters.

3.3 Knowledge-State Estimate Network and Predictor

Because we use the predicted knowledge state as the prior knowledge for the next time step for students, and for learners with different past answer sequences, their understanding of the same question and the knowledge gained through practice may differ. Therefore, we process the entire previous learning sequence of the students through the transformer before predicting their knowledge state. By feeding all historical interactions into the Transformer model, the model can perform global modeling and analysis of the entire learning process, and the model can capture the knowledge and learning patterns accumulated by students in past interactions, as well as the evolution and changes in the learning process. After the Transformer, we obtain the new question embedding and question-response embedding as input to the knowledge state prediction module to obtain the student's current knowledge state. To simulate the forgetting behavior in the learning process, we design an attention mechanism with exponential decay based on the Ebbinghaus forgetting curve [8]. The Ebbinghaus forgetting curve is typically described by an exponential decay function:

$$R_t = R_0 e^{-\lambda t} \tag{12}$$

where R_t is the memory retention at time t, R_0 is the initial memory retention, and λ is the decay rate.The decay rate λ is for the entire value and is determined through the training process. We incorporate this decay function into our attention mechanism by multiplying the original attention scores by the decay function to obtain a new set of attention scores. These new attention scores are then used to compute the student's knowledge state:

$$K_t = Softmax(\frac{e^{-\lambda t} \cdot q^\top \cdot k}{\sqrt{D_k}}) \cdot v \tag{13}$$

$$q = k = w_{l_2} \cdot X_t + b_2 \tag{14}$$

$$v = w_{l_3} \cdot Y_t + b_3 \tag{15}$$

Here $K_t \in \mathbb{R}^D$ represents the knowledge state of the student at time t as predicted by the model. After obtaining the student's knowledge state, we concatenate x_t and K_t and pass them through a fully connected layer, followed by a sigmoid function [5], to obtain the probability $\hat{r}_t \in [0, 1]$ that the student will answer the current question correctly. All learnable parameters in the entire method are trained end-to-end by minimizing the binary cross-entropy loss of all learners' responses:

$$\ell = \sum_i \sum_t - (r_t^i \log \hat{r}_t^i + (1 - r_t^i) \log (1 - r_t^i)) \tag{16}$$

4   Experimental Study

In this section, we first introduce the real-world dataset utilized in our experiments and the baseline models we will be comparing, followed by an overview of the experimental settings employed throughout the study. Finally, we present experiments designed based on the following research questions and demonstrate our experimental results:

- **RQ1**: Does the model exhibit strong predictive performance in estimating students' future responses?
- **RQ2**: What are the individual contributions of each component to the overall knowledge tracing performance?
- **RQ3**: Does our model demonstrate enhanced capability in capturing the sequential nature of the learning process?
- **RQ4**: By incorporating time information, does the prediction of student knowledge state become more stable?

4.1   Datasets

We tested our model on four real-world datasets to effectively predict students' future responses and compared it with several baseline models. We will discuss our experimental results later. Below, we introduce the four datasets used in this experiment:

- **ASSISTments2009**[1] dataset: This dataset was collected by the ASSISTment online teaching platform during the 2009–2010 academic year.

---

[1] https://sites.google.com/site/assistmentsdata/home/2009-2010-assistment-data.

- **ASSISTments2017**[2] dataset: Another dataset collected by ASSISTment. Compared to ASSISTments2009, students have longer learning sequences in this dataset because they are allowed to continuously attempt the same question until they answer it correctly.
- **Statics2011**[3] dataset: This dataset contains interaction data from students enrolled in the Engineering Statics course at Carnegie Mellon University during the 2011 academic year.
- **Algebra05** (see Footnote 3) dataset: This dataset was published in the KDD-cup 2010 Educational Data Mining challenge and is based on a cognitive algebra tutor system course conducted from 2005 to 2006.

4.2   Baseline Methods

We compared our model with several baseline models, including:

- **DKT** [10]: DKT employs a recurrent neural network(RNN) and a Long Short Term Memory(LSTM) to predicate the probability of correctly answering a question at each time step. It represents a pioneering approach in utilizing deep learning for knowledge tracing.
- **DKT+** [12]: DKT+ employs two additional regularization terms to augment the original DKT loss function, specifically targeting the reconstruction and consistency issues encountered by DKT when predicting student knowledge states.
- **DKVMN** [15]: The DKVMN utilizes two memory matrices, termed *key* and *value* to respectively store the representations of knowledge concepts and the proficiency levels of students. In this framework, the *key* matrix remains static, while the *value* matrix is dynamic, updating in response to students' answers to reflect changes in their knowledge states.
- **SAKT** [9]: SAKT utilizes an attention mechanism to explore long-term dependencies between students' learning sequences. It marks the first application of self-attention mechanisms in knowledge tracing.
- **AKT** [2]: AKT employs two encoders equipped with Monotonic Attention Mechanisms and a knowledge state prediction module to forecast students' knowledge states.
- **DTransformer** [13]: DTransformer introduces contrastive learning into knowledge tracing, enabling the model to comprehend knowledge state evolution. This approach achieves better performance prediction accuracy and more stable knowledge tracing results.

4.3   Experimental Setup

To assess the performance of our proposed model, we conducted a 5-fold cross-validation evaluation against state-of-the-art methods on the aforementioned

---

[2] https://sites.google.com/view/assistmentsdatamining.
[3] https://pslcdatashop.web.cmu.edu/DatasetInfo?datasetId=507.

datasets. We divided the datasets into a 20% test set, a 20% validation set, and a 60% training set based on the individual students within the dataset. All hyperparameters were tuned based on the standard 5-fold cross-validation procedure. We employed the Adam optimizer [4] to train all models with a batch size of 24 learners. We also reimplemented DKT, DKT+, and SAKT, as incorporating question IDs necessitates new dataset partitioning and would introduce new experimental results. For AKT, DKT, DKT+, and SAKT, we utilized the Xavier parameter initialization method [3]. For DKVMN, we followed their work and initialized parameters using samples from a normal distribution. All our models were trained on an NVIDIA GeForce RTX 3090 GPU. We did not reimplement DTransformer, and its performance on various datasets is reported from [13].

4.4   Overall Performance (RQ1)

To assess the effectiveness of our model in predicting students' future responses, we conducted a comprehensive evaluation across four aforementioned datasets. We employed a range of evaluation metrics to compare our model against state-of-the-art methods, including Mean Absolute Error (MAE), Accuracy (ACC), and Area Under the Curve (AUC). The results, summarized in Table 1, reveal several noteworthy findings. Our model consistently outperforms the baseline methods on assist09 and assist17, achieving significant performance gains of 2.94% and 2.64%, respectively. This demonstrates the superior predictive capability of our model in these two datasets. On static and algebra05, while our model did not consistently achieve the top performance across all metrics, the margins between our model and the best-performing methods were relatively narrow. For instance, in static, DTransformer marginally outperforms our model in AUC by 0.41%, while in algebra05, DTransformer edges out our model in ACC by 0.03%. These results suggest that our model is highly competitive with the state-of-the-art on these datasets, often exhibiting comparable or even superior performance.

4.5   Ablation Study(RQ2)

To delve into the contributions of each component within our model to its overall predictive performance, we conducted ablation experiments. These experiments were carried out on the assist09, assist17, static and algebra05 datasets, utilizing AUC and ACC as the performance evaluation metric. The results of the ablation experiments are shown in Table 2. We began by removing the Temporal-Aware Question Encoder (TPKT-NT) and directly employing the question embedding from Rasch embedding as input for subsequent modules. Next, we disabled the model's Knowledge-Adaptive Response Encoder (TPKT-NP) and directly used the questions-responses embedding from Rasch embedding as input for subsequent modules. Finally, we removed the Ebbinghaus forgetting curve decay function from the attention mechanism within the Knowledge-State Estimate Network (TPKT-NF). We observe that the removal of any single module results

Table 1. Performance of all KT methods on all datasets in predicting future learner responses.

Dataset	Metrics	DKT	DKT+	DKVMN	SAKT	AKT	DTransformer	ours
assist09	ACC	0.6352	0.7366	0.7534	0.7513	0.7565	0.7632	**0.7865**
	MAE	0.4068	0.3645	0.3214	0.3421	0.3443	0.3097	**0.2135**
	AUC	0.7954	0.7839	0.7865	0.7657	0.7893	0.8146	**0.8440**
assist17	ACC	0.6998	0.6701	0.6783	0.6745	0.7044	0.7078	**0.7232**
	MAE	0.4201	0.4367	0.4081	0.4267	0.3823	0.376	**0.2768**
	AUC	0.6843	0.6578	0.7062	0.6749	0.7458	0.7506	**0.7770**
static	ACC	0.7376	0.7782	0.7937	0.7861	0.776	0.7962	**0.8147**
	MAE	0.3804	0.3256	0.2649	0.2591	0.3047	0.2612	**0.1853**
	AUC	0.8147	0.7861	0.8277	0.8319	0.7987	**0.8382**	0.8341
algebra05	ACC	0.8234	0.8346	0.8319	0.8344	0.8357	**0.8424**	0.8421
	MAE	0.3479	0.2761	0.2317	0.2316	0.2352	0.2201	**0.1579**
	AUC	0.7569	0.7133	0.7892	0.7826	0.7783	0.7946	**0.8000**

in a degradation of the model's performance, indicating that each of our modules contributes to enhancing the model's capabilities to some extent. Notably, the TPKT-NP model exhibits the most significant performance decline. This finding underscores the importance of our model's approach, which involves extracting prior knowledge related to the current KC from the predicted knowledge state of the preceding time step, in improving model performance.

Table 2. Our model performance after removing several major parts of the model.

Dataset	TPKT		TPKT-NT		TPKT-NP		TPKT-NF	
	ACC	AUC	ACC	AUC	ACC	AUC	ACC	AUC
assist09	0.7865	0.8440	0.7838	0.8417	0.7735	0.8321	0.7795	0.8364
assist17	0.7232	0.7770	0.7192	0.7716	0.7124	0.7654	0.7162	0.7691
static	0.8147	0.8341	0.8102	0.8299	0.8024	0.8222	0.8066	0.8251
algebra05	0.8421	0.8000	0.8367	0.7963	0.8321	0.7877	0.8345	0.7896

4.6   Capability in Capturing the Sequential(RQ3)

To assess whether our model exhibits enhanced sensitivity to the order of interactions within students' learning sequences, we conducted experiments involving the randomization of student data. We systematically disrupted the sequence of interactions in the datasets by varying the proportion of data shuffled. We employed the assist09 dataset for this investigation and utilized AUC as the evaluation metric. The randomization process involved randomly selecting a specified percentage of interactions from all interaction sequences of all students. These selected interactions were then shuffled in order, effectively disrupting the original learning sequence. As depicted in the Fig. 2[a], the AUC of our model exhibits a steeper decline with increasing randomization proportions compared to AKT. This observation suggests that our model is more sensitive to the order of interactions in students' learning sequences.

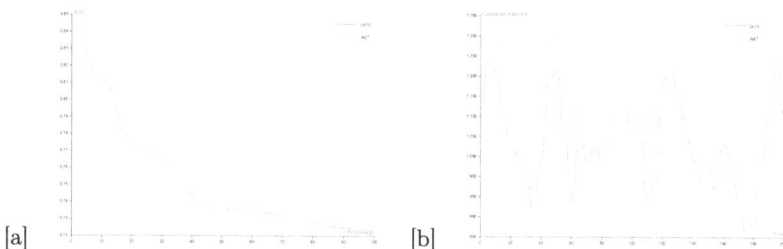

[a]   [b]

Fig. 2. [a] When we disrupt the order of the students' learning sequences, as the proportion of disruption increases, both our model and the AKT experience a certain degree of performance degradation, but our model's performance declines more rapidly. [b] The Euclidean distance between the knowledge states predicted by our model at two consecutive time steps is always less than the Euclidean distance between the knowledge states predicted by AKT.

4.7 Predictive Stability(RQ4)

In our model, a student's knowledge state at a given time step is represented by a vector of length 256. To investigate whether the predicted knowledge states by our model are more stable, we calculated the Euclidean distance [1] between the predicted knowledge states at adjacent time steps for the same student. A smaller Euclidean distance indicates greater similarity between the two vectors. In our experiments, we limited the length of the students' learning sequences to 200 interactions, so Fig. 2[b] in our study shows the Euclidean distance between the predicted knowledge states before and after 200 interactions for the same student by both our model and AKT. From the figure, it can be seen that the trends of the curves are the same, which indicates that both our model and AKT can capture the trend of changes in students' knowledge states. However, the Euclidean distance between the predicted knowledge states by our model is always smaller than that predicted by AKT, which suggests that our model can predict students' knowledge states more stably.

5 Conclusions and Future Work

In this study, we have introduced a new KT model that improves upon the state-of-the-art by considering the temporal dynamics and individual learning rates of students. Our model's architecture, which includes the Temporal-Aware Question Encoder and the Knowledge-Adaptive Response Encoder, allows for a nuanced understanding of student knowledge states. The incorporation of an exponential forgetting curve within our Transformer model provides a more accurate simulation of the forgetting behavior observed in the learning process. Our experimental results on four diverse datasets validate the effectiveness of our model, showing improved predictive accuracy and stability in knowledge state tracing. The ablation study further confirms the importance of each component in our model's architecture. The visualization of our model's performance on a learning sequence demonstrates its sensitivity to the order of interactions, a testament to its capability to capture the sequential nature of learning.Although our model has shown some improvement in performance, there are still many areas where the model can be optimized and improved, such as, for example, whether there are better ways of fusing information to enhance representations, or more intuitive and interpretable ways of using this information in knowledge tracing methods. In the future, we hope to explore more meaningful information to enhance the accuracy and interpretability of response prediction in knowledge tracing, or to better model students' forgetting behavior by introducing time lags between interactions.

References

1. Deza, E., Deza, M.M., Deza, M.M., Deza, E.: Encyclopedia of Distances. Springer, Heidelberg (2009). https://doi.org/10.1007/978-3-642-00234-2
2. Ghosh, A., Heffernan, N., Lan, A.S.: Context-aware attentive knowledge tracing. In: Proceedings of the 26th ACM SIGKDD International Conference on Knowledge Discovery & Data Mining, pp. 2330–2339 (2020)
3. Glorot, X., Bengio, Y.: Understanding the difficulty of training deep feedforward neural networks. In: Proceedings of the Thirteenth International Conference on Artificial Intelligence and Statistics, pp. 249–256. JMLR Workshop and Conference Proceedings (2010)
4. Kingma, D.: Adam: a method for stochastic optimization. In: International Conference Learn Represent (2014)
5. LeCun, Y., Bengio, Y., Hinton, G.: Deep learning. Nature **521**(7553), 436–444 (2015)
6. Ma, H., et al.: HD-KT: advancing robust knowledge tracing via anomalous learning interaction detection. In: Proceedings of the ACM on Web Conference 2024, pp. 4479–4488 (2024)
7. Mao, S., Zhan, J., Wang, Y., Jiang, Y.: Improving knowledge tracing via considering two types of actual differences from exercises and prior knowledge **16**(3), 324–338 (2023). https://doi.org/10.1109/TLT.2023.3259013. conference Name: IEEE Transactions on Learning Technologies
8. Murre, J.M., Dros, J.: Replication and analysis of ebbinghaus' forgetting curve. PLoS ONE **10**(7), e0120644 (2015)
9. Pandey, S., Karypis, G.: A self-attentive model for knowledge tracing. In: 12th International Conference on Educational Data Mining, EDM 2019, pp. 384–389. International Educational Data Mining Society (2019)

10. Piech, C., et al.: Deep knowledge tracing. In: Advances in Neural Information Processing Systems, vol. 28 (2015)
11. Rasch, G.: Probabilistic models for some intelligence and attainment tests. ERIC (1993)
12. Yeung, C.K., Yeung, D.Y.: Addressing two problems in deep knowledge tracing via prediction-consistent regularization. In: Proceedings of the Fifth Annual ACM Conference on Learning at Scale, pp. 1–10 (2018)
13. Yin, Y., et al.: Tracing knowledge instead of patterns: stable knowledge tracing with diagnostic transformer. In: Proceedings of the ACM Web Conference 2023, pp. 855–864. ACM. https://doi.org/10.1145/3543507.3583255, https://dl.acm.org/doi/10.1145/3543507.3583255
14. Zeng, A., Chen, M., Zhang, L., Xu, Q.: Are transformers effective for time series forecasting?. http://arxiv.org/abs/2205.13504
15. Zhang, J., Shi, X., King, I., Yeung, D.Y.: Dynamic key-value memory networks for knowledge tracing. In: Proceedings of the 26th International Conference on World Wide Web, pp. 765–774 (2017)

Position-Aware Dynamic Graph Convolutional Recurrent Network for Traffic Forecasting

Rui Mao, Xufei Zhuang$^{(\boxtimes)}$, Xudong Gao, Haitao Zhang, Qing-Dao-Er-Ji Ren, Bao Shi, Yatu Ji, and Nier Wu

School of Information Engineering, Inner Mongolia University of Technology, Hohhot 010080, China

{20221100131,20221800107,20221800126,MLjyt,wunier04}@imut.edu.cn

Abstract. Traffic forecasting is a typical spatio-temporal data forecasting task with complex spatio-temporal dependencies. Recent works use predefined static graphs and adaptive graphs to reflect real-world traffic patterns. However, traffic networks often suffer from unexpected changes, and the graph structures learned during training phases are not always applicable during testing phases. To cope with this issue, we propose a Position-Aware Dynamic Graph Convolutional Recurrent Network (PADGCRN) for traffic forecasting. First, we design a novel position-aware dynamic graph learning method to obtain dynamic spatial representations. Unlike previous methods, our approach generates dynamic graphs based on the spatio-temporal position embeddings, which more effectively capture hidden spatial correlations. Then, by integrating dynamic graph diffusion convolution into gated recurrent unit, our method is able to capture synchronous spatio-temporal dependencies. Experiments on two real traffic speed datasets verify that effectiveness and efficiency of PADGCRN compared to 12 baselines.

Keywords: Traffic forecasting · Dynamic graph learning · Graph convolutional network · Gated recurrent unit

1 Introduction

Spatio-temporal data mining problem has attracted widespread attention in the field of deep learning [13], playing a crucial role in applications including weather observation, natural disaster detection, and traffic forecasting. Traffic forecasting problems draw interest of researchers due to their complex spatio-temporal dependencies and great practical value [16].

Deep learning methods like RNNs and CNNs are extensively used in traffic forecasting. RNNs model temporal dependencies through gated memory units, while CNNs use 1D convolutions [7] to extract temporal correlations. Unfortunately, these approaches are not effective for modeling spatial relationships of

R. Hadfi et al. (Eds.): PRICAI 2024, LNAI 15281, pp. 416–428, 2025.
https://doi.org/10.1007/978-981-96-0116-5_35

urban networks. Therefore, some researchers divided traffic networks into regular grids and used CNNs to extract spatial dependencies among these grids [9]. However, CNNs, which are suitable for Euclidean spaces, overlook the topological relationships in traffic networks. Currently, Graph Neural Networks (GNNs) model the traffic network as a graph and sensors as nodes. GNNs use convolution operations to aggregate information from neighboring nodes and update the central node's features, thereby learning the underlying spatial topologies. DCRNN [8] employs diffusion convolution to model traffic changes as a bidirectional random walk on graphs combined with a GRU-based encoder-decoder to capture spatio-temporal correlations. STGCN [19] replaces RNN with gated CNNs and integrates graph convolution to extract spatio-temporal dependencies. STGODE [5] addresses excessive smoothing in GCNs through Ordinary Differential Equations (ODEs). GMAN [22] captures spatio-temporal correlations using self-attention mechanisms. MTGNN [17] extracts sparse graph adjacency matrices from data and mitigates over-smoothing problem of GCNs. However, hidden factors like regional functions (commercial, industrial, office areas), road types (multiple intersections, one-way streets), and the distribution of Points of Interest (POIs) may also influence spatial relationships between areas. For example, commercial areas often become congested during holidays, while industrial areas are comparatively clear, despite their proximity. Conversely, schools and office areas exhibit similar traffic patterns during peak hours, even if they are far apart. Therefore, graphs constructed based on predefined rules or learnable parameters, may not effectively capture dynamic traffic patterns, ignoring the time-varying spatio-temporal heterogeneity.

To solve the these issues, we present a novel spatio-temporal traffic forecasting model, Position-Aware Dynamic Graph Convolutional Recurrent Network, (PADGCRN). The main contributions of this paper are summarized as follows.

1. We propose a novel position-aware dynamic graph learning method to obtain the dynamic spatial representation. First, the method constructs an embedding matrix based on spatio-temporal position information. Then, the position embeddings are combined with the dynamic filters to generate dynamic position-aware embeddings, which are used to generate position-aware dynamic graph.
2. We present an efficient framework PADGCRN for traffic forecasting, which combines gated recurrent unit with dynamic diffusion convolution networks to model spatio-temporal correlations and uses a general RNN training strategy to overcome the shortcomings of time and memory consumption.
3. Experiments on two real-world datasets demonstrate that PADGCRN achieves the best prediction performance compared with 12 baselines in benchmark.

2   Related Work

2.1   Traffic Forecasting

Traffic data is recorded as time-series by a series of sensors at fixed intervals. Early approaches to handling univariate time-series tasks primarily employed knowledge-driven statistical approaches, like VAR [2] and ARIMA [14], as well as data-driven machine learning approaches, like SVR [15] and KNN [21]. These approaches rely on the assumption of a stationary linear dependence in time-series data. However, traffic data often exhibits complex and highly nonlinear variations, and traditional methods only consider temporal correlations while neglecting spatial effects. Therefore, they struggle to cope with the complex spatio-temporal correlations in traffic data. Deep learning methods have achieved significant success in natural language processing, attracting increasing attention from scholars in the field of traffic forecasting. FC-LSTM [11] combines CNN with LSTM to model traffic data. TCN [20] employs dilated convolutions to achieve an exponentially increasing receptive field. These approaches have achieved positive outcomes but are still not ideal for handling spatial topologies.

2.2   Spatio-Temporal Graph Neural Networks

Currently, Spatio-Temporal Graph Neural Networks (STGNNs) have achieved excellent performance in modeling spatio-temporal correlations, DCRNN [8], STGCN [19], and STGODE [5], models based on predefined graphs structures, which are limited by the availability of graphs and heavily rely on the acquisition of prior knowledge. To cope with this issues, models like Graph WaveNet [18], AGCRN [1], and MTGNN [17], which are based on learnable parameters, construct adaptive graph structures and have achieved better results. However, these graph structures defined during the training phase may not be suitable for the validation and testing phases, ignoring time-varying spatial features. Therefore, recent works have focused on dynamically how to generate graph structures, adaptively updating the spatial correlations among nodes during the testing phase. Z-GCNETs [3] incorporates the concept of jagged persistence to generate jagged persistent graphs that capture dynamic spatial topology. ASTGNN [6] dynamically adjusts the weights of nodes using self-attention. PGCN [10] and Ada-STNet [12] constructs spatio-temporal adaptive graphs by mining historical traffic data.

3   Preliminaries

Definition 1 (Traffic Road Network). The traffic road network is defined as a weighted graph $\mathcal{G} = (\mathcal{V}, \mathcal{E}, A)$, the sensors information is represented by a set $\mathcal{V} = \{v_1, v_2, \cdots, v_N\}$. The graph edges set $\mathcal{E} = \{e_1, e_2, \cdots, e_M\}$ represent the connectivity between sensors, and $A \in R^{N \times N}$ is the graph adjacency matrix.

Definition 2 (Traffic graph signal). Given the road network at time t, the traffic data collected by N sensor nodes is considered a graph signal, defined as $X_t = [x_t^1, x_t^2, \cdots, x_t^N] \in R^{N \times C}$, $x_t^i \in R^C$ denotes the feature vector of v_i, and C represents traffic features. The input tensor for all nodes over the historical time steps T is denoted as $X = [X_1, X_2, \cdots, X_T] \in R^{T \times N \times C}$.

Definition 3 (Problem Definition). The purpose of traffic forecasting is to predict future traffic conditions using historical observational data. The prediction problem can be viewed as to learn a function Φ, which maps the traffic data from historical time steps T to a future signal over time steps P, represented by:

$$[X_{t-T+1}, X_{t-T+2}, \cdots, X_t; \mathcal{G}] \xrightarrow{\Phi} \left[\hat{X}_{t+1}, \hat{X}_{t+2}, \cdots, \hat{X}_{t+P}\right] \tag{1}$$

4 Methodology

This section introduces a detailed overview of PADGCRN. The overall architecture of PADGCRN is shown in Fig. 1.

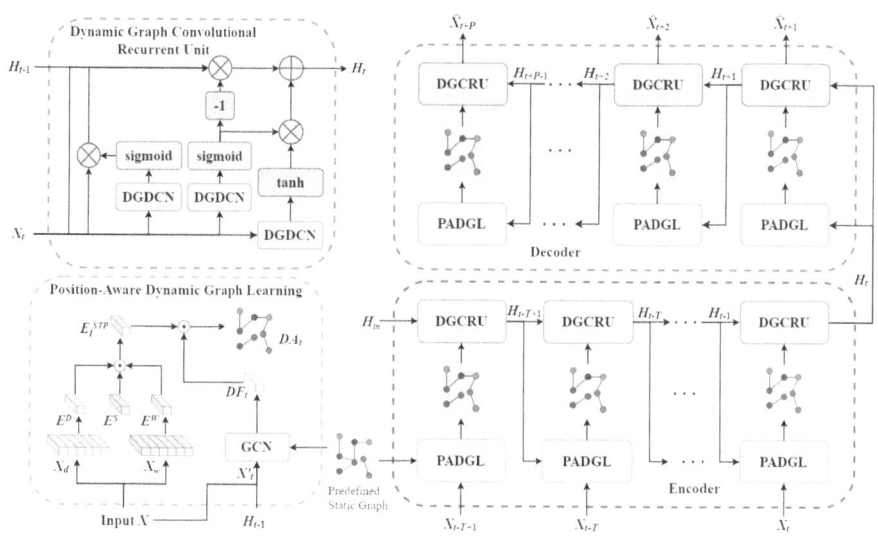

Fig. 1. The overall architecture and modules of PADGCRN

4.1 Position-Aware Dynamic Graph Learning

The predefined graph structure represents stable spatial relationships among nodes. We represent the message passing process of dynamic node states through the graph convolution operation. The output is a dynamic filtering tensor $DF_t \in R^{N \times d}$:

$$X'_t = X_t \| H_{t-1} \tag{2}$$

$$DF_t = \Theta_{*\mathcal{G}}(X_t; A) = \sum_{k=0}^{K} AX'_t W^k \tag{3}$$

where $\|$ represents a concatenation operation. $*\mathcal{G}$ denotes the graph convolutions, Θ or W^k is the kernel parameter, K is the graph depth.

To fully consider spatio-temporal dependencies on different scales, we design a spatio-temporal position embedding constructor. Specifically, weekly and daily features are encoded to obtain time embedding vectors $T_w^{(w_t)}$, $T_d^{(d_t)} \in R^d$, where d represents the embedding dimension ($d > C$), the week index $w_t \in [0, 7)$ indicates a specific day of the week, and the day index $d_t \in [0, 288)$ represents a specific minute of the day. The embeddings for all T time slices are concatenated to form the periodic embedding matrices E^W, $E^D \in R^{T \times d}$. To explicitly model spatial heterogeneity, we assign an additional embedding vector to each node, obtaining the spatial position embedding matrix E^{STP}. Then, we perform an Hadamard product between the temporal embedding and the spatial position embedding to obtain spatio-temporal position embedding matrix as follows:

$$E^{STP} = E^S \odot E^W \odot E^D \tag{4}$$

where $\odot$ represents the Hadamard product. Subsequently, we perform Hadamard product and nonlinear transformation of the dynamic filtering tensor DF_t with the spatio-temporal position embedding matrix, dynamically adjusting the spatial correlations of nodes to generate the spatio-temporal position-aware dynamic embedding matrix DE_t^1. Finally, we compute the dynamic graph DA_t based on the similarity between spatio-temporal position-aware dynamic embeddings, defined by:

$$\begin{aligned} DE_t^1 &= \tanh\left(\delta\left(DF_t^1 \odot E_t^{STP}\right)\right) \\ DE_t^2 &= \tanh\left(\delta\left(DF_t^2 \odot E_t^{STP}\right)\right) \end{aligned} \tag{5}$$

$$DA_t = \text{ReLU}\left(\tanh\left(\delta\left(DE_t^1 DE_t^{2^T} - DE_t^2 DE_t^{1^T}\right)\right)\right) \tag{6}$$

where DA_t represents the position-aware dynamic graph at time t, $\tanh(\cdot)$ is the activation function, $\text{ReLU}(\cdot)$ is used for graph sparsification, the hyperparameter δ is used to control the saturation rate of activation function.

4.2   Dynamic Graph Diffusion Convolution

In traffic prediction, DCRNN [8] uses bidirectional diffusion convolution to model spatial correlation, capturing traffic dynamics based on the diffusion process. Specifically, the K-order bidirectional diffusion process in the directed graph, defined by:

$$Z = \Theta_{*\mathcal{G}}(X; A) = \sum_{k=0}^{K} P_f^k X W_f^k + P_b^k X W_b^k \tag{7}$$

where $P_f = D_f^{-1}A, P_b = D_b^{-1}A$ represent the forward and backward diffusion process, respectively. W_f^k, W_b^k are learnable parameters. Considering the impact of bidirectional traffic flows, we use the dynamic graph in a bidirectional diffusion convolution network, defined as follows:

$$Z_t = \Theta_{*\mathcal{G}}^1 \left(X_t'; A, \widetilde{DA}_{t,f} \right) + \Theta_{*\mathcal{G}}^2 \left(X_t'; A^T, \widetilde{DA}_{t,b} \right) \tag{8}$$

$$\widetilde{DA}_t = DA_t + I \tag{9}$$

where $\widetilde{DA}_t = \left(\sum_{J=0}^N \widetilde{DA}_{t,(i,j)} \right)^{-1}$ represent the dynamic transition matrices. Furthermore, to reduce noise signals and error propagation caused by stacked graph convolution layers, we use a gating mechanism to adaptively fuse the output Z_t and the input X_t' of the dynamic graph diffusion convolution.

$$z = \sigma \left(X_t' W_z^1 + Z_t W_z^2 + b_z \right) \tag{10}$$

$$Z_t^{\text{out}} = z \odot X_t' + (1 - z) \odot Z_t \tag{11}$$

where W_z^1, W_z^2, and b_z are weight parameters, $\sigma(\cdot)$ denotes the sigmoid nonlinear activation. Z_t^{out} is the output of gated dynamic graph convolution module.

4.3   Dynamic Graph Convolutional Recurrent Module

Traffic data exhibits complex spatio-temporal dependencies. RNNs can effectively model temporal correlations but suffer from gradient vanishing issues and ignore spatial impact. To address these issues, we replace the linear transformation in the gated recurrent unit (GRU) [4] with dynamic graph diffusion convolution, capturing synchronous temporal contextual information and spatial correlations. The computation of each gated recurrent unit can be expressed as:

$$\begin{aligned}
r_t &= \sigma \left(\Theta_{*\mathcal{G}}^r \left[X_t \| H_{t-1}, E_t^{STP} \right] \right) \\
u_t &= \sigma \left(\Theta_{*\mathcal{G}}^u \left[X_t \| H_{t-1}, E_t^{STP} \right] \right) \\
C_t &= \tanh \left(\Theta_{*\mathcal{G}}^C \left[X_t \| r_t \odot H_{t-1}, E_t^{STP} \right] \right) \\
H_t &= u_t \odot H_{t-1} + (1 - u_t) \odot C_t
\end{aligned} \tag{12}$$

where H_t is the hidden state output at time t. u_t, r_t represent the update gate and reset gate of GRU, respectively. Θ^r, Θ^u, and Θ^C are the kernel parameters. We combine the dynamic graph diffusion convolution network with GRU to infer the spatio-temporal position-aware embeddings and generate dynamic graphs, enhancing the capability of model to handle fine-grained spatio-temporal patterns.

4.4   Segmented Training Strategy

RNN shows advantages in modeling sequence tasks. However, as the sequence length increases, the forgetting mechanism in memory units selectively stores historical information, leading to insensitivity to long-range temporal dependencies. Based on segmented learning approach, we employ an efficient RNN training strategy. We calculate the only first i lengths of the sequence in early training. As the training input sequence length increases, the decoder can achieve better performance over longer ranges. Therefore, the segmented training strategy can effectively alleviate time and memory consumption issues during the early stages of training.

5   Experiments

5.1   Datasets

Table 1. Dataset information summary.

Datasets	Samples	Sensors	Edges	Time Span
METR-LA	34272	207	1515	2012/3/1 - 2012/6/30
PEMS-BAY	52116	325	2691	2017/1/1 - 2017/5/31

The performance of PADGCRN is validated on two real traffic speed datasets [8], METR-LA and PEMS-BAY. METR-LA consists of speed data recorded every five minutes by 207 detectors located on Los Angeles highways, PEMS-BAY collected by 325 sensors located on the San Francisco Bay Area. Table 1 provides the description of each dataset.

5.2   Baseline Methods

We compare the proposed method with 12 baselines. Below is a brief overview of critical baselines: (1) HA predicts future data by calculating the average of historical data. (2) ARIMA [14] uses autoregressive and moving average methods for prediction. (3) VAR [2] utilizes support vector machines to predict time series. (4) FC-LSTM [11] embeds a fully connected network into the LSTM unit. (5) STGCN [19] integrates graph convolutional networks and causal convolutional networks to model temporal and spatial correlations. (6) DCRNN [8] combines bidirectional diffusion convolution and RNN in an encoder-decoder framework. (7) GraphWaveNet [18] captures spatial dependencies in the data using an adaptive graph and processed long-term temporal features using dilated causal convolution. (8) AGCRN [1] generates an adaptive graph by learnable parameters and extracts spatio-temporal correlations using GRU. (9) GMAN [22] focuses on critical parts of traffic data at different times using multiple spatio-temporal attention mechanisms. (10) MTGNN [17] employs a graph learning module to capture latent spatial correlations between variables and dilated 1D convolutions to extract temporal correlations. (11) Ada-STNet [12] guides optimal adaptive graph learning using node attributes and extracts spatio-temporal dependencies using dilated causal convolutions and diffusion convolutions. (12) PGCN [10] constructs progressive graphs by learning the trend similarities between nodes.

5.3   Experimental Settings

PADGCRN utilizes the encoder-decoder architecture, the hidden state dimension for each GRU is set 64, and the spatio-temporal embedding dimension d is set 40. The graph diffusion convolution depth K is set to 2, and δ is set to 3. We employ the Adam optimizer with an initial learning rate of 0.001 for model training. An early stopping strategy is used during training to avoid overfitting, stopping when the loss fails to decrease for 20 consecutive iterations or after 150 epochs. We selected the Mean Absolute Error (MAE) as the loss function.

5.4   Experimental Comparison Results

Table 2. Experimental comparison results on two real-word datasets.

Datasets	Models	15 min			30 min			60 min		
		MAE	RMSE	MAPE	MAE	RMSE	MAPE	MAE	RMSE	MAPE
METR-LA	HA	4.16	7.80	13.00%	4.16	7.80	13.00%	4.16	7.80	13.00%
	ARIMA	3.99	8.21	9.60%	5.15	10.45	12.70%	6.90	13.25	17.40%
	VAR	4.42	7.89	10.20%	5.41	9.13	12.70%	6.52	10.11	15.80%
	FC-LSTM	3.44	6.30	9.60%	3.77	7.23	10.90%	4.37	8.69	13.20%
	STGCN	2.88	5.74	7.62%	3.47	7.24	9.57%	4.59	9.40	12.70%
	DCRNN	2.77	5.38	7.30%	3.15	6.45	8.80%	3.60	7.60	10.50%
	GraphWaveNet	2.69	5.15	6.90%	3.07	6.22	8.37%	3.53	7.37	10.01%
	AGCRN	2.87	5.58	7.70%	3.23	6.58	9.00%	3.62	7.51	10.38%
	GMAN	2.80	5.55	7.41%	3.12	6.49	8.73%	3.44	7.35	10.07%
	MTGNN	2.69	5.18	6.86%	3.05	6.17	8.19%	3.49	7.23	9.87%
	Ada-STNet	2.65	5.06	6.80%	3.03	6.08	8.20%	3.47	7.18	**9.80%**
	PGCN	2.69	5.15	6.90%	3.07	6.22	8.37%	3.53	7.36	9.94%
	PADGCRN	**2.62**	**5.03**	**6.70%**	**2.98**	**6.01**	8.17%	**3.43**	7.18	9.82%
PEMS-BAY	HA	2.88	5.59	6.80%	2.88	5.59	6.80%	2.88	5.59	6.80%
	ARIMA	1.62	3.30	3.50%	2.33	4.76	5.40%	3.38	6.50	8.30%
	VAR	1.74	3.16	3.60%	2.32	4.25	5.00%	2.93	5.44	6.50%
	FC-LSTM	2.05	4.19	4.80%	2.20	4.55	5.20%	2.37	4.96	5.70%
	STGCN	1.36	2.96	2.90%	1.81	4.27	4.17%	2.49	5.69	5.79%
	DCRNN	1.38	2.95	2.90%	1.74	3.97	3.90%	2.07	4.74	4.90%
	GraphWaveNet	1.30	2.74	2.73%	1.63	3.70	3.67%	1.95	4.52	4.63%
	AGCRN	1.37	2.87	2.94%	1.69	3.85	3.87%	1.96	4.54	4.64%
	GMAN	1.34	2.91	2.86%	1.63	3.76	3.68%	**1.86**	**4.32**	**4.37%**
	MTGNN	1.32	2.79	2.77%	1.65	3.74	3.69%	1.94	4.49	4.53%
	Ada-STNet	1.30	2.73	2.70%	1.62	3.67	3.60%	1.89	4.36	4.50%
	PGCN	1.30	2.73	2.72%	1.62	3.67	3.63%	1.92	4.45	4.45%
	PADGCRN	**1.28**	**2.69**	**2.68%**	**1.60**	**3.61**	**3.57%**	1.87	4.33	4.49%

Table 2 shows the forecasting performance of PADGCRN compared to baseline methods under the same experimental conditions for various horizons. The best performing results are in bold, and the second best are underlined in the table. Compared with other baselines, PADGCRN achieves the best overall accuracy. Evidently, statistical models like HA, ARIMA, and VAR handle nonlinear time series with difficulty, producing larger errors. Deep learning models such as FC-LSTM perform better but ignore spatial influences. Models based on predefined graphs, like STGCN and DCRNN, capture more complex spatio-temporal relationships and achieve better performance but may not adequately represent dynamic traffic conditions. GWNET, AGCRN, and MTGNN adaptively construct graph structures based on initialization parameters, overcoming the limitations of predefined graphs. However, the adaptive graph is still static and may fail to adapt to dynamic traffic patterns. GMAN utilizes the self-attention mechanism to achieve a global receptive field, which has advantages in capturing long-term spatio-temporal dependencies. However, it falls short in extracting local temporal dependencies and has difficulty with the attention mechanism in handling large-scale nodes. Ada-STNet and PGCN use node attributes to guide adaptive graph learning, effectively modeling dynamic spatial dependencies, but Ada-STNet requires two-stage training for the adaptive graph, leading to extra time consumption.

To clearly illustrate the differences in prediction performance, we plot a visual comparison of the predicted and actual values for a specific sensor on a given day. As shown in Fig. 2, both PADGCRN and Ada-STNet fit well speed changes during most periods. However, our method demonstrates superior prediction performance in complex scenes, such as traffic peak hours or periods with significant fluctuations. For example, the blue magnified area shows that our method responds to dynamic changes and sudden fluctuations in peak traffic more quickly and accurately than the baseline methods. Thus, PADGCRN more effectively captures complex spatio-temporal dependencies and models dynamic changes in real-time traffic conditions with greater accuracy.

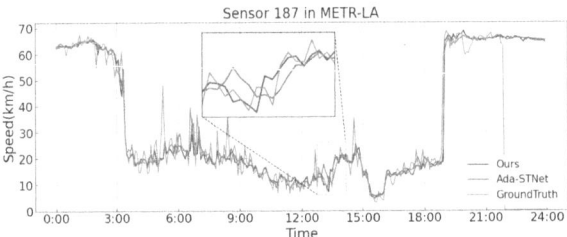

Fig. 2. The comparison of forecasting curves within one day on METR-LA.

5.5   Ablation Experiment

In order to validate the impact of key components on PADGCRN prediction performance, we perform an ablation experiment on METR-LA. Our model is transformed into four variants: (1) Rem-DG: The dynamic graph convolution branch is removed, using only the predefined graph for bidirectional diffusion convolution to capture spatial correlations; (2) Rem-STPE: The spatio-temporal position embedding is removed, using only the randomly initialize node embedding matrix to generate dynamic graph; (3) Rem-DGL: Replace the graph convolutional message passing process in the dynamic graph learning layer with a fully connected network to measure the dependencies between nodes. (4) Rem-STS: Disregard the concept of RNN segmented training and directly use the sequence maximum length as input.

Table 3. Ablation study results on METR-LA.

Models	15 min			30 min			60 min		
	MAE	RMSE	MAPE	MAE	RMSE	MAPE	MAE	RMSE	MAPE
Rem-DG	2.73	5.20	7.11%	3.11	6.23	8.53%	3.58	7.47	10.23%
Rem-DGL	2.65	5.08	6.86%	3.01	6.08	8.28%	3.45	7.18	9.93%
Rem-STPE	2.67	5.04	6.77%	3.03	6.09	8.19%	3.50	7.26	10.05%
Rem-STS	2.64	5.07	6.75%	3.00	6.08	8.21%	3.44	7.21	**9.79%**
PADGCRN	**2.62**	**5.03**	**6.70%**	**2.98**	**6.01**	**8.17%**	**3.43**	**7.18**	9.82%

Table 3 shows the results of different variants. Rem-DG lacks the dynamic graph convolution branch, which leads to inadequate consideration of global spatial correlations and results in significantly reduced prediction performance. Similarly, Rem-DGL lacks the guidance of graph convolution in the message passing process, making it ineffective in describing dynamic spatial topologies. Rem-STPE generates dynamic graphs through the initialization of node embeddings, overlooking the impact of spatio-temporal positions, which leads to decreased performance. Rem-STS indicates that the segmented learning strategy significantly reduces memory and time consumption during training without affecting prediction performance. Overall, PADGCRN outperforms these variants, confirming the effectiveness of each component.

5.6   Interpretability Study

To demonstrate the effectiveness of the position-aware dynamic graph, we visualize the spatial relationships of certain nodes on METR-LA in the dynamic graph obtained by training and the predefined graph as heatmaps.

As shown in Fig. 3(a), the heatmap of the predefined graph is sparse and single except for the diagonal. In contrast, Fig. 3(b) shows that the dynamic graph learned through spatio-temporal position embedding matrices contains rich and diverse information. Some nodes in the marked box do not reflect correlation in the Fig. 3(a). But in fact, as shown in Fig. 3(c), the speed fluctuations of two of the nodes are very similar during the same time period. Therefore, the dynamic graph can preserve latent spatial dependencies at discrete time steps, effectively complementing the predefined graph.

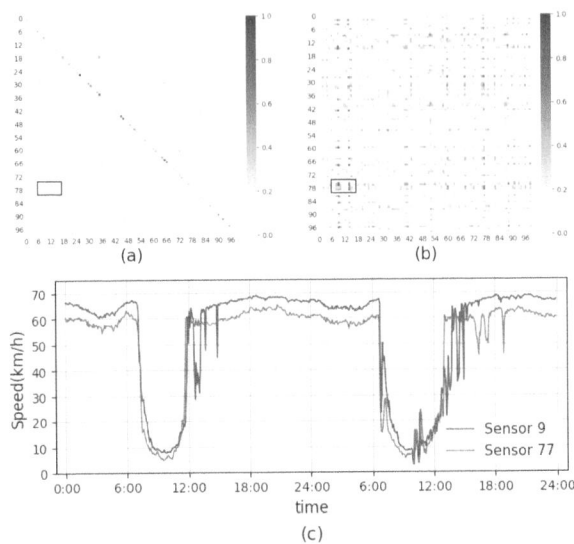

Fig. 3. Interpretability study of the heatmap visualization for predefined graph and position-aware dynamic graph on METR-LA.

6 Conclusion

In this paper, we propose a position-aware dynamic graph convolutional recurrent network (PADGCRN) for traffic forecasting. First, the model combines spatio-temporal position embedding matrices with graph convolution networks to capture spatial relationships among nodes, generating discrete-time dynamic graphs. Then, we integrate diffusion convolution with GRU to capture synchronous spatio-temporal correlations, and an RNN-based training strategy is utilized to effectively reduce time and memory consumption. Experiments on two traffic speed datasets show that our method outperforms most comparison methods in prediction intervals. Furthermore, to enhance the interpretability of our proposed method, we visualize the node correlations under predefined graph and dynamic graph as heatmaps.

Acknowledgments. This study was supported by the Science and Technology Plan Projects of Inner Mongolia Autonomous Region (Grant No. 2020GG0104), the Inner Mongolia Natural Science Foundation (Grant Nos. 2023MS06021), the Universities Directly under the Autonomous Region Funded by the Fundamental Research Fund Project (Grant Nos. JY20230065 and JY20240062).

References

1. Bai, L., Yao, L., Li, C., Wang, X., Wang, C.: Adaptive graph convolutional recurrent network for traffic forecasting. Adv. Neural. Inf. Process. Syst. **33**, 17804–17815 (2020)
2. Chandra, S.R., Al-Deek, H.: Predictions of freeway traffic speeds and volumes using vector autoregressive models. J. Intell. Transp. Syst. **13**(2), 53–72 (2009)
3. Chen, Y., Segovia, I., Gel, Y.R.: Z-GCNETs: time zigzags at graph convolutional networks for time series forecasting. In: International Conference on Machine Learning, pp. 1684–1694. PMLR (2021)
4. Cho, K., Van Merriënboer, B., Gulcehre, C., Bahdanau, D., Bougares, F., Schwenk, H., Bengio, Y.: Learning phrase representations using RNN encoder-decoder for statistical machine translation. arXiv preprint arXiv:1406.1078 (2014)
5. Fang, Z., Long, Q., Song, G., Xie, K.: Spatial-temporal graph ode networks for traffic flow forecasting. In: Proceedings of the 27th ACM SIGKDD Conference on Knowledge Discovery & Data Mining, pp. 364–373 (2021)
6. Guo, S., Lin, Y., Wan, H., Li, X., Cong, G.: Learning dynamics and heterogeneity of spatial-temporal graph data for traffic forecasting. IEEE Trans. Knowl. Data Eng. **34**(11), 5415–5428 (2021)
7. Li, D., Zhang, J., Zhang, Q., Wei, X.: Classification of ECG signals based on 1d convolution neural network. In: 2017 IEEE 19th International Conference on e-Health Networking, Applications and Services (Healthcom), pp. 1–6. IEEE (2017)
8. Li, Y., Yu, R., Shahabi, C., Liu, Y.: Diffusion convolutional recurrent neural network: data-driven traffic forecasting. arXiv preprint arXiv:1707.01926 (2017)
9. Lin, Z., Feng, J., Lu, Z., Li, Y., Jin, D.: DeepSTN+: context-aware spatial-temporal neural network for crowd flow prediction in metropolis. In: Proceedings of the AAAI Conference on Artificial Intelligence, vol. 33, pp. 1020–1027 (2019)
10. Shin, Y., Yoon, Y.: PGCN: progressive graph convolutional networks for spatial-temporal traffic forecasting. IEEE Trans. Intell. Transp. Syst. **25**(7), 7633–7644 (2024)
11. Sutskever, I., Vinyals, O., Le, Q.V.: Sequence to sequence learning with neural networks. In: Advances in Neural Information Processing Systems, vol. 27 (2014)
12. Ta, X., Liu, Z., Hu, X., Yu, L., Sun, L., Du, B.: Adaptive spatio-temporal graph neural network for traffic forecasting. Knowl. Based Syst. **242**, 108199 (2022)
13. Wang, S., Cao, J., Philip, S.Y.: Deep learning for spatio-temporal data mining: a survey. IEEE Trans. Knowl. Data Eng. **34**(8), 3681–3700 (2020)
14. Williams, B.M., Hoel, L.A.: Modeling and forecasting vehicular traffic flow as a seasonal ARIMA process: theoretical basis and empirical results. J. Transp. Eng. **129**(6), 664–672 (2003)
15. Wu, C.H., Ho, J.M., Lee, D.T.: Travel-time prediction with support vector regression. IEEE Trans. Intell. Transp. Syst. **5**(4), 276–281 (2004)
16. Wu, Z., Pan, S., Chen, F., Long, G., Zhang, C., Philip, S.Y.: A comprehensive survey on graph neural networks. IEEE Trans. Neural Netw. Learn. Syst. **32**(1), 4–24 (2020)
17. Wu, Z., Pan, S., Long, G., Jiang, J., Chang, X., Zhang, C.: Connecting the dots: multivariate time series forecasting with graph neural networks. In: Proceedings of the 26th ACM SIGKDD International Conference on Knowledge Discovery & Data Mining, pp. 753–763 (2020)
18. Wu, Z., Pan, S., Long, G., Jiang, J., Zhang, C.: Graph WaveNet for deep spatial-temporal graph modeling. arXiv preprint arXiv:1906.00121 (2019)

19. Yu, B., Yin, H., Zhu, Z.: Spatio-temporal graph convolutional networks: a deep learning framework for traffic forecasting. arXiv preprint arXiv:1709.04875 (2017)
20. Yu, F., Koltun, V.: Multi-scale context aggregation by dilated convolutions. arXiv preprint arXiv:1511.07122 (2015)
21. Zhang, L., Liu, Q., Yang, W., Wei, N., Dong, D.: An improved k-nearest neighbor model for short-term traffic flow prediction. Procedia. Soc. Behav. Sci. **96**, 653–662 (2013)
22. Zheng, C., Fan, X., Wang, C., Qi, J.: GMAN: a graph multi-attention network for traffic prediction. In: Proceedings of the AAAI Conference on Artificial Intelligence, vol. 34, pp. 1234–1241 (2020)

Pose Preserving Landmark Guided Neural Radiation Fields for Talking Portrait Synthesis

Zhen Xiong, Haozhi Huang$^{(\boxtimes)}$, Jundong Tan, and Guanghua Yang

Jinan University, Guangzhou, China
{hzhuang,ghyang}@jnu.edu.cn

Abstract. Talking portrait synthesis is a challenging task of synthesizing an image sequence of portraits with accurate lip synchronization and head pose estimation which correspond to a given audio clip of speech. Recently, the dynamic Neural Radiance Field(NeRF) has achieved real-time synthesizing and high-fidelity 3D modeling of talking portraits, and becomes a hot topic within the research community. In this work, we propose a pose preserving prior and a prior-guided NeRF rendering method for talking portrait synthesis. The prior is a fusion of the facial landmark and the input audio, where the facial landmark is composed of a unified lip-synced landmark and the pose landmark. The unified lip-synced landmarks are generated by a Transformer-like network trained by a large lip-reading corpus, which is suppose to learn the correspondence between the phoneme of an audio and the overall lip motion via its landmark. Lip-synced landmark along with the pose landmark compose the facial landmark for pose preserving. Relying on the uniqueness of the facial landmark and facial action correspondences, it aims to optimize the stability between the synthesized portrait and the driving information. The prior-guided NeRF renderer is to generate the synthesizing portraits according to the input audio and pose preserving prior that learn. Extensive experiments show that our method outperforms existing methods in terms of fidelity and synchronization of speech and video.

Keywords: talking portrait synthesis · landmark guided nerf · pose preserving prior · neural rendering · lip-synced landmark generation

1 Introduction

With the liberation of computing power and the development of 3D rendering models, NeRF-based rendering methods [8,17] have been a certain range of interest and has been applied to talking portrait synthesis, while previous work related to the task generates the sequence of portraits by applying the Generative Adversarial Network (GAN) [14]. The GAN-based rendering advantages in predicting the lip motions, however, as is known to all that synthesizing video with GAN is challenge [2], eliminating the inconsistent between consecutive frames synthesized by GAN is still an open problem.

© The Author(s), under exclusive license to Springer Nature Singapore Pte Ltd. 2025
R. Hadfi et al. (Eds.): PRICAI 2024, LNAI 15281, pp. 429–440, 2025.
https://doi.org/10.1007/978-981-96-0116-5_36

The NeRF-based rendering methods map audios into radiation fields for a latent audio-voice correspondences and achieve high-fidelity 3D modeling of talking portraits, therefore outperform the GAN-based methods and retain more details. Recently, the proposed RAD-NeRF [19] has shown its success in real-time synthesizing of talking portraits. Since the computational resources consumed by the neural network are limited, the training data for talking portrait synthesis are typically a single-person talking video of a few minutes. This might cause few-shot learning problems. In general, the main challenges of the talking portrait synthesis are concluded as follows: 1) shortage of training data, as there is no unified oral movements for a certain speech audio, therefore, generality of the model is the key to addressed this problem. However, the shortage of training data is insufficient to guarantee a trained neural network model which is in good generalization; 2) the many-to-many relationship [16] among audios and the synthesizing portraits. Due to variations in psychological or physiological states, individuals may exhibit different lip movements for the same audio. Conversely, the same lip shape can correspond to a range of sounds. As a result, relying solely on audio data for inference can compromise the accuracy of the predicted lip shapes, leading to blurred or flickering character movements.

In this work, we propose a method along with the pose preserving prior module (LA-NeRF). We propose to use facial landmark [11] and audio to compose the pose preserving prior for synthesizing portraits. The facial landmark is composed of a unified lip-synced landmark and the pose landmark. Since facial landmarks are uniquely matched to facial movements. We add them to training to increase the stability of driving information and synthetic sequences, while also improving the generalization problem caused by training with only a small amount of audio. Specifically, in order to obtain landmarks corresponding to arbitrary audio. We implemented a Transformer encoder based on the cross-attention mechanism, which fuses the features of the two modalities of posture landmark embedding and audio embedding, and finally decodes and synthesizes lip synchronization landmark. In the radiation field network part, in order to improve the sampling accuracy and convergence speed, we use tri-plane hash coding sampling to obtain spatial information. Using audio and landmark as dynamic input, we also use the attention mechanism to fuse audio and facial landmark to extract driving feature information, and finally connect it with spatial information as training data input into the portrait radiation field. The main contributions of this paper are summarized as follows:

1. We propose a two-stage framework that combines pose-preserving priors and NeRF rendering for synthesizing high-fidelity audio-driven portrait sequences with better rendering quality.
2. We integrate the cross-attention mechanism between facial landmark and audio to improve the fusion of feature information from different modal data.
3. Extensive experiments show that our LA-NeRF outperforms other existing methods from the perspective of both objective and subjective metrics.

2   Related Work

Data-driven Talking Head Synthesis. The goal of data-driven talking portrait synthesis is to achieve a specific person synchronized with given arbitrary input data. Currently breakthroughs are mainly based on audio data [10,21]. Nowadays, methods to achieve speech synchronization mouth shape have been mainly divided into two categories: model-based methods and data-driven methods. Model-based methods [3,18] need to define the relationship between audio and facial motion, and use a 3D deformed facial model (3DMM) or auxiliary information for synthesizing of the talking portrait. 3DMM is mostly used in digital technologies such as movies and the metaverse. Due to hardware and cost limitations, this method is difficult to expand. Early methods applying deep learning are the GAN-based methods [7,14] through restricting the latent parameters such as facial landmark [5]. Recently, some NeRF-based works have achieved success in audio-driven 3D talking face synthesis, which can achieve more realistic talking faces compared to GAN-based methods.

Neural Radiation Field. The implicit neural radiation field [13] was proposed in 2020 and has attracted a lot of interests in the field of neural rendering and neural reconstruction. Recent works have also been applied to NeRF in audio-driven portrait synthesis. AD-NeRF [8] firstly proposed an end-to-end audio data-driven method to train the dynamic radiation field of talking portraits on several-minute-long audio and synthesizing video of talking portraits. DFRF [17] introduce a learned portrait prior to achieve few-shot learning. RAD-NeRF [19] further reducing training costs by applying small networks to encode spatial coordinates and audio information to achieve real-time synthesizing. Geneface [20] proposed a landmark-driven model for synthesizing talking portraits, where the three-dimensional facial landmark are substitute for the input audio data. The current efforts of NeRF are focusing on reducing the training costs and enhancing the generalization ability. We combine multiple modal inputs as reference factors for facial movement, slightly increasing the computational complexity while obtaining a high-quality dynamic feature expression that improves both facial reconstruction and lip synchronization confidence.

3   Method

In this section, we present the LA-NeRF framework, as shown in (Fig. 1). Our LA-NeRF consists of two parts: (Sect. 3.1) the LANDMARK GENERATOR, which learns the speech-to-landmark relationship for synced-lip synthesis. (Section 3.2) the NERF-BASED RENDERER, which is a modified NeRF model processing the prior feature concatenated by the facial landmark and the audio.

3.1   Landmark Generator

Typically we can easily obtain audio clips. As our model synthesize talking portraits by referencing the input audio and the corresponding facial landmark.

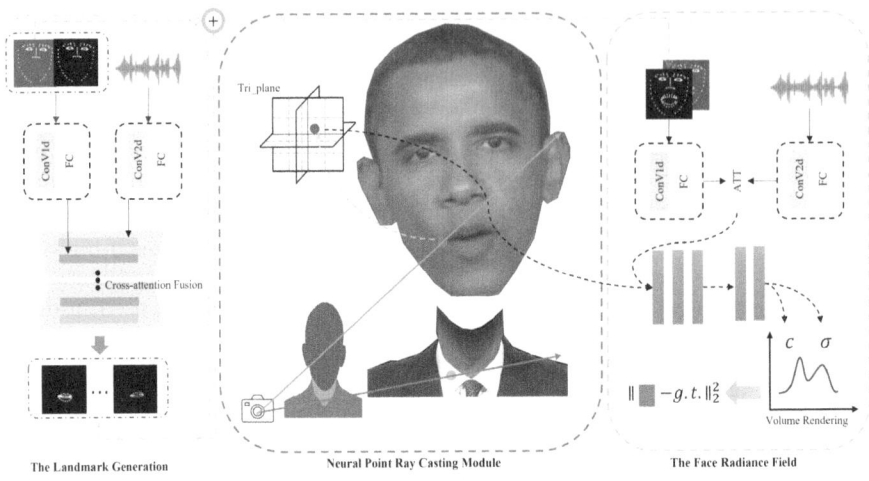

Fig. 1. Network Architecture of LA-NeRF.

Since the original image sequences that provided are irrelevant to the input audio. Therefore, we need a generator for synthesizing the lip-synced landmark correspond to the audio. Arbitrary audio clips are easy to obtain, however, obtaining the corresponding facial landmark of the talking portraits are challenging.

To obtain audio-corresponded facial landmark, we introduced a landmark generator inspired by IP-LAP [23] to obtain the facial landmark. We use multi-frame pose prior landmark information and multi-frame audio information as input data. Pose prior landmark $\{l_t^p \in \mathbb{R}^{2 \times n_p}\}_{t=1}^T$ and input audio $\{m_t \in \mathbb{R}^{h \times w}\}_{t=1}^T$. The output of the synthetic landmark generator is the generated lip sync landmark, expressed as $\{l_t^o \in \mathbb{R}^{2 \times n_o}\}_{t=1}^T$. Among them, n_o, n_p are the number of landmark representing lips and poses, respectively.

We use two-dimensional convolution operations to extract features from audio and obtain audio features a_t. In addition, the size of the landmark is $\{l \in \mathbb{R}^{2 \times n_p}\}$. For point set data, it is essentially a one-dimensional list, so we use one-dimensional convolution to extract the potential representation of the landmark and obtain the landmark feature p_t.

Subsequently, we use the Transformer module to learn the relationship between the two types of data, audio a_t and pose landmark variables p_t, align the encoded data, and obtain the initial audio token $\{Z_a \in \mathbb{R}^T\}$ and pose landmark token $\{Z_p \in \mathbb{R}^T\}$. The details are as follows:

$$Z_a, Z_p = \gamma(a_t), \gamma(p_t) \tag{1}$$

where $\gamma(\cdot)$ represents the positional encoding.

Considering that the two data are in different modalities, the simple concatenation and self-attention mechanism cannot well learn the information between the two. In this regard, we propose to use the cross-attention mechanism to improve the model's ability to understand and express the information of audio features and landmark features. For the task of generating facial landmark motion, we usually use audio as the basic motion condition. So we use audio data as the key (K) and value (V). This is because we hope to guide the generation or adjustment of facial landmark based on audio information, which provides the necessary context or features to help the model understand how facial landmark should change under specific audio input. As the landmark is the target of generation, we regard the information carried by the pose landmark as the core of the query, and we use the pose landmark sequence as the query (Q):

$$CrossAttn(Z_p, Z_a) = Attention(Q, K, V) \tag{2}$$

When decoding, we use the pose landmark as the query and the CrossAttn output by the Encoder as the key and value. We perform cross-attention fusion again and finally get the mouth landmark.

$$\bar{l}_t^o = Decoder(Z_p, CrossAttn(Z_p, Z_a)) \tag{3}$$

Among them, $\bar{l}_t^o \in \mathbb{R}^{2 \times n_o}$ represents the predicted the synced-lip landmark of frame t.

We consider the loss function for landmark synthesizing a linear combination of the L_1 error of the predicted lip-synced landmark, and the L_2 loss for time consistency [23]. Therefore the final loss function is written as:

$$\mathcal{L}_{landmark} = \frac{1}{T} \sum_{t=1}^{T} \left(\|\bar{l}_t^o - l_t^o\|_1 \right)$$
$$+ \frac{1}{T-1} \sum_{t=1}^{T-1} \left(\|(\bar{l}_{t+1}^o - \bar{l}_t^o) - (l_{t+1}^o - l_t^o)\|_2 \right) \tag{4}$$

where l_t^o represents the ground truth landmark of the lip.

3.2   NERF-Based Renderer

The landmark synthesizing module generate pose preserving prior from the input audio. And a NeRF-based portrait radiance field model guided by pose preserving prior is then proposed for synthesizing portrait images, where the prior is composed of the facial landmark and the input audio in the form of potential codes as the guidance of the NeRF rendering.

Pose preserving prior along with the input image sequence compose the inputs of NeRF, where the image sequence are parameterized by the 3D position X and viewing direction d. To prevent hash collisions from affecting training

[12], we use tri-plane hash coding to sample spatial information. Therefore, the implicit function $\mathcal{F}$ [13] is formulated as follows:

$$\mathcal{F} : (X, d, l, a; H) \rightarrow (c, \sigma) \tag{5}$$

where c and σ represent the color and density in the radiation field. H is the result of tri-plane hash coding. We extract features from multiple consecutive frames of the driving data (audio and landmark) to infer the temporal consistency of the synthesized faces. Therefore, $\{l \in \mathbb{R}^{T \times 2 \times n_L}\}$ and $\{a \in \mathbb{R}^{T \times h \times w}\}$, where them, n_L represents the number of facial landmark, and T represents the number of consecutive frames.

The hash algorithm in Instant-NGP treats every position in 3D space equally, which enhances the expressiveness of static complex scenes. However, for dynamic scenes, when the MLP decoder needs to process multiple dynamic features at the same time, the increase in hash conflicts will bring the burden of resolving conflicting gradients to the MLP. With the introduction of some work [12], the adoption of plane decomposition can handle this problem well. For each coordinate $X \in \mathbb{R}^{x \times y \times z}$ of each frame, we perform two-dimensional projections in three directions and obtain its spatial information $H(X)$ by splicing the projections:

$$H(X) = \mathcal{H}^{xy}(X) + \mathcal{H}^{yz}(X) + \mathcal{H}^{xz}(X) \tag{6}$$

where $\mathcal{H}$ represents the plane direction projection.

Each input is a data consisting of multiple frames. Based on the convolutional network of the first module, we implemented the feature extraction of audio and landmark, represented as E_l^t (extracted landmark embedding) and E_a^t (extracted audio embedding). In order to better extract information of different modal features, we also use the attention mechanism to fuse audio and landmark:

$$Att(l, a) = CrossAttn(E_l^t, E_a^t) \tag{7}$$

For volume rendering settings:

$$C(r, l, a) = \int_{t_0}^{t_1} \sigma(r(t), Att(l, a)) \\ \cdot c(r(t), Att(l, a), d) \cdot T(t) dt \tag{8}$$

where t_0 and t_1 are the near and far boundaries of ray r, c and σ are the outputs of the implicit function $\mathcal{F}$, and $T(t)$ is the cumulative transmittance of rays from t_0 to t, which is defined as:

$$T(t) = \exp(-\int_{t_0}^{t} \sigma(r(\tau))d\tau) \tag{9}$$

Since the NeRF model for talking portrait synthesis consider the head and the torso two individual part to be rendered, we therefore train two independent NeRFs to render the head and the torso part respectively [8,19]. First, a head

NeRF is trained through audio, landmark and head pose. Taking the radiation field rendered by this part of NeRF as a condition, we assume that the trunk part is located in the canonical space, and use the head posture h as a driver to achieve the prediction of trunk motion. Consequently, the rendering process for the torso of the synthesizing portrait also adapt the head pose Π and the head color C_{head} as restricts to guide the radiation field of the torso:

$$F_{torso} : (X, d, \Pi, l, a; C_{head}) \rightarrow (c, \sigma) \tag{10}$$

The optimization goal of NeRF is to reduce photogrammetric reconstruction errors between rendered images and ground truth images. Specifically, the loss function can be formulated as:

$$\mathcal{L}_{face} = \sum_{r \in \mathcal{R}} ||C(r, l, a) - C_{gt}||_2^2 \tag{11}$$

where $\mathcal{R}$ is the set of camera rays and C_{gt} is the color of the ground truth images.

4   Experiment

4.1   Implementation Details

Dataset Preparation. We choose a large-scale lip-reading corpus to learn the mapping of audio to facial landmarks. Therefore, we use LRS2 [1] to train our landmark generator. In addition, we train the radiance field on the dataset collected in a previous work [8].

Data Preprocessing. Firstly, when collecting landmark, we use the mediapipe tool to detect facial landmark from each video frame, and set the facial landmark for each frame to be 131. For audio data, we calculate the corresponding Mel spectrogram from the speech wave, or use Wav2vec2 for feature extraction.

4.2   Experimental Setup

Compare to baseline. We compare our LA-NeRF with several excellent works: 1) Wav2Lip [15], a pre-trained synchronization expert to improve lip synchronization performance; 2) AD-NeRF [8], the first Use NeRF to generate talking heads. 3) RAD-NeRF [19] realizes rapid training of nerf rendering avatars. 4) Geneface [20]. The concept of three-dimensional facial landmark is introduced to NeRF for the first time. 5) Makeittalk [24]. Enables inference of arbitrary audio and arbitrary characters.6) ER-NeRF [12]. Optimising spatial coding methods and attention mechanisms based on RAD-NeRF.

We train LA-NeRF on 1 NVIDIA A100 GPU. For the landmark generator module, it takes about 10 h to converge. For the NeRF-based renderer, we performed about 6 h of convergence for each model.

4.3 Quantitative Evaluation

Evaluation indicators. We use peak signal-to-noise ratio (PSNR), image feature distance (FID) [9], boundary distance (LMD) [4] and learned perceptual image patch similarity (LPIPS) [22] to measure Similarity between generated and real images. Additionally, we use the synchronization network confidence score (Sync) [6] to evaluate lip synchronization.

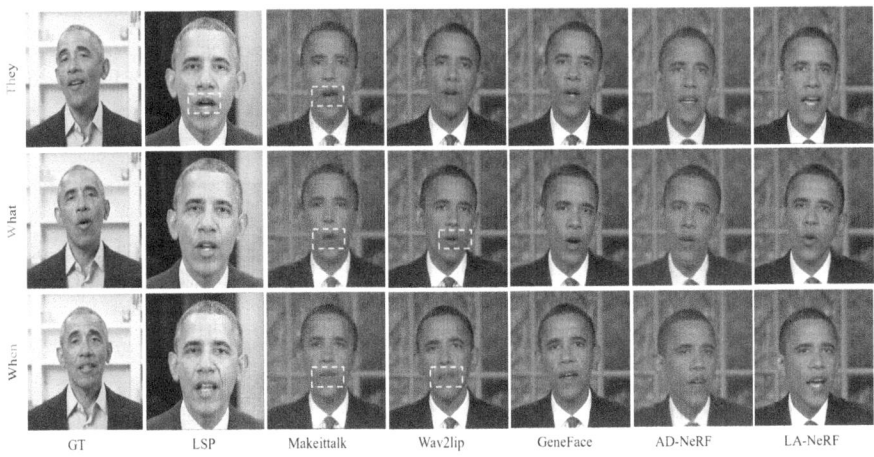

Fig. 2. Comparison of generated keyframes. Compare the visual mouth shape and digital human reconstruction effects of different algorithms under the same audio. Among them, yellow boxes indicate low-quality phenomena such as blur, artifacts, or inaccurate mouth shapes. (Color figure online)

Evaluation Results. The evaluation results are shown in Table 1. Compared with recent best-performing methods, Therefore: (1) Our method shows excellent quality in most metrics. (2) Specifically, from the perspective of video reconstruction, our rendering effect maintains the best visual quality. We observed that the wav2lip and makeittalk algorithms have low fidelity for image reconstruction and perform poorly on FID and LPIPS. ER-NeRF alleviates the impact of high-dimensional hash conflicts in sampling point encoding, has better face reconstruction results, and performs better in LMD. (3) In terms of mouth synchronization, since Wav2lip is jointly trained with SyncNet, it tends to maintain the best and closest to the real video synchronization confidence score. Our method is slightly inferior to it, but also maintains a higher confidence level overall.

4.4 Qualitative Evaluation

In order to compare the results generated by different methods, we show in Fig. 2 the digital human inferred by each algorithm under three key frames under self-drive. Our results are more accurate and clearer, and can achieve more accurate

Table 1. Quantitative evaluation with different methods. We conducted data-driven synthesis on the same identity test set and compared the quality of portrait reconstruction. Best results are in **bold**.

Methods	PSNR↑	FID↓	Sync↑	LPIPS↓	LMD↓
Ground Truth	N/A	0	8.514	0	0)
Wav2Lip [15]	30.94	53.05	**8.380**	0.0639	4.285
MakeitTalk [24]	–	–	4.980	–	10.138
AD-NeRF [8]	30.06	41.99	3.678	0.0901	3.896
RAD-NeRF [19]	36.28	36.30	6.003	0.0336	2.195
GeneFace [20]	33.64	43.82	5.063	0.0401	3.957
ER-NeRF [12]	36.41	39.23	6.416	0.03279	**2.14**
LA-NeRF	**36.44**	**34.67**	6.419	**0.0295**	2.225

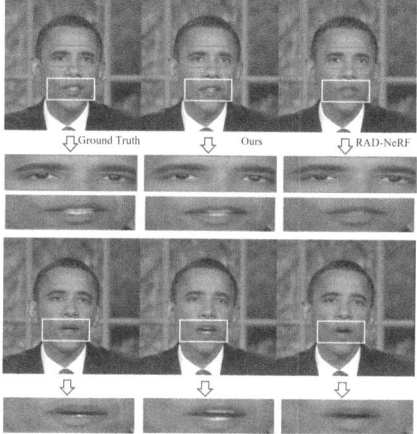

Fig. 3. Quality comparison of detail reconstructions. We compare with ground truth images on the test set.

Fig. 4. Additional digital human data reconstruction. Visualize their partial frame landmark and facial avatar images

reconstruction results in lip reconstruction. This phenomenon also proves that there is a many-to-many phenomenon between audio and mouth movements, and this phenomenon will lead to blurred mouth reconstruction. A more detailed comparison with RAD-NeRF is shown in Fig. 3, when there are large movements of the mouth, such as pouting or opening the mouth wide, our method can synthesize the mouth motion more robustly and reconstruct more details. Since the pose is fixed, what really drives the digital human is the mouth feature point in the landmark. As shown in Fig. 4, we use arbitrary audio as the driver, and the generated landmark and corresponding NeRF are inferred. of digital people for visual display. In multi-syllable movements, the landmark of the mouth and the character's mouth shape can remain relatively consistent.

Table 2. User study. Rating is from 1-5, higher is better.

Methods	Wav2Lip	MakeitTalk	AD-NeRF	RAD-NeRF	GeneFace	LA-NeRF
Audio-Lips Sync	**4.05**	2.67	2.97	3.31	3.54	3.78
Image Quality	2.52	2.16	2.85	3.57	**4.13**	3.85
Video Realness	2.33	2.24	3.09	3.75	3.91	**3.93**

User Study. To better evaluate subjective portrait quality, we conducted user studies to test the effectiveness. We compared the above six algorithms and asked 20 participants to rate the video from three aspects: lip synchronization accuracy, image reconstruction quality, and video authenticity. The final table is shown in Table 2. We have good evaluations in three aspects, and perform better in the authenticity of the video. However, the lip synchronization and picture reconstruction quality are not as good as Wav2lip and Geneface. Geneface provides additional mapping encodings when processing arbitrary landmark. The landmark in any audio are modified to landmark that are similar to the training data, which also makes the algorithm have better generalization ability when processing any data.

4.5   Ablation Study

In order to prove the necessity of each component in LA-NeRF. We tested four settings on the portrait Radiation Field: (1) w/o landmark-driven, in which we removed landmark data as input, consistent with most previous NeRF work, and only used audio as the driver. The results are shown in the third row of Table 3. The year-on-year score has declined to a certain extent. This phenomenon verifies that the unstable mapping between audio and mouth shape is the reason for the large performance degradation in the confidence and similarity of the mouth. (2) w/o audio-driven, in which we remove the audio data input and rely only on landmark information as the driver. The results show that all scores have dropped significantly, which also shows that audio is still the main carrier of action information. When driven by a digital human, audio information and landmark information can be used as input data to better train realistic character

Table 3. Ablation experiment statistics table.

Method	PSNR↑	LPIPS↓	Sync↑
LA-NeRF	36.44	0.02954	6.419
w/o landmark-driven	36.28	0.03362	6.003
w/o audio-driven	36.33	0.03541	3.829
w/o cross-attention	36.40	0.03164	5.903
w/o Tri-plane	36.23	0.03001	5.829

portraits. (3) w/o cross-attention mechanism, we adopted the concatenation of audio and landmark features and directly fed them into MLP for training. (4) w/o tri-plane, we retained the original hash code and sampled the space. Both the attention mechanism and the code have a small decrease.

5 Conclusion

In this paper, we propose a pose preserving landmark guided neural radiation fields talking portrait synthesis method. In order to solve the problem of weak generalization ability of input data, we use audio signals and facial landmark simultaneously as the driving data for digital human NeRF synthesizing. Experiments show that the use of landmark data, cross attention and tri-plane hashing mechanisms also improves the model's expressiveness and training speed, and better captures the correspondence between out-of-domain audio and facial movements.

Acknowledgments. This work was supported by the Fundamental Research Funds for the Central Universities (11623347).

Disclosure of Interests. The authors have no competing interests to declare that are relevant to the content of this article.

References

1. Afouras, T., Chung, J.S., Senior, A., Vinyals, O., Zisserman, A.: Deep audio-visual speech recognition. IEEE Trans. Pattern Anal. Mach. Intell. **44**(12), 8717–8727 (2018)
2. Aldausari, N., Sowmya, A., Marcus, N., Mohammadi, G.: Video generative adversarial networks: a review. ACM Comput. Surv. (CSUR) **55**(2), 1–25 (2022)
3. Chen, L., et al.: Talking-head generation with rhythmic head motion. In: Vedaldi, A., Bischof, H., Brox, T., Frahm, J.-M. (eds.) ECCV 2020. LNCS, vol. 12354, pp. 35–51. Springer, Cham (2020). https://doi.org/10.1007/978-3-030-58545-7_3
4. Chen, L., Li, Z., Maddox, R.K., Duan, Z., Xu, C.: Lip movements generation at a glance. In: Ferrari, V., Hebert, M., Sminchisescu, C., Weiss, Y. (eds.) ECCV 2018. LNCS, vol. 11211, pp. 538–553. Springer, Cham (2018). https://doi.org/10.1007/978-3-030-01234-2_32
5. Chen, L., Maddox, R.K., Duan, Z., Xu, C.: Hierarchical cross-modal talking face generation with dynamic pixel-wise loss. In: Proceedings of the IEEE/CVF Conference on Computer Vision and Pattern Recognition, pp. 7832–7841 (2019)
6. Chung, J.S., Zisserman, A.: Out of time: automated lip sync in the wild. In: Chen, C.-S., Lu, J., Ma, K.-K. (eds.) ACCV 2016. LNCS, vol. 10117, pp. 251–263. Springer, Cham (2017). https://doi.org/10.1007/978-3-319-54427-4_19
7. Doukas, M.C., Zafeiriou, S., Sharmanska, V.: Headgan: Video-and-audio-driven talking head synthesis, **1**(2) . arXiv preprint arXiv:2012.08261 (2020)
8. Guo, Y., Chen, K., Liang, S., Liu, Y.J., Bao, H., Zhang, J.: Ad-nerf: audio driven neural radiance fields for talking head synthesis. In: Proceedings of the IEEE/CVF International Conference on Computer Vision, pp. 5784–5794 (2021)

9. Heusel, M., Ramsauer, H., Unterthiner, T., Nessler, B., Hochreiter, S.: Gans trained by a two time-scale update rule converge to a local nash equilibrium. Adv. Neural Inform. Process. Syst. **30** (2017)

10. Ji, X., et al.: Audio-driven emotional video portraits. In: Proceedings of the IEEE/CVF Conference on Computer Vision and pattern recognition, pp. 14080–14089 (2021)

11. Koestinger, M., Wohlhart, P., Roth, P.M., Bischof, H.: Annotated facial landmarks in the wild: A large-scale, real-world database for facial landmark localization. In: 2011 IEEE international conference on computer vision workshops (ICCV workshops), pp. 2144–2151. IEEE (2011)

12. Li, J., Zhang, J., Bai, X., Zhou, J., Gu, L.: Efficient region-aware neural radiance fields for high-fidelity talking portrait synthesis. In: Proceedings of the IEEE/CVF International Conference on Computer Vision, pp. 7568–7578 (2023)

13. Mildenhall, B., Srinivasan, P.P., Tancik, M., Barron, J.T., Ramamoorthi, R., Ng, R.: Nerf: representing scenes as neural radiance fields for view synthesis. Commun. ACM **65**(1), 99–106 (2021)

14. Prajwal, K., Mukhopadhyay, R., Namboodiri, V.P., Jawahar, C.: A lip sync expert is all you need for speech to lip generation in the wild. In: Proceedings of the 28th ACM International Conference on Multimedia, pp. 484–492 (2020)

15. Pumarola, A., Corona, E., Pons-Moll, G., Moreno-Noguer, F.: D-nerf: neural radiance fields for dynamic scenes. In: Proceedings of the IEEE/CVF Conference on Computer Vision and Pattern Recognition, pp. 10318–10327 (2021)

16. Ren, Y., Liu, J., Zhao, Z.: Portaspeech: portable and high-quality generative text-to-speech. Adv. Neural. Inf. Process. Syst. **34**, 13963–13974 (2021)

17. Shen, S., Li, W., Zhu, Z., Duan, Y., Zhou, J., Lu, J.: Learning dynamic facial radiance fields for few-shot talking head synthesis. In: European Conference on Computer Vision, pp. 666–682. Springer (2022). https://doi.org/10.1007/978-3-031-19775-8_39

18. Suwajanakorn, S., Seitz, S.M., Kemelmacher-Shlizerman, I.: Synthesizing obama: learning lip sync from audio. ACM Trans. Graph. (ToG) **36**(4), 1–13 (2017)

19. l Tang, J., et al.: Real-time neural radiance talking portrait synthesis via audio-spatial decomposition. arXiv preprint arXiv:2211.12368 (2022)

20. Ye, Z., Jiang, Z., Ren, Y., Liu, J., He, J., Zhao, Z.: Geneface: Generalized and high-fidelity audio-driven 3d talking face synthesis. arXiv preprint arXiv:2301.13430 (2023)

21. Yi, R., Ye, Z., Zhang, J., Bao, H., Liu, Y.J.: Audio-driven talking face video generation with learning-based personalized head pose. arXiv preprint arXiv:2002.10137 (2020)

22. Zhang, R., Isola, P., Efros, A.A., Shechtman, E., Wang, O.: The unreasonable effectiveness of deep features as a perceptual metric. In: Proceedings of the IEEE Conference on Computer Vision and Pattern Recognition, pp. 586–595 (2018)

23. Zhong, W., et al.: Identity-preserving talking face generation with landmark and appearance priors. In: Proceedings of the IEEE/CVF Conference on Computer Vision and Pattern Recognition, pp. 9729–9738 (2023)

24. Zhou, Y., Han, X., Shechtman, E., Echevarria, J., Kalogerakis, E., Li, D.: Makelttalk: speaker-aware talking-head animation. ACM Trans. Graph. (TOG) **39**(6), 1–15 (2020)

Adaptive Optimisation of PyTorch Memory Pools for DNNs

Leilei Li[1], Jun Luo[1]([envelope]), Pan Dong[1], Xiaoxiang Fang[1], Axin Yu[1], and Zhe Jiang[2]

[1] National University of Defense Technology, Changsha 410073, China
junluo@nudt.edu.cn
[2] SouthEast University, Nanjing 214135, China

Abstract. With the growth of the scale of deep neural learning models and the increasing amount of data, training Deep Neural Networks (DNNs) within the confines of GPU limitations has become a significant challenge. Existing techniques, including data compression, recomputation, and memory swapping, can facilitate training larger DNN models or increasing their batch sizes under constrained memory conditions. However, these methods often overlook the performance impact caused by the memory management strategies employed by the operating system or deep learning framework.This work is motivated by our observations that when the batch size of DNN model training exceeds a certain threshold, the PyTorch memory management triggers the OOM (Out of Memory) mechanism, therefore leading to substantial training performance losses. In light of this, we propose an adaptive memory pool for DNN training, which is mainly characterized by making a memory pool design based on runtime-tracking tensor memory allocation to optimize the global memory layout. The adaptive memory pool implements effective memory management based on the recognized patterns. Experimental results show that compared to native PyTorch framework large-batch DNN training, the adaptive memory pool can achieve up to a 1.24x performance acceleration.

Keywords: DNN · Adaptive optimisation · Memory pool

1 Introduction

During the training process of Deep Neural Network (DNN) models, significant memory resources are required to store the intermediate results of forward propagation, backward propagation, gradient information, etc. Additionally, further memory resources are required for the process of parameter updates. As DNN models continue to develop, the demands for GPU memory and computing power increase correspondingly. Usually, deeper and wider DNN models offer better performance [4,7,11], and in order to achieve shorter training time, larger batch sizes are used for training [8,23], which means higher memory consumption. Therefore, training large-scale models under device memory constraints is becoming increasingly challenging.

In coping with this problem, many related techniques have been studied, e.g., data compression [3,6,10,14,16], data re-computation [5,9,22], and memory swapping [2,3,12,13,15,18–22], which aim to optimize the memory requirements of model computations. However, these works often overlook the performance impact introduced by the memory management methods of the operating system or deep learning frameworks. For example, when training DNNs using GPUs, popular deep learning frameworks (e.g., TensorFlow [1] or PyTorch [17]) will establish their own managed GPU memory pools to reduce the time of memory allocation/release and simultaneously reduce memory fragmentation. When the memory resource requirements of the model and batch size reach the threshold of device memory, the memory allocation operation may cause an OOM (Out Of Memory) situation. The framework itself will trigger the OOM exception handler, which will perform defragmentation or memory release operations. After the OOM exception handling is completed, the framework will attempt memory allocation again. The normal overhead of memory allocation is usually in the range of a few microseconds to hundreds of microseconds, while the overhead of memory reallocation through the OOM exception handler reaches hundreds or even thousands of milliseconds(the data can be seen in Table 1 of Sect. 3). When frequency of OOM occurrences in each iteration process of DNN training is too high, it will have a non-negligible training performance loss which can reach up to 30%. Therefore, when memory of acceleration devices such as GPUs is limited, it is of great significance to reasonably avoid or reduce OOM exceptions in large-batch training of DNN models to improve training performance.

However, in real-world scenarios, such as large-batch training of DNN models in the PyTorch framework, due to PyTorch's use of dynamic computing graphs, which cannot predict the operations to be performed in advance, and the processing is completely based on tensor computations, its memory management optimization faces two main challenges:(i) How to achieve dynamic adjustment of tensor allocation during runtime. (ii) To avoid or reduce OOM exceptions, which requires adaptation to the model and batch size. Moreover, there is significant uncertainty regarding the triggering of the OOM exception handling mechanism for different models and different batch sizes during training.

The work in this paper is based on two observations: (i) DNN model training is a process of multiple iterations, similar to the reuse and locality characteristics of memory access in traditional iterative programs, the memory allocation of tensors in each iteration of DNN training also shows a relatively fixed pattern. (ii) The PyTorch framework has built-in monitoring mechanisms for memory information during the training process, which can promptly detect and locate OOM issues. Utilizing this mechanism can track the memory allocation information of tensors and plan global memory usage.

In this paper, we establish an adaptive memory pool that enables DNN computations to adapt to the characteristics of DNN network structures and batch sizes, and further reduces memory fragmentation which decreasing the frequency of OOM. Experimental results show that compared to the native framework, PyTorch after adopting the method in this paper can reduce the runtime overhead by 14% - 24% for ResNet50, 8% - 21% for ResNet101, and 8% - 15% for ResNet152 under large-batch training.

The contributions of this paper are summarized as follows:

1. Deeply analyze and summarize the reasons for triggering OOM when training DNN models in large batches under the PyTorch framework, helping developers to predict and avoid OOM problems in advance, and reduce training time and resource waste.
2. Propose a memory pool design method based on statistical principles to control the use of memory more precisely.
3. Design a scheme for the adaptation of memory block parameters in the memory pool of the PyTorch memory management mechanism to the characteristics of DNN models and batch sizes, and evaluate the performance of the scheme, prove that the scheme can well reduce the performance loss caused by the deep learning framework itself due to the large batch training of training DNN models.

2   Related Work

In order to alleviate the model size limitation caused by limited GPU memory, a lot of research has been conducted, mainly including three aspects:data compression, data recomputation, and memory swapping.

In the training stage of deep learning models, the memory space occupied by variables can be effectively reduced by using compression algorithms, and the occupation of the memory of the accelerator device can be reduced. In the inference stage, in order to deploy the trained model on the edge device with limited memory, methods such as model pruning and quantization have been proposed to compress neural network models by optimizing the model structure and reducing the memory space occupied by model parameters. FlashNeuron [3] is the first DNN training system to use NVMe SSD as virtual memory. It references an offload scheduler to selectively offload a set of intermediate compressed format data to the SSD without increasing the DNN evaluation time, making full use of the limited SSD write bandwidth. Buddy Compression [6] divides each compressed 128B memory entry between high-bandwidth GPU memory and slower but larger Buddy memory. Compressible memory entries can be fully accessed from GPU memory, and uncompressible entries can obtain part of the data from off-GPU. It ensures that compressibility changes do not cause expensive page movement and reallocation.

Data recomputation is a method to save memory space through computing. It utilizes the repeatability of computing to avoid storing certain intermediate results during the forward propagation process and dynamically recalculate these intermediate results when needed, thereby reducing memory usage. Tianqi Chen et al. [5] proposed that a neural network is divided into several parts. The algorithm only retains the intermediate results output by each part and deletes the other intermediate results. For the results that are deleted and need to be used in the backpropagation process, they are recalculated through the retained intermediate result information of each part. On this basis, it is realized that by adding an additional forward calculation to each layer of the neural network, an n-layer linear DNN with only $O\sqrt{n}$ memory overhead can be trained. SuperNeurons [22] proposes a cost-aware recomputation module, which releases tensors in the low-cost computing layer at runtime and recomputes them during backpropagation, saving an additional 50% of memory consumption.

Memory swapping is a method of exchanging data between the memory of an accelerator device and the main memory to alleviate memory pressure on the accelerator device. When a variable is no longer in use, it can be temporarily stored in the main memory and restored to the accelerator device's memory when needed again. FlashNeuron [3] offloads tensors to NVMe SSD. SwapAdvisor [13] uses a genetic algorithm to schedule operator and memory allocation and swapping decisions based on a given dataflow graph. Capuchin [18] makes memory management decisions based on dynamically traced tensor access patterns, evicting and prefetching tensors. DeepSpeed [19] provides a memory swapping mechanism between GPUs and CPU memory or NVMe SSD through a lightweight API compatible with PyTorch. vDNN [21] is the first method to introduce GPU memory swapping for DNN workloads and only supports convolutional neural networks. SuperNeurons [22] implements unified tensor pooling, taking DNN models as input and exporting the optimal tensor offloading plan.

The above-mentioned works focus on addressing the memory capacity bottleneck and do not take into account the performance impact introduced by memory management approaches of operating system or deep learning frameworks. In contrast, they often introduce significant performance overhead, resulting in longer training cycles. However, this paper specifically focuses on the time overhead introduced by the OOM mechanism triggered due to memory allocation when the memory capacity reaches its limit. We aim to uncover its underlying risks and challenges and provide valuable insights and solutions to optimize program performance and enhance system reliability.

3   Related Concept and Analysis of PyTorch Memory Management Mechanism

3.1   Related Concept

Memory Fragmentation and Mechanism of OOM. During DNN training, tensors in the computational graph are frequently created and released. This dynamic nature leads to irregularities in memory allocation and release, which easily cause memory fragmentation. As shown in Fig. 1, suppose 500MB of memory needs to be allocated currently, although the total free memory is 800MB, the free memory consists of two 400MB blocks with non-contiguous addresses, not enough to allocate this 500MB memory. However, if the addresses of the two

400MB free blocks are contiguous, they can be consolidated into an 800MB free block through memory defragmentation. The situation in the upper part of Fig. 1 is prone to triggering the OOM mechanism. OOM refers to the situation when the system memory is exhausted. When the system is unable to allocate more memory to meet new memory requests, the OOM exception handling mechanism will be triggered. In the operating system, the OOM mechanism is to prevent the system from becoming unstable or crashing due to memory exhaustion. For example, the OOM exception handling in the Linux system is that the OOM Killer terminates some processes to release memory. In the PyTorch memory management, there is also an OOM mechanism to handle. When there is insufficient memory allocation, an error report will be generated. CUDA will capture the error report and execute the CUDA error handling program, and reallocate memory. This process has several orders of magnitude more time overhead compared to normal allocation, which is a significant performance loss.

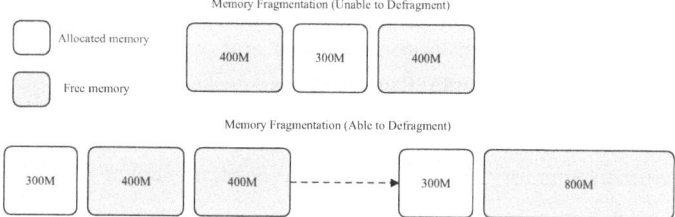

Fig. 1. Explanation about memory fragmentation.

3.2   Analysis of PyTorch Memory Management Mechanism

To reduce memory fragmentation and avoid OOM errors, PyTorch adopts the hierarchical memory management mechanism shown in Fig. 2(a). PyTorch uses memory pool technology. After obtaining memory from the GPU, it does not release it and return it to the GPU immediately after use, but remains in PyTorch for subsequent reuse, reducing the overhead of memory allocation and release. When PyTorch needs to allocate new memory, it first looks in the memory pool to see if there is enough available memory. If there is, it allocates directly from the memory pool; if not, it requests new memory from the GPU and adds it to the memory pool. This can improve the utilization efficiency of memory, reduce the generation of memory fragmentation, and thereby improve the performance of the program. To further reduce memory fragmentation, the memory pool implements automatic defragmentation, which has two key operations: splitting and merging. Figure 2(b) shows a continuous address block, which is internally organized as a doubly linked list (arrows are omitted). Usually, the memory resources applied for are more than the actual needs. In order to avoid waste, the memory block will be split. Figure 2(b) shows a 200M memory block being split into multiple memory blocks of different sizes. When the memory blocks are released, it will check whether the adjacent blocks are free blocks, and merge them according to the inspection results. For example, if the memory block 5 in Fig. 2(b) is released, the memory blocks 4–6 will be merged into a large block.

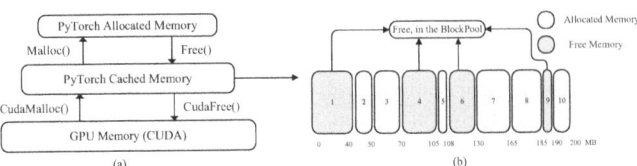

Fig. 2. PyTorch memory management mechanism and splitting-merging features.

Although PyTorch memory management mechanism reduces the time of memory allocation/releasing to a certain extent, and also reduces memory fragmentation, when dealing with large-scale data and complex models, due to the accumulation of enough memory fragments, it cannot find a complete memory block to meet the memory allocation requirements, which will cause OOM. The reason behind this situation is related to internal layout of memory pool. The steps for acquiring memory blocks in memory pool, as shown in Fig. 3.

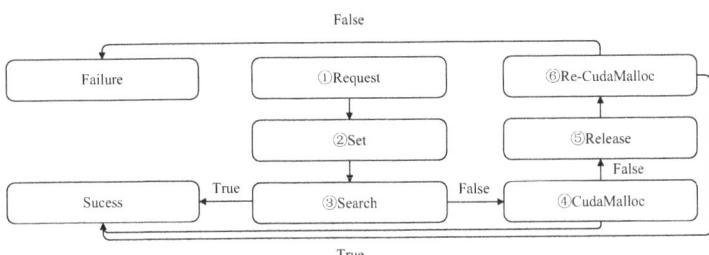

Fig. 3. Memory block acquiring steps.①Memory request,②Set the corresponding memory block size for the memory application, ③Try to find a free memory block of appropriate size in the memory pool maintained by the PyTorch allocator,④Request memory allocation from the GPU, ⑤Release, mainly to release some memory blocks in the memory pool maintained by the PyTorch allocator and return them to the GPU, ⑥Request memory allocation from the GPU again. In the case of failed memory block acquisition, it will lead to program crashes, and the step that triggers the OOM mechanism is ④.

Deeper and wider DNN models generally provide better performance [4,7, 11], and larger batch sizes are used to reduce training time [8,23]. However, in this study, we found that when the batch size of DNN training in PyTorch reaches a certain size, the training time does not decrease but increases instead. By using torch.cuda.memory.summary(), it was observed that CUDA OOM errors and cudaMalloc retries occurred thousands of times during 10 training iterations. Although the program can still run without crashing, it significantly affects training performance negatively. Therefore, it is of great significance to mitigate or reduce OOM exceptions in large-batch DNN training to improve training performance. In conclusion, increasing the batch size in DNN training using PyTorch can lead to an increase in training time and significantly impact training performance, as evidenced by a high frequency of CUDA OOM errors and cudaMalloc retries. Thus, it is important to take measures to avoid or minimize OOM exceptions in large-batch DNN training to enhance training efficiency. Due to PyTorch's memory management principle, when the PyTorch allocator acquires excessive GPU memory, the available free memory on the CUDA GPU may not be sufficient to create new blocks. In this case, memory blocks are released from the PyTorch allocator back to CUDA, and then CUDA creates new blocks. This leads to frequent execution of steps ⑤ and ⑥ in Fig. 3 for acquiring PyTorch memory blocks, resulting in an increased number of memory reallocations, which affects the time overhead of training DNN models. This impact is particularly significant during the training process, which typically involves thousands or even tens of thousands of iterations to ensure model accuracy. The time overhead introduced by steps ⑤ and ⑥ cannot be ignored. We compared the memory allocation time for triggering the OOM mechanism among three models, as shown in Table 1 below.

This study focuses on the native PyTorch memory management mechanism to identify the conditions triggering CUDA OOM and cudaMalloc retries. The hard constraint is the limitation of GPU memory capacity, which is an unavoidable consequence based on the hardware itself. The study primarily considers the flexible conditions. By using the function torch.cuda.memory.dump.snapshot() in PyTorch, the address, allocation size, and allocation/release sequence of each memory allocation request can be obtained. Observation reveals that for a fixed memory allocation sequence, step ② in Fig. 3 determines the global memory layout based on the memory block size setting, which is a static parameter. However, this memory block size setting may not be the most suitable for different models or different batch sizes during training. In conclusion, this study looks at the conditions triggering CUDA OOM and cudaMalloc retries from the perspective of the native PyTorch memory management mechanism. While the hard constraint is the limitation of GPU memory capacity, the study focuses on the flexible conditions. The analysis reveals that the static parameter of memory

Table 1. Comparison of memory allocation overhead.

DNN Models	Nomal	Trigger the OOM mechanism
ResNet50	47 - 358 us	1045 - 1056 ms
ResNet101	54 - 368 us	368 - 807 ms
ResNet152	32 - 406 us	246 - 406 ms

block size setting in step ② of Fig. 3 determines the global memory layout, which may not be optimal for different models or batch sizes during training.

4   Memory Block Design Based on Statistical Principles

According to Code 1, the native PyTorch memory management mechanism has three cases for setting the size of memory blocks, the minimum granularity of PyTorch memory block requests (i.e., requests to CUDA) is 2MB and 10MB respectively, which causes some allocation requests larger than 1MB to allocate a 10MB block from CUDA. That means that too small data structures occupy too large linear contiguous physical addresses, and the probability of this physical address being released and reused will be relatively low, which increases the failure probability of requesting a large contiguous address block from CUDA. Therefore, reducing the block size requested from CUDA as much as possible can reduce the probability of OOM when requesting large contiguous physical addresses from CUDA, but too small block allocation will increase the number of small fragments, so it is necessary to find a partitioning strategy suitable for the characteristics of the model.

```
1   //Code1 :
2   static size_t get_allocation_size(size_t size) {
3       if (size <= kSmallSize) {  // kSmallSize:1MB
4           return kSmallBuffer;}  // kSmallBuffer:2MB
5       else if (size < kMinLargeAlloc) {
6           return kLargeBuffer;}  // kMinLargeAlloc:10MB
7       else {  // kLargeBuffer:20MB
8           return kRoundLarge
9           *((size + kRoundLarge - 1) / kRoundLarge);}
10  }  // kRoundLarge:2MB
```

```
1   /*Code2.The parameter names that are
2   the same as Code1 have the same values.*/
3   static size_t get_allocation_size(size_t size) {
4       if (size <= kSmallSize) {return kSmallBuffer;}
5       else if (size <= kBasic) {
6           return n*kBasic;}  // Group 1
7       else if (size <= n*kBasic) {
8           return n*n*kBasic;}  // Group 2
9       ...  // Group 3 to Group m-1
10      else { return kRoundLarge
11          * ((size+kRoundLarge-1)/kRoundLarge);}}  // Group m
```

The design principle of the buddy algorithm is that the kernel frequently requests and releases a group of contiguous page frames of different sizes, which will inevitably lead to the dispersion of many small free page frames within the already allocated blocks. The problem is that even if there are enough free page frames to meet the request, it is impossible to allocate a large contiguous page frame, and the PyTorch memory management mechanism also has such a problem. The buddy algorithm is a robust and efficient allocation strategy to solve this kind of problem. This article adopts a strategy similar to the buddy algorithm. The buddy algorithm divides the free pages into m groups. The first group stores memory blocks of 2^0 unit, the second group stores memory blocks of 2^1 units, the third group stores memory blocks of 2^2 units, and the fourth group stores memory blocks of 2^3 units, and so on, until the m-th group, which stores memory blocks of 2^{m-1} units. Each group is a linked list used to connect memory blocks of the same size. The sizes of buddy blocks are equal, and the first block and the second block are buddies, the third block and the fourth block are buddies, and so on. The difference from the buddy algorithm is that our design divides memory requests greater than 1MB into m groups according to intervals. The size of the memory block in the second group is n times the size of the memory block in the first group until group $m - 1$. For the m-th group, the memory alignment method is still used because the mth group is basically the largest batch of memory requests. For the m-th group, still using n times the size allocation will cause excessive allocation of memory, and still use the memory alignment method for allocation. The specific mode shows in Code 2.

Algorithm 1

Input: An array of memory allocation sequence obtained through one iteration of training, M,the array has l elements;

Output: Obtain three parameter values, m, n , $kBasic$;

1: Filter the elements in M that are greater than 1MB, sort them in ascending order, obtain array M_1, which has k elements, $M_1 = \{X_1, X_2, ..., X_k\}$;

2: Calculate the mean to obtain $E(X)$;

3: Calculate the standard deviation to obtain $\sigma(X)$;

4: Calculate the coefficient of variation CV, where CV is equal to the standard deviation $\sigma(X)$ divided by the mean $E(X)$;

5: If CV is less than 0.3, m equals 8; otherwise, m equals 4;

6: The value of n is determined based on experience and ranges from 2 to 4;

7: $kBasic = [X[(k(m - 1)/m) + 1]/m/n]$;

8: **return** m, n , $kBasic$;

Since the size variation range of memory blocks smaller than 1MB is relatively small, we can divide all memory block sizes smaller than 1MB into one interval, which is (0, 1 MB). Generally speaking, when the coefficient of variation $CV \geq 0.3$, it can be considered that the data has a high degree of dispersion. For the value of m, according to the fixed characteristics of the DNN model, the data shows a concentrated trend locally. Therefore, we use the method of quartiles and octiles in statistics for the value of m, that is, the value of m is 4 or 8. For the value of n, we consider two constraining factors. First, when setting the parameters of the memory block is too large, since the memory block will be split, some of the split memory blocks cannot be released before being used up, which will cause the entire memory block to be unable to be released. For new memory requests, although the total amount of remaining blocks meets the size of the memory block request, the remaining memory blocks cannot be merged, and in fact, it cannot be met, and a new memory block needs to be applied for again, which will result in excessive allocation of memory blocks. Second, if the set parameters of the memory block are too small, it can only meet the current memory request, and new memory requests still need to allocate a new memory block, resulting in waste of the remaining amount of the original memory block. According to the debugging experience, the value of n is in the interval [2,4]. For kBasic, according to the grouping form of Algorithm 1, $kBasic = [X[(k(m-1)/m)+1]/m/n]$, and then $kBasic$ is rounded. The experimental results prove the effectiveness of our method. Among them, $kBasic$ is the unit memory block larger than 1MB. As long as we determine the three values of m, n, and $kBasic$, the allocation mode can be determined. We use the principle of statistics to determine these three values. The specific operation is shown in Algorithm 1.

5   Experiment

The experiment is run on a single host, which is configured with Ubuntu 20.04.1, GPU model is NVIDIA GeForce GTX 1660, and the memory capacity is 6GB. The PyTorch version is 2.1, and the CUDA version is V11.8.89. In Table 2, the parameter values corresponding to the model and batch size are determined by utilizing our method, among which the batch size is the largest batch size that can trigger the out-of-memory mechanism in the existing experimental environment. The dataset used is uniformly CIFAR-10, because any dataset will be transformed to make the input meet the requirements of the model, and the input size is fixed, so the dataset has no impact on the experiments in this paper. We uniformly adopt ten iterations for training.

Table 2. The parameters corresponding to the model.

DNN Models	m	n	kBasic	Batchsize
ResNet50	8	2.5	4 MB	2560
ResNet101	8	2	4 MB	1792
ResNet152	4	4	2 MB	1312

Firstly, we evaluated training performance by training ResNet50, ResNet101, and ResNet152 without triggering OOM mechanism of Bathsize. Compared with native PyTorch, the method in this paper does not have a cost loss, and it is found that with larger batch training, training time will also be reduced. However, once the batch size reaches the batch size that triggers the OOM mechanism, the training time under native PyTorch will increase significantly, as shown in Fig. 4. Compared with native PyTorch, the method in this paper can reduce the running time overhead of ResNet50 by 14% - 24%, ResNet101 by 8% - 21%, and ResNet152 by 8% - 15% in this case. Secondly, we compared the number of OOMs triggered in large-scale training of DNNs and the number of CudaMalloc retries between the method in this paper and native PyTorch. As shown in Table 3, compared with native PyTorch, the method in this paper can significantly reduce the number of OOMs and the number of CudaMalloc retries.

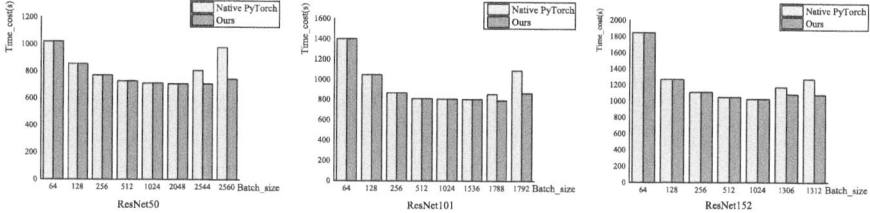

Fig. 4. Comparison of the training times of the three models.

Table 3. Comparison of OOM occurrences and CudaMalloc retries.

DNN Models	Batchsize	Native PyTorch		Ours	
		OOMs	CudaMalloc retries	OOMs	CudaMalloc retries
ResNet50	2544	772	776	0	1
	2560	2233	2238	18	19
ResNet101	1788	1028	1054	1	5
	1792	1300	1684	1	5
ResNet152	1306	3792	4551	1542	2301
	1312	10692	11457	3028	3788

6   Conclusion

In this paper, we focus on the problem of the training performance loss caused by the OOM exception in the large-batch training of the DNN model under the device memory limitation. We establish an adaptive memory pool for DNN training to solve this problem, and we compare the training results of Three DNN models through this method to the training under the native PyTorch framework. Experimental results show that the method in this paper has better performance.

References

1. Abadi, M., et al.: TensorFlow: a system for Large-Scale machine learning. In: 12th USENIX symposium on operating systems design and implementation (OSDI 2016), pp. 265-283. USENIX, Savannah, GA (2016)

2. Awan, A.A., et al.: Oc-dnn: Exploiting advanced unified memory capabilities in cuda 9 and volta gpus for out-of-core dnn training. In: 2018 IEEE 25th International Conference on High Performance Computing (HiPC), pp. 143-152. IEEE, Bengaluru, INDIA (2018)

3. Bae, J., et al.: Flash neuron: SSD-enabled large-batch training of very deep neural networks. In: 19th USENIX Conference on File and Storage Technologies (FAST 2021), pp. 387-401. USENIX, Electr Network (2021)

4. Brown, T., et al.: Language models are few-shot learners. Adv. Neural. Inf. Process. Syst. **33**, 1877–1901 (2020)

5. Chen, T., et al.: Training deep nets with sublinear memory cost. arxiv preprint arxiv:1604.06174 (2016)

6. Choukse, E., et al.: Buddy compression: Enabling larger memory for deep learning and hpc workloads on gpus. In: 2020 ACM/IEEE 47th Annual International Symposium on Computer Architecture (ISCA), pp. 926-939. IEEE, Electr Network (2020)

7. Devlin, J., Chang, M.-W., Lee, K., Toutanova, K.: BERT: Pre-training of Deep Bidirectional Transformers for Language Understanding. In: 2019 Conference Of The North American Chapter of the Association for Computational Linguistics: Human Language Technologies (NAACL HLT 2019), pp. 4171-4186. ACL, Minneapolis, MN (2019)

8. Goyal, P., et al.: Accurate, large minibatch sgd: Training imagenet in 1 hour. arxiv preprint arxiv:1706.02677 (2017)

9. Gruslys, A., et al.: Memory-efficient backpropagation through time. In: Advances in Neural Information Processing Systems 29 (NIPS 2016), pp. 4132-4140. NIPS, Barcelona, Spain (2016)

10. Han, S et al.: Learning both weights and connections for efficient neural network. In: Advances in Neural Information Processing Systems 28 (NIPS 2015), pp. 1135-1143. NIPS, Montreal, CANADA (2015)

11. He, K., et al.: Deep residual learning for image recognition. In: Proceedings of the IEEE Conference on Computer Vision and Pattern Recognition, pp. 770-778. IEEE, Seattle, WA (2016)

12. Hildebrand, M., et al.: Autotm: automatic tensor movement in heterogeneous memory systems using integer linear programming. In: Proceedings of the Twenty-Fifth International Conference on Architectural Support for Programming Languages and Operating Systems, pp. 875-890. ACM, Lausanne, Switzerland (2020)

13. Huang, C.0C., Jin, G., Li, J.: SwapAdvisor: pushing Deep Learning Beyond the GPU Memory Limit via Smart Swapping. In: Proceedings of the Twenty-Fifth International Conference on Architectural Support for Programming Languages and Operating Systems, pp. 1341-1355. ACM, Lausanne, Switzerland (2020)

14. Jain, A., et al.: Gist: efficient data encoding for deep neural network training. In: 2018 ACM/IEEE 45th Annual International Symposium on Computer Architecture (ISCA), pp. 776-789. IEEE, Los Angeles, CA (2018)

15. Le, T.D., et al.: Tflms: Large model support in tensorflow by graph rewriting. arxiv preprint arxiv:1807.02037 (2018)

16. Li, C., et al.: A framework for memory oversubscription management in graphics processing units. In: Proceedings of the Twenty-Fourth International Conference on Architectural Support for Programming Languages and Operating Systems, pp. 49-63. ACM, Brown Univ, Providence, RI (2019)

17. Paszke, A., et al.: Pytorch: an imperative style, high-performance deep learning library. In: Advances in Neural Information Processing Systems 32 (NIPS 2019), pp. 8024-8035. NIPS, Vancouver, canada (2019)

18. Peng, X., et al.: Capuchin: tensor-based gpu memory management for deep learning. In: Proceedings of the Twenty-Fifth International Conference on Architectural Support for Programming Languages and Operating Systems, pp. 891-905. ACM, Lausanne, switzerland (2020)

19. Rasley, J., et al.: Deepspeed: system optimizations enable training deep learning models with over 100 billion parameters. In: Proceedings of the 26th ACM SIGKDD International Conference on Knowledge Discovery & Data Mining, pp. 3505-3506. ACM, Electr Network (2020)

20. Ren, J., et al.: Sentinel: efficient tensor migration and allocation on heterogeneous memory systems for deep learning. In: 2021 IEEE International Symposium on High-Performance Computer Architecture (HPCA), pp. 598-611. IEEE, Electr Network (2021)

21. Rhu, M., et al.: vDNN: virtualized deep neural networks for scalable, memory-efficient neural network design. In: 2016 49th Annual IEEE/ACM International Symposium on Microarchitecture (MICRO), pp. 1-13. IEEE, Taipei, Taiwan (2016)

22. Wang, L., et al.: Superneurons: dynamic GPU memory management for training deep neural networks. In: Proceedings of the 23rd ACM SIGPLAN symposium on principles and practice of parallel programming, pp. 41-53. ACM, Vienna, Austria (2018)

23. You, Y., et al.: Large batch optimization for deep learning: Training bert in 76 minutes. arxiv preprint arxiv:1904.00962 (2019)

Detaching Range from Depth: Personalized Recommendation Meets Personalized PageRank

Jiahui Hu[1], Jie Xu[1(✉)], Jiakun Chen[1], Liqiang Qiao[1], Jilu Wang[1], Feiran Huang[2], and Chaozhuo Li[3]

[1] School of Information Science and Technology, Beijing Foreign Studies University, Beijing, China
jxu@bfsu.edu.cn
[2] College of Cyber Security/College of Information Science and Technology, Jinan University, Guangzhou, China
[3] Key Laboratory of Trustworthy Distributed Computing and Service (MoE), Beijing University of Posts and Telecommunications, Beijing, China

Abstract. Recommendation systems chiefly rely on Collaborative Filtering techniques to depict user inclinations by analyzing historical interactions. This traditional approach has seen significant improvements with recent advancements that leverage Graph Neural Networks (GNNs). GNNs enhance CF by exploiting high-order interactions within user-item bipartite graphs [1]. However, existing GNN-based CF models face a critical limitation: the entanglement of depth and range, where increasing GNN layers simultaneously enlarges the receptive field, complicating the model and increasing computational demands. To address this, we propose a framework that decouples range from depth, using Personalized PageRank (PPR) to extract localized subgraphs with bounded ranges, allowing for deeper GNN layers without expanding the receptive field. Additionally, we introduce a learnable aggregation function that optimally integrates sum, max, and mean operations for improved message aggregation. Experiments on multiple datasets demonstrate our approach's superior performance. The results indicate that our framework not only addresses the depth and range entanglement issue but also significantly boosts the effectiveness of GNN-based CF models.

Keywords: Personalized recommendation · Collaborative filtering · Graph convolution networks · Personalized PageRank

1 Introduction

With the rapid advancement of information technology, data has surged exponentially, leading to the challenge of information overload [7]. Recommender systems have emerged as a crucial tool in many domains, including e-commerce and targeted ads, by harnessing user preferences through historical engagement and Collaborative Filtering (CF). These systems personalize recommendations based on individual interests, creating a tailored list of items for each user.

Learning representations that accurately reflect the user's personalized preferences has been a central theme of research. Various methods like matrix factorization [11] and deep neural networks [6] have been proposed to learn desirable embeddings from the historical user-item interactions. Recently, Graph Neural Networks (GNNs), leveraging deep learning techniques on graph data, have demonstrated great potential to advance recommendations. User-item interactions over time naturally construct a bipartite graph linking users to items. The high-order interactions from ℓ-hop neighbors in the bipartite graph can be explicitly perceived by the central node via the stacked ℓ GNN layers, leading to the powerful expressive representations.

The success of GNN-based CF models depends on their powerful modeling capacity of multiple-order interactions, including two crucial aspects: the *range* denotes the scale of the receptive field, and the *depth* indicates the expressivity in modeling the attended localized structures [29–31]. CF models with wider ranges are capable of gathering more copious collaborative signals from long-distance interactions, while greater depths equip CF models with more powerful capability in modeling the latent intent factors beneath the perceived interactions. Consequently, both range and depth are indispensable for GNN-based CF models to achieve desirable performance. However, for most existing GNN-based CF models [7,24], the range and depth are bound together. Namely, as the number of GNN layers (i.e., depth) increase, the scope of the receptive field (i.e., range) grows synchronously. Users may exhibit distinct behavioral patterns due to the diverse interests, resulting in the sophisticated non-linear topological structures [12,13,23]. Enhancing CF models with deeper GNN layers can better capture collaborative signals in complex structures, but this deepenning results in an exponential receptive field expansion and more complex topologies.

In view of this limitation of existing GNN-based CF models, a natural question arises here: *is there a framework to detach the range from the depth in the neighborhood aggregating process?* Our motivation lies in increasing the modeling capacity (i.e., depth) on the localized user-item interactions while avoiding the cumbersome challenges introduced by the enlarged range. We propose to first extract a localized subgraph with the bounded range by Personalized PageRank(PPR), and thus GNN layers with arbitrary depth can be employed on top of such subgraphs. The critical collaborative signals are preserved in the sampled subgraphs, while the arbitrary layers ensure the modeling capacity and flexibility of our proposal. Since the localized subgraph has the bounded-size range independent of the depth, the range can be naturally detached from the depth. In addition, we also propose a learnable aggregation function to better capture and aggregate the messages between individual nodes. We find that different aggregation functions have an impact on the GNN's performance. Additionally, a universal aggregator SAF we proposed could automatically adjust to find the optimal message aggregation function through parameter learning. In summary, this work makes the following contributions:

1) We focus on an overlooked factor in GNN-based recommendation: the entanglement of depth and range. We propose to detach the range from the depth to alleviate these problems efficiently.
2) We introduce Personalized PageRank (PPR) into the user-item recommendation and derive a closed-form expression for rating computation.
3) Experiments results on three mainstream datasets illustrate our work's effectiveness.

2   Preliminaries

This subsection introduces some useful notations and definitions, starting with the matrix notations. In this paper, we use a_i to indicate the i-th entry of a vector $\boldsymbol{a}$, A_{ij} or $A_{i,j}$ to indicate the (i, j) entry of a matrix $\boldsymbol{A}$, with the index starting at 1. $\boldsymbol{A}_{i:j,p:q}$ is a submatrix of the matrix $\boldsymbol{A}$ with rows $i \sim j$ and columns $p \sim q$ of $\boldsymbol{A}$ remained. $\mathcal{U}$ is the user set and $\mathcal{I}$ is the item set. This work considers the recommendation problem with latent feedback. We use $\boldsymbol{R} \in \mathbb{R}^{N \times M}$ to indicate the latent feedback matrix, where $N = |\mathcal{U}|$ and $M = |\mathcal{I}|$ indicate the user and item count, separately. A non-zero entry R_{ui} of $\boldsymbol{R}$ denotes that the individual u, who is a member of the user set U, has previously engaged with the item i, which belongs to the item set I; if not, the corresponding value is recorded as zero. A user-item interaction network $G = (\mathcal{V}, \mathcal{E})$ is constructed from the interaction matrix R, with $\mathcal{V} = \{\mathcal{U}, \mathcal{I}\}$ representing the vertices that include both users and items, and E denoting the edges of the network. The adjacency matrix of the user-item interaction graph G is given by

$$\boldsymbol{A} = \begin{bmatrix} \boldsymbol{O}_{N \times N} & \boldsymbol{R} \\ \boldsymbol{R}^{\top} & \boldsymbol{O}_{M \times M} \end{bmatrix} \in \mathbb{R}^{(N+M) \times (N+M)}$$

where $\boldsymbol{O}_{N \times N}$ denotes a zero matrix in $\mathbb{R}^{N \times N}$. Let $\boldsymbol{D}$ be a diagonal matrix, also known as the *degree matrix*, with the diagonal entry $D_{ii} = \sum_{j=1}^{N+M} A_{ij} = |\mathcal{N}(i)|$. Here $\mathcal{N}(i)$ denotes node i's 1-hop neighbors.

Following mainstream GNN-based recommendation models [7], the user u and item i can be depicted by a representation $\boldsymbol{e}_u \in \mathbb{R}^d$ and $\boldsymbol{e}_i \in \mathbb{R}^d$, separately, in which d is the vector scale. The corresponding representation matrix can be defined as follows:

$$\boldsymbol{E} = [\underbrace{\boldsymbol{e}_{u_1}, \cdots, \boldsymbol{e}_{u_N}}_{\text{user embeddings}}, \underbrace{\boldsymbol{e}_{i_1}, \cdots, \boldsymbol{e}_{i_M}}_{\text{item embeddings}}]^{\top} \in \mathbb{R}^{(N+M) \times d}$$

Initially, every user or item is related to a one-hot ID encoding $\boldsymbol{e}_u^{(0)}$ or $\boldsymbol{e}_i^{(0)}$, separately. The corresponding starting representation matrix $\boldsymbol{E}^{(0)} \in \mathbb{R}^{(N+M) \times d}$ is learnable.

3   Detaching the Range from Depth

In this section, we present our proposed methods in detail. An illustration of the proposed DetachGCN is provided in Fig. 1. To generate the embedding $\boldsymbol{e}_v$

of an arbitrary node v, DetachGCN proceeds as follows: 1) We first exploit a subgraph extraction process to extract a localized subgraph $G[v]$ for each node v. 2) We then apply a GCN-based recommendation model to $G[v]$ by treating it as the new full graph and ignoring all nodes and edges not in $G[v]$. Hence the range of node v is restricted by $G[v]$ and detached from the model depth. 3) We finally apply a READOUT function on the subgraph $G[v]$ to generate the representation of subgraph $G[v]$ as the embedding of node v.

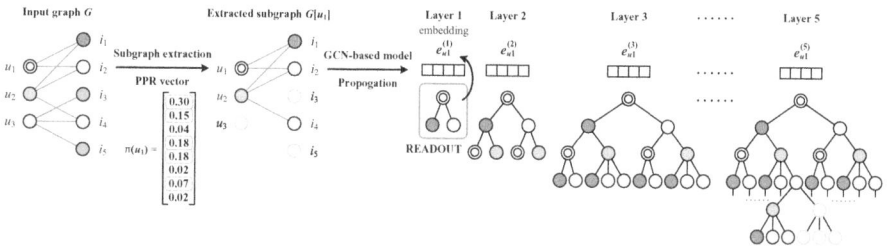

Fig. 1. A visual representation of the proposed DetachGCN.

3.1 Overall Framework

Consider the traditional GCN-based recommendation models, a model with ℓ layers has the range of full ℓ-hop neighborhood. Consequently, any two nodes in the interaction graph G can finally receive information from each other after multiple propagations, no matter how far away they are. As discussed in Sect. 1, such a paradigm that indistinguishably exploits high-order information is problematic and even harmful. Hence we propose to detach the range from the model depth to overcome this obstacle. Specifically, we first design a subgraph extraction process to extract a localized subgraph for each node v, comprising a limited set of key neighbors surrounding it while excluding extraneous ones. Let $G[v]$ indicate the subgraph extracted for vertex v as well as $\mathcal{V}[v]$ indicate the vertex set of $G[v]$. In this way, the vertex v's neighbors is defined by $\mathcal{V}[v]$, a subset of the vertex set $\mathcal{V}$ instead of the full one. If $u \notin \mathcal{V}[v]$, v will never consider u as a neighbor and never receive information from it. Hence the range of node v is an informative subgraph $G[v]$ regardless of the model depth and naturally detached from the depth.

To express vertex v, we then apply a GCN-based recommendation model, such as LightGCN [7], of arbitrary depth on the extracted subgraph $G[v]$. For example, the embedding of a user u is iteratively defined as:

$$e_u^{(\ell+1)} = \sum_{i \in \mathcal{N}_{G[u]}(u)} \frac{1}{\sqrt{|\mathcal{N}_{G[u]}(u)|}\sqrt{|\mathcal{N}_{G[u]}(i)|}} e_i^{(\ell)}$$

$$e_i^{(\ell+1)} = \sum_{u \in \mathcal{N}_{G[u]}(i)} \frac{1}{\sqrt{|\mathcal{N}_{G[u]}(i)|}\sqrt{|\mathcal{N}_{G[u]}(u)|}} e_u^{(\ell)} \qquad (1)$$

in which $e_u^{(\ell)}$ and $e_i^{(\ell)}$ are the user u and item i's embeddings, and ℓ is the model layer. $\mathcal{N}_{G[u]}(i)$ is the 1-hop neighborhood of node i *in subgraph* $G[u]$. Since the detachment makes the subgraph extraction and model depth naturally separated and independent, the number of layers of the model can be flexibly chosen. When we stack more layers than the diameter of subgraph $G[v]$ (the maximum distance between any pair of nodes), each pair of nodes in $G[v]$ could exchange their information multiple times, thereby helping this method better capture the features of the subgraph $G[v]$. After deep propagation passing of L layers, we finally apply a READOUT function, the Self-learning Aggregate Function (SAF) we proposed on the subgraph $G[v]$ to generate the representation of $G[v]$ as the embedding of node v:

$$e_v = \text{READOUT} \left(\left\{ e_z^{(L)} \mid z \in G[v] \right\} \right) \tag{2}$$

In the worst-case scenario, the model could also suffer from the *over-smoothing* problem [2,14,28], node embeddings in the subgraph become similar even indistinguishable, and become representative of the global subgraph and a property of the subgraph [10,26]. However, note that we ultimately hope that the embedding of node v can capture the characteristics of subgraph $G[v]$. In essence, the embedding learning of node v is transformed into the representation learning of subgraph $G[v]$. In this case, the over-smoothing phenomenon is resolved.

3.2   Personalized Recommendation Meets Personalized PageRank

PageRank [18] is a famous algorithm for rating Web pages. It measures the relative importance of nodes in a graph and assigns a numerical weighting to each node. Personalized PageRank (PPR) [3,8], a variant of PageRank, emphasizes the comparative importance of a objective node to a starting node of the graph. We propose to exploit PPR to reflect the significance of other nodes with respect to each target node and then design a subgraph extraction algorithm by such importance. In order to apply it in practical application, we resort to Approximate PPR (APPR) [15,17,20] to ensure the efficiency and scalability without degrading the recommendation performance. Moreover, PPR applied to personalized recs without training/learning outperforms many classical models and matches state-of-the-art performance [3,4].

Theoretical Derivation. Considering a graph, the PPR (Personalized PageRank) score $\pi_t(s)$ for one concrete vertex t in light of a starting vertex s is calculated as the probability that a random walk originating from s will eventually reach t. At each step, the walk either teleports back to the source node s with the teleport (restart) probability α and continues from there, or traverses to a stochastic neighboring node of the present node using the probability $1 - \alpha$. Based on above process, the computation of PPR value $\pi_t(s)$ can be defined as the following iteration formula:

$$\pi_t(s) = (1 - \alpha) \sum_{j \in \mathcal{N}(t)} \frac{\pi_j(s)}{|\mathcal{N}(j)|} + \alpha \delta_{ts} \tag{3}$$

where δ_{ts} is the Kronecker delta, whose value is 1 if $t = s$, and 0 otherwise. The PPR value $\pi_t(s)$ reflects the related node significance t in regard to the source node s in the graph. Similarly, given a user-item interaction graph, we can generalize Eq. (3) to the personalized recommendation to reflect the node significance z on respect to the source node v in this user-item interaction graph:

$$\pi_z(v) = (1 - \alpha) \sum_{j \in \mathcal{N}(z)} \frac{\pi_j(v)}{\sqrt{|\mathcal{N}(z)||\mathcal{N}(j)|}} + \alpha \delta_{zv} \tag{4}$$

Here we use the symmetric normalization term $1/\sqrt{|\mathcal{N}(z)||\mathcal{N}(j)|}$ instead of the random walk normalization term $1/|\mathcal{N}(j)|$ in Eq. (3) to consider the role of both z and j on edge (z, j).

Next, we provide the matrix form of Eq. (4) and derive the closed-form expression of PPR matrix in personalized recommendation to facilitate the implementation. We denote the source node v via a one-hot indicator i_v, whose v-th entry is 1. Let $\pi(i_v)$ denote the PPR vector of node v, whose z-th entry is the PPR value $\pi_z(v)$ reflecting the node significance z on respect to the source node v. Thus the matrix form of Eq. (4) is formulated as:

$$\pi(i_v) = (1 - \alpha)\hat{A}\pi(i_v) + \alpha i_v \tag{5}$$

where $\hat{A} = D^{-\frac{1}{2}}AD^{-\frac{1}{2}}$. Solving Eq. (5), we obtain:

$$\pi(i_v) = \alpha \left(I_{M+N} - (1 - \alpha)\hat{A} \right)^{-1} i_v \tag{6}$$

This vector is different for different source node v. Substituting the one-hot indicator $i_1, i_2, \cdots, i_{M+N}$ into Eq. (6) and stacking $\pi(i_1), \pi(i_2), \cdots, \pi(i_{M+N})$ as a PPR matrix $\Pi \in \mathbb{R}^{(N+M) \times (N+M)}$:

$$\begin{aligned}
\Pi &= [\Pi(i_1), \Pi(i_2), \cdots, \Pi(i_{M+N})] \\
&= \alpha \left(I_{M+N} - (1 - \alpha)\hat{A} \right)^{-1} [i_1, i_2, \cdots, i_{M+N}] \\
&= \alpha \left(I_{M+N} - (1 - \alpha)\hat{A} \right)^{-1} I_{M+N} \\
&= \alpha \left(I_{M+N} - (1 - \alpha)\hat{A} \right)^{-1}
\end{aligned} \tag{7}$$

Equation (7) gives the closed-form expression of PPR matrix in personalized recommendation. The (i, j) entry of Π, i.e., the PPR value $\Pi_i(j)$, represents the node significance i with respect to node j in the user-item interaction graph. Actually since Π is a symmetric matrix, i.e., $\Pi_{i,j} = \Pi_{j,i}$, the relative importance of i on j is equivalent to that of j on i.

Taking the PPR value as the metric, we can design a PPR-based subgraph extractor for each node v. The PPR vector $\boldsymbol{\Pi}(\boldsymbol{i}_v)$ should be computed first according to Eq. (6), or compute the PPR matrix $\boldsymbol{\Pi}$ according to Eq. (7) and take the v-th column. Then we select $V[v]$ by taking k nodes corresponding to the top-k values in $\boldsymbol{\Pi}(\boldsymbol{i}_v)$ and filter out other $N + M - k$ nodes. Now we can extract the subgraph $G[v]$ induced by these k nodes as the range of node v. Moreover, note that the PPR values are unrelated to vertex content but solely the location in the whole structure. Similarly, in the historical interaction diagram for personalized recommendation, every vertex of users or items v could be also represented through one featureless one-hot ID $\boldsymbol{i}_v$. Consequently, the predicted ratings for personalized recommendation is closely relevant to the global graph structure. Thus we are naturally motivated to apply the PPR to personalized recommendation. We start by partitioning the PPR matrix $\boldsymbol{\Pi}$ into four blocks as follows:

$$\boldsymbol{\Pi} = \left[\begin{array}{c|c} \boldsymbol{\Pi}_{1:N,1:N} & \boldsymbol{\Pi}_{1:N,(N+1):(N+M)} \\ \hline \boldsymbol{\Pi}_{(N+1):(N+M),1:N} & \boldsymbol{\Pi}_{(N+1):(N+M),(N+1):(N+M)} \end{array} \right]$$

Let $\boldsymbol{R}_{\text{PPR}} = \boldsymbol{\Pi}_{1:N,(N+1):(N+M)} \in \mathbb{R}^{N \times M}$, then $\boldsymbol{\Pi}_{(N+1):(N+M),1:N} = \boldsymbol{R}_{\text{PPR}}^{\top}$. Since $\boldsymbol{R}_{\text{PPR}}$ is a block of $\boldsymbol{\Pi}$, the (i, j) entry of $\boldsymbol{R}_{\text{PPR}}$ plays the same role as the $(i, N + j)$ entry of $\boldsymbol{\Pi}$, representing the relative importance of node i on respect to node $N + j$ in the user-item interaction graph. Moreover, $\boldsymbol{R}_{\text{PPR}}$ exactly lies in the $(1 \sim N)$-th rows of $\boldsymbol{\Pi}$ that represent the users, the $(N + 1 \sim N + M)$-th columns of $\boldsymbol{\Pi}$ that represent the items. Hence the (i, j) entry of $\boldsymbol{R}_{\text{PPR}}$ also acts as the estimated score of user i to item j. The $\boldsymbol{R}_{\text{PPR}}$ matrix directly gives every user's preferences towards all items drawn individually from the structure of interaction diagram *without any training and learning process*. We directly name this approach as "PPR". The performance of PPR is shown in Table 1.

3.3 Self-learning Aggregate Function

To enhance the robustness of deep graph neural networks (GNNs), recent studies highlight the significance of invariance and equivariance properties [9,16,27]. In GNNs, invariance to input transformations like node order or properties allows models to focus on task-relevant features by disregarding irrelevant information. Equivariance ensures that input transformations correspond to output transformations, preserving data integrity and adaptability. We explore achieving these properties through common GNN aggregation functions: mean, max, and sum.

We propose an adaptive aggregation function, SAF, for deep GNNs that outperforms basic functions (mean, max, sum). SAF learns the optimal aggregation through a continuous parameter p, encompassing various functions and optimizing aggregation by targeting specific states in parameter space.

For simplicity, we first propose the formula that incorporates only two simple aggregate functions which we have chosen *mean* and *max* as follows,

$$SAF_{mean,max}(e_z^{(L)}|z \in G[v]) = \sum_{z \in G[v]} \frac{exp(\beta e_z)}{\sum\limits_{z' \in G[v]} exp(\beta e_{z'})} e_z \qquad (8)$$

where β is a continuous parameter to learn the best aggregate state. In other words, when $\beta = 0$, the molecular is equivalent to 1 and the denominator is equivalent to the user's neighbors count, and so the formula is equivalent to a *mean* function. When $\beta = \infty$, the max node message is equal to itself, and the rest is equal to 0, and so it is equivalent to a *max* function.

For a *mean* function, we only need to multiplied by the number of nodes, and this function becomes a *sum* function. So we introduce a parameter γ on the formula $SAF_{mean,max}$, and multiply it by $|G[v]|^\gamma$ to build a bridge ranging from mean to sum, where $G[v]$ is the number of the user's neighbors, and the γ as the power of the number of node numbers can maintain all message features as positive values. Consequently, the generalized aggregate function that we have proposed can be formally defined as:

$$SAF(e_z^{(L)}|z \in G[v]) = |G[v]|^\gamma \sum_{z \in G[v]} \frac{exp(\beta e_z)}{\sum\limits_{z' \in G[v]} exp(\beta e_{z'})} e_z \qquad (9)$$

where γ is also a continuous parameter to learn the best aggregate state. When $\gamma = 0$, the SAF function is still a *mean-max* function. And when $\gamma = 1$ and $\beta = 0$, the SAF function is a *sum* aggregation.

3.4 Model Training

We estimate the propensity between one user and the objective item through inner product:

$$\hat{r}_{ui} = e_u^\top e_i \qquad (10)$$

DetachGCN applies Bayesian Personalized Ranking loss on prioritizing the prediction of known users or items over unknown ones:

$$\mathcal{L}_{BPR} = -\sum_{u=1}^{N} \sum_{i \in \mathcal{N}(u)} \sum_{j \notin \mathcal{N}(u)} \ln \sigma(\hat{r}_{ui} - \hat{r}_{uj}) \qquad (11)$$

where $\sigma(\cdot)$ is the sigmoid function. And the Adam optimizer is employed.

4 Experiments

4.1 Experimental Setting

To lighten the experiment burden while maintaining a level playing field for comparison, we closely replicate the experimental setup of the LightGCN work

[7]. We have acquired all the datasets from the authors. The assessment criteria consist of recall@20 and ndcg@20, which are determined using the all-ranking methodology, where all items that a user has not engaged with are considered as potential candidates.

The main competing method is LightGCN, which outperforms several recommendation methods including NGCF [21], LR-GCCF [5], NIA-GCN [19], DGCF [22] and SGL-ED [25].

Similar to LightGCN, we make the embedding dimension be 64. Glorot's initialization is used on embedding parameters. And we utilized the Adam SGD optimizer to train DetachGCN where the initial learning rate is 0.001. And we set default mini-batch size as 2048. The teleport (restart) probability α is searched in $0.05, 0.10, 0.15, \ldots, 0.45, 0.50$, and in every scenario, the most favorable value is 0.15 or 0.20 for DetachGCN, but varies with datasets for PPR and APPR.

4.2   Performance Comparison

The performance metrics of the baseline models in Table 1 are extracted from the original research papers, except LR-GCCF and NIA-GCN are tested by us. The best achievable score for each method is presented. It is evident that DetachGCN consistently outperform other models on all three datasets, showcasing its superiority for its sensible design approach. Especially on Amazon-Book, the recall and NDCG have improved 29.2% and 36.2% respectively compared to LightGCN.

Table 1. Model Performance Comparison: Cross-Dataset Evaluation Results.

Model	Gowalla		Yelp2018		Amazon-Book	
	Recall	NDCG	Recall	NDCG	Recall	NDCG
NGCF	0.1570	0.1327	0.0579	0.0477	0.0344	0.0263
LR-GCCF	0.1519	0.1285	0.0561	0.0343	0.0335	0.0265
NIA-GCN	0.1359	0.1106	0.0599	0.0491	0.0369	0.0287
LightGCN	0.1830	0.1554	0.0649	0.0530	0.0411	0.0315
DGCF	0.1842	0.1561	0.0654	0.0534	0.0422	0.0324
SGL-ED	N/A	N/A	0.0675	0.0555	0.0478	0.0379
PPR	0.1718	0.1399	0.0639	0.0525	0.0622	0.0518
APPR	0.1723	0.1402	0.0640	0.0527	0.0621	0.0516
DetachGCN	**0.1894**	**0.1599**	**0.0704**	**0.0571**	**0.0635**	**0.0542**

4.3   Effectiveness Analysis

In this subsection, the effectiveness of DetachGCN will be verified. For traditional GCN-based recommendation models, as outlined in Table 2, we provide a summary of the mean protection ratio of the nodes' count that a objective node can reach during propagating, with varying layers' count stacked for each dataset. Table 2 shows the average number of nodes touched within 3-hop exceeds 10,000, corresponding to around 20% of the full graph size. When the range comes to 4-hop, the percent rapidly increases to around 60% or even 70%. Since traditional GCN-based recommendation models [7, 21, 22] generally stack 3 or 4 layers, this phenomenon indicates that they need to propagate features from the huge neighborhood to construct the embedding of a single objective node. Nevertheless, most nodes in the huge neighborhood would be irrelevant to the target node, hence such propagation can be inefficient or even harmful.

Table 2. Average number and percent of nodes touched by the DetachGCN based computation, each hop is *accumulative*.

Range	Gowalla		Yelp2018		Amazon-Book	
	#Nodes	Percent	#Nodes	Percent	#Nodes	Percent
1-hop	22.9	0.03%	35.5	0.05%	33.0	0.02%
2-hop	1154.0	1.63%	2058.2	2.95%	3147.3	2.18%
3-hop	12330.0	17.41%	16766.7	24.05%	34634.9	24.01%
4-hop	39693.7	56.03%	46824.4	67.16%	103578.0	71.81%
5-hop	62609.6	88.38%	66637.6	95.58%	138845.7	96.26%
∞-hop	70839.0	100.00%	69716.0	100.00%	144242.0	100.00%

Table 3. Average number and percent of nodes touched by the DetachGCN based computation, each hop is *accumulative*.

Range	Gowalla		Yelp2018		Amazon-Book	
	#Nodes	Percent	#Nodes	Percent	#Nodes	Percent
1-hop	22.8	2.28%	35.5	3.55%	32.9	3.29%
2-hop	512.0	51.20%	722.3	72.23%	701.5	70.15%
3-hop	919.1	91.91%	982.7	98.27%	984.4	98.44%
4-hop	997.4	99.74%	999.9	99.99%	999.9	99.99%
5-hop	999.9	99.99%	1000.0	100.00%	1000.0	100.00%
∞-hop	1000.0	100.00%	1000.0	100.00%	1000.0	100.00%

In contrast, Table 3 details the mean protection ratio of the nodes' count that a objective node can reach during the propagating process using DetachGCN. Since DetachGCN only takes 1000 nodes in the extracted subgraph, the maximum number of nodes reached within infinite-hop is bounded in 1,000. When the range comes to 3-hop, the percent rapidly increases to more than 90%. And when the range comes to 4-hop, the percent is approximately 100%. To generate the embedding of a single target node, DetachGCN only needs to propagate features from the small but informative neighborhood, thereby avoiding the defects of the traditional GCN-based recommendation model.

5 Conclusion

In this work, we argued the synchronization between the model depth of Graph Convolutional Networks (GCNs) and the range of their receptive fields. This indicates that in traditional GCNs, depth and range are bound, and as the depth increases, the model's receptive field also expands. However, indiscriminate expansion of the receptive field can be detrimental to model performance. We then propose DetachGCN, which utilizes Personalized PageRank (PPR) to delineate reasonable ranges for the model, successfully decoupling the depth from the range. This effectively alleviates the over-smoothing problem in GCN models.

Acknowledgement. This work was supported by the Fundamental Research Funds for the Central Universities (No. 2021QD014, No.2024JJ039, 2024TD001).

References

1. Abu-El-Haija, S., et al.: MixHop: higher-order graph convolutional architectures via sparsified neighborhood mixing. In: Proceedings of the 36th International Conference on ML, pp. 21–29 (2019)
2. Alon, U., Yahav, E.: On the bottleneck of graph neural networks and its practical implications. In: Proceedings of the 9th International Conference on LR (2021)
3. Andersen, R., Chung, F., Lang, K.: Local graph partitioning using PageRank vectors. In: Proceedings of the 47th Annual IEEE Symposium on FCS, pp. 475–486 (2006)
4. Bojchevski, A., et al.: Scaling graph neural networks with approximate PageRank. In: Proceedings of the 26th ACM SIGKDD Conference on KDDM, pp. 2464–2473 (2020)
5. Chen, L., Wu, L., Hong, R., Zhang, K., Wang, M.: Revisiting graph based collaborative filtering: a linear residual graph convolutional network approach. In: Proceedings of the 34th AAAI Conference on AI, pp. 27–34 (2020)
6. He, K., Zhang, X., Ren, S., Sun, J.: Deep residual learning for image recognition. In: Proceedings of the IEEE Conference on CVPR, pp. 770–778 (2016)
7. He, X., Deng, K., Wang, X., Li, Y., Zhang, Y., Wang, M.: LightGCN: simplifying and powering graph convolution network for recommendation. In: Proceedings of the 43rd International ACM SIGIR Conference on RDIR, pp. 639–648 (2020)
8. Jeh, G., Widom, J.: Scaling personalized web search. In: Proceedings of the 12th International Conference on WWW, pp. 271–279 (2003)
9. Keriven, N., Peyré, G.: Universal invariant and equivariant graph neural networks. Adv. NIPS **32** (2019)
10. Klicpera, J., Bojchevski, A., Günnemann, S.: Predict then propagate: Graph neural networks meet personalized PageRank. In: Proceedings of the 7th International Conference on LR (2019)

11. Koren, Y., Bell, R., Volinsky, C.: Matrix factorization techniques for recommender systems. Computer **42**(8), 30–37 (2009)
12. Li, C., et al.: Adversarial learning for weakly-supervised social network alignment. In: Proceedings of the AAAI Conference on Artificial Intelligence, vol. 33, pp. 996–1003 (2019)
13. Li, C., et al.: PPNE: Property Preserving Network Embedding. In: Candan, S., Chen, L., Pedersen, T.B., Chang, L., Hua, W. (eds.) DASFAA 2017. LNCS, vol. 10177, pp. 163–179. Springer, Cham (2017). https://doi.org/10.1007/978-3-319-55753-3_11
14. Li, Q., Han, Z., Wu, X.M.: Deeper insights into graph convolutional networks for semi-supervised learning. In: Proceedings of the 32nd AAAI Conference on AI, pp. 3538–3545 (2018)
15. Lofgren, P., Banerjee, S., Goel, A.: Personalized pagerank estimation and search: a bidirectional approach. In: Proceedings of the 9th ACM International Conference on WSDM, pp. 163–172 (2016)
16. Maron, H., Fetaya, E., Segol, N., Lipman, Y.: On the universality of invariant networks. In: International Conference on ML, pp. 4363–4371. PMLR (2019)
17. Nassar, H., Kloster, K., Gleich, D.F.: Strong localization in personalized PageRank vectors. In: Proceedings of the 12th International Workshop on AMW, pp. 190–202 (2015)
18. Page, L., Brin, S., Motwani, R., Winograd, T.: The PageRank citation ranking: Bringing order to the web. Tech. rep, Stanford InfoLab (1999)
19. Sun, J., et al.: Neighbor interaction aware graph convolution networks for recommendation. In: Proceedings of the 43rd International ACM SIGIR Conference on RDIR, pp. 1289–1298 (2020)
20. Wang, S., Yang, R., Xiao, X., Wei, Z., Yang, Y.: FORA: simple and effective approximate single-source personalized PageRank. In: Proceedings of the 23rd ACM SIGKDD Conference on KDDM, pp. 505–514 (2017)
21. Wang, X., He, X., Wang, M., Feng, F., Chua, T.S.: Neural graph collaborative filtering. In: Proceedings of the 42nd International ACM SIGIR Conference on RDIR, pp. 165–174 (2019)
22. Wang, X., Jin, H., Zhang, A., He, X., Xu, T., Chua, T.S.: Disentangled graph collaborative filtering. In: Proceedings of the 43rd International ACM SIGIR Conference on RDIR, pp. 1001–1010 (2020)
23. Wang, Y., et al.: An adaptive graph pre-training framework for localized collaborative filtering. ACM Trans. Inform. Syst. **41**(2), 1–27 (2022)
24. Wu, F., Souza, A., Zhang, T., Fifty, C., Yu, T., Weinberger, K.: Simplifying graph convolutional networks. In: Proceedings of the 36th International Conference on ML, pp. 6861–6871 (2019)
25. Wu, J., et al.: Self-supervised graph learning for recommendation. In: Proceedings of the 44th International ACM SIGIR Conference on RDIR, pp. 726–735 (2021)
26. Xu, K., Li, C., Tian, Y., Sonobe, T., Kawarabayashi, K.i., Jegelka, S.: Representation learning on graphs with jumping knowledge networks. In: Proceedings of the 35th International Conference on ML, pp. 5453–5462 (2018)
27. Yan, H., et al.: A comprehensive study on text-attributed graphs: benchmarking and rethinking. In: Thirty-seventh Conference on Neural Information Processing Systems Datasets and Benchmarks Track (2023)
28. Zeng, H., et al.: Decoupling the depth and scope of graph neural networks (2021)
29. Zhang, P., et al.: Efficiently leveraging multi-level user intent for session-based recommendation via atten-mixer network. In: Proceedings of the Sixteenth ACM International Conference on Web Search and Data Mining, pp. 168–176 (2023)

30. Zhao, J., et al.: Learning on large-scale text-attributed graphs via variational infer-
    ence. arXiv preprint arXiv:2210.14709 (2022)
31. Zhao, Y., et al.: Beyond the overlapping users: cross-domain recommendation via
    adaptive anchor link learning. In: Proceedings of the 46th International ACM
    SIGIR Conference on Research and Development in Information Retrieval, pp.
    1488–1497 (2023)

Context-Aware Structural Adaptive Graph Neural Networks

Jiakun Chen[1], Jie Xu[1]([✉]), Jiahui Hu[1], Liqiang Qiao[1], Shuo Wang[2],
Feiran Huang[3], and Chaozhuo Li[4]

[1] School of Information Science and Technology, Beijing Foreign Studies University,
Beijing, China
`jxu@bfsu.edu.cn`
[2] China Mobile Communications Group Shandong Co., Ltd. Weihai Branch, Weihai,
China
[3] College of Cyber Security/College of Information Science and Technology,
Jinan University, Guangzhou, China
[4] Key Laboratory of Trustworthy Distributed Computing and Service (MoE),
Beijing University of Posts and Telecommunications, Beijing, China

Abstract. Graph-based data structures are prevalent in various real-world applications, for example, protein molecules and social connection networks, necessitating effective representation learning techniques. Graph Neural Networks (GNNs) have demonstrated significant advancements in tasks like node classification and social network analysis through recursive information aggregation. However, current GNN approaches are predominantly static, lacking adaptability to specific graph structures. Inspired by Neural Architecture Search (NAS) in designing dataset-specific architectures, we propose Context-Aware Structure Adaptive Graph Neural Networks (CAS-GNN). This framework is capable of automatically selecting the appropriate aggregator for each node which is determined by both node attributes and local contextual information. The selection is formulated as the Markov Decision Process (MDP) optimized via Deep-Q-Network (DQN) training. Our contributions include a flexible framework incorporating various aggregators for individual nodes based on their attributes and local context, improved performance through node-specific aggregator selection, and extensive experimental validation demonstrating the effectiveness of CAS-GNN on multiple real-world datasets.

Keywords: Graph Neural Networks · Node Classification · Deep Reinforcement Learning

1 Introduction

Enormous amount of real-world data could be formulated into graphs, such as the connections between atoms in protein molecules and the links between users in social networks. Consequently, the study of representation learning specifically

R. Hadfi et al. (Eds.): PRICAI 2024, LNAI 15281, pp. 467–479, 2025.
https://doi.org/10.1007/978-981-96-0116-5_39

on graphs has garnered growing attention. Recently, the research in Graph Neural Networks (GNNs) have thrived in the node classification task [5,14], social network analysis [19,23],, and recommendation systems [7,8,16,20,21].

The impressive representational power of GNNs primarily stems from recursive information aggregation through layers. GraphSage has introduced several aggregators, including the GCN and LSTM aggregators, demonstrating that different aggregators yield varying performances on specific datasets. However, most current GNN-based methods are static, focusing on designing general GNN architectures suitable for any graph rather than building structure-adaptive models tailored to specific graphs. Although these methods have achieved satisfactory performances on several datasets, their expressive power has not been fully exploited because static models do not adapt to different graphs. The impressive success of Neural Architecture Search (NAS) has provided a powerful tool for designing neural network architectures that adapt to datasets, sparking interest in the automatic design of aggregators and GNN architectures for specific graphs. GraphNAS [2] proposes an RNN-based controller to sample certain variable-length architecture strings to serve GNNs, using a reinforced strategy to update the controller. To enhance efficiency, Auto-GNN [17,22,24,25] introduced a parameter-sharing method and a reinforced conservative controller. However, these NAS-based models only slightly improve performance on node classification tasks, and their architecture search does not consider the unique properties of individual nodes.

To address this issue, PolicyGNN [6] introduced a meta-policy method which can be used to learn the amount of the aggregated layers for each node. In PolicyGNN, the final representations of different nodes are obtained through varying numbers of GNN layers, leading to notable improvements in node classification tasks. Despite its success, PolicyGNN is suboptimal as it uses only node attributes to determine the aggregated layer number, ignoring the local contextual information around the node. We believe that both node attributes and contextual topology information are crucial in deciding the appropriate architecture for a given node. Given two nodes, a and b, with the same attributes but differ in their higher-order neighbors' labels, PolicyGNN would assign the same aggregated layer number to both, which is suboptimal. Moreover, the number of aggregated layers is essential but not the only factor, and other components such as the aggregator and activation function also play significant roles, which PolicyGNN fails to design automatically.

To overcome these limitations, we propose Context-Aware Structure Adaptive Graph Neural Networks (CAS-GNN), a unified framework that automatically selects the appropriate aggregator for each node based on the node's representation and its neighbors' representations. We define an aggregator space where a reinforcement learning (RL) agent can be applied to choose the optimal one efficiently for each node. Additionally, we formulate the layer-by-layer aggregator selection which is defined as a Markov Decision Process (MDP). The chosen architecture benefits the RL agent through Deep-Q-Network (DQN) training. This iterative process updates both GNN and DQN parameters to achieve better performance.

Our main contributions are listed as follows:

- We propose a unified framework that is flexible with various aggregators. Our framework can integrate any new aggregators easily and hence enhance the model's performance.
- We demonstrate that applying different aggregators to different nodes improves model performance, which is capable of adapting different aggregators for individual nodes within a single graph.
- We carry out extensive experiments on several real-world datasets for the node classification task. Compared to state-of-the-art models, the experiment results highlight the effectiveness of the proposed method.

2   Related Work

Graph Neural Networks. The idea of Graph Neural Networks (GNNs) and its architecture was first introduced by Scarselli et al. [3]. There are two major subsequent developments in GNNs: *spectral-based* and *spatial-based*. Specifically, the spectral-based methods treat the graph holistically, which can define spectral convolution operators in the Fourier domain, which necessitates the eigenvalue decomposition of the Laplacian matrix [1]. The Graph Convolutional Network (GCN) [5] recursively aggregates features from one-hop neighbors to collect information from the source of multi-hop neighbors. The Graph Attention Network (GAT) [14] introduces an mechanism that aggregate node features. Beyond that, this attention mechanism uses learned edge weights. GraphSAGE [4] expands upon this by proposing various aggregation functions such as MAX, MEAN, and LSTM aggregators. In this study, we aim to integrate these state-of-the-art aggregators to develop a node-specific GNN architecture, thereby enhancing performance. **Deep Reinforcement Learning.** The remarkable success of Deep Neural Networks (DNNs) has paved the way for the Reinforcement Learning (RL) algorithms leveraging DNNs. Mnih et al. [15] introduced the Deep Q-Network (DQN), which trains agents to surpass the performance of most linear models in Atari games. They further proposed a main network-target network structure to enhance training stability. Beyond gaming, Deep Reinforcement Learning has found extensive applications in Neural Architecture Search (NAS) [12,26] and has been employed to optimize GNN architectures [2,6,25]. In this research, we incorporate DQN to determine the ideal aggregator for nodes in each layer, facilitating the design of a node-specific GNN architecture.

3   Preliminaries

Consider an undirected graph $\mathcal{G} = (\mathcal{V}, \mathcal{E})$. In the graph, there are n nodes $v_i \in \mathcal{V}$, and edges $(v_i, v_j) \in \mathcal{E}$. Usually we use the adjacency matrix $\mathbf{A} \in \mathbb{R}^{n \times n}$ to denote the graph $\mathcal{G}$, in which $\mathbf{A}_{ij} = 1$ denotes an edge $(v_i, v_j) \in \mathcal{E}$, otherwise, if $\mathbf{A}_{ij} = 0$, then $(v_i, v_j) \notin \mathcal{E}$. We mark $\tilde{\mathbf{A}} = \mathbf{A} + \mathbf{I}$ as the graph that has self-loop, $\tilde{\mathbf{D}} = diag\left(\sum_{i=1}^{n} \tilde{\mathbf{A}}_{1i}, \ldots, \sum_{i=1}^{n} \tilde{\mathbf{A}}_{ni}\right)$ as the degree matrix. $\hat{\mathbf{A}}$ is the re-normalization of the adjacency matrix $\mathbf{A}$ which usually takes form of row normalization $\tilde{\mathbf{D}}^{-1}\tilde{\mathbf{A}}$ or symmetric normalization $\tilde{\mathbf{D}}^{-\frac{1}{2}}\tilde{\mathbf{A}}\tilde{\mathbf{D}}^{-\frac{1}{2}}$. Besides, there is an attribute matrix $\mathbf{X} \in \mathbb{R}^{n \times m}$ to describe nodes' attribute. For each node $v_i \in \mathcal{V}$, there i^{th} row of $\mathbf{X}$ is its attribute vector $\mathbf{x}_i \in \mathbb{R}^m$. And label matrix $\mathbf{Y} \in \{0,1\}^{n \times C}$. The aim of graph representation learning is searching for a low-dimensional vector that preserves both node's attribute information and its local topology information, therefore we can use the learned representation vector in downstream tasks. We mainly work on node classification task in our experiment. Formally, we aim to learn a mapping $f : \mathbf{A}, \mathbf{X} \rightarrow \mathbf{Y}$. Table 1 lists the main notations in the paper.

Table 1. Main notations used in this paper

Notation	Description
$\mathcal{G}$	A graph consists of edges and nodes
$\mathcal{V}$	Node set of $\mathcal{G}$
$\mathcal{E}$	Edge set of $\mathcal{G}$
$\mathbf{A}$	Adjacency matrix of $\mathcal{G}$
$\tilde{\mathbf{A}}$	Adjacency matrix of $\mathcal{G}$ with self-loop
$\tilde{\mathbf{D}}$	Degree matrix of $\mathcal{G}$ with self-loop
$\hat{\mathbf{A}}$	re-normalized adjacency matrix of $\mathcal{G}$ with self-loop
$\mathbf{X}$	Feature matrix of $\mathcal{G}$
$\mathbf{Y}$	Feature matrix of $\mathcal{G}$
$N(v)$	The set of neighbor nodes of v
$\mathbf{h}_v^k$	The representation of node v at the kth GNN layer
$\mathcal{D}_{tr}, \mathcal{D}_{val}, \mathcal{D}_{te}$	Training set, validation set, test set
$\mathcal{S}$	The set of all possible states in MDP
$\mathcal{A}$	The set of all possible actions in MDP
$\mathcal{P}$	The transition distribution in MDP
$\mathcal{R}$	The reward function in MDP
$Q(s, a)$	The value estimation of state s taking the action a
s_t^v	The state of node v at the tth timestep

Graph Neural Networks. It has been noted that graph neural network (GNN) does a terrific job to generate graph representation. The mainstream of GNNs can be written in a message-passing fashion, in which for each layer of GNN, the node cam aggregates its own representation and neighbor's representations together to generate a new representation:

$$\mathbf{h}_v^k = AGG(\mathbf{h}_v^{k-1}, \{\mathbf{h}_u^{k-1} | u \in N(v)\}, \mathbf{W}^k) \tag{1}$$

Since our framework consists of several different kinds of GNN layers, we will briefly go over some GNN models which will be utilize in this paper. Note that our model is flexible to extend to any exisiting GNN layers, and will not be limited to the GNN layers below.

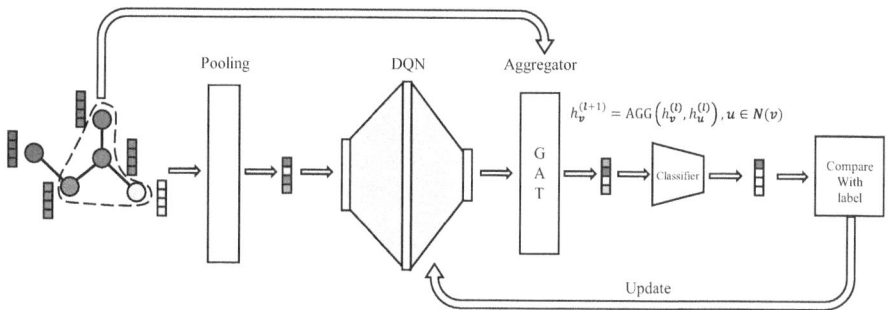

Fig. 1. A one-layer example of CAS-GNN. In each layer, a DQN decides which aggregator a certain node will pass according to its state s, take the red node as an example, The DQN decides the aggregator is GAT according to the result of the pooling of the subgraph centered by the red node. If the red node belongs to validation set, the classification result of the last layer will be used as reward. (Color figure online)

– Graph Convolutional Network (GCN) [5]:

$$h_v^k = \sigma \left(\sum_{u \in \{v\} \cup N(v)} \hat{a}_{vu} \mathbf{W}^k \mathbf{h}_u^{k-1} \right) \qquad (2)$$

where $\hat{\mathbf{A}} = (\hat{a}_{vu}) \in \mathbb{R}^{n \times n}$ is the re-normalization of the adjacency matrix $\mathbf{A}$ with self-loops. Here we use symmetric normalization. $\mathbf{W}^k$ is the trainable parameter at k^{th} layer.
– Graph Attention Network (GAT) [14]:

$$h_v^k = \sigma \left(\sum_{u \in \{v\} \cup N(v)} a_{vu} \mathbf{W}^k \mathbf{h}_u^{k-1} \right) \qquad (3)$$

where a_{vu} is the attention score indicating the importance from u to v. GAT will assign different attention score according to node representation similarity. $\mathbf{W}^k$ is the trainable parameter at k^{th} layer.
– GraphSAGE [4]:

$$\mathbf{h}_{N(v)}^k = AGGREGATE_k \left(\{ \mathbf{h}_u^{k-1} | u \in N(v) \} \right)$$
$$\mathbf{h}_v^k = \sigma \left(\mathbf{W}^k \cdot CONCAT(\mathbf{h}_v^{k-1}, \mathbf{h}_{N(v)}^k) \right) \qquad (4)$$

where MAX, MEAN and LSTM-aggregator are the candidates of feature aggregation. GraphSAGE follows a two-step process, first, it aggregates the representation over node v's neighbor $N(v)$, then it combines v and the aggregated representation to obtain the final version of the representation of the layer. $\mathbf{W}^k$ is the trainable parameter at k^{th} layer.

Markov Decision Process. In our framework, the aggregators choosing process, which is also known as a Markov Decision Process (MDP), will be formulated as a sequential decision issue. There is a quintuple $(\mathcal{S}, \mathcal{A}, \mathcal{P}, \mathcal{R}, \gamma)$ in MDP. In the quintuple, $\mathcal{S}$ is a set of possible states. $\mathcal{A}$ is a set of possible actions. $\mathcal{P} : \mathcal{S} \times \mathcal{A} \times \mathcal{S} \rightarrow [0,1]$ indicates the distribution of the next state $s' \in \mathcal{S}$ of current state $s \in \mathcal{S}$ taking an action $a \in \mathcal{A}$. There is also the reward function $\mathcal{R} : \mathcal{S} \rightarrow \mathbb{R}$. When an agent at the state s_t takes an action a_t, the agent will be transited to next state s_{t+1} according to $\mathcal{P}$. At the same time, a reward signal $r = \mathcal{R}(s_{t+1})$ will be sent. γ is a discount factor, larger γ that is related to a larger impact of future reward. And our objective to obtain an optimal policy $\pi^* : \mathcal{S} \rightarrow \mathcal{A}$ maximizing the discounted cumulative reward $\mathbb{E}_\pi [\sum_{t=0}^{\infty} \gamma^t r_t]$.

Solving MDP with Deep-Q Network. Deep-Q Network (DQN) [10,15] is a powerful tool for solving MDP. In DQN, there is a neural network $Q(s, a)$ to estimate the Q-value of the current state s taking the action a. And the Q-Network satisfies the following equation:

$$Q(s, a) = \mathbb{E}_{s'} \left[\mathcal{R}(s') + \gamma \max_{a'}(Q(s', a')) \right] \tag{5}$$

where s' and a' respectively denotes the next state and action. We approximate $Q(s, a)$ by Eq. 5. In practice, we often stabilize the training process by using a reply buffer and target network trick [10].

4   Method

The goal of our framework **C**ontext-**A**ware **S**tructure Adaptive **G**raph **N**eural **N**etworks (CAS-GNN) is to formulate a framework which is capable of automatically choose the proper aggregator for each node according to its neighbor nodes' representation and its own representation. Unlike most GNN models whose architecture are static and same for different nodes, CAS-GNN seeks an adaptive aggregation strategy based on DQN, which can fully exploit neighbors' information and obtain a better representation under this fashion. We illustrate the framework of CAS-GNN in Fig. 1.

In this section, we will make a detailed description of our framework. We will explain how the MDP is formulated in this specific problem first, then we will show how the algorithm works and how to train DQN and GNN iteratively.

4.1   The Formulation of MDP on Graph

As the component of a well-defined MDP with a quintuple $(\mathcal{S}, \mathcal{A}, \mathcal{P}, \mathcal{R}, \gamma)$, we will define the components in this certain problem and explain the intuitions.

– State $\mathcal{S}$. As we mentioned, the state s is supposed to contain both node's information and neighbor's information, we assume that with these two components, a DQN is sufficient enough to decide which aggregator is the most suitable. Thus we define the state as

$$s_t^v = \mathbf{h}_v^t \parallel POOL(\mathbf{h}_u^t | u \in N(v)) \tag{6}$$

where $\parallel$ is concatenation operator, $POOL(\cdot)$ is a permute invariant operation on sets, we simply take average operation, more complicated graph pooling methods are left for future exploration.

For the initial state s_0, to make the dimension consistent, we project the node attribute into the hidden dimension then through a non-linear transform, i.e. $\mathbf{h}_v^0 = \sigma(\mathbf{W}^0 \mathbf{x}_v)$, where $\mathbf{W}^0 \in \mathbb{R}^{m \times h}$ and m, h are the dimension of raw attribute and hidden representation respectively. Then get s_0^v according to Eq. 6.

In our settings, there is an maximum layer number T as a hyperparameter.

– Action $\mathcal{A}$. $\mathcal{A}$ is a set of all possible aggregators. A special aggregator $IDENTITY$ is included, this is an aggregator that keeps the representation of the node unchanged. Here, we set $\mathcal{A} = \{GCN, GAT, MEANSage, IDENTITY\}$. Note that our model is not limited to the aggregators above, any GNN aggregators can be easily added in our framework. Note that for different layers, the parameters of the same kind of aggregator will not be shared, that is, we will have $|\mathcal{A}| \times T$ GNN aggregators with different parameters. When picking the action by DQN, ϵ-greedy strategy will be applied for exploration-exploitation trade off: with the probability ϵ randomly pick an action a_t, otherwise $a_t = \mathrm{argmax}_a Q(s_t, a)$.

– Transition $\mathcal{P}$. The transition $\mathcal{P}$ describes what the next state s_{t+1}^v is when a current state s_t^v takes an action a_t^v. Here, we set $\mathbf{h}_v^{t+1}$ as the result of the aggregation operator a_t^v under current representations, thus we have

$$\begin{aligned} \mathbf{h}_v^{t+1} &= ReLU(a_t^v(\mathbf{h}_v^t, \{\mathbf{h}_u^t | u \in N(v)\}) \\ s_{t+1}^v &= \mathbf{h}_v^{t+1} \parallel POOL(\mathbf{h}_u^{t+1} | u \in N(v))) \end{aligned} \tag{7}$$

– Reward $\mathcal{R}$. In our settings, the reward is used to reflect whether the sequential decision process really benefit the result of node classification, therefore, we set the reward as whether the prediction is correct at the last layer. That is

$$r_t^v = \begin{cases} 1 & t = T \text{ and node } v \text{ is classified correctly} \\ 0 & t < T \text{ or node } v \text{ is classified incorrectly} \end{cases} \tag{8}$$

With the well defined MDP on graphs, we are able to generate node-specific GNN architectures for all nodes on the graph. Compared with previous work PolicyGNN [6], our model is more advantageous in three aspects. 1) More flexible to provide GNN architectures, since PolicyGNN can only decide the number of layers for a certain aggregator, but our model can automatically choose aggregators. 2) Consider neighbor information when choosing GNN architecture, since PolicyGNN only consider node's raw feature when choosing aggregated layers. 3) Defines a more task-related MDP. The MDP defined in PolicyGNN is less related to the specific task and even somehow confusing.

4.2   Training of CAS-GNN

Next, with the pipeline defined before, we will go through the training process of CAS-GNN. Specifically, we will describe the training objective for both GNN and DQN, and explain the iterative training process of these two modules.

As for GNN training, we take the representation at layer T into a linear classifier for its label prediction, i.e. $\hat{\mathbf{y}}_v = \text{Softmax}(\mathbf{W}^c \mathbf{h}_v^T)$. Then we minimize cross entropy loss over training set for the GNN parameters training:

$$\mathcal{L}_{GNN} = -\frac{1}{|\mathcal{D}_{tr}|} \sum_{i=1}^{|\mathcal{D}_{tr}|} \sum_{c=1}^{C} \mathbf{y}_{i,c} \log \hat{\mathbf{y}}_{i,c} \tag{9}$$

where C is total number of label classes. The update of GNN parameters enables the learning a node presentation with better precision as well as classifier in the proposed model.

As for DQN training, in each time step t, we record (s_t, a_t, s_{t+1}, r_t) into a replay buffer B, when the buffer size b is attained, we throw the earliest item and record a new one. And a batch of items is picked randomly from the replay buffer, then we apply this batch to do the DQN training according to the MSE loss:

$$\mathcal{L}_{DQN} = \frac{1}{|\mathcal{S}|} \sum_{(s,a,s',r) \in \mathcal{S}} \left(r + \gamma \max_{a'} Q\left(s', a'; \bar{\theta}\right) - Q\left(s, a; \theta\right) \right)^2 \tag{10}$$

where $\mathcal{S}$ is the sampled item set from the replay buffer $\mathcal{B}$, $\bar{\theta}$ and θ are parameters from the target and original network. And we update $\bar{\theta}$ equals to θ every K steps. This is the target network trick so as to better stabilize the DQN training [10].

5   Experiment

In this section, we will evaluate the effectiveness of our CAS-GNN model.

5.1   Datasets

Here, we adopt the commonly used citation networks, namely Cora, Citeseer and Pubmed for our node classification task [13]. For these citation networks, each node represent a published document, and the bag-of-words vector represents its attributes. The undirected edges denote citation relations. And the label denotes

Algorithm 1. CAS-GNN

1: **Input:** Max layer T, DQN batch size $|\mathcal{S}|$, total training epoch N, ϵ
2: Initialize all GNN layers Θ_{GNN}, DQN parameters Θ_{DQN}, replay buffer $\mathcal{B}$, $\mathbf{W}^0, \mathbf{W}^c$
3: **for** $epoch \leftarrow 1$ **to** n **do**
4:     initialize states for all nodes: $\mathbf{h}_v^0 = \sigma(\mathbf{W}^0 \mathbf{x}_v)$ and get s_0^v
5:     **for** $t \leftarrow 0$ **to** $T - 1$ **do**
6:         Get a_t^v for all nodes according to ϵ-greedy strategy
7:         Generate next state s_{t+1}^v for all nodes according to Eq. 7
8:         For $v \in \mathcal{D}_{val}$ compute r_t^v and store the quadruples in $\mathcal{B}$
9:     **end for**
10: **end for**
11: Update $\Theta_{GNN}, \mathbf{W}^0, \mathbf{W}^c$ via Eq. 9
12: Sample $|\mathcal{S}|$ items from $\mathcal{B}$, update Θ_{DQN} via Eq. 10

the category of a certain document. The statistics of these datasets are in Table 2. As for data splitting, we implement the previous works [5,14,18], which takes 20 nodes per class for training. For the validation, we use 500 nodes. And we take 1000 nodes for test. We compare the accuracy of node classification as the performance metric.

Table 2. Statistics of Cora, Citeseer and Pubmed

Dataset	Cora	Citeseer	Pubmed
Nodes	2708	3327	19717
Features	1433	3703	500
Classes	7	6	3
Training Nodes	140	120	60
Validation Nodes	500	500	500
Testing Nodes	1000	1000	1000

5.2 Baselines

To show the effectiveness of our method, we compare this method with the following state-of-the-art methods.

– **DeepWalk** [11]. This is a model that learns node embeddings by walking randomly over graph, and optimizes the embeddings by Skip-Gram method [9].
– **GCN** [5]. This is a model that performs information aggregation on a Laplacian adjacency matrix over the whole graph.
– **GraphSAGE** [4]. This is a model that aggregates the information over sampled nodes and combines the aggregated information and center node's information together to produce the next representation.

- **GAT** [14]. This model utilizes multi-head attention mechanism to treat different neighbors with different weights in aggregation phase.
- **SGC** [18]. This model removes non-linear activate function in GCN, thus more computational efficient and parameter-saving compared to vanilla GCN.
- **GraphNAS** [2]. It proposes an RNN-based controller to sample variable-length architectural strings for GNNs, and use a reinforced strategy to update the controller.

5.3   Experimental Settings

In our experiments, as described above, we set the action space as $\mathcal{A} = \{GCN, GAT, MEANSage, IDENTITY\}$. We apply *Relu* as the activation function after aggregation in each layer. For GNN training, we adopt Adam optimizer in which the learning rate is set to 0.001 and weight decay is set to 0.0005. We set the hidden dimension as 16 and the maximum layer as 2. For DQN settings, we set the hidden layer of DQN as $\{32, 64, 128, 64, 32\}$, and the replay buffer size as 640. ϵ decreases from 1 to 0.01 in 1000000 steps. We set the discount factor as $\gamma = 0.99$. The learning rate of DQN is 0.0005, and the parameters are optimized by Adam optimizer. We trained the DQN together with GNN for 10000 episodes, and report the test accuracy on validation set by the performance (Table 3).

Table 3. Node classification accuracy on Cora, Citeseer and Pubmed

Model	Cora	Citeseer	Pubmed
DeepWalk	0.672	0.432	0.653
GCN	0.815	0.703	0.790
GraphSAGE	0.745	0.672	0.768
GAT	0.830	0.725	0.790
SGC	0.810	0.719	0.789
GraphNAS	0.833	0.735	0.781
CAS-GNN	**0.887**	**0.753**	**0.833**

5.4   Effect of Different Activation Function

In this section, we evaluate what effect do various activation functions have on the performance of CAS-GNN by performing an ablation study. The models in Table 4 represent the removal of specific activation function models from the candidate set. The experimental results are presented in Table 4. On analyzing the results, we have the following observations: The performance of all models declines after the removal of any single activation function model. The GCN and GAT activation functions are more critical than the other two functions. This is expected, as GCN and GAT can aggregate neighborhood information through learnable parameters, whereas the other two functions rely on heuristic settings for information aggregation.

Table 4. Ablation study on Cora, Citeseer and Pubmed

Model	Cora	Citeseer	Pubmed
-GCN	0.855	0.706	0.803
-GAT	0.861	0.702	0.801
-MEANSAGE	0.874	0.738	0.811
-IDENTITY	0.872	0.741	0.815
CAS-GNN	**0.887**	**0.753**	**0.833**

6   Conclusion

In this paper, we introduced Context-Aware Structure Adaptive Graph Neural Networks (CAS-GNN). We design this model to enhance the adaptability and performance of GNNs by selecting appropriate aggregators for individual nodes based on their attributes and local context. By framing the aggregator selection process as a Markov Decision Process (MDP) and utilizing Deep-Q-Network (DQN) training, our method dynamically optimizes the architecture for each node, resulting in significant improvements in node classification tasks. Our real-world-datasets experiments demonstrate that CAS-GNN outperforms state-of-the-art architectures by effectively leveraging node-specific contextual information. The flexibility of our framework allows for the easy integration of new aggregators, further enhancing its applicability and robustness across different graph-based applications.

Acknowledgement. This work was supported by the Fundamental Research Funds for the Central Universities (No. 2021QD014, No.2024JJ039, 2024TD001).

References

1. Bruna, J., Zaremba, W., Szlam, A., Lecun, Y.: Spectral networks and locally connected networks on graphs. In: International Conference on Learning Representations (ICLR2014), CBLS (April 2014)
2. Gao, Y., Yang, H., Zhang, P., Zhou, C., Hu, Y.: Graph neural architecture search. In: Bessiere, C. (ed.) Proceedings of the 29th AJCAI, IJCAI 2020, pp. 1403–1409. IJCAI (July 2020), main track
3. Gori, M., Monfardini, G., Scarselli, F.: A new model for learning in graph domains. In: Proceedings. 2005 IEEE IJCNN 2005, vol. 2, pp. 729–734 (2005)

4. Hamilton, W.L., Ying, R., Leskovec, J.: Inductive representation learning on large graphs. In: NIPS (2017)

5. Kipf, T.N., Welling, M.: Semi-supervised classification with graph convolutional networks. In: International Conference on Learning Representations (ICLR) (2017)

6. Lai, K.H., Zha, D., Zhou, K., Hu, X.: Policy–gnn: aggregation optimization for graph neural networks. In: KDD 2020, pp. 461-471. Association for Computing Machinery, New York (2020)

7. Li, C., et al.: Adversarial learning for weakly-supervised social network alignment. In: Proceedings of the AAAI Conference on Artificial Intelligence, vol. 33, pp. 996–1003 (2019)

8. Li, C., et al.: PPNE: property preserving network embedding. In: Candan, S., Chen, L., Pedersen, T.B., Chang, L., Hua, W. (eds.) DASFAA 2017. LNCS, vol. 10177, pp. 163–179. Springer, Cham (2017). https://doi.org/10.1007/978-3-319-55753-3_11

9. Mikolov, T., Sutskever, I., Chen, K., Corrado, G.S., Dean, J.: Distributed representations of words and phrases and their compositionality. In: Burges, C.J.C., Bottou, L., Welling, M., Ghahramani, Z., Weinberger, K.Q. (eds.) Advances in NIPS, vol. 26, pp. 3111–3119. Curran Associates, Inc. (2013)

10. Mnih, V., et al.: Human-level control through deep reinforcement learning. Nature **518**(7540), 529–533 (2015)

11. Perozzi, B., Al-Rfou, R., Skiena, S.: Deepwalk: online learning of social representations. In: Proceedings of the 20th ACM SIGKDD International Conference on KDDM, KDD 2014, pp. 701–710. ACM, New York (2014)

12. Pham, H., Guan, M.Y., Zoph, B., Le, Q.V., Dean, J.: Efficient neural architecture search via parameter sharing. In: ICML (2018)

13. Sen, P., et al.: Collective classification in network data. AI Mag. **29**(3), 93 (2008)

14. Veličković, P., Cucurull, G., Casanova, A., Romero, A., Liò, P., Bengio, Y.: Graph Attention Networks. In: International Conference on Learning Representations (2018)

15. Volodymyr, M., et al.: Playing atari with deep reinforcement learning. In: NIPS Deep Learning Workshop (2013)

16. Wang, X., He, X., Wang, M., Feng, F., Chua, T.: Neural graph collaborative filtering. In: Proceedings of the 42nd International ACM SIGIR Conference on RDIR, SIGIR 2019, Paris, France, 21-25 July 2019, pp. 165–174 (2019)

17. Wang, Y., et al.: An adaptive graph pre-training framework for localized collaborative filtering. ACM Trans. Inform. Syst. **41**(2), 1–27 (2022)

18. Wu, F., Souza, A., Zhang, T., Fifty, C., Yu, T., Weinberger, K.: Simplifying graph convolutional networks. In: Chaudhuri, K., Salakhutdinov, R. (eds.) Proceedings of the 36th ICML. Proceedings of Machine Learning Research, 09–15 Jun, vol. 97, pp. 6861–6871. PMLR (2019)

19. Wu, Y., Lian, D., Jin, S., Chen, E.: Graph convolutional networks on user mobility heterogeneous graphs for social relationship inference. In: Proceedings of the 28th, IJCAI 2019, pp. 3898–3904. IJCAI (July2019)

20. Yan, H., et al.: A comprehensive study on text-attributed graphs: Benchmarking and rethinking. In: Thirty-seventh Conference on Neural Information Processing Systems Datasets and Benchmarks Track (2023)

21. Ying, R., He, R., Chen, K., Eksombatchai, P., Hamilton, W.L., Leskovec, J.: Graph convolutional neural networks for web-scale recommender systems. In: Proceedings of the 24th ACM SIGKDD International Conference on KDDM, KDD 2018, pp. 974-983. Association for Computing Machinery, New York (2018)

22. Zhang, P., et al.: Efficiently leveraging multi-level user intent for session-based recommendation via atten-mixer network. In: Proceedings of the Sixteenth ACM International Conference on Web Search and Data Mining, pp. 168–176 (2023)
23. Zhao, J., et al.: Learning on large-scale text-attributed graphs via variational inference. arXiv preprint arXiv:2210.14709 (2022)
24. Zhao, Y., et al.: Beyond the overlapping users: cross-domain recommendation via adaptive anchor link learning. In: Proceedings of the 46th International ACM SIGIR Conference on Research and Development in Information Retrieval, pp. 1488–1497 (2023)
25. Zhou, K., Song, Q., Huang, X., Hu, X.: Auto-gnn: Neural architecture search of graph neural networks (2019)
26. Zoph, B., Le, Q.V.: Neural architecture search with reinforcement learning. In: ICLR (2016)

multi-GAT: Integrative Analysis of scRNA-seq and scATAC-seq Data Using Graph Attention Networks for Cell Annotation

Shangru Jia[1]([📧]) [iD], Tatsuhiko Tsunoda[1,2,3] [iD], and Alok Sharma[2,3,4,5]([📧]) [iD]

[1] Laboratory for Medical Science Mathematics, Department of Computational Biology and Medical Sciences, Graduate School of Frontier Sciences, The University of Tokyo, Tokyo, Japan
jiashangru@g.ecc.u-tokyo.ac.jp
[2] Laboratory for Medical Science Mathematics, Department of Biological Sciences, School of Science, The University of Tokyo, Tokyo, Japan
[3] Laboratory for Medical Science Mathematics, RIKEN Center for Integrative Medical Sciences, Yokohama, Japan
[4] Institute for Integrated and Intelligent Systems, Griffith University, Nathan, Brisbane QLD4111, Australia
[5] College of Informatics, Korea University, Seoul, South Korea

Abstract. Single-cell RNA sequencing (scRNA-seq) and single-cell Assay for Transposase-Accessible Chromatin using sequencing (scATAC-seq) provide complementary views of cellular states by capturing transcriptomic and chromatin accessibility landscapes, respectively [1]. Combining these modalities offers a comprehensive understanding of cellular functions and regulatory mechanisms. Here, we present multi-GAT, a model specifically designed for integrative analysis of scRNA-seq and scATAC-seq data using Canonical Correlation Analysis (CCA) followed by Graph Attention Network (GAT) to predict cell types. This approach leverages shared nearest neighbors and contrastive learning to enhance model performance. Multi-GAT effectively captures the complex relationships between transcriptomic and chromatin accessibility data, achieving robust cell type annotation across different single-cell modalities. The experimental results demonstrate that multi-GAT surpasses several baseline methods in accuracy, precision, and F1-score on the benchmark dataset.

Keywords: Graph Attention Networks · Single-cell transcriptomics · Canonical Correlation Analysis · Cell Annotation · Contrastive Learning

1 Introduction

Recent advancements in computational methodologies have led to innovative strategies that address the inherent challenges of integrating Single-cell RNA

R. Hadfi et al. (Eds.): PRICAI 2024, LNAI 15281, pp. 480–486, 2025.
https://doi.org/10.1007/978-981-96-0116-5_40

sequencing (scRNA-seq) and single-cell Assay for Transposase-Accessible Chromatin using sequencing (scATAC-seq) data. These challenges primarily arise from the distinct nature of transcriptomic and chromatin accessibility datasets, requiring advanced techniques for effective integration. One promising approach is Canonical Correlation Analysis (CCA), a statistical method that identifies and quantifies linear relationships between high-dimensional datasets [2]. CCA is particularly effective in aligning scRNA-seq and scATAC-seq data by identifying shared components that represent common underlying biological signals, simplifying the complex and high-dimensional nature of the data for more meaningful integrative analyses.

After aligning the datasets via CCA, Graph Attention Networks (GAT) are employed. GAT, designed for graph-structured data [3], are well-suited for modeling the intricate relationships in single-cell multi-omics data. By assigning varying levels of attention to nodes in a graph, GAT captures complex interactions and dependencies that traditional methods may miss. This is crucial for accurately modeling relationships between gene expression profiles and chromatin accessibility patterns, leading to more precise cell type predictions and functional annotations.

In this study, we introduce multi-GAT, a novel framework for integrative analysis of scRNA-seq and scATAC-seq data. Unlike other annotation methods, such as SingleR and scType, which heavily depend on the quality and completeness of reference datasets or known marker genes, multi-GAT uses CCA to align these datasets in a common latent space, followed by GAT to model complex cell relationships. This approach outperforms traditional methods, particularly in noisy and sparse environments, by leveraging shared nearest neighbors and contrastive learning to distinguish between similar and dissimilar cells. By preserving local data structures and capturing intricate relationships between transcriptomic and chromatin accessibility data, multi-GAT achieves robust and accurate cell type annotation across various single-cell modalities.

2   Methods

2.1   The Proposed Workflow

The proposed workflow integrates scRNA-seq and scATAC-seq data using Canonical Correlation Analysis (CCA) followed by Graph Attention Networks (GAT) to predict cell types. Initially, scRNA-seq and scATAC-seq data are normalized and log-transformed. CCA is then applied to align these datasets in a common latent space, resulting in canonical variables representing the CCA components. A shared nearest neighbor graph is constructed from the CCA-transformed data, connecting each cell to its 10 nearest neighbors based on Euclidean distance. GAT computes hidden states of each node by attending over its neighbors using self-attention, with attention coefficients determining their importance. Contrastive learning [4] enhances model performance by encouraging similar cells to have similar embeddings and dissimilar cells to have distinct embeddings. The GAT model is trained on combined graph data, minimizing a combined loss function of cross-entropy and contrastive loss to ensure robust cell type annotation (Fig. 1).

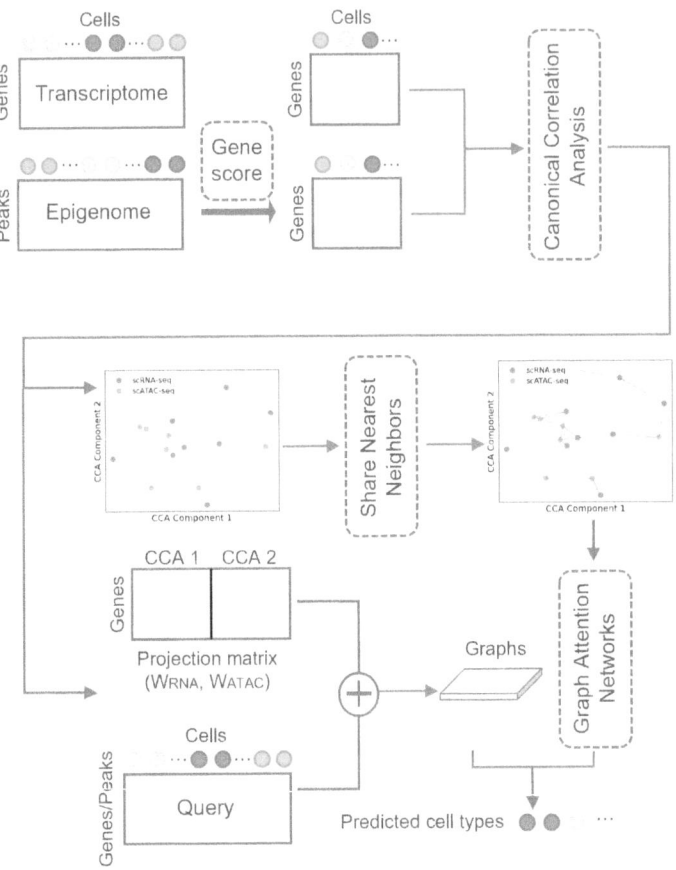

Fig. 1. The workflow of multi-GAT

2.2   Data Preprocessing

The preprocessing steps for scRNA-seq data include normalization to a total count of 10,000 reads per cell and log-transformation. Highly variable genes are identified using the variance stabilizing transformation, and the top 2,000 most variable genes are selected. These thresholds are commonly used in the literature to ensure a balance between noise reduction and information retention, facilitating effective downstream analysis. The data are then scaled to unit variance and zero mean:

$$\mathbf{X}_{\text{norm}} = \log_2 \left(\frac{\mathbf{X}}{\sum \mathbf{X}} \times 10,000 + 1 \right) \tag{1}$$

Similar to scRNA-seq, scATAC-seq data are normalized, log-transformed, and scaled. Additionally, peak calling is performed on the scATAC-seq data to identify open chromatin regions, which are then associated with corresponding genes for integration.

2.3   Canonical Correlation Analysis

CCA is employed to align the scRNA-seq and scATAC-seq data in a common latent space. CCA finds linear combinations of variables in each dataset that are maximally correlated. Given two datasets $\mathbf{X}_{\text{RNA}}$ and $\mathbf{X}_{\text{ATAC}}$, CCA solves:

$$\max_{\mathbf{W}_{\text{RNA}}, \mathbf{W}_{\text{ATAC}}} \text{corr}(\mathbf{U}_{\text{RNA}}, \mathbf{U}_{\text{ATAC}}) \tag{2}$$

$$\mathbf{U}_{\text{RNA}} = \mathbf{X}_{\text{RNA}} \mathbf{W}_{\text{RNA}}, \quad \mathbf{U}_{\text{ATAC}} = \mathbf{X}_{\text{ATAC}} \mathbf{W}_{\text{ATAC}} \tag{3}$$

subject to:

$$\mathbf{W}_{\text{RNA}}^{\top} \mathbf{X}_{\text{RNA}}^{\top} \mathbf{X}_{\text{RNA}} \mathbf{W}_{\text{RNA}} = 1, \quad \mathbf{W}_{\text{ATAC}}^{\top} \mathbf{X}_{\text{ATAC}}^{\top} \mathbf{X}_{\text{ATAC}} \mathbf{W}_{\text{ATAC}} = 1 \tag{4}$$

This results in two sets of canonical variables, $\mathbf{U}_{\text{RNA}}$ and $\mathbf{U}_{\text{ATAC}}$, representing the CCA components.

2.4   Graph Construction

Using the CCA-transformed data, we constructed a shared nearest neighbor graph. Each cell is connected to its 10 nearest neighbors based on Euclidean distance in the CCA space. The adjacency matrix is constructed such that $A_{ij} = 1$ if cell i and cell j are neighbors, and $A_{ij} = 0$ otherwise.

2.5   Graph Attention Networks

GAT extends GNNs by incorporating attention mechanisms, which allow the model to weigh the importance of different neighbors. The GAT layer computes the hidden states of each node by attending over its neighbors, using self-attention. To enhance the model's capacity, multi-head attention is employed.

For a node i, its hidden representation $\mathbf{h}_i$ using multi-head attention is computed as:

$$\mathbf{h}_i' = \Big\|_{m=1}^{M} \sigma \left(\sum_{j \in \mathcal{N}(i)} \alpha_{ij}^{(m)} \mathbf{W}^{(m)} \mathbf{h}_j \right) \tag{5}$$

where $\mathcal{N}(i)$ denotes the set of neighbors of node i, M is the number of attention heads, $\mathbf{W}^{(m)}$ is the weight matrix for the m-th attention head, and $\alpha_{ij}^{(m)}$ are the attention coefficients computed as:

$$\alpha_{ij}^{(m)} = \frac{\exp\left(\text{LeakyReLU}\left(\mathbf{a}^{(m)\top}[\mathbf{W}^{(m)}\mathbf{h}_i||\mathbf{W}^{(m)}\mathbf{h}_j]\right)\right)}{\sum_{k \in \mathcal{N}(i)} \exp\left(\text{LeakyReLU}\left(\mathbf{a}^{(m)\top}[\mathbf{W}^{(m)}\mathbf{h}_i||\mathbf{W}^{(m)}\mathbf{h}_k]\right)\right)} \tag{6}$$

where $\mathbf{a}^{(m)}$ is the learnable weight vector for the m-th attention head, and $||$ denotes concatenation. During the training, three attention heads are used.

2.6 Contrastive Learning

To enhance the model's performance, we incorporated contrastive loss, which encourages similar cells to have similar embeddings. Loss L is defined as:

$$L = \frac{1}{N} \sum_{i,j} \left(y_{ij} D(\mathbf{h}_i, \mathbf{h}_j)^2 + (1 - y_{ij}) \max(0, m - D(\mathbf{h}_i, \mathbf{h}_j))^2\right) \tag{7}$$

where $y_{ij} = 1$ if cells i and j are of the same type, $y_{ij} = 0$ otherwise, $D(\cdot)$ denotes Euclidean distance, and m is a margin parameter.

2.7 Training the GAT Model

The GAT model is trained using the combined graph data. The input features are the CCA components, and the labels are the known cell types. The model is trained to minimize cross-entropy loss, combined with the contrastive loss.

$$L_{\text{total}} = L_{\text{cross-entropy}} + \lambda L_{\text{contrastive}} \tag{8}$$

where λ is a weighting parameter balancing the two loss components. In the training process, λ is set to be 0.4.

3 Model Performance

We use the reference dataset [5] containing 35,882 scRNA-seq samples and 35,038 scATAC-seq samples to train the multi-GAT model. Then the performance of cell type annotation is tested on an independent multi-omics peripheral blood mononuclear cell (PBMC) query datasets containing 9,631 cells [6]. The GAT model demonstrated high accuracy in predicting cell types, with an average accuracy of 0.86 across 19 different cell types. The model's effectiveness stems from its ability to integrate transcriptomic and chromatin data via CCA, enhancing signal detection and mitigating noise and sparsity issues. The GAT's attention mechanism further refines cell relationships, improving robustness. Comparisons with methods like SingleR and scType demonstrate that multi-GAT achieves superior accuracy, precision, and F1-score, especially in noisy or sparse data. Ablation studies further validate that contrastive learning boosts performance (Table 1).

Table 1. Performance of cell type annotation on the query PBMC dataset

Methods	Accuracy	Precision	F1-score
multi-GAT (proposed)	0.86	0.85	0.83
multi-GAT (without contrastive learning)	0.83	0.79	0.80
SingleR [7]	0.81	0.77	0.80
scType [8]	0.79	0.75	0.79
cellassign [9]	0.76	0.72	0.77
scPred [10]	0.73	0.71	0.71
SCINA [11]	0.70	0.65	0.72

4   Conclusion

The integration of scRNA-seq and scATAC-seq data using CCA and GAT offers a powerful approach for comprehensive single-cell analysis. CCA effectively aligns the datasets in a common latent space, while GAT leverage graph structure to capture complex relationships between cells. The contrastive loss further enhances the model's ability to distinguish between different cell types.

This method can be extended to other multi-omics data types, providing a flexible framework for integrative single-cell analysis. The ongoing refinement of these techniques holds promise for advancing our understanding of cellular heterogeneity and the underlying regulatory mechanisms at a single-cell resolution.

References

1. Elisabetta Mereu, A.L., et al.: Benchmarking single-cell RNAsequencing protocols for cell atlas projects. Nat.Biotechnol. **38**(6), 747–755 (2020). https://doi.org/10.1038/s41587-020-0469-4
2. Stuart, T., et al.: Comprehensive Integration of Single-Cell Data. Cell **177**(7) 1888–1902.e21 (2019). https://doi.org/10.1016/j.cell.2019.05.031
3. Veličković, P., et al.: Graph Attention Networks (2018)
4. Chen, T., et al.: A Simple Framework for Contrastive Learning of Visual Representations (2020)
5. Granja, J.M., Klemm, S., et al.: Single-cell multiomic analysis identifies regulatory programs in mixed-phenotype acute leukemia. Nat. Biotechnol. **37**(12), 1458–1465 (2019). https://doi.org/10.1038/s41587-019-0332-7
6. Cao, Z.-J., Gao, G.: Multi-omics single-cell data integration and regulatory inference with graph-linked embedding. Nat. Biotechnol. **40**(10), 1458–1466 (2022). https://doi.org/10.1038/s41587-022-01284-4
7. Aran, D., Looney, A.P., et al.: Reference-based analysis of lung single-cell sequencing reveals a transitional profibrotic macrophage. Nat. Immunol. **20**(2), 163–172 (2019). https://doi.org/10.1038/s41590-018-0276-y
8. Ianevski, A., Giri, A.K., Aittokallio, T.: Fully-automated and ultra-fast cell-type identification using specific marker combinations from single-cell transcriptomic data. Nat. Commun. **13**(1), 1246 (2022). https://doi.org/10.1038/s41467-022-28803-w

9. Zhang, A.W., et al.: Probabilistic cell-type assignment of single-cell RNA-seq for tumor microenvironment profiling. Nat. Methods **16**(10), 1007–1015 (2019). https://doi.org/10.1038/s41592-019-0529-1

10. Alquicira-Hernandez, J., et al.: scPred: accurate supervised method for cell-type classification from single-cell RNA-seq data. Genome Biol. **20**(1), 264 (2019). https://doi.org/10.1186/s13059-019-1862-5

11. Zhang, Z., et al.: SCINA: a semi-supervised subtyping algorithm of single cells and bulk samples. Genes **10**(7), 531 (2019). https://doi.org/10.3390/genes10070531

Author Index

A

Abe, Yoshia 3

C

Cai, Songtao 403
Cao, Yong 221
Chaudhari, Tejas 16
Chen, Huaming 93
Chen, Jiakun 454, 467
Chen, Jun 257
Chen, Ruiqi 309
Chen, Xiao 194
Cheng, Songsong 396
Chowdhury, Mashfiqul Huq 29
Colonna, Juan Gabriel 375
Cui, Lizhen 269

D

Daikoku, Tatsuya 3
Dong, Feiyang 297
Dong, Pan 441

E

El Bolock, Alia 134

F

Fang, Xiaoxiang 441
Fu, Wei 348

G

Gao, Chao 158, 236
Gao, Junjie 41
Gao, Xudong 416
Geng, Xiaoke 170
Gong, Lei 348
Guo, Bing 328
Guo, Jingfeng 194

H

He, Hangwei 54
Hirose, Yuichi 29
Hou, Jian 69
Hu, Jiahui 454, 467
Hu, Tao 170
Huang, Chongwei 69
Huang, Danni 81
Huang, Feiran 454, 467
Huang, Haozhi 429
Huang, Yiyun 93
Huang, Zhixiang 41

I

Ike, Yuichi 243

J

Ji, Yatu 416
Jia, Shangru 480
Jiang, Yuncheng 81
Jiang, Zhe 441
Jin, Jizhong 297
Jin, Zhibo 93
Jun, Tanimoto 158, 236

K

Kanamori, Kentaro 243
Kobayashi, Ken 243
Kuniyoshi, Yasuo 3

L

Lai, Yantong 361
Lan, Yuqing 221
Li, Chaozhuo 454, 467
Li, Heyang 297
Li, Hongao 383
Li, Jiawei 81

© The Editor(s) (if applicable) and The Author(s), under exclusive license
to Springer Nature Singapore Pte Ltd. 2025
R. Hadfi et al. (Eds.): PRICAI 2024, LNAI 15281, pp. 487–489, 2025.
https://doi.org/10.1007/978-981-96-0116-5

Li, Jie   322
Li, Kai   170
Li, Lei   297
Li, Leilei   441
Li, Li   403
Li, Ruirui   182
Li, Teng   396
Li, Weiling   119
Li, Xianghua   236
Liang, Xiaolong   106
Liu, Bin   194
Liu, Jia   383
Liu, Zhigang   119
Lou, Wenqi   348
Luo, Haiyong   341
Luo, Jun   441

M

Manwani, Naresh   16
Mao, Rui   416
Mao, Shun   81
Marsland, Stephen   29
Mei, Yi   309
Meng, Qianwen   269
Mi, Yongqing   383

N

Nakata, Kazuhide   243
Niu, Guanchen   396

O

Ouyang, Mingxing   209

P

Pan, Xiao   194

Q

Qiao, Liqiang   454, 467
Qin, Yunji   348

R

Rasmy, Mohamad   134
Ren, Qing-Dao-Er-Ji   416

S

Sabty, Caroline   134
Sakr, Nourhan   134
Shariat, Raad   146
Sharma, Alok   480

Shen, Zhiqi   269
Shi, Bao   416
Sun, Junzheng   282
Sun, Xin   383

T

Takagi, Takuya   243
Tan, Jundong   429
Teng, Min   158
Tsunoda, Tatsuhiko   480

W

Wang, Chao   348
Wang, DongDong   41
Wang, Enshu   54
Wang, Hui   170
Wang, Jilu   454
Wang, Naihao   182
Wang, Nianbin   282
Wang, Shuo   467
Wang, Tianci   361
Wang, Xingwei   322
Wang, Xinyi   93
Wáng, Yì N.   106
Wang, Yifan   322
Wang, Yimin   257
Wang, Yixi   257
Wang, Yiyuan   361
Wang, Yizhou   54
Wang, Yuxia   322
Wang, Zhen   158, 236
Wu, Fan   341
Wu, Libing   54
Wu, Nier   416
Wu, You   194

X

Xia, Xiao-Lei   209
Xiang, Ji   361
Xie, Jie   375
Xing, Zhihuan   221
Xiong, Zhen   429
Xu, Haowei   236
Xu, Jie   454, 467
Xu, Yonghui   269

Y

Yamao, Shoki   243
Yan, Hao   119

Yang, Guanghua   429
Yang, Haoning   257
Yang, Xiaoyi   221
Yao, Yuan   29
Yu, Axin   441
Yu, Dan   221
Yu, Jicheng   81
Yu, Ruiyun   322
Yu, Yichun   221
Yu, Yin   221
Yuan, Huaqiang   69

Z

Zhang, Fangfang   309
Zhang, Haitao   416
Zhang, Jiayu   93
Zhang, John Z.   146
Zhang, Mengjie   309

Zhang, Yangfan   328
Zhang, Yixin   269
Zhang, Yucheng   297
Zhang, Zhengchao   282
Zhao, Fang   341
Zhao, Yu   54
Zheng, Bangqi   41
Zheng, Xiangyu   41
Zhong, Yurong   119
Zhou, Bo   341
Zhou, Lianke   282
Zhou, Xin   269
Zhou, Xuehai   348
Zhou, Zineng   341
Zhu, Fanglin   269
Zhu, Mingying   375
Zhu, Zhiyu   93
Zhuang, Xufei   416

GPSR Compliance

The European Union's (EU) General Product Safety Regulation (GPSR) is a set of rules that requires consumer products to be safe and our obligations to ensure this.

If you have any concerns about our products, you can contact us on ProductSafety@springernature.com

In case Publisher is established outside the EU, the EU authorized representative is:

Springer Nature Customer Service Center GmbH
Europaplatz 3
69115 Heidelberg, Germany

The manufacturer's authorised representative in the EU is Springer
Nature Customer Service Centre GmbH, Europaplatz 3, 69115 Heidelberg,
Germany. If you have any concerns regarding our products, please
contact ProductSafety@springernature.com

Printed and bound by CPI Group (UK) Ltd, Croydon, CR0 4YY
29/04/2026
02099533-0004